Lecture Notes in Computer Science **10806**

Commenced Publication in 1973
Founding and Former Series Editors:
Gerhard Goos, Juris Hartmanis, and Jan van Leeuwen

Advanced Research in Computing and Software Science
Subline of Lecture Notes in Computer Science

More information about this series at http://www.springer.com/series/7407

Dirk Beyer · Marieke Huisman (Eds.)

Tools and Algorithms for the Construction and Analysis of Systems

24th International Conference, TACAS 2018
Held as Part of the European Joint Conferences
on Theory and Practice of Software, ETAPS 2018
Thessaloniki, Greece, April 14–20, 2018
Proceedings, Part II

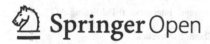

Editors
Dirk Beyer
Ludwig-Maximilians-Universität München
Munich
Germany

Marieke Huisman
University of Twente
Enschede
The Netherlands

ISSN 0302-9743   ISSN 1611-3349   (electronic)
Lecture Notes in Computer Science
ISBN 978-3-319-89962-6   ISBN 978-3-319-89963-3   (eBook)
https://doi.org/10.1007/978-3-319-89963-3

Library of Congress Control Number: 2018940138

LNCS Sublibrary: SL1 – Theoretical Computer Science and General Issues

Printed on acid-free paper

This Springer imprint is published by the registered company Springer International Publishing AG
part of Springer Nature
The registered company address is: Gewerbestrasse 11, 6330 Cham, Switzerland

ETAPS Foreword

Welcome to the proceedings of ETAPS 2018! After a somewhat coldish ETAPS 2017 in Uppsala in the north, ETAPS this year took place in Thessaloniki, Greece. I am happy to announce that this is the first ETAPS with gold open access proceedings. This means that all papers are accessible by anyone for free.

ETAPS 2018 was the 21st instance of the European Joint Conferences on Theory and Practice of Software. ETAPS is an annual federated conference established in 1998, and consists of five conferences: ESOP, FASE, FoSSaCS, TACAS, and POST. Each conference has its own Program Committee (PC) and its own Steering Committee. The conferences cover various aspects of software systems, ranging from theoretical computer science to foundations to programming language developments, analysis tools, formal approaches to software engineering, and security. Organizing these conferences in a coherent, highly synchronized conference program facilitates participation in an exciting event, offering attendees the possibility to meet many researchers working in different directions in the field, and to easily attend talks of different conferences. Before and after the main conference, numerous satellite workshops take place and attract many researchers from all over the globe.

ETAPS 2018 received 479 submissions in total, 144 of which were accepted, yielding an overall acceptance rate of 30%. I thank all the authors for their interest in ETAPS, all the reviewers for their peer reviewing efforts, the PC members for their contributions, and in particular the PC (co-)chairs for their hard work in running this entire intensive process. Last but not least, my congratulations to all authors of the accepted papers!

ETAPS 2018 was enriched by the unifying invited speaker Martin Abadi (Google Brain, USA) and the conference-specific invited speakers (FASE) Pamela Zave (AT & T Labs, USA), (POST) Benjamin C. Pierce (University of Pennsylvania, USA), and (ESOP) Derek Dreyer (Max Planck Institute for Software Systems, Germany). Invited tutorials were provided by Armin Biere (Johannes Kepler University, Linz, Austria) on modern SAT solving and Fabio Somenzi (University of Colorado, Boulder, USA) on hardware verification. My sincere thanks to all these speakers for their inspiring and interesting talks!

ETAPS 2018 took place in Thessaloniki, Greece, and was organised by the Department of Informatics of the Aristotle University of Thessaloniki. The university was founded in 1925 and currently has around 75 000 students; it is the largest university in Greece. ETAPS 2018 was further supported by the following associations and societies: ETAPS e.V., EATCS (European Association for Theoretical Computer Science), EAPLS (European Association for Programming Languages and Systems), and EASST (European Association of Software Science and Technology). The local organization team consisted of Panagiotis Katsaros (general chair), Ioannis Stamelos,

Lefteris Angelis, George Rahonis, Nick Bassiliades, Alexander Chatzigeorgiou, Ezio Bartocci, Simon Bliudze, Emmanouela Stachtiari, Kyriakos Georgiadis, and Petros Stratis (EasyConferences).

The overall planning for ETAPS is the main responsibility of the Steering Committee, and in particular of its Executive Board. The ETAPS Steering Committee consists of an Executive Board and representatives of the individual ETAPS conferences, as well as representatives of EATCS, EAPLS, and EASST. The Executive Board consists of Gilles Barthe (Madrid), Holger Hermanns (Saarbrücken), Joost-Pieter Katoen (chair, Aachen and Twente), Gerald Lüttgen (Bamberg), Vladimiro Sassone (Southampton), Tarmo Uustalu (Tallinn), and Lenore Zuck (Chicago). Other members of the Steering Committee are: Wil van der Aalst (Aachen), Parosh Abdulla (Uppsala), Amal Ahmed (Boston), Christel Baier (Dresden), Lujo Bauer (Pittsburgh), Dirk Beyer (Munich), Mikolaj Bojanczyk (Warsaw), Luis Caires (Lisbon), Jurriaan Hage (Utrecht), Rainer Hähnle (Darmstadt), Reiko Heckel (Leicester), Marieke Huisman (Twente), Panagiotis Katsaros (Thessaloniki), Ralf Küsters (Stuttgart), Ugo Dal Lago (Bologna), Kim G. Larsen (Aalborg), Matteo Maffei (Vienna), Tiziana Margaria (Limerick), Flemming Nielson (Copenhagen), Catuscia Palamidessi (Palaiseau), Andrew M. Pitts (Cambridge), Alessandra Russo (London), Dave Sands (Göteborg), Don Sannella (Edinburgh), Andy Schürr (Darmstadt), Alex Simpson (Ljubljana), Gabriele Taentzer (Marburg), Peter Thiemann (Freiburg), Jan Vitek (Prague), Tomas Vojnar (Brno), and Lijun Zhang (Beijing).

I would like to take this opportunity to thank all speakers, attendees, organizers of the satellite workshops, and Springer for their support. I hope you all enjoy the proceedings of ETAPS 2018. Finally, a big thanks to Panagiotis and his local organization team for all their enormous efforts that led to a fantastic ETAPS in Thessaloniki!

February 2018   Joost-Pieter Katoen

Preface

TACAS 2018 is the 24th edition of the International Conference on Tools and Algorithms for the Construction and Analysis of Systems conference series. TACAS 2018 is part of the 21st European Joint Conferences on Theory and Practice of Software (ETAPS 2018). The conference is held in the hotel Makedonia Palace in Thessaloniki, Greece, during April 16–19, 2018.

Conference Description. TACAS is a forum for researchers, developers, and users interested in rigorously based tools and algorithms for the construction and analysis of systems. The conference aims to bridge the gaps between different communities with this common interest and to support them in their quest to improve the utility, reliability, flexibility, and efficiency of tools and algorithms for building systems. TACAS solicits five types of submissions:

- Research papers, identifying and justifying a principled advance to the theoretical foundations for the construction and analysis of systems, where applicable supported by experimental validation
- Case-study papers, reporting on case studies and providing information about the system being studied, the goals of the study, the challenges the system poses to automated analysis, research methodologies and approaches used, the degree to which goals were attained, and how the results can be generalized to other problems and domains
- Regular tool papers, presenting a new tool, a new tool component, or novel extensions to an existing tool, with an emphasis on design and implementation concerns, including software architecture and core data structures, practical applicability, and experimental evaluations
- Tool-demonstration papers (6 pages), focusing on the usage aspects of tools
- Competition-contribution papers (4 pages), focusing on describing software-verification systems that participated at the International Competition on Software Verification (SV-COMP), which has been affiliated with our conference since TACAS 2012

New Items in the Call for Papers. There were three new items in the call for papers, which we briefly discuss.

- *Focus on Replicability of Research Results.* We consider that reproducibility of results is of the utmost importance for the TACAS community. Therefore, we encouraged all authors of submitted papers to include support for replicating the results of their papers.
- *Limit of 3 Submissions.* A change of the TACAS bylaws requires that each individual author is limited to a maximum of three submissions as an author or co-author. Authors of co-authored submissions are jointly responsible for respecting this policy. In case of violations, all submissions of this (co-)author would be desk-rejected.

– *Artifact Evaluation.* For the first time, TACAS 2018 included an optional artifact evaluation (AE) process for accepted papers. An artifact is any additional material (software, data sets, machine-checkable proofs, etc.) that substantiates the claims made in a paper and ideally makes them fully replicable. The evaluation and archival of artifacts improves replicability and traceability for the benefit of future research and the broader TACAS community.

Paper Selection. This year, 154 papers were submitted to TACAS, among which 115 were research papers, 6 case-study papers, 26 regular tool papers, and 7 were tool-demonstration papers. After a rigorous review process, with each paper reviewed by at least 3 program committee (PC) members, followed by an online discussion, the PC accepted 35 research papers, 2 case-study papers, 6 regular tool papers, and 2 tool-demonstration papers (45 papers in total).

Competition on Software Verification (SV-COMP). TACAS 2018 also hosted the 7th International Competition on Software Verification (SV-COMP), chaired and organized by Tomas Vojnar. The competition again had a high participation: 21 verification systems with developers from 11 countries were submitted for the systematic comparative evaluation, including two submissions from industry. This volume includes short papers describing 9 of the participating verification systems. These papers were reviewed by a separate program committee (PC); each of the papers was assessed by four reviewers. One session in the TACAS program was reserved for the presentation of the results: the summary by the SV-COMP chair and the participating tools by the developer teams.

Artifact-Evaluation Process. The authors of each of the 45 accepted papers were invited to submit an artifact immediately after the acceptance notification. An artifact evaluation committee (AEC), chaired by Arnd Hartmanns and Philipp Wendler, reviewed these artifacts, with 2 reviewers assigned to each artifact. The AEC received 33 artifact submissions, of which 24 were successfully evaluated (73% acceptance rate) and have been awarded the TACAS AEC badge, which is added to the title page of the respective paper. The AEC used a two-phase reviewing process: Reviewers first performed an initial check of whether the artifact was technically usable and whether the accompanying instructions were consistent, followed by a full evaluation of the artifact. In addition to the textual reviews, reviews also provided scores for consistency, completeness, and documentation. The main criterion for artifact acceptance was consistency with the paper, with completeness and documentation being handled in a more lenient manner as long as the artifact was useful overall. Finally, TACAS provided authors of all submitted artifacts the possibility to publish and permanently archive a "camera-ready" version of their artifact on https://springernature.figshare.com/tacas, with the only requirement being an open license assigned to the artifact. This possibility was used for 20 artifacts, while 2 more artifacts were archived independently by the authors.

Acknowledgments. We would like to thank all the people who helped to make TACAS 2018 successful. First, the chairs would like to thank the authors for submitting their papers to TACAS 2018. The reviewers did a great job in reviewing papers: They contributed informed and detailed reports and took part in the discussions during the virtual PC meeting. We also thank the steering committee for their advice.

Special thanks go to the general chair, Panagiotis Katsaros, and his overall organization team, to the chair of the ETAPS 2018 executive board, Joost-Pieter Katoen, who took care of the overall organization of ETAPS, to the EasyConference team for the local organization, and to the publication team at Springer for solving all the extra problems that our introduction of the new artifact-evaluation process caused.

March 2018

Dirk Beyer
Marieke Huisman
(PC Chairs)
Goran Frehse
(Tools Chair)
Tomas Vojnar
(SV-COMP Chair)
Arnd Hartmanns
Philipp Wendler
(AEC Chairs)

Organization

Program Committee

Wolfgang Ahrendt	Chalmers University of Technology, Sweden
Dirk Beyer (Chair)	Ludwig-Maximilians-Universität München, Germany
Armin Biere	Johannes Kepler University Linz, Austria
Lubos Brim	Masaryk University, Czech Republic
Franck Cassez	Macquarie University, Australia
Alessandro Cimatti	FBK-irst, Italy
Rance Cleaveland	University of Maryland, USA
Goran Frehse	University of Grenoble Alpes – Verimag, France
Jan Friso Groote	Eindhoven University of Technology, The Netherlands
Gudmund Grov	Norwegian Defence Research Establishment (FFI), Norway
Orna Grumberg	Technion — Israel Institute of Technology, Israel
Arie Gurfinkel	University of Waterloo, Canada
Klaus Havelund	Jet Propulsion Laboratory, USA
Matthias Heizmann	University of Freiburg, Germany
Holger Hermanns	Saarland University, Germany
Falk Howar	TU Clausthal/IPSSE, Germany
Marieke Huisman (Chair)	University of Twente, The Netherlands
Laura Kovacs	Vienna University of Technology, Austria
Jan Kretinsky	Technical University of Munich, Germany
Salvatore La Torre	Università degli studi di Salerno, Italy
Kim Larsen	Aalborg University, Denmark
Axel Legay	IRISA/Inria, Rennes, France
Yang Liu	Nanyang Technological University, Singapore
Rupak Majumdar	MPI-SWS, Germany
Tiziana Margaria	Lero, Ireland
Rosemary Monahan	National University of Ireland Maynooth, Ireland
David Parker	University of Birmingham, UK
Corina Pasareanu	CMU/NASA Ames Research Center, USA
Alexander K. Petrenko	ISP RAS, Russia
Zvonimir Rakamaric	University of Utah, USA
Kristin Yvonne Rozier	Iowa State University, USA
Natasha Sharygina	USI Lugano, Switzerland
Stephen F. Siegel	University of Delaware, USA
Bernhard Steffen	University of Dortmund, Germany
Stavros Tripakis	University of California, Berkeley, USA
Frits Vaandrager	Radboud University, The Netherlands
Tomas Vojnar	Brno University of Technology, Czech Republic

Heike Wehrheim   University of Paderborn, Germany
Thomas Wies   New York University, USA
Damien Zufferey   MPI-SWS, Germany

Program Committee and Jury — SV-COMP

Tomáš Vojnar (Chair)
Peter Schrammel (representing 2LS)
Jera Hensel (representing AProVE)
Michael Tautschnig (representing CBMC)
Vadim Mutilin (representing CPA-BAM-BnB)
Mikhail Mandrykin (representing CPA-BAM-Slicing)
Thomas Lemberger (representing CPA-Seq)
Hussama Ismail (representing DepthK)
Felipe Monteiro (representing ESBMC-incr)
Mikhail R. Gadelha (representing ESBMC-kind)
Martin Hruska (representing Forester)
Zhao Duan (representing InterpChecker)
Herbert Oliveira Rocha (representing Map2Check)
Veronika Šoková (representing PredatorHP)
Franck Cassez (representing Skink)
Marek Chalupa (representing Symbiotic)
Matthias Heizmann (representing UAutomizer)
Alexander Nutz (representing UKojak)
Daniel Dietsch (representing UTaipan)
Priyanka Darke (representing VeriAbs)
Pritom Rajkhowa (representing VIAP)
Liangze Yin (representing Yogar-CBMC)

Artifact Evaluation Committee (AEC)

Arnd Hartmanns (Chair)
Philipp Wendler (Chair)
Pranav Ashok
Maryam Dabaghchian
Daniel Dietsch
Rohit Dureja
Felix Freiberger
Karlheinz Friedberger
Frederik Gossen
Samuel Huang
Antonio Iannopollo
Omar Inverso
Nils Jansen
Sebastiaan Joosten

Eunsuk Kang
Sean Kauffman
Ondrej Lengal
Tobias Meggendorfer
Malte Mues
Chris Novakovic
David Sanan

Additional Reviewers

Aarssen, Rodin	Dureja, Rohit	Hoenicke, Jochen
Alzuhaibi, Omar	Dvir, Nurit	Holik, Lukas
Andrianov, Pavel	Ehlers, Rüdiger	Horne, Ross
Asadi, Sepideh	Elrakaiby, Yehia	Hou, Zhe Hou
Ashok, Pranav	Enea, Constantin	Hyvärinen, Antti
Bacci, Giovanni	Faella, Marco	Inverso, Omar
Bainczyk, Alexaner	Falcone, Ylies	Irfan, Ahmed
Baranowski, Marek	Fedotov, Alexander	Jabbour, Fadi
Barringer, Howard	Fedyukovich, Grigory	Jacobs, Swen
Ben Said, Najah	Fox, Gereon	Jansen, Nils
Benerecetti, Massimo	Freiberger, Felix	Jensen, Peter Gjøl
Benes, Nikola	Frenkel, Hadar	Joshi, Rajeev
Bensalem, Saddek	Frohme, Markus	Jovanović, Dejan
Berzish, Murphy	Genaim, Samir	Kan, Shuanglong
Biewer, Sebastian	Getman, Alexander	Kang, Eunsuk
Biondi, Fabrizio	Given-Wilson, Thomas	Kauffman, Sean
Blahoudek, František	Gleiss, Bernhard	Klauck, Michaela
Blicha, Martin	Golden, Bat-Chen	Kopetzki, Dawid
Bosselmann, Steve	González De Aledo, Pablo	Kotelnikov, Evgenii
Bruttomesso, Roberto	Goodloe, Alwyn	Krishna, Siddharth
Butkova, Yuliya	Gopinath, Divya	Krämer, Julia
Casagrande, Alberto	Gossen, Frederik	Kumar, Rahul
Caulfield, Benjamin	Graf-Brill, Alexander	König, Jürgen
Ceska, Milan	Greitschus, Marius	Lahav, Ori
Chen, Wei	Griggio, Alberto	Le Coent, Adrien
Chimento, Jesus Mauricio	Guthmann, Ofer	Lengal, Ondrej
Cleophas, Loek	Habermehl, Peter	Leofante, Francesco
Cordeiro, Lucas	Han, Tingting	Li, Jianwen
Dabaghchian, Maryam	Hao, Jianye	Lime, Didier
Darulova, Eva	Hark, Marcel	Lin, Yuhui
de Vink, Erik	Hartmanns, Arnd	Lorber, Florian
Delzanno, Giorgio	Hashemi, Vahid	Maarek, Manuel
Dietsch, Daniel	He, Shaobo	Mandrykin, Mikhail
Du, Xiaoning	Heule, Marijn	Marescotti, Matteo

Markey, Nicolas
Meggendorfer, Tobias
Meyer, Philipp
Meyer, Roland
Micheli, Andrea
Mjeda, Anila
Moerman, Joshua
Mogavero, Fabio
Monniaux, David
Mordan, Vitaly
Murtovi, Alnis
Mutilin, Vadim
Myreen, Magnus O.
Navas, Jorge A.
Neele, Thomas
Nickovic, Dejan
Nies, Gilles
Nikolov, Nikola S.
Norman, Gethin
Nyman, Ulrik
Oortwijn, Wytse
Pastva, Samuel
Pauck, Felix
Pavlinovic, Zvonimir
Pearce, David
Peled, Doron

Poulsen, Danny Bøgsted
Power, James
Putot, Sylvie
Quilbeuf, Jean
Rasin, Dan
Reger, Giles
Reynolds, Andrew
Ritirc, Daniela
Robillard, Simon
Rogalewicz, Adam
Roveri, Marco
Ročkai, Petr
Rüthing, Oliver
Šafránek, David
Salamon, Andras Z.
Sayed-Ahmed, Amr
Schieweck, Alexander
Schilling, Christian
Schmaltz, Julien
Seidl, Martina
Sessa, Mirko
Shafiei, Nastaran
Sharma, Arnab
Sickert, Salomon
Simon, Axel
Sloth, Christoffer

Spoto, Fausto
Sproston, Jeremy
Stan, Daniel
Taankvist, Jakob Haahr
Tacchella, Armando
Tetali, Sai Deep
Toews, Manuel
Tonetta, Stefano
Traonouez, Louis-Marie
Travkin, Oleg
Trostanetski, Anna
van den Bos, Petra
van Dijk, Tom
van Harmelen, Arnaud
Vasilev, Anton
Vasilyev, Anton
Veanes, Margus
Vizel, Yakir
Widder, Josef
Wijs, Anton
Willemse, Tim
Wirkner, Dominik
Yang, Fei
Zakharov, Ilja
Zantema, Hans

Contents – Part II

Static and Dynamic Program Analysis

Hybrid and Stochastic Systems

Temporal Logic and Mu-calculus

7th Competition on Software Verification (SV-COMP)

Contents – Part I

Software Verification and Optimisation

Model Checking

Machine Learning

Concurrent and Distributed Systems

Computing the Concurrency Threshold of Sound Free-Choice Workflow Nets

Philipp J. Meyer[1]([✉]), Javier Esparza[1][ID], and Hagen Völzer[2]

[1] Technical University of Munich, Munich, Germany
{meyerphi,esparza}@in.tum.de
[2] IBM Research, Zurich, Switzerland
hvo@zurich.ibm.com

Abstract. Workflow graphs extend classical flow charts with concurrent fork and join nodes. They constitute the core of business processing languages such as BPMN or UML Activity Diagrams. The activities of a workflow graph are executed by humans or machines, generically called resources. If concurrent activities cannot be executed in parallel by lack of resources, the time needed to execute the workflow increases. We study the problem of computing the minimal number of resources necessary to fully exploit the concurrency of a given workflow, and execute it as fast as possible (i.e., as fast as with unlimited resources).

We model this problem using free-choice Petri nets, which are known to be equivalent to workflow graphs. We analyze the computational complexity of two versions of the problem: computing the resource and concurrency thresholds. We use the results to design an algorithm to approximate the concurrency threshold, and evaluate it on a benchmark suite of 642 industrial examples. We show that it performs very well in practice: It always provides the exact value, and never takes more than 30 ms for any workflow, even for those with a huge number of reachable markings.

1 Introduction

A *workflow graph* is a classical control-flow graph (or flow chart) extended with concurrent fork and join. Workflow graphs represent the core of workflow languages such as BPMN (Business Process Model and Notation), EPC (Event-driven Process Chain), or UML Activity Diagrams.

In many applications, the activities of an execution workflow graph have to be carried out by a fixed number of *resources* (for example, a fixed number of computer cores). Increasing the number of cores can reduce the minimal runtime of the workflow. For example, consider a simple deterministic workflow (a workflow without choice or merge nodes), which forks into k parallel activities, all of duration 1, and terminates after a join. With an optimal assignment of resources to activities, the workflow takes time k when executed with one resource, time $\lceil k/2 \rceil$ with two resources, and time 1 with k resources; additional resources

D. Beyer and M. Huisman (Eds.): TACAS 2018, LNCS 10806, pp. 3–19, 2018.
https://doi.org/10.1007/978-3-319-89963-3_1

bring no further reduction. We call k the *resource threshold*. In a deterministic workflow that forks into two parallel chains of k sequential activities each, one resource leads to runtime $2k$, and two resources to runtime k. More resources do not improve the runtime, and so the resource threshold is 2. Clearly, the resource threshold of a deterministic workflow with k activities is a number between 1 and k. Determining this number can be seen as a scheduling problem. However, most scheduling problems assume a fixed number of resources and study how to optimize the makespan [11,17], while we study how to minimize the number of resources. Other works on resource/machine minimization [5,6] consider interval constraints instead of the partial-order constraints given by a workflow graph.

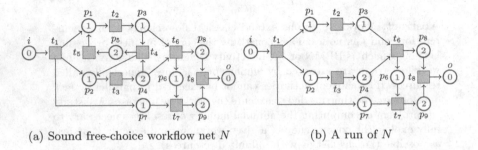

(a) Sound free-choice workflow net N (b) A run of N

Fig. 1. A sound free-choice workflow net and one of its runs (Color figure online)

Following previous work, we do not directly work with workflow graphs, but with their equivalent representation as *free-choice workflow Petri nets*, which has been shown to be essentially the same model [10] and allows us to directly use a wealth of results of free-choice Petri nets [7]. Figure 1(a) shows a free-choice workflow net. The actual workflow activities, also called *tasks*, which need a resource to execute and which consume time are modeled as the places of the net: Each place p of the net is assigned a time $\tau(p)$, depicted in blue. Intuitively, when a token arrives in p, it must execute a task that takes $\tau(p)$ time units before it can be used to fire a transition. A free choice exists between transitions t_4 and t_6, which is a representation of a choice node (if-then-else or loop condition) in the workflow.

If no choice is present or all choices are resolved, we have a deterministic workflow such as the one in Fig. 1(b). In Petri net terminology, deterministic workflows correspond to the class of marked graphs. Deterministic workflows are common in practice: in the standard suite of 642 industrial workflows that we use for experiments, 63.7% are deterministic. We show that already for this restricted class, deciding if the threshold exceeds a given bound is NP-hard. Therefore, we investigate an over-approximation of the resource threshold, already introduced in [4]: the *concurrency threshold*. This is the maximal number of task places that can be simultaneously marked at a reachable marking. Clearly, if a workflow with concurrency threshold k is executed with k resources, then we can always start the task of a place immediately after a token arrives, and this schedule already

achieves the fastest runtime achievable with unlimited resources. We show that
the concurrency threshold can be computed in polynomial time for deterministic
workflows.

For workflows with nondeterministic choice, corresponding to free-choice
nets, we show that computing the concurrency threshold of free-choice workflow
nets is NP-hard, solving a problem left open in [4]. We even prove that the problem remains NP-hard for sound free-choice workflows. Soundness is the dominant
behavioral correctness notion for workflows, which rules out basic control-flow
errors such as deadlocks. NP-hardness in the sound case is remarkable, because
many analysis problems that have high complexity in the unsound case can be
solved in polynomial time in the sound case (see e.g. [1,7,8]).

After our complexity analysis, we design an algorithm to compute bounds
on the concurrency threshold using a combination of linear optimization and
state-space exploration. We evaluate it on a benchmark suite of 642 sound free-
choice workflow nets from an industrial source (IBM) [9]. The bounds can be
computed in a total of 7 s (over all 642 nets). On the contrary, the computation
of the exact value by state-space exploration techniques times out for the three
largest nets, and takes 7 min for the rest. (Observe that partial-order reduction
techniques cannot be used, because one may then miss the interleaving realizing
the concurrency threshold.)

The paper is structured as follows. Section 2 contains preliminaries. Sections 3
and 4 study the resource and concurrency thresholds, respectively. Section 5
presents our algorithms for computing the concurrency bound, and experimental
results. Finally, Sect. 6 contains conclusions.

2 Preliminaries

Petri Nets. A *Petri net* N is a tuple (P, T, F) where P is a finite set of places,
T is a finite set of transitions $(P \cap T = \emptyset)$, and $F \subseteq (P \times T) \cup (T \times P)$ is a
set of arcs. The *preset* of $x \in P \cup T$ is $^{\bullet}x \stackrel{\text{def}}{=} \{y \mid (y, x) \in F\}$ and its *postset* is
$x^{\bullet} \stackrel{\text{def}}{=} \{y \mid (x, y) \in F\}$. We extend the definition of presets and postsets to sets of
places and transitions $X \subseteq P \cup T$ by $^{\bullet}X \stackrel{\text{def}}{=} \bigcup_{x \in X} {}^{\bullet}x$ and $X^{\bullet} \stackrel{\text{def}}{=} \bigcup_{x \in X} x^{\bullet}$. A net
is *acyclic* if the relation F^* is a partial order, denoted by $\preceq$ and called the *causal
order*. A node x of an acyclic net is *causally maximal* if no node y satisfies $x \prec y$.

A *marking* of a Petri net is a function $M : P \to \mathbb{N}$, representing the number of
tokens in each place. For a set of places $S \subseteq P$, we define $M(S) \stackrel{\text{def}}{=} \sum_{p \in S} M(p)$.
Further, for a set of places $S \subseteq P$, we define by M_S the marking with $M_S(p) = 1$
for $p \in S$ and $M_S(p) = 0$ for $p \notin S$.

A transition t is *enabled* at a marking M if for all $p \in {}^{\bullet}t$, we have $M(p) \geq 1$.
If t is enabled at M, it may *occur*, leading to a marking M' obtained by removing
one token from each place of $^{\bullet}t$ and then adding one token to each place of $t^{\bullet}$.
We denote this by $M \stackrel{t}{\to} M'$. Let $\sigma = t_1 t_2 \ldots t_n$ be a sequence of transitions.
For a marking M_0, σ is an *occurrence sequence* if $M_0 \stackrel{t_1}{\to} M_1 \stackrel{t_2}{\to} \ldots \stackrel{t_n}{\to} M_n$
for some markings $M_1, \ldots, M_n$. We say that M_n is reachable from M_0 by σ and

denote this by $M_0 \xrightarrow{\sigma} M_n$. The set of all markings reachable from M in N by some occurrence sequence σ is denoted by $\mathcal{R}^N(M)$. A *system* is a pair (N, M) of a Petri net N and a marking M. A system (N, M) is *live* if for every $M' \in \mathcal{R}^N(M)$ and every transition t some marking $M'' \in \mathcal{R}^N(M')$ enables t. The system is *1-safe* if $M'(p) \leq 1$ for every $M' \in \mathcal{R}^N(M)$ and every place $p \in P$.

Convention: Throughout this paper we assume that systems are 1-safe, i.e., we identify "system" and "1-safe system".

Net Classes. A net $N = (P, T, F)$ is a *marked graph* if $|{}^{\bullet}p| \leq 1$ and $|p^{\bullet}| \leq 1$ for every place $p \in P$, and a *free-choice net* if for any two places $p_1, p_2 \in P$ either $p_1^{\bullet} \cap p_2^{\bullet} = \emptyset$ or $p_1^{\bullet} = p_2^{\bullet}$.

Non-sequential Processes of Petri Nets. An (A, B)-*labeled Petri net* is a tuple $N = (P, T, F, \lambda, \mu)$, where $\lambda \colon P \to A$ and $\mu \colon T \to B$ are *labeling functions* over alphabets A, B. The nonsequential processes of a 1-safe system (N, M) are acyclic, (P, T)-labeled marked graphs. Say that a set P'' of places of a (P, T)-labeled acyclic net *enables* $t \in T$ if all the places of P'' are causally maximal, carry pairwise distinct labels, and $\lambda(P'') = {}^{\bullet}t$.

Definition 1. *Let $N = (P, T, F)$ be a Petri net and let M be a marking of N. The set $\mathcal{NP}(N, M)$ of nonsequential processes of (N, M) (processes for short) is the set of (P, T)-labeled Petri nets defined inductively as follows:*

- *The (P, T)-labeled Petri net containing for each place $p \in P$ marked at M one place $\widehat{p}$ labeled by p, no other places, and no transitions, belongs to $\mathcal{NP}(N, M)$.*
- *If $\Pi = (P', T', F', \lambda, \mu) \in \mathcal{NP}(N, M)$ and $P'' \subseteq P'$ enables some transition t of N, then the (P, T)-labeled net $\Pi_t = (P' \uplus \widehat{P}, T' \uplus \{\widehat{t}\}, F' \uplus \widehat{F}, \lambda \uplus \widehat{\lambda}, \mu \uplus \widehat{\mu})$, where*
  - $\widehat{P} = \{\widehat{p} \mid p \in t^{\bullet}\}$, *with* $\widehat{\lambda}(\widehat{p}) = p$, *and* $\widehat{\mu}(\widehat{t}) = t$;
  - $\widehat{F} = \{(p'', \widehat{t}) \mid p'' \in P''\} \cup \{(\widehat{t}, \widehat{p}) \mid \widehat{p} \in \widehat{P}\}$;
  also belongs to $\mathcal{NP}(N, M)$. We say that Π_t extends Π.

We denote the minimal and maximal places of a process Π w.r.t. the causal order by $\min(\Pi)$ and $\max(\Pi)$, respectively.

As usual, we say that two processes are *isomorphic* if they are the same up to renaming of the places and transitions (notice that we rename only the names of the places and transitions, not their labels).

Figure 2 shows two processes of the workflow net in Fig. 1(a). (The figure does not show the names of places and transitions, only their labels.) The net containing the white and grey nodes only is already a process, and the grey places are causally maximal places that enable t_6. Therefore, according to the definition we can extend the process with the green nodes to produce another process. On the right we extend the same process in a different way, with the transition t_4.

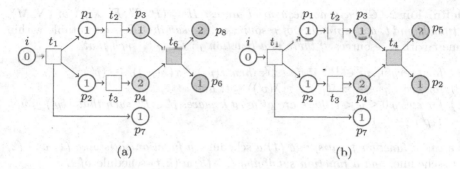

(a)   (b)

Fig. 2. Nonsequential processes of the net of Fig. 1(a) (Color figure online)

The following is well known. Let $(P', T', F', \lambda, \mu)$ be a process of (N, M):

- For every linearization $\sigma = t_1' \dots t_n'$ of T' respecting the causal order $\preceq$, the sequence $\mu(\sigma) = \mu(t_1') \dots \mu(t_n')$ is a firing sequence of (N, M). Further, all these firing sequences lead to the same marking. We call it the *final marking* of Π, and say that Π leads from M to its final marking.

  For example, in Fig. 2 the sequences of the right process labeled by $t_1 t_2 t_3 t_4$ and $t_1 t_3 t_2 t_4$ are firing sequences leading to the marking $M = \{p_2, p_5, p_7\}$.
- For every firing sequence $t_1 \cdots t_n$ of (N, M) there is a process $(P', T', F', \lambda, \mu)$ such that $T' = \{t_1', \dots, t_n'\}$, $\mu(t_i') = t_i$ for every $1 \leq i \leq n$, and $\mu(t_i') \preceq \mu(t_j')$ implies $i \leq j$.

Workflow Nets. We slightly generalize the definition of workflow net as presented in e.g. [1] by allowing multiple initial and final places. A *workflow* net is a Petri net with two distinguished sets I and O of *input places* and *output places* such that (a) $^\bullet I = \emptyset = O^\bullet$ and (b) for all $x \in P \cup T$, there exists a path from some $i \in I$ to some $o \in O$ passing through x. The markings M_I and M_O are called initial and final markings of N. A workflow net N is *sound* if

- $\forall M \in \mathcal{R}^N (M_I) : M_O \in \mathcal{R}^N (M)$,
- $\forall M \in \mathcal{R}^N (M_I) : (M(O) \geq |O|) \Rightarrow (M = M_O)$, and
- $\forall t \in T : \exists M \in \mathcal{R}^N (M_I) : t$ is enabled at M.

It is well-known that every sound free-choice workflow net is a 1-safe system with the initial marking M_I [2,7]. Given a workflow net according to this definition one can construct another one with one single input place i and output place o and two transitions t_i, t_o with $^\bullet t_i = \{i\}, t_i^\bullet = I$ and $^\bullet t_o = O, t_o^\bullet = \{o\}$. For all purposes of this paper these two workflow nets are equivalent.

Given a workflow net N, we say that a process Π of (N, M_I) is a *run* if it leads to M_O. For example, the net in Fig. 1(b) is a run of the net in Fig. 1(a).

Petri Nets with Task Durations. We consider Petri nets in which, intuitively, when a token arrives in a place p it has to execute a task taking $\tau(p)$ time units before the token can be used to fire any transition. Formally, we consider tuples $N = (P, T, F, \tau)$ where (P, T, F) is a net and $\tau : P \to \mathbb{N}$.

Definition 2. *Given a nonsequential process* $\Pi = (P', T', F', \lambda, \mu)$ *of* (N, M), *a time bound t, and a number of resources k, we say that Π is executable within time t with k resources if there is a function $f \colon P' \to \mathbb{N}$ such that*

(1) for every $p'_1, p'_2 \in P'$: if $p'_1 \prec p'_2$ then $f(p'_1) + \tau(\lambda(p'_1)) \leq f(p'_2)$;
(2) for every $p' \in P'$: $f(p') + \tau(\lambda(p')) \leq t$; and
(3) for every $0 \leq u < t$ there are at most k places $p' \in P'$ such that $f(p') \leq u < f(p') + \tau(p')$.

We call a function f satisfying (1) a schedule, *a function satisfying (1) and (2) a t-schedule, and a function satsifying (1)–(3) a (k,t)-schedule of Π.*

Intuitively, $f(p')$ describes the starting time of the task executed at p'. Condition (1) states that if $p'_1 \preceq p'_2$, then the task associated to p'_2 can only start after the task for p'_1 has ended; condition (2) states that all tasks are done by time t, and condition (3) that at any moment in time at most k tasks are being executed. As an example, the process in Fig. 1(b) can be executed with two resources in time 6 with the schedule $i, p_1, p_2 \mapsto 0$; $p_3, p_4 \mapsto 1$; $p_7, p_6 \mapsto 3$, and $p_8, p_9 \mapsto 4$.

   Given a process $\Pi = (P', T', F', \lambda, \mu)$ of (N, M) we define the schedule $f_{\min}$ as follows: if $p' \in \min(\Pi)$ then $f_{\min}(p') = 0$, otherwise define $f_{\min}(p') = \max\{f_{\min}(p'') + \tau(\lambda(p'')) \mid p'' \preceq p'\}$. Further, we define the *minimal execution time* $t_{\min}(\Pi) = \max\{f(p') + \tau(\lambda(p'')) \mid p' \in \max(\Pi)\}$. In the process in Fig. 1(b), the schedule $f_{\min}$ is the function that assigns $i, p_1, p_2, p_7 \mapsto 0$, $p_3, p_4 \mapsto 1$, $p_6, p_8 \mapsto 3$, $p_9 \mapsto 4$, and $o \mapsto 6$, and so $t_{\min}(\Pi) = 6$. We have:

Lemma 1. *A process $\Pi = (P', T', F', \lambda, \mu)$ of (N, M) can be executed within time $t_{\min}(\Pi)$ with $|P'|$ resources, and cannot be executed faster with any number of resources.*

Proof. For $k \geq |P'|$ resources condition (3) of Definition 2 holds vacuously. Π is executable within time t iff conditions (1) and (2) hold. Since $f_{\min}$ satisfies (1) and (2) for $t = t_{\min}(\Pi)$, Π can be executed within time $t_{\min}(\Pi)$. Further, $t_{\min}(\Pi)$ is the smallest time for which (1) and (2) can hold, and so Π cannot be executed faster with any number of resources.

3   Resource Threshold

We define the resource threshold of a run of a workflow net, and of the net itself. Intuitively, the resource threshold of a run is the minimal number of resources that allows one to execute it as fast as with unlimited resources, and the resource threshold of a workflow net is the minimal number of resources that allows one to execute *every run* as fast as with unlimited resources.

Definition 3. *Let N be a workflow net, and let Π be a run of N. The* resource threshold of Π, *denoted by $RT(\Pi)$ is the smallest number k such that Π can be executed in time $t_{\min}(\Pi)$ with k resources. A schedule of Π realizes the resource threshold if it is a $(RT(\Pi), t_{\min}(\Pi))$-schedule.*

The resource threshold *of* N, *denoted by* $RT(N)$, *is defined by* $RT(N) =$ $\max\{RT(\Pi) \mid \Pi$ *is a run of* $(N, M_I)\}$. *A* schedule of N *is a function that assigns to every process* $\Pi \in \mathcal{NP}(N, M)$ *a schedule of* Π. *A schedule of* N *is a* (k, t)-*schedule if it assigns to every run* Π *a* (k, t)-*schedule of* Π. *A schedule of* N *realizes the resource threshold if it assigns to every run* Π *a* $(RT(N), t_{\min}(\Pi))$-*schedule.*

Example 1. We have seen in the previous section that for the process in Fig. 1(b) we have $t_{\min}(\Pi) = 6$, and a schedule with two resources already achieves this time. So the resource bound is 2. The workflow net of Fig. 1 has infinitely many runs, in which loosely speaking, the net executes t_4 arbitrarily many times, until it "exits the loop" by choosing t_6, followed by t_7 and t_8. It can be shown that all processes have resource threshold 2, and so that is also the resource threshold of the net.

In the rest of the section we obtain two negative results about the result threshold. First, it is difficult to compute: Determining if the resource threshold exceeds a given threshold is NP-complete even for acyclic marked graphs, a very simple class of workflows. Second, we show that even for acyclic free-choice workflow nets the resource threshold may not be realized by any online scheduler.

3.1 Resource Threshold Is NP-complete for Acyclic Marked Graphs

We prove that deciding if the resource threshold exceeds a given bound is NP-complete even for acyclic sound marked graphs. The proof proceeds by reduction from the following classical scheduling problem, proved NP-complete in [18]:

> **Given:** a finite, partially ordered set of jobs with non-negative integer durations, and non-negative integers t and k.
> **Decide:** Can all jobs can be executed with k machines within t time units in a way that respects the given partial order, i.e., a job is started only after all its predecessors have been finished?

More formally, the problem is defined as follows: Given jobs $\mathcal{J} = \{J_1, \ldots, J_n\}$, where J_i has duration $\tau(J_i)$ for every $1 \le i \le n$, and a partial order $\preceq$ on $\mathcal{J}$, does there exist a function $f \colon \mathcal{J} \to \mathbb{N}$ such that

(1) for every $1 \le i, j \le n$: if $J_i \prec J_j$ then $f(J_i) + \tau(J_i) \le f(J_j)$;
(2) for every $1 \le i \le n$: $f(J_i) + \tau(J_i) \le t$; and
(3) for every $0 \le u < t$ there are at most k indices i such that $f(J_i) \le u < f(J_i) + \tau(J_i)$.

These conditions are almost identical to the ones we used to define if a nonsequential process can be executed within time t with k resources. We exploit this to construct an acyclic workflow marked graph that "simulates" the scheduling problem. For the detailed proof, we refer to the full version of this paper [15].

Theorem 1. *The following problem is NP-complete:*

> **Given:** *An acyclic, sound workflow marked graph* N, *and a number* k.
> **Decide:** *Does* $RT(N) \le k$ *hold?*

3.2 Acyclic Free-Choice Workflow Nets May Have no Optimal Online Schedulers

A resource threshold of k guarantees that every run *can* be executed without penalty with k resources. In other words, *there exists* a schedule that achieves optimal runtime. However, in many applications the schedule must be determined at runtime, that is, the resources must be allocated without knowing how choices will be resolved in the future. In order to formalize this idea we define the notion of an *online schedule* of a workflow net N.

Definition 4. *Let N be a Petri net, and let Π and Π' be two processes of (N, M). We say that Π is a* prefix *of Π', denoted by $\Pi \lhd \Pi'$, if there is a sequence $\Pi_1, \ldots, \Pi_n$ of processes such that $\Pi_1 = \Pi$, $\Pi_n = \Pi'$, and Π_{i+1} extends Π_i by one transition for every $1 \leq i \leq n-1$.*

Let f be a schedule of (N, M), i.e., a function assigning a schedule to each process. We say that f is an online schedule *if for every two runs Π_1, Π_2, and for every two prefixes $\Pi'_1 \lhd \Pi_1$ and $\Pi'_2 \lhd \Pi_2$: If Π'_1 and Π'_2 are isomorphic, then $f(\Pi'_1) = f(\Pi'_2)$.*

Intuitively, if Π'_1 and Π'_2 are isomorphic then they are the same process Π, which in the future can be extended to either Π_1 or Π_2, depending on which transitions occur. In an online schedule, Π is scheduled in the same way, independently of whether it will become Π_1 or Π_2 in the future. We show that even for acyclic free-choice workflow nets there may be no online schedule that realizes the resource threshold. That is, even though for every run it is possible to schedule the tasks with $RT(N)$ resources to achieve optimal runtime, this requires knowing how it will evolve before the execution of the workflow.

Proposition 1. *There is an acyclic, sound free-choice workflow net for which no online schedule realizes the resource threshold.*

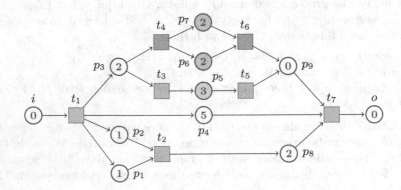

Fig. 3. A workflow net with two runs. No online scheduler for three resources achieves the minimal runtime in both runs. (Color figure online)

Proof. Consider the sound free-choice workflow net (N, M_I) of Fig. 3. It has two runs: Π_g, which executes the grey and green transitions, and Π_r, which executes the grey and red transitions. Their resource thresholds are $RT(\Pi_g) = RT(\Pi_r) = 3$, realized by the schedules f_g and f_r in Fig. 4:

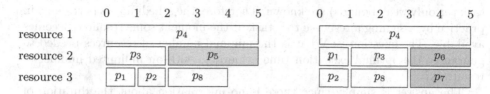

Fig. 4. Schedules f_g and f_r for the two runs Π_g and Π_r of the net of Fig. 3.

Indeed, observe that f_g and f_r execute Π_g and Π_r within time 5, and even with unlimited resources no schedule can be faster because of the task p_4, while two or fewer resources are insufficient to execute either run within time 5.

The schedule of (N, M_I) that assigns f_g and f_r to Π_g and Π_r is not an online schedule. Indeed, the process containing one single transition labeled by t_1 and places labeled by i, p_1, p_2, p_3 is isomorphic to prefixes of Π_g and Π_r. However, we have $f_g(p_3) = 0 \neq 1 = f_r(p_3)$. We now claim:

(a) Every schedule f_g of Π_g that realizes the resource threshold (time 5 with 3 resources) satisfies $f_g(p_3) = 0$.

   Indeed, if $f_g(p_3) \geq 1$, then $f_g(p_5) \geq 3$, $f_g(p_9) \geq 6$, and finally $f_g(o) \geq 6$, so f_g does not meet the time bound.

(b) Every schedule f_r of Π_r that realizes the resource threshold (time 5 with 3 resources) satisfies $f_r(p_3) > 0$.

   Observe first that we necessarily have $f_r(p_4) = 0$, and so a resource, say R_1, is bound to p_4 during the complete execution of the workflow, leaving two resources left. Assume $f_r(p_3) = 0$, i.e., a second resource, say R_2, is bound to p_3 at time 0, leaving one resource left, say R_3. Since both p_1 and p_2 must be executed before p_8, and only R_3 is free until time 2, we get $f_r(p_8) \geq 2$. So at time 2 we still have to execute p_6, p_7, p_8 with resources R_2, R_3. Therefore, two out of p_6, p_7, p_8 must be executed sequentially by the same resource. Since p_6, p_7, p_8 take 2 time units each, one of the two resources needs time 4, and we get $f_r(o) \geq 6$.

By this claim, at time 0, an online schedule has to decide whether to allocate a resource to p_3 or not, without knowing which of t_3 or t_4 will be executed in the future. If it schedules $f(p_3) = 0$ and later t_4 occurs, then Π_r is executed and the deadline of 5 time units is not met. The same occurs if it schedules $f(p_3) > 0$, and later t_3 occurs.

4   Concurrency Threshold

Due to the two negative results presented in the previous section, we study a different parameter, introduced in [4], called the concurrency threshold. During execution of a business process, information on the resolution of future choices is often not available, and further no information on the possible duration of a task (or only weak bounds) are known. Therefore, the scheduling is performed in practice by assigning a resource to a task at the moment some resource becomes available. The question is: What is the minimal number of resources needed to guarantee the optimal execution time achievable with an unlimited number of resources?

The answer is simple: since there is no information about the duration of tasks, every reachable marking of the workflow net without durations may be also reached for some assignment of durations. Let M be a reachable marking with a maximal number of tokens, say k, in places with positive duration, and let $d_1 \leq d_2 \leq \cdots \leq d_k$ be the durations of their associated tasks. If less than k resources are available, and we do not assign a resource to the task with duration d_k, we introduce a delay with respect to the case of an unlimited number of resources. On the contrary, if the number of available resources is k, then the scheduler for k resources can always simulate the behaviour of the scheduler for an unlimited number of resources.

Definition 5. *Let $N = (P, T, F, I, O, \tau)$ be a workflow Petri net. For every marking M of N, define the* concurrency *of M as* $\mathrm{conc}(M) \stackrel{def}{=} \sum_{p \in D} M(p)$, *where $D \subseteq P$ is the set of places $p \in P$ such that $\tau(p) > 0$. The* concurrency threshold *of$N$ is defined by*

$$CT(N) \stackrel{def}{=} \max \left\{ \mathrm{conc}(M) \mid M \in \mathcal{R}^N(M) \right\}.$$

The following lemma follows easily from the definitions.

Lemma 2. *For every workflow net N: $RT(N) \leq CT(N)$.*

Proof. Follows immediately from the fact that for every schedule f of a run of N, there is a schedule g with $CT(N)$ machines such that $g(p) \leq f(p)$ for every place p.

In the rest of the paper we study the complexity of computing the concurrency threshold. In [4], it was shown that the threshold can be computed in polynomial time for regular workflows, a class with a very specific structure, and the problem for the general free-choice case was left open. In Sect. 4.1 we prove that the concurrency threshold of marked graphs can be computed in polynomial time by reduction to a linear programming problem over the rational numbers. In Sect. 4.2 we study the free-choice case. We show that deciding if the threshold exceeds a given value is NP-complete for acyclic, sound free-choice workflow nets. Further, it can be computed by solving the same linear programming problem as in the case of marked graphs, but over the integers. Finally, we show that in the cyclic case the problem remains NP-complete, but the integer linear programming problem does not necessarily yield the correct solution.

4.1 Concurrency Threshold of Marked Graphs

The concurrency threshold of marked graphs can be computed using a standard technique based on the *marking equation* [16]. Given a net $N = (P,T,F)$, define the *incidence matrix* of N as the $|P| \times |T|$ matrix $\boldsymbol{N}$ given by:

$$\boldsymbol{N}(p,t) = \begin{cases} 1 & \text{if } p \in t^\bullet \setminus {}^\bullet t \\ -1 & \text{if } p \in {}^\bullet t \setminus t^\bullet \\ 0 & \text{otherwise} \end{cases}$$

In the following, we denote by $\boldsymbol{M}$ the representation of a marking M as a vector of dimension $|P|$. Let N be a Petri net, and let M_1, M_2 be markings of N. The following results are well known from the literature (see e.g. [16]):

- If M_2 is reachable from M_1 in N, then $\boldsymbol{M_2} = \boldsymbol{M_1} + \boldsymbol{N} \cdot \boldsymbol{X}$ for some integer vector $\boldsymbol{X} \geq 0$.
- If N is a marked graph and $\boldsymbol{M_2} = \boldsymbol{M_1} + \boldsymbol{N} \cdot \boldsymbol{X}$ for some *rational* vector $\boldsymbol{X} \geq 0$, then M_2 is reachable from M_1 in N.
- If N is acyclic and $\boldsymbol{M_2} = \boldsymbol{M_1} + \boldsymbol{N} \cdot \boldsymbol{X}$ for some *integer* vector $\boldsymbol{X} \geq 0$, then M_2 is reachable from M_1 in N.

Given a workflow net $N = (P,T,F,I,O,\tau)$, let $\boldsymbol{D}: P \mapsto \mathbb{N}$ be the vector defined by $\boldsymbol{D}(p) = 1$ if $p \in D$ and $\boldsymbol{D}(p) = 0$ if $p \notin D$, where D is the set of places with positive duration. We define the linear optimization problem

$$\ell^N = \max\{\boldsymbol{D} \cdot \boldsymbol{M} \mid \boldsymbol{M} = \boldsymbol{M_I} + \boldsymbol{N} \cdot \boldsymbol{X}, \boldsymbol{M} \geq 0, \boldsymbol{X} \geq 0\} \qquad (1)$$

Since the solutions of $\boldsymbol{M} = \boldsymbol{M_I} + \boldsymbol{N} \cdot \boldsymbol{X}$ contain all the reachable markings of (N, M_I), we have $\ell^N \geq CT(N)$. Further, using these results above, we obtain:

Theorem 2. *Let N be a workflow net, and let $\ell_{\mathbb{Q}}^N$ and $\ell_{\mathbb{Z}}^N$ be the solution of the linear optimization problem (1) over the rationals and over the integers, respectively. We have:*

- $\ell_{\mathbb{Q}}^N \geq \ell_{\mathbb{Z}}^N \geq CT(N)$;
- *If N is a marked graph, then $\ell_{\mathbb{Q}} = \ell_{\mathbb{Z}} = CT(N)$.*
- *If N is acyclic, then $\ell_{\mathbb{Q}} \geq \ell_{\mathbb{Z}} = CT(N)$.*

In particular, it follows that $CT(N)$ can be computed in polynomial time for marked graphs, acyclic or not. (The result about acyclic nets is used in the next section.)

4.2 Concurrency Threshold of Free-Choice Nets

We study the complexity of computing the concurrency threshold of free-choice workflow nets. We first show that, contrary to numerous other properties for which there are polynomial algorithms, deciding if the concurrency threshold exceeds a given value is NP-complete.

Theorem 3. *The following problem is NP-complete:*

Given: *A sound, free-choice workflow net* $N = (P, T, F, I, O)$, *and a number* $k \leq |T|$.
Decide: *Is the concurrency threshold of* N *at least* k?

Proof. A detailed proof can be found in the full version of this paper [15], here we only sketch the argument. Membership in NP is nontrivial, and follows from results of [1,7]. We prove NP-hardness by means of a reduction from Maximum Independent Set (MIS):

Given: An undirected graph $G = (V, E)$, and a number $k \leq |V|$.
Decide: Is there a set $In \subseteq V$ such that $|In| \geq k$ and $\{v, u\} \notin E$ for every $u, v \in In$?

Given a graph $G = (V, E)$, we construct a sound free-choice workflow net N_G in polynomial time as follows:

– For each $e = \{v, u\} \in E$ we add to N_G the "gadget net" N_e shown in Fig. 5(a), and for every node v we add the gadget net N_v shown in Fig. 5(b).
– For every $e = \{v, u\} \in E$, we add an arc from the place $[e, v]^4$ of N_e to the transition v^1 of N_v, and from $[e, u]^4$ to the transition u^1 of N_u.
– The set I of initial places contains the place e^0 of N_e for every edge e; the set O of output places contains the places v^2 of the nets N_v.

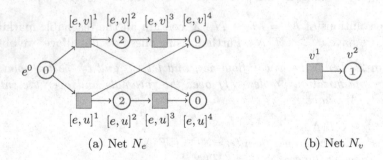

(a) Net N_e (b) Net N_v

Fig. 5. Gadgets for the proof of Theorem 3.

It is easy to see that N_G is free-choice and sound, and in [15] we show the result of applying the reduction to a small graph and prove that G has an independent set of size at least k iff the concurrency threshold of (N_G, M_I) is at least $2|E| + k$. The intuition is that for each edge $e \in E$, we fire the transition $[e, u]^1$ where $u \notin In$, and for each $v \in In$, we fire the transition v^1, thus marking one of $[e, u]^2$ or $[e, v]^2$ for each edge $e \in E$ and the place v^2 for each $v \in In$.

4.3   Approximating the Concurrency Threshold

Recall that the solution of problem (1) over the rationals or the integers is always an upper bound on the concurrency threshold for any Petri net (Theorem 2). The question is whether any stronger result holds when the workflows are sound and free-choice. Since computing the concurrency threshold is NP-complete, we cannot expect the solution over the rationals, which is computable in polynomial time, to provide the exact value. However, it could still be the case that the solution over the integers is always exact. Unfortunately, this is not true, and we can prove the following results:

Theorem 4. *Given a Petri net N, let $\ell_{\mathbb{Q}}^N$ and $\ell_{\mathbb{Z}}^N$ be as in Theorem 2.*

(a) There is an acyclic sound free-choice workflow net N such that $CT(N) < \ell_{\mathbb{Q}}^N$.
(b) There is a sound free-choice workflow net N such that and let $CT(N) < \ell_{\mathbb{Z}}^N$.

Proof. For (a), we can take the net obtained by adding to the gadget in Fig. 5(a) a new transition with input places $[e, v]^4$ and $[e, u]^4$, and an output place o with weight 2. We take e^0 as input place. The concurrency threshold is clearly 2, reached, for example, after firing $[e, v]^1$. However, we have $\ell_{\mathbb{Q}}^N = 3$, reached by the rational solution $\boldsymbol{X} = (1/2, 1/2, \ldots, 1/2)$. Indeed, the marking equation then yields the marking M satisfying $M([e, v]^2) = M([e, u]^2) = M(o) = 1/2$.

For (b), we can take the workflow net of Fig. 6. It is easy to see that the concurrency threshold is equal to 1. The marking $\boldsymbol{M}$ that puts one token in each of the two places with weight 1, and no token in the rest of the places, is not reachable from M_I. However, it is a solution of the marking equation, even when solved over the integers. Indeed, we have $\boldsymbol{M} = \boldsymbol{M_I} + \boldsymbol{N} \cdot \boldsymbol{X}$ for $\boldsymbol{X} = (1,0,1,1,0,0,1)$. Therefore, the upper bound derived from the marking equation is 2.

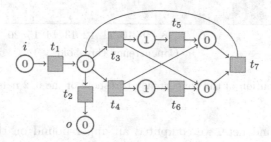

Fig. 6. A sound free-choice workflow net for which the linear programming problem derived from the marking equation does not yield the exact value of the concurrency bound, even when solved over the integers.

5 Concurrency Threshold: A Practical Approach

We have implemented a tool[1] to compute an upper bound on the concurrency threshold by constructing a linear program and solving it by calling the mixed-integer linear programming solver Cbc from the COIN-OR project [14]. Additionally, fixing a number k, we used the state-of-the art Petri net model checker LoLA [19] to both establish a lower bound, by querying LoLA for existence of a reachable marking M with $\text{conc}(M) \geq k$; and to establish an upper bound, by querying LoLA if all reachable markings M' satisfy $\text{conc}(M') \leq k$.

We evaluated the tool on a set of 1386 workflow nets extracted from a collection of five libraries of industrial business processes modeled in the IBM WebSphere Business Modeler [9]. For the concurrency threshold, we set $D = P \setminus O$. These nets also have multiple output places, however with a slightly different semantics for soundness allowing unmarked output places in the final marking. We applied the transformation described in [12] to ensure all output places will be marked in the final marking. This transformation preserves soundness and the concurrency threshold.

All of the 1386 nets in the benchmark libraries are free-choice nets. We selected the sound nets among them, which are 642. Out of those 642 nets, 409 are marked graphs. Out of the remaining 233 nets, 193 are acyclic and 40 cyclic. We determined the exact concurrency threshold of all sound nets with LoLA using state-space exploration. Figure 7 shows the distribution of the threshold.

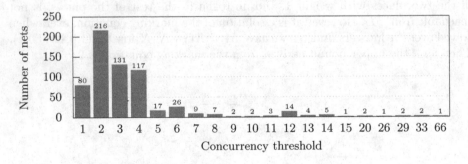

Fig. 7. Distribution of the concurrency threshold of the 642 nets analyzed.

On all 642 sound nets, we computed an upper bound on the concurrency threshold using our tool, both using rational and integer variables. We computed lower and upper bounds using LoLA with the value $k = CT(N)$ of the concurrency threshold. We report the results for computing the lower and upper bound separately.

All experiments were performed on the same machine equipped with an Intel Core i7-6700K CPU and 32 GB of RAM. The results are shown in Table 1.

---

[1] The tool is available from https://gitlab.lrz.de/i7/macaw.

Using the linear program, we were able to compute an upper bound for all nets in total in less than 7 s, taking at most 30 ms for any single net. LoLA could compute the lower bound for all nets in 6 s. LoLA fails to compute the upper bound in three cases due to reaching the memory limit of 32 GB. For the remaining 639 nets, LoLA could compute the upper bound within 7 min in total.

We give a detailed analysis for the 9 nets with a state space of over one million. For three nets with state space of sizes 10^9, 10^{10} and 10^{17}, LoLa reaches the memory limit. For four nets with state spaces between 10^6 and 10^8 and concurrency threshold above 25, LoLA takes 2, 10, 48 and 308 s each. For two nets with a state space of 10^8 and a concurrency threshold of just 11, LoLA can establish the upper bound in at most 20 ms. The solution of the linear program can be computed in all 9 cases in less than 30 ms.

Table 1. Statistics on the size and analyis time for the 642 nets analyzed. The times marked with * exclude the 3 nets where LoLA reaches the memory limit.

	Net size				Analysis time (sec)			
	$|P|$	$|T|$	$|\mathcal{R}^N|$	$CT(N)$	$\ell_{\mathbb{Q}}^N$	$\ell_{\mathbb{Z}}^N$	$CT(N) \geq k$	$CT(N) \leq k$
Median	21	14	16	3	0.01	0.01	0.01	0.01
Mean	28.4	18.6	$3 \cdot 10^{14}$	3.7	0.01	0.01	0.01	0.58*
Max	262	284	$2 \cdot 10^{17}$	66	0.03	0.03	1.18	307.76*

Comparing the values of the upper bound, first we observed that we obtained the same value using either rational or integer variables. The time difference between both was however negligible. Second, quite surprisingly, we noticed that the upper bound obtained from the linear program is exact in all of our cases, even for the cyclic ones. Further, it can be computed much faster in several cases than the upper bound obtained by LoLA and it gives a bound in all cases, even when the state-space exploration reaches its limit. By combining linear programming for the upper bound and state-space exploration for the lower bound, an exact bound can always be computed within a few seconds.

6   Conclusion

Planning sufficient execution resources for a business or production process is a crucial part of process engineering [3,13,20]. We considered a simple version of this problem in which resources are uniform and tasks are not interruptible. We studied the complexity of computing the resource threshold, i.e., the minimal number of resources allowing an optimal makespan. We showed that deciding if the resource threshold exceeds a given bound is NP-hard even for acyclic marked graphs. For this reason, we investigated the complexity of computing the concurrency threshold, an upper bound of the resource threshold introduced in [4]. Solving a problem left open in [4], we showed that deciding if the concurrency threshold exceeds a given bound is NP-hard for general sound free-choice workflow nets. We then presented a polynomial-time approximation algorithm, and showed experimentally that it computes the *exact* value of the concurrency threshold for all benchmarks of a standard suite of free-choice workflow nets.

References

1. van der Aalst, W.M.P.: Verification of workflow nets. In: Azéma, P., Balbo, G. (eds.) ICATPN 1997. LNCS, vol. 1248, pp. 407–426. Springer, Heidelberg (1997). https://doi.org/10.1007/3-540-63139-9_48
2. van der Aalst, W.M.P.: Workflow verification: finding control-flow errors using Petri-net-based techniques. In: van der Aalst, W., Desel, J., Oberweis, A. (eds.) Business Process Management. LNCS, vol. 1806, pp. 161–183. Springer, Heidelberg (2000). https://doi.org/10.1007/3-540-45594-9_11
3. Bessai, K., Youcef, S., Oulamara, A., Godart, C., Nurcan, S.: Resources allocation and scheduling approaches for business process applications in cloud contexts. In: 4th IEEE International Conference on Cloud Computing Technology and Science Proceedings, CloudCom 2012, Taipei, Taiwan, 3–6 December 2012, pp. 496–503 (2012)
4. Botezatu, M., Völzer, H., Thiele, L.: The complexity of deadline analysis for workflow graphs with multiple resources. In: La Rosa, M., Loos, P., Pastor, O. (eds.) BPM 2016. LNCS, vol. 9850, pp. 252–268. Springer, Cham (2016). https://doi.org/10.1007/978-3-319-45348-4_15
5. Chuzhoy, J., Codenotti, P.: Resource minimization job scheduling. In: Dinur, I., Jansen, K., Naor, J., Rolim, J. (eds.) APPROX/RANDOM -2009. LNCS, vol. 5687, pp. 70–83. Springer, Heidelberg (2009). https://doi.org/10.1007/978-3-642-03685-9_6
6. Chuzhoy, J., Guha, S., Khanna, S., Naor, J.: Machine minimization for scheduling jobs with interval constraints. In: 45th Symposium on Foundations of Computer Science (FOCS 2004), 17–19 October 2004, Rome, Italy, Proceedings, pp. 81–90 (2004)
7. Desel, J., Esparza, J.: Free Choice Petri Nets. Cambridge University Press, Cambridge (1995)
8. Esparza, J., Hoffmann, P., Saha, R.: Polynomial analysis algorithms for free choice probabilistic workflow nets. In: Agha, G., Van Houdt, B. (eds.) QEST 2016. LNCS, vol. 9826, pp. 89–104. Springer, Cham (2016). https://doi.org/10.1007/978-3-319-43425-4_6
9. Fahland, D., Favre, C., Jobstmann, B., Koehler, J., Lohmann, N., Völzer, H., Wolf, K.: Instantaneous soundness checking of industrial business process models. In: Dayal, U., Eder, J., Koehler, J., Reijers, H.A. (eds.) BPM 2009. LNCS, vol. 5701, pp. 278–293. Springer, Heidelberg (2009). https://doi.org/10.1007/978-3-642-03848-8_19
10. Favre, C., Fahland, D., Völzer, H.: The relationship between workflow graphs and free-choice workflow nets. Inf. Syst. **47**, 197–219 (2015)
11. Hall, N.G., Sriskandarajah, C.: A survey of machine scheduling problems with blocking and no-wait in process. Oper. Res. **44**(3), 510–525 (1996)
12. Kiepuszewski, B., ter Hofstede, A.H.M., van der Aalst, W.M.P.: Fundamentals of control flow in workflows. Acta Inf. **39**(3), 143–209 (2003)

13. Liu, L., Zhang, M., Lin, Y., Qin, L.: A survey on workflow management and scheduling in cloud computing. In: 14th IEEE/ACM International Symposium on Cluster, Cloud and Grid Computing, CCGrid 2014, Chicago, IL, USA, 26–29 May 2014, pp. 837–846 (2014)
14. Lougee-Heimer, R.: The common optimization interface for operations research: promoting open-source software in the operations research community. IBM J. Res. Dev. **47**(1), 57–66 (2003)
15. Meyer, P.J., Esparza, J., Völzer, H.: Computing the concurrency threshold of sound free-choice workflow nets. arXiv:1802.08064 [cs.LO] (2018)
16. Murata, T.: Petri nets: properties, analysis, and applications. Proc. IEEE **77**(4), 541–576 (1989)
17. Pinedo, M.L.: Scheduling: Theory, Algorithms, and Systems. Springer, New York (2016). https://doi.org/10.1007/978-1-4614-2361-4
18. Ullman, J.: NP-complete scheduling problems. J. Comput. Syst. Sci. **10**(3), 384–393 (1975)
19. Wolf, K.: Generating Petri net state spaces. In: Kleijn, J., Yakovlev, A. (eds.) ICATPN 2007. LNCS, vol. 4546, pp. 29–42. Springer, Heidelberg (2007). https://doi.org/10.1007/978-3-540-73094-1_5
20. Xu, J., Liu, C., Zhao, X.: Resource allocation vs. business process improvement: how they impact on each other. In: Dumas, M., Reichert, M., Shan, M.-C. (eds.) BPM 2008. LNCS, vol. 5240, pp. 228–243. Springer, Heidelberg (2008). https://doi.org/10.1007/978-3-540-85758-7_18

Fine-Grained Complexity of Safety Verification

Peter Chini$^{(\boxtimes)}$, Roland Meyer$^{(\boxtimes)}$, and Prakash Saivasan$^{(\boxtimes)}$

TU Braunschweig, Braunschweig, Germany
{p.chini,roland.meyer,p.saivasan}@tu-bs.de

Abstract. We study the fine-grained complexity of Leader Contributor Reachability (LCR) and Bounded-Stage Reachability (BSR), two variants of the safety verification problem for shared-memory concurrent programs. For both problems, the memory is a single variable over a finite data domain. We contribute new verification algorithms and lower bounds based on the Exponential Time Hypothesis (ETH) and kernels.

LCR is the question whether a designated leader thread can reach an unsafe state when interacting with a certain number of equal contributor threads. We suggest two parameterizations: (1) By the size of the data domain D and the size of the leader L, and (2) by the size of the contributors C. We present two algorithms, running in $\mathcal{O}^*((L \cdot (D+1))^{L \cdot D} \cdot D^D)$ and $\mathcal{O}^*(4^C)$ time, showing that both parameterizations are fixed-parameter tractable. Further, we suggest a modification of the first algorithm suitable for practical instances. The upper bounds are complemented by (matching) lower bounds based on ETH and kernels.

For BSR, we consider programs involving t different threads. We restrict the analysis to computations where the write permission changes s times between the threads. BSR asks whether a given configuration is reachable via such an s-stage computation. When parameterized by P, the maximum size of a thread, and t, the interesting observation is that the problem has a large number of difficult instances. Formally, we show that there is no polynomial kernel, no compression algorithm that reduces D or s to a polynomial dependence on P and t. This indicates that symbolic methods may be harder to find for this problem.

A full version of the paper is available as [9].

1 Introduction

We study the fine-grained complexity of two safety verification problems [1,16, 27] for shared-memory concurrent programs. The motivation to reconsider these problems are recent developments in fine-grained complexity theory [6,10,30,33]. They suggest that classifications such as NP or even FPT are too coarse to explain the success of verification methods. Instead, it should be possible to identify the precise influence that parameters of the input have on the verification time. Our contribution confirms this idea. We give new verification algorithms for the two problems that, for the first time, can be proven optimal in the sense of fine-grained complexity theory. To state the results, we need some background. As we proceed, we explain the development of fine-grained complexity theory.

© The Author(s) 2018
D. Beyer and M. Huisman (Eds.): TACAS 2018, LNCS 10806, pp. 20–37, 2018.
https://doi.org/10.1007/978-3-319-89963-3_2

There is a well-known gap between the success that verification tools see in practice and the judgments about computational hardness that worst case complexity is able to give. The applicability of verification tools steadily increases by tuning them towards industrial instances. The complexity estimation is stuck with considering the input size (or at best assumes certain parameters to be constant, which does not mean much if the runtime is then n^k, where n is the input size and k the parameter).

The observation of a gap between practical algorithms and complexity theory is not unique to verification but made in every field that has to solve computationally hard problems. Complexity theory has taken up the challenge to close the gap. So-called *fixed-parameter tractability* (FPT) [11, 13] proposes to identify parameters k so that the runtime is $f(k)poly(n)$, where f is a computable function. These parameters are powerful in the sense that they dominate the complexity.

For an FPT result to be useful, function f should only be mildly exponential, and of course k should be small in the instances of interest. Intuitively, they are what one needs to optimize. *Fine-grained complexity* is the study of upper and lower bounds on function f. Indeed, the fine-grained complexity of a problem is written as $O^*(f(k))$, emphasizing f and k and suppressing the polynomial part. For upper bounds, the approach is still to come up with an algorithm.

For lower bounds, fine-grained complexity has taken a new and very pragmatic perspective. For the problem of n-variable 3-SAT the best known algorithm runs in 2^n, and this bound has not been improved since 1970. The idea is to take improvements on this problem as unlikely, known as the exponential-time hypothesis (ETH) [30]. ETH serves as a lower bound that is reduced to other problems [33]. An even stronger assumption about n-variable SAT, called SETH [6, 30], and a similar one about *Set Cover* [10] allow for lower bounds like the absence of $(2 - \varepsilon)^n$ algorithms.

In this work, we contribute fine-grained complexity results for verification problems on concurrent programs. The first problem is reachability for a leader thread that is interacting with an unbounded number of contributors (LCR) [16, 27]. We show that, assuming a parameterization by the size of the leader L and the size of the data domain D, the problem can be solved in $O^*((L \cdot (D+1))^{L \cdot D} \cdot D^D)$. At the heart of the algorithm is a compression of computations into witnesses. To check reachability, our algorithm then iterates over candidates for witnesses and checks each of them for being a proper witness. Interestingly, we can formulate a variant of the algorithm that seems to be suited for large state spaces.

Using ETH, we show that the algorithm is (almost) optimal. Moreover, the problem is shown to have a large number of hard instances. Technically, there is no polynomial kernel [4, 5]. Experience with kernel lower bounds is still limited. This notion of hardness seems to indicate that symbolic methods are hard to apply to the problem. The lower bounds that we present share similarities with the reductions from [7, 24, 25].

If we consider the size of the contributors a parameter, we obtain a singly exponential upper bound that we also prove to be tight. The saturation-based technique that we use is inspired by thread-modular reasoning [20,21,26,29].

The second problem we study generalizes bounded context switching. Bounded-stage reachability (BSR) asks whether a state is reachable if there is a bound s on the number of times the write permission is allowed to change between the threads [1]. Again, we show the new form of kernel lower bound. The result is tricky and highlights the power of the computation model.

The results are summarized by the table below. Two findings stand out, we highlight them in gray. We present a new algorithm for LCR. Moreover, we suggest kernel lower bounds as hardness indicators for verification problems. The lower bound for BSR is particularly difficult to achieve.

Problem	Upper Bound	Lower Bound	Kernel
LCR(D, L)	$\mathcal{O}^*((L \cdot (D+1))^{L \cdot D} \cdot D^D)$	$2^{o(\sqrt{L \cdot D} \cdot \log(L \cdot D))}$	No poly.
LCR(C)	$\mathcal{O}^*(4^C)$	$2^{o(C)}$	No poly.
BSR(P, t)	$\mathcal{O}^*(P^{2t})$	$2^{o(t \cdot \log(P))}$	No poly.

Related Work. Concurrent programs communicating through a shared memory and having a fixed number of threads have been extensively studied [2,14,22,28]. The leader contributor reachability problem as considered in this paper was introduced as parametrized reachability in [27]. In [16], it was shown to be NP-complete when only finite-state programs are involved and PSPACE-complete for recursive programs. In [31], the parameterized pairwise-reachability problem was considered and shown to be decidable. Parameterized reachability under a variant of round-robin scheduling was proven decidable in [32].

The bounded-stage restriction on the computations of concurrent programs as considered here was introduced in [1]. The corresponding reachability problem was shown to be NP-complete when only finite-state programs are involved. The problem remains in NEXP-time and PSPACE-hard for a combination of counters and a single pushdown. The bounded-stage restriction generalizes the concept of bounded context switching from [34], which was shown to be NP-complete in that paper. In [8], FPT algorithms for bounded context switching were obtained under various parameterization. In [3], networks of pushdowns communicating through a shared memory were analyzed under various topological restrictions.

There have been few efforts to obtain fixed-parameter-tractable algorithms for automata and verification-related problems. FPT algorithms for automata problems have been studied in [18,19,35]. In [12], model-checking problems for synchronized executions on parallel components were considered and proven intractable. In [15], the notion of conflict serializability was introduced for the TSO memory model and an FPT algorithm for checking serializability was provided. The complexity of predicting atomicity violations on concurrent systems was considered in [17]. The finding is that FPT solutions are unlikely to exist.

2   Preliminaries

We introduce our model for programs, which is fairly standard and taken from [1, 16,27], and give the basics on fixed-parameter tractability.

Programs. A program consists of finitely many threads that access a shared memory. The memory is modeled to hold a single value at a time. Formally, a *(shared-memory) program* is a tuple $\mathcal{A} = (D, a^0, (P_i)_{i \in [1..t]})$. Here, D is the data domain of the memory and $a^0 \in D$ is the initial value. Threads are modeled as control-flow graphs that write values to or read values from the memory. These operations are captured by $Op(D) = \{!a, ?a \mid a \in D\}$. We use the notation $W(D) = \{!a \mid a \in D\}$ for the write operations and $R(D) = \{?a \mid a \in D\}$ for the read operations. A thread P_{id} is a non-deterministic finite automaton $(Op(D), Q, q^0, \delta)$ over the alphabet of operations. The set of states is Q with $q^0 \in Q$ the initial state. The final states will depend on the verification task. The transition relation is $\delta \subseteq Q \times (Op(D) \cup \{\varepsilon\}) \times Q$. We extend it to words and also write $q \xrightarrow{w} q'$ for $q' \in \delta(q, w)$. Whenever we need to distinguish between different threads, we add indices and write Q_{id} or δ_{id}.

The semantics of a program is given in terms of labeled transitions between configurations. A *configuration* is a pair $(pc, a) \in (Q_1 \times \cdots \times Q_t) \times D$. The program counter pc is a vector that shows the current state $pc(i) \in Q_i$ of each thread P_i. Moreover, the configuration gives the current value in memory. We call $c^0 = (pc^0, a^0)$ with $pc^0(i) = q_i^0$ for all $i \in [1..t]$ the initial configuration. Let C denote the set of all configurations. The transition relation among configurations $\rightarrow \subseteq C \times (Op(D) \cup \{\varepsilon\}) \times C$ is obtained by lifting the transition relations of the threads. To define it, let $pc_1 = pc[i = q_i]$, meaning thread P_i is in state q_i and otherwise the program counter coincides with pc. Let $pc_2 = pc[i = q_i']$. If thread P_i tries to read with the transition $q_i \xrightarrow{?a} q_i'$, then $(pc_1, a) \xrightarrow{?a} (pc_2, a)$. Note that the memory is required to hold the desired value. If the thread has the transition $q_i \xrightarrow{!b} q_i'$, then $(pc_1, a) \xrightarrow{!b} (pc_2, b)$. Finally, $q_i \xrightarrow{\varepsilon} q_i'$ yields $(pc_1, a) \xrightarrow{\varepsilon} (pc_2, a)$. The program's transition relation is generalized to words, $c \xrightarrow{w} c'$. We call such a sequence of consecutive labeled transitions a *computation*. To indicate that there is a word that justifies a computation from c to c', we write $c \rightarrow^* c'$. We may use an index $\xrightarrow{w}_i$ to indicate that the computation was induced by thread P_i. Where appropriate, we also use the program as an index, $\xrightarrow{w}_\mathcal{A}$.

Fixed-Parameter Tractability. We wish to study the fine-grained complexity of safety verification problems for the above programs. This means our goal is to identify parameters of these problems that have two properties. First, in practical instances they are small. Second, assuming that these parameters are small, show that there are efficient verification algorithms. *Parametrized complexity* makes precise the idea of an algorithm being efficient relative to a parameter.

A *parameterized problem* L is a subset of $\Sigma^* \times \mathbb{N}$. The problem is *fixed-parameter tractable* if there is a deterministic algorithm that, given $(x, k) \in \Sigma^* \times \mathbb{N}$, decides $(x, k) \in L$ in time $f(k) \cdot |x|^{O(1)}$. We use FPT for the class of all fixed-parameter-tractable problems and say *a problem is* FPT to mean it is in that class. Note that f is a computable function that only depends on the parameter k. It is common to denote the runtime by $\mathcal{O}^*(f(k))$ and suppress the polynomial part. We will be interested in the precise dependence on the parameter, in upper and lower bounds on the function f. This study is often referred to as *fine-grained complexity*.

Lower bounds on f are obtained by the *Exponential Time Hypothesis* (ETH). It assumes that there is no algorithm solving n-variable 3-SAT in $2^{o(n)}$ time. The reasoning is as follows: If f dropped below a certain bound, ETH would fail.

While many parameterizations of NP-hard problems were proven to be fixed-parameter tractable, there are problems that are unlikely to be FPT. Such problems are hard for the complexity class W[1]. The appropriate notion of reduction for a theory of relative hardness in parameterized complexity is called *parameterized reduction*.

3   Leader Contributor Reachability

We consider the *leader contributor reachability problem* for shared-memory programs. The problem was introduced in [27] and shown to be NP-complete in [16] for the finite-state case.[1] We contribute two new verification algorithms that target two parameterizations of the problem. In both cases, our algorithms establish fixed-parameter tractability. Moreover, with matching lower bounds we prove them to be optimal even in the fine-grained sense.

An instance of the leader contributor reachability problem is given by a shared-memory program of the form $\mathcal{A} = (D, a^0, (P_L, (P_i)_{i\in[1..t]}))$. The program has a designated *leader* thread P_L and several *contributor* threads $P_1, \ldots, P_t$. In addition, we are given a set of unsafe states for the leader. The task is to check whether the leader can reach an unsafe state when interacting with a number of instances of the contributors. It is worth noting that the problem can be reduced to having a single contributor. Let the corresponding thread P_C be the union of $P_1, \ldots, P_t$ (constructed using an initial ε-transition). We base our complexity analysis on this simplified formulation of the problem.

For the definition, let $\mathcal{A} = (D, a^0, (P_L, P_C))$ be a program with two threads. Let $F_L \subseteq Q_L$ be a set of unsafe states of the leader. For $t \in \mathbb{N}$, define the program $\mathcal{A}^t = (D, a^0, (P_L, (P_C)_{i\in[1..t]}))$ to have t copies of P_C. Further, let C^f be the set of configurations where the leader is in an unsafe state (from F_L). The problem of interest is as follows:

Leader Contributor Reachability (LCR)
Input: A program $\mathcal{A} = (D, a^0, (P_L, P_C))$ and a set of states $F_L \subseteq Q_L$.
Question: Is there a $t \in \mathbb{N}$ such that $c^0 \rightarrow^*_{\mathcal{A}^t} c$ for some $c \in C^f$?

---

[1] The problem is called parameterized reachability in these works. We renamed it to avoid confusion with parameterized complexity.

We consider two parameterizations of LCR. First, we parameterize by D, the size of the data domain D, and L, the number of states of the leader P_L. We denote the parameterization by LCR(D, L). While for LCR(D, L) we obtain an FPT algorithm, it is not likely that LCR(D) and LCR(L) admit the same. These parameterizations are W[1]-hard. For details, we refer to the full version [9].

The second parameterization that we consider is LCR(C), a parameterization by the number of states of the contributor P_C. We prove that the parameter is enough to obtain an FPT algorithm.

3.1   Parameterization by Memory and Leader

We give an algorithm that solves LCR in time $\mathcal{O}^*((L \cdot (D+1))^{L \cdot D} \cdot D^D)$, which means LCR(D, L) is FPT. We then show how to modify the algorithm to solve instances of LCR as they are likely to occur in practice. Interestingly, the modified version of the algorithm lends itself to an efficient implementation based on off-the-shelf sequential model checkers. We conclude with lower bounds for LCR(D, L).

Upper Bound. We give an algorithm for the parameterization LCR(D, L). The key idea is to compactly represent computations that may be present in an instance of the given program. To this end, we introduce a domain of so-called witness candidates. The main technical result, Lemma 4, links computations and witness candidates. It shows that reachability of an unsafe state holds in an instance of the program if and only if there is a witness candidate that is valid (in a precise sense). With this, our algorithm iterates over all witness candidates and checks each of them for being valid. To state the overall result, let $Wit(L, D) = (L \cdot (D+1))^{L \cdot D} \cdot D^D \cdot L$ be the number of witness candidates and let $Valid(L, D, C) = L^3 \cdot D^2 \cdot C^2$ be the time it takes to check validity of a candidate. Note that it is polynomial.

Theorem 1. LCR *can be solved in time* $\mathcal{O}(Wit(L, D) \cdot Valid(L, D, C))$.

Let $\mathcal{A} = (D, a^0, (P_L, P_C))$ be the program of interest and F_L be the set of unsafe states in the leader. Assume we are given a computation ρ showing that P_L can reach a state in F_L when interacting with a number of contributors. We explain the main ideas to find an efficient representation for ρ that still allows for the reconstruction of a similar computation. To simplify the presentation, we assume the leader never writes ($!a$) and immediately reads ($?a$) the same value. If this is the case, the read can be replaced by ε.

In a first step, we delete most of the moves in ρ that were carried out by contributors. We only keep *first writes*. For each value a, this is the write transition $fw(a) = c \xrightarrow{!a} c'$ where a is written by a contributor for the first time. The reason we can omit subsequent writes of a is the following: If $fw(a)$ is carried out by contributor P_1, we can assume that there is an arbitrary number of other contributors that all mimicked the behavior of P_1. This means whenever P_1 did a transition, they copycatted it right away. Hence, there are arbitrarily many contributors pending to write a. Phrased differently, the symbol a is available for the leader whenever P_L needs to read it. The idea goes back to the *Copycat Lemma* stated in [16]. The reads of the contributors are omitted as well. We will make sure they can be served by the first writes and the moves done by P_L.

After the deletion, we are left with a shorter expression ρ'. We turn it into a word w over the alphabet $Q_L \cup D_\perp \cup \bar{D}$ with $D_\perp = D \cup \{\perp\}$ and $\bar{D} = \{\bar{a} \mid a \in D\}$. Each transition $c \xrightarrow{!a/?a/\varepsilon}_L c'$ in ρ' that is due to the leader moving from q to q' is mapped (i) to $q.a.q'$ if it is a write and (ii) to $q.\perp.q'$ otherwise. A first write $fw(a) = c \xrightarrow{a} c'$ of a contributor is mapped to $\bar{a}$. We may assume that the resulting word w is of the form $w = w_1.w_2$ with $w_1 \in ((Q_L.D_\perp)^*.\bar{D})^*$ and $w_2 \in (Q_L.D_\perp)^*.F_L$. Note that w can still be of unbounded length.

In order to find a witness of bounded length, we compress w_1 and w_2 to w_1' and w_2'. Between two first writes $\bar{a}$ and $\bar{b}$ in w_1, the leader can perform an unbounded number of transitions, represented by a word in $(Q_L.D_\perp)^*$. Hence, there are states $q \in Q_L$ repeating between $\bar{a}$ and $\bar{b}$. We contract the word between the first and the last occurrence of q into just a single state q. This state now represents a loop on P_L. Since there are L states in the leader, this bounds the number of contractions. Furthermore, we know that the number of first writes is bounded by D, each symbol can be written for the first time at most once. Thus, the compressed string w_1' is in the language $((Q_L.D_\perp)^{\leq L}.\bar{D})^{\leq D}$.

The word w_2 is of the form $w_2 = q.u$ for a state $q \in Q_L$ and a word u. We truncate the word u and only keep the state q. Then we know that there is a computation leading from q to a state in F_L where P_L can potentially write any symbol but read only those symbols which occurred as a first write in w_1'. Altogether, we are left with a word of bounded length.

Definition 2. *The set of witness candidates is* $\mathcal{E} = ((Q_L.D_\perp)^{\leq L}.\bar{D})^{\leq D}.Q_L$.

To characterize computations in terms of witness candidates, we define the notion of validity. This needs some notation. Consider a word $w = w_1 \ldots w_\ell$ over some alphabet Γ. For $i \in [1..\ell]$, we set $w[i] = w_i$ and $w[1..i] = w_1 \ldots w_i$. If $\Gamma' \subseteq \Gamma$, we use $w \downarrow_{\Gamma'}$ for the projection of w to the letters in Γ'.

Consider a witness candidate $w \in \mathcal{E}$ and let $i \in [1..|w|]$. We use $\bar{D}(w,i)$ for the set of all first writes that occurred in w up to position i. Formally, $\bar{D}(w,i) = \{a \mid \bar{a}$ is a letter in $w[1..i] \downarrow_{\bar{D}}\}$. We abbreviate $\bar{D}(w,|w|)$ as $\bar{D}(w)$. Let $q \in Q_L$ and $S \subseteq D$. Recall that the state represents a loop in P_L. The set of all letters written within a loop from q to q when reading only symbols from S is $\text{Loop}(q,S) = \{a \mid a \in D$ and $\exists v_1, v_2 \in (W(D) \cup R(S))^* : q \xrightarrow{v_1!av_2}_L q\}$.

The definition of validity is given next. The three requirements are made precise in the text below.

Definition 3. *A witness candidate* $w \in \mathcal{E}$ *is valid if it satisfies the following properties: (1) First writes are unique. (2) The word w encodes a run in P_L. (3) There are supportive computations on the contributors.*

(1) If $w \downarrow_{\bar{D}} = \bar{c}_1 \ldots \bar{c}_\ell$, then the $\bar{c}_i$ are pairwise different.

(2) Let $w \downarrow_{Q_L \cup D_\perp} = q_1 a_1 q_2 a_2 \ldots a_\ell q_{\ell+1}$. If $a_i \in D$, then $q_i \xrightarrow{!a_i}_L q_{i+1} \in \delta_L$ is a write transition of P_L. If $a_i = \perp$, then we have an ε-transition $q_i \xrightarrow{\varepsilon}_L q_{i+1}$.

Alternatively, there is a read $q_i \xrightarrow{?a}_L q_{i+1}$ of a symbol $a \in \bar{D}(w, \text{pos}(a_i))$ that already occurred within a first write (the leader does not read the own writes). Here, we use $\text{pos}(a_i)$ to access the position of a_i in w. State $q_1 = q_L^0$ is initial. There is a run from $q_{\ell+1}$ to a state $q_f \in F_L$. During this run, reading is restricted to symbols that occurred as first writes in w. Formally, there is a $v \in (W(D) \cup R(\bar{D}(w)))^*$ such that $q_{\ell+1} \xrightarrow{v}_L q_f$.

(3) For each prefix $v\bar{a}$ of w with $\bar{a} \in \bar{D}$ there is a computation $q_C^0 \xrightarrow{u!a}_C q$ on P_C so that the reads in u can be obtained from v. Formally, let $u' = u{\downarrow}_{R(D)}$. Then there is an embedding of u' into v, a monotone map $\mu : [1..|u'|] \rightarrow [1..|v|]$ that satisfies the following. Let $u'[i] = ?a$ with $a \in D$. The read is served in one of the following three ways. We may have $v[\mu(i)] = a$, which corresponds to a write of a by P_L. Alternatively, $v[\mu(i)] = q \in Q_L$ and $a \in \text{Loop}(q, \bar{D}(w, \mu(i)))$. This amounts to reading from a leader's write that was executed in a loop. Finally, we may have $a \in \bar{D}(w, \mu(i))$, corresponding to reading from another contributor.

Lemma 4. *There is a $t \in \mathbb{N}$ so that $c^0 \rightarrow_{\mathcal{A}^t}^* c$ with $c \in C^f$ if and only if there is a valid witness candidate $w \in \mathcal{E}$.*

Our algorithm iterates over all witness candidates $w \in \mathcal{E}$ and tests whether w is valid. The number of candidates $Wit(\text{L}, \text{D})$ is given by $(\text{L} \cdot (\text{D} + 1))^{\text{L} \cdot \text{D}} \cdot \text{D}^\text{D} \cdot \text{L}$. This is due to the fact that we can force a witness candidate to have maximum length via inserting padding symbols. The number of candidates constitutes the first factor of the runtime stated in Theorem 1. The polynomial factor $Valid(\text{L}, \text{D}, \text{C})$ is due to the following Lemma. Details are given in the full version of the paper [9].

Lemma 5. *Validity of $w \in \mathcal{E}$ can be checked in time $\mathcal{O}(L^3 \cdot D^2 \cdot C^2)$.*

Practical Algorithm. We improve the above algorithm so that it should work well on practical instances. The idea is to factorize the leader along its *strongly connected components* (SCCs), the number of which is assumed to be small in real programs. Technically, our improved algorithm works with *valid SCC-witnesses*. They symbolically represent SCCs rather than loops in the leader. To state the complexity, we define the *straight-line depth*, the number of SCCs the leader may visit during a computation. The definition needs a graph construction.

Let $\mathcal{V} \subseteq \bar{D}^{\leq \text{D}}$ contain only words that do not repeat letters. Let $r = \bar{c}_1 \ldots \bar{c}_\ell \in \mathcal{V}$ and $i \in [0..\ell]$. By $P_L {\downarrow}_i$ we denote the automaton obtained from P_L by removing all transitions that read a value outside $\{c_1, \ldots, c_i\}$. Let $\text{SCC}(P_L {\downarrow}_i)$ denote the set of all SCCs in this automaton. We construct the directed graph $G(P_L, r)$ as follows. The vertices are the SCCs of all $P_L {\downarrow}_i$, $i \in [0..\ell]$. There is an edge between $S, S' \in \text{SCC}(P_L {\downarrow}_i)$, if there are states $q \in S, q' \in S'$ with $q \rightarrow q'$ in $P_L {\downarrow}_i$. If $S \in \text{SCC}(P_L {\downarrow}_{i-1})$ and $S' \in \text{SCC}(P_L {\downarrow}_i)$, we only get an edge if we can get from S to S' by reading c_i. Note that the graph is acyclic.

The depth $d(r)$ of P_L relative to r is the length of the longest path in $G(P_L, r)$. The *straight-line depth* is $\text{d} = \max\{d(r) \mid r \in \mathcal{V}\}$. The *number of SCCs* s is the size of $\text{SCC}(P_L {\downarrow}_0)$. With these values at hand, the number of SCC-witness candidates (the definition of which can be found in the full version [9]) can be bounded by $Wit_{SCC}(\mathsf{s}, \mathsf{D}, \mathsf{d}) \leq (\mathsf{s} \cdot (\mathsf{D} + 1))^{\mathsf{d}} \cdot \mathsf{D}^{\mathsf{D}} \cdot 2^{\mathsf{D}+\mathsf{d}}$. The time needed to test whether a candidate is valid is $Valid_{SCC}(\mathsf{L}, \mathsf{D}, \mathsf{C}, \mathsf{d}) = \mathsf{L}^2 \cdot \mathsf{D} \cdot \mathsf{C}^2 \cdot \mathsf{d}^2$.

Theorem 6. LCR *can be solved in time* $\mathcal{O}(Wit_{SCC}(\mathsf{s}, D, \mathsf{d}) \cdot Valid_{SCC}(L, D, C, \mathsf{d}))$.

For this algorithm, what matters is that the leader's state space is strongly connected. The number of states has limited impact on the runtime.

Lower Bound. We prove that the algorithm from Theorem 1 is only a root factor away from being optimal: A $2^{o(\sqrt{\mathsf{L} \cdot \mathsf{D}} \cdot \log(\mathsf{L} \cdot \mathsf{D}))}$-time algorithm for LCR would contradict ETH. We achieve the lower bound by a reduction from $\mathsf{k} \times \mathsf{k}$ Clique, the problem of finding a clique of size k in a graph the vertices of which are elements of a $k \times k$ matrix. Moreover, the clique has to contain one vertex from each row. Unless ETH fails, the problem cannot be solved in time $2^{o(k \cdot \log(k))}$ [33].

Technically, we construct from an instance (G, k) of $\mathsf{k} \times \mathsf{k}$ Clique an instance $(\mathcal{A} = (D, a^0, (P_L, P_C)), F_L)$ of LCR such that $\mathsf{D} = \mathcal{O}(k)$ and $\mathsf{L} = \mathcal{O}(k)$. Furthermore, we show that G contains the desired clique of size k if and only if there is a $t \in \mathbb{N}$ such that $c^0 \rightarrow^*_{\mathcal{A}^t} c$ with $c \in C^f$. Suppose we had an algorithm for LCR running in time $2^{o(\sqrt{\mathsf{L} \cdot \mathsf{D}} \cdot \log(\mathsf{L} \cdot \mathsf{D}))}$. Combined with the reduction, this would yield an algorithm for $\mathsf{k} \times \mathsf{k}$ Clique with runtime $2^{o(\sqrt{k^2} \cdot \log(k^2))} = 2^{o(k \cdot \log k)}$. But unless ETH fails, such an algorithm cannot exist.

Proposition 7. LCR *cannot be solved in time* $2^{o(\sqrt{L \cdot D} \cdot \log(L \cdot D))}$ *unless* ETH *fails.*

We assume that the vertices V of G are given by tuples (i, j) with $i, j \in [1..k]$, where i denotes the row and j denotes the column. In the reduction, we need the leader and the contributors to communicate on the vertices of G. However, we cannot store tuples (i, j) in the memory as this would cause a quadratic blow-up $\mathsf{D} = \mathcal{O}(k^2)$. Instead, we communicate a vertex (i, j) as a string $\mathtt{row}(i).\mathtt{col}(j)$. We distinguish between row and column symbols to avoid stuttering, the repeated reading of the same symbol. With this, it cannot happen that a thread reads a row symbol twice and takes it for a column.

The program starts its computation with each contributor choosing a vertex (i, j) to store. For simplicity, we denote a contributor storing (i, j) by $P_{(i,j)}$. Note that there can be copies of $P_{(i,j)}$.

Since there are arbitrarily many contributors, the chosen vertices are only a superset of the clique we want to find. To cut away the false vertices, the leader P_L guesses for each row the vertex belonging to the clique. To this end, the program performs for each $i \in [1..k]$ the following steps: If (i, j_i) is the vertex of interest, P_L first writes $\mathtt{row}(i)$ to the memory. Each contributor that is still active reads the symbol and moves on for one state. Then P_L communicates the column by writing $\mathtt{col}(j_i)$. Again, the active contributors $P_{(i',j')}$ read.

A contributor can react to the read symbol in three different ways: (1) If $i' \neq i$, the contributor $P_{(i',j')}$ stores a vertex of a different row. The computation in $P_{(i',j')}$ can only go on if (i', j') is connected to (i, j_i) in G. Otherwise it will stop. (2) If $i' = i$ and $j' = j_i$, then $P_{(i',j')}$ stores exactly the vertex guessed by P_L. In this case, $P_{(i',j')}$ can continue its computation. (3) If $i' = i$ and $j' \neq j_i$, thread $P_{(i',j')}$ stores a different vertex from row i. The contributor has to stop its computation.

After k such rounds, there are only contributors left that store vertices guessed by P_L. Furthermore, each two of these vertices are connected. Hence, they form a clique. To transmit this information to P_L, each $P_{(i,j_i)}$ writes $\#_i$ to the memory, a special symbol for row i. After P_L has read the string $\#_1 \ldots \#_k$, it moves to its final state. A formal construction can be found in the full version [9].

Absence of a Polynomial Kernel. A kernelization of a parameterized problem is a compression algorithm. Given an instance, it returns an equivalent instance the size of which is bounded by a function only in the parameter. From an algorithmic perspective, kernels put a bound on the number of hard instances of the problem. Indeed, the search for small kernels is a key interest in algorithmics, similar to the search for fast FPT algorithms. Even more, it can be shown that kernels exist if and only if a problem admits an FPT algorithm [11].

Let Q be a parameterized problem. A *kernelization* of Q is an algorithm that transforms, in polynomial time, a given instance (B, k) into an equivalent instance (B', k') such that $|B'| + k' \leq g(k)$, where g is a computable function. If g is a polynomial, we say that Q admits a *polynomial kernel*.

Unfortunately, for many problems the community failed to come up with polynomial kernels. This lead to the contrary approach, namely disproving their existence [4,5,23]. Such a result constitutes an exponential lower bound on the number of hard instances. Like computational hardness results, such a bound is seen as an indication of general hardness of the problem. Technically, the existence of a polynomial kernel for the problem of interest is shown to imply $\mathsf{NP} \subseteq \mathsf{coNP/poly}$. But this inclusion is unlikely as it would cause a collapse of the polynomial hierarchy to the third level [36].

In order to link the occurrence of a polynomial kernel for $\mathsf{LCR(D, L)}$ with the above inclusion, we follow the framework developed in [5]. Let Γ be an alphabet. A *polynomial equivalence relation* is an equivalence relation $\mathcal{R}$ on Γ^* with the following properties: Given $x, y \in \Gamma^*$, it can be decided in time polynomial in $|x| + |y|$ whether $(x, y) \in \mathcal{R}$. Moreover, for each n there are at most polynomially many equivalence classes in $\mathcal{R}$ restricted to $\Gamma^{\leq n}$.

The key tool for proving kernel lower bounds are cross-compositions: Let $L \subseteq \Gamma^*$ be a language and $Q \subseteq \Gamma^* \times \mathbb{N}$ be a parameterized language. We say that L *cross-composes* into Q if there exists a polynomial equivalence relation $\mathcal{R}$ and an algorithm $\mathcal{C}$, the *cross-composition*, with the following properties: $\mathcal{C}$ takes as input $\varphi_1, \ldots, \varphi_I \in \Gamma^*$, all equivalent under $\mathcal{R}$. It computes in time polynomial in $\sum_{\ell=1}^{I} |\varphi_\ell|$ a string $(y, k) \in \Gamma^* \times \mathbb{N}$ such that $(y, k) \in Q$ if and only if there is an $\ell \in [1..I]$ with $\varphi_\ell \in L$. Furthermore, $k \leq p(\max_{\ell \in [1..I]} |\varphi_\ell| + \log(I))$ for a polynomial p.

It was shown in [5] that a cross-composition of any NP-hard language into a parameterized language Q prohibits the existence of a polynomial kernel for

Q unless $NP \subseteq coNP/poly$. In order to make use of this result, we show how to cross-compose 3-SAT into $LCR(D, L)$. This yields the following:

Theorem 8. $LCR(D, L)$ *does not admit a poly. kernel unless* $NP \subseteq coNP/poly$.

The difficulty of finding a cross-composition is in the restriction on the size of the parameters. This affects D and L: Both parameters are not allowed to depend polynomially on I, the number of given 3-SAT-instances. We resolve the polynomial dependence by encoding the choice of a 3-SAT-instance into the contributors via a binary tree.

Proof (Idea). Assume some encoding of Boolean formulas as strings over a finite alphabet. We use the polynomial equivalence relation $\mathcal{R}$ defined as follows: Two strings φ and ψ are equivalent under $\mathcal{R}$ if both encode 3-SAT-instances, and the numbers of clauses and variables coincide. On strings of bounded length, $\mathcal{R}$ has polynomially many equivalence classes.

Let the given 3-SAT-instances be $\varphi_1, \ldots, \varphi_I$. Every two of them are equivalent under $\mathcal{R}$. This means that all φ_ℓ have the same number of clauses m and use the same set of variables $\{x_1, \ldots, x_n\}$. We assume that $\varphi_\ell = C_1^\ell \wedge \cdots \wedge C_m^\ell$.

We construct a program proceeding in three phases. First, it chooses an instance φ_ℓ, then it guesses a valuation for all variables, and in the third phase it verifies that the valuation satisfies φ_ℓ. While the second and the third phase do not cause a dependence of the parameters on I, the first phase does. It is not possible to guess a number $\ell \in [1..I]$ and communicate it via the memory as this would provoke a polynomial dependence of D on I.

To implement the first phase without a polynomial dependence, we transmit the indices of the 3-SAT-instances in binary. The leader guesses and writes tuples $(u_1, 1), \ldots, (u_{\log(I)}, \log(I))$ with $u_\ell \in \{0, 1\}$ to the memory. This amounts to choosing an instance φ_ℓ with binary representation $\texttt{bin}(\ell) = u_1 \ldots u_{\log(I)}$.

It is the contributors' task to store this choice. Each time, the leader writes a tuple (u_i, i), the contributors read and branch either to the left, if $u_i = 0$, or to the right, if $u_i = 1$. Hence, in the first phase, the contributors are binary trees with I leaves, each leaf storing the index of an instance φ_ℓ. Since we did not assume that I is a power of 2, there may be computations arriving at leaves that do not represent proper indices. In this case, the computation deadlocks.

The size of D and P_L in the first phase is $\mathcal{O}(\log(I))$. This satisfies the size-restrictions of a cross-composition.

For guessing the valuation in the second phase, the system communicates on tuples (x_i, v) with $i \in [1..n]$ and $v \in \{0, 1\}$. The leader guesses such a tuple for each variable and writes it to the memory. Any participating contributor is free to read one of the tuples. After reading, it stores the variable and the valuation.

In the third phase, the satisfiability check is performed as follows: Each contributor that is still active has stored in its current state the chosen instance φ_ℓ, a variable x_i, and its valuation v_i. Assume that x_i when evaluated to v_i satisfies C_j^ℓ, the j-th clause of φ_ℓ. Then the contributor loops in its current state while writing the symbol $\#_j$. The leader waits to read the string $\#_1 \ldots \#_m$. If P_L succeeds, we are sure that the m clauses of φ_ℓ were satisfied by the chosen valuation. Thus, φ_ℓ is satisfiable and P_L moves to its final state. For details of the construction, we refer to the full version of the paper [9]. □

3.2 Parameterization by Contributors

We show that the size of the contributors C has a wide influence on the complexity of LCR. We give an algorithm singly exponential in C, provide a matching lower bound, and prove the absence of a polynomial kernel.

Upper Bound. Our algorithm is based on saturation. We keep the states reachable by the contributors in a set and saturate it. This leads to a more compact representation of the program. Technically, we reduce LCR to a reachability problem on a finite automaton. The result is as follows.

Proposition 9. LCR *can be solved in time* $\mathcal{O}(4^C \cdot L^4 \cdot D^3 \cdot C^2)$.

The main observation is that keeping one set of states for all contributors suffices to represent a computation. Let $S \subseteq Q_C$ be the set of states reachable by the contributors in a given computation. By the *Copycat Lemma* [16], we can assume for each $q \in S$ an arbitrary number of contributors that are currently in state q. This means that we do not have to distinguish between different contributor instances.

Formally, we reduce the search space to $Q_L \times D \times \mathcal{P}(Q_C)$. Instead of storing explicit configurations, we store tuples (q_L, a, S), where $q_L \in Q_L$, $a \in D$, and $S \subseteq Q_C$. Between such tuples, the transition relation is as follows. Transitions of the leader change the state and the memory as expected. The contributors also change the memory but saturate S instead of changing the state. Formally, if there is a transition from $q \in S$ to q', we add q' to S.

Lemma 10. *There is a* $t \in \mathbb{N}$ *so that* $c^0 \rightarrow^*_{\mathcal{A}^t} c$ *with* $c \in C^f$ *if and only if there is a run from* $(q_L^0, a^0, \{q_C^0\})$ *to a state in* $F_L \times D \times \mathcal{P}(Q_C)$.

The dominant factor in the complexity estimation of Proposition 9 is the time needed to construct the state space. It takes time $\mathcal{O}(4^C \cdot L^4 \cdot D^3 \cdot C^2)$. For the definition and the proof of Lemma 10, we refer to the full version [9].

Lower Bound and Absence of a Polynomial Kernel. We present two lower bounds for LCR. The first is based on ETH: We show that there is no $2^{o(C)}$-time algorithm for LCR unless ETH fails. This indicates that the above algorithm is asymptotically optimal. Technically, we give a reduction from n-variable 3-SAT to LCR such that the size of the contributor in the constructed instance is $\mathcal{O}(n)$. Then a $2^{o(C)}$-time algorithm for LCR yields a $2^{o(n)}$-time algorithm for 3-SAT, a contradiction to ETH.

With a similar reduction, one can cross-compose 3-SAT into LCR(C). This shows that the problem does not admit a polynomial kernel. The precise constructions and proofs can be found in the full version [9].

Proposition 11

(a) LCR *cannot be solved in time* $2^{o(C)}$ *unless* ETH *fails.*
(b) LCR(C) *does not admit a polynomial kernel unless* NP $\subseteq$ coNP/poly.

4   Bounded-Stage Reachability

The *bounded-stage reachability problem* is a simultaneous reachability problem. It asks whether all threads of a program can reach an unsafe state when restricted to s-stage computations. These are computations where the write permission changes s times. The problem was first analyzed in [1] and shown to be NP-complete for finite-state programs. We give matching upper and lower bounds in terms of fine-grained complexity and prove the absence of a polynomial kernel.

Let $\mathcal{A} = (D, a^0, (P_i)_{i \in [1..t]})$ be a program. A *stage* is a computation in $\mathcal{A}$ where only one of the threads writes. The remaining threads are restricted to reading the memory. An s-*stage computation* is a computation that can be split into s parts, each of which forming a stage.

Bounded-Stage Reachability (BSR)
Input: A program $\mathcal{A} = (D, a^0, (P_i)_{i \in [1..t]})$, a set $C^f \subseteq C$, and $s \in \mathbb{N}$.
Question: Is there an s-stage computation $c^0 \rightarrow^*_{\mathcal{A}} c$ for some $c \in C^f$?

We focus on a parameterization of BSR by P, the maximum number of states of a thread, and t, the number of threads. Let it be denoted by BSR(P, t). We prove that the parameterization is FPT and present a matching lower bound. The main result in this section is the absence of a polynomial kernel for BSR(P, t). The result is technically involved and reveals hardness of the problem.

Parameterizations of BSR involving D and s, the number of stages, are not interesting for fine-grained complexity theory. We can show that BSR is NP-hard even for constant D and s. This immediately rules out FPT algorithms in these parameters. For details, we refer to the full version of the paper [9].

Upper Bound. We show that BSR(P, t) is fixed-parameter tractable. The idea is to reduce to reachability on a product automaton. The automaton stores the configurations, the current writer, and counts up to the number of stages s. To this end, it has $\mathcal{O}^*(P^t)$ many states. Details can be found in the full version [9].

Proposition 12. BSR *can be solved in time* $\mathcal{O}^*(P^{2t})$.

Lower Bound. By a reduction from k × k Clique, we show that a $2^{o(t \cdot \log(P))}$-time algorithm for BSR would contradict ETH. The above algorithm is optimal.

Proposition 13. BSR *cannot be solved in time* $2^{o(t \cdot \log(P))}$ *unless* ETH *fails.*

The reduction maps an instance of k × k Clique to an equivalent instance $(\mathcal{A} = (D, a^0(P_i)_{i \in [1..t]}), C^f, s)$ of BSR. Moreover, it keeps the parameters small. We have that $P = \mathcal{O}(k^2)$ and $t = \mathcal{O}(k)$. As a consequence, a $2^{o(t \cdot \log(P))}$-time algorithm for BSR would yield an algorithm for k × k Clique running in time $2^{o(k \cdot \log(k^2))} = 2^{o(k \cdot \log(k))}$. But this contradicts ETH.

Proof (Idea). For the reduction, let $V = [1..k] \times [1..k]$ be the vertices of G. We define $D = V \cup \{a^0\}$ to be the domain of the memory. We want the threads to communicate on the vertices of G. For each row we introduce a reader thread P_i that is responsible for storing a particular vertex of the row. We also add one writer, P_{ch}, that is used to steer the communication between the P_i. Our program $\mathcal{A}$ is given by $(D, a^0, ((P_i)_{i \in [1..k]}, P_{ch}))$.

Intuitively, the program proceeds in two phases. In the first phase, each P_i non-deterministically chooses a vertex from the i-th row and stores it in its state space. This constitutes a clique candidate $(1, j_1), \ldots, (k, j_k) \in V$. In the second phase, thread P_{ch} starts to write a random vertex $(1, j_1')$ of the first row to the memory. The first thread P_1 reads $(1, j_1')$ from the memory and verifies that the read vertex is actually the one from the clique candidate. The computation in P_1 will deadlock if $j_1' \neq j_1$. The threads P_i with $i \neq 1$ also read $(1, j_1')$ from the memory. They have to check whether there is an edge between the stored vertex (i, j_i) and $(1, j_1')$. If this fails in some P_i, the computation in that thread will also deadlock. After this procedure, the writer P_{ch} guesses a vertex $(2, j_2')$ and writes it to the memory. Now the verification steps repeat. After k repetitions of the procedure, we can ensure that the guessed clique candidate is indeed a clique. Note that the whole communication takes one stage. Details are given in [9]. □

Absence of a Polynomial Kernel. We show that BSR(P, t) does not admit a polynomial kernel. To this end, we cross-compose 3-SAT into BSR(P, t).

Theorem 14. BSR(P, t) *does not admit a poly. kernel unless* NP $\subseteq$ coNP/poly.

In the present setting, coming up with a cross-composition is non-trivial. Both parameters, P and t, are not allowed to depend polynomially on the number I of given 3-SAT-instances. Hence, we cannot construct an NFA that distinguishes the I instances by branching into I different directions. This would cause a polynomial dependence of P on I. Furthermore, it is not possible to construct an NFA for each instance as this would cause such a dependence of t on I. To circumvent the problems, some deeper understanding of the model is needed.

Proof (Idea). Let $\varphi_1, \ldots, \varphi_I$ be given 3-SAT-instances, where each two are equivalent under $\mathcal{R}$, the polynomial equivalence relation of Theorem 8. Then each φ_ℓ has m clauses and n variables $\{x_1, \ldots, x_n\}$. We assume $\varphi_\ell = C_1^\ell \wedge \cdots \wedge C_m^\ell$.

In the program that we construct, the communication is based on 4-tuples of the form (ℓ, j, i, v). Intuitively, such a tuple transports the following information: The j-th clause in instance φ_ℓ, C_j^ℓ, can be satisfied by variable x_i with valuation v. Hence, our data domain is $D = ([1..I] \times [1..m] \times [1..n] \times \{0, 1\}) \cup \{a^0\}$.

For choosing and storing a valuation of the x_i, we introduce so-called variable threads $P_{x_1}, \ldots, P_{x_n}$. In the beginning, each P_{x_i} non-deterministically chooses a valuation for x_i and stores it in its states.

We further introduce a writer P_w. During a computation, this thread guesses exactly m tuples $(\ell_1, 1, i_1, v_1), \ldots, (\ell_m, m, i_m, v_m)$ in order to satisfy m clauses of potentially different instances. Each (ℓ_j, j, i_j, v_j) is written to the memory by P_w. All variable threads then start to read the tuple. If P_{x_i} with $i \neq i_j$ reads it, then the thread will just move one state further since the suggested tuple does not affect the variable x_i. If P_{x_i} with $i = i_j$ reads the tuple, the thread will only continue its computation if v_j coincides with the value that P_{x_i} guessed for x_i and, moreover, x_i with value v_j satisfies clause $C_j^{\ell_j}$.

Now suppose the writer did exactly m steps while each variable thread did exactly $m + 1$ steps. This proves the satisfiability of m clauses by the chosen valuation. But these clauses can be part of different instances: It is not ensured that the clauses were chosen from one formula φ_ℓ. The major difficulty of the cross-composition lies in how to ensure exactly this.

We overcome the difficulty by introducing so-called bit checkers P_b, where $b \in [1..\log(I)]$. Each P_b is responsible for the b-th bit of $\text{bin}(\ell)$, the binary representation of ℓ, where φ_ℓ is the instance we want to satisfy. When P_w writes a tuple $(\ell_1, 1, i_1, v_1)$ for the first time, each P_b reads it and stores either 0 or 1, according to the b-th bit of $\text{bin}(\ell_1)$. After P_w has written a second tuple $(\ell_2, 2, i_2, v_2)$, the bit checker P_b tests whether the b-th bit of $\text{bin}(\ell_1)$ and $\text{bin}(\ell_2)$ coincide, otherwise it will deadlock. This will be repeated any time P_w writes a new tuple to the memory.

Assume, the computation does not deadlock in any of the P_b. Then we can ensure that the b-th bit of $\text{bin}(\ell_j)$ with $j \in [1..m]$ never changed during the computation. This means that $\text{bin}(\ell_1) = \cdots = \text{bin}(\ell_m)$. Hence, the writer P_w has chosen clauses of just one instance φ_ℓ and with the current valuation, it is possible to satisfy the formula. Since the parameters are bounded, $\text{P} \in \mathcal{O}(m)$ and $\text{t} \in \mathcal{O}(n + \log(I))$, the construction constitutes a proper cross-composition. For a formal construction and proof, we refer to the full version [9]. $\square$

5 Conclusion

We studied several parameterizations of LCR and BSR, two safety verification problems for shared-memory concurrent programs. For LCR, we identified the parameters D, L, and C. Our first algorithm showed that LCR(D, L) is FPT. Then, we used a modification of the algorithm to obtain a verification procedure valuable for practical instances. The main insight was that due to a factorization along strongly connected components, the impact of L can be reduced to a polynomial factor in the time complexity. We also proved the absence of a polynomial kernel for LCR(D, L) and presented a lower bound which is a root factor away from the upper bound. For LCR(C) we gave a tight upper and lower bound.

The parameters of interest for BSR are P and t. We have shown that BSR(P, t) is FPT and gave a matching lower bound. The main contribution was to prove it unlikely that a polynomial kernel exists for BSR(P, t). The proof relies on a technically involved cross-composition that avoids a polynomial dependence of the parameters on the number of given 3-SAT-instances.

References

1. Atig, M.F., Bouajjani, A., Kumar, K.N., Saivasan, P.: On bounded reachability analysis of shared memory systems. In: FSTTCS, LIPIcs, vol. 29, pp. 611–623. Schloss Dagstuhl (2014)
2. Atig, M.F., Bouajjani, A., Qadeer, S.: Context-bounded analysis for concurrent programs with dynamic creation of threads. In: Kowalewski, S., Philippou, A. (eds.) TACAS 2009. LNCS, vol. 5505, pp. 107–123. Springer, Heidelberg (2009). https://doi.org/10.1007/978-3-642-00768-2_11
3. Atig, M.F., Bouajjani, A., Touili, T.: On the reachability analysis of acyclic networks of pushdown systems. In: van Breugel, F., Chechik, M. (eds.) CONCUR 2008. LNCS, vol. 5201, pp. 356–371. Springer, Heidelberg (2008). https://doi.org/10.1007/978-3-540-85361-9_29
4. Bodlaender, H.L., Downey, R.G., Fellows, M.R., Hermelin, D.: On problems without polynomial kernels. JCSS 75(8), 423–434 (2009)
5. Bodlaender, H.L., Jansen, B.M.P., Kratsch, S.: Kernelization lower bounds by cross-composition. SIDAM 28(1), 277–305 (2014)
6. Calabro, C., Impagliazzo, R., Paturi, R.: The complexity of satisfiability of small depth circuits. In: Chen, J., Fomin, F.V. (eds.) IWPEC 2009. LNCS, vol. 5917, pp. 75–85. Springer, Heidelberg (2009). https://doi.org/10.1007/978-3-642-11269-0_6
7. Cantin, J.F., Lipasti, M.H., Smith, J.E.: The complexity of verifying memory coherence. In: SPAA, pp. 254–255. ACM (2003)
8. Chini, P., Kolberg, J., Krebs, A., Meyer, R., Saivasan, P.: On the complexity of bounded context switching. In: ESA, LIPIcs, vol. 87, pp. 27:1–27:15. Schloss Dagstuhl (2017)
9. Chini, P., Meyer, R., Saivasan, P.: Fine-grained complexity of safety verification. CoRR, abs/1802.05559 (2018)
10. Cygan, M., Dell, H., Lokshtanov, D., Marx, D., Nederlof, J., Okamoto, Y., Paturi, R., Saurabh, S., Wahlström, M.: On problems as hard as CNF-SAT. ACM TALG 12(3), 41:1–41:24 (2016)
11. Cygan, M., Fomin, F.V., Kowalik, Ł., Lokshtanov, D., Marx, D., Pilipczuk, M., Pilipczuk, M., Saurabh, S.: Parameterized Algorithms. Springer, Cham (2015). https://doi.org/10.1007/978-3-319-21275-3
12. Demri, S., Laroussinie, F., Schnoebelen, P.: A parametric analysis of the state explosion problem in model checking. In: Alt, H., Ferreira, A. (eds.) STACS 2002. LNCS, vol. 2285, pp. 620–631. Springer, Heidelberg (2002). https://doi.org/10.1007/3-540-45841-7_51
13. Downey, R.G., Fellows, M.R.: Fundamentals of Parameterized Complexity. TCS. Springer, London (2013). https://doi.org/10.1007/978-1-4471-5559-1
14. Durand-Gasselin, A., Esparza, J., Ganty, P., Majumdar, R.: Model checking parameterized asynchronous shared-memory systems. In: Kroening, D., Păsăreanu, C.S. (eds.) CAV 2015. LNCS, vol. 9206, pp. 67–84. Springer, Cham (2015). https://doi.org/10.1007/978-3-319-21690-4_5
15. Enea, C., Farzan, A.: On atomicity in presence of non-atomic writes. In: Chechik, M., Raskin, J.-F. (eds.) TACAS 2016. LNCS, vol. 9636, pp. 497–514. Springer, Heidelberg (2016). https://doi.org/10.1007/978-3-662-49674-9_29

16. Esparza, J., Ganty, P., Majumdar, R.: Parameterized verification of asynchronous shared-memory systems. In: Sharygina, N., Veith, H. (eds.) CAV 2013. LNCS, vol. 8044, pp. 124–140. Springer, Heidelberg (2013). https://doi.org/10.1007/978-3-642-39799-8_8

17. Farzan, A., Madhusudan, P.: The complexity of predicting atomicity violations. In: Kowalewski, S., Philippou, A. (eds.) TACAS 2009. LNCS, vol. 5505, pp. 155–169. Springer, Heidelberg (2009). https://doi.org/10.1007/978-3-642-00768-2_14

18. Fernau, H., Heggernes, P., Villanger, Y.: A multi-parameter analysis of hard problems on deterministic finite automata. JCSS **81**(4), 747–765 (2015)

19. Fernau, H., Krebs, A.: Problems on finite automata and the exponential time hypothesis. In: Han, Y.-S., Salomaa, K. (eds.) CIAA 2016. LNCS, vol. 9705, pp. 89–100. Springer, Cham (2016). https://doi.org/10.1007/978-3-319-40946-7_8

20. Flanagan, C., Freund, S.N., Qadeer, S.: Thread-modular verification for shared-memory programs. In: Le Métayer, D. (ed.) ESOP 2002. LNCS, vol. 2305, pp. 262–277. Springer, Heidelberg (2002). https://doi.org/10.1007/3-540-45927-8_19

21. Flanagan, C., Qadeer, S.: Thread-modular model checking. In: Ball, T., Rajamani, S.K. (eds.) SPIN 2003. LNCS, vol. 2648, pp. 213–224. Springer, Heidelberg (2003). https://doi.org/10.1007/3-540-44829-2_14

22. Fortin, M., Muscholl, A., Walukiewicz, I.: Model-checking linear-time properties of parametrized asynchronous shared-memory pushdown systems. In: Majumdar, R., Kunčak, V. (eds.) CAV 2017. LNCS, vol. 10427, pp. 155–175. Springer, Cham (2017). https://doi.org/10.1007/978-3-319-63390-9_9

23. Fortnow, L., Santhanam, R.: Infeasibility of instance compression and succinct PCPs for NP. JCSS **77**(1), 91–106 (2011)

24. Furbach, F., Meyer, R., Schneider, K., Senftleben, M.: Memory model-aware testing - a unified complexity analysis. In: ACSD, pp. 92–101. IEEE (2014)

25. Gibbons, P.B., Korach, E.: Testing shared memories. SIAM J. Comput. **26**(4), 1208–1244 (1997)

26. Gotsman, A., Berdine, J., Cook, B., Sagiv, M.: Thread-modular shape analysis. In: PLDI, pp. 266–277. ACM (2007)

27. Hague, M.: Parameterised pushdown systems with non-atomic writes. In: FSTTCS, LIPIcs, vol. 13, pp. 457–468. Schloss Dagstuhl (2011)

28. Hague, M., Lin, A.W.: Synchronisation- and reversal-bounded analysis of multi-threaded programs with counters. In: Madhusudan, P., Seshia, S.A. (eds.) CAV 2012. LNCS, vol. 7358, pp. 260–276. Springer, Heidelberg (2012). https://doi.org/10.1007/978-3-642-31424-7_22

29. Holík, L., Meyer, R., Vojnar, T., Wolff, S.: Effect summaries for thread-modular analysis. In: Ranzato, F. (ed.) SAS 2017. LNCS, vol. 10422, pp. 169–191. Springer, Cham (2017). https://doi.org/10.1007/978-3-319-66706-5_9

30. Impagliazzo, R., Paturi, R.: On the complexity of k-SAT. JCSS **62**(2), 367–375 (2001)

31. Kahlon, V.: Parameterization as abstraction: a tractable approach to the dataflow analysis of concurrent programs. In: LICS, pp. 181–192. IEEE (2008)

32. La Torre, S., Madhusudan, P., Parlato, G.: Model-checking parameterized concurrent programs using linear interfaces. In: Touili, T., Cook, B., Jackson, P. (eds.) CAV 2010. LNCS, vol. 6174, pp. 629–644. Springer, Heidelberg (2010). https://doi.org/10.1007/978-3-642-14295-6_54

33. Lokshtanov, D., Marx, D., Saurabh, S.: Slightly superexponential parameterized problems. In: SODA, pp. 760–776. SIAM (2011)

34. Qadeer, S., Rehof, J.: Context-bounded model checking of concurrent software. In: Halbwachs, N., Zuck, L.D. (eds.) TACAS 2005. LNCS, vol. 3440, pp. 93–107. Springer, Heidelberg (2005). https://doi.org/10.1007/978-3-540-31980-1_7
35. Todd Wareham, H.: The parameterized complexity of intersection and composition operations on sets of finite-state automata. In: Yu, S., Păun, A. (eds.) CIAA 2000. LNCS, vol. 2088, pp. 302–310. Springer, Heidelberg (2001). https://doi.org/10.1007/3-540-44674-5_26
36. Yap, C.K.: Some consequences of non-uniform conditions on uniform classes. TCS **26**, 287–300 (1983)

Parameterized Verification
of Synchronization in Constrained
Reconfigurable Broadcast Networks

A. R. Balasubramanian[1], Nathalie Bertrand[2], and Nicolas Markey[2(✉)]

[1] Chennai Mathematical Institute, Chennai, India
[2] Univ. Rennes, Inria, CNRS, IRISA, Rennes, France
nicolas.markey@irisa.fr

Abstract. Reconfigurable broadcast networks provide a convenient formalism for modelling and reasoning about networks of mobile agents broadcasting messages to other agents following some (evolving) communication topology. The parameterized verification of such models aims at checking whether a given property holds irrespective of the initial configuration (number of agents, initial states and initial communication topology). We focus here on the synchronization property, asking whether all agents converge to a set of target states after some execution. This problem is known to be decidable in polynomial time when no constraints are imposed on the evolution of the communication topology (while it is undecidable for static broadcast networks).

In this paper we investigate how various constraints on reconfigurations affect the decidability and complexity of the synchronization problem. In particular, we show that when bounding the number of reconfigured links between two communications steps by a constant, synchronization becomes undecidable; on the other hand, synchronization remains decidable in PTIME when the bound grows with the number of agents.

1 Introduction

There are numerous application domains for networks formed of an arbitrary number of anonymous agents executing the same code: prominent examples are distributed algorithms, communication protocols, cache-coherence protocols, and biological systems such as populations of cells or individuals, etc. The automated verification of such systems is challenging [3,8,12,15]: its aim is to validate at once all instances of the model, independently of the (parameterized) number of agents. Such a problem can be phrased in terms of infinite-state-system verification. Exploiting symmetries may lead to efficient algorithms for the verification of relevant properties [7].

Different means of interactions between agents can be considered in such networks, depending on the application domain. Typical examples are shared

---

This work has been supported by the Indo-French research unit UMI Relax, and by ERC project EQualIS (308087).

D. Beyer and M. Huisman (Eds.): TACAS 2018, LNCS 10806, pp. 38–54, 2018.
https://doi.org/10.1007/978-3-319-89963-3_3

variables [4,10,13], *rendez-vous* [12], and broadcast communications [6,9]. In this paper, we target ad hoc networks [6], in which the agents can broadcast messages simultaneously to all their neighbours, *i.e.*, to all the agents that are within their radio range. The number of agents and the communication topology are fixed once and for all at the beginning of the execution. Parameterized verification of broadcast networks checks if a specification is met independently of the number of agents and communication topology. It is usually simpler to reason about the dual problem of the existence of an initial configuration (consisting of a network size, an initial state for each agent, and a communication topology) from which some execution violates the given specification.

Several types of specifications have been considered in the literature. We focus here on coverability and synchronization: *does there exist an initial configuration from which some agent (resp. all agents at the same time) may reach a particular set of target states*. Both problems are undecidable; decidability of coverability can be regained by bounding the length of simple paths in the communication topology [6].

In the case of mobile ad hoc networks (MANETs), agents are mobile, so that the communication links (and thus the neighbourhood of each agent) may evolve over time. To reflect the mobility of agents, Delzanno *et al.* studied *reconfigurable broadcast networks* [5,6]. In such networks, the communication topology can change arbitrarily at any time. Perhaps surprisingly, this modification not only allows for a more faithful modelling of MANETs, but it also leads to decidability of both the coverability and the synchronization problems [6]. A probabilistic extension of reconfigurable broadcast networks has been studied in [1,2] to model randomized protocols.

A drawback of the semantics of reconfigurable broadcast networks is that they allow arbitrary changes at each reconfiguration. Such arbitrary reconfigurations may not be realistic, especially in settings where communications are frequent enough, and mobility is slow and not chaotic. In this paper, we limit the impact of reconfigurations in several ways, and study how those limitations affect the decidability and complexity of parameterized verification of synchronization.

More specifically, we restrict reconfigurations by limiting the number of changes in the communication graph, either by considering *global* constraints (on the total number of edges being modified), or by considering *local* constraints (on the number of updates affecting each individual node). We prove that synchronization is decidable when imposing constant local constraints, as well as when imposing global constraints depending (as a divergent function) on the number of agents. On the other hand, imposing a constant global bound makes synchronization undecidable. We recover decidability by bounding the maximal degree of each node by 1.

2   Broadcast Networks with Constrained Reconfiguration

In this section, we first define reconfigurable broadcast networks; we then introduce several constraints on reconfigurations along executions, and investigate how they compare one to another and with unconstrained reconfigurations.

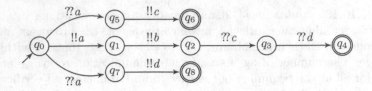

Fig. 1. Example of a broadcast protocol

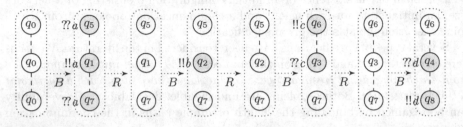

Fig. 2. Sample execution under reconfigurable semantics, synchronizing to $\{q_4, q_6, q_8\}$ (*B*-transitions are communications steps, *R* are reconfiguration steps.)

2.1 Reconfigurable Broadcast Networks

Definition 1. *A broadcast protocol is a tuple* $\mathcal{P} = (Q, I, \Sigma, \Delta)$ *where* Q *is a finite set of control states;* $I \in Q$ *is the set of initial control states;* Σ *is a finite alphabet; and* $\Delta \subseteq (Q \times \{!!a, ??a \mid a \in \Sigma\} \times Q)$ *is the transition relation.*

A (reconfigurable) broadcast network is a system made of several copies of a single broadcast protocol $\mathcal{P}$. Configurations of such a network are undirected graphs whose each node is labelled with a state of $\mathcal{P}$. Transitions between configurations can either be reconfigurations of the communication topology (*i.e.*, changes in the edges of the graph), or a communication via broadcast of a message (*i.e.*, changes in the labelling of the graph). Figures 1 and 2 respectively display an example of a broadcast protocol and of an execution of a network made of three copies of that protocol.

Formally, we first define undirected labelled graphs. Given a set $\mathcal{L}$ of labels, an $\mathcal{L}$-*graph* is an undirected graph $\mathsf{G} = (\mathsf{N}, \mathsf{E}, \mathsf{L})$ where N is a finite set of nodes; $\mathsf{E} \subseteq \mathcal{P}_2(\mathsf{N})^1$ (notice in particular that such a graph has no self-loops); finally, $\mathsf{L} \colon \mathsf{N} \to \mathcal{L}$ is the labelling function. We let $\mathcal{G}_{\mathcal{L}}$ denote the (infinite) set of $\mathcal{L}$-labelled graphs. Given a graph $\mathsf{G} \in \mathcal{G}_{\mathcal{L}}$, we write $\mathsf{n} \sim \mathsf{n}'$ whenever $\{\mathsf{n}, \mathsf{n}'\} \in \mathsf{E}$ and we let $\mathsf{Neigh}_{\mathsf{G}}(\mathsf{n}) = \{\mathsf{n}' \mid \mathsf{n} \sim \mathsf{n}'\}$ be the neighbourhood of n, *i.e.* the set of nodes adjacent to n. For a label ℓ, we denote by $|\mathsf{G}|_{\ell}$ the number of nodes in G labelled by ℓ. Finally $\mathsf{L}(\mathsf{G})$ denotes the set of labels appearing in nodes of G.

The semantics of a reconfigurable broadcast network based on broadcast protocol $\mathcal{P}$ is an infinite-state transition system $\mathcal{T}(\mathcal{P})$. The configurations of $\mathcal{T}(\mathcal{P})$ are Q-labelled graphs. Intuitively, each node of such a graph runs protocol $\mathcal{P}$,

---

[1] For a finite set S and $1 \leq k \leq |S|$, we let $\mathcal{P}_k(S) = \{T \subseteq S \mid |T| = k\}$.

and may send/receive messages to/from its neighbours. A configuration (N, E, L) is said *initial* if $L(N) \subseteq I$. From a configuration $G = (N, E, L)$, two types of steps are possible. More precisely, there is a step from (N, E, L) to (N', E', L') if one of the following two conditions holds:

(reconfiguration step) $N' = N$ and $L' = L$: a reconfiguration step does not change the set of nodes and their labels, but may change the edges arbitrarily;

(communication step) $N' = N$, $E' = E$, and there exists $n \in N$ and $a \in \Sigma$ such that $(L(n), !!a, L'(n)) \in \Delta$, and for every n', if $n' \in \text{Neigh}_G(n)$, then $(L(n'), ??a, L'(n')) \in \Delta$, otherwise $L'(n') = L(n')$: a communication step reflects how nodes evolve when one of them broadcasts a message to its neighbours.

An *execution* of the reconfigurable broadcast network is a sequence $\rho = (G_i)_{0 \leq i \leq r}$ of configurations such that for any $i < r$, there is a step from G_i to G_{i+1} and ρ strictly alternates communication and reconfiguration steps (the latter possibly being trivial). An execution is *initial* if it starts from an initial configuration.

An important ingredient that we heavily use in the sequel is *juxtaposition* of configurations and *shuffling* of executions. The juxtaposition of two configurations $G = (N, E, L)$ and $G' = (N', E', L')$ is the configuration $G \uplus G' = (N \uplus N', E \uplus E', L_\oplus)$, in which $L_\oplus$ extends both L and L': $L_\oplus(n) = L(n)$ if $n \in N$ and $L_\oplus(n) = L'(n)$ if $n \in N'$. We write G^2 for the juxtaposition of G with itself, and, inductively, G^N for the juxtaposition of G^{N-1} with G. A shuffle of two executions $\rho = (G_i)_{0 \leq i \leq r}$ and $\rho' = (G'_j)_{0 \leq j \leq r'}$ is an execution $\rho_\oplus$ from $G_0 \oplus G'_0$ to $G_r \oplus G'_{r'}$, obtained by interleaving ρ and ρ'. Note that a reconfiguration step in $\rho_\oplus$ may be composed of reconfigurations from both ρ and ρ'. We write $\rho \oplus \rho'$ for the set of shuffle executions obtained from ρ and ρ'.

Natural decision problems for reconfigurable broadcast networks include checking whether some node may reach a target state, or whether all nodes may synchronize to a set of target states. More precisely, given a broadcast protocol $\mathcal{P}$ and a subset $F \subseteq Q$, the *coverability* problem asks whether there exists an initial execution ρ that visits a configuration G with $L(G) \cap F \neq \emptyset$, and the *synchronization* problem asks whether there exists an initial execution ρ that visits a configuration G with $L(G) \subseteq F$. For unconstrained reconfigurations, we have:

Theorem 2 ([5,6,11]). *The coverability and synchronization problems are decidable in* **PTIME** *for reconfigurable broadcast protocols.*

Remark 1. The synchronization problem was proven decidable in [6], and **PTIME** membership was given in [11, p. 41]. The algorithm consists in computing the set of states of $\mathcal{P}$ that are both reachable (*i.e.*, coverable) from an initial configuration and co-reachable from a target configuration. This can be performed by applying iteratively the algorithm of [5] for computing the set of reachable states (with reversed transitions for computing co-reachable states).

Example 1. Consider the broadcast protocol of Fig. 1 with $I = \{q_0\}$. From each state, unspecified message receptions lead to an (omitted) sink state; this way, each broadcast message triggers a transition in all the neighbouring copies.

For that broadcast protocol, one easily sees that it is possible to synchronize to the set $\{q_4, q_6, q_8\}$. Moreover, three copies are needed and sufficient for that objective, as witnessed by the execution of Fig. 2. The initial configuration has three copies and two edges. If the central node broadcasts a, the other two nodes receive, one proceeding to q_5 and the other to q_7. Then, we assume the communication topology is emptied before the same node broadcasts b, moving to q_2. Finally the node in q_5 connects to the one in q_2 to communicate on c and then disconnects, followed by a similar communication on d initiated by the node in q_7.

2.2   Natural Constraints for Reconfiguration

Allowing arbitrary changes in the network topology may look unrealistic. In order to address this issue, we introduce several ways of bounding the number of reconfigurations after each communication step. For this, we consider the following natural pseudometric between graphs, which for simplicity we call *distance*.

Definition 3. *Let* $G = (N, E, L)$ *and* $G' = (N', E', L')$ *be two* $\mathcal{L}$*-labelled graphs. The distance between* G *and* G' *is defined as*

$$\mathsf{dist}(G, G') = |E \cup E' \setminus (E \cap E')|$$

when $N = N'$ *and* $L = L'$, *and* $\mathsf{dist}(G, G') = 0$ *otherwise.*

Setting the "distance" to 0 for two graphs that do not agree on the set of nodes or on the labelling function might seem strange at first. This choice is motivated by the definition of constraints on executions (see below) and of the number of reconfigurations along an execution (see Sect. 2.3). Other distances may be of interest in this context; in particular, for a fixed node $n \in N$, we let $\mathsf{dist}_n(G, G')$ be the number of edges involving node n in the symmetric difference of E and E' (still assuming $N = N'$ and $L = L'$).

Constant Number of Reconfigurations per Step. A first natural constraint on reconfiguration consists in bounding the number of changes in a reconfiguration step by a constant number. Recall that along executions, communication and reconfiguration steps strictly alternate.

Definition 4. *Let* $k \in \mathbb{N}$. *An execution* $\rho = (G_i)_{0 \le i \le r}$ *of a reconfigurable broadcast network is* k*-constrained if for every index* $i < r$, *it holds* $\mathsf{dist}(G_i, G_{i+1}) \le k$.

Example 1 (Contd). For the synchronization problem, bounding the number of reconfigurations makes a difference. The sample execution from Fig. 2 is not 1-constrained, and actually no 1-constrained executions of that broadcast protocol can synchronize to $\{q_4, q_5, q_6\}$. This can be shown by exhibiting and proving an invariant on the reachable configurations (see Lemma 10).

Beyond Constant Number of Reconfigurations per Step. Bounding the number of reconfigurations per step by a constant is somewhat restrictive, especially when this constant does not depend on the size of the network. We introduce other kinds of constraints here, for instance by bounding the number of reconfigurations by k *on average* along the execution, or by having a bound that depends on the number of nodes executing the protocol.

For a finite execution $\rho = (G_i)_{0 \leq i \leq r}$ of a reconfigurable broadcast network, we write $\mathtt{nb\_comm}(\rho)$ for the number of communication steps along ρ (notice that $\lfloor r/2 \rfloor \leq \mathtt{nb\_comm}(\rho) \leq \lceil r/2 \rceil$ since we require strict alternation between reconfiguration and communication steps), and $\mathtt{nb\_reconf}(\rho)$ for the total number of edge reconfigurations in ρ, that is $\mathtt{nb\_reconf}(\rho) = \sum_{i=0}^{r-2} \mathrm{dist}(G_i, G_{i+1})$.

Definition 5. *Let $k \in \mathbb{N}$. An execution ρ of a reconfigurable broadcast network is said k-balanced if it starts and ends with a communication step, and satisfies $\mathtt{nb\_reconf}(\rho) \leq k \cdot (\mathtt{nb\_comm}(\rho) - 1)$.*

This indeed captures our intuition that along a k-balanced execution, reconfigurations *on average* update less than k links.

Finally, we will also consider two relevant ways to constrain reconfigurations depending on the size of the network: first locally, bounding the number of reconfigurations *per node* by a constant; second globally, bounding the total number of reconfigurations by a function of the number of nodes.

We first bound reconfigurations locally.

Definition 6. *Let $k \in \mathbb{N}$. An execution $\rho = (G_i)_{0 \leq i \leq r}$ of a reconfigurable broadcast network is k-locally-constrained, if, for every node n and for every index $i < r$, $\mathrm{dist}_n(G_i, G_{i+1}) \leq k$.*

One may also bound the number of reconfigurations globally using bounding functions, that depend on the number of nodes in the network:

Definition 7. *Let $f \colon \mathbb{N} \to \mathbb{N}$ be a function. An execution $\rho = (G_i)_{0 \leq i \leq r}$ of a reconfigurable broadcast network is f-constrained, if, writing n for the number of nodes in G_0, it holds $\mathrm{dist}(G_i, G_{i+1}) \leq f(n)$ for any $i < r$.*

Notice that if f is the constant function $n \in \mathbb{N} \mapsto k$ for some $k \in \mathbb{N}$, f-constrained executions coincide with k-constrained ones, so that our terminology is non-ambiguous. Other natural bounding functions are non-decreasing and *diverging*. This way, the number of possible reconfigurations tends to infinity when the network size grows, *i.e.* $\forall n. \exists k. f(k) \geq n$.

Remark 2. Coverability under constrained reconfigurations is easily observed to be equivalent to coverability with unconstrained reconfigurations: from an unconstrained execution, we can simply juxtapose extra copies of the protocol, which would perform extra communication steps so as to satisfy the constraint. When dealing with synchronization, this technique does not work since the extra copies would also have to synchronize to a target state. As a consequence, we only focus on synchronization in the rest of this paper.

2.3 Classification of Constraints

In this section, we compare our restrictions. We prove that, for the synchronization problem, k-locally-constrained and f-constrained reconfigurations, for diverging functions f, are equivalent to unconstrained reconfigurations. On the other hand, we prove that k-constrained reconfigurations are equivalent to k-balanced reconfigurations, and do not coincide with unconstrained reconfigurations.

Equivalence Between Unconstrained and Locally-Constrained Reconfigurations.

Lemma 8. *Let $\mathcal{P}$ be a broadcast protocol, $F \subseteq Q$ be a target set, and f be a non-decreasing diverging function. If the reconfigurable broadcast network defined by $\mathcal{P}$ has an initial execution synchronizing in F, then it has an f-constrained initial execution synchronizing in F.*

Proof. We first prove the lemma for the identity function Id. More precisely, we prove that for an execution $\rho = (G_i)_{0 \leq i \leq n}$, of the reconfigurable broadcast network, there exists a Id-constrained execution $\rho' = (G'_j)_{0 \leq j \leq m}$, whose last transition (if any) is a communication step, and such that for any control state q, $|G_n|_q = |G'_m|_q$. We reason by induction on the length of the execution. The claim is obvious for $n = 0$. Suppose the property is true for all naturals less than or equal to some $n \in \mathbb{N}$, and consider an execution $\rho = (G_i)_{0 \leq i \leq n+1}$. The induction hypothesis ensures that there is an f-constrained execution $\rho' = (G'_j)_{0 \leq j \leq m}$ with $|G_n|_q = |G'_m|_q$ for all q. If the last transition from G_n to G_{n+1} in ρ is a reconfiguration step, then the execution ρ' witnesses our claim. Otherwise, the transition from G_n to G_{n+1} is a communication step, involving a broadcasting node n of G_n labelled with q, and receiving nodes n_1 to n_r of G_n, respectively labelled with q_1 to q_r. By hypothesis, G'_m also contains a node n' labelled with q and r nodes n'_1 to n'_r, labelled with q_1 to q_r. We then add two steps after G'_m in ρ': we first reconfigure the graph so that $\mathsf{Neigh}_{G'_{m+1}}(n') = \{n'_i \mid 0 \leq i \leq r\}$, which requires changing at most $|G_0| - 1$ links, and then perform the same broadcast/receive transitions as between G_n and G_{n+1}.

For the general case of the lemma, suppose f is a non-decreasing diverging function. Further, let $\rho = (G_i)_{0 \leq i \leq n}$ be an Id-constrained execution, and pick k such that $f(k \cdot |G_0|) \geq |G_0|$. Consider the initial configuration G_0^k, made of k copies of G_0, and the execution, denoted ρ^k, made of k copies of ρ running independently from each of the k copies of G_0 in G_0^k. Each reconfiguration step involves at most $|G_0|$ links, so that ρ^k is f-constrained. $\square$

Lemma 9. *Let $\mathcal{P}$ be a broadcast protocol with $F \subseteq Q$ a target set. If the reconfigurable broadcast network defined by $\mathcal{P}$ has an initial execution synchronizing in F, then it has a 1-locally-constrained initial execution synchronizing in F.*

k-Constrained and k-Balanced Reconfigurations. We prove here that k-constrained and k-balanced reconfigurations are equivalent w.r.t. synchronization, and that they are strictly stronger than our other restrictions. We begin with the latter:

Lemma 10. *There exists a broadcast protocol* $\mathcal{P}$ *and a set* $F \subseteq Q$ *of target states for which synchronization is possible from some initial configuration when unconstrained reconfigurations are allowed, and impossible, from every initial configuration when only 1-constrained reconfigurations are allowed.*

A protocol with this property is the one from Example 1, for which we exhibited a 2-constrained synchronizing execution. It can be proved that no 1-constrained synchronizing executions exist for this protocol, whatever the number of copies. We now prove the main result of this section:

Theorem 11. *Let* $\mathcal{P}$ *be a broadcast protocol and* $F \subseteq Q$. *There exists a k-constrained initial execution synchronizing in F if, and only if, there exists a k-balanced initial execution synchronizing in F.*

Proof. The left-to-right implication is simple: if there is a k-constrained initial execution synchronizing in F, w.l.o.g. we can assume that this execution starts and ends with a communication step; moreover, each reconfiguration step contains at most k edge reconfigurations, so that the witness execution is k-balanced.

Let $\rho = (\mathsf{G}_i)_{0 \leq i \leq n}$ be a k-balanced execution synchronizing in F and starting and ending with communication steps (hence n is odd). We define the potential $(p_i)_{0 \leq i \leq n}$ of ρ as the sequence of $n+1$ integers obtained as follows:

- $p_0 = 0$;
- $p_{2i+1} = p_{2i} + k$ for $i \leq (n-1)/2$ (this corresponds to a communication step);
- $p_{2i+2} = p_{2i+1} - \mathsf{dist}(\mathsf{G}_{2i+1}, \mathsf{G}_{2i+2})$ for $i \leq (n-1)/2 - 1$ (reconfiguration step).

That ρ is k-balanced translates as $p_{n-1} \geq 0$: the sequence $(p_i)_{0 \leq i \leq n}$ stores the value of $k \cdot \mathtt{nb\_comm}(\rho_{\leq i}) - \mathtt{nb\_reconf}(\rho_{\leq i})$ for each prefix $\rho_{\leq i}$ of ρ; being k-balanced means that $p_n \geq k$, and since the last step is a communication step, this in turn means $p_{n-1} \geq 0$. On the other hand, in order to be k-constrained, it is necessary (but not sufficient) to have $p_i \geq 0$ for all $0 \leq i \leq n$.

We build a k-constrained execution by shuffling several copies of ρ. We actually begin with the case where $k = 1$, and then extend the proof to any k. We first compute how many copies we need. For this, we split ρ into several phases, based on the potential $(p_i)_{0 \leq i \leq n}$ defined above. A phase is a maximal segment of $\rho_{\leq n-1}$ (the prefix of ρ obtained by dropping the last (communication) step) along which the sign of the potential is constant (or zero): graphs G_i and G_j are in the same phase if, and only if, for all $i \leq l \leq l' \leq j$, it holds $p_l \cdot p_{l'} \geq 0$. We decompose ρ as the concatenation of phases $(\rho_j)_{0 \leq j \leq m}$; since ρ is k-balanced, m is even, and ρ_0, ρ_m, and all even-numbered phases are *non-negative* phases (*i.e.*, the potential is non-negative along those executions), while all odd-numbered executions are *non-positive* phases. Also, all phases end with potential zero, except possibly for ρ_m. See Fig. 3 for an example of a decomposition into phases.

Lemma 12. *For any phase $\rho_i = \mathsf{G}_{b_i} \cdots \mathsf{G}_{e_i}$ of a 1-balanced execution $\rho = \mathsf{G}_0 \cdots \mathsf{G}_n$, there exists $\kappa_i \leq (e_i - b_i)/2$ such that for any $N \in \mathbb{N}$, there exists a 1-constrained execution from $\mathsf{G}_0^{\kappa_i} \oplus \mathsf{G}_{b_i}^{N}$ to $\mathsf{G}_1^{\kappa_i} \oplus \mathsf{G}_{e_i}^{N}$.*

Proof. We handle non-negative and non-positive phases separately. In a non-negative phase, we name *repeated reconfiguration step* any reconfiguration step that immediately follows another (possibly from the previous phase) reconfiguration step (so that if there are four consecutive reconfiguration steps, the last three are said repeated); similarly, we name *repeated communication step* any communication step that is immediately followed (possibly in the next phase) by another communication step (hence the first three of fours consecutive communication steps are repeated).

We first claim that any non-negative phase contains at least as many repeated communication steps as it contains repeated reconfiguration steps. Indeed, any non-repeated communication step in a non-negative phase is necessarily followed by a non-repeated reconfiguration step, and conversely, and non-negative phases have at least as many communication steps as they have reconfiguration steps.

As a consequence, we can number all repeated reconfiguration steps from 1 (earliest) to κ_i (latest), for some κ_i, and similarly for repeated communication steps. Clearly enough, in a non-negative phase, for any $1 \leq j \leq \kappa_i$, the repeated communication step numbered j occurs before the repeated reconfiguration step carrying the same number.

We now build our 1-constrained execution from $G_0^{\kappa_i} \oplus G_{b_i}^N$ to $G_1^{\kappa_i} \oplus G_{e_i}^N$. We begin with a first part, where only the components starting from G_{b_i} move:

- the first copy starting in G_{b_i} follows the execution ρ_i until reaching the repeated reconfiguration step number 1. That reconfiguration step cannot be performed immediately as it follows another reconfiguration step. Notice that during this stage, this copy has taken at least one repeated communication step, numbered 1;
- the second copy then follows ρ_i until reaching its first repeated communication step (which must occur before the first repeated reconfiguration step). It takes this communication step, then allowing the first copy to perform its first repeated reconfiguration step;
- this simulation continues, each time having the $l + 1$-st copy of the system taking its j-th repeated communication step in order to allow the l-th copy to perform its j-th repeated reconfiguration step. Non-repeated steps can always be performed individually by each single copy. Also, the first copy may always take repeated communication steps not having a corresponding reconfiguration step, as in the first stage of this part.

Notice that the number of copies involved in this process is arbitrary. The process lasts as long as some copies may advance within phase ρ_i. Hence, when the process stops, all copies of the original system either have reached the end of ρ_i, or are stopped before a repeated reconfiguration step. For the copies in the latter situation, we use the copies starting from G_0. It remains to prove that having κ_i such copies is enough to make all processes reach the end of ρ_i.

For this, we first assume that the potential associated with ρ_i ends with value zero. This must be the case of all phases except the last one, which we handle after the general case. We first notice that in the execution we are currently building, any repeated communication step performed by any (but the

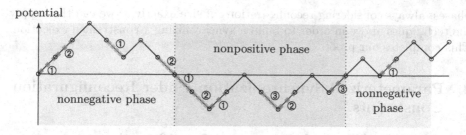

Fig. 3. Phases of a 1-balanced execution, and correspondence between repeated communication steps (loosely dotted blue steps) and repeated reconfiguration steps (densely dotted red steps) (Color figure online)

very first) copy that started from G_{b_i} is always followed by a repeated reconfiguration step. Similarly, non-repeated communication steps of any copy is followed by a non-repeated broadcast step of the same copy. As a consequence, the potential associated with the global execution we are currently building never exceeds the total number of repeated communication steps of performed by the first copy; hence it is bounded by κ_i, whatever the number N of copies involved. As a consequence, at most κ_i communication steps are sufficient in order to advance all copies that started from G_{b_i} to the end of ρ_i.

Finally, the case of the last phase ρ_m (possibly ending with positive potential) is easily handled, since it has more communication steps than reconfiguration steps.

The proof for non-positive phases is similar.

Pick a 1-balanced execution $\rho = G_0 \cdots G_n$, and decompose it into phases $\rho_1 \cdots \rho_m$. For each phase ρ_i, we write κ_i for the total number of repeated reconfiguration steps, and we let $\kappa = \sum_{1 \leq i \leq m} \kappa_i$ for the total number of repeated reconfiguration steps along ρ. Notice that $\kappa \leq n/2$.

Lemma 13. *For every 1-balanced execution $\rho = G_0 \cdots G_n$, and for every $N \in \mathbb{N}$, there exists a 1-constrained execution from $G_1^N \oplus G_{e_m}^{\kappa N}$ to $G_n^{N+\kappa N}$.*

Combining the above two lemmas, we obtain the following proposition, which refines the statement of the Theorem 11:

Proposition 14. *For every 1-balanced execution $\rho = G_0 \cdots G_n$ and every $N \geq \kappa^2 + \kappa$, there exists a 1-constrained execution from G_0^N to G_n^N.*

We finally extend this result to $k > 1$. In this case, splitting ρ into phases is not as convenient as when $k = 1$: indeed, a non-positive phase might not end with potential zero (because communication steps make the potential jump by k units). Lemma 12 would not hold in this case.

We circumvent this problem by first shuffling k copies of ρ in such a way that reconfigurations can be gathered into groups of size exactly k. This way, we can indeed split the resulting execution into non-negative and non-positive phases, always considering reconfigurations of size exactly k; we can then apply the techniques above in order to build a synchronizing k-constrained execution. This completes our proof.   □

3 Parameterized Synchronization Under Reconfiguration Constraints

3.1 Undecidability for k-Constrained Reconfiguration

Although synchronization is decidable in PTIME [6,11] for reconfigurable broadcast networks, the problem becomes undecidable when reconfigurations are k-constrained.

Theorem 15. *The synchronization problem is undecidable for reconfigurable broadcast networks under k-constrained reconfigurations.*

Proof. We prove this undecidability result for 1-constrained reconfigurations, by giving a reduction from the halting problem for Minsky machines [14]. We begin with some intuition. The state space of our protocol has two types of states:

- *control states* encode the control state of the 2-counter machine;
- *counter states* are used to model counter values: for each counter $c_j \in \{c_1, c_2\}$, we have a state zero_j and a state one_j. The value of counter c_j in the simulation will be encoded as the number of edges in the communication topology between the *control node* and *counter nodes* in state one_j; moreover, we will require that control nodes have no communication links with counter nodes in state zero_j.

  Incrementations and decrementations can then be performed by creating a link with a node in zero_j and sending this node to one_j, or sending a one_j-node to zero_j and removing the link.

In order to implement this, we have to take care of the facts that we may have several control nodes in our network, that we may have links between two control nodes or between two counter nodes, or that links between control nodes and counter nodes may appear or disappear at random. Intuitively, those problems will be handled as follows:

- we cannot avoid having several control nodes; instead, given a synchronizing execution of the broadcast protocol, we will select one control node and show that it encodes a correct execution of the 2-counter machine;
- in order to reach a synchronizing configuration, the selected control node will have to perform at least as many reconfiguration steps as broadcast steps. Because we consider 1-constrained runs, it will perform exactly the same number of reconfiguration steps as broadcast steps, so that no useless/ unexpected reconfigurations may take place during the simulation;

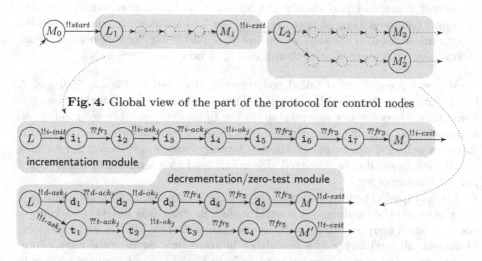

Fig. 4. Global view of the part of the protocol for control nodes

Fig. 5. Modules for simulating incrementation and decrementation/zero test

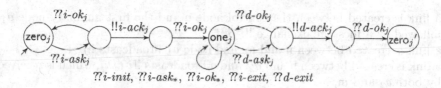

Fig. 6. The part of the protocol for counter nodes

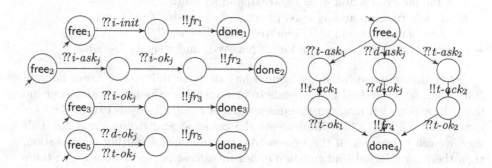

Fig. 7. Parts of the protocol for auxiliary nodes

- control nodes will periodically run special broadcasts that would send any connected nodes (except nodes in state one_j) to a sink state, thus preventing synchronization. This way, we ensure that particular control node is *clean*. Initially, we require that control nodes have no connections at all.

We now present the detailed construction, depicted at Figs. 4, 5, 6 and 7. Each state of the protocol is actually able to synchronize with all the messages. Some transitions are not represented on the figures, to preserve readability: all nodes with no outgoing transitions (i.e., state L_{halt} corresponding to the halting state, as well as states $\mathsf{zero}_j{}'$ and done_i) actually carry a self-loop synchronizing on all messages; all other omitted transitions lead to a sink state, which is not part of the target set.

Let us explain the intended behaviour of the incrementation module of Fig. 5: when entering the module, our control node n in state L is linked to c_1 counter nodes in state one_1 and to c_2 counter nodes in state one_2; it has no other links. Moreover, all auxiliary nodes are either in state free_i or in state done_i. Running through the incrementation module from L will use one counter node m in state zero_j (which is used to effectively encode the increase of counter c_j) and four auxiliary nodes a_1 (initially in state free_1), a_2 (in state free_2), and a_3 and a_3' (in state free_3).

The execution then runs as follows:

- a link is created between the control node n and the first auxiliary node a_1, followed by a message exchange $!!i\text{-}init$;
- a link is created between n and m, and node a_1 broadcasts $!!fr_1$;
- a link is created between n and a_2, and n broadcasts $!!i\text{-}ask_j$, which is received by both a_2 and m;
- a link is created between n and a_3; node m sends its acknowledgement $!!i\text{-}ack_j$ to n;
- a link is created between n and a_3'; node n sends $!!i\text{-}ok_j$, received by m, a_2, a_3 and a_3';
- the link between n and a_1 is removed, and a_2 sends $!!fr_2$;
- the link between n and a_2 is removed, and a_3 sends $!!fr_3$;
- the link between n and a_3 is removed, and a_3' sends $!!fr_4$;
- finally, the link between n and a_3' is removed, and n sends $!!i\text{-}exit$.

After this sequence of steps, node n has an extra link to a counter node in state one_j, which indeed corresponds to incrementing counter c_j. Moreover, no nodes have been left in an intermediary state. A similar analysis can be done for the second module, which implements the zero-test and decrementation. This way, we can prove that if the two-counter machine has a halting computation, then there is an initial configuration of our broadcast protocol from which there is an execution synchronizing in the set F formed of the halting control state and states one_j, $\mathsf{zero}_j{}'$ and done_i.

It now remains to prove the other direction. More precisely, we prove that from a 1-constrained synchronizing execution of the protocol, we can extract a synchronizing execution in some normal form, from which we derive a halting execution of the two-counter machine.

Fix a 1-constrained synchronizing execution of the broadcast network. First notice that when a control node n reaches some state L (the first node of an incrementation or decrementation module), it may only be linked to counter nodes in state one_j: this is because states L can only be reached by sending $!!i\text{-}exit$, $!!d\text{-}exit$, $!!t\text{-}exit$, or $!!start$. The former two cases may only synchronize with counter nodes in state one_j; in the other two cases, node n may be linked to no other node. Hence, for a control node n to traverse an incrementation module, it must get links to four auxiliary nodes (in order to receive the four fr messages), those four links must be removed (to avoid reaching the sink state), and an extra link has to be created in order to receive message $i\text{-}ack_j$. In total, traversing an incrementation module takes nine communication steps and at least nine reconfiguration steps. Similarly, traversing a decrementation module via any of the two branches takes at least as many reconfiguration steps as communication steps. In the end, taking into account the initial $!!start$ communication step, if a control node n is involved in B_n communication steps, it must be involved in at least $B_n - 1$ reconfiguration steps.

Assume that every control node n is involved in at least B_n reconfiguration steps: then we would have at least as many reconfiguration steps as communication steps, which in a 1-constrained execution is impossible. Hence there must be a control node n_0 performing B_{n_0} communication steps and exactly $B_{n_0} - 1$ reconfiguration steps. As a consequence, when traversing an incrementation module, node n_0 indeed gets connected to exactly one new counter node, which indeed must be in state one_j when n_0 reaches the first state of the next module. Similarly, traversing a decrementation/zero-test module indeed performs the expected changes. It follows that the sequence of steps involving node n_0 encodes a halting execution of the two-counter machines.   □

The 1-constrained executions in the proof of Theorem 15 have the additional property that all graphs describing configurations are 2-bounded-path configurations. For $K \in \mathbb{N}$ a configuration G is a K-bounded-path configuration if the length of all simple paths in G is bounded by K. Note that a constant bound on the length of simple paths implies that the diameter (i.e. the length of the longest shortest path between any pair of vertices) is itself bounded. The synchronization problem was proved to be undecidable for broadcast networks without reconfiguration when restricting to K-bounded-path configurations [6]. In comparison, for reconfigurable broadcast networks under k-constrained reconfigurations, the undecidability result stated in Theorem 15 can be strengthened into:

Corollary 16. *The synchronization problem is undecidable for reconfigurable broadcast networks under k-constrained reconfigurations when restricted either to bounded-path configurations, or to bounded-diameter configurations.*

3.2 Decidability Results

f-Constrained and k-Locally-Constrained Reconfigurations. From the equivalence (w.r.t. synchronization) of k-locally-constrained, f-constrained and unconstrained executions (Lemmas 8 and 9), and thanks to Theorem 2, we immediately get:

Corollary 17. *Let $k \in \mathbb{N}$ and $f \colon \mathbb{N} \to \mathbb{N}$ be a non-decreasing diverging function. The synchronization problem for reconfigurable broadcast networks under k-locally-constrained (resp. f-constrained) reconfigurations is decidable in* PTIME.

Bounded Degree Topology. We now return to k-constrained reconfigurations, and explore restrictions that allow one to recover decidability of the synchronization problem. We further restrict k-constrained reconfigurations by requiring that the degree of nodes remains bounded, by 1; in other terms, communications correspond to *rendez-vous* between the broadcasting node and its single neighbour.

Theorem 18. *The synchronization problem is decidable for reconfigurable broadcast networks under k-constrained reconfiguration when restricted to 1-bounded-degree topologies.*

Sketch of Proof. The proof consists in transforming the synchronization problem above into a reachability problem for some Petri net. The Petri net has two kinds of places (plus a few auxiliary places): one place for each state of the protocol, representing isolated nodes (*i.e.*, nodes having no neighbours), and one place for each pair of states of the protocol, representing pairs of connected nodes. Since we restrict to degree-1 topologies, any node of the network is in one of those two configurations. Places representing isolated nodes are simply called *isolated places* in the sequel, while places corresponding to pairs of connects nodes are called *connected places*.

An initialization phase stores tokens in the places described above, so as to represent the initial configuration. In a second phase, the Petri net simulates an execution of the reconfigurable broadcast network: communication steps and (k-constrained) reconfiguration steps are easily encoded as transitions of this Petri net: communication steps correspond to moving tokens from one place to the place obtained by updating the states as prescribed by the transitions of the broadcast protocol. Atomic reconfigurations may create or remove links, either consuming two tokens in isolated places and adding a token in the corresponding connected place, or the other way around. We use k auxiliary places in order to count the number of atomic reconfigurations, in order to enforce the k-constraint.

Finally, the Petri net may enter a terminal phase, where it checks synchronization by absorbing all tokens that lie in (isolated or connected) places corresponding to target states. In the end, the simulated execution has been synchronizing if, and only if, no tokens remain in any of the main states.

4   Conclusion

Restricting reconfigurations in reconfigurable broadcast networks is natural to better reflect mobility when communications are frequent enough and the movement of nodes is not chaotic. In this paper, we studied how constraints on the number of reconfigurations (at each step and for each node, at each step and globally, or along an execution) change the semantics of networks, in particular with respect to the synchronization problem, and affect its decidability. Our main results are the equivalence of k-constrained and k-balanced semantics, the undecidability of synchronization under k-constrained reconfigurations, and its decidability when restricting to 1-bounded-degree topologies.

As future work, we propose to investigate, beyond the coverability and synchronization problems, richer objectives such as cardinality reachability problems as in [5]. Moreover, for semantics with constrained reconfigurations that are equivalent to the unconstrained one as far as the coverability and synchronization problems are concerned, it would be worth studying the impact of the reconfiguration restrictions (e.g. k-locally-constrained or f-constrained) on the minimum number of nodes for which a synchronizing execution exists, and on the minimum number of steps to synchronize.

References

1. Bertrand, N., Fournier, P., Sangnier, A.: Playing with probabilities in reconfigurable broadcast networks. In: Muscholl, A. (ed.) FoSSaCS 2014. LNCS, vol. 8412, pp. 134–148. Springer, Heidelberg (2014). https://doi.org/10.1007/978-3-642-54830-7_9
2. Bertrand, N., Fournier, P., Sangnier, A.: Distributed local strategies in broadcast networks. In: CONCUR 2015, LIPIcs, vol. 42, pp. 44–57. LZI (2015). http://dx.doi.org/10.4230/LIPIcs.CONCUR.2015.44
3. Bloem, R., Jacobs, S., Khalimov, A., Konnov, I., Rubin, S., Veith, H., Widder, J.: Decidability of parameterized verification. In: Synthesis Lectures on Distributed Computing Theory. Morgan & Claypool Publishers (2015)
4. Bouyer, P., Markey, N., Randour, M., Sangnier, A., Stan, D.: Reachability in networks of register protocols under stochastic schedulers. In: ICALP 2016, LIPIcs, vol. 55, pp. 106:1–106:14. LZI (2016). http://dx.doi.org/10.4230/LIPIcs.ICALP.2016.106
5. Delzanno, G., Sangnier, A., Traverso, R., Zavattaro, G.: On the complexity of parameterized reachability in reconfigurable broadcast networks. In: FSTTCS 2012, LIPIcs, vol. 18, pp. 289–300. LZI (2012). http://dx.doi.org/LIPIcs.FSTTCS.2012.289
6. Delzanno, G., Sangnier, A., Zavattaro, G.: Parameterized verification of ad hoc networks. In: Gastin, P., Laroussinie, F. (eds.) CONCUR 2010. LNCS, vol. 6269, pp. 313–327. Springer, Heidelberg (2010). https://doi.org/10.1007/978-3-642-15375-4_22
7. Emerson, E.A., Sistla, A.P.: Symmetry and model checking. Formal Methods Syst. Des. 9(1–2), 105–131 (1996). https://doi.org/10.1007/FBF00625970

8. Esparza, J.: Keeping a crowd safe: on the complexity of parameterized verification (invited talk). In: STACS 2014, LIPIcs, vol. 25, pp. 1–10. LZI (2014). http://dx.doi.org/10.4230/LIPIcs.STACS.2014.1

9. Esparza, J., Finkel, A., Mayr, R.: On the verification of broadcast protocols. In: LICS 1999, pp. 352–359. IEEE Computer Society Press (1999). http://dx.doi.org/10.1109/LICS.1999.782630

10. Esparza, J., Ganty, P., Majumdar, R.: Parameterized verification of asynchronous shared-memory systems. In: Sharygina, N., Veith, H. (eds.) CAV 2013. LNCS, vol. 8044, pp. 124–140. Springer, Heidelberg (2013). https://doi.org/10.1007/978-3-642-39799-8_8

11. Fournier, P.: Parameterized verification of networks of many identical processes. Thèse de doctorat, Université Rennes 1, France (2015)

12. German, S.M., Sistla, A.P.: Reasoning about systems with many processes. J. ACM 39(3), 675–735 (1992). https://doi.org/10.1145/146637.146681

13. Hague, M.: Parameterised pushdown systems with non-atomic writes. In: FSTTCS 2011, LIPIcs, vol. 13, pp. 457–468. LZI (2011). http://dx.doi.org/10.4230/LIPIcs.FSTTCS.2011.457

14. Minsky, M.: Computation: Finite and Infinite Machines. Prentice Hall, Englewood Cliffs (1967)

15. Suzuki, I.: Proving properties of a ring of finite-state machines. Inf. Process. Lett. 28(4), 213–214 (1988). https://doi.org/10.1016/0020-0190(88)90211-6

EMME: A Formal Tool for ECMAScript Memory Model Evaluation

Cristian Mattarei[1]([⊠]), Clark Barrett[1]⓪, Shu-yu Guo[2], Bradley Nelson[3], and Ben Smith[3]

[1] Stanford University, Stanford, CA, USA
{mattarei,barrett}@cs.stanford.edu
[2] Mozilla, Mountain View, USA
shu@rfrn.org
[3] Google Inc., Mountain View, USA
{bradnelson,binji}@google.com

Abstract. Nearly all web-based interfaces are written in JavaScript. Given its prevalence, the support for high performance JavaScript code is crucial. The ECMA Technical Committee 39 (TC39) has recently extended the ECMAScript language (i.e., JavaScript) to support shared memory accesses between different threads. The extension is given in terms of a natural language memory model specification. In this paper we describe a formal approach for validating both the memory model and its implementations in various JavaScript engines. We first introduce a formal version of the memory model and report results on checking the model for consistency and other properties. We then introduce our tool, EMME, built on top of the Alloy analyzer, which leverages the model to generate all possible valid executions of a given JavaScript program. Finally, we report results using EMME together with small test programs to analyze industrial JavaScript engines. We show that EMME can find bugs as well as missed opportunities for optimization.

1 Introduction

As web-based applications written in JavaScript continue to increase in complexity, there is a corresponding need for these applications to interact efficiently with modern hardware architectures. Over the last decade, processor architectures have moved from single-core to multi-core, with the latter now present in the vast majority of both desktop and mobile platforms. In 2012, an extension to JavaScript was standardized [20] which supports the creation of multi-threaded parallel Web Workers with message-passing. More recently, the committee responsible for JavaScript standardization extended the language to support shared memory access [10]. This extension integrates a new datatype

---

Mozilla—At the time this work was done.

C. Mattarei—This work was supported by a research grant from Google. We would also like to thank JF Bastien from Apple for his support of this project.

D. Beyer and M. Huisman (Eds.): TACAS 2018, LNCS 10806, pp. 55–71, 2018.
https://doi.org/10.1007/978-3-319-89963-3_4

called *SharedArrayBuffer* which allows for concurrent memory accesses, thus enabling more efficient multi-threaded program interaction.

Given a multi-threaded program that uses shared memory, there can be several possible valid executions of the program, given that reads and writes may concurrently operate on the same shared memory and that every thread can have a different view of it. However, not all behaviors are allowed, and the separation between valid and invalid behaviors is defined by a *memory model*. In one common approach, memory models are specified using axioms, and the correctness of a program execution is determined by checking its consistency with the axioms in the memory model. Given a set of memory operations (i.e., reads and writes) over shared memory, the memory model defines which combinations of written values each read event can observe. Because many different programs can have the same behaviors, the memory model is also particularly important for helping to determine the set of possible optimizations that a compiler can apply to a given program. As an example, a memory model could specify that the only allowed multi-threaded executions are those that are equivalent to a sequential program composed of some interleaving of the events in each thread. This model is the most stringent one and is called sequential consistency. With this approach, all threads observe the same total order of events. However, this model has significant performance limitations. In particular, it requires all cores/processors to synchronize their local cache with each other in order to maintain a coherent order of the memory events. In order to overcome such limitations, weaker memory models have been introduced. The ECMAScript Memory Model is a weak model.

Memory models are notoriously challenging to analyze with conventional testing alone, due to their non-intuitive semantics and formal axiomatic definitions. As a result, formal methods are frequently used in order to verify and validate the correctness of memory models [4–7,18]. Some of these models apply to instruction set architectures, whereas others apply to high-level programming languages. In this work, we use formal methods to validate the ECMAScript Memory Model and to analyze the correctness and performance of different implementations of ECMAScript engines. JavaScript is usually regarded as a high-level programming language, but its memory model is decidedly low-level and more closely matches that of instruction set architectures than that of other languages. The analyses that we provide are based on a formalization of the memory model using the Alloy language [12], which is then combined with a formal translation of the program to be analyzed in order to compute its set of valid executions. This result can then be used to automatically generate litmus tests that can be run on a concrete ECMAScript engine, allowing the developers to evaluate its correctness. The concrete executions observed when running the ECMAScript engine can either be a subset of, be equivalent to, or be a superset of the valid executions. Standard litmus test analyses usually target the latter case (incorrect engine behavior), providing little information in the other cases. However, when the concrete engine's observed executions are a relatively small subset of the valid executions, (e.g., 1/5 the size), this can indicate a missed opportunity for code optimization. As part of our work, we introduce a novel approach in such cases that is able to identify specific predicates over the memory model that are always consistent with the executions of the concrete engine, thus providing guidance about where potential optimization opportunities might exist.

The analyses proposed in this paper have been implemented in a tool called **ECMAScript Memory Model Evaluator** (EMME), which has been used to validate the memory model and to test the compliance of all major ECMAScript engines, including Google's V8 [1], Apple's JSC [2], and Mozilla's SpiderMonkey [3].

The rest of the paper is organized as follows: Sect. 2 covers related work on formal analysis of memory models; Sect. 3 describes the ECMAScript Memory Model and its formal representation; Sect. 4 characterizes the analyses that are presented in this paper; Sect. 5 provides an overview of the Alloy translation; Sect. 6 concentrates on the tool implementation and the design choices that were made; Sect. 7 provides an evaluation of the performance of the different techniques proposed in this paper; Sect. 8 describes the results of the analyses performed on the ECMAScript Memory Model and several specific engine implementations; and Sect. 9 provides concluding remarks.

2 Related Work

Most modern multiprocessor systems implement relaxed memory models, enabling them to deliver better performance when compared to more strict models. Well known approaches such as Sequential Consistency (SC), Processor Consistency (PC), Relaxed-Memory Order (RMO), Total Store Order (TSO), and Partial Store Order (PSO) are mainly directed towards relaxing the constraints on when read and write operations can be reordered.

The formal analysis of weak memory model hardware implementations has typically been done using SAT-based techniques [5,9]. In [4], a formal analysis based on Coq is used in order to evaluate SC, TSO, PSO, and RMO memory models. The DIY tool developed in [4] generates assembly programs to run against Power and x86 architectures. In contrast, in this work we concentrate on the analysis of the ECMAScript memory model, assuming the processor behavior is correct.

MemSAT [19] is a formal tool, based on Alloy [12], that allows for the verification of axiomatic memory models. Given a program enriched with assertions, MemSAT finds a trace execution (if it exists) where both assertions and the axioms in the memory model are satisfied.

An analysis of the C++ memory model is presented in [6]. The formalization is based on the LEM language [17], and the CPPMem software provides all possible interpretations of a C/C++ program consistent with the memory model. More recently, an approach based on Alloy and oriented towards synthesizing litmus tests is proposed in [14].

In this paper, we build on ideas present in MemSAT and CPPMem to build a tool for JavaScript. Our EMME tool can provide the set of valid executions for a given input JavaScript program, and it can also generate litmus tests suitable for evaluating the correctness of JavaScript engine implementations. In contrast to previous work, we also analyze situations where the litmus tests provide correct results but expose a discrepancy between the number of observed behaviors in the implementation and what is possible given the specification.

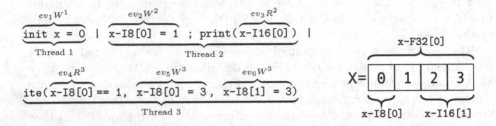

Fig. 1. Concurrent program example   **Fig. 2.** Shared memory views

3   The ECMAScript Memory Model

The objective of the ECMAScript Memory Model is to precisely define when an execution of a concurrent program that relies on shared memory is valid. From the point of view of the Memory Model, a JavaScript program can be abstracted as a set of threads, each of them composed of an ordered set of shared memory events. Each memory event has a set of attributes that specify its: operation (*Read, Write,* or *ReadModifyWrite*); ordering (*SeqCst, Unordered,* or *Init*); tear type (whether a single read operation can read from two different writes to the same location); (source or destination) memory block and address; payload value; and modify operation (in the case of a *ReadModifyWrite*). The shared memory is essentially an array of bytes, and a memory operation reads, writes, or modifies it. In these operations, the bytes can be interpreted either as *signed/unsigned integer* values or as *floating point* values. For instance, in Fig. 2, the notation x-I16[1] represents an access to the memory block x starting at index 1, where the bytes are interpreted as 16-bit signed integers (i.e., I16), while x-F32[0] stands for a 32-bit floating point value starting at byte 0.

Formally, a program is defined as a set of events E and a partial order between them, namely the *Agent Order*, that encodes the thread structure. For the example in Fig. 1, the set of events is defined as $E = \{ev_1W^1, ev_2W^2, ev_3R^2, ev_4R^3, ev_5W^3, ev_6W^3\}$, with agent order $AO = AO^1 \cup AO^2 \cup AO^3$, where AO^1, AO^2, and AO^3 are the agent orders for each thread: $AO^1 = \{\}$, $AO^2 = \{(ev_2W^2, ev_3R^2)\}$, and $AO^3 = \{(ev_4R^3, ev_5W^3), (ev_4R^3, ev_6W^3), (ev_5W^3, ev_6W^3)\}$.

The execution semantics of a program is given by the *Reads Bytes From* (RBF) relation, a trinary relation which relates two events and a single byte index i, with the interpretation that the first event reads the byte at index i which was written by the second event. Looking again at the example in Fig. 1, one of the possible valid assignments to the RBF relation is $\{(ev_4R^3, ev_1W^1, 0),$ $(ev_3R^2, ev_2W^2, 0), (ev_3R^2, ev_6W^3, 1)\}$, meaning that the *Read* event ev_4R^3 reads byte 0 from ev_1W^1 (taking the else branch), and ev_3R^2 reads byte 0 from ev_2W^2 and 1 from ev_6W^3.

The combination of a (finite) set of events $E = \{e_1, \ldots, e_n\}$, an agent order $AO \in E \times E$, and a *Reads Bytes From RBF* $\in E \times E \times \mathbb{N}$ relation identify a *Candidate Execution*, and the purpose of the Memory Model is to partition this set into *Valid* and *Invalid* executions. The separation is defined as a formula that is satisfiable if and only if the *Candidate Execution* is *Valid*. Given a *Candidate Execution*, the Memory Model constructs a set of supporting relations in order to assess its validity:

- *Reads From* (RF): a binary relation that generalizes RBF by dropping the byte location;
- *Synchronizes With* (SW): the synchronization relation between sequentially consistent writes and reads;
- *Happens Before* (HB): a partial order relation between all events;
- *Memory Order* (MO): a total order relation between sequentially consistent events.

Finally, a *Candidate Execution* is valid when the following predicates hold:

- *Coherent Reads* (CR): RF and HB relations are consistent;
- *Tear Free Reads* (TFR): for reads and writes for which the tear attribute is false, a single read event cannot read from two different write events (both of which are to the same memory address);
- *Sequential Consistent Atomics* (SCA): the MO relation is not empty.

3.1   Formal Representation

The formalization of the ECMAScript Memory Model is based on the formal definition of a *Memory Operation*, shown in Definition 1.

Definition 1 (Memory Operation). *A Memory Operation is a tuple $\langle ID,$ $O, T, R, B, M, A \rangle$ where:*

- *ID is a unique event identifier;*
- *$O \in \{Read\ (R), Write\ (W), ReadModifyWrite\ (M)\}$ is the operation;*
- *$T \in \mathbb{B}$ is the Tear attribute;*
- *$R \in \{Init\ (I), SeqCst\ (SC), Unordered\ (U)\}$ is the order attribute;*
- *B is the name of a Shared Data Block;*
- *M is a set of integers representing the memory addresses in B accessed by the operation O, with the requirement that $M = \{i \in \mathbb{N} \mid ByteIndex \leq i < ByteIndex + ElementSize\}$, for some $ByteIndex, ElementSize \in \mathbb{N}$*
- *$A \in \mathbb{B}$ is an Activation attribute.*

Note that this definition differs slightly from the one used in [10] (though the underlying semantics are the same). The differences make the model easier to reason about formally and include:

- In [10], the memory address range for an operation is represented by two numbers, the *ByteIndex* and the *ElementSize*, whereas in Definition 1, we represent the memory address range explicitly as a set of bytes (which must contain some set of consecutive numbers, so the two representations are equivalent). This representation allows for a simpler encoding of some operators like computing the intersection of two address ranges.
- Definition 1 omits the payload and modify operation attributes, as these are only needed to compute the concrete value(s) of the data being read or written. The formal model does not need to reason about such concrete values in order to partition candidate executions into valid and invalid ones. Furthermore, for any specific candidate execution of a JavaScript program, these values can be computed from the original program using the RBF relation.
- The activation attribute A is an extension used to encode whether an event should be considered active based on the control flow path taken in an execution. In particular, we model *if-then-else* statements by enabling or disabling the events in the then and else branches depending on the value of the condition.

All relations in [10] (i.e., RBF, RF, SW, HB, and MO) are included in the formal model, and their semantics are defined using set operations, while the predicates (i.e., CR, TFR, and SCA) are expressed as formulas. The resulting formulation of the Memory Model, combining all constraints and predicates, is shown in Eq. (1). Details of our implementation of this formulation are given in Sect. 5.

$$
\begin{aligned}
MM(E, AO, RF, RBF, SW, HB, MO) := {} & \varphi_{RBF}(RBF, E) \land \varphi_{RF}(RF, E, RBF) \\
& \land \varphi_{SW}(SW, E, RF) \land \varphi_{HB}(HB, E, AO, SW) \land \varphi_{MO}(MO, E, HB, SW) \\
& \land CR(E, HB, RBF) \land TFR(E, RF) \land SCA(MO)
\end{aligned}
\tag{1}
$$

4 Formal Analyses

The design and development of a critical (software or hardware) system often follows a process in which high-level requirements (such as the standards committee's specification of the memory model) are used to guide an actual implementation. This process can be integrated with different formal analyses to ensure that the result is a faithful implementation with respect to the requirements. In this section, we describe the set of analyses that we used to validate the requirements and implementations of the ECMAScript Memory Model. Results of our analyses are reported in Sect. 8.

4.1   Formal Requirements Validation

The ECMAScript Memory Model defines a set of *constraints* which together make up a formula (Eq. (1)). The solutions of this formula are the valid executions. The Memory Model also lists a number of *assertions*, formulas that are expected to be true in every valid execution (and thus must follow from the constraints). Complete formal requirements validation would require checking two things: (i) the constraints are consistent with each other, i.e. they contain no contradictions; and (ii) each assertion is logically entailed by the set of constraints in the Memory Model. However, because we used Alloy (see Sect. 5) we were unable to show full logical entailment, as Alloy can only reason about a finite number of events. So we instead showed that for finite sets of events up to a certain size, (i) and (ii) hold. In future work, we plan to explore using an SMT solver to see if we can prove unbounded entailment in some cases. When (i) or (ii) do not hold, there is a bug in either the requirements or the formal modeling of the requirements. To help debug problems with (i), we used the unsat core feature of Alloy, which identifies a subset of the constraints that are inconsistent. To further aid debugging, we labeled each constraint c_i with a Boolean activation variable av_i (i.e. we replaced c_i with $(av_i \rightarrow c_i) \land av_i$). This allowed us to inspect the unsat core for activation variables and immediately discern which constraints were active in producing the unsatisfiable result.

4.2   Implementation Testing

The *Implementation testing* phase analyzes whether a specific JavaScript engine correctly implements the ECMAScript Memory Model. In particular, given a program with shared memory operations, we generate: (1) the set of valid executions, (2) a litmus test, and (3) behavioral coverage constraints.

Valid Executions. This analysis lists all of (and only) the behaviors that the (provided) program can exhibit that are consistent with the Memory Model specification. The encoding of the problem is based on the following definition:

$$VE(E, AO) := \{(RBF, HB, MO, SW) \mid$$
$$MM(E, AO, RF, RBF, SW, HB, MO) \text{ is SAT}\}$$

where $VE(E, AO)$ is the complete (and finite because the program itself is finite) set of possible assignments to the RBF, HB, MO, and SW relations. Each assignment corresponds to a *valid* execution.

Litmus Tests. *Litmus test generation* uses the generated list of valid executions to construct a JavaScript program enriched with an assertion that is violated if the output of the program does not match any of the valid executions. A litmus test is executed multiple times (e.g., millions), in order to increase the chance of exposing a problem if there is one.

The result of running a litmus test many times can (in general) have one of three outcomes: the assertion is violated at least once, the assertion is not violated and all possible executions are observed, and the assertion is not violated and only some of the possible executions are observed. More specifically, given a program P, the set of its valid executions $VE(P)$, and the set of concrete executions $E_N(P)$ (obtained by running the JavaScript program on engine E some number of times N), the possible results can be respectively expressed as $E_N(P) \backslash VE(P) \neq \emptyset$, $E_N(P) = VE(P)$, and $E_N(P) \subset VE(P)$.

Behavioral Coverage Constraints. Though they can expose bugs, the litmus tests do not provide a guarantee of implementation correctness. In fact, even when a "bug" is found, it could be that the specification is too tight (i.e., it is incompatible with some intended behaviors) rather than that the implementation wrong. On the other hand, when $E_N(P) \subset VE(P)$, and especially if the cardinality of $E_N(P)$ is significantly smaller than that of $VE(P)$, it might be the case that the implementation is too simple: it is not taking sufficient advantage of the weak memory model and is therefore unnecessarily inefficient.

Whenever $E_N(P) \subset VE(P)$, this situation can be analyzed by the generation of *Behavioral Coverage Constraints*. The goal of this analysis is to synthesize the formulae Σ_{OBS} and Σ_{UNOBS}, for observed and unobserved outputs, that restrict the behavior of the memory model in order to match $E_N(P)$ and $VE(P) \backslash E_N(P)$.

Our approach to doing this relies on first choosing a set $\Pi = \{\pi_1, \ldots, \pi_n\}$ of predicates over which the formula will be constructed. One choice for Π might be all atomic predicates appearing in Eq. (1). Now, let $\Delta(\Pi)$ be the set of all cubes of size n over Π. Formally,

$$\Delta(\Pi) = \{l_1 \wedge \cdots \wedge l_n \mid \forall 1 \leq i \leq n.\, l_i \in \{\pi_i, \neg\pi_i\}\}.$$

Further, define the observed and unobserved executions as:

$$EX_{OBS} \quad = \bigvee_{\langle RBF,\, HB,\, MO,\, SW\rangle \in E_N(P)} (RBF \wedge HB \wedge MO \wedge SW)$$
$$EX_{UNOBS} = \bigvee_{\langle RBF,\, HB,\, MO,\, SW\rangle \in VE(P) \backslash E_N(P)} (RBF \wedge HB \wedge MO \wedge SW)$$

We compute those cubes in $\Delta(\Pi)$ that are consistent with the observed and unobserved executions as follows:

$$\delta_{OBS}(\Pi) \quad = \{\delta \in \Delta(\Pi) \mid MM \wedge EX_{OBS} \wedge \delta \text{ is satisfiable}\}$$
$$\delta_{UNOBS}(\Pi) = \{\delta \in \Delta(\Pi) \mid MM \wedge EX_{UNOBS} \wedge \delta \text{ is satisfiable}\}$$

The cubes are then combined to generate the formulae for matched and unmatched executions:

$$\Sigma_{OBS} = \bigvee_{\delta \in \delta_{OBS}} \delta, \quad \Sigma_{UNOBS} = \bigvee_{\delta \in \delta_{UNOBS}} \delta.$$

For example, let $(R2H := \forall_{e_1, e_2 \in E} : RF(e_1, e_2) \rightarrow HB(e_1, e_2)) \in \Pi$ be a predicate expressing that every tuple in *Reads From* is also in *Happens Before*. If the behavioral coverage constraints analysis generates $\Sigma_{OBS} = R2H$ and $\Sigma_{UNOBS} = \neg R2H$, it means that the JavaScript engine always aligns the read from relation with the HB relation, thus identifying a possible path for optimization in order to take advantage of the (weak) memory model.

5   Alloy Formalization

Alloy is a widely used modelling language that can be used to describe data structures. The Alloy language is based on relational algebra and has been successfully used in many applications, including the analysis of memory models [14].

We used Alloy to formalize the memory model discussed in Sect. 3.1. We followed the formalization given in Definition 1, using sets and relations to represent each concept.[1] For instance, an `operation_type` is defined as an (abstract) set with three disjoint subsets (R for *Read*, W for *Write*, and M for *ReadModifyWrite*), one for each possible operation. In contrast, `blocks` and `bytes` are represented as sets. A memory operation is modeled as a relation which links all of the attributes necessary to describe a memory event.

6.3.1.14 happens-before

4. For each pair of events E and D in EventSet(execution):
   a. If E is agent-order before D then E happens-before D.
   b. If E synchronizes-with D then E happens-before D.
   c. ...

Fig. 3. Excerpt of the *Happens Before* definition [10]

The formalization of a natural language specification usually requires multiple attempts and iterations before the intended semantics become clear. In the case of the ECMAScript Memory Model, this process was crucial for disambiguating some of the stated constraints. An example is the *Happens Before* relation. Figure 3 shows an excerpt of its definition, expressing how it is related to the *Agent Order* and *Synchronizes With* relations. One might expect that the formal interpretation would be something like: $\forall (e_1, e_2). (AO(e_1, e_2) \rightarrow HB(e_1, e_2)) \wedge (SW(e_1, e_2) \rightarrow HB(e_1, e_2)) \wedge (\ldots)$

```
1    fact hb_def {all ee,ed : mem_events | Active2 [ee,ed] =>
        (HB [ee,ed] <=> ((ee != ed) and (AO [ee,ed] or SW [ee,ed] or ... ))))}
```

Fig. 4. Excerpt of the *Happens Before* definition

However, further analysis and discussions with the people responsible for the Memory Model revealed that the correct interpretation is: $\forall (e_1, e_2).HB(e_1, e_2) \leftrightarrow (AO(e_1, e_2) \vee SW(e_1, e_2) \vee \ldots)$. The Alloy formalization of the *Happens Before* relation is shown in Fig. 4. The `Active2` predicate evaluates to true when both events are active.

---

[1] The complete Alloy model is available at https://github.com/FMJS/EMME/blob/master/model/memory_model.als.

Once the Memory Model has been formalized, the next step is to combine it with the encoding of the program under analysis. This requires modeling the memory events present in each thread. In the Alloy model, each event in a program extends the set of memory events, and its values are defined as a series of facts. Figure 5 shows an example of the Alloy model for the event ev_5W^3 from Fig. 1. A notable aspect of this example is the fact that its activation is dependent on the value of id1_cond which symbolically represents the condition of the *if-then-else* statement.

```
1    one sig ev5_W_t3 extends mem_events{}
2    fact ev5_W_t3_def {(ev5_W_t3.O = W) and
                         (ev5_W_t3.T = NT) and
4                        (ev5_W_t3.R = U) and
                         (ev5_W_t3.M = {byte_0}) and
6                        ((ev5_W_t3.A = ENABLED) <=> ((id1_cond.value = TRUE))) and
                         (ev5_W_t3.B = x)}
8    fact ev5_W_t3_in_mem_events {ev5_W_t3 in mem_events}
```

Fig. 5. Event ev_5W^3 encoding (w.r.t. Fig. 1)

6 Implementation

The techniques described in this paper have been implemented in a tool called EMME: **E**CMAScript **M**emory **M**odel **E**valuator [15]. The tool is written in Python, is open source, and its usage is regulated by a modified BSD license. The input to EMME is a program with shared memory accesses. The tool interacts with the Alloy Analyzer [13] to perform the formal analyses described in Sect. 4, which include the enumeration of valid executions and the generation of behavioral coverage constraints.

Input Format and Encoding. The input format of EMME uses a simplified JavaScript-like syntax. It supports the definition of *Read, Write*, and *ReadModifyWrite* events, allows events to be atomic or not atomic, and supports operations on integer or floating point values. The input format also supports *if-then-else* and bounded *for-loop* statements, as well as parametric values. An example of an input program is shown in Fig. 6. The program is encoded in Alloy and combined with the memory model in order to provide the input formula for the formal analyses.

```
1    var x = new SharedArrayBuffer();
2
     Thread t1 {
4        x-I8[0] = 1;
         print(x-I16[0]);
6    }

8    Thread t2 {
         if (x-I8[0] == 1) {
10           x-I8[0] = 3;
         } else {
12           x-I8[1] = 3;
         }
14   }
```

Fig. 6. EMME input for the program from Fig. 1.

Generation of All Valid Executions. The generation of all valid executions is computed by using Alloy to solve the AllSAT problem. In this case, the distinguishing models of the formula are the assignments to the RBF relation. Thus, after each satisfiability check iteration of the Alloy Analyzer, an additional constraint is added in order to block the current assignment to the RBF relation. This procedure is performed until the model becomes unsatisfiable.

As described in Sect. 3.1, our formal model does not encode the concrete values of each memory operation; thus, the extraction of a valid execution, given a satisfiable assignment to the formula, requires an additional step. This step is to reconstruct the values of each read or modify operation based on the program and the assignment to the RBF relation. For example, given the program in Fig. 1, and assuming that the RBF relation contains the tuples $(ev_3R^2, ev_2W^2, 0)$ and $(ev_3R^2, ev_6W^3, 1)$, the reconstruction of the value read by ev_3R^2 depends on the fact that ev_2W^2 writes 1 with an 8-bit integer encoding at position 0, while ev_6W^3 writes 3 at position 1. The composition of byte 0 and byte 1 from those two writes is the input for the decoding of a 16-bit integer for the event ev_3R^2, resulting in a read of the value 769. Clearly, each event could also have a different size and format (i.e., integer, unsigned integer, or float); thus, the reconstruction of the correct value must also take this into account.

When interpreting a program containing *if-then-else* statements, the possible outcomes must be filtered to exclude executions that break the semantics of *if-then-else*. In particular, it might be the case that the Boolean condition in the model does not match the concrete value, given the read values. For instance, consider the example in Fig. 6 in which the conditional is encoded as a Boolean variable id1_cond representing the statement x-I8[0] == 1. However, the tool may assign id1_cond to false even though the event x-I8[0] turns out to read a value different from 1 based on the information in the RBF relation. In this case, this execution is discarded since it is not possible given the semantics of the *if-then-else* statement.

Graph Representation of the Results. For each valid execution, EMME will produce a graphviz file that provides a graphical representation of the assignments to main relations and read values. An example of this graphical representation is shown in Fig. 7. The default setup removes some redundant information such as the explicit transitive closure of the HB relation, while RF and AO are not represented, and the total order MO is reported in the top right corner. Black arrows are used to represent the HB relation, while red and blue are respectively used for RBF and SW. Figure 7(a) represents an execution where event ev4_R_t3 reads value 1 from ev2_W_t2, thus executing the *THEN* branch in the *if-then-else* statement. In contrast, Fig. 7(b) reports an execution where it reads 0, thus taking the *ELSE* branch.

Litmus Test Generation. The generation of all valid executions also constructs a JavaScript litmus test that can be used to evaluate whether the engine respects the semantics of the Memory Model. The structure of the litmus test mirrors that of the input program, but the syntax follows the official TEST262 ECMAScript conformance standard [11].

To check whether a test produced a valid result, the results of memory operations must be collected. The basic idea consists of printing the values of each read and collecting them all at the thread level. The main thread is then responsible

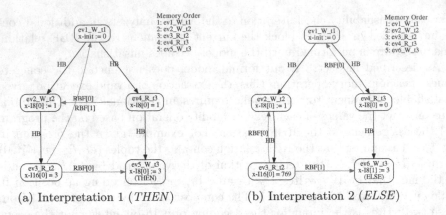

(a) Interpretation 1 (*THEN*)   (b) Interpretation 2 (*ELSE*)

Fig. 7. Memory model interpretations of the program in Fig. 6.

for collecting all the results. The sorted report is then compared with the set of expected outputs using an assertion. Moreover, the test contains a part that is parsed by the Litmus script, which is provided along with the EMME tool, and provides a list of expected outputs. The Litmus script is used to facilitate the execution of multiple runs of the same test, and it will provide a summary of the results as well as a warning whenever one of the executions observed is a not valid according to the standard.

Generation of the Behavioral Coverage Constraints. As described in Sect. 6, for each assignment to the RBF relation, it is possible to construct a concrete value for each memory event. Thus, for each RBF assignment in a set of valid executions for a given program, we can determine the output of the corresponding litmus test. Thus, running the litmus test many times on a JavaScript engine, it is possible to determine which assignments to the RBF relation have been matched. We denote these $MA\_rbf_1, \ldots, MA\_rbf_n$. The unmatched assignments to RBF can also be determined simply by removing the matched ones from the set of all valid executions. We denote the unmatched ones UN_rbf_1, $\ldots$, UN_rbf_m.

As described in Sect. 4, the generation of separation constraints that distinguish between matched and unmatched executions first requires the definition of a set of predicates Π. The extraction of the separation constraints is based on an AllSAT call for matched and unmatched results. The former is shown in (2), and consists of extracting all assignments to the predicates Π such that the models of the RBF relation are consistent with MA_rbf_i.

$$\text{ALLSAT}_{\Pi}[MM(E, AO, RBF, \ldots) \wedge (E = BE_E) \wedge (AO = BE_{AO})$$
$$\wedge (\bigvee_{i=1,\ldots,k} RBF = MA\_rbf_i)] \qquad (2)$$

Similarly, the evaluation for the unmatched executions performs an AllSAT analysis for the formula reported in (3). The results of these two calls to the solver produce respectively the formula Σ_{OBS} and Σ_{UNOBS} as described in Sect. 4.

$$\text{ALLSAT}_{\Pi}[MM(E, AO, RBF, \ldots) \wedge (E = BE_E) \wedge (AO = BE_{AO})$$

$$\wedge \, (\bigvee_{i=1,\ldots,k} RBF = \text{UN\_rbf}_i)] \qquad (3)$$

The results from the two AllSAT queries can then be manipulated using a BDD [8] package that produces in most cases a smaller formula. After this step, the tool provides a set of formal comparisons that can be done between these two formulas such as implication, intersection, and disjunction, in order to understand the relation between Σ_{OBS} and Σ_{UNOBS}.

7   Experimental Evaluations

In this section, we evaluate the performance of EMME over a set of programs, each containing up to 8 memory events. The analyses can be reproduced using the package available at [16].

Programs Under Analysis. In this work, we rely on programs from previous work [6] as well as handcrafted and automatically generated programs. The handcrafted examples are part of the EMME [15] distribution, and they cover a variety of different configurations with 1 to 8 memory events, if-statements, for-loops, and parametric definitions.

The programs from previous work as well as the handcrafted examples cover an interesting set of examples, but provide no particular guarantees on the space of programs that are covered. To overcome this limitation, we implemented a tool that enumerates all possible programs of a fixed size, thus giving us the possibility of generating programs to entirely cover the space of configurations, given a fixed set of events.

The sizes of the programs considered in this evaluation allow us to cover a representative variety of possible event interactions, while preserving a reasonable level of readability of the results. In fact, a program with 8 memory events can have hundreds of valid executions that often require extensive manual effort to understand.

All Valid Executions. As described in Sect. 6, the generation of all valid executions is based on a single AllSAT procedure. Figure 8 shows a scalability evaluation when generating all valid executions of 1200 program instances, each with from 3 to 8 memory events (200 programs for each configuration). The x-axis refers to the program number, ordered first by number of memory events, and then by increasing execution time, while the y-axis reports the execution time (in seconds on an

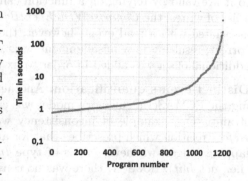

Fig. 8. Generation of all valid executions (form 3 to 8 memory events).

Intel i7-6700 @ 3.4 GHz) on a logarithmic scale. The results show that the proposed approach is able to analyze programs with 7 memory events in fewer than 10 s, providing reasonable responsiveness to deal with small, but informative, programs.

Behavioral Coverage Constraints. For the coverage constraints analysis, we first extracted a subset of the 1200 tests, considering only the ones that could produce at least 5 different outputs. There were 288 such tests. For each test, we ran the JavaScript engine 500 times, and performed an analysis using 11 predicates, each of which corresponds to a sub-part of the Memory Model, as well as some additional formulae. During this evaluation, the average computation time required to perform the behavioral coverage constraints analysis was 3.25 s, with a variance of 0.37 s.

8   Results of the Formal Analyses

In this Section we provide an overview of the results of the formal analyses for the ECMAScript Memory Model.

Circular relations definition. In the original Memory Model, a subset of the relations were specified using circular definitions. More specifically, using the notation a → b as "the definition of a depends on b", the loop was *Synchronizes With → Reads From → Reads Bytes From → Happens Before → Synchronizes With.* Cyclic definitions can result in vacuous constraints, and in the case of binary relations, this manifests as solutions with unconstrained tuples that belong to all relations involved in the cycle. In order to solve this problem, the definition of *Reads Bytes From* was changed so that it no longer depends on *Happens Before.* In addition, the memory model was extended with a property called *Valid Coherent Reads* that constrains the possible tuples belonging to the *Reads Bytes From* relation.

Misalignment of the ComposeWriteEventBytes. The memory model defines a *Reads Bytes From* relation, and checks whether the tuples belonging to it are valid by relying on a function called *ComposeWriteEventBytes.* Given a list of writes, the *ComposeWriteEventBytes* function creates a vector of values associated with a read event; however, the index for each write event was not correct, resulting in a misalignment w.r.t. the *Reads Bytes From* relation. An additional offset was added in order to fix the problem.

Distinct events quantification. Another problem encountered while analyzing the ECMAScript memory model was caused by a series of inconsistent constraints. One example of inconsistency was in the definition of the *Happens Before* relation which prescribes that for any two events ev_1 and ev_2 with overlapping ranges, whenever ev_1 is of type *Init*, ev_2 should be of a different type (i.e., not *Init*). However, there was no constraint stating that ev_1 and ev_2 have to be distinct, and certainly, whenever ev_1 and ev_2 are not distinct then this expression is unsatisfiable.

A similar inconsistency was found in the definition of the *Memory Order* relation. In this case, if the SW relation contains the pair (ev_1, ev_2), and $(cv_1, ev_2) \in$ HB, then the MO should contain (ev_1, ev_2). However, this is inconsistent with another constraint requiring that no event ev_3 should exist operating on the same memory addresses as ev_2 such that both $(ev_1, ev_3) \in$ MO and $(ev_3, ev_2) \in$ MO. This constraint is false when $ev_1 = ev_2 = ev_3$. Both the *Happens Before* and the *Memory Order* relations initially permitted any pairs of elements to be related (including two equal elements). The solution was to only allow pairs of distinct events in these relations.

The definition of the *Reads Bytes From* relation stated that each read or modify event $ev_1 R$ is associated with a list of pairs of byte indices and write or modify events. The definition did not specifically preclude allowing modify events to read from themselves. This does not cause any particular issues at the formal model level, but it is not clear what the implication at the JavaScript engine implementation level would be. In order to resolve this issue, the definition of the *Reads Bytes From* relation was modified to allow only events that are distinct to be related by *Reads Bytes From*.

Outputs coverage on ECMAScript engines. As described in Sect. 4, the litmus test analysis can result in three possible outcomes, e.g., $E_x(P) \backslash VE(P) \neq \emptyset$ when the engine violates the specification, $E_x(P) = VE(P)$ when the engine matches the specification, and $E_x(P) \subset VE(P)$ when the engine is more restrictive than the specification. Typically, such an analysis is designed to find bugs in the software implementation of the memory model [4, 6], focusing on the first case $(E_x(P) \backslash VE(P) \neq \emptyset)$. However, in this project, the last case was most prevalent, where $E_x(P)$ is significantly smaller than $VE(P)$.

For instance, when we ran the 288 examples with at least 5 possible outputs (from Sect. 7) 1000 times for each combination of program and JavaScript engine, the overall output coverage reached 75%, but for 1/6 of the examples, the coverage did not exceed 50%, and some were even below 15%[2].

This situation (frequently having far fewer observed behaviors than allowed behaviors) guided our development of alternative analyses, such as the generation of the behavioral coverage constraints, to help developers understand the relationship between an engine's implementation and the memory model specification. Future improvements of JavaScript engines will likely be less conservative, meaning that more behaviors will be covered. The tests produced in this project will be essential to ensure that no bugs are introduced. Currently, we are in the process of adapting the litmus tests so that they can be included as part of the official TEST262 test suite for the ECMAScript Memory Model.

9   Conclusion

Extending JavaScript, the language used by nearly all web-based interfaces, to support shared memory operations warrants the use of extensive verification techniques. In this work, we have presented a tool that has been developed

---

[2] On an x86 machine, and with the latest version of the engines available on October 1st, 2017.

in order to support the design and development of the ECMAScript Memory Model. The formal analysis of the original specification allowed us to identify a number of potential issues and inconsistencies. The evaluation of the valid executions and litmus tests coverage analysis identified a conservative level of optimization in current engine implementations. This situation motivated us to develop a specific technique for understanding differences between the Memory Model specification and JavaScript engine implementations.

Future extensions to this work will consider providing additional techniques to help developers improve code optimizations in JavaScript engines. Techniques such as the synthesis of equivalent programs, and automated value instantiation given a parametric program will provide additional analytical capabilities able to identify possible directions for code optimization. Moreover, we will also consider integration with other constraint solving engines in order to deal with more complex programs.

References

1. Chrome V8: Google's High Performance, Open Source, JavaScript Engine (2017). https://developers.google.com/v8/
2. JavaScriptCore: Is the Built-in JavaScript Engine for WebKit (2017). https://developer.apple.com/reference/javascriptcore
3. SpiderMonkey: Mozilla's JavaScript Engine (2017). https://developer.mozilla.org/en-US/docs/Mozilla/Projects/SpiderMonkey
4. Alglave, J.: A shared memory poetics. Ph.D. thesis, lUniversitè Paris 7 Denis Diderot, Paris, France, 11 2010
5. Atig, M.F., Bouajjani, A., Burckhardt, S., Musuvathi, M.: On the verification problem for weak memory models. ACM SIGPLAN Not. **45**(1), 7–18 (2010)
6. Batty, M.: The C11 and C++11 concurrency model. Ph.D. thesis, University of Kent, Canterbury, UK, 1 2015
7. Batty, M., Owens, S., Sarkar, S., Sewell, P., Weber, T.: Mathematizing C++ concurrency. ACM SIGPLAN Not. **46**, 55–66 (2011)
8. Bryant, R.E.: Symbolic Boolean manipulation with ordered binary-decision diagrams. ACM Comput. Surv. **24**(3), 293–318 (1992)
9. Burckhardt, S., Alur, R., Martin, M.M.: Checkfence: checking consistency of concurrent data types on relaxed memory models. ACM SIGPLAN Not. **42**, 12–21 (2007)
10. ECMA TC39 Committee: ECMAScript Shared Memory and Atomics (2016). https://tc39.github.io/ecmascript_sharedmem/shmem.html
11. ECMA TC39 Committee: Official ECMAScript Conformance Test Suite (2017). https://github.com/tc39/test262
12. Jackson, D.: Alloy: a lightweight object modelling notation. ACM Trans. Softw. Eng. Methodol. **11**(2), 256–290 (2002)
13. Jackson, D.: Alloy: A Language & Tool for Relational Models (2017). http://alloy.mit.edu/alloy/
14. Lustig, D., Wright, A., Papakonstantinou, A., Giroux, O.: Automated synthesis of comprehensive memory model litmus test suites. In: Proceedings of the Twenty-Second International Conference on Architectural Support for Programming Languages and Operating Systems, ASPLOS 2017, pp. 661–675. ACM, New York (2017)

15. Mattarei, C.: EMME: ECMAScript Memory Model Evaluator (2017). https:// github.com/fmjs/EMME
16. Mattarei, C., Barrett, C., Guo, S.-Y., Nelson, B., Smith, B.: Artifact Evaluation for the ECMAScript Memory Model Evaluator (EMME) Tool (2018). https://doi. org/10.6084/m9.figshare.5923312.v1
17. Owens, S., Böhm, P., Zappa Nardelli, F., Sewell, P.: Lem: a lightweight tool for heavyweight semantics. In: van Eekelen, M., Geuvers, H., Schmaltz, J., Wiedijk, F. (eds.) ITP 2011. LNCS, vol. 6898, pp. 363–369. Springer, Heidelberg (2011). https://doi.org/10.1007/978-3-642-22863-6_27
18. ten Dijke, N.: Comparison of verification methods for weak memory models (2014)
19. Torlak, E., Vaziri, M., Dolby, J.: MemSAT: checking axiomatic specifications of memory models. ACM SIGPLAN Not. **45**, 341–350 (2010)
20. W3C Web Application Working Group. Web Workers Specification (2012). https:// www.w3.org/TR/2012/CR-workers-20120501

SAT and SMT II

What a Difference a Variable Makes

Marijn J. H. Heule[1]([✉])[iD] and Armin Biere[2][iD]

[1] Department of Computer Science, The University of Texas, Austin, USA
`marijn@heule.nl`
[2] Institute for Formal Models and Verification, JKU, Linz, Austria

Abstract. We present an algorithm and tool to convert derivations from the powerful recently proposed PR proof system into the widely used DRAT proof system. The PR proof system allows short proofs without new variables for some hard problems, while the DRAT proof system is supported by top-tier SAT solvers. Moreover, there exist efficient, formally verified checkers of DRAT proofs. Thus our tool can be used to validate PR proofs using these verified checkers. Our simulation algorithm uses only one new Boolean variable and the size increase is at most quadratic in the size of the propositional formula and the PR proof. The approach is evaluated on short PR proofs of hard problems, including the well-known pigeon-hole and Tseitin formulas. Applying our tool to PR proofs of pigeon-hole formulas results in short DRAT proofs, linear in size with respect to the size of the input formula, which have been certified by a formally verified proof checker.

1 Introduction

Satisfiability (SAT) solvers are powerful tools for many applications in formal methods and artificial intelligence [3,9]. Arguably the most effective new techniques in recent years are based on *inprocessing* [21,25]: Interleaving preprocessing techniques and conflict-driven clause learning (CDCL) [26]. Several powerful inprocessing techniques, such as symmetry breaking [1,6] and blocked clause addition [23], do not preserve logical equivalence and cannot be expressed compactly using classical resolution proofs [30]. The RAT proof system [14] was designed to express such techniques succinctly and facilitate efficient proof validation. All top-tier SAT solvers support proof logging in the DRAT proof system [12], which extends the RAT proof system with clause deletion.

More recently a ground-breaking paper [8] presented at TACAS'17 showed how to efficiently certify huge propositional proofs of unsatisfiability by proof checkers, which are formally verified by theorem provers, such as ACL2 [7], Coq [7,8], and Isabelle/HOL [24]. These developments are clearly a breakthrough in SAT solving. They allow us to have the same trust in the correctness of the results produced by a highly tuned state-of-the-art SAT solver as into

---

Supported by the National Science Foundation (NSF) under grant CCF-1526760 and by the Austrian Science Fund (FWF) under project S11409-N23 (RiSE).

D. Beyer and M. Huisman (Eds.): TACAS 2018, LNCS 10806, pp. 75–92, 2018.
https://doi.org/10.1007/978-3-319-89963-3_5

those claims deduced with proof producing theorem provers. We can now use SAT solvers as part of such fully trusted proof generating systems.

On the other hand, with even more powerful proof systems we can produce even smaller proofs. The goal in increasing the power of proof systems is to cover additional not yet covered but existing reasoning techniques compactly, e.g., algebraic reasoning, but also to provide a framework for investigating new inprocessing techniques. If proofs are required, then this is a necessary condition for solving certain formulas faster. However it makes proof checking more challenging. The recently proposed PR proof system [17] (best paper at CADE'17) is such a generalization of the RAT proof system, actually an instance of the most general way of defining a clausal proof system based on clause redundancy.

There are short PR proofs without new variables for some hard formulas [17]. Some of them can be found automatically [18]. The PR proof system can therefore reveal new powerful inprocessing techniques. Short proofs for hard formulas in the RAT proof system likely require many new variables, making it difficult to find them automatically. The question whether PR proofs can efficiently be converted into proofs in the RAT and DRAT proof systems has been open. In this paper, we give a positive answer and present a conversion algorithm that in the worst case results in a quadratic blowup in size. Surprisingly only a single new Boolean variable is required to convert PR proofs into DRAT proofs.

At this point there exists only an unverified checker to validate PR proofs, written in C. In order to increase the trust in the correctness of PR proofs, we implemented a tool, called PR2DRAT, to convert PR proofs into DRAT proofs, which in turn can be validated using verified proof checkers. Thanks to various optimizations, the size increase during conversion is rather modest on available PR proofs, thereby making this a useful certification approach in practice.

Contributions

- We show that the RAT and DRAT proof systems are as strong as the recently introduced PR proof system by giving an efficient simulation algorithm of PR proofs by RAT and DRAT proofs.
- We implemented a proof conversion tool including various optimizations, which allow us to obtain linear size DRAT proofs from PR proofs for the well-known pigeon-hole formulas. These new DRAT proofs are significantly smaller than the most compact known DRAT proof for these formulas.
- We validated short PR proofs of hard formulas by converting them into DRAT proofs and certified these using a formally verified proof checker.

Structure

After preliminaries in Sect. 2 we elaborate on clausal proof systems in Sect. 3 also taking the idea of deletion steps into account. Then Sect. 4 describes and analyzes our simulation algorithm. In Sect. 5 we present how to optimize our new algorithm for special cases followed by alternative simulation algorithms in Sect. 6. Experiments are presented in Sect. 7 before we conclude with Sect. 8.

2 Preliminaries

Below we present the most important background concepts related to this paper.

Propositional Logic. Propositional formulas in *conjunctive normal form* (CNF) are the focus of this paper. A *literal* is either a variable x (a *positive literal*) or the negation $\bar{x}$ of a variable x (a *negative literal*). The *complementary literal* $\bar{l}$ of a literal l is defined as $\bar{l} = \bar{x}$ if $l = x$ and $\bar{l} = x$ if $l = \bar{x}$. A *clause* C is a disjunction of literals. A *formula* F is a conjunction of clauses. For a literal, clause, or formula ϕ, $var(\phi)$ denotes the variables in ϕ. We treat $var(\phi)$ as a variable if ϕ is a literal, and as a set of variables otherwise.

Satisfiability. An *assignment* is a (partial) function from a set of variables to the truth values 1 (*true*) and 0 (*false*). An assignment is *total* w.r.t. a formula if it assigns a truth value to all variables occurring in the formula. We extend a given α to an assignment over literals, clauses and formulas in the natural way. Let ϕ be either a literal, clause or formula ϕ. Then ϕ is *satisfied* if $\alpha(\phi) = 1$ and *falsified* if $\alpha(\phi) = 0$. Otherwise ϕ is *unassigned*. In particular, we have $\bar{x}$ is satisfied if x is falsified by α and vice versa. A clause is satisfied by α if it contains a literal that is satisfied by α and falsified if all its literals are falsified. Finally a formula is satisfied by α if all its clauses are satisfied by α. We often denote assignments by sequences of literals they satisfy. For instance, $x\,\bar{y}$ denotes the assignment that assigns 1 to x and 0 to y. For an assignment α, $var(\alpha)$ denotes the variables assigned by α. Further, α_l denotes the assignment obtained from α by flipping the truth value of literal l assuming it is assigned. A formula is *satisfiable* if there exists an assignment that satisfies it and *unsatisfiable* otherwise.

Formula Simplification. We denote the empty clause by $\perp$ and by $\top$ the valid and always satisfied clause. A clause is a *tautology* if it contains a literal l and its negation $\bar{l}$. Given assignment α and clause C, we define $C|\alpha = \top$ if α satisfies C; otherwise, $C|\alpha$ denotes the result of removing from C all the literals falsified by α. For a formula F, we define $F|\alpha = \{C|\alpha \mid C \in F \text{ and } C|\alpha \neq \top\}$. We say that an assignment α *touches* a clause C if $var(\alpha) \cap var(C) \neq \emptyset$. A *unit clause* is a clause with only one literal. The result of applying the *unit clause rule* to a formula F is the formula $F|l$ where (l) is a unit clause in F. The iterated application of the unit clause rule to a formula, until no unit clauses are left, is called *unit propagation*. If unit propagation yields the empty clause $\perp$, we say that it derived a *conflict*. Given two clauses $(l \vee C)$ and $(\bar{l} \vee D)$ their *resolvent* is $C \vee D$. If further $D \subseteq C$, *self-subsuming literal elimination* (SSLE) allows removing l from $(l \vee C)$. Notice that C is the resolvent of $(l \vee C)$ and $(\bar{l} \vee D)$. So an SSLE step can be seen as two operations, learning the resolvent C followed by the removal of $(l \vee C)$, which is subsumed by C. The reverse of SSLE is *self-subsuming literal addition* (SSLA), which can add a literal l to a clause C in the presence of a clause $(\bar{l} \vee D)$ with $D \subseteq C$. The notion of SSLE first appeared in [10] and is a special case of *asymmetric literal elimination* (ALE), which in turn is the inverse of *asymmetric literal addition* (ALA) [16].

   Clause C is *blocked* on literal $l \in C$ w.r.t. a formula F, if all resolvents of C and $D \in F$ with $\bar{l} \in D$ are tautologies. If a clause $C \in F$ is blocked w.r.t. F,

C can be removed from F while preserving satisfiability. If a clause $C \notin F$ is blocked w.r.t. F, then C can be added to F while preserving satisfiability.

Formula Relations. Two formulas are *logically equivalent* if they are satisfied by the same assignments. Two formulas are *satisfiability equivalent* if they are either both satisfiable or both unsatisfiable. Given two formulas F and F', we denote by $F \vDash F'$ that F implies F', i.e., all assignments satisfying F also satisfy F'. Furthermore, by $F \vdash_1 F'$ we denote that for every clause $(l_1 \vee \cdots \vee l_n) \in F'$, unit propagation on $F \wedge (\bar{l}_1) \wedge \cdots \wedge (\bar{l}_n)$ derives a conflict. If $F \vdash_1 F'$, we say that F implies F' through unit propagation. For example, $(x) \wedge (y) \vdash_1 (x \vee z) \wedge (y)$, since unit propagation of the unit clauses $(\bar{x})$ and $(\bar{z})$ derives a conflict with (x), and unit propagation of $(\bar{y})$ derives a conflict with (y).

3   Clausal Proof Systems

In this section, we introduce a formal notion of clause redundancy and demonstrate how it provides the basis for clausal proof systems. We start by introducing clause redundancy [22]:

Definition 1. *A clause C is* redundant *w.r.t. a formula F if F and $F \cup \{C\}$ are satisfiability equivalent.*

For instance, the clause $C = (x \vee y)$ is redundant w.r.t. $F = (\bar{x} \vee \bar{y})$ since F and $F \cup \{C\}$ are satisfiability equivalent (although they are not logically equivalent). Since this notion of redundancy allows us to add redundant clauses to a formula without affecting its satisfiability, it gives rise to clausal proof systems.

Definition 2. *For $n \in \mathbb{N}$ a derivation of a formula F_n from a formula F_0 is a sequence of n triples $(d_1, C_1, \omega_1), \ldots, (d_n, C_n, \omega_n)$, where each clause C_i for $1 \le i \le n$ is redundant w.r.t. $F_{i-1} \setminus \{C_i\}$ with $F_i = F_{i-1} \cup \{C_i\}$ if $d_i = 0$ and $F_i = F_{i-1} \setminus \{C_i\}$ if $d_i = 1$. The assignment ω_i acts as (arbitrary) witness of the redundancy of C_i w.r.t. F_{i-1} and we call the number n of steps also the* length *of the derivation. A derivation is a* refutation *of F_0 if $d_n = 0$ and $C_n = \bot$. A derivation is a* proof of satisfaction *of F_0 if F_n equals the empty formula.*

If there exists such a derivation of a formula F' from a formula F, then F and F' are satisfiability equivalent. Further a refutation of a formula F, as defined above, obviously certifies the unsatisfiability of F since any F' containing the empty clause is unsatisfiable. Note that at this point these ω_i are still place-holders used in refinements, i.e., in the RAT and PR proof systems defined below, where these ω_i are witnesses for the redundancy of C_i w.r.t. F_{i-1}. In these specialized proof systems this redundancy can be *checked efficiently*, i.e., in polynomial time w.r.t. the size of C_i, F_{i-1} and ω_i.

3.1   The RAT Proof System

The RAT proof system allows the addition of a redundant clause, which is a so-called *resolution asymmetric tautology* [21] (RAT, defined below). It can be efficiently checked whether a clause is a RAT. The following definition of RAT is equivalent to the original one in [21] based on resolvents using results from [17].

Definition 3. *Let F be a formula, C a clause, and α the smallest assignment that falsifies C. Then, C is a* resolution asymmetric tautology (RAT) *with respect to F if there exists a literal $l \in C$ such that $F|\alpha \vdash_1 F|\alpha_l$. We say that C is a* RAT *on l w.r.t. F. The empty clause $\bot$ is a* RAT *w.r.t. F iff $F \vdash_1 \bot$.*

Informally, $F|\alpha \vdash_1 F|\alpha_l$ means that $F|\alpha_l$ is at least as satisfiable compared to $F|\alpha$. We know that α_l satisfies C as $l \in C$, thus $F|\alpha_l = (F \wedge C)|\alpha_l$. Hence, if F has a satisfying assignment β that falsifies C, which necessarily is an extension of α, then it also satisfies $(F \wedge C)|\alpha_l$, and thus there exists a satisfying assignment of F that satisfies C, obtained from β by flipping the assigned value of l.

Example 1. Let $F = (x \vee y) \wedge (\overline{x} \vee y) \wedge (\overline{x} \vee z)$ and $C = (x \vee \overline{z})$. Then, $\alpha = \overline{x}\, z$ is the smallest assignment that falsifies C. Observe that C is a RAT clause on literal x w.r.t. F. First, $\alpha_x = x\, z$. Now, consider $F|\alpha = (y)$ and $F|\alpha_x - (y)$. Clearly, unit propagation on $F|\alpha \wedge (\overline{y})$ derives a conflict, thus $F|\alpha \vdash_1 F|\alpha_x$. □

In a RAT derivation $(d_1, C_1, \omega_1), \ldots, (d_n, C_n, \omega_n)$ all d_i's are zero (additions). Let α_i denote the smallest assignment that falsifies C_i and let $l_i \in C_i$ be a literal on which C_i is a RAT on l_i w.r.t F_{i-1}. Each witness ω_i in a RAT derivation equals $(\alpha_i)_{l_i}$, which is obtained from α_i by flipping the value of l_i.

3.2   The PR Proof System

As discussed, addition of PR clauses (short for *propagation-redundant clauses*) to a formula can lead to short proofs for hard formulas without the introduction of new variables. Although PR as well as RAT clauses are not necessarily implied by the formula, their addition preserves satisfiability [17]. The intuitive reason for this is that the addition of a PR clause prunes the search space of possible assignments in such a way that there still remain assignments under which the formula is as satisfiable as under the pruned assignments.

Definition 4. *Let F be a formula, C a non-empty clause, and α the smallest assignment that falsifies C. Then, C is* propagation redundant (PR) *with respect to F if there exists an assignment ω which satisfies C, such that $F|\alpha \vdash_1 F|\omega$.*

The clause C can be seen as a constraint that "prunes" from the search space all assignments that extend α. Note again, that in our setting assignments are in general partial functions. Since $F|\alpha$ implies $F|\omega$, every assignment that satisfies $F|\alpha$ also satisfies $F|\omega$, meaning that F is at least as satisfiable under ω as it is under α. Moreover, since ω satisfies C, it must disagree with α on at least one variable. We refer to ω as the *witness*, since it witnesses the propagation-redundancy of the clause. Consider the following example from [17].

Example 2. Let $F = (x \lor y) \land (\overline{x} \lor y) \land (\overline{x} \lor z)$, $C = (x)$, and let $\omega = x\,z$ be an assignment. Then, $\alpha = \overline{x}$ is the smallest assignment that falsifies C. Now, consider $F|\alpha = (y)$ and $F|\omega = (y)$. Clearly, unit propagation on $F|\alpha \land (\overline{y})$ derives a conflict. Thus, $F|\alpha \vdash_1 F|\omega$ and C is propagation redundant w.r.t. F. Notice that C is not RAT w.r.t F as $(y) = F|\alpha \not\vdash_1 F|\alpha_x = (y)(z)$.   □

Most known types of redundant clauses are PR clauses [17], including *blocked clauses* [23], *set-blocked clauses* [22], *resolution asymmetric tautologies*, etc.

3.3   The Power of Deletion

The clausal proof system DRAT [29] is the de-facto standard for proofs of unsatisfiability (refutations) in practice. It extends RAT by allowing the deletion of clauses. The main purpose of clause deletion is to reduce computation cost to validate proofs of unsatisfiability. Note, that SAT solvers not only learn clauses, but also aggressively delete clauses to speed up reasoning. Integrating deletion information in proofs is crucial to speed up proof checking.

In principle, while deleted clause information has to be taken into account to update the formula after a deletion step, one does not need to check the validity of clause deletion steps in order to refute a propositional formula. Simply removing deleted clauses during proof checking trivially preserves unsatisfiability.

Proofs of satisfiability only exist in proof systems that allow and enforce valid deletion steps, because they are required to reduce a formula to the empty formula. In case of propositional formulas, the notion of proofs of satisfiability is probably not useful as a satisfying assignment can be used to certify satisfiability. However, for richer logics, such as quantified Boolean formulas, the proof of satisfiability can be exponentially smaller compared to alternatives [19,20].

4   Conversion Algorithm

This section presents our main algorithm, which describes how to convert a PR derivation $(0, C_1, \omega_1), \ldots, (0, C_n, \omega_n)$ of a formula F_n from a formula F_0 into a DRAT derivation $(d_1, D_1, \omega_1'), \ldots, (d_m, D_m, \omega_m')$ of $G_m = F_n$ from $G_0 = F_0$. Each PR proof step adds a clause to the formula. Let G_0 be a copy of F_0 and $F_i := F_{i-1} \land C_i$ for $1 \le i \le n$. Each proof step in a DRAT proof either deletes or adds a clause depending on whether d_i is 1 or 0 (respectively). For $1 \le j \le m$ we either have $G_i := G_{i-1} \setminus \{D_i\}$ if d_i is 1 or $G_i := G_{i-1} \land D_i$ if d_i is 0.

Each single PR derivation step $(0, C_i, \omega_i)$ is also a PR derivation of F_i from F_{i-1} and our conversion algorithm simply translates each such PR derivation step separately into a DRAT derivation of F_i from F_{i-1}. The conversion of the whole PR derivation is then obtained as concatenation of these individual DRAT derivations, which gives a DRAT derivation of F_n from F_0. We will first offer an informal top-down description of converting a single PR derivation step into a sequence of DRAT steps.

4.1 Top-Down

Consider a formula F and a clause C which has PR w.r.t. F with witness ω, i.e., a single PR derivation step. The central question addressed in this paper is how to construct a DRAT derivation of $F \wedge C$ from F. The constructed DRAT derivation $(d_1, C_1, \omega_1), \ldots, (d_q, C_q, \omega_q), (d_{q+1}, C_{q+1}, \omega_{q+1}), \ldots, (d_p, C_p, \omega_p)$ of $F \wedge C$ from F consists of three parts. It also requires to introduce a (new) Boolean variable x that does not occur in F.

1. Construct a DRAT derivation $(d_1, C_1, \omega_1), \ldots, (d_q, C_q, \omega_q)$ of F' from F where
   a. the clause $(x \vee C)$ is a RAT on x w.r.t. F' and
   b. there exists a DRAT derivation from $F' \wedge (x \vee C)$ to $F \wedge C$.
2. In step $q + 1$, clause $C_{q+1} = (x \vee C)$ is added to F'.
3. The steps after step $q + 1$ transform $F' \wedge (x \vee C)$ into $F \wedge C$.

Notice that $(x \vee C)$ is blocked w.r.t. F and could therefore be added to F as a first step. However, it is very hard to eliminate literal x from $F \wedge (x \vee C)$. Instead, we transform F into F', before the addition and reverse the transformation afterwards. Below we describe the details of our simulation algorithm in five phases of which phase (I) and (II) correspond to the transformation (part 1.) and phase (IV) and (V) corresponds to the reverse transformation (part 3.).

4.2 Five Phases

We will show a transformation of how F_{i+1} is derived from F_i using PR step $(0, C_{i+1}, \omega_{i+1})$ into a sequence of p DRAT proof steps from G_j to G_{j+p} such that $G_j = F_i$ and $G_{j+p} = F_{i+1}$. In the description below, F refers to F_i, C refers to C_{i+1}, and ω refers to ω_{i+1}. Further let x be a new Boolean variable, i.e., x does not occur in F. We can assume that $var(C) \subseteq var(F)$. Otherwise there exists a literal $l \in C$ and $var(l) \notin var(F)$. Thus C is blocked on l w.r.t. F and can be added to F using a single RAT step.

(I) *Add shortened copies of clauses that are reduced, but not satisfied by ω.*
   The first phase of the conversion algorithm extends F by adding the clauses $(\overline{x} \vee D)$ with $D \in F|\omega \setminus F$. The literal x does not occur in F. All clauses $(\overline{x} \vee D)$ are blocked on $\overline{x}$ w.r.t. F as no resolution on x is possible. We denote with $G^{(I)}$ the formula F after these clause additions.

(II) *Weaken the clauses that are reduced and satisfied by ω.*
   A clause $E \in F$ is called *involved* if it is both reduced by ω as well as satisfied by ω. The second phase weakens all involved clauses by replacing E with $(x \vee E)$ as follows. First, we add the implication $x \Rightarrow \omega$, or in clauses $(\overline{x} \vee l)$ with $l \in \omega$. These clauses are blocked because $G^{(I)}$ does not contain clauses with literal x. Second, we weaken the involved clauses using self-subsuming literal addition (SSLA), since they all contain at least one $l \in \omega$. Third, we remove the implication $x \Rightarrow \omega$. When this implication was added, the clauses $(\overline{x} \vee l)$ with $l \in \omega$ were blocked on x. Now we can remove them, because they have RAT on l, which can be seen as follows. Consider

a clause containing $\bar{l}$. If it is a weakened clauses $(x \vee E)$ of E where $E \in F$ is satisfied by ω, then x occurs in opposite phase and the resolvent is a tautology (same condition as for blocked clauses). Otherwise the resolvent on l of $(\bar{x} \vee l)$ with the clause containing $\bar{l}$ is subsumed by a clause $(\bar{x} \vee D)$ with $D \in F|\omega \setminus F$ added in first step above. The resulting formula, where all involved clauses in $G^{(I)}$ are weakened, is denoted by $G^{(II)}$.

(III) *Add the weakened* PR *clause.*

Add the clause $(x \vee C)$ to $G^{(II)}$, resulting in $G^{(III)}$. The key observation related to this phase is that $(x \vee C)$ has RAT on x w.r.t. $G^{(II)}$: The only clauses in $G^{(II)}$ that contain literal $\bar{x}$ are the ones that were added in the first phase. We need to show that $G^{(II)}$ implies every clause $(x \vee C \vee D)$ with $D \in F|\omega \setminus F$ by unit propagation. Let α be the smallest assignment that falsifies C. Since C has PR w.r.t. F using witness ω, we know that $F|\alpha \vdash_1 D$ with $D \in F|\omega \setminus F$. This is equivalent to $F \vdash_1 (C \vee D)$ with $D \in F|\omega \setminus F$. Furthermore $G^{(II)}|\bar{x} \supseteq F$. Hence, $G^{(II)}|\bar{x} \vdash_1 (C \vee D)$ or equivalently, $G^{(II)} \vdash_1 (x \vee C \vee D)$.

(IV) *Strengthen all weakened clauses.*

The fourth phase removes all occurrences of the literal x from clauses in $G^{(III)}$, thereby reversing the second phase *and* strengthening $(x \vee C)$ to C. This phase consists of three parts. First, we reintroduce the implication $x \Rightarrow \omega$, or in clauses $(\bar{x} \vee l)$ with $l \in \omega$. These clauses have RAT on l w.r.t. $G^{(III)}$ by the same reasoning used to remove them in the second phase above and in case $(\bar{x} \vee l)$ can be resolved on l with the only clause $(x \vee C)$ added in the third phase, thus $\bar{l} \in C$, the resolvent is a tautology (contains x and $\bar{x}$). Afterwards, we strengthen all clauses $(x \vee E) \in G^{(III)}$ to E as follows. Note that this also strengthens clause $(x \vee C)$ to C. Observe that all clauses $(x \vee E) \in G^{(III)}$ including $(x \vee C)$ are satisfied by ω and therefore there exists a clause $(\bar{x} \vee l)$ with $l \in E$. Self-subsuming literal elimination (SSLE) can now eliminate all literals x. Finally, the implication $x \Rightarrow \omega$ is no longer required. The clauses $(\bar{x} \vee l)$ with $l \in \omega$ added twice already can be removed again since literal $\bar{x}$ has become pure due to the strengthening of all clauses containing literal x. The resulting formula obtained from $G^{(III)}$ by removing all occurrences of literal x is denoted by $G^{(IV)}$.

(V) *Remove the shortened copies.*

The fifth phase reverses the first phase, and actually uses the same argument as the fourth phase. All clauses in $G^{(III)}$ that contained a literal x were strengthened by removing these literals in phase four. As a consequence, the literal $\bar{x}$ is (still) pure in $G^{(IV)}$. The only clauses that still contain literal $\bar{x}$ are exactly the clauses that have been added in the first phase. Since they are all blocked on $\bar{x}$ w.r.t. $G^{(IV)}$, they can be eliminated, while preserving satisfiability. After removing these clauses we obtain $G^{(V)}$ which equals $F \wedge C$.

4.3   Complexity

In this section we analyze the worst case complexity of converting a PR derivation $(0, C_1, \omega_1), \ldots, (0, C_n, \omega_n)$ of a formula F_n from a formula F_0 into a DRAT derivation $(d_1, D_1, \omega'_1), \ldots, (d_1, D_m, \omega'_m)$ of $G_m = F_n$ from $G_0 = F_0$ using the presented simulation algorithm. The number of DRAT steps that are required to simulate a single PR addition step depends on the size of the formula. Let $N = |F_n|$ be the number of clauses in the last F_n and $V = |var(F_n)|$ the number of its variables. Since a PR derivation does not remove clauses, we have $|F_i| = |F_{i-1}| + 1$ and $|var(F_i)| \geq |var(F_{i-1})|$. Therefore for $i \in \{1..n\}$, $|F_i| \leq N$ and $|var(F_i)| \leq V$. In the analysis we ignore clause deletion, since the number of clause deletions is bounded by the number of added clauses.

In phase (I) of the conversion algorithm, copies of clauses that are reduced but not satisfied by ω_i are added, while phase (II) clauses are weakened which are reduced and satisfied by ω_i. Since a clause is either satisfied, not satisfied, or untouched by ω_i, the sum of the number of copies and weakened clauses is at most $|F_i| \leq N$. Also the implication $x \Rightarrow \omega_i$ is added in phase (II), meaning at most $|var(\omega_i)| \leq |var(F_i)| \leq V$ clause addition steps. Phase (III) adds a single clause. Phase (IV) adds again the implication $x \Rightarrow \omega_i$ (at most V steps) and strengthens all weakened clauses (at most N steps). Phase (V) only deletes clauses. Thus the total number of clause additions for all phases in the conversion of a single PR step is bounded by $2V + 2N + 1$.

There are $n \leq N$ additions in the PR proof and for each addition we apply the conversion algorithm. Hence the total number of clause addition steps in the DRAT derivation is at most $2NV + 2N^2 + N$. Since $V \leq N$ for any interesting PR derivation, the number of steps in the resulting DRAT derivation is in $\mathcal{O}(N^2)$.

5   Optimizations

The simulation algorithm described in the prior section was designed to result in compact DRAT derivations using a single new variable, while focussing on converting any PR derivation into a DRAT derivation. The algorithm can be further optimized to reduce the size of the resulting DRAT derivations.

5.1   Refutations

In practice, most PR derivations are refutations, i.e., they include adding the empty clause. When converting PR refutations, one can ignore the justification of any weakening steps as such steps trivially preserve unsatisfiability. The only weakening steps in the simulation algorithm are performed in phase (II). The purpose of the addition of the implication $x \Rightarrow \omega$ in phase (II) is to allow the weakening via self-subsuming literal addition (SSLA). This justification is no longer required for PR refutations. Without the addition of $x \Rightarrow \omega$, one can also discard its removal. So both the first and third part of phase (II) can be omitted.

5.2 Witness Minimization

In some situations, only a subset of the involved clauses needs to be weakened (phase (II)) and later strengthened (phase (IV)). Weakening of involved clauses is required to make sure that the clauses $(\overline{x} \vee l)$ with $l \in \omega$ are RAT on l w.r.t. $G^{(\text{III})}$ in phase (IV) of the simulation algorithm. However, some of the clauses $(\overline{x} \vee l)$ may be unit implied by others (and do not require to be a RAT on l). This situation occurs when a subset of the witness implies the full witness via unit propagation. We minimize the witness by searching for the smallest witness $\omega' \subseteq \omega$ such that ω' implies ω via unit propagation. Only clauses reduced by ω' and satisfied by ω need to be weakened in phase (II) and strengthened in (IV).

5.3 Avoiding Copying

In some quite specific case, one can avoid copying the clauses that are reduced, but not satisfied by the witness altogether. In other words skip phase (I) and (V) of the simulation algorithm. This case, however, occurred frequently in our PR proofs. Let α denote the smallest assignment that falsifies the PR clause C to be added. Furthermore, let ω be the witness and ω' the minimized witness as discussed above. The condition for avoiding clause copying consists of two parts. First, there is no literal $l \in \alpha$ such that $\overline{l} \in \omega'$. Recall that there always exists a literal $l \in \alpha$ such that $\overline{l} \in \omega$. So witness minimization is necessary. Second, for each literal $l \in \omega'$, the unit clause (l) should be a RAT on l w.r.t. the current formula without the involved clauses under α. Although both conditions are very restrictive, they apply often in the PR proofs used in the evaluation.

Basically, this optimization removes phases (I) and (V), and modifies (II), (III), and (IV). The modified phases are named phase (i), (ii), and (iii), resp.

(i) *Weaken the clauses that are reduced by ω' and satisfied by ω.*
    Clause $E \in F$ is called *involved* if it is reduced by the reduced witness ω' and satisfied by the original ω. The first phase weakens all involved clauses E to $(x \vee E)$ as follows. First, we add the implication $x \Rightarrow \omega' \cup \alpha$, or in clauses $(\overline{x} \vee l)$ with $l \in \omega' \cup \alpha$. These clauses are blocked because G does not contain clauses with literal x. Now we can weaken the involved clauses using SSLA. Then we remove the implication part $x \Rightarrow \omega'$, but keep $x \Rightarrow \alpha$. When adding this implication, the clauses $(\overline{x} \vee l)$ with $l \in \omega'$ were blocked on x. Now we can remove them, because they have RAT on l as all clauses containing $\overline{l}$ have been either weakened (if they were satisfied by ω) or are implied by α by the second condition. The resulting formula, G in which all involved clauses are weakened and includes $x \Rightarrow \alpha$, is denoted by $G^{(\text{i})}$.

(ii) *Add the weakened PR clause.*
    Add the clause $(x \vee C)$, which is equivalent to the implication $x \Leftarrow \alpha$, to $G^{(\text{i})}$, resulting in $G^{(\text{ii})}$. The only clauses containing literal $\overline{x}$ are the ones that originate from $x \Rightarrow \alpha$. As a consequence, $(x \vee C)$ is blocked on x w.r.t. $G^{(\text{i})}$.

(iii) *Strengthen all weakened clauses.*

The third phase removes all occurrences of the literal x from clauses in $G^{(ii)}$, thereby reversing the second phase *and* strengthening $(x \vee C)$ to C. This phase consists of four parts. First, we reintroduce the implication part $x \Rightarrow \omega'$, or in clauses $(\overline{x} \vee l)$ with $l \in \omega'$. Again, these clauses have RAT on l w.r.t. $G^{(ii)}$. Second, we remove the implication part $x \Rightarrow \alpha$, i.e. the clauses $(\overline{x} \vee l)$ with $l \in \alpha$. Afterwards, we strengthen $(x \vee C)$ to C and all clauses $(x \vee E) \in G^{(ii)}$ to E. Observe that all clauses $(x \vee E) \in G^{(ii)}$ including $(x \vee C)$ are satisfied by ω and therefore there exists a clause $(\overline{x} \vee l)$ with $l \in F$. SSLE can therefore remove all literals x. Finally, the implication $x \Rightarrow \omega'$ is no longer required. The clauses $(\overline{x} \vee l)$ with $l \in \omega'$ can be eliminated because literal $\overline{x}$ has become pure due to the strengthening of all clauses containing literal x. The resulting formula, i.e., $G^{(ii)}$ after removing all occurrences of literal x, is denoted by $G^{(iii)}$ and equals $G \wedge C$.

In case the PR derivation is a refutation, we can further optimize this case, by changing phase (i) as follows: Instead of adding the implication $x \Rightarrow \omega' \cup \alpha$, the implication $x \Rightarrow \alpha$ is added. Without the addition of the implication part $x \Rightarrow \omega'$, we can also discard removing that part at the end of phase (i).

6 Alternative Simulation Algorithms

Even though the conversion from PR derivations to DRAT derivations is arguably the most useful one in practice, one can also consider the following alternatives.

6.1 Limiting the Number of RAT Steps

Most steps in the simulation algorithm are "basic" steps, i.e., self-subsuming literal addition or elimination and blocked clause addition or elimination. There are only few "full" RAT addition steps: The removal of the implication in phase (II), the addition of the weakened PR clause in phase (III) and the addition of the implication in phase (IV). It is interesting to explore the option to reduce the number of these "full" RAT addition steps. Eliminating "full" RAT addition steps brings us close to a simulation algorithm with only basic steps.

It is easy to eliminate all but one "full" RAT addition step. In order to eliminate the RAT steps in phase (II), one can weaken the clauses (i.e., add a literal x using SSLA) that are reduced but not satisfied by the witness using the shortened copies of clauses that are reduced, but not satisfied by ω. After the weakening, we can remove the implication $x \Rightarrow \omega$ using blocked clause elimination (instead of RAT), because now all clauses that are touched by ω have a literal x. Therefore all clauses $(\overline{x} \vee l)$ with $l \in \omega$ are blocked on l. The weakening also allows adding the implication $x \Rightarrow \omega$ in phase (IV) using blocked clause addition steps (instead of RAT). The strengthening of the newly weakened clause can be performed in phase (IV) using SSLE (after adding the implication). It is not obvious how to replace the only remaining RAT addition in phase (III) using basic steps.

6.2   Converting DPR Proofs into DRAT Proofs

So far we only considered converting a PR clause addition as a sequence of
DRAT steps and ignored deletion of PR clauses from a formula. In most cases,
clause deletion steps in a proof facilitate more efficient checking of a proof of
unsatisfiability and can therefore be deleted without any checking. However,
there are situations in which one wants to check the validity of clause deletion
steps. In particular for proofs of satisfiability, i.e., a sequence of proof steps that
show that a given formula is equivalent to the empty formula and thus satisfiable.

The DPR proof system is a clausal proof system that allows the addition
and deletion of PR clauses. Conversion of a PR clause addition step into DRAT
proof steps is equivalent to the conversion of such a step in the PR proof system.
The conversion of a PR clause deletion step is slightly different. Given a formula
F and a clause $C \in F$, which is a PR clause w.r.t. F with witness ω. The first
phase of the conversion is exactly the same as phase (I) of the PR clause addition
conversion. The second phase of the conversion is slightly different compared to
phase (II) of the PR clause addition conversion: Instead of weakening all clauses
reduced and satisfied by ω, we weaken all clauses satisfied by ω. Notice that this
includes weakening C to $(x \vee C)$. The third phase consists of deleting $(x \vee C)$ from
the current formula. Recall that phase (III) of the PR clause addition conversion
added $(x \vee C)$. The final phase corresponds to phases (IV) and (V).

6.3   Converting PR Refutations into RAT Refutations

The presented simulation algorithm converts PR derivations into DRAT derivations. We selected the DRAT proof system as target, because it is the most
widely-supported proof system by top-tier SAT solvers and it allows step-wise
simulation using deletion steps. The question arises whether deletion steps are
required when converting a PR refutation. In short, the answer is *no* when allowing the introduction of arbitrary many new Boolean variables. Converting a deletion step can be realized as follows. Let C be the clause that is deleted from a
formula F. For each $x \in var(C)$, add to F the equivalence $x' \Leftrightarrow x$ with x' being
a new variable. Afterwards, copy all clauses in F —apart from C— that contain
at least one literal l with $var(l) \in var(C)$ using the new x' variables instead of
the old x variables. Finally replace all occurrences of old literals x and $\overline{x}$ in the
remaining proof by literals x' and $\overline{x}'$, respectively.

In order to limit the number of copy operations, one can group (consecutive) deletion steps and use the same variables x' for the group. The simulation
algorithm can be partitioned into two groups of (consecutive) clause addition
steps that are followed each by groups of consecutive clause deletion steps: The
first group of addition steps consists of phase (I) and the first half of phase (II),
i.e., adding the implication $x \Rightarrow \omega$ and the weakened involved clauses. The first
group of deletion steps consists of the remaining part of phase (II), i.e., deletion of the involved clauses and deletion of the implication $x \Rightarrow \omega$. The second
group of consecutive addition steps consists of phase (III) and the first half of
phase (IV), i.e, adding the implication $x \Rightarrow \omega$ and adding back the involved

clauses. The second group of consecutive deletion steps consists of the remaining part of phase (IV), i.e., removal of the weakened involved clauses and the implication $x \Rightarrow \omega$, and phase (V). By grouping the deletion steps, one can convert PR refutations into RAT refutations with at most a quadratic blowup, so the same worst case complexity as converting PR derivations into DRAT derivations.

7   Evaluation

We implemented a tool, called PR2DRAT, to convert PR proofs into DRAT proofs[1] and evaluated the tool on short PR proofs for hard formulas from three families:

(1) pigeon-hole,   (2) two-pigeons-per-hole [2], and   (3) Tseitin formulas [4,27].

Every resolution proof of a formula in these families is exponential in the size of the formula [11,28]. As a consequence, any CDCL solver without dedicated special reasoning techniques, such as cardinality or XOR reasoning, is unable to solve these benchmarks in reasonable time. In contrast, our PR proofs are smaller than the formulas, so linear in size. The PR proofs of the pigeon-hole formulas and two-pigeons-per-hole formulas have been constructed manually in earlier work [17]. The proofs of the Tseitin formulas have been manually constructed by expressing Gaussian elimination in the PR system. Applying Gaussian elimination —after syntactically extracting XOR constraints from the CNF formulas— is enough to solve these formulas. We will first evaluate the size of the conversion. Afterwards we certify for the first time the short PR proofs by converting them into DRAT proofs which are checked by a formally verified checker.

7.1   Proof Simulation and Optimization

We will compare three kinds of DRAT proofs for the benchmarks used in the experiments: the most compact existing ones [14,15], the proofs obtained from using our plain conversion algorithm, and the proofs obtained from our optimized algorithm. The most compact existing ones originate from expressing symmetry breaking as DRAT proof steps. Table 1 shows the comparison. All proofs have been trimmed using the DRAT-trim tool [12] once. Applying DRAT-trim multiple rounds (using the output proof as input proof for the next round) allows further reduction of the proof size, but typically these extra reductions are small.

For pigeon-hole formulas over n pigeons, the most compact existing proofs have $\mathcal{O}(n^4)$ proof steps. This is also the case for the DRAT proofs obtained through our basic conversion algorithm as well as for the extended resolution proofs by Cook [5]. However, DRAT proofs obtained with our optimized algorithm have only $\mathcal{O}(n^3)$ proof steps. Notice that the size of pigeon-hole formulas as well as the size of PR proofs are both in $\mathcal{O}(n^3)$. In other words, our optimized conversion algorithm cannot only produce DRAT proofs, but for pigeon-hole formulas it generates the first DRAT proofs of linear size.

---

[1] The tool, checkers, formulas, and proofs discussed in this section are available at http://www.cs.utexas.edu/~marijn/pr2drat/.

Table 1. Comparison of the size of trimmed, generated DRAT proofs for hard formulas. The size of proofs is measured in the number of clause addition steps (#add). We denote with "—" that no DRAT proof is available. Bold is used for the smallest DRAT proofs.

	input		PR proofs	DRAT proofs (#add)		
formula	#var	#cls	#add	existing [14,15]	plain	optimized
hole20	420	4,221	2,870	49,410	94,901	**26,547**
hole30	930	13,981	9,455	234,195	422,101	**89,827**
hole40	1,640	32,841	22,140	715,030	1,241,126	**213,107**
hole50	2,550	63,801	42,925	1,708,915	2,893,476	**416,387**
tph8	136	5,457	1,156	253,958	86,216	**25,204**
tph12	300	27,625	3,950	1,966,472	612,108	**127,296**
tph16	528	87,329	9,416	—	2,490,672	**401,004**
tph20	820	213,241	18,450	—	7,440,692	**976,376**
Urquhart-s5-b1	106	714	620	—	30,235	**28,189**
Urquhart-s5-b2	107	742	606	—	34,535	**32,574**
Urquhart-s5-b3	121	1,116	692	—	44,117	**41,230**
Urquhart-s5-b4	114	888	636	—	40,598	**37,978**

The results for the two-pigeons-per-hole formulas are similar, but more pronounced: There exist only DRAT proofs of the formulas up to 12 holes and 25 pigeons (tph12) [15]. Our plain simulation algorithm can produce DRAT proofs of the formulas up to 20 holes and 41 pigeons (tph20). Moreover, our optimized simulation algorithm is able to produce proofs that are linear in size of the formulas, although not linear in the size of the PR proofs.

We are unaware of any DRAT proofs of hard Tseitin formulas, e.g., from the Urquhart-s5-b* family [4], nor of any tool able to produce such DRAT proofs. However, we succeeded to manually produce short PR proofs without new variables for these formulas and convert them into DRAT proofs. The resulting DRAT proofs, with and without optimizations, are relatively large compared to the PR proofs. The blowup is close to the quadratic worse case. We observed that DRAT-trim was able to remove many (around 70%) of clause additions, which suggests that there could be an optimization to generate shorter DRAT proofs.

7.2   Verified PR Proof Checking

Our proof simulation approach can be used to validate PR proofs with formally verified tools and thereby increasing the confidence in their correctness. The tool chain works as follows: Given a formula F and an alleged PR proof P_{PR} of F, our tool PR2DRAT converts P_{PR} into a DRAT proof P_{DRAT}. Afterwards, we use the DRAT-trim tool to convert P_{DRAT} into a CLRAT (compressed linear RAT) proof P_{CLRAT}. CLRAT proofs can be efficiently checked using formally verified checkers [7]. We used the verified checker ACL2check [13] to certify that P_{CLRAT} is a valid proof of unsatisfiability of F. Notice that the tools PR2DRAT and DRAT-trim are unverified and thus may turn an invalid proof into a valid proof or vice versa.

Figure 1 shows the results of applying this tool chain on the benchmark suite. The PR2DRAT tool was able to convert each PR proof into a DRAT proof in less

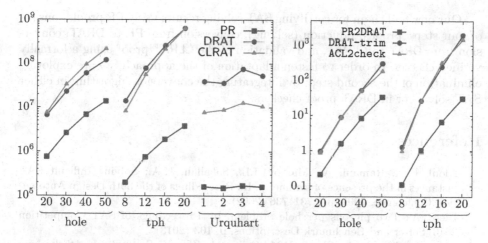

Fig. 1. Certification of PR proofs using PR2DRAT, DRAT-trim, and the formally verified checker ACL2check. Left the sizes of proofs in the PR, DRAT, and CLRAT formats are shown in bytes and right the proof conversion and checking times are in seconds. No times are shown for the Urquhart instances as all times were less than a second.

than a minute and half of the proofs in less than a second. The runtimes of DRAT-trim and ACL2check are one to two orders of magnitude higher than for PR2DRAT. Thus our tool adds little overhead to the tool chain. The sizes of the DRAT and CLRAT proofs are comparable. However, these proofs are different: DRAT-trim (A) removes redundant clause additions; (B) includes hints to speedup verified checking; (C) compresses proofs. The effect of (A) depends on proof quality; (B) increases the size of proofs of small hard problems by roughly a factor of four; (C) reduces size to 30% of the uncompressed proofs. The difference between the DRAT and CLRAT proofs therefore indicate how much redundancy was removed: for pigeon-hole proofs hardly anything, for two-pigeons-per-hole proofs a modest amount, and for Tseitin proofs a lot. Notice that runtimes of the verified checker ACL2check are comparable to the C-based checker DRAT-trim.

8   Conclusions and Future Work

We showed how to convert PR proofs into DRAT proofs using only a single new variable with an at most quadratic blowup in proof size. This result suggests that it might also be possible to construct DRAT proofs without new variables using one variable elimination step and reusing the eliminated variable. The optimizations implemented in our conversion tool PR2DRAT made it possible to produce DRAT proofs for hard problems that are significantly smaller compared to existing DRAT proofs of those problems. The main open question is whether PR proofs can be converted into RAT proofs (i.e., not allowing the deletion steps) with a small number of new variables. Without deletion steps, it seems that copying the formula using new variables is required.

Our new tool chain for certifying SAT solving results using PR proofs consists of four steps: proof production (solving), conversion from PR to DRAT, conversion from DRAT to CLRAT, and validation of the CLRAT proof using a formally verified checker. In order to fasten adaptation of the approach, we are exploring elimination of the second step, by integrating the conversion algorithm in either SAT solvers or in DRAT proof checkers.

References

1. Aloul, F.A., Ramani, A., Markov, I.L., Sakallah, K.A.: Solving difficult SAT instances in the presence of symmetry. In: Proceedings of the 39th Design Automation Conference, 2002, pp. 731–736 (2002)
2. Biere, A.: Two pigeons per hole problem. In: Proceedings of SAT Competition 2013: Solver and Benchmark Descriptions, p. 103 (2013)
3. Biere, A., Cimatti, A., Clarke, E.M., Fujita, M., Zhu, Y.: Symbolic model checking using SAT procedures instead of BDDs. In: DAC, pp. 317–320 (1999)
4. Chatalic, P., Simon, L.: Multi-resolution on compressed sets of clauses. In: 12th IEEE International Conference on Tools with Artificial Intelligence (ICTAI 2000), 13–15 November 2000, Vancouver, BC, Canada, pp. 2–10 (2000)
5. Cook, S.A.: A short proof of the pigeon hole principle using extended resolution. SIGACT News 8(4), 28–32 (1976)
6. Crawford, J.M., Ginsberg, M.L., Luks, E.M., Roy, A.: Symmetry-breaking predicates for search problems. In: Knowledge Representation and Reasoning – KR 1996, pp. 148–159. Morgan Kaufmann (1996)
7. Cruz-Filipe, L., Heule, M.J.H., Hunt Jr., W.A., Kaufmann, M., Schneider-Kamp, P.: Efficient certified RAT verification. In: de Moura, L. (ed.) CADE 2017. LNCS (LNAI), vol. 10395, pp. 220–236. Springer, Cham (2017)
8. Cruz-Filipe, L., Marques-Silva, J., Schneider-Kamp, P.: Efficient certified resolution proof checking. In: Legay, A., Margaria, T. (eds.) TACAS 2017. LNCS, vol. 10205, pp. 118–135. Springer, Heidelberg (2017)
9. D'Silva, V., Kroening, D., Weissenbacher, G.: A survey of automated techniques for formal software verification. IEEE Trans. CAD Integr. Circuits Syst. 27(7), 1165–1178 (2008)
10. Eén, N., Biere, A.: Effective preprocessing in SAT through variable and clause elimination. In: Bacchus, F., Walsh, T. (eds.) SAT 2005. LNCS, vol. 3569, pp. 61–75. Springer, Heidelberg (2005)
11. Haken, A.: The intractability of resolution. Theor. Comput. Sci. 39, 297–308 (1985)
12. Heule, M.J.H.: The DRAT format and DRAT-trim checker. CoRR, abs/1610.06229 (2016)
13. Heule, M.J.H., Hunt Jr., W.A., Kaufmann, M., Wetzler, N.D.: Efficient, verified checking of propositional proofs. In: Ayala-Rincón, M., Muñoz, C.A. (eds.) ITP 2017. LNCS, vol. 10499, pp. 269–284. Springer, Cham (2017)
14. Heule, M.J.H., Hunt Jr., W.A., Wetzler, N.D.: Verifying refutations with extended resolution. In: Bonacina, M.P. (ed.) CADE 2013. LNCS (LNAI), vol. 7898, pp. 345–359. Springer, Heidelberg (2013)
15. Heule, M.J.H., Hunt Jr., W.A., Wetzler, N.D.: Expressing symmetry breaking in DRAT proofs. In: Felty, A.P., Middeldorp, A. (eds.) CADE 2015. LNCS (LNAI), vol. 9195, pp. 591–606. Springer, Cham (2015)

16. Heule, M.J.H., Järvisalo, M., Lonsing, F., Seidl, M., Biere, A.: Clause elimination for SAT and QSAT. J. Artif. Intell. Res. **53**, 127–168 (2015)
17. Heule, M.J.H., Kiesl, B., Biere, A.: Short proofs without new variables. In: de Moura, L. (ed.) CADE 2017. LNCS (LNAI), vol. 10395, pp. 130–147. Springer, Cham (2017)
18. Heule, M.J.H., Kiesl, B., Seidl, M., Biere, A.: PRuning through satisfaction. In: Strichman, O., Tzoref-Brill, R. (eds.) HVC 2017. LNCS, vol. 10629, pp. 179–194. Springer, Cham (2017)
19. Heule, M.J.H., Seidl, M., Biere, A.: A unified proof system for QBF preprocessing. In: Demri, S., Kapur, D., Weidenbach, C. (eds.) IJCAR 2014. LNCS (LNAI), vol. 8562, pp. 91–106. Springer, Cham (2014)
20. Heule, M.J.H., Seidl, M., Biere, A.: Solution validation and extraction for QBF preprocessing. J. Autom. Reason. **58**(1), 97–125 (2017)
21. Järvisalo, M., Heule, M.J.H., Biere, A.: Inprocessing rules. In: Gramlich, B., Miller, D., Sattler, U. (eds.) IJCAR 2012. LNCS (LNAI), vol. 7364, pp. 355–370. Springer, Heidelberg (2012)
22. Kiesl, B., Seidl, M., Tompits, H., Biere, A.: Super-blocked clauses. In: Olivetti, N., Tiwari, A. (eds.) IJCAR 2016. LNCS (LNAI), vol. 9706, pp. 45–61. Springer, Cham (2016)
23. Kullmann, O.: On a generalization of extended resolution. Discrete Appl. Math. **96–97**, 149–176 (1999)
24. Lammich, P.: Efficient verified (UN)SAT certificate checking. In: de Moura, L. (ed.) CADE 2017. LNCS (LNAI), vol. 10395, pp. 237–254. Springer, Cham (2017)
25. Luo, M., Li, C., Xiao, F., Manyà, F., Lü, Z.: An effective learnt clause minimization approach for CDCL SAT solvers. In: Proceedings of the Twenty-Sixth International Joint Conference on Artificial Intelligence, IJCAI 2017, pp. 703–711 (2017)
26. Marques-Silva, J.P., Lynce, I., Malik, S.: Conflict-driven clause learning SAT solvers. In: FAIA, vol. 185, Chap. 4, pp. 131–153. IOS Press, February 2009
27. Tseitin, G.S.: On the complexity of derivation in propositional calculus. In: Siekmann, J.H., Wrightson, G. (eds.) Automation of Reasoning 2, pp. 466–483. Springer, Heidelberg (1983)
28. Urquhart, A.: Hard examples for resolution. J. ACM **34**(1), 209–219 (1987)
29. Wetzler, N.D., Heule, M.J.H., Hunt Jr., W.A.: DRAT-trim: efficient checking and trimming using expressive clausal proofs. In: Sinz, C., Egly, U. (eds.) SAT 2014. LNCS, vol. 8561, pp. 422–429. Springer, Cham (2014)
30. Zhang, L., Malik, S.: Validating SAT solvers using an independent resolution-based checker: practical implementations and other applications. In: DATE, pp. 10880–10885 (2003)

Abstraction Refinement for Emptiness Checking of Alternating Data Automata

Radu Iosif[(✉)] and Xiao Xu

CNRS, Verimag, Université de Grenoble Alpes, Grenoble, France
{Radu.Iosif,Xiao.Xu}@univ-grenoble-alpes.fr

Abstract. Alternating automata have been widely used to model and
verify systems that handle data from finite domains, such as communication protocols or hardware. The main advantage of the alternating model
of computation is that complementation is possible in linear time, thus
allowing to concisely encode trace inclusion problems that occur often in
verification. In this paper we consider alternating automata over infinite
alphabets, whose transition rules are formulae in a combined theory of
Booleans and some infinite data domain, that relate past and current values of the data variables. The data theory is not fixed, but rather it is a
parameter of the class. We show that union, intersection and complementation are possible in linear time in this model and, though the emptiness problem is undecidable, we provide two efficient semi-algorithms,
inspired by two state-of-the-art abstraction refinement model checking
methods: lazy predicate abstraction [8] and the IMPACT semi-algorithm
[17]. We have implemented both methods and report the results of an
experimental comparison.

1 Introduction

The language inclusion problem is recognized as being central to verification of
hardware, communication protocols and software systems. A property is a specification of the correct executions of a system, given as a set $\mathcal{P}$ of executions,
and the verification problem asks if the set $\mathcal{S}$ of executions of the system under
consideration is contained within $\mathcal{P}$. This problem is at the core of widespread
verification techniques, such as automata-theoretic model checking [23], where
systems are specified as finite-state automata and properties defined using Linear
Temporal Logic [21]. However the bottleneck of this and other related verification techniques is the intractability of language inclusion (PSPACE-complete for
finite-state automata over finite alphabets).

Alternation [3] was introduced as a generalization of nondeterminism, introducing universal, in addition to existential transitions. For automata over finite
alphabets, the language inclusion problem can be encoded as the emptiness
problem of an alternating automaton of linear size. Moreover, efficient exploration techniques based on antichains are shown to perform well for alternating
automata over finite alphabets [5].

© The Author(s) 2018
D. Beyer and M. Huisman (Eds.): TACAS 2018, LNCS 10806, pp. 93–111, 2018.
https://doi.org/10.1007/978-3-319-89963-3_6

Using finite alphabets for the specification of properties and models is however very restrictive, when dealing with real-life computer systems, mostly because of the following reasons. On one hand, programs handle data from very large domains, that can be assumed to be infinite (64-bit integers, floating point numbers, strings of characters, etc.) and their correctness must be specified in terms of the data values. On the other hand, systems must respond to strict deadlines, which requires temporal specifications as timed languages [1].

Although being convenient specification tools, automata over infinite alphabets lack the decidability properties ensured by finite alphabets. In general, when considering infinite data as part of the input alphabet, language inclusion is undecidable and, even complementation becomes impossible, for instance, for timed automata [1] or finite-memory register automata [13]. One can recover theoretical decidability, by restricting the number of variables (clocks) in timed automata to one [20], or forbidding relations between current and past/future values, as with symbolic automata [24]. In such cases, also the emptiness problem for the alternating versions becomes decidable [4,14].

In this paper, we present a new model of alternating automata over infinite alphabets consisting of pairs (a, ν) where a is an input event from a finite set and ν is a valuation of a finite set $\mathbf{x}$ of variables that range over an infinite domain. We assume that, at all times, the successive values taken by the variables in $\mathbf{x}$ are an observable part of the language, in other words, there are no hidden variables in our model. The transition rules are specified by a set of formulae, in a combined first-order theory of Boolean control states and data, that relate past with present values of the variables. We do not fix the data theory a priori, but rather consider it to be a parameter of the class.

A run over an input word $(a_1, \nu_1) \ldots (a_n, \nu_n)$ is a sequence $\phi_0(\mathbf{x}_0) \Rightarrow \phi_1(\mathbf{x}_0, \mathbf{x}_1) \Rightarrow \ldots \Rightarrow \phi_n(\mathbf{x}_0, \ldots, \mathbf{x}_n)$ of rewritings of the initial formula by substituting Boolean states with time-stamped transition rules. The word is accepted if the final formula $\phi_n(\mathbf{x}_0, \ldots, \mathbf{x}_n)$ holds, when all time-stamped variables $\mathbf{x}_1, \ldots, \mathbf{x}_n$ are substituted by their values in $\nu_1, \ldots, \nu_n$, all non-final states replaced by false and all final states by true.

The Boolean operations of union, intersection and complement can be implemented in linear time in this model, thus matching the complexity of performing these operations in the finite-alphabet case. The price to be paid is that emptiness becomes undecidable, for which reason we provide two efficient semi-algorithms for emptiness, based on lazy predicate abstraction [8] and the IMPACT method [17]. These algorithms are proven to terminate and return a word from the language of the automaton, if one exists, but termination is not guaranteed when the language is empty.

We have implemented the Boolean operations and emptiness checking semi-algorithms and carried out experiments with examples taken from array logics [2], timed automata [9], communication protocols [25] and hardware verification [22].

Related Work. Data languages and automata have been defined previously, in a classical nondeterministic setting. For instance, Kaminski and Francez [13] consider languages, over an infinite alphabet of data, recognized by automata with a finite number of registers, that store the input data and compare it using equality. Just as the timed languages recognized by timed automata [1], these languages, called quasi-regular, are not closed under complement, but their emptiness is decidable. The impossibility of complementation here is caused by the use of hidden variables, which we do not allow. Emptiness is however undecidable in our case, mainly because counting (incrementing and comparing to a constant) data values is allowed, in many data theories.

Another related model is that of predicate automata [6], which recognize languages over integer data by labeling the words with conjunctions of uninterpreted predicates. We intend to explore further the connection with our model of alternating data automata, in order to apply our method to the verification of parallel programs.

The model presented in this paper stems from the language inclusion problem considered in [11]. There we provide a semi-algorithm for inclusion of data languages, based on an exponential determinization procedure and an abstraction refinement loop using lazy predicate abstraction [8]. In this work we consider the full model of alternation and rely entirely on the ability of SMT solvers to produce interpolants in the combined theory of Booleans and data. Since determinisation is not needed and complementation is possible in linear time, the bulk of the work is carried out by the solver.

The emptiness check for alternating data automata adapts similar semi-algorithms for nondeterministic infinite-state programs to the alternating model of computation. In particular, we considered the state-of-the-art IMPACT procedure [17] that is shown to outperform lazy predicate abstraction [8] in the nondeterministic case, and generalized it to cope with alternation. More recent approaches for interpolant-based abstraction refinement target Horn systems [10,18], used to encode recursive and concurrent programs [7]. However, the emptiness of alternating word automata cannot be directly encoded using Horn clauses, because all the branches of the computation synchronize on the same input, which cannot be encoded by a finite number of local (equality) constraints. We believe that the lazy annotation techniques for Horn clauses are suited for branching computations, which we intend to consider in a future tree automata setting.

2 Preliminaries

A *signature* $S = (S^s, S^f)$ consists of a set S^s of sort *symbols* and a set S^f of sorted *function symbols*. To simplify the presentation, we assume w.l.o.g. that $S^s = \{\mathsf{Data}, \mathsf{Bool}\}^1$ and each function symbol $f \in S^f$ has $\#(f) \geq 0$ arguments of sort Data and return value $\sigma(f) \in S^s$. If $\#(f) = 0$ then f is a *constant*. We consider constants $\top$ and $\bot$ of sort Bool.

---

[1] The generalization to more than two sorts is without difficulty, but would unnecessarily clutter the technical presentation.

Let Var be an infinite countable set of *variables*, where each $x \in$ Var has an associated sort $\sigma(x)$. A *term* t of sort $\sigma(t) = S$ is a variable $x \in$ Var where $\sigma(x) = S$, or $f(t_1, \ldots, t_{\#(f)})$ where $t_1, \ldots, t_{\#(f)}$ are terms of sort Data and $\sigma(f) = S$. An *atom* is a term of sort Bool or an equality $t \approx s$ between two terms of sort Data. A *formula* is an existentially quantified combination of atoms using disjunction $\vee$, conjunction $\wedge$ and negation $\neg$ and we write $\phi \to \psi$ for $\neg\phi \vee \psi$.

We denote by $\mathrm{FV}^\sigma(\phi)$ the set of free variables of sort σ in ϕ and write $\mathrm{FV}(\phi)$ for $\bigcup_{\sigma \in \mathsf{S}^s} \mathrm{FV}^\sigma(\phi)$. For a variable $x \in \mathrm{FV}(\phi)$ and a term t such that $\sigma(t) = \sigma(x)$, let $\phi[t/x]$ be the result of replacing each occurrence of x by t. For indexed sets $\mathbf{t} = \{t_1, \ldots, t_n\}$ and $\mathbf{x} = \{x_1, \ldots, x_n\}$, we write $\phi[\mathbf{t}/\mathbf{x}]$ for the formula obtained by simultaneously replacing x_i with t_i in ϕ, for all $i \in [1, n]$. The size $|\phi|$ is the number of symbols occuring in ϕ.

An *interpretation* $\mathcal{I}$ maps (1) the sort Data into a non-empty set $\mathsf{Data}^\mathcal{I}$, (2) the sort Bool into the set $\mathbb{B} = \{\mathtt{true}, \mathtt{false}\}$, where $\top^\mathcal{I} = \mathtt{true}$, $\bot^\mathcal{I} = \mathtt{false}$, and (3) each function symbol f into a total function $f^\mathcal{I} : (\mathsf{Data}^\mathcal{I})^{\#(f)} \to \sigma(f)^\mathcal{I}$, or an element of $\sigma(f)^\mathcal{I}$ when $\#(f) = 0$. Given an interpretation $\mathcal{I}$, a *valuation* ν maps each variable $x \in$ Var into an element $\nu(x) \in \sigma(x)^\mathcal{I}$. For a term t, we denote by $t_\nu^\mathcal{I}$ the value obtained by replacing each function symbol f by its interpretation $f^\mathcal{I}$ and each variable x by its valuation $\nu(x)$. For a formula ϕ, we write $\mathcal{I}, \nu \models \phi$ if the formula obtained by replacing each term t in ϕ by the value $t_\nu^\mathcal{I}$ is logically equivalent to true.

A formula ϕ is *satisfiable* in the interpretation $\mathcal{I}$ if there exists a valuation ν such that $\mathcal{I}, \nu \models \phi$, and *valid* if $\mathcal{I}, \nu \models \phi$ for all valuations ν. The *theory* $\mathbb{T}(\mathsf{S}, \mathcal{I})$ is the set of valid formulae written in the signature S, with the interpretation $\mathcal{I}$. A *decision procedure* for $\mathbb{T}(\mathsf{S}, \mathcal{I})$ is an algorithm that takes a formula ϕ in the signature S and returns yes iff $\phi \in \mathbb{T}(\mathsf{S}, \mathcal{I})$.

Given formulae φ and ψ, we say that ϕ *entails* ψ, denoted $\phi \models^\mathcal{I} \psi$ iff $\mathcal{I}, \nu \models \varphi$ implies $\mathcal{I}, \nu \models \psi$, for each valuation ν, and $\phi \Leftrightarrow^\mathcal{I} \psi$ iff $\phi \models^\mathcal{I} \psi$ and $\psi \models^\mathcal{I} \phi$. We omit mentioning the interpretation $\mathcal{I}$ when it is clear from the context.

3   Alternating Data Automata

In the rest of this section we fix an interpretation $\mathcal{I}$ and a finite alphabet Σ of *input events*. Given a finite set $\mathbf{x} \subset$ Var of variables of sort Data, let $\mathbf{x} \mapsto \mathsf{Data}^\mathcal{I}$ be the set of valuations of the variables $\mathbf{x}$ and $\Sigma[\mathbf{x}] = \Sigma \times (\mathbf{x} \mapsto \mathsf{Data}^\mathcal{I})$ be the set of *data symbols*. A *data word* (word in the sequel) is a finite sequence $(a_1, \nu_1)(a_2, \nu_2) \ldots (a_n, \nu_n)$ of data symbols, where $a_1, \ldots, a_n \in \Sigma$ and $\nu_1, \ldots, \nu_n : \mathbf{x} \to \mathsf{Data}^\mathcal{I}$ are valuations. We denote by ε the empty sequence, by Σ^* the set of finite sequences of input events and by $\Sigma[\mathbf{x}]^*$ the set of data words over $\mathbf{x}$.

This definition generalizes the classical notion of words from a finite alphabet to the possibly infinite alphabet $\Sigma[\mathbf{x}]$. Clearly, when $\mathsf{Data}^\mathcal{I}$ is sufficiently large or infinite, we can map the elements of Σ into designated elements of $\mathsf{Data}^\mathcal{I}$ and use a special variable to encode the input events. However, keeping Σ explicit in the following simplifies several technical points below, without cluttering the presentation.

Given sets of variables $\mathbf{b}, \mathbf{x} \subset \mathsf{Var}$ of sort Bool and Data, respectively, we denote by $\mathsf{Form}(\mathbf{b}, \mathbf{x})$ the set of formulae ϕ such that $\mathsf{FV}^{\mathsf{Bool}}(\phi) \subseteq \mathbf{b}$ and $\mathsf{FV}^{\mathsf{Data}}(\phi) \subseteq \mathbf{x}$. By $\mathsf{Form}^+(\mathbf{b}, \mathbf{x})$ we denote the set of formulae from $\mathsf{Form}(\mathbf{b}, \mathbf{x})$ in which each Boolean variable occurs under an even number of negations.

An *alternating data automaton* (ADA or automaton in the sequel) is a tuple $\mathcal{A} = \langle \mathbf{x}, Q, \iota, F, \Delta \rangle$, where:

- $\mathbf{x} \subset \mathsf{Var}$ is a finite set of variables of sort Data,
- $Q \subset \mathsf{Var}$ is a finite set of variables of sort Bool (*states*),
- $\iota \in \mathsf{Form}^+(Q, \emptyset)$ is the *initial configuration*,
- $F \subseteq Q$ is a set of *final states*, and
- $\Delta : Q \times \Sigma \to \mathsf{Form}^+(Q, \overline{\mathbf{x}} \cup \mathbf{x})$ is a *transition function*, where $\overline{\mathbf{x}}$ denotes $\{\overline{x} \mid x \in \mathbf{x}\}$.

In each formula $\Delta(q, a)$ describing a transition rule, the variables $\overline{\mathbf{x}}$ track the previous and $\mathbf{x}$ the current values of the variables of $\mathcal{A}$. Observe that the initial values of the variables are left unconstrained, as the initial configuration does not contain free data variables. The size of $\mathcal{A}$ is defined as $|\mathcal{A}| = |\iota| + \sum_{(q,a) \in Q \times \Sigma} |\Delta(q, a)|$.

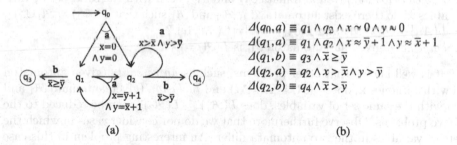

$$\Delta(q_0, a) \equiv q_1 \wedge q_2 \wedge x \sim 0 \wedge y \approx 0$$
$$\Delta(q_1, a) \equiv q_1 \wedge q_2 \wedge x \approx \overline{y} + 1 \wedge y \approx \overline{x} + 1$$
$$\Delta(q_1, b) \equiv q_3 \wedge \overline{x} \geq \overline{y}$$
$$\Delta(q_2, a) \equiv q_2 \wedge x > \overline{x} \wedge y > \overline{y}$$
$$\Delta(q_2, b) \equiv q_4 \wedge \overline{x} > \overline{y}$$

(a)   (b)

Fig. 1. Alternating data automaton example

Example. Figure 1(a) depicts an ADA with input alphabet $\Sigma = \{a, b\}$, variables $\mathbf{x} = \{x, y\}$, states $Q = \{q_0, q_1, q_2, q_3, q_4\}$, initial configuration q_0, final states $F = \{q_3, q_4\}$ and transitions given in Fig. 1(b), where missing rules, such as $\Delta(q_0, b)$, are assumed to be $\bot$. Rules $\Delta(q_0, a)$ and $\Delta(q_1, a)$ are universal and there are no existential nondeterministic rules. Rules $\Delta(q_1, a)$ and $\Delta(q_2, a)$ compare past $(\overline{x}, \overline{y})$ with present (x, y) values, $\Delta(q_0, a)$ constrains the present and $\Delta(q_1, b)$, $\Delta(q_2, b)$ the past values, respectively.   □

Formally, let $\mathbf{x}_k = \{x_k \mid x \in \mathbf{x}\}$, for any $k \geq 0$, be a set of time-stamped variables. For an input event $a \in \Sigma$ and a formula ϕ, we write $\Delta(\phi, a)$ (respectively $\Delta^k(\phi, a)$) for the formula obtained from ϕ by simultaneously replacing each state $q \in \mathsf{FV}^{\mathsf{Bool}}(\phi)$ by the formula $\Delta(q, a)$ (respectively $\Delta(q, a)[\mathbf{x}_k / \overline{\mathbf{x}}, \mathbf{x}_{k+1} / \mathbf{x}]$, for $k \geq 0$). Given a word $w = (a_1, \nu_1)(a_2, \nu_2) \ldots (a_n, \nu_n)$, the *run* of $\mathcal{A}$ over w is the sequence of formulae:

$$\phi_0(Q) \Rightarrow \phi_1(Q, \mathbf{x}_0 \cup \mathbf{x}_1) \Rightarrow \ldots \Rightarrow \phi_n(Q, \mathbf{x}_0 \cup \ldots \cup \mathbf{x}_n)$$

where $\phi_0 \equiv \iota$ and, for all $k \in [1, n]$, we have $\phi_k \equiv \Delta^k(\phi_{k-1}, a_k)$. Next, we slightly abuse notation and write $\Delta(\iota, a_1, \ldots, a_n)$ for the formula $\phi_n(\mathbf{x}_0, \ldots, \mathbf{x}_n)$ above. We say that $\mathcal{A}$ *accepts* w iff $I, \nu \models \Delta(\iota, a_1, \ldots, a_n)$, for some valuation ν that maps:(1) each $x \in \mathbf{x}_k$ to $\nu_k(x)$, for all $k \in [1, n]$, (2) each $q \in \mathrm{FV}^{\mathsf{Bool}}(\phi_n) \cap F$ to $\top$ and (3) each $q \in \mathrm{FV}^{\mathsf{Bool}}(\phi_n) \setminus F$ to $\bot$. The language of $\mathcal{A}$ is the set $L(\mathcal{A})$ of words from $\Sigma[\mathbf{x}]^*$ accepted by $\mathcal{A}$.

Example. The following sequence is a non-accepting run of the ADA from Fig. 1 on the word $(a, \langle 0, 0 \rangle), (a, \langle 1, 1 \rangle), (b, \langle 2, 1 \rangle)$, where $\mathsf{Data}^I = \mathbb{Z}$ and the function symbols have standard arithmetic interpretation:

$$q_0 \overset{(a,\langle 0,0\rangle)}{\Longrightarrow} \underbrace{q_1 \wedge q_2 \wedge x_1 \approx 0 \wedge y_1 \approx 0}_{} \overset{(a,\langle 1,1\rangle)}{\Longrightarrow} \underbrace{q_1 \wedge q_2 \wedge x_2 \approx y_1 + 1 \wedge y_2 \approx x_1 + 1}_{q_1} \wedge \underbrace{q_2 \wedge x_2 > x_1 \wedge y_2 > y_1 \wedge x_1 \approx 0 \wedge y_1 \approx 0}_{q_2} \overset{(b,\langle 2,1\rangle)}{\Longrightarrow}$$

$$\underbrace{q_3 \wedge x_2 \geq y_2 \wedge q_4 \wedge x_2 > y_2 \wedge x_2 \approx y_1 + 1 \wedge}_{q_1} \underbrace{y_2 \approx x_1 + 1 \wedge q_4 \wedge x_2 > y_2 \wedge x_2 > x_1 \wedge y_2 > y_1 \wedge x_1 \approx 0 \wedge y_1 \approx 0}_{q_2} \qquad \square$$

In this paper we tackle the following problems:

1. *Boolean closure*: given automata $\mathcal{A}_1$ and $\mathcal{A}_2$, both with the same set of variables $\mathbf{x}$, do there exist automata $\mathcal{A}_\cup$, $\mathcal{A}_\cap$ and $\overline{\mathcal{A}_1}$ such that $L(\mathcal{A}_\cup) = \mathcal{A}_1 \cup \mathcal{A}_2$, $L(A_\cap) = \mathcal{A}_1 \cap \mathcal{A}_2$ and $L(\overline{\mathcal{A}_1}) = \Sigma[\mathbf{x}]^* \setminus L(\mathcal{A}_1)$?
2. *emptiness*: given an automaton $\mathcal{A}$, is $L(\mathcal{A}) = \emptyset$?

It is well known that other problems, such as *universality* (given automaton $\mathcal{A}$ with variables $\mathbf{x}$, does $L(\mathcal{A}) = \Sigma[\mathbf{x}]^*$?) and *inclusion* (given automata $\mathcal{A}_1$ and $\mathcal{A}_2$ with the same set of variables, does $L(\mathcal{A}_1) \subseteq L(\mathcal{A}_2)$?) can be reduced to the above problems. Observe furthermore that we do not consider cases in which the sets of variables in the two automata differ. An interesting problem in this case would be: given automata $\mathcal{A}_1$ and $\mathcal{A}_2$, with variables $\mathbf{x}_1$ and $\mathbf{x}_2$, respectively, such that $\mathbf{x}_1 \subseteq \mathbf{x}_2$, does $L(\mathcal{A}_1) \subseteq L(\mathcal{A}_2)\downarrow_{\mathbf{x}_1}$, where $L(\mathcal{A}_2)\downarrow_{\mathbf{x}_1}$ is the projection of the set of words $L(\mathcal{A}_2)$ onto the variables $\mathbf{x}_1$? This problem is considered as future work.

3.1 Boolean Closure

Given a set Q of Boolean variables and a set $\mathbf{x}$ of variables of sort Data, for a formula $\phi \in \mathsf{Form}^+(Q, \mathbf{x})$, with no negated occurrences of the Boolean variables, we define the formula $\overline{\phi} \in \mathsf{Form}^+(Q, \mathbf{x})$ recursively on the structure of ϕ:

$$\overline{\phi_1 \vee \phi_2} \equiv \overline{\phi_1} \wedge \overline{\phi_2} \qquad\qquad \overline{\phi_1 \wedge \phi_2} \equiv \overline{\phi_1} \vee \overline{\phi_2}$$
$$\overline{\neg \phi} \equiv \neg \overline{\phi} \text{ if } \phi \text{ not atom} \qquad\qquad \overline{\phi} \equiv \phi \text{ if } \phi \in Q$$
$$\overline{\phi} \equiv \neg \phi \text{ if } \phi \notin Q \text{ atom}$$

We have $|\overline{\phi}| = |\phi|$, for every formula $\phi \in \mathsf{Form}^+(Q, \mathbf{x})$.

In the following let $\mathcal{A}_i = \langle \mathbf{x}, Q_i, \iota_i, F_i, \Delta_i \rangle$, for $i = 1, 2$, where w.l.o.g. we assume that $Q_1 \cap Q_2 = \emptyset$. We define:

$$\mathcal{A}_\cup = \langle \mathbf{x}, Q_1 \cup Q_2, \iota_1 \vee \iota_2, F_1 \cup F_2, \Delta_1 \cup \Delta_2 \rangle$$
$$\mathcal{A}_\cap = \langle \mathbf{x}, Q_1 \cup Q_2, \iota_1 \wedge \iota_2, F_1 \cup F_2, \Delta_1 \cup \Delta_2 \rangle$$
$$\overline{\mathcal{A}_1} = \langle \mathbf{x}, Q_1, \overline{\iota_1}, Q_1 \setminus F_1, \overline{\Delta_1} \rangle$$

where $\overline{\Delta_1}(q, a) \equiv \overline{\Delta_1(q, a)}$, for all $q \in Q_1$ and $a \in \Sigma$. The following lemma shows the correctness of the above definitions:

Lemma 1. *Given automata* $\mathcal{A}_i = \langle \mathbf{x}, Q_i, \iota_i, F_i, \Delta_i \rangle$, *for* $i = 1, 2$, *such that* $Q_1 \cap Q_2 = \emptyset$, *we have* $L(\mathcal{A}_\cup) = L(\mathcal{A}_1) \cup L(\mathcal{A}_2)$, $L(\mathcal{A}_\cap) = L(\mathcal{A}_1) \cap L(\mathcal{A}_2)$ *and* $L(\overline{\mathcal{A}_1}) = \Sigma[\mathbf{x}]^* \setminus L(\mathcal{A}_1)$.

It is easy to see that $|\mathcal{A}_\cup| = |\mathcal{A}_\cap| = |\mathcal{A}_1| + |\mathcal{A}_2|$ and $|\overline{\mathcal{A}}| = |\mathcal{A}|$, thus the automata for the Boolean operations, including complementation, can be built in linear time. This matches the linear-time bounds for intersection and complementation of alternating automata over finite alphabets [3].

4 Antichains and Interpolants for Emptiness

The emptiness problem for ADA is undecidable, even in very simple cases. For instance, if $\text{Data}^{\mathcal{I}}$ is the set of positive integers, an ADA can simulate an Alternating Vector Addition System with States (AVASS) using only atoms $x \geq k$ and $x - \overline{x} \mid k$, for $k \in \mathbb{Z}$, with the classical interpretation of the function symbols on integers. Since reachability of a control state is undecidable for AVASS [15], ADA emptiness is undecidable.

Consequently, we give up on the guarantee for termination and build semi-algorithms that meet the requirements below:

(i) given an automaton $\mathcal{A}$, if $L(\mathcal{A}) \neq \emptyset$, the procedure will terminate and return a word $w \in L(\mathcal{A})$, and

(ii) if the procedure terminates without returning such a word, then $L(\mathcal{A}) = \emptyset$.

Let us fix an automaton $\mathcal{A} = \langle \mathbf{x}, Q, \iota, F, \Delta \rangle$ whose (finite) input event alphabet is Σ, for the rest of this section. Given a formula $\phi \in \text{Form}^+(Q, \mathbf{x})$ and an input event $a \in \Sigma$, we define the *post-image* function $\text{Post}_{\mathcal{A}}(\phi, a) \equiv \exists \overline{\mathbf{x}}.\Delta(\phi[\overline{\mathbf{x}}/\mathbf{x}], a) \in \text{Form}^+(Q, \mathbf{x})$, mapping each formula in $\text{Form}^+(Q, \mathbf{x})$ to a formula defining the effect of reading the event a. We generalize the post-image function to finite sequences of input events, as follows:

$$\text{Post}_{\mathcal{A}}(\phi, \varepsilon) \equiv \phi \quad \text{Post}_{\mathcal{A}}(\phi, ua) \equiv \text{Post}_{\mathcal{A}}(\text{Post}_{\mathcal{A}}(\phi, u), a)$$
$$\text{Acc}_{\mathcal{A}}(u) \equiv \text{Post}_{\mathcal{A}}(\iota, u) \wedge \bigwedge_{q \in Q \setminus F}(q \to \bot), \text{ for any } u \in \Sigma^*$$

Then the emptiness problem for $\mathcal{A}$ becomes: does there exist $u \in \Sigma^*$ such that the formula $\text{Acc}_{\mathcal{A}}(u)$ is satisfiable? Observe that, since we ask a satisfiability query, the final states of $\mathcal{A}$ need not be constrained[2]. A naïve semi-algorithm enumerates all finite sequences and checks the satisfiability of $\mathsf{Acc}_{\mathcal{A}}(u)$ for each $u \in \Sigma^*$, using a decision procedure for the theory $\mathbb{T}(\mathsf{S}, \mathcal{I})$.

Since no Boolean variable from Q occurs under negation in ϕ, it is easy to prove the following monotonicity property: given two formulae $\phi, \psi \in \mathsf{Form}^+(Q, \mathbf{x})$ if $\phi \models \psi$ then $\mathsf{Post}_{\mathcal{A}}(\phi, u) \models \mathsf{Post}_{\mathcal{A}}(\psi, u)$, for any $u \in \Sigma^*$. This suggest an improvement of the above semi-algorithm, that enumerates and stores only a set $U \subseteq \Sigma^*$ for which $\{\mathsf{Post}_{\mathcal{A}}(\phi, u) \mid u \in U\}$ forms an *antichain*[3] w.r.t. the entailment partial order. This is because, for any $u, v \in \Sigma^*$, if $\mathsf{Post}_{\mathcal{A}}(\iota, u) \models \mathsf{Post}_{\mathcal{A}}(\iota, v)$ and $\mathsf{Acc}_{\mathcal{A}}(uw)$ is satisfiable for some $w \in \Sigma^*$, then $\mathsf{Post}_{\mathcal{A}}(\iota, uw) \models \mathsf{Post}_{\mathcal{A}}(\iota, vw)$, thus $\mathsf{Acc}_{\mathcal{A}}(vw)$ is satisfiable as well, and there is no need for u, since the non-emptiness of $\mathcal{A}$ can be proved using v alone. However, even with this optimization, the enumeration of sequences from Σ^* diverges in many real cases, because infinite antichains exist in many interpretations, e.g. $q \wedge x \approx 0$, $q \wedge x \approx 1, \ldots$ for $\mathsf{Data}^{\mathcal{I}} = \mathbb{N}$.

A *safety invariant* for $\mathcal{A}$ is a function $\mathsf{I} : (Q \mapsto \mathbb{B}) \to 2^{\mathbf{x} \mapsto \mathsf{Data}^{\mathcal{I}}}$ such that, for every Boolean valuation $\beta : Q \to \mathbb{B}$, every valuation $\nu : \mathbf{x} \mapsto \mathsf{Data}^{\mathcal{I}}$ of the data variables and every finite sequence $u \in \Sigma^*$ of input events, the following hold:

1. $\mathcal{I}, \beta \cup \nu \models \mathsf{Post}_{\mathcal{A}}(\iota, u) \Rightarrow \nu \in \mathsf{I}(\beta)$, and
2. $\nu \in \mathsf{I}(\beta) \Rightarrow \mathcal{I}, \beta \cup \nu \not\models \mathsf{Acc}_{\mathcal{A}}(u)$.

If I satisfies only the first point above, we call it an *invariant*. Intuitively, a safety invariant maps every Boolean valuation into a set of data valuations, that contains the initial configuration $\iota \equiv \mathsf{Post}_{\mathcal{A}}(\iota, \varepsilon)$, whose data variables are unconstrained, over-approximates the set of reachable valuations (point 1) and excludes the valuations satisfying the acceptance condition (point 2). A formula $\phi(Q, \mathbf{x})$ is said to *define* I iff for all $\beta : Q \to \mathbb{B}$ and $\nu : \mathbf{x} \to \mathsf{Data}^{\mathcal{I}}$, we have $\mathcal{I}, \beta \cup \nu \models \phi$ iff $\nu \in \mathsf{I}(\beta)$.

Lemma 2. *For any automaton $\mathcal{A}$, we have $L(\mathcal{A}) = \emptyset$ if and only if $\mathcal{A}$ has a safety invariant.*

Turning back to the issue of divergence of language emptiness semi-algorithms in the case $L(\mathcal{A}) = \emptyset$, we can observe that an enumeration of input sequences $u_1, u_2, \ldots \in \Sigma^*$ can stop at step k as soon as $\bigvee_{i=1}^{k} \mathsf{Post}_{\mathcal{A}}(\iota, u_i)$ defines a safety invariant for $\mathcal{A}$. Although this condition can be effectively checked using a decision procedure for the theory $\mathbb{T}(\mathsf{S}, \mathcal{I})$, there is no guarantee that this check will ever succeed.

The solution we adopt in the sequel is abstraction to ensure the termination of invariant computations. However, it is worth pointing out from the start that abstraction alone will only allow us to build invariants that are not necessarily

---

[2] Since each state occurs positively in $\mathsf{Acc}_{\mathcal{A}}(u)$, this formula has a model iff it has a model with every $q \in F$ set to true.

[3] Given a partial order $(D, \preceq)$ an antichain is a set $A \subseteq D$ such that $a \not\preceq b$ for any $a, b \in A$.

safety invariants. To meet the latter condition, we resort to counterexample guided abstraction refinement (CEGAR).

Formally, we fix a set of formulae $\Pi \subseteq \mathsf{Form}(Q, \mathbf{x})$, such that $\bot \in \Pi$ and refer to these formulae as *predicates*. Given a formula ϕ, we denote by $\phi^\sharp \equiv \bigwedge \{\pi \in \Pi \mid \phi \models \pi\}$ the abstraction of ϕ w.r.t. the predicates in Π. The abstract versions of the post-image and acceptance condition are defined as follows:

$$\mathsf{Post}^\sharp_{\mathcal{A}}(\phi, \varepsilon) \equiv \phi \quad \mathsf{Post}^\sharp_{\mathcal{A}}(\phi, ua) \equiv (\mathsf{Post}_{\mathcal{A}}(\mathsf{Post}^\sharp_{\mathcal{A}}(\phi, u), a))^\sharp$$
$$\mathsf{Acc}^\sharp_{\mathcal{A}}(u) \equiv \mathsf{Post}^\sharp_{\mathcal{A}}(\iota, u) \wedge \bigwedge_{q \in Q \setminus F}(q \rightarrow \bot), \text{ for any } u \in \Sigma^*$$

Lemma 3. *For any bijection $\mu : \mathbb{N} \rightarrow \Sigma^*$, there exists $k > 0$ such that $\bigvee_{i=0}^{k} \mathsf{Post}^\sharp_{\mathcal{A}}(\iota, \mu(i))$ defines an invariant $\mathsf{I}^\sharp$ for $\mathcal{A}$.*

We are left with fulfilling point (2) from the definition of a safety invariant. To this end, suppose that, for a given set Π of predicates, the invariant $\mathsf{I}^\sharp$, defined by the previous lemma, meets point (1) but not point (2), where $\mathsf{Post}_{\mathcal{A}}$ and $\mathsf{Acc}_{\mathcal{A}}$ replace $\mathsf{Post}^\sharp_{\mathcal{A}}$ and $\mathsf{Acc}^\sharp_{\mathcal{A}}$, respectively. In other words, there exists a finite sequence $u \in \Sigma^*$ such that $\nu \in \mathsf{I}^\sharp(\beta)$ and $\mathcal{I}, \beta \cup \nu \models \mathsf{Acc}^\sharp_{\mathcal{A}}(u)$, for some Boolean $\beta : Q \rightarrow \mathbb{B}$ and data $\nu : \mathbf{x} \rightarrow \mathsf{Data}^\mathcal{I}$ valuations. Such a $u \in \Sigma^*$ is called a *counterexample*.

Once a counterexample u is discovered, there are two possibilities. Either (i) $\mathsf{Acc}_{\mathcal{A}}(u)$ is satisfiable, in which case u is *feasible* and $L(\mathcal{A}) \neq \emptyset$, or (ii) $\mathsf{Acc}_{\mathcal{A}}(u)$ is unsatisfiable, in which case u is *spurious*. In the first case, our semi-algorithm stops and returns a witness for non-emptiness, obtained from the satisfying valuation of $\mathsf{Acc}_{\mathcal{A}}(u)$ and in the second case, we must strenghten the invariant by excluding from $\mathsf{I}^\sharp$ all pairs (β, ν) such that $\mathcal{I}, \beta \cup \nu \models \mathsf{Acc}^\sharp_{\mathcal{A}}(u)$. This strengthening is carried out by adding to Π several predicates that are sufficient to exclude the spurious counterexample.

Given an unsatisfiable conjunction of formulae $\psi_1 \wedge \ldots \wedge \psi_n$, an *interpolant* is a tuple of formulae $\langle I_1, \ldots, I_{n-1}, I_n \rangle$ such that $I_n \equiv \bot$, $I_i \wedge \psi_i \models_\mathcal{T} I_{i+1}$ and I_i contains only variables and function symbols that are common to ψ_i and ψ_{i+1}, for all $i \in [n-1]$. Moreover, by Lyndon's Interpolation Theorem [16], we can assume without loss of generality that every Boolean variable with at least one positive (negative) occurrence in I_i has at least one positive (negative) occurrence in both ψ_i and ψ_{i+1}. In the following, we shall assume the existence of an interpolating decision procedure for $\mathbb{T}(S, \mathcal{I})$ that meets the requirements of Lyndon's Interpolation Theorem.

A classical method for abstraction refinement is to add the elements of the interpolant obtained from a proof of spuriousness to the set of predicates. This guarantees progress, meaning that the particular spurious counterexample, from which the interpolant was generated, will never be revisited in the future. Though not always, in many practical test cases this progress property eventually yields a safety invariant.

Given a non-empty spurious counterexample $u = a_1 \ldots a_n$, where $n > 0$, we consider the following interpolation problem:

$$\Theta(u) \equiv \theta_0(Q_0) \wedge \theta_1(Q_0 \cup Q_1, \mathbf{x}_0 \cup \mathbf{x}_1) \wedge \ldots \tag{1}$$
$$\wedge\, \theta_n(Q_{n-1} \cup Q_n, \mathbf{x}_{n-1} \cup \mathbf{x}_n) \wedge \theta_{n+1}(Q_n)$$

where $Q_k = \{q_k \mid q \in Q\}$, $k \in [0, n]$ are time-stamped sets of Boolean variables corresponding to the set Q of states of $\mathcal{A}$. The first conjunct $\theta_0(Q_0) \equiv \iota[Q_0/Q]$ is the initial configuration of $\mathcal{A}$, with every $q \in \mathrm{FV}^{\mathsf{Bool}}(\iota)$ replaced by q_0. The definition of θ_k, for all $k \in [1, n]$, uses *replacement sets* $R_\ell \subseteq Q_\ell$, $\ell \in [0, n]$, which are defined inductively below:

- $R_0 = \mathrm{FV}^{\mathsf{Bool}}(\theta_0)$,
- $\theta_\ell \equiv \bigwedge_{q_{\ell-1} \in R_{\ell-1}} (q_{\ell-1} \rightarrow \Delta(q, a_\ell)[Q_\ell/Q, \mathbf{x}_{\ell-1}/\overline{\mathbf{x}}, \mathbf{x}_\ell/\mathbf{x}])$ and $R_\ell = \mathrm{FV}^{\mathsf{Bool}}(\theta_\ell) \cap Q_\ell$, for each $\ell \in [1, n]$.
- $\theta_{n+1}(Q_n) \equiv \bigwedge_{q \in Q \setminus F} (q_n \rightarrow \bot)$.

The intuition is that $R_0, \ldots, R_n$ are the sets of states replaced, $\theta_0, \ldots, \theta_n$ are the sets of transition rules fired on the run of $\mathcal{A}$ over u and θ_{n+1} is the acceptance condition, which forces the last remaining non-final states to be false. We recall that a run of $\mathcal{A}$ over u is a sequence:

$$\phi_0(Q) \Rightarrow \phi_1(Q, \mathbf{x}_0 \cup \mathbf{x}_1) \Rightarrow \ldots \Rightarrow \phi_n(Q, \mathbf{x}_0 \cup \ldots \cup \mathbf{x}_n)$$

where ϕ_0 is the initial configuration ι and for each $k > 0$, ϕ_k is obtained from ϕ_{k-1} by replacing each state $q \in \mathrm{FV}^{\mathsf{Bool}}(\phi_{k-1})$ by the formula $\Delta(q, a_k)[\mathbf{x}_{k-1}/\overline{\mathbf{x}}, \mathbf{x}_k/\mathbf{x}]$, given by the transition function of $\mathcal{A}$. Observe that, because the states are replaced with transition formulae when moving one step in a run, these formulae lose track of the control history and are not suitable for producing interpolants that relate states and data.

The main idea behind the above definition of the interpolation problem is that we would like to obtain an interpolant $\langle \top, I_0(Q), I_1(Q, \mathbf{x}), \ldots, I_n(Q, \mathbf{x}), \bot \rangle$ whose formulae *combine states with the data constraints that must hold locally*, whenever the control reaches a certain Boolean configuration. This association of states with data valuations is tantamount to defining efficient semi-algorithms, based on lazy abstraction [8]. Furthermore, the abstraction defined by the interpolants generated in this way can also *over-approximate the control structure* of an automaton, in addition to the sets of data values encountered throughout its runs.

The correctness of this interpolation-based abstraction refinement setup is captured by the progress property below, which guarantees that adding the formulae of an interpolant for $\Theta(u)$ to the set Π of predicates suffices to exclude the spurious counterexample u from future searches.

Lemma 4. *For any sequence* $u = a_1 \ldots a_n \in \Sigma^*$, *if* $\mathsf{Acc}_{\mathcal{A}}(u)$ *is unsatisfiable, the following hold:*

1. $\Theta(u)$ *is unsatisfiable, and*
2. *if* $\langle \top, I_0, \ldots, I_n, \bot \rangle$ *is an interpolant for* $\Theta(u)$ *such that* $\{I_i \mid i \in [0, n]\} \subseteq \Pi$ *then* $\mathsf{Acc}_{\mathcal{A}}^{\#}(u)$ *is unsatisfiable.*

5 Lazy Predicate Abstraction for ADA Emptiness

We have now all the ingredients to describe the first emptiness checking semi-algorithm for alternating data automata. Algorithm[4] 1 builds an *abstract reachability tree* (ART) whose nodes are labeled with formulae over-approximating the concrete sets of configurations, and a covering relation between nodes in order to ensure that the set of formulae labeling the nodes in the ART forms an antichain. Any spurious counterexample is eliminated by computing an interpolant and adding its formulae to the set of predicates (cf. Lemma 4). Formally, an ART is tuple $\mathcal{T} = \langle N, E, \mathbf{r}, \Lambda, R, T, \lhd \rangle$, where:

- N is a set of nodes,
- $E \subseteq N \times \Sigma \times N$ is a set of edges,
- $\mathbf{r} \in N$ is the root of the directed tree (N, E),
- $\Lambda : N \to \mathsf{Form}(Q, \mathbf{x})$ is a labeling of the nodes with formulae, such that $\Lambda(\mathbf{r}) = \iota$,
- $R : N \to 2^Q$ is a labeling of nodes with replacement sets, such that $R(\mathbf{r}) = \mathrm{FV}^{\mathsf{Bool}}(\iota)$,
- $T : E \to \bigcup_{i=0}^{\infty} \mathsf{Form}^+(Q_i, \mathbf{x}_i, Q_{i+1}, \mathbf{x}_{i+1})$ is a labeling of edges with time-stamped formulae, and
- $\lhd \subseteq N \times N$ is a set of *covering edges*.

Each node $n \in N$ corresponds to a unique path from the root to n, labeled by a sequence $\lambda(n) \in \Sigma^*$ of input events. The *least infeasible suffix* of $\lambda(n)$ is the smallest sequence $v = a_1 \ldots a_k$, such that $\lambda(n) = wv$, for some $w \in \Sigma^*$ and the following formula is unsatisfiable:

$$\Psi(v) \equiv \Lambda(p)[Q_0/Q] \wedge \theta_1(Q_0 \cup Q_1, \mathbf{x}_0 \cup \mathbf{x}_1) \wedge \ldots \wedge \theta_{k+1}(Q_k) \qquad (2)$$

where $\theta_1, \ldots, \theta_{k+1}$ are defined as in (1) and $\theta_0 \equiv \Lambda(p)[Q_0/Q]$. The *pivot* of n is the node p corresponding to the start of the least infeasible suffix. We assume the existence of two functions $\mathrm{FINDPIVOT}(u, \mathcal{T})$ and $\mathrm{LEASTINFEASIBLESUFFIX}(u, \mathcal{T})$ that return the pivot and least infeasible suffix of a sequence $u \in \Sigma^*$ in an ART $\mathcal{T}$, without detailing their implementation.

With these considerations, Algorithm 1 uses a worklist iteration to build an ART. We keep newly expanded nodes of $\mathcal{T}$ in a queue WorkList, thus implementing a breadth-first exploration strategy, which guarantees that the shortest counterexamples are explored first. When the search encounters a counterexample candidate u, it is checked for spuriousness. If the counterexample is feasible, the procedure returns a data word $w \in L(\mathcal{A})$, which interleaves the input events of u with the data valuations from the model of $\mathrm{Acc}_{\mathcal{A}}(u)$ (since u is feasible, clearly $\mathrm{Acc}_{\mathcal{A}}(u)$ is satisfiable). Otherwise, u is spurious and we compute its pivot p (line 12), add the interpolants for the least unfeasible suffix of u to Π, remove and recompute the subtree of $\mathcal{T}$ rooted at p.

Termination of Algorithm 1 depends on the ability of a given interpolating decision procedure for the combined Boolean and data theory $\mathbb{T}(\mathsf{S}, \mathcal{I})$ to provide

---

[4] Though termination is not guaranteed, we call it algorithm for conciseness.

Algorithm 1. Lazy Predicate Abstraction for ADA Emptiness

---

input: an ADA $\mathcal{A} = \langle \mathbf{x}, Q, \iota, F, \Delta \rangle$ over the alphabet Σ of input events
output: true if $L(\mathcal{A}) = \emptyset$ and a data word $w \in L(\mathcal{A})$ otherwise

1: let $\mathcal{T} = \langle N, E, \mathbf{r}, \Lambda, \lhd \rangle$ be an ART
2: initially $N = E = \lhd = \emptyset$, $\Lambda = \{(\mathbf{r}, \iota)\}$, $\Pi = \{\bot\}$, WorkList $= \langle \mathbf{r} \rangle$,
3: **while** WorkList $\neq \emptyset$ **do**
4:     dequeue n from WorkList
5:     $N \leftarrow N \cup \{n\}$
6:     let $\lambda(n) = a_1 \ldots a_k$ be the label of the path from $\mathbf{r}$ to n
7:     **if** $\mathsf{Post}^\sharp_{\mathcal{A}}(\lambda(n))$ is satisfiable **then**   ▷ counterexample candidate
8:         **if** $\mathsf{Acc}_{\mathcal{A}}(u)$ is satisfiable **then**   ▷ feasible counterexample
9:             get model $(\beta, \nu_1, \ldots, \nu_k)$ of $\mathsf{Acc}_{\mathcal{A}}(\lambda(n))$
10:            **return** $w = (a_1, \nu_1) \ldots (a_k, \nu_k)$ ▷ $w \in L(\mathcal{A})$ by construction
11:        **else**   ▷ spurious counterexample
12:            $p \leftarrow \textsc{FindPivot}(\lambda(n), \mathcal{T})$
13:            $v \leftarrow \textsc{LeastInfeasibleSuffix}(\lambda(n), \mathcal{T})$
14:            $\Pi \leftarrow \Pi \cup \{I_0, \ldots, I_\ell\}$, where $\langle \top, I_0, \ldots, I_\ell, \bot \rangle$ is an interpolant for $\Psi(v)$
15:            let $\mathcal{S} = \langle N', E', p, \Lambda', \lhd' \rangle$ be the subtree of $\mathcal{T}$ rooted at p
16:            **for** $(m, q) \in \lhd$ such that $q \in N'$ **do**
17:                remove m from N and enqueue m into WorkList
18:                remove $\mathcal{S}$ from $\mathcal{T}$
19:                enqueue p into WorkList   ▷ recompute the subtree rooted at p
20:    **else**
21:        **for** $a \in \Sigma$ **do**   ▷ expand n
22:            $\phi \leftarrow \mathsf{Post}^\sharp_{\mathcal{A}}(\Lambda(n), a)$
23:            **if** exist $m \in N$ such that $\phi \models \Lambda(m)$ **then**
24:                $\lhd \leftarrow \lhd \cup \{(n, m)\}$ ▷ m covers n
25:            **else**
26:                let s be a fresh node
27:                $E \leftarrow E \cup \{(n, a, s)\}$
28:                $\Lambda \leftarrow \Lambda \cup \{(s, \phi)\}$
29:                $R \leftarrow \{m \in \text{WorkList} \mid \Lambda(m) \models \phi\}$ ▷ worklist nodes covered by s
30:                **for** $r \in R$ **do**
31:                    **for** $m \in N$ such that $(m, b, r) \in E$, $b \in \Sigma$ **do**
32:                        $\lhd \leftarrow \lhd \cup \{(m, s)\}$ ▷ redirect covered children from R into s
33:                    **for** $(m, r) \in \lhd$ **do**
34:                        $\lhd \leftarrow \lhd \cup \{(m, s)\}$ ▷ redirect covered nodes from R into s
35:                remove R from $\mathcal{T}$
36:                enqueue s into WorkList
37: **return** true

---

interpolants that yield a safety invariant, whenever $L(\mathcal{A}) = \emptyset$. In this case, we use the covering relation $\lhd$ to ensure that, when a newly generated node is covered by a node already in N, it is not added to the worklist, thus cutting the current branch of the search.

Formally, for any two nodes $n, m \in N$, we have $n \lhd m$ iff $\mathsf{Post}^\sharp_{\mathcal{A}}(\Lambda(n), a) \models \Lambda(m)$ for some $a \in \Sigma$, in other words, if n has a successor whose label entails the label of m.

Example. Consider the automaton given in Fig. 1. First, Algorithm 1 fires the sequence a, and since there are no other formulae than $\bot$ in Π, the successor of $\iota \equiv q_0$ is $\top$, in Fig. 2(a). The spuriousness check for a yields the root of the ART as pivot and the interpolant $\langle q_0, q_1 \rangle$, which is added to the set Π. Then the $\top$ node is removed and the next time a is fired, it creates a node labeled q_1. The second sequence aa creates a successor node q_1, which is covered by the first, depicted with a dashed arrow, in Fig. 2(b). The third sequence is ab, which results in a new uncovered node $\top$ and triggers a spuriousness check. The new predicate obtained from this check is $x \leq 0 \wedge q_2 \wedge y \geq 0$ and the pivot is again the root. Then the entire ART is rebuilt with the new predicates and the fourth sequence aab yields an uncovered node $\top$, in Fig. 2(c). The new pivot is the endpoint of a and the newly added predicates are $q_1 \wedge q_2$ and $y > x - 1 \wedge q_2$. Finally, the ART is rebuilt from the pivot node and finally all nodes are covered, thus proving the emptiness of the automaton, in Fig. 2(d).   □

The correctness of Algorithm 1 is proved below:

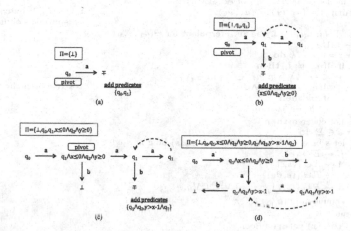

Fig. 2. Proving emptiness of the automaton from Fig. 1 by Algorithm 1

Theorem 1. *Given an automaton $\mathcal{A}$, such that $L(\mathcal{A}) \neq \emptyset$, Algorithm 1 terminates and returns a word $w \in L(\mathcal{A})$. If Algorithm 1 terminates reporting* **true**, *then $L(\mathcal{A}) = \emptyset$.*

6   Checking ADA Emptiness with IMPACT

As pointed out by a number of authors, the bottleneck of predicate abstraction is the high cost of reconstructing parts of the ART, subsequent to the refinement of the set of predicates. The main idea of the IMPACT procedure [17] is that this can be avoided and the refinement (strengthening of the node labels of the ART) can be performed in-place. This refinement step requires an update of the covering relation, because a node that used to cover another node might not cover it after the strengthening of its label.

We consider a total alphabetical order $\prec$ on Σ and lift it to the total lexicographical order $\prec^*$ on Σ^*. A node $n \in N$ is *covered* if $(n, p) \in \vartriangleleft$ or it has an ancestor m such that $(m, p) \in \vartriangleleft$, for some $p \in N$. A node n is *closed* if it is covered, or $\Lambda(n) \not\models \Lambda(m)$ for all $m \in N$ such that $\lambda(m) \prec^* \lambda(n)$. Observe that we use the coverage relation $\vartriangleleft$ here with a different meaning than in Algorithm 1.

The execution of Algorithm 2 consists of three phases[5]: *close*, *refine* and *expand*. Let n be a node removed from the worklist at line 4. If $\mathsf{Acc}_{\mathcal{A}}(\lambda(n))$

---

[5] Corresponding to the CLOSE, REFINE and EXPAND in [17].

Algorithm 2. IMPACT for ADA Emptiness

input: an ADA $\mathcal{A} = \langle \mathbf{x}, Q, \iota, F, \Delta \rangle$ over the alphabet Σ of input events
output: true if $L(\mathcal{A}) = \emptyset$ and a data word $w \in L(\mathcal{A})$ otherwise

1: let $\mathcal{T} = \langle N, E, \mathbf{r}, \Lambda, R, T, \lhd \rangle$ be an ART
2: initially $N = E = T = \lhd = \emptyset$, $\Lambda = \{(\mathbf{r}, \iota)\}$, $R = \mathrm{FV}^{\mathsf{Bool}}(\iota[Q_0/Q])$, WorkList $= \{\mathbf{r}\}$
3: **while** WorkList $\neq \emptyset$ **do**
4:     dequeue n from WorkList
5:     $N \leftarrow N \cup \{n\}$
6:     let $(\mathbf{r}, a_1, n_1), (n_1, a_2, n_2), \ldots, (n_{k-1}, a_k, n)$ be the path from $\mathbf{r}$ to n
7:     **if** $\mathsf{Acc}_{\mathcal{A}}(a_1 \ldots a_k)$ is satisfiable **then**   ▷ counterexample is feasible
8:        get model $(\beta, \nu_1, \ldots, \nu_k)$ of $\mathsf{Acc}_{\mathcal{A}}(\lambda(n))$
9:        **return** $w = (a_1, \nu_1) \ldots (a_k, \nu_k)$ ▷ $w \in L(\mathcal{A})$ by construction
10:     **else**   ▷ spurious counterexample
11:        let $\langle \top, I_0, \ldots, I_k, \bot \rangle$ be an interpolant for $\Theta(a_1 \ldots a_k)$
12:        $b \leftarrow$ **false**
13:        **for** $i = 0, \ldots, k$ **do**
14:           **if** $\Lambda(n_i) \not\models I_i$ **then**
15:              $\lhd \leftarrow \lhd \setminus \{(m, n_i) \in \lhd \mid m \in N\}$
16:              $\Lambda(n_i) \leftarrow \Lambda(n_i) \wedge I_i$ ▷ strenghten the label of n_i
17:              **if** $\neg b$ **then**
18:                 $b \leftarrow \mathrm{CLOSE}(n_i)$
19:     **if** n is not covered **then**
20:        **for** $a \in \Sigma$ **do**   ▷ expand n
21:           let s be a fresh node and $e = (n, a, s)$ be a new edge
22:           $E \leftarrow E \cup \{e\}$
23:           $\Lambda \leftarrow \Lambda \cup \{(s, \top)\}$
24:           $T \leftarrow T \cup \{(e, \theta_k)\}$
25:           $R \leftarrow R \cup \{(s, \bigcup_{q \in R(n)} \mathrm{FV}^{\mathsf{Bool}}(\Delta(q, a)))\}$
26:           enqueue s into WorkList
27: **return** true

1: **function** $\mathrm{CLOSE}(x)$ **returns** Bool
2:     **for** $y \in N$ such that $\lambda(y) \prec^* \lambda(x)$ **do**
3:        **if** $\Lambda(x) \models \Lambda(y)$ **then**
4:           $\lhd \leftarrow (\lhd \setminus \{(p, q) \in \lhd \mid q \text{ is } x \text{ or a successor of } x\}) \cup \{(x, y)\}$
5:           **return** true
6:     **return** false

---

is satisfiable, the counterexample $\lambda(n)$ is feasible, in which case a model of $\mathsf{Acc}_{\mathcal{A}}(\lambda(n))$ is obtained and a word $w \in L(\mathcal{A})$ is returned. Otherwise, $\lambda(n)$ is a spurious counterexample and the procedure enters the refinement phase (lines 11–18). The interpolant for $\Theta(\lambda(n))$ (cf. formula 1) is used to strenghten the labels of all the ancestors of n, by conjoining the formulae of the interpolant to the existing labels.

In this process, the nodes on the path between $\mathbf{r}$ and n, including n, might become eligible for coverage, therefore we attempt to close each ancestor of n that is impacted by the refinement (line 18). Observe that, in this case the call to CLOSE must uncover each node which is covered by a successor of n (line 4 of the CLOSE function). This is required because, due to the over-approximation of the sets of reachable configurations, the covering relation is not transitive, as explained in [17]. If CLOSE adds a covering edge (n_i, m) to $\lhd$, it does not have to be called for the successors of n_i on this path, which is handled via the Boolean flag b.

Finally, if n is still uncovered (it has not been previously covered during the refinement phase) we expand n (lines 20–26) by creating a new node for each successor s via the input event $a \in \Sigma$ and inserting it into the worklist.

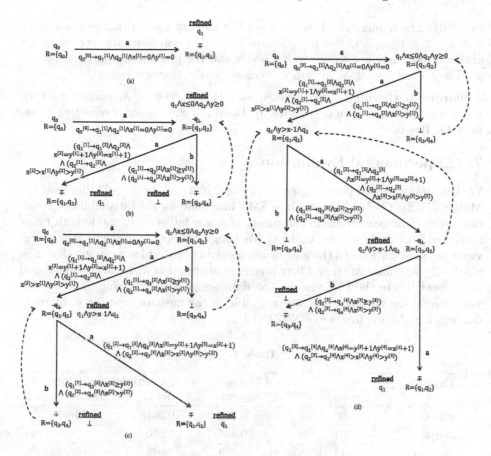

Fig. 3. Proving emptiness of the automaton from Fig. 1 by Algorithm 2

Example. We show the execution of Algorithm 2 on the automaton from Fig. 1. Initially, the procedure fires the sequence a, whose endpoint is labeled with $\top$, in Fig. 3(a). Since this node is uncovered, we check the spuriousness of the counterexample a and refine the label of the node to q_1. Since the node is still uncovered, two successors, labeled with $\top$ are computed, corresponding to the sequences aa and ab, in Fig. 3(b). The spuriousness check for aa yields the interpolant $\langle q_0, x \leq 0 \wedge q_2 \wedge y \geq 0 \rangle$ which strengthens the label of the endpoint of a from q_1 to $q_1 \wedge x \leq 0 \wedge q_2 \wedge y \geq 0$. The sequence ab is also found to be spurious, which changes the label of its endpoint from $\top$ to $\bot$, and also covers it (depicted with a dashed edge). Since the endpoint of aa is not covered, it is expanded to aaa and aab, in Fig. 3(c). Both sequences aaa and aab are found to be spurious, and the enpoint of aab, whose label has changed from $\top$ to $\bot$, is now covered. In the process, the label of aa has also changed from q_1 to $q_1 \wedge y > x - 1 \wedge q_2$, due to the sstrengthening with the interpolant from aab. Finally, the only uncovered node aaa is expanded to $aaaa$ and $aaab$, both found to be spurious, in

Fig. 3(d). The refinement of $aaab$ causes the label of aaa to change from q_1 to $q_1 \wedge y > x - 1 \wedge q_2$ and this node is now covered by aa. Since its successors are also covered, there are no uncovered nodes and the procedure returns true. □

The correctness of Algorithm 2 is coined by the theorem below:

Theorem 2. *Given an automaton $\mathcal{A}$, such that $L(\mathcal{A}) \neq \emptyset$, Algorithm 2 terminates and returns a word $w \in L(\mathcal{A})$. If Algorithm 2 terminates reporting* true, *then $L(\mathcal{A}) = \emptyset$.*

7   Experimental Evaluation

We have implemented both Algorithms 1 and 2 in a prototype tool[6] that uses the MathSAT5 SMT solver[7] via the Java SMT interface[8] for the satisfiability queries and interpolant generation, in the theory of linear integer arithmetic with uninterpreted Boolean functions (UFLIA). We compared both algorithms with a previous implementation of a trace inclusion procedure, called INCLUDER[9], that uses on-the-fly determinisation and lazy predicate abstraction with interpolant-based refinement [11] in the LIA theory. The datasets generated during and/or analysed during the current study are available in the figshare repository: https://doi.org/10.6084/m9.figshare.5925472.v1 [12].

Table 1.

Example	$|\mathcal{A}|$ (bytes)	$L(\mathcal{A}) = \emptyset$?	Algorithm 1 (sec)	Algorithm 2 (sec)	INCLUDER (sec)
simple1	309	No	0.774	0.064	0.076
simple2	504	Yes	0.867	0.070	0.070
simple3	214	Yes	0.899	0.095	0.095
array_shift	874	Yes	2.889	0.126	0.078
array_simple	3440	Yes	Timeout	9.998	7.154
array_rotation1	1834	Yes	7.227	0.331	0.229
array_rotation2	15182	Yes	Timeout	Timeout	31.632
abp	6909	No	9.492	0.631	2.288
train	1823	Yes	19.237	0.763	0.678
hw1	322	Yes	1.861	0.163	0.172
hw2	674	Yes	24.111	0.308	0.473

The results of the experiments are given in Table 1. We applied the tool first to several array logic entailments, which occur as verification conditions for imperative programs with arrays [2] (array_shift, array_simple, array_rotation1+2)

---

[6] The implementation is available at https://github.com/cathiec/JAltImpact.
[7] http://mathsat.fbk.eu/.
[8] https://github.com/sosy-lab/java-smt.
[9] http://www.fit.vutbr.cz/research/groups/verifit/tools/includer/.

available online [19]. Next, we applied it on proving safety properties of hardware circuits (hw1+2) [22]. Finally, we considered two timed communication protocols, consisting of systems that are asynchronous compositions of timed automata, whom correctness specifications are given by timed automata monitors: a timed version of the Alternating Bit Protocol (abp) [25] and a controller of a railroad crossing (train) [9]. All results were obtained on x86_64 Linux Ubuntu virtual machine with 8 GB of RAM running on an Intel(R) Xeon(R) CPU E5-2683 v3 @ 2.00 GHz. The automata sizes are given in bytes needed to store their ASCII description on file and the execution times are in seconds.

As in the case of non-alternating nondeterministic integer programs [17], the alternating version of IMPACT (Algorithm 2) outperforms lazy predicate abstraction for checking emptiness by at least one order of magnitude. Moreover, IMPACT is comparable, on average, to the previous implementation of INCLUDER, which uses also MathSAT5 via the C API. We believe the reason for which INCLUDER outperforms IMPACT on some examples is the hardness of the UFLIA entailment checks used in Algorithm 2 (lines 14 and 3 in the function CLOSE) as opposed to the pure LIA entailment checks used in INCLUDER. According to our statistics, Algorithm 2 spends more than 50% of the time waiting for the SMT solver to finish answering entailment queries.

References

1. Alur, R., Dill, D.L.: A theory of timed automata. Theor. Comput. Sci. **126**(2), 183–235 (1994)
2. Bozga, M., Habermehl, P., Iosif, R., Konečný, F., Vojnar, T.: Automatic verification of integer array programs. In: Bouajjani, A., Maler, O. (eds.) CAV 2009. LNCS, vol. 5643, pp. 157–172. Springer, Heidelberg (2009). https://doi.org/10.1007/978-3-642-02658-4_15
3. Chandra, A.K., Kozen, D.C., Stockmeyer, L.J.: Alternation. J. ACM **28**(1), 114–133 (1981)
4. D'Antoni, L., Kincaid, Z., Wang, F.: A symbolic decision procedure for symbolic alternating finite automata. CoRR, abs/1610.01722 (2016)
5. De Wulf, M., Doyen, L., Maquet, N., Raskin, J.-F.: Antichains: alternative algorithms for LTL satisfiability and model-checking. In: Ramakrishnan, C.R., Rehof, J. (eds.) TACAS 2008. LNCS, vol. 4963, pp. 63–77. Springer, Heidelberg (2008). https://doi.org/10.1007/978-3-540-78800-3_6
6. Farzan, A., Kincaid, Z., Podelski, A.: Proof spaces for unbounded parallelism. SIGPLAN Not. **50**(1), 407–420 (2015)
7. Grebenshchikov, S., Lopes, N.P., Popeea, C., Rybalchenko, A.: Synthesizing software verifiers from proof rules. SIGPLAN Not. **47**(6), 405–416 (2012)
8. Henzinger, T.A., Jhala, R., Majumdar, R., Sutre, G.: Lazy abstraction. SIGPLAN Not. **37**(1), 58–70 (2002)
9. Henzinger, T.A., Nicollin, X., Sifakis, J., Yovine, S.: Symbolic model checking for real-time systems. Inf. Comput. **111**, 394–406 (1992)
10. Hoder, K., Bjørner, N.: Generalized property directed reachability. In: Cimatti, A., Sebastiani, R. (eds.) SAT 2012. LNCS, vol. 7317, pp. 157–171. Springer, Heidelberg (2012). https://doi.org/10.1007/978-3-642-31612-8_13

11. Iosif, R., Rogalewicz, A., Vojnar, T.: Abstraction refinement and antichains for trace inclusion of infinite state systems. In: Chechik, M., Raskin, J.-F. (eds.) TACAS 2016. LNCS, vol. 9636, pp. 71–89. Springer, Heidelberg (2016). https:// doi.org/10.1007/978-3-662-49674-9_5

12. Iosif, R., Xu, X.: Artifact related to abstraction refinement for emptiness checking of alternating data automata. In: TACAS 2018 (2018). https://doi.org/10.6084/ m9.figshare.5925472.v1

13. Kaminski, M., Francez, N.: Finite-memory automata. Theor. Comput. Sci. **134**(2), 329–363 (1994)

14. Lasota, S., Walukiewicz, I.: Alternating timed automata. In: Sassone, V. (ed.) FoSSaCS 2005. LNCS, vol. 3441, pp. 250–265. Springer, Heidelberg (2005). https:// doi.org/10.1007/978-3-540-31982-5_16

15. Lincoln, P., Mitchell, J., Scedrov, A., Shankar, N.: Decision problems for propositional linear logic. Ann. Pure Appl. Logic **56**(1), 239–311 (1992)

16. Lyndon, R.C.: An interpolation theorem in the predicate calculus. Pacific J. Math. **9**(1), 129–142 (1959)

17. McMillan, K.L.: Lazy abstraction with interpolants. In: Ball, T., Jones, R.B. (eds.) CAV 2006. LNCS, vol. 4144, pp. 123–136. Springer, Heidelberg (2006). https://doi. org/10.1007/11817963_14

18. McMillan, K.L.: Lazy annotation revisited. In: Biere, A., Bloem, R. (eds.) CAV 2014. LNCS, vol. 8559, pp. 243–259. Springer, Cham (2014). https://doi.org/10. 1007/978-3-319-08867-9_16

19. Numerical Transition Systems Repository (2012). http://nts.imag.fr/index.php/ Flata

20. Ouaknine, J., Worrell, J.: On the language inclusion problem for timed automata: closing a decidability gap. In: Proceedings of LICS 2004, pp. 54–63 (2004)

21. Pnueli, A.: The temporal logic of programs. In: Proceedings of the 18th Annual Symposium on Foundations of Computer Science, SFCS 1977, pp. 46–57. IEEE (1977)

22. Smrcka, A., Vojnar, T.: Verifying parametrised hardware designs via counter automata. In: HVC 2007, pp. 51–68 (2007)

23. Vardi, M., Wolper, P.: Reasoning about infinite computations. Inf. Comput. **115**(1), 1–37 (1994)

24. Veanes, M., Hooimeijer, P., Livshits, B., Molnar, D., Bjorner, N.: Symbolic finite state transducers: algorithms and applications. In: Proceedings of POPL 2012. ACM (2012)

25. Zbrzezny, A., Polrola, A.: Sat-based reachability checking for timed automata with discrete data. Fundamenta Informaticae **79**, 1–15 (2007)

Revisiting Enumerative Instantiation

Andrew Reynolds[1]([✉]), Haniel Barbosa[1,2]([✉]), and Pascal Fontaine[2]([✉])

[1] University of Iowa, Iowa City, USA
`andrew.j.reynolds@gmail.com`
[2] Université de Lorraine, CNRS, Inria, LORIA,
Nancy, France
{`haniel.barbosa,pascal.fontaine`}`@inria.fr`

Abstract. Formal methods applications often rely on SMT solvers to automatically discharge proof obligations. SMT solvers handle quantified formulas using incomplete heuristic techniques like E-matching, and often resort to model-based quantifier instantiation (MBQI) when these techniques fail. This paper revisits enumerative instantiation, a technique that considers instantiations based on exhaustive enumeration of ground terms. Although simple, we argue that enumerative instantiation can supplement other instantiation techniques and be a viable alternative to MBQI for valid proof obligations. We first present a stronger Herbrand Theorem, better suited as a basis for the instantiation loop used in SMT solvers; it furthermore requires considering less instances than classical Herbrand instantiation. Based on this result, we present different strategies for combining enumerative instantiation with other instantiation techniques in an effective way. The experimental evaluation shows that the implementation of these new techniques in the SMT solver CVC4 leads to significant improvements in several benchmark libraries, including many stemming from verification efforts.

1 Introduction

In many formal methods applications, such as verification, it is common to represent proof obligations in terms of the *Satisfiability Modulo Theories* (SMT) problem. SMT solvers have thus become popular backends for such applications. They have been primarily designed to be decision procedures for quantifier-free problems, on which they are highly efficient and capable of handling large formulas over background theories. Quantified formulas are generally handled with instantiation techniques that are often incomplete, even on decidable or semi-decidable fragments. Heavily relying on incomplete heuristics however leads to instability and unpredictability on the solver's behavior, which is undesirable for the tools relying on them. To address these issues some systems use model-based

© The Author(s) 2018
D. Beyer and M. Huisman (Eds.): TACAS 2018, LNCS 10806, pp. 112–131, 2018.
https://doi.org/10.1007/978-3-319-89963-3_7

instantiation (MBQI) [19], a complete technique for first-order logic with equality and for several restricted fragments containing theories, which can be used as a fallback strategy to the incomplete techniques.

In this paper we introduce a novel enumerative instantiation technique which can serve as a simpler alternative to model-based instantiation. Similar to MBQI, our technique can be used as a secondary strategy when incomplete techniques fail. Our experiments show that a careful implementation of this technique in the state-of-the-art SMT solver CVC4 leads to noticeable gains in performance on unsatisfiable problems.

Background. Some of the earliest tools for theorem proving in first-order logic come from the work by Skolem and Herbrand. The Herbrand Theorem states that if a closed formula in Skolem normal form, i.e. a prenex formula without existential quantifiers, is unsatisfiable, then there is an unsatisfiable finite conjunction of Herbrand instances of the formula, that is, instances on terms from the *Herbrand universe*, i.e. the set of all possible well-sorted ground terms in the formula's signature. The first theorem provers for first-order logic to be implemented based on Herbrand's theorem employed a completely unguided search on the Herbrand Universe (e.g. Gilmore [20] and Davis et al. [11] early efforts). Such systems were only capable of dealing with very simple formulas and were soon put aside. Techniques which would only generate Herbrand instances when needed were first introduced by Prawitz [24] and later refined by Davis and Putnam [12], culminating in the resolution calculus introduced by Robinson [30]. The most successful techniques for handling pure first-order logic have been based on resolution and ordering criteria [3]. More recently, techniques based on instantiation have shown promise for first-order logic as well [13,17,28]. Inspired by early work on the subject, this paper revisits whether modern implementations of the latter class of techniques can benefit from enumerative instantiation.

Outline. We first give preliminaries in Sect. 2. Then, we introduce a stronger Herbrand Theorem as the basis for making enumerative instantiation practical so that it can be used in modern systems in Sect. 3. We formalize the different instantiation strategies used by state-of-the-art SMT solvers, discuss their strengths and weaknesses, and present a schematization of how to combine such strategies in Sect. 4, with a focus on a new strategy for enumerative instantiation. An extensive experimental evaluation of enumerative instantiation as implemented in CVC4 is presented in Sect. 5.

2   Preliminaries

We work in the context of many-sorted first-order logic with equality (see e.g. [16]) and assume the reader is familiar with the notions of signature, term, (quantified and ground) formula, atom, literal, free and bound variable, and substitution.

We consider signatures Σ containing a Bool sort and constants $\top$, $\bot$ and a family of predicate symbols ($\approx : \tau \times \tau \to$ Bool) interpreted as equality for each sort τ. Without loss of generality, we assume $\approx$ is the only predicate in Σ. We use $=$ for syntactic equality. The set of all terms occurring in a formula φ (resp. term t) is denoted by $\mathbf{T}(\varphi)$ (resp. $\mathbf{T}(t)$). We write $\bar{t}$ for the sequence of terms $t_1, \ldots, t_n$ for an unspecified $n \in \mathbb{N}^+$ that is either irrelevant or deducible from the context.

An *interpretation* is a triple $\mathcal{M} = (\mathcal{D}, \mathcal{I}, \mathcal{V})$ in which $\mathcal{D}$ is a collection of non-empty *domain sets* for all sorts in Σ, $\mathcal{I}$ interprets symbols by mapping them into functions over domain sets according to the symbol sort, and $\mathcal{V}$ maps free variables to elements of their respective domain sets. A *theory* is a pair $\mathcal{T} = (\Sigma, \Omega)$ in which Σ is a signature and Ω is a class of interpretations denoted the *models of* $\mathcal{T}$. The *empty theory* is the theory for which the class of interpretations Ω is unrestricted, which coincides with first-order logic with equality. Throughout this paper we assume a fixed background theory $\mathcal{T}$, which unless otherwise stated is the empty theory. A formula φ is *satisfiable* (resp. *unsatisfiable*) *in* $\mathcal{T}$ if it is satisfied by some (resp. no) interpretation $\mathcal{M} \in \Omega$, written $\mathcal{M} \models_{\mathcal{T}} \varphi$. A formula φ *entails in* $\mathcal{T}$ a formula ψ, written $\varphi \models_{\mathcal{T}} \psi$, if every interpretations in Ω satisfying φ also satisfies ψ. For these notions of model satisfaction and entailment in the empty theory, we omit the subscript.

A substitution σ maps variables to terms and its domain, $\mathsf{dom}(\sigma)$, is finite. We write $\mathsf{ran}(\sigma)$ to denote its range. Throughout the paper, conjunctions may be written as sets or tuples, and vice-versa, whenever convenient and unambiguous. All definitions are assumed to be lifted in the expected way from formulas into sets or tuples of formulas.

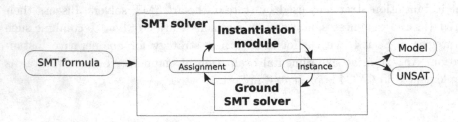

Fig. 1. The SMT instantiation loop for quantified formulas

Instantiation-Based SMT Solvers

Quantifiers in formulas are generally handled by SMT solvers through instantiation-based techniques, which capitalize on their capability to handle large ground formulas. In this approach, an input formula ψ is given to the ground SMT solver, which will abstract all atoms and quantified formulas and treat them as if they were propositional variables. The solver for ground formulas will provide an assignment $E \cup Q$, where E is a set of ground literals and Q is a set of quantified formulas appearing in ψ, such that $E \sqcup Q$ propositionally entails ψ. We assume that all quantified formulas in ψ are of the form $\forall \bar{x}. \varphi$ with φ quantifier-free. This can be achieved by prenex form transformation and Skolemization. The instantiation module of the solver will then generate new ground formulas of the form $\forall \bar{x}. \varphi \Rightarrow \varphi\sigma$ where $\forall \bar{x}. \varphi$ is a quantified formula in Q and σ is a substitution from the variables in φ to ground terms. These instances will be added conjunctively to the input of the ground solver, hence refining its knowledge of the quantified formulas. The ground solver may then provide another assignment $E' \cup Q'$, where this is a set that entails both φ and the newly added instances. This new assignment might either be the previous one, augmented by new ground literals coming from the new instances, or if the previous E has been refuted by the new instances, a completely different set. On the other hand, the process may terminate if the newly added instances suffice to prove the unsatisfiability of the original formula. We will refer to the game between the ground solver that provides assignments for the abstraction of the formula and the instantiation module that provides instances added conjunctively to the formula, as the instantiation loop of the SMT solver (see Fig. 1).

3   Herbrand Theorem and Beyond

The Herbrand Theorem (see e.g. [16]) for pure first-order logic with equality[1] provides a refutationally complete procedure to check the satisfiability of a formula ψ, or more specifically of a set of literals and quantifiers $E \cup Q$. Indeed, $E \cup Q$ is satisfiable if and only if $E \cup Q_g$ is satisfiable, where Q_g is the set of all (Herbrand) instances one can build from the quantifiers in Q by instantiation with the Herbrand universe, i.e. all the possible well-sorted terms built on the signature used in $E \cup Q$. Based on this, an instantiation module has a simple refutationally complete strategy for pure first-order logic with equality: it suffices to enumerate Herbrand instances. The major drawback of this strategy is that the Herbrand universe is large. For instance, as soon as there is a function with the range sort also used as an argument, the Herbrand universe is infinite.

---

[1] The Herbrand Theorem is generally presented in pure first-order logic without equality, but it also holds for equality: it suffices to consider the equality axioms conjunctively with formulas.

Fortunately, a stronger variant of the Herbrand Theorem holds. Using this variant, the instantiation module does not need to consider all possible well-sorted terms (i.e. the full Herbrand universe), but only the terms already available in $E \cup Q$, and those subsequently generated.

Theorem 1. *Consider the conjunctive sets E and Q of ground literals and universally quantified clauses respectively where $\mathbf{T}(E)$ contains at least one term of each sort. The set $E \cup Q$ is unsatisfiable in pure first-order logic if and only if there exists a series Q_i of finite sets of instances of Q such that*

- *for some number n, the finite set of formulas $E \cup \bigcup_{i=1}^{n} Q_i$ is unsatisfiable;*
- $Q_{i+1} \subseteq \left\{ \varphi\sigma \mid \forall \bar{x}.\, \varphi \in Q,\, \mathsf{ran}(\sigma) \subseteq \mathbf{T}(E \cup \bigcup_{j=1}^{i} Q_j) \right\}.$

Proof. All proofs for this section are included in [26].   □

The above theorem is stronger than the classical Herbrand theorem in the sense that the set of instances considered above is smaller (or equal) than the set of instances considered in the classical Herbrand theorem. As a trivial example, if a function f appears only in $E \cup Q$ in ground terms, no new applications of f are considered. The theorem does not consider all arbitrary terms from the signature, but only those that are generated by the successive instantiations with only already available ground terms. Note the theorem holds for pure first-order logic with equality, and in any theory that preserves the compactness property. It is also necessary however to consider the axioms of the theory for the generation of new terms, that might lead to other instances.

In the Bernays-Schönfinkel-Ramsey fragment of first-order logic (also know as the EPR class) formulas do not contain non constant function symbols, therefore the Herbrand universe of any formula is a finite set. Since the above sets of terms are a subset of the Herbrand universe, the enumeration will always terminate, even when the formula is satisfiable. Therefore, the resulting ground problem is decidable, and the above method comprises a decision procedure for this fragment, just like some variant of model-based quantifier instantiation.

Theorem 1 implies that an instantiation module only has to consider terms occurring within assignments, and not all possible terms. To show refutational completeness (termination on unsatisfiable input) and model soundness (termination without declaring unsatisfiability implies that the input is satisfiable), it is however necessary to account for the successive assignments produced by the ground SMT solver and the consecutive generation of instances. This is achieved using the following lemma.

Lemma 1. *Consider the conjunctive sets E and Q of ground literals and universally quantified clauses respectively where $\mathbf{T}(E)$ contains at least one term of each sort. If there exists an infinite series of finite satisfiable sets of ground literals E_i and of finite sets of ground instances Q_i of Q such that*

- $Q_i = \{\varphi\sigma \mid \forall \bar{x}.\, \varphi \in Q,\, \mathsf{dom}(\sigma) = \{\bar{x}\} \wedge \mathsf{ran}(\sigma) \subseteq \mathbf{T}(E_i)\};$
- $E_0 = E,\, E_{i+1} \models E_i \cup Q_i;$

then $E \cup Q$ is satisfiable in the empty theory with equality.

The above lemma has two direct consequences on the instantiation loop of SMT solvers, where instances are generated from the set of available terms in the ground assignment provided by the ground SMT solver. The following two corollaries state the model soundness and the refutational completeness of the instantiation loop respectively.

Corollary 1. *Given a formula ψ, if there exists a satisfiable set of literals E and a set of quantified clauses Q such that $E \cup Q \models \psi$ and the instantiation module of the SMT solver cannot generate any new instance, i.e. E already entails all instances of Q for substitutions built with terms $\mathbf{T}(E)$, then ψ is satisfiable.*

Proof. A formal statement of the corollary and a proof is available in [26].   □

Corollary 2. *Given an unsatisfiable formula, if the generation of instances is fair the instantiation loop of the SMT solver terminates.*

Proof. A formal statement of the corollary and a proof is available in [26].   □

$\mathbf{c}(\,E, \forall \bar{x}.\varphi\,)$: 1. Either return $\{\sigma\}$ where $E, \varphi\sigma \models \bot$, or return $\emptyset$.

$\mathbf{e}(\,E, \forall \bar{x}.\varphi\,)$: 1. Select a set of triggers $\{\bar{t}_1, \ldots \bar{t}_n\}$ for $\forall \bar{x}.\varphi$.
  2. For each $i = 1, \ldots, n$, select a set of substitutions S_i such that
     for each $\sigma \in S_i$, $E \models \bar{t}_i\sigma \approx \bar{g}_i$ for some tuple $\bar{g}_i \in \mathbf{T}(E)$.
  3. Return $\bigcup_{i=1}^{n} S_i$.

$\mathbf{m}(\,E, \forall \bar{x}.\varphi\,)$: 1. Construct a model $\mathcal{M}$ for E.
  2. Return $\{\{\bar{x} \mapsto \bar{t}\}\}$ where $\bar{t} \in \mathbf{T}(E)$ and $\mathcal{M} \not\models \varphi\{\bar{x} \mapsto \bar{t}\}$, or $\emptyset$ if none exists.

$\mathbf{u}(\,E, \forall \bar{x}.\varphi\,)$: 1. Choose an ordering $\preceq$ on tuples of quantifier-free terms.
  2. Return $\{\{\bar{x} \mapsto \bar{t}\}\}$ where $\bar{t}$ is a minimal tuple of terms w.r.t $\preceq$ such that
     $\bar{t} \in \mathbf{T}(E)$ and $E \not\models \varphi\{\bar{x} \mapsto \bar{t}\}$, or $\emptyset$ if none exist.

Fig. 2. Quantifier Instantiation strategies: Conflict-based Instantiation ($\mathbf{c}$), E-matching instantiation ($\mathbf{e}$), Model-based Instantiation ($\mathbf{m}$) and Enumerative Instantiation ($\mathbf{u}$).

4   Quantifier Instantiation in CDCL($\mathcal{T}$)

This section overviews recent techniques used by SMT solvers for quantifier instantiation, and comments on their relative strengths and weaknesses. We will focus on enumerative quantifier instantiation, a technique which has received little attention in recent work, but has several compelling advantages with respect to current techniques.

Definition 1 (Instantiation Strategy). *An instantiation strategy takes as input:*

1. *A $\mathcal{T}$-satisfiable set of ground literals* E, *and*
2. *A quantified formula* $\forall \bar{x}. \varphi$.

It outputs a set of substitutions $\{\sigma_1, \ldots, \sigma_n\}$ *where* $\mathsf{dom}(\sigma_i) = \bar{x}$ *for each* $i = 1, \ldots, n$.

Figure 2 gives four instantiation strategies used by modern SMT solvers, each that have the interface given in Definition 1. The first three have been described in detail in previous works (see [25] for a recent overview). We briefly review these techniques in this section. The fourth, enumerative quantifier instantiation, is the subject of this paper.

Conflict-based instantiation (**c**) was introduced in [28] as a technique for improving the performance of SMT solvers for unsatisfiable problems. In this strategy, we return a substitution σ such that $\varphi\sigma$ together with E is unsatisfiable, We refer to $\varphi\sigma$ as a *conflicting instance* (for E). Typical implementations of this strategy do not insist that a conflicting instance be returned if one exists, and hence the strategy may choose to return the empty set of substitutions. Recent work [4,5] gives a strategy for conflict-based instantiation that has refutational completeness guarantees for the empty theory with equality, that is, when a conflict instance exists for a quantified formula in this theory, the strategy is guaranteed to return it.

E-matching instantiation (**e**) is the most commonly used strategy for quantifier instantiation in modern SMT solvers [13,15,18]. In this strategy, we first heuristically choose a set of *triggers* for a quantified formula $\forall \bar{x}. \varphi$, where a trigger is a tuple of terms whose free variables are $\bar{x}$. In practice, triggers can be selected using user-provided annotations, or selected automatically by the SMT solver. For each trigger $\bar{t}_i$, we select a set of substitutions S_i such that for each σ in this set, E entails that $\bar{t}_i\sigma$ is equal to a tuple of ground terms g_i in E. We return the union of these sets S_i for each selected trigger. E-matching instantiation is generally incomplete, but works well in practice for unsatisfiable problems, and hence is a key component of most SMT solvers that support quantified formulas.

Model-based quantifier instantiation (**m**) was introduced in [19], and has also been used for improving the performance of finite model finding [29]. In this strategy, we first construct a model $\mathcal{M}$ for the quantifier-free portion of our input E, where typically the interpretations of functions for values not constrained by E are chosen heuristically. Notice that $\mathcal{M}$ does not necessarily satisfy the quantified formula $\forall \bar{x}.\, \varphi$. If it does not, we return a single substitution σ for which $\mathcal{M}$ does not satisfy $\varphi\sigma$, where typically σ maps variables from $\bar{x}$ to terms that occur in $\mathbf{T}(\mathsf{E})$. With respect to conflict-based and E-matching instantiation, model-based quantifier instantiation has the advantage that it is model sound: when it returns $\emptyset$, then $\mathsf{E} \cup \{\forall \bar{x}.\, \varphi\}$ is satisfiable.

This paper revisits enumerative quantifier instantiation ($\mathbf{u}$) as a viable alternative to model-based quantifier instantiation. In this strategy, we assume an ordering $\preceq$ on quantifier-free terms. This ordering is not related to the usual term ordering one generally uses for saturation theorem proving, but rather determines which instance will be generated first. The strategy returns the substitution $\{\bar{x} \mapsto \bar{t}\}$, where $\bar{t}$ is the minimal tuple of terms with respect to $\preceq$ from $\mathbf{T}(\mathsf{E})$ such that $\varphi\{\bar{x} \mapsto \bar{t}\}$ is not entailed by E. We refer to this strategy as enumerative instantiation since in the worst case it generates instantiations by enumerating tuples of all terms of the proper sort from E, according to the ordering $\preceq$. In practice, the number of instantiations produced by this strategy is kept small by interleaving it with other strategies like $\mathbf{c}$ or $\mathbf{e}$, or due to the fact that a small number of instances may already allow the SMT solver to conclude the input is unsatisfiable. Moreover, thanks to the results in Sect. 3, this strategy is refutationally complete and model sound for quantified formulas in the empty theory with equality.

Example 1. Consider the set of ground literals $\mathsf{E} = \{\neg P(a), \neg P(b), P(c), \neg R(b)\}$. For the input $(\mathsf{E}, \forall x.\, P(x) \vee R(x))$, the strategies in this section will do the following.

1. Conflict based: Since E, $P(b) \vee R(b) \models \bot$, this strategy will return $\{\{x \mapsto b\}\}$.
2. E-matching: This strategy may choose the singleton set of triggers $\{(P(x))\}$. Based on this trigger, since $\mathsf{E} \models P(x)\{x \mapsto t\} \approx P(t)$ where $P(t) \in \mathbf{T}(\mathsf{E})$ for $t = a, b, c$, this strategy may return $\{\{x \mapsto a\}, \{x \mapsto b\}, \{x \mapsto c\}\}$.
3. Model-based: This strategy will construct a model $\mathcal{M}$ for E, where assume that $P^{\mathcal{M}} = \lambda x.\, \mathrm{ite}(x \approx c, \top, \bot)$ and $R^{\mathcal{M}} = \lambda x.\, \bot$. Since $\mathcal{M}$ does not satisfy $P(a) \vee R(a)$, this strategy may return $\{\{x \mapsto a\}\}$.
4. Enumerative instantiation: This strategy chooses an ordering on tuples of terms, say the lexicographic extension of $\preceq$ where $a \prec b \prec c$. Since E does not entail $P(a) \vee R(a)$, this strategy returns $\{\{x \mapsto a\}\}$. □

In the previous example, clearly $\{x \mapsto b\}$ is the most useful substitution, since it leads to an instance $P(b) \vee R(b)$ which together with E is unsatisfiable. The substitution $\{x \mapsto c\}$ is definitely not a useful substitution, since it is already entailed by $P(c) \in \mathsf{E}$. The substitution $\{x \mapsto a\}$ is potentially useful since it forces the solver to satisfy $P(a) \vee R(a)$. Here, we point out that the effect of enumerative instantiation and model-based instantiation is essentially the same, as both return an instance that is not entailed by E. However, the substitutions produced by enumerative instantiation often have advantages with respect to model-based instantiation on unsatisfiable problems.

Example 2. Consider the set of ground literals $E = \{\neg P(a), R(b), S(c)\}$ and the quantified clauses $Q = \{\forall x.\ R(x) \vee S(x),\ \forall x.\ \neg R(x) \vee P(x),\ \forall x.\ \neg S(x) \vee P(x)\}$ in a mono-sorted signature. Notice that $E \cup Q$ is unsatisfiable: it suffices to consider the instances of the three quantified formulas in Q with $x \mapsto a$. On such an input, model-based instantiation will first construct a model for E. Assume this model $\mathcal{M}$ is such that $P^{\mathcal{M}} = \lambda x.\ \bot$, $R^{\mathcal{M}} = \lambda x.\ \mathrm{ite}(x \approx b, \top, \bot)$, and $S^{\mathcal{M}} = \lambda x.\ \mathrm{ite}(x \approx c, \top, \bot)$. Assuming enumerative instantiation chooses the lexicographic extension of a term ordering $\preceq$ where $a \prec b \prec c$. The following table summarizes the result of running the two strategies.

φ	x s.t. $\mathcal{M} \not\models \varphi$	x s.t. $E \not\models \varphi$	$\mathbf{m}(E, \forall x.\ \varphi)$	$\mathbf{u}(E, \forall x.\ \varphi)$
$R(x) \vee S(x)$	a	a	$\{\{x \mapsto a\}\}$	$\{\{x \mapsto a\}\}$
$\neg R(x) \vee P(x)$	b	a, b, c	$\{\{x \mapsto b\}\}$	$\{\{x \mapsto a\}\}$
$\neg S(x) \vee P(x)$	c	a, b, c	$\{\{x \mapsto c\}\}$	$\{\{x \mapsto a\}\}$

The second and third columns show the sets of possible values of x that are considered with model-based and enumerative instantiation respectively, and the third and fourth columns show one possible selection. The instances corresponding to the three substitutions returned by enumerative instantiation $R(a) \vee S(a)$, $\neg R(a) \vee P(a)$ and $\neg S(a) \vee P(a)$ when conjoined with $\neg P(a)$ from E are unsatisfiable, whereas the instances produced by model-based instantiation do not suffice to show that E is unsatisfiable. Hence, the latter will consider an extension of E that satisfies the instances $R(a) \vee S(a)$, $\neg R(b) \vee P(b)$ and $\neg S(c) \vee P(c)$ and guess another model for this extension.   □

A key observation is that useful instantiations can be obscured by guesses made when constructing models $\mathcal{M}$. Here, since we decided $R(a)^{\mathcal{M}} = \bot$, the substitution $\{x \mapsto a\}$ was not considered when applying model-based instantiation to the second quantified formula, and since $S(a)^{\mathcal{M}} = \bot$, the substitution $\{x \mapsto a\}$ was not considered when applying it to the third. In implementations of model-based instantiation, certain values in models are chosen heuristically, leading to this behavior. This is done out of necessity, since determining whether there exists a model that satisfies quantified formulas, even for a fixed context, is a challenging problem.

On the other hand, the range of substitutions considered by enumerative instantiation in the previous example include all terms that correspond to instances that are not entailed by E. The substitutions it considers are "minimally diverse", that is, in the previous example they introduce new predicates on term a only, whereas model-based instantiation introduces new predicates on a, b and c. Reducing the number of new terms introduced by instantiations can have a significant positive impact on performance in practice. Furthermore, enumerative instantiation has the advantage that a term ordering allows fine-grained heuristics better suited for unsatisfiable problems, which we comment on in Sect. 4.1.

Example 3. Consider the sets $E = \{a \not\approx b,\ b \not\approx c,\ a \not\approx c\}$ and $Q = \{\forall x.P(x)\}$. For the input $(E, \forall x.P(x))$, model-based quantifier instantiation will first construct a model $\mathcal{M}$ for E, where assume that $P^{\mathcal{M}} = \lambda x.\top$. It is easy to see $\mathcal{M} \models \varphi\{x \mapsto t\}$ for $a, b, c \in \mathbf{T}(E)$, and hence it returns the empty set of substitutions, indicating that $E \cup Q$ is satisfiable. On the other hand, assume enumerative instantiation chooses the lexicographic extension of a term ordering $\preceq$ where $a \prec b \prec c$. Since $E \not\models P(a)$ and a is smaller than b and c according to $\preceq$, $\mathbf{u}(E, P(x))$ returns the set containing $\{x \mapsto a\}$. Subsequently and for similar reasons, two more iterations of this strategy will be invoked, resulting in the instances $P(b)$ and $P(c)$ before it terminates with the empty set.   □

  In this example, model-based instantiation was able to terminate on the first iteration, since it guessed the correct interpretation for P, whereas enumerative instantiation considered substitutions mapping x to each ground term a, b, c from E. For this reason, model-based instantiation is typically better suited for satisfiable problems.

4.1   Implementing Enumerative Instantiation

We comment on several important details concerning the implementation of enumerative quantifier instantiation in the SMT solver CVC4.

Term Ordering. Given a term ordering $\preceq$, CVC4 considers the extension to tuples of terms such that:

$$(t_1, \ldots, t_n) \prec (s_1, \ldots, s_n) \text{ if } \begin{cases} \max_{i=1}^{n} t_i \prec \max_{i=1}^{n} s_i, \text{ or} \\ \max_{i=1}^{n} t_i = \max_{i=1}^{n} s_i \text{ and } (t_1, \ldots, t_n) \prec_{\text{lex}} (s_1, \ldots, s_n) \end{cases}$$

where $\prec_{\text{lex}}$ is the lexicographic extension of $\prec$. For example, if $a \prec b \prec c$, then we have that $(a, a) \prec (a, b) \prec (b, a) \prec (b, b) \prec (a, c) \prec (c, b) \prec (c, c)$. By this ordering, we consider substitutions involving c only after all combinations of substitutions involving a and b are considered. This choice is important since it leads to instantiations that introduce fewer terms, and are thus more likely to lead to conflicts at the ground level.

  The underlying term ordering is determined dynamically based on the current set of assertions E. At all times, we maintain a finite list of quantifier-free terms such that we have fixed the ordering $t_1 \prec \ldots \prec t_n$. Then, if all combinations of instantiations for $t_1, \ldots, t_n$ are currently entailed by E, we choose a term

$t \in \mathbf{T}(\mathsf{E})$ that is such that $\mathsf{E} \not\models t \approx t_i$ for $i = 1, \ldots, n$ if one exists, and append it to our ordering so that $t_n \prec t$. The particular choice of t beyond this criteria is arbitrary. An experimental evaluation of more sophisticated term orderings, such as those inspired by first-order automated theorem proving [2] is the subject of future work.

Entailment Checks. For a set of ground equalities and disequalities E, quantified formula $\forall \bar{x}.\varphi$ and substitution $\{\bar{x} \mapsto \bar{t}\}$, CVC4 implements a two-layered method for checking whether the entailment $\mathsf{E} \models \varphi\{\bar{x} \mapsto \bar{t}\}$ holds. First, we maintain a cache of instantiations that have already been returned on previous iterations. Hence if E satisfies a set of formulas containing $\varphi\{\bar{x} \mapsto \bar{s}\}$, where $\mathsf{E} \models \bar{t} \approx \bar{s}$, then the entailment clearly holds.

Second, we use an incomplete and fast method for inferring when an entailment holds. We first compute from E congruence classes over $\mathbf{T}(\mathsf{E})$. For each $t \in \mathbf{T}(\mathsf{E})$, let $[t]$ be the representative of term t in this equivalence relation. For each function f, we use a *term index* data structure $\mathscr{I}_f$ that stores an entry of the form $([t_1], \ldots, [t_n]) \rightarrow [f(t_1, \ldots, t_n)] \in \mathscr{I}_f$ for each uninterpreted function application $f(t_1, \ldots, t_n) \in \mathbf{T}(\mathsf{E})$. To check the entailment of $\mathsf{E} \models \ell$ where ℓ is a literal, we update ℓ based on the iterative process until a fixed point is reached:

1. Replace each constant t in ℓ with $[t]$.
2. Replace each function term $f(t_1, \ldots, t_n)$ in ℓ with s if $(t_1, \ldots, t_n) \rightarrow s \in \mathscr{I}_f$.
3. If ℓ is $t \approx t$, replace it by $\top$.
4. If ℓ is $t \not\approx s$ and $t' \not\approx s' \in \mathsf{E}$ where $[t'] = t$ and $[s'] = s$, replace it by $\top$.

Then, if the resultant ψ is $\top$, then the entailment holds. Although not shown here, the above process is extended in a straightforward way to handle Boolean structure, and also can be extended in the presence of other background theories in a straightforward way by incorporating theory-specific rewriting steps.

Restricting Enumeration Space. Enumerative instantiation can be refined further by noticing that only a subset of the set of terms $\mathbf{T}(E)$ will ever be relevant for showing unsatisfiability of a quantified formula. An approach in this spirit was used by Ge and de Moura [19], where decidable fragments were identified by noticing that the *relevant domains* of quantified formulas in these fragments are guaranteed to be finite. In that work, the relevant domain of a quantified formula $\forall \bar{x}.\psi$ is computed based on the terms in E and the structure of its body ψ. For example, t is in the relevant domain of function f for all ground terms $f(t)$, the relevant domain of x for a quantified formula containing the term $f(x)$ is equal to the relevant domain of f, and so on. A related approach is to use *sort inference* [8,9,22], to compute more precise sort information and thus decrease the number of possible instantiations.

Example 4. Say $E \cup Q = \{a \not\approx b, f(a) \approx c\} \cup \{\forall x. P(f(x))\}$, where a, b, c, x are of sort τ, f is a unary function $\tau \to \tau$, and P is a predicate on τ. It can be shown that $E \cup Q$ is equivalent to $E^s \cup Q^s = \{a_1 \not\approx b_1, f_{12}(a_1) \approx c_2\} \cup \{P_2(f_{12}(x_1))\}$, where a_1, b_1, x_1 are of sort τ_1, c_2 is of sort τ_2, f_{12} is of sort $\tau_1 \to \tau_2$, and P_2 is a predicate on τ_2. □

Sorts can be inferred in this manner using a linear traversal on the input formula (for details, see for instance Sect. 4 of [22]). This technique narrows the set of terms considered by enumerative instantiation. In the above example, whereas enumerative instantiation for $E \cup Q$ might consider the substitutions $\{x \mapsto c\}$ or $\{x \mapsto f(c)\}$, for $E^s \cup Q^s$ it would not consider $\{x_1 \mapsto c_2\}$ since their sorts are different, nor would it consider $\{x_1 \mapsto f_{12}(c_2)\}$ since $f_{12}(c_2)$ is not a well-sorted term. Moreover, the Herbrand universe of an inferred subsort may be finite when the universe of its parent sort is infinite. In the above example, the Herbrand universe of τ_1 is $\{a_1, b_1\}$ and τ_2 is $\{f_{12}(a_1), f_{12}(b_1), c_2\}$, whereas the Herbrand universe of τ is infinite.

Compound Strategies. Since the instantiation strategies from this section have their respective strengths and weaknesses, it is valuable to combine them. We consider two ways of combining strategies which we refer as *priority* instantiation and *interleaved* instantiation. For base strategies s_1 and s_2, priority instantiation $(s_1; s_2)$ first invokes s_1. If this strategy returns a non-empty set of substitutions, it returns that set, otherwise it returns the instances returned by s_2. On the other hand, interleaved instantiation $(s_1 + s_2)$ returns the union of the substitutions returned by the two strategies.

Enumerative instantiation is the most effective when used as a complement to heuristic strategies. In particular, we will see in the next section that the strategies c;e;u and c;e+u are the most effective strategies for unsatisfiable problems in CVC4.

5   Experiments

This section reports on our experimental evaluation of different strategies based on enumerative instantiation as implemented in the SMT solver CVC4.[2] We present an extensive analysis of enumerative instantiation and compare it with implementations of model-based instantiation on both unsatisfiable and satisfiable benchmarks. Experiments were performed on untyped first-order benchmarks from the TPTP library [33][3], version 6.4.0, and from SMT-LIB [7], as of October 2017, on logics having quantifiers and either uninterpreted functions or arrays. For the latter, we considered also logics containing other theories such as

---

[2] For details, see http://matryoshka.gforge.inria.fr/pubs/fol_enumerative_inst/.
[3] In SMT parlance, the logic of these benchmarks is quantified EUF.

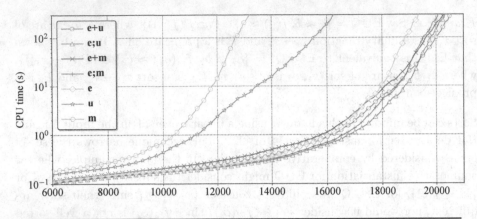

Library	#	u	e;u	e+u	e	m	e;m	e+m	uport	mport	port
TPTP	14731	4426	6125	6273	5396	4369	6066	6151	6674	6566	6859
UF	7293	2607	2906	2961	2862	2418	2898	2972	3119	3045	3159
UFDT	4384	1783	1977	1998	1958	1642	1954	1993	2091	2070	2113
UFLIA	7745	3622	5022	5037	4867	2638	4966	4989	5253	5132	5279
UFNIA	3213	1788	1947	1978	1937	1169	1860	1865	2107	2064	2138
Others	4699	2019	2348	2288	2320	966	2338	2312	2400	2363	2404
Total	42065	16245	20325	20535	19340	13202	20082	20282	21644	21240	21952

Fig. 3. CVC4 configurations on unsatisfiable benchmarks with a 300 s timeout.

arithmetic and datatypes. Some benchmarks are solved by all considered configurations of solvers in less than 0.1 s. We discarded those 25 580 benchmarks. In total, 42 065 problems were selected, 14 731 from TPTP and 27 334 from SMT-LIB. All results were produced on StarExec [32], a public execution service for running comparative evaluations of solvers, with a timeout of 300 s.

We follow the convention in Sect. 4 for identifying configurations based on their instantiation strategy. All configurations of CVC4 use conflict-based instantiation [5,28] with highest priority, so we omit the prefix "c;" from the names of CVC4 configurations e.g. **e+u** in fact means **c;e+u**. Sort inference, as discussed in Sect. 4.1, is also used by all configurations of CVC4.

5.1 Impact of Enumerative Instantiation in CVC4

In this section, we highlight the impact of enumerative instantiation in CVC4 for unsatisfiable benchmarks. Where applicable, we contrast the difference in the impact of enumerative instantiation and model-based instantiation on the performance of CVC4 on unsatisfiable benchmarks.[4]

---

[4] There are technical details that influence the comparison of these techniques (see [26]).

The comparison of various instantiation strategies supported by CVC4 is summarized in Fig. 3. In the table, each row is dedicated to a library and logic. SMT-LIB is shown in more granularity than TPTP to highlight comparisons of individual strategies. The first column identifies the subset and the second shows its total number of benchmarks. The next seven columns show the number of benchmarks found to be unsatisfiable by each configuration. The last three columns show the results of virtual portfolio solvers, with **uport** combining **e**, **u**, **e;u**, and **e+u**; and **mport** combining **e**, **m**, **e;m**, and **e+m**; while **port** combines all seven configurations.

First, we can see that **u** outperforms **m**, as it solves 3 043 more benchmarks overall. While this is not close to the performance of E-matching (**e**), it should be noted that **u** is highly orthogonal to **e**, solving 1 737 benchmarks that could not be solved by **e**[5]. Combining **e** with either **u** or **m**, using either priority or interleaving instantiation, leads to significant gains in performance. Overall the best configuration is **e+u**, that is, the interleaving of enumerative instantiation and E-matching, which solves 20 535 benchmarks, that is, 253 more than its counterpart **e+m** interleaving model-based instantiation and E-matching, and 1 295 more than E-matching alone. In the UFLIA logic, the enumerative techniques are specially effective in comparison with the model-based ones. In particular, they enable CVC4 to solve previously intractable problems, e.g. the family "sexpr" with 32 problems. These are notoriously hard problems involving the verification of C# programs using Spec# [6]. Z3 can solve 31 of them thanks to its advanced optimizations of E-matching [13]. CVC4 previously could solve at most 16 using techniques combining **e** and **m**, but **u** alone could solve 27, and all of 32 are solved by **e+u**. Another example is the family "vcc-havoc" in UFNIA, stemming from the verification of concurrent C with VCC [10]. The strategy **e+u** solves 940 out of 984 problems, outperforming **e** and its combinations with **m**, which solve at most 860 problems[6].

The portfolio columns of the table in Fig. 3 highlight the improvement due to enumerative instantiation for CVC4 on the number of solved problems: there are 712 more problems overall solved when adding enumerative instantiation in the strategies (see columns **mport** and **port**). The cactus plot of Fig. 3 shows that while the priority strategies are initially quicker, the interleaving ones scale better, solving more hard problems than their priority counterparts. Overall, we conclude that in addition to being much simpler to implement[7] instantiation strategies that combine E-matching with enumerative instantiation in CVC4 have a noticeable advantage over those that combine E-matching with model-based instantiation on unsatisfiable problems.

---

[5] Number of uniquely solved benchmarks between configurations are available in [26].

[6] A detailed comparison by families can be seen in [26].

[7] As a rough estimate, the implementation of enumerative instantiation in CVC4 is around 500 lines of code, whereas model-based instantiation is around 4500 lines of code.

5.2 Comparison Against Other SMT Solvers

In this section, we compare our implementation of enumerative instantiation in CVC4 against another state-of-the-art SMT solver: Z3 [14] (version 4.5.1) which, like CVC4, also relies on E-matching instantiation for handling unsatisfiable problems. Before making the comparison, we first summarize the main differences between Z3 and CVC4 here. Z3 uses several optimizations for E-matching that are not implemented in CVC4, including the use of code trees and techniques for applying instantiation incrementally during the CDCL($\mathcal{T}$) search (see Sect. 5 of [13]). It also implements techniques for removing previously considered instantiations from its set of known clauses (see Sect. 7 of [13]). The main advantage of CVC4 with respect to Z3 is its use of conflict-based instantiation **c** [28], which is enabled by default in all strategies we considered. It also supports interleaved instantiation strategies as described in Sect. 4.1, whereas Z3 does not. In addition to these differences, Z3 implements model-based instantiation **m** as described in [19], whereas CVC4 implements model-based instantiation as described in [29]. Finally, CVC4 implements enumerative instantiation as described in this paper, which we compare as an alternative to these implementations.

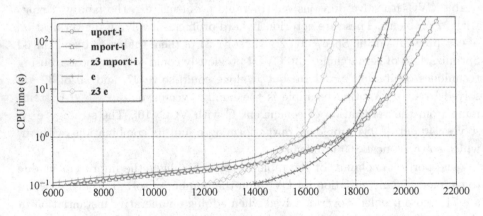

Library	#	z3 m	z3 e	z3 e;m	z3 mport-i	e	uport-i	mport-i
TPTP	14731	2382	4098	5288	5519	5396	6519	6396
UF	7293	1192	2428	2516	2600	2862	3076	2982
UFDT	4384	838	1702	1721	1781	1958	2062	2036
UFLIA	7745	2460	4751	4841	4923	4867	5164	5049
UFNIA	3213	1089	2074	2112	2238	1937	2091	2015
Others	4699	990	2226	2332	2346	2320	2393	2357
Total	42065	8951	17279	18810	19407	19340	21305	20835

Fig. 4. Z3 and CVC4 on unsatisfiable benchmarks with a 300 s timeout.

Figure 4 summarizes the performance of Z3 on our benchmark set. First, like CVC4, using model-based instantiation to complement E-matching leads to significant gains in Z3, as **z3 e;m** solves a total of 1731 more benchmarks than solved by E-matching alone **z3 e**. In comparison with CVC4, the configuration **z3 e** outperforms **e** in the logics with non-linear arithmetic and other theories, while **e** is better in the others. Finally, Z3's implementation of model-based quantifier instantiation by itself **z3 m** is not effective for unsatisfiable benchmarks, solving only 8951 overall.

To further compare Z3 and CVC4, the third column from the left is the number of benchmarks solved by CVC4's E-matching strategy (**e**), which we gave in Fig. 3. The second to last column **uport-i** gives the number of benchmarks solved by at least one of **u**, **e**, or **e;u** in CVC4, where we intentionally omit the interleaved strategy **e+u**, since Z3 does not support a similar strategy. The column **mport-i** is computed similarly. We compare these with the fifth column, **z3 mport-i**, i.e. the number of benchmarks solved by either **z3 m**, **z3 e** or **z3 e;m**. A comparison of these is given in the cactus plot of Fig. 4. We can see that due to Z3's highly optimized implementations, **z3 mport-i** solves the highest number of problems in less than one second (around 13000), whereas the portfolio strategies of CVC4 solve more for larger timeouts. Overall, the best portfolio strategy is enumerative instantiation in CVC4, which solves a total of 21305 unsatisfiable benchmarks overall, which is 1965 more benchmarks than **z3 mport-i**, and 470 more benchmarks than **mport-i**. We thus conclude that the use of enumerative instantiation when paired with E-matching and conflict-based instantiation in CVC4 improves the state-of-the-art of instantiation-based SMT solvers for unsatisfiable benchmarks.

Comparison with Automated Theorem Provers. Automated theorem provers like Vampire [23] and E [31] use substantially different techniques based on super-position, hence we do not provide an extensive comparison here. However, we do remark that the gains provided by enumerative instantiation were one of the main reasons for CVC4 being more competitive in the 2017 CASC competition of automatic theorem provers [34]. CVC4 placed third in the category with unsatisfiable problems on the empty theory, as in previous years, behind superposition-based theorem provers Vampire and E, which implement complete strategies. There was, however, a 23% reduction in the number of problems that E solves and CVC4 does not, w.r.t. the previous competition, reducing the gap between the two systems.

Satisfiable Benchmarks. For satisfiable benchmarks[8], **m** solves 1350 benchmarks across all theories. As expected, this is much higher than the number solved by

---

[8] For further details, see [26].

u, which solves 510 benchmarks, all from the empty theory. Nevertheless, there are 13 satisfiable problems solved by u and not by m, which shows that enumerative instantiation has some orthogonality on satisfiable benchmarks as well. We conclude that enumeration not only has superior performance to MBQI on unsatisfiable benchmarks, but also can be an alternative for satisfiable benchmarks in the empty theory.

5.3   Artifact

We have produced an artifact [27] to reproduce the experimental results presented in this paper. The artifact contains the binaries of the SMT solvers CVC4 and Z3, the benchmarks on which they were evaluated, and the running scripts for each configuration evaluated. Detailed instructions are given to perform tests on the various benchmark families with all configurations within the time limits, as well as for retrieving the respective results in CSV format. The artifact has been tested in the virtual machine available at [21].

6   Conclusion

We have presented a strengthening of the Herbrand Theorem, and used it to devise an efficient technique for enumerative instantiation. The implementation of this technique in the state-of-the-art SMT solver CVC4 increases its success rate and outperforms existing implementations of MBQI on unsatisfiable problems with quantified formulas. Given its relatively simple implementation, this technique is well poised as an alternative to MBQI for being integrated in an instantiation based SMT solver to achieve completeness in first-order logic with the empty theory and equality, as well as perform improvements also when theories are considered.

Future work includes further restricting the enumeration space, for instance with ordering criteria in the spirit of resolution-based theorem proving [3]. Another direction is lifting the techniques seen here to reasoning in higher-order logic. To handle quantification over functions it is often necessary to enumerate expressions, and so performing such an enumeration in a principled manner is paramount for this domain. Techniques from syntax-guided function synthesis [1] could be combined with enumerative instantiation to pursue this goal.

Data Availability Statement and Acknowledgments. The datasets generated and analyzed during the current study are available in the figshare repository: https://doi.org/10.6084/m9.figshare.5917384.v1.

This work was partially funded by the National Science Foundation under Award 1656926, by the H2020-FETOPEN-2016-2017-CSA project SC^2 (712689), and by the European Research Council (ERC) starting grant Matryoshka (713999). We would like to thank the anonymous reviewers for their comments. We are grateful to Jasmin C. Blanchette for discussions, encouragements and financial support through his ERC grant.

References

1. Alur, R., Bodík, R., Juniwal, G., Martin, M.M.K., Raghothaman, M., Seshia, S.A., Singh, R., Solar-Lezama, A., Torlak, E., Udupa, A.: Syntax-guided synthesis. In: Formal Methods in Computer-Aided Design (FMCAD), pp. 1–8. IEEE (2013)
2. Baader, F., Nipkow, T.: Term Rewriting and All That. Cambridge University Press, New York (1998)
3. Bachmair, L., Ganzinger, H.: Resolution theorem proving. In: Robinson, A., Voronkov, A. (eds.) Handbook of Automated Reasoning, vol. 1, pp. 19–99 (2001)
4. Barbosa, H.: New techniques for instantiation and proof production in SMT solving. Ph.D. thesis, Université de Lorraine, Universidade Federal do Rio Grande do Norte (2017)
5. Barbosa, H., Fontaine, P., Reynolds, A.: Congruence closure with free variables. In: Legay, A., Margaria, T. (eds.) TACAS 2017. LNCS, vol. 10206, pp. 214–230. Springer, Heidelberg (2017). https://doi.org/10.1007/978-3-662-54580-5_13
6. Barnett, M., DeLine, R., Fähndrich, M., Jacobs, B., Leino, K.R.M., Schulte, W., Venter, H.: The Spec# programming system: challenges and directions. In: Meyer, B., Woodcock, J. (eds.) VSTTE 2005. LNCS, vol. 4171, pp. 144–152. Springer, Heidelberg (2008). https://doi.org/10.1007/978-3-540-69149-5_16
7. Barrett, C., Fontaine, P., Tinelli, C.: The SMT-LIB Standard: Version 2.5. Technical report, Department of Computer Science, The University of Iowa (2015). www.SMT-LIB.org
8. Claessen, K., Lillieström, A., Smallbone, N.: Sort it out with monotonicity. In: Bjørner, N., Sofronie-Stokkermans, V. (eds.) CADE 2011. LNCS (LNAI), vol. 6803, pp. 207–221. Springer, Heidelberg (2011). https://doi.org/10.1007/978-3-642-22438-6_17
9. Claessen, K., Sörensson, N.: New techniques that improve MACE-style finite model finding. In: Proceedings of the CADE-19 Workshop: Model Computation - Principles, Algorithms, Applications (2003)
10. Cohen, E., Dahlweid, M., Hillebrand, M., Leinenbach, D., Moskal, M., Santen, T., Schulte, W., Tobies, S.: VCC: a practical system for verifying concurrent C. In: Berghofer, S., Nipkow, T., Urban, C., Wenzel, M. (eds.) TPHOLs 2009. LNCS, vol. 5674, pp. 23–42. Springer, Heidelberg (2009). https://doi.org/10.1007/978-3-642-03359-9_2
11. Davis, M., Logemann, G., Loveland, D.: A machine program for theorem-proving. Commun. ACM 5(7), 394–397 (1962)
12. Davis, M., Putnam, H.: A computing procedure for quantification theory. J. ACM 7(3), 201–215 (1960)
13. de Moura, L., Bjørner, N.: Efficient E-matching for SMT solvers. In: Pfenning, F. (ed.) CADE 2007. LNCS (LNAI), vol. 4603, pp. 183–198. Springer, Heidelberg (2007). https://doi.org/10.1007/978-3-540-73595-3_13

14. de Moura, L., Bjørner, N.: Z3: an efficient SMT solver. In: Ramakrishnan, C.R., Rehof, J. (eds.) TACAS 2008. LNCS, vol. 4963, pp. 337–340. Springer, Heidelberg (2008). https://doi.org/10.1007/978-3-540-78800-3_24

15. Detlefs, D., Nelson, G., Saxe, J.B.: Simplify: a theorem prover for program checking. J. ACM **52**(3), 365–473 (2005)

16. Enderton, H.B.: A Mathematical Introduction to Logic, 2nd edn. Academic Press, Burlington (2001)

17. Ganzinger, H., Korovin, K.: New directions in instantiation-based theorem proving. In: Symposium on Logic in Computer Science, p. 55 (2003)

18. Ge, Y., Barrett, C., Tinelli, C.: Solving quantified verification conditions using satisfiability modulo theories. In: Pfenning, F. (ed.) CADE 2007. LNCS (LNAI), vol. 4603, pp. 167–182. Springer, Heidelberg (2007). https://doi.org/10.1007/978-3-540-73595-3_12

19. Ge, Y., de Moura, L.: Complete instantiation for quantified formulas in satisfiabiliby modulo theories. In: Bouajjani, A., Maler, O. (eds.) CAV 2009. LNCS, vol. 5643, pp. 306–320. Springer, Heidelberg (2009). https://doi.org/10.1007/978-3-642-02658-4_25

20. Gilmore, P.C.: A proof method for quantification theory: its justification and realization. IBM J. Res. Dev. **4**(1), 28–35 (1960)

21. Hartmanns, A., Wendler, P.: figshare (2018). https://doi.org/10.6084/m9.figshare.5896615

22. Korovin, K.: Non-cyclic sorts for first-order satisfiability. In: Fontaine, P., Ringeissen, C., Schmidt, R.A. (eds.) FroCoS 2013. LNCS (LNAI), vol. 8152, pp. 214–228. Springer, Heidelberg (2013). https://doi.org/10.1007/978-3-642-40885-4_15

23. Kovács, L., Voronkov, A.: First-order theorem proving and VAMPIRE. In: Sharygina, N., Veith, H. (eds.) CAV 2013. LNCS, vol. 8044, pp. 1–35. Springer, Heidelberg (2013). https://doi.org/10.1007/978-3-642-39799-8_1

24. Prawitz, D.: An improved proof procedure1. Theoria **26**(2), 102–139 (1960)

25. Reynolds, A.: Conflicts, models and heuristics for quantifier instantiation in SMT. In: Kovács, L., Voronkov, A. (eds.) Vampire Workshop, EPiC Series in Computing, pp. 1–15. EasyChair (2016)

26. Reynolds, A., Barbosa, H., Fontaine, P.: Revisiting enumerative instantiation. Technical report, University of Iowa, Inria (2018). https://hal.inria.fr/hal-01744956

27. Reynolds, A., Barbosa, H., Fontaine, P.: Revisiting enumerative instantiation - Artifact (2018). figshare https://doi.org/10.6084/m9.figshare.5917384.v1

28. Reynolds, A., Tinelli, C., de Moura, L.M.: Finding conflicting instances of quantified formulas in SMT. In: Formal Methods In Computer-Aided Design (FMCAD), pp. 195–202. IEEE (2014)

29. Reynolds, A., Tinelli, C., Goel, A., Krstić, S., Deters, M., Barrett, C.: Quantifier instantiation techniques for finite model finding in SMT. In: Bonacina, M.P. (ed.) CADE 2013. LNCS (LNAI), vol. 7898, pp. 377–391. Springer, Heidelberg (2013). https://doi.org/10.1007/978-3-642-38574-2_26

30. Robinson, J.A.: A machine-oriented logic based on the resolution principle. J. ACM **12**(1), 23–41 (1965)

31. Schulz, S.: E - A brainiac theorem prover. AI Commun. **15**(2,3), 111–126 (2002)
32. Stump, A., Sutcliffe, G., Tinelli, C.: StarExec: a cross-community infrastructure for logic solving. In: Demri, S., Kapur, D., Weidenbach, C. (eds.) IJCAR 2014. LNCS (LNAI), vol. 8562, pp. 367–373. Springer, Cham (2014). https://doi.org/10.1007/978-3-319-08587-6_28
33. Sutcliffe, G.: The TPTP problem library and associated infrastructure. J. Autom. Reasoning **43**(4), 337–362 (2009)
34. Sutcliffe, G.: The CADE ATP system competition - CASC. AI Mag. **37**(2), 99–101 (2016)

A Non-linear Arithmetic Procedure
for Control-Command Software
Verification

Pierre Roux[1]([✉]), Mohamed Iguernlala[2,3], and Sylvain Conchon[3,4]

[1] ONERA, DTIS, 31055 Toulouse, France
pierre.roux@onera.fr
[2] OCamlPro SAS, 91190 Gif-sur-Yvette, France
[3] LRI, Université Paris-Sud, 91405 Orsay, France
[4] INRIA Saclay – Ile-de-France, Toccata,
91893 Orsay, France

Abstract. State-of-the-art (semi-)decision procedures for non-linear real arithmetic address polynomial inequalities by mean of symbolic methods, such as quantifier elimination, or numerical approaches such as interval arithmetic. Although (some of) these methods offer nice completeness properties, their high complexity remains a limit, despite the impressive efficiency of modern implementations. This appears to be an obstacle to the use of SMT solvers when verifying, for instance, functional properties of control-command programs.

Using off-the-shelf convex optimization solvers is known to constitute an appealing alternative. However, these solvers only deliver approximate solutions, which means they do not readily provide the soundness expected for applications such as software verification. We thus investigate a-posteriori validation methods and their integration in the SMT framework. Although our early prototype, implemented in the Alt-Ergo SMT solver, often does not prove competitive with state of the art solvers, it already gives some interesting results, particularly on control-command programs.

Keywords: SMT · Non-linear real arithmetic
Polynomial inequalities · Convex optimization

1 Introduction

Systems of non-linear polynomial constraints over the reals are known to be solvable since Tarski proved that the first-order theory of the real numbers is decidable, by providing a quantifier elimination procedure. This procedure has then been much improved, particularly with the cylindrical algebraic decomposition. Unfortunately, its doubly exponential complexity remains a serious limit to its

This work has been partially supported by the French ANR projects ANR-12-INSE-0007 Cafein and ANR-14-CE28-0020 Soprano and the project SEFA IKKY.

D. Beyer and M. Huisman (Eds.): TACAS 2018, LNCS 10806, pp. 132–151, 2018.
https://doi.org/10.1007/978-3-319-89963-3_8

scalability. It is now integrated into SMT solvers [23]. Although it demonstrates very good practical results, symbolic quantifier elimination seems to remain an obstacle to scalability on some problems. In some cases, branch and bound with interval arithmetic constitutes an interesting alternative [17].

We investigate the use of numerical optimization techniques, called semi-definite programming, as an alternative. We show in this paper how solvers based on these techniques can be used to design a sound semi-decision procedure that outperforms symbolic and interval-arithmetic methods on problems of practical interest. A noticeable characteristic of the algorithms implemented in these solvers is to only compute approximate solutions.

We explain this by making a comparison with linear programming. There are two competitive methods to optimize a linear objective under linear constraints: the interior point and the simplex algorithms. The interior point algorithm starts from some initial point and performs steps towards an optimal value. These iterations converge to the optimum but not in finitely many steps and have to be stopped at some point, yielding an approximate answer. In contrast, the simplex algorithm exploits the fact that the feasible set is a polyhedra and that the optimum is achieved on one of its vertices. The number of vertices being finite, the optimum can be exactly reached after finitely many iterations. Unfortunately, this nice property does not hold for spectrahedra, the equivalent of polyhedra for semi-definite programming. Thus, all semi-definite programming solvers are based on the interior-point algorithm, or a variant thereof.

To illustrate the consequences of these approximate solutions, consider the proof of $e \leq c$ with e a complicated ground expression and c a constant. $e \leq c$ can be proved by exactly computing e, giving a constant c', and checking that $c' \leq c$. However, if e is only approximately computed: $e \in [c' - \epsilon, c' + \epsilon]$, this is conclusive only when $c' + \epsilon \leq c$. In particular, if e is equal to c, an exact computation is required. This inability to prove inequalities that are not satisfied with some margin is a well known property of numerical verification methods [42] which can then be seen as a trade-off between completeness and computation cost.

The main point of this paper is that, despite their incompleteness, numerical verification methods remain an interesting option when they enable to practically solve problems for which other methods offer an untractable complexity. Our contributions are:

(1) a comparison of two sound semi-decision procedures for systems of non-linear constraints, which rely on off-the-shelf numerical optimization solvers,
(2) an integration of these procedures in the Alt-Ergo SMT solver,
(3) an experimental evaluation of our approach on a set of benchmarks coming from various application domains.

The rest of this paper is organized as follows: Sect. 2 gives a practical example of a polynomial problem, coming from control-command program verification, better handled by numerical methods. Section 3 is dedicated to preliminaries. It introduces basic concepts of sum of squares polynomials and semi-definite programming. In Sect. 4, we compare two methods to derive sound solutions to polynomial problems from approximate answers of semi-definite programming

```
typedef struct { double x0, x1, x2; } state;
/*@ predicate inv(state *s) = 6.04 * s->x0 * s->x0 - 9.65 * s->x0 * s->x1
  @   - 2.26 * s->x0 * s->x2 + 11.36 * s->x1 * s->x1
  @   + 2.67 * s->x1 * s->x2 + 3.76 * s->x2 * s->x2 <= 1; */

/*@ requires \valid(s) && inv(s) && -1 <= in0 <= 1;
  @ ensures inv(s); */
void step(state *s, double in0) {
  double pre_x0 = s->x0, pre_x1 = s->x1, pre_x2 = s->x2;
  s->x0 = 0.9379 * pre_x0 - 0.0381 * pre_x1 - 0.0414 * pre_x2 + 0.0237 * in0;
  s->x1 = -0.0404 * pre_x0 + 0.968 * pre_x1 - 0.0179 * pre_x2 + 0.0143 * in0;
  s->x2 = 0.0142 * pre_x0 - 0.0197 * pre_x1 + 0.9823 * pre_x2 + 0.0077 * in0;
}
```

Fig. 1. Example of a typical control-command code in C.

solvers. Section 5 provides some implementation details and discuss experimental results. Finally, Sect. 6 concludes with some related and future works.

2   Example: Control-Command Program Verification

Control-command programs usually iterate linear assignments periodically over time. These assignments take into account a measure (via some *sensor*) of the state of the physical system to control (called *plant* by control theorists) to update an internal state and eventually output orders back to the physical system (through some *actuator*). Figure 1 gives an example of such an update, in0 being the input and s the internal state. The comments beginning by @ in the example are annotations in the ACSL language [12]. They specify that before the execution of the function (requires) s must be a valid pointer satisfying the predicate inv and $|in0| \leq 1$ must hold. Under these hypotheses, s still satisfies inv after executing the function (ensures).

To prove that the internal state remains bounded over any execution of the system, a quadratic polynomial[1] can be used as invariant[2]. Checking the validity of these invariants then leads to arithmetic verification conditions (VCs) involving quadratic polynomials. Such VCs can for instance be generated from the program of Fig. 1 by the Frama-C/Why3 program verification toolchain [12,16]. Unfortunately, proving the validity of these VCs seem out of reach for current state-of-the-art SMT solvers. For instance, although Z3 [13] can solve smaller examples with just two internal state variables in a matter of seconds, it ran for a few days on the three internal state variable example of Fig. 1 without reaching a conclusion[3]. In contrast, our prototype can prove it in a fraction of second, as well as other examples with up to a dozen variables.

---

[1] For instance, the three variables polynomial in *inv* in Fig. 1.

[2] Control theorists call these invariants sublevel sets of a quadratic Lyapunov function. Such functions exist for linear systems if and only if they do not diverge.

[3] This is the case even on a simplified version with just arithmetic constructs, i.e., expurgated of all the reasoning about pointers and the C memory model.

Verification of control-command programs is a good candidate for numerical methods. These systems are designed to be robust to many small errors, which means that the verified properties are usually satisfied with some margin. Thus, the incompleteness of numerical methods is not an issue for this kind of problems.

3   Preliminaries

3.1   Emptiness of Semi-algebraic Sets

Our goal is to prove that conjunctions of polynomial inequalities are unsatisfiable, that is, given some polynomials with real coefficients $p_1, \ldots, p_m \in \mathbb{R}[x]$, we want to prove that there does not exist any assignment for the n variables $x_1, \ldots, x_n \in \mathbb{R}^n$ such that all inequalities $p_1(x_1, \ldots, x_n) \geq 0, \ldots, p_m(x_1, \ldots, x_n) \geq 0$ hold simultaneously. In the rest of this paper, the notation $p \geq 0$ (resp. $p > 0$) means that for all $x \in \mathbb{R}^n$, $p(x) \geq 0$ (resp. $p(x) > 0$).

Theorem 1. *If there exist polynomials $r_i \in \mathbb{R}[x]$ such that*

$$-\sum_i r_i\, p_i > 0 \quad and \quad \forall i, r_i \geq 0 \tag{1}$$

then the conjunction $\bigwedge_i p_i \geq 0$ is unsatisfiable[4].

Proof. Assume there exist $x \in \mathbb{R}^n$ such that for all i, $p_i(x) \geq 0$. Then, since $r_i \geq 0$, we have $r_i(x)\, p_i(x) \geq 0$ hence $\left(\sum_i r_i\, p_i\right)(x) \geq 0$ which contradicts $-\sum_i r_i\, p_i > 0$.

In fact, under some hypotheses[5] on the p_i, the condition (1) is not only sufficient but also necessary, as stated by the Putinar's Positivstellensatz [27, Sect. 2.5.1]. Unfortunately, no practical bound is known on the degrees of the polynomials r_i. In our prototype, we restrict the degrees of each r_i to[6] $d - \deg(p_i)$ where $d := \max_i(\deg(p_i))$, so that $\sum_i r_i\, p_i$ is a polynomial of degree d. This is a first source of incompleteness, although benchmarks show that it already enables to solve many interesting problems.

The sum of squares (SOS) technique [26, 36] is an efficient way to numerically solve polynomial problems such as (1). The next sections recall its main ideas.

3.2   Sum of Squares (SOS) Polynomials

A polynomial $p \in \mathbb{R}[x]$ is said to be SOS if there exist polynomials $h_i \in \mathbb{R}[x]$ such that for all x,

$$p(x) = \sum_i h_i^2(x).$$

Although not all non negative polynomials are SOS, being SOS is a sufficient condition to be non negative.

---

[4] Or, with different words, the semi-algebraic set $\{x \in \mathbb{R}^n \mid \forall i, p_i(x) \geq 0\}$ is empty.
[5] For instance, when one of the sets $\{x \in \mathbb{R}^n \mid p_i(x) \geq 0\}$ is bounded.
[6] More precisely to $2\left\lceil \frac{d-\deg(p_i)}{2} \right\rceil$ as $deg(r_i)$ is necessarily even since $r_i \geq 0$.

Example 1 (from [36]). Considering $p(x_1, x_2) = 2x_1^4 + 2x_1^3 x_2 - x_1^2 x_2^2 + 5x_2^4$, there exist $h_1(x_1, x_2) = \frac{1}{\sqrt{2}}\left(2x_1^2 - 3x_2^2 + x_1 x_2\right)$ and $h_2(x_1, x_2) = \frac{1}{\sqrt{2}}\left(x_2^2 + 3x_1 x_2\right)$ such that $p = h_1^2 + h_2^2$. This proves that for all $x_1, x_2 \in \mathbb{R}$, $p(x_1, x_2) \geq 0$.

Any polynomial p of degree $2d$ (a non negative polynomial is necessarily of even degree) can be written as a quadratic form in the vector of all monomials of degree less or equal to d:

$$p(x) = z^T Q z \tag{2}$$

where $z = \left[1, x_1, \ldots, x_n, x_1 x_2, \ldots, x_n^d\right]^T$ and Q is a constant symmetric matrix.

Example 2. For $p(x_1, x_2) = 2x_1^4 + 2x_1^3 x_2 - x_1^2 x_2^2 + 5x_2^4$, we have[7]

$$p(x_1, x_2) = \begin{bmatrix} x_1^2 \\ x_2^2 \\ x_1 x_2 \end{bmatrix}^T \begin{bmatrix} q_{11} & q_{12} & q_{13} \\ q_{12} & q_{22} & q_{23} \\ q_{13} & q_{23} & q_{33} \end{bmatrix} \begin{bmatrix} x_1^2 \\ x_2^2 \\ x_1 x_2 \end{bmatrix}$$

$$= q_{11} x_1^4 + 2q_{13} x_1^3 x_2 + (q_{33} + 2q_{12}) x_1^2 x_2^2 + 2q_{23} x_1 x_2^3 + q_{22} x_2^4.$$

Thus $q_{11} = 2$, $2q_{13} = 2$, $q_{33} + 2q_{12} = -1$, $2q_{23} = 0$ and $q_{22} = 5$. Two possible examples for the matrix Q are shown below:

$$Q = \begin{bmatrix} 2 & 1 & 1 \\ 1 & 5 & 0 \\ 1 & 0 & -3 \end{bmatrix}, \qquad Q' = \begin{bmatrix} 2 & -3 & 1 \\ -3 & 5 & 0 \\ 1 & 0 & 5 \end{bmatrix}.$$

The polynomial p is then SOS if and only if there exists a positive semi-definite matrix Q satisfying (2). A matrix Q is called positive semi-definite, noted $Q \succeq 0$, if, for all vector x, $x^T Q x \geq 0$. Just as a scalar $q \in \mathbb{R}$ is non negative if and only if $q = r^2$ for some $r \in \mathbb{R}$ (typically $r = \sqrt{q}$), $Q \succeq 0$ if and only if $Q = R^T R$ for some matrix R (then, for all x, $x^T Q x = (Rx)^T (Rx) = \|Rx\|_2^2 \geq 0$). The vector Rz is then a vector of polynomials h_i such that $p = \sum_i h_i^2$.

Example 3. In the previous example, the matrix Q is not positive semi-definite (for $x = [0, 0, 1]^T$, $x^T Q x = -3$). In contrast, $Q' \succeq 0$ as $Q' = R^T R$ with

$$R = \frac{1}{\sqrt{2}} \begin{bmatrix} 2 & -3 & 1 \\ 0 & 1 & 3 \end{bmatrix}$$

giving the decomposition of Example 1.

3.3 Semi-Definite Programming (SDP)

Given symmetric matrices $C, A_1, \ldots, A_m \in \mathbb{R}^{s \times s}$ and scalars $a_1, \ldots, a_m \in \mathbb{R}$, the following optimization problem is called *semi-definite programming*

$$\begin{aligned} \text{minimize} \quad & \text{tr}(CQ) \\ \text{subject to} \quad & \text{tr}(A_1 Q) = a_1 \\ & \quad \vdots \\ & \text{tr}(A_m Q) = a_m \\ & Q \succeq 0 \end{aligned} \tag{3}$$

---

[7] All monomials of p are of degree 4, so z does not need to contain 1, x_1 and x_2.

where the symmetric matrix $Q \in \mathbb{R}^{s \times s}$ is the variable, $\mathrm{tr}(M) = \sum_i M_{i,i}$ denotes the trace of the matrix M and $Q \succeq 0$ means Q positive semi definite.

Remark 1. Since the matrices are symmetric, $\mathrm{tr}(AQ) = \mathrm{tr}(A^T Q) = \sum_{i,j} A_{i,j} Q_{i,j}$. The constraints $\mathrm{tr}(AQ) = a$ are then affine constraints between the entries of Q.

As we have just seen in Sect. 3.2, existence of a SOS decomposition amounts to existence of a positive semi-definite matrix satisfying a set of affine constraints, that is a solution of a semi-definite program. Semi-definite programming is a convex optimization problem for which there exist efficient numerical solvers [7, 44], thus enabling to solve problems involving polynomial inequalities over the reals.

3.4 Parametric Problems

Up to now, we have only seen how to check whether a given polynomial p with fixed coefficients is SOS (which implies its non negativeness). However, according to Sect. 3.1, we need to solve problems in which polynomials p have coefficients that are not fixed but parameters. One of the great strengths of SOS programming is its ability to solve such problems.

An unknown polynomial $p \in \mathbb{R}[x]$ of degree d with n variables can be written

$$p = \sum_{\alpha_1 + \cdots + \alpha_n \le d} p_\alpha x_1^{\alpha_1} \ldots x_n^{\alpha_n}$$

where the p_α are scalar parameters. A constraint such as $r_i \ge 0$ in (1) can then be replaced by r_i is SOS, that is: $\exists Q \succeq 0, r_i = z^T Q z$, which is a set of affine equalities between the coefficients of Q and the coefficients $r_{i,\alpha}$ of r_i. This can be cast as a semi-definite programming problem[8].

Thus, problems with unknown polynomials p, as the one presented in Sect. 3.1, can be numerically solved through SOS programming.

Remark 2 (Complexity). The number s of monomials in n variables of degree less than or equal to d, i.e., the size of the vector z in the decomposition $p(x) = z^T Q z$, is $s := \binom{n+d}{d}$. This is polynomial in n for a fixed d (and vice versa). In practice, current SDP solvers can solve problems where s is about a few hundreds. This makes the SOS relaxation tractable for small values of n and d ($n \sim 10$ and $d \sim 3$, for instance). Our benchmarks indicate this is already enough to solve some practical problems that remain out of reach for other methods.

---

[8] By encoding the $r_{i,\alpha} \in \mathbb{R}$ as $r_{i,\alpha}^+ - r_{i,\alpha}^-$ with $r_{i,\alpha}^+, r_{i,\alpha}^- \ge 0$ and putting the new variables in a block diagonal matrix variable $Q' := \mathrm{diag}(Q, \ldots, r_{i,\alpha}^+, r_{i,\alpha}^-, \ldots)$.

4   Numerical Verification of SOS

According to Sect. 3.1, a conjunction of polynomial constraints can be proved unsatisfiable by exhibiting other polynomials satisfying some constraints. Section 3.4 shows that such polynomials can be efficiently found by some numerical optimization solvers. Unfortunately, due to the algorithms they implement, we cannot directly trust the results of these solvers. This section details this issue and reviews two a-posteriori validation methods, with their respective weaknesses.

4.1   Approximate Solutions from SDP Solvers

In practice, the matrix Q returned by SDP solvers upon solving an SDP problem (3) does not precisely satisfy the equality constraints, due both to the algorithms used and their implementation with floating-point arithmetic. Therefore, although the SDP solver returns a positive answer for a SOS program, this does not constitute a valid proof that a given polynomial is SOS.

Most SDP solvers start from some $Q \succeq 0$ not satisfying the equality constraints (for instance the identity matrix) and iteratively modify it in order to reduce the distance between $\mathrm{tr}(A_i Q)$ and a_i while keeping Q positive semidefinite. This process is stopped when the distance is deemed small enough. This final distance ϵ is called the *primal infeasibility*, and is one of the result quality measures displayed by SDP solvers[9]. Therefore, we do not obtain a Q satisfying $\mathrm{tr}(A_i Q) = a_i$ but rather $\mathrm{tr}(A_i Q) = a_i + \epsilon_i$ for some small ϵ_i such that $|\epsilon_i| \leq \epsilon$.

4.2   Proving Existence of a Nearby Solution

This primal infeasibility has a simple translation in terms of our original SOS problem. The polynomial equality $p = z^T Q z$ is encoded as one scalar constraint $\mathrm{tr}(A_i Q) = a_i$ for each coefficient a_i of the polynomial p (c.f., Examples 2). coefficients of the polynomials p and $z^T Q z$ differ by some ϵ_i and, since $|\epsilon_i| \leq \epsilon$, there exists a matrix $E \in \mathbb{R}^{s \times s}$ such that, for all i, j, $|E_{i,j}| \leq \epsilon$ and

$$p = z^T (Q + E) z. \tag{4}$$

Proving that $Q + E \succeq 0$ is now enough to prove that the polynomial p is SOS, hence non negative. A sufficient condition is to check[10] $Q - s\epsilon I \succeq 0$.

As seen in Sect. 3.2, checking that a matrix M is positive semi-definite amounts to exhibiting a matrix R such that $M = R^T R$. The Cholesky decomposition algorithm [45, Sect. 1.4] computes such a matrix R. Given a matrix $M \in \mathbb{R}^{s \times s}$, it attempts to compute R such that $M = R^T R$ and when M is not positive semi-definite, it fails by attempting to take the square root of a negative value or perform a division by zero.

---

[9] Typically, $\epsilon \sim 10^{-8}$.

[10] In order to get good likelihood for this to hold, we ask the SDP solver for $Q - 2s\epsilon I \succeq 0$ rather than $Q \succeq 0$, as solvers often return matrices Q slightly not positive definite.

Due to rounding errors, a simple floating-point Cholesky decomposition would produce a matrix R not exactly satisfying the equality $M = R^T R$, hence not proving $M \succeq 0$. However, these rounding errors can be bounded by a matrix B so that, when the floating-point Cholesky decomposition of $M - B$ succeeds, then $M \succeq 0$ is guaranteed to hold. Moreover, B can be easily computed from the matrix M and the characteristics of the floating-point format used [41].

To sum up, the following verification procedure can prove that a given polynomial p is SOS[11].

Let $Q \in \mathbb{R}^{s \times s}$ be the approximate solution returned by an SDP solver for the problem $p = z^T Q z \wedge Q \succeq 0$. Then,

1. Compute a bound ϵ on the coefficients of $p - z^T Q z$.
2. Check that $Q - s\epsilon I \succeq 0$.

Complexity. Note that step 1 can be achieved using floating-point interval arithmetic in $\Theta(s^2)$ operations while the Cholesky decomposition in step 2 requires $\Theta(s^0)$ floating-point operations. Thus, the whole verification method takes $\Theta(s^3)$ floating-point operations which, in practice, constitutes a very small overhead compared to the time required by the SDP solver to compute Q.

Soundness. It is interesting to notice that the soundness of the method does not rely on the SDP solver. Thanks to this pessimistic method, the trusted codebase remains small, and efficient off-the-shelf solvers can be used as untrusted oracles. The method was even verified [31,38] within the Coq proof assistant.

Incompleteness. Numerical verification methods can only prove inequalities satisfied with some margin. Here, if the polynomial p to prove SOS (hence $p \geq 0$) reaches the value 0, this usually means that the feasible set of the SDP problem $\{Q \mid p = z^T Q z, Q \succeq 0\}$ has an empty relative interior (i.e., there is no point Q in this set such that a small ball centered on Q is included in $\{M \mid M \succeq 0\}$) and the method does not work, as illustrated on Fig. 2. This is a second source of incompleteness of our approach, that adds to the limitation of degrees of polynomials searched for, as presented in Sect. 3.1.

Remark 3. The floating-point Cholesky decomposition is theoretically a third source of incompleteness. However, it is negligible as the entries of the bound matrix B are, in practice, orders of magnitude smaller than the accuracy ϵ of the SDP solvers [40].

---

[11] It is worth noting that the value reported by the solver for ϵ, being just computed with floating-point arithmetic, cannot be formally trusted. It must then be recomputed.

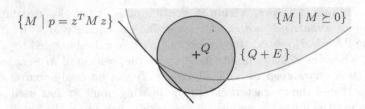

$\{M \mid p = z^T M z\}$ $\{M \mid M \succeq 0\}$

$+Q$ $\{Q + E\}$

Fig. 2. When the feasible set has an empty interior, the subspace $\{M \mid p = z^T M z\}$ is tangent to $\{M \mid M \succeq 0\}$. Thus the ball $\{Q + E\}$ intersecting the subspace almost never lies in $\{M \mid M \succeq 0\}$, making the proof fail.

4.3   Rounding to an Exact Rational Solution

The most common solution to verify results of SOS programming is to round the output of the SDP solver to an exact rational solution [19,24,33].

To sum up, the matrix Q returned by the SDP solver is first projected to the subspace $\{M \mid p = z^T M z\}$ then all its entries are rounded to rationals with small denominators (first integers, then multiples of $\frac{1}{2}, \frac{1}{3}, \ldots$)[12]. For each rounding, positive semi-definiteness of the resulting matrix Q is tested using a complete check, based on a LDLT decomposition[13] [19]. The rationale behind this choice is that problems involving only simple rational coefficients can reasonably be expected to admit simple rational solutions[14].

Using exact solutions potentially enables to verify SDP problems with empty relative interiors. This means the ability to prove inequalities without margin, to distinguish strict and non-strict inequalities and even to handle (dis)equalities. All of this nevertheless requires a different relaxation scheme than (1).

Example 4. To prove $x_1 \geq 0 \wedge x_2 \geq 0 \wedge q_1 = 0 \wedge q_2 = 0 \wedge p > 0$ unsatisfiable, with $q_1 := x_1^2 + x_2^2 - x_3^2 - x_4^2 - 2$, $q_2 := x_1 x_3 + x_2 x_4$ and $p := x_3 x_4 - x_1 x_2$, one can look for polynomials l_1, l_2 and SOS polynomials $s_1, \ldots, s_8$ such that $l_1 q_1 + l_2 q_2 + s_1 + s_2 p + s_3 x_1 + s_4 x_1 p + s_5 x_2 + s_6 x_2 p + s_7 x_1 x_2 + s_8 x_1 x_2 p + p = 0$.

Rounding the result of an SDP solver yields $l_1 = -\frac{1}{2}(x_1 x_2 - x_3 x_4)$, $l_2 = -\frac{1}{2}(x_2 x_3 + x_1 x_4)$, $s_2 = \frac{1}{2}(x_3^2 + x_4^2)$, $s_7 = \frac{1}{2}(x_1^2 + x_2^2 + x_3^2 + x_4^2)$ and $s_1 = s_3 = s_4 = s_5 = s_6 = s_8 = 0$. This problem has no margin, since when replacing $p > 0$ by $p \geq 0$, $(x_1, x_2, x_3, x_4) = (0, \sqrt{2}, 0, 0)$ becomes a solution.

Under some hypotheses, this relaxation scheme is complete, as stated by a theorem from Stengle [27, Theorem 2.11]. However, similarly to Sect. 3.1, no practical bound is known on the degrees of the relaxation polynomials.

---

[12] In practice, to ensure that the rounded matrix Q still satisfy the equality $p = z^T Q z$, a dual SDP encoding is used, that differs from the encoding introduced in Sect. 3. This dual encoding is also called image representation [36, Sect. 6.1].

[13] The LDLT decomposition expresses a positive semi-definite matrix M as $M = LDL^T$ with L a lower triangular matrix and D a diagonal matrix.

[14] However, there exist rational SDP problems that do not admit any rational solution.

Complexity. The relaxation scheme involves products of all polynomials appearing in the original problem constraints. The number of such products, being exponential in the number of constraints, limits the scalability of the approach.

Moreover, to actually enjoy the benefits of exact solutions, the floating-point Cholesky decomposition introduced in Sect. 4.2 cannot be used and has to be replaced by an exact rational decomposition[15]. Computing decompositions of large matrices can then become particularly costly as the size of the involved rationals can blow up exponentially during the computation.

Soundness. The exact solutions make for an easy verification. The method is thus implemented in the HOL Light [19] and Coq [4] proof assistants.

Incompleteness. Although this verification method can work for some SDP problems with an empty relative interior, the rounding heuristic is not guaranteed to provide a solution. In practice, it tends to fail on large problems or problems whose coefficients are not rationals with small numerators and denominators.

5   Experimental Results

5.1   The OSDP Library

The SOS to SDP translation described in Sect. 3, as well as the validation methods described in Sect. 4 have been implemented in our OCaml library OSDP. This library offers a common interface to the SDP solvers[16] Csdp [6], Mosek [2] and SDPA [46], giving simple access to SOS programming in contexts where soundness matters, such as SMT solvers or program static analyzers. It is composed of 5 kloc of OCaml and 1 kloc of C (interfaces with SDP solvers) and is available under LGPL license at https://cavale.enseeiht.fr/osdp/.

5.2   Integration of OSDP in Alt-Ergo

Alt-Ergo [5] is a very effective SMT solver for proving formulas generated by program verification frameworks. It is used as a back-end of different tools and in various settings, in particular via the Why3 [16] platform. For instance, the Frama-C [12] suite relies on it to prove formulas generated from C code, and the SPARK [21] toolset uses it to check formulas produced from Ada programs. It is also used by EasyCrypt [3] to prove formulas issued from cryptographic protocols verification, from the Cubicle [10] model-checker, and from Atelier-B [1].

---

[15] The Cholesky decomposition, involving square roots, cannot be computed in rational arithmetic, however its LDLT variant can.

[16] Csdp is used for the following benchmarks as it provides the best results.

Alt-Ergo's native input language is a polymorphic first-order logic *à la ML* modulo theories, a very suitable language for expressing formulas generated in the context of program verification. Its reasoning engine is built on top of a SAT solver that interacts with a combination of decision procedures to look for a model for the input formula. Universally quantified formulas, that naturally arise in program verification, are handled via E-matching techniques. Currently, Alt-Ergo implements decision procedures for the free theory of equality with uninterpreted symbols, linear arithmetic over integers and rationals, fragments of non-linear arithmetic, enumerated and records datatypes, and the theory of associative and commutative function symbols (hereafter AC).

Figure 3 shows the simplified architecture of arithmetic reasoning framework in Alt-Ergo, and the OSDP extension. The first component in the figure is a completion-like algorithm AC(LA) that reasons modulo associativity and commutativity properties of non-linear multiplication, as well as its distributivity over addition[17]. AC(LA) is a modular extension of ground AC completion with a decision procedure for reasoning modulo equalities of linear integer and rational arithmetic [9]. It builds and maintains a convergent term-rewriting system modulo arithmetic equalities and the AC properties of the non-linear multiplication symbol. The rewriting system is used to update a union-find data-structure.

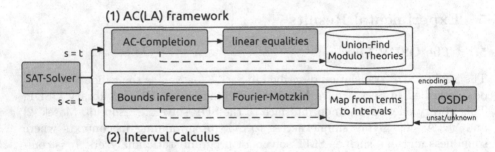

Fig. 3. Alt-Ergo's arithmetic reasoning framework with OSDP integration.

The second component is an Interval Calculus algorithm that computes bounds of (non-linear) terms: the initial non-linear problem is first relaxed by abstracting non-linear parts, and a Fourier-Motzkin extension[18] is used to infer bounds on the abstracted linear problem. In a second step, axioms of non-linear arithmetic are internally applied by intervals propagation. These two steps allow to maintain a map associating the terms of the problems (that are normalized *w.r.t.* the union-find) to unions of intervals.

Finally, the last part is the SAT solver that dispatches equalities and inequalities to the right component and performs case-split analysis over finite domains. Of course, this presentation is very simplified and the exact architecture of Alt-Ergo is much more complicated.

---

[17] Addition and multiplication by a constant is directly handled by the LA module.
[18] We can also use a simplex-based algorithm [8] for bounds inference.

$p_1' := (p_1 - a_1)(b_1 - p_1), \ldots, p_k' := (p_k - a_k)(b_k - p_k)$
// or $p_i' := p_i - a_i$ when $b_i = +\infty$ or $p_i' := b_i - p_i$ when $a_i = -\infty$
$d := \max_i \{\, \deg(p_i') \,\}$

encode $-\sum_{i=1}^{k} r_i p_i'$ is SOS, r_1 is SOS, $\ldots r_k'$ is SOS

as an SDP problem $-\sum r_i p_i' = z_0^T Q_0 z_0$, $r_1 = z_1^T Q_1 z_1, \ldots, r_k = z_k^T Q_k z_k$
with $\deg(r_i) := 2 \left\lceil \frac{d - \deg(p_i')}{2} \right\rceil$
call an SDP solver and retrieve r_1, r_k and Q_0, Q_1, $\ldots$, Q_k

overapproximate $\epsilon_i := \max_\alpha \left\{\, |c_\alpha| \,\middle|\, r_i - z_i^T Q_1 z_i = \sum_\alpha c_\alpha x^\alpha \right\}$

if $1 \in z_0 \wedge Q_0 - \#|z_0|\epsilon_0 I \succ 0 \wedge Q_1 - \#|z_1|\epsilon_1 I \succ 0 \wedge \ldots \wedge Q_k - \#|z_k|\epsilon_k I \succ 0$ **then**
  return Unsat
else
  return Unknown
end if

Fig. 4. Semi-decision procedure to prove $\bigwedge_{i=1}^{k} p_i \in [a_i, b_i]$ unsat. $\#|z|$ is the size of the vector z and $\succ 0$ is tested with a floating-point Cholesky decomposition [41].

The integration of OSDP in Alt-Ergo is achieved via the extension of the Interval Calculus component of the solver, as shown in Fig. 3: terms that are polynomials, and their corresponding interval bounds, form the problem (1) which is given to OSDP. OSDP attempts to verify its result with the method of Sect. 4.2. When it succeeds, the original conjunction of constraints is proved unsat. Otherwise, (dis)equalities are added and OSDP attempts a new proof by the method of Sect. 4.3. In case of success, unsat is proved, otherwise satisfiability or unsatisfiability cannot be deduced. Outlines of the first algorithm are given in Fig. 4 whereas the second one follows the original implementation [19].

Our modified version of Alt-Ergo is available under CeCILL-C license at https://cavale.enseeiht.fr/osdp/aesdp/.

Incrementality. In the SMT context, our theory solver is often succesively called with the same problem with a few additional constraints each time. It would then be interesting to avoid doing the whole computation again when a constraint is added, as is usually done with the simplex algorithm for linear arithmetic.

Some SDP solvers do offer to provide an initial point. Our experiments however indicated that this significantly speeds up the computation only when the provided point is extremely close to the solution. A bad initial point could even slow down the computation or, worse, make it fail. This is due to the very different nature of the interior point algorithms, compared to the simplex, and their convergence properties [7, Part III]. Thus, speed ups could only be obtained when the previous set of constraints was already unsatisfiable, i.e. a useless case.

Small Conflict Sets. When a set of constraints is unsatisfiable, some of them may not play any role in this unsatisfiability. Returning a small subset of unsatisfiable constraints can help the underlying SAT solver. Such useless constraints can easily be identified in (1) when the relaxation polynomial r_i is 0. A common heuristic to maximize their number is to ask the SDP solver to minimize (the sum of) the traces of the matrices Q_i.

When using the exact method of Sect. 4.3, the appropriate r_i are exactly 0. Things are not so clear when using the approximate method of Sect. 4.2 since the r_i are only *close to* 0. A simple solution is to rank the r_i by decreasing trace of Q_i before performing a dichotomy search for the smallest prefix of this sequence proved unsatisfiable. Thus, for n constraints, $\log(n)$ SDPs are solved.

5.3   Experimental Results

We compared our modified version of Alt-Ergo (v. 1.30) to the SMT solvers ran in both the QF_NIA and QF_NRA sections of the last SMT-COMP. We ran the solvers on two sets of benchmarks. The first set comes from the QF_NIA and QF_NRA benchmarks for the last SMT-COMP. The second set contains four subsets. The C problems are generated by Frama-C/Why3 [12,16] from control-command C programs such as the one from Sect. 2, with up to a dozen variables [11,39]. To distinguish difficulties coming from the handling of the memory model of C, for which Alt-Ergo was particularly designed, and from the actual non-linear arithmetic problem, the quadratic benchmarks contain simplified versions of the C problems with a purely arithmetic goal. To demonstrate that the interest of our approach is not limited to this initial target application, the flyspeck benchmarks come from the benchmark sets of dReal[19] [18] and global-opt are global optimization benchmarks [34]. All these benchmarks are available at https://cavale.enseeiht.fr/osdp/aesdp/. Since our solver only targets unsat proofs, benchmarks known sat were removed from both sets.

All experiments were conducted on an Intel Xeon 2.30 GHz processor, with individual runs limited to 2 GB of memory and 900 s. The results are presented in Tables 1, 2 and 3. For each subset of problems, the first column indicates the number of problems that each solver managed to prove unsat and the second presents the cumulative time (in seconds) for these problems. AE is the original Alt-Ergo, AESDP our new version, AESDPap the same but using only the approximate method of Sect. 4.2 and AESDPex using only the exact method of Sect. 4.3. All solvers were run with default options, except CVC4 which was run with all its --nl-ext* options.

As seen in Tables 1 and 2, despite an improvement over Alt-Ergo alone, our development is not competitive with state-of-the-art solvers on the QF_NIA and QF_NRA benchmarks. In fact, the set of problems solved by any of our Alt-Ergo versions is strictly included in the set of problems solved by at least one of the other solvers. The most commonly observed source of failure for AESDPap here comes from SDPs with empty relative interior. Although AESDPex can handle such problems, it is impaired by its much higher complexity.

---

[19] Removing problems containing functions sin and cos, not handled by our tool.

Table 1. Experimental results on benchmarks from QF_NIA.

		AE	AESDP	AESDPap	AESDPex	CVC4	Smtrat	Yices2	Z3
AProVE (746)	unsat	103	319	359	318	586	185	**709**	252
	time	7387	23968	7664	22701	10821	3879	**1982**	5156
calypto (97)	unsat	92	88	88	89	87	89	**97**	95
	time	357	679	489	816	7	754	**409**	613
LassoRanker (102)	unsat	57	62	64	63	72	20	**84**	84
	time	9	959	274	878	27	12	**595**	2538
LCTES (2)	unsat	0	0	0	0	1	0	0	0
	time	0	0	0	0	**0**	0	0	0
leipzig (5)	unsat	0	0	0	0	0	0	1	0
	time	0	0	0	0	0	0	**0**	0
mcm (161)	unsat	0	0	0	0	4	0	0	4
	time	0	0	0	0	**2489**	0	0	2527
UltimateAutom (7)	unsat	1	7	7	7	6	1	**7**	7
	time	0.35	0.73	0.62	0.69	0.03	7.22	**0.04**	0.31
UltimateLasso (26)	unsat	26	26	26	26	4	26	**26**	26
	time	118	212	126	215	66	177	**6**	21
total (1146)	unsat	270	502	544	503	780	321	**924**	468
	time	7872	25818	8553	24611	13411	4829	**2993**	10855

However good results are obtained on the more numerical[20] second set of benchmarks. In particular, control-command programs with up to a dozen variables are verified while other solvers remain limited to two variables. Playing a key point in this result, the inequalities in these benchmarks are satisfied with some margin. For control command programs, this comes from the fact that they are designed to be robust to many small errors. This opens new perspectives for the verification of functional properties of control-command programs, particularly in the aerospace domain, our main application field at ONERA[21].

Although solvers such as dReal, based on branch and bound with interval arithmetic could be expected to perform well on these numerical benchmarks, dReal solves less benchmarks than most other solvers. Geometrically speaking, the C benchmarks require to prove that an ellipsoid is included in a slightly larger one, i.e., the borders of both ellipsoids are close from one another. This requires to subdivide the space between the two borders in many small boxes so that none of them intersects both the interior of the first ellipsoid and the exterior of the second one. Whereas this can remain tractable for small dimensional ellipsoids, the number of required boxes grows exponentially with the dimension, which explains the poor results of dReal. This issue is unfortunately shared, to a large extent, by any linear relaxation, including more elaborate ones [30].

---

[20] Involving polynomials with a few dozen monomials or more and whose coefficients are not integers or rationals with small numerators and denominators.

[21] French public agency for aerospace research.

Table 2. Experimental results on benchmarks from QF_NRA.

		AE	AESDP	AESDPap	AESDPex	CVC4	Smtrat	Yices2	Z3
Sturm-MBO (300)	unsat	155	155	155	155	285	**285**	2	47
	time	12950	13075	13053	12973	1403	**620**	0	21
Sturm-MGC (7)	unsat	0	0	0	0	1	1	0	**7**
	time	0	0	0	0	7	0	0	**0**
Heizmann (68)	unsat	0	0	0	0	1	1	**11**	3
	time	0	0	0	0	16	0	**2083**	41
hong (20)	unsat	1	20	20	20	20	**20**	8	9
	time	0	28	24	27	1	**0**	240	6
hycomp (2494)	unsat	1285	1266	1271	1265	2184	1588	2182	**2201**
	time	15351	15857	16080	14909	208	13784	1241	**4498**
keymaera (320)	unsat	261	291	278	291	249	307	270	**318**
	time	36	356	97	360	4	13	359	**2**
LassoRanker (627)	unsat	0	0	0	0	**441**	0	236	119
	time	0	0	0	0	**32786**	0	30835	1733
meti-tarski (2615)	unsat	1882	2273	2267	2241	1643	2520	2578	**2611**
	time	10	91	65	73	804	3345	2027	**337**
UltimateAutom (13)	unsat	0	0	0	0	5	0	12	**13**
	time	0	0	0	0	0.52	0	57.19	**19.23**
zankl (85)	unsat	14	24	24	24	24	19	**32**	27
	time	1.00	15.46	16.09	15.67	9.40	13.47	**7.22**	0.43
total (6549)	unsat	3571	4029	4015	3996	4853	4740	5331	**5355**
	time	28348	29423	29334	28357	35239	17775	36849	**6658**

Table 3. Experimental results on benchmarks from [11,18,34,39].

		AE	AESDP	AESDPap	AESDPex	CVC4	Smtrat	Yices2	Z3	dReal
C (67)	unsat	11	**63**	63	13	0	0	0	0	0
	time	0.05	**39.78**	40.01	1.18	0	0	0	0	0
quadratic (67)	unsat	13	**67**	67	15	14	18	25	25	13
	time	0.06	**14.68**	15.44	0.08	2.46	1.26	357.20	257.39	23.36
flyspeck (20)	unsat	1	**19**	19	3	6	9	10	9	16
	time	0.00	**26.35**	26.62	0.01	695.59	36.54	0.05	0.05	11.77
global-opt (14)	unsat	2	**14**	14	5	5	12	12	13	9
	time	0.01	**8.72**	8.83	0.20	0.12	41.18	0.16	683.45	0.05
total (168)	unsat	27	**163**	163	36	25	39	47	47	38
	time	0.12	**89.53**	90.90	1.47	698.17	78.98	357.41	940.89	35.18

6   Related Work and Conclusion

Related work. MONNIAUX and CORBINEAU [33] improved the rounding heuristic of HARRISON [19]. This has unfortunately no impact on the complexity of the relaxation scheme. PLATZER et al. [37] compared their early versions with the symbolic methods based on quantifier elimination and Gröbner basis. An intermediate solution is offered by MAGRON et al. [29] but only handling a restricted class of parametric problems.

Branch-and-bound and interval arithmetic constitute another numerical approach to non-linear arithmetic, as implemented in the SMT solver dReal by GAO et al. [17,18]. These methods easily handle non-linear functions such as the trigonometric functions sin or cos, not yet considered in our prototype[22]. In the case of polynomial inequalities MUÑOZ and NARKAWICZ [34] offer Bernstein polynomials as an improvement to simple interval arithmetic.

Finally, VSDP [20,22] is a wrapper to SDP solvers offering a similar method to the one of Sect. 4.2. Moreover, an implementation is also offered by LÖFBERG [28] in the popular Matlab interface Yalmip but remains unsound, since all computations are performed with floating-point arithmetic, ignoring rounding errors.

Using convex optimization into an SMT solver was already proposed by NUZZO et al. [35,43]. However, they intentionally made their solver unsound in order to lean toward completeness. While this can make sense in a bounded model checking context, soundness is required for many applications, such as program verification. Moreover, this proposal was limited to convex formulas. Although this enables to provide models for satisfiable formulas, while only unsat formulas are considered in this paper, and whereas this seems a perfect choice for bounded model checking applications, non convex formulas are pervasive in applications such as program verification[23].

The use of numerical off-the-shelf solvers in SMT tools has also been studied in the framework of linear arithmetic [15,32]. Some comparison with state-of-the-art exact simplex procedures show mitigated results [14] but better results can be obtained by combining both approaches [25].

Conclusion. We presented a semi-decision procedure for non-linear polynomial constraints over the reals, based on numerical optimization solvers. Since these solvers only compute approximate solutions, a-posteriori soundness checks were investigated. Our first prototype implemented in the Alt-Ergo SMT solver shows that, although the new numerical method does not strictly outperform state-of-the-art symbolic methods, it enables to solve practical problems that are out of reach for other methods. In particular, this is demonstrated on the verification of functional properties of control-command programs. Such properties are of significant importance for critical cyber-physical systems.

It could thus be worth studying the combination of symbolic and numerical methods in the hope to benefit from the best of both worlds.

---

[22] Polynomial approximations such as Taylor expansions should be investigated.

[23] Typically, to prove a convex loop invariant I for a loop body f, one need to prove $I \Rightarrow I(f)$, that is $\neg I \vee I(f)$ which is likely non convex ($\neg I$ being concave).

Data Availability Statement and Acknowledgements. The source code, benchmarks and instructions to replicate the results of Sect. 5 are available in the figshare repository: http://doi.org/10.6084/m9.figshare.5900260.v1.

The authors thank Rémi Delmas for insightful discussions and technical help, particularly with the dReal solver.

References

1. Abrial, J.-R.: The B-Book - Assigning Programs to Meanings. Cambridge University Press, Cambridge (2005)
2. MOSEK ApS: The MOSEK C Optimizer API Manual Version 7.1 (Rev. 40) (2015)
3. Barthe, G., Dupressoir, F., Grégoire, B., Kunz, C., Schmidt, B., Strub, P.-Y.: EasyCrypt: a tutorial. In: Aldini, A., Lopez, J., Martinelli, F. (eds.) FOSAD 2012-2013. LNCS, vol. 8604, pp. 146–166. Springer, Cham (2014). https://doi.org/10.1007/978-3-319-10082-1_6
4. Besson, F.: Fast reflexive arithmetic tactics the linear case and beyond. In: Altenkirch, T., McBride, C. (eds.) TYPES 2006. LNCS, vol. 4502, pp. 48–62. Springer, Heidelberg (2007). https://doi.org/10.1007/978-3-540-74464-1_4
5. Bobot, F., Conchon, S., Contejean, E., Iguernlala, M., Lescuyer, S., Mebsout, A.: Alt-Ergo, Version 0.99.1. CNRS, Inria, Université Paris-Sud 11, and OCamlPro, December 2014. http://alt-ergo.lri.fr/
6. Borchers, B.: CSDP, A C Library for Semidefinite Programming. Optimization Methods and Software (1999)
7. Boyd, S., Vandenberghe, L.: Convex Optimization. Cambridge University Press, Cambridge (2004)
8. Bobot, F., Conchon, S., Contejean, E., Iguernelala, M., Mahboubi, A., Mebsout, A., Melquiond, G.: A simplex-based extension of Fourier-Motzkin for solving linear integer arithmetic. In: Gramlich, B., Miller, D., Sattler, U. (eds.) IJCAR 2012. LNCS (LNAI), vol. 7364, pp. 67–81. Springer, Heidelberg (2012). https://doi.org/10.1007/978-3-642-31365-3_8
9. Conchon, S., Contejean, É., Iguernelala, M.: Canonized rewriting and ground AC completion modulo Shostak theories: design and implementation. In: Logical Methods in Computer Science, Selected Papers of TACAS (2012)
10. Conchon, S., Goel, A., Krstić, S., Mebsout, A., Zaïdi, F.: Cubicle: a parallel SMT-based model checker for parameterized systems. In: Madhusudan, P., Seshia, S.A. (eds.) CAV 2012. LNCS, vol. 7358, pp. 718–724. Springer, Heidelberg (2012). https://doi.org/10.1007/978-3-642-31424-7_55
11. Cox, A., Sankaranarayanan, S., Chang, B.-Y.E.: A bit too precise? Bounded verification of quantized digital filters. In: Flanagan, C., König, B. (eds.) TACAS 2012. LNCS, vol. 7214, pp. 33–47. Springer, Heidelberg (2012). https://doi.org/10.1007/978-3-642-28756-5_4
12. Cuoq, P., Kirchner, F., Kosmatov, N., Prevosto, V., Signoles, J., Yakobowski, B.: Frama-C - a software analysis perspective. In: Eleftherakis, G., Hinchey, M., Holcombe, M. (eds.) SEFM 2012. LNCS, vol. 7504, pp. 233–247. Springer, Heidelberg (2012). https://doi.org/10.1007/978-3-642-33826-7_16
13. de Moura, L., Bjørner, N.: Z3: an efficient SMT solver. In: Ramakrishnan, C.R., Rehof, J. (eds.) TACAS 2008. LNCS, vol. 4963, pp. 337–340. Springer, Heidelberg (2008). https://doi.org/10.1007/978-3-540-78800-3_24

14. de Oliveira, D.C.B., Monniaux, D.: Experiments on the feasibility of using a floating-point simplex in an SMT solver. In: PAAR@IJCAR (2012)
15. Faure, G., Nieuwenhuis, R., Oliveras, A., Rodríguez-Carbonell, E.: SAT modulo the theory of linear arithmetic: exact, inexact and commercial solvers. In: Kleine Büning, H., Zhao, X. (eds.) SAT 2008. LNCS, vol. 4996, pp. 77–90. Springer, Heidelberg (2008). https://doi.org/10.1007/978-3-540-79719-7_8
16. Filliâtre, J.-C., Paskevich, A.: Why3—Where programs meet provers. In: Felleisen, M., Gardner, P. (eds.) ESOP 2013. LNCS, vol. 7792, pp. 125–128. Springer, Heidelberg (2013). https://doi.org/10.1007/978-3-642-37036-6_8
17. Gao, S., Avigad, J., Clarke, E.M.: δ-Complete decision procedures for satisfiability over the reals. In: Gramlich, B., Miller, D., Sattler, U. (eds.) IJCAR 2012. LNCS (LNAI), vol. 7364, pp. 286–300. Springer, Heidelberg (2012). https://doi.org/10.1007/978-3-642-31365-3_23
18. Gao, S., Kong, S., Clarke, E.M.: dReal: an SMT solver for nonlinear theories over the reals. In: Bonacina, M.P. (ed.) CADE 2013. LNCS (LNAI), vol. 7898, pp. 208–214. Springer, Heidelberg (2013). https://doi.org/10.1007/978-3-642-38574-2_14
19. Harrison, J.: Verifying nonlinear real formulas via sums of squares. In: Schneider, K., Brandt, J. (eds.) TPHOLs 2007. LNCS, vol. 4732, pp. 102–118. Springer, Heidelberg (2007). https://doi.org/10.1007/978-3-540-74591-4_9
20. Härter, V., Jansson, C., Lange, M.: VSDP: verified semidefinite programming. http://www.ti3.tuhh.de/jansson/vsdp/
21. Hoang, D., Moy, Y., Wallenburg, A., Chapman, R.: SPARK 2014 and gnatprove - a competition report from builders of an industrial-strength verifying compiler. In: STTT (2015)
22. Jansson, C., Chaykin, D., Keil, C.: Rigorous error bounds for the optimal value in semidefinite programming. SIAM J. Numer. Anal. **46**(1), 180–200 (2007)
23. Jovanović, D., de Moura, L.: Solving non-linear arithmetic. In: Gramlich, B., Miller, D., Sattler, U. (eds.) IJCAR 2012. LNCS (LNAI), vol. 7364, pp. 339–354. Springer, Heidelberg (2012). https://doi.org/10.1007/978-3-642-31365-3_27
24. Kaltofen, E., Li, B., Yang, Z., Zhi, L.: Exact certification in global polynomial optimization via sums-of-squares of rational functions with rational coefficients. J. Symb. Comput. **47**(1), 1–15 (2012)
25. King, T., Barrett, C.W., Tinelli, C.: Leveraging linear and mixed integer programming for SMT. In: FMCAD (2014)
26. Lasserre, J.B.: Global optimization with polynomials and the problem of moments. SIAM J. Optim. **11**(3), 796–817 (2001)
27. Lasserre, J.B.: Moments, Positive Polynomials and Their Applications. Imperial College Press Optimization. Imperial College Press, World Scientific, Singapore (2009)
28. Löfberg, J.: Pre- and post-processing sum-of-squares programs in practice. IEEE Trans. Autom. Control **5**, 1007–1011 (2009)
29. Magron, V., Allamigeon, X., Gaubert, S., Werner, B.: Formal proofs for nonlinear optimization. J. Formalized Reason. **8**(1), 1–24 (2015)
30. Maréchal, A., Fouilhé, A., King, T., Monniaux, D., Périn, M.: Polyhedral approximation of multivariate polynomials using handelman's theorem. In: Jobstmann, B., Leino, K.R.M. (eds.) VMCAI 2016. LNCS, vol. 9583, pp. 166–184. Springer, Heidelberg (2016). https://doi.org/10.1007/978-3-662-49122-5_8
31. Martin-Dorel, É., Roux, P.: A reflexive tactic for polynomial positivity using numerical solvers and floating-point computations. In: CPP (2017)

32. Monniaux, D.: On using floating-point computations to help an exact linear arithmetic decision procedure. In: Bouajjani, A., Maler, O. (eds.) CAV 2009. LNCS, vol. 5643, pp. 570–583. Springer, Heidelberg (2009). https://doi.org/10.1007/978-3-642-02658-4_42

33. Monniaux, D., Corbineau, P.: On the generation of positivstellensatz witnesses in degenerate cases. In: van Eekelen, M., Geuvers, H., Schmaltz, J., Wiedijk, F. (eds.) ITP 2011. LNCS, vol. 6898, pp. 249–264. Springer, Heidelberg (2011). https://doi.org/10.1007/978-3-642-22863-6_19

34. Muñoz, C., Narkawicz, A.: Formalization of Bernstein polynomials and applications to global optimization. J. Autom. Reason. **51**(2), 151–196 (2013)

35. Nuzzo, P., Puggelli, A., Seshia, S.A., Sangiovanni-Vincentelli, A.L.: CalCS: SMT solving for non-linear convex constraints. In: FMCAD (2010)

36. Parrilo, P.A.: Semidefinite programming relaxations for semialgebraic problems. Math. Program. **96**(2), 293–320 (2003)

37. Platzer, A., Quesel, J.-D., Rümmer, P.: Real world verification. In: Schmidt, R.A. (ed.) CADE 2009. LNCS (LNAI), vol. 5663, pp. 485–501. Springer, Heidelberg (2009). https://doi.org/10.1007/978-3-642-02959-2_35

38. Roux, P.: Formal proofs of rounding error bounds - with application to an automatic positive definiteness check. J. Autom. Reasoning **57**(2), 135–156 (2016)

39. Roux, P., Jobredeaux, R., Garoche, P.-L., Féron, É: A generic ellipsoid abstract domain for linear time invariant systems. In: HSCC (2012)

40. Roux, P., Voronin, Y.-L., Sankaranarayanan, S.: Validating numerical semidefinite programming solvers for polynomial invariants. In: Rival, X. (ed.) SAS 2016. LNCS, vol. 9837, pp. 424–446. Springer, Heidelberg (2016). https://doi.org/10.1007/978-3-662-53413-7_21

41. Rump, S.M.: Verification of positive definiteness. BIT Num. Math. **46**(2), 433–452 (2006)

42. Rump, S.M.: Verification methods: rigorous results using floating-point arithmetic. Acta Numerica **19**, 287–449 (2010)

43. Shoukry, Y., Nuzzo, P., Sangiovanni-Vincentelli, A.L., Seshia, S.A., Pappas, G.J., Tabuada, P.: SMC: satisfiability modulo convex optimization. In: HSCC (2017)

44. Vandenberghe, L., Boyd, S.: Semidefinite programming. SIAM Rev. **38**(1), 49–95 (1996)

45. Watkins, D.S.: Fundamentals of matrix computations. Wiley, New York (2004)

46. Yamashita, M., Fujisawa, K., Nakata, K., Nakata, M., Fukuda, M., Kobayashi, K., Goto, K.: A high-performance software package for semidefinite programs: SDPA 7. Technical report B-460, Tokyo Institute of Technology, Tokyo (2010)

Security and Reactive Systems

Approximate Reduction of Finite Automata for High-Speed Network Intrusion Detection

Milan Češka, Vojtěch Havlena, Lukáš Holík, Ondřej Lengál[✉],
and Tomáš Vojnar

FIT, IT4Innovations Centre of Excellence,
Brno University of Technology,
Brno, Czech Republic
lengal@fit.vutbr.cz

Abstract. We consider the problem of *approximate reduction of non-deterministic automata* that appear in hardware-accelerated network intrusion detection systems (NIDSes). We define an error *distance* of a reduced automaton from the original one as the probability of packets being incorrectly classified by the reduced automaton (wrt the probabilistic distribution of packets in the network traffic). We use this notion to design an *approximate reduction procedure* that achieves a great size reduction (much beyond the state-of-the-art language preserving techniques) with a controlled and small error. We have implemented our approach and evaluated it on use cases from SNORT, a popular NIDS. Our results provide experimental evidence that the method can be highly efficient in practice, allowing NIDSes to follow the rapid growth in the speed of networks.

1 Introduction

The recent years have seen a boom in the number of security incidents in computer networks. In order to alleviate the impact of network attacks and intrusions, Internet providers want to detect malicious traffic at their network's entry points and on the backbones between sub-networks. Software-based network intrusion detection systems (NIDSes), such as the popular open-source system SNORT [1], are capable of detecting suspicious network traffic by testing (among others) whether a packet payload matches a regular expression (regex) describing known patterns of malicious traffic. NIDSes collect and maintain vast databases of such regexes that are typically divided into groups according to types of the attacks and target protocols.

Regex matching is the most computationally demanding task of a NIDS as its cost grows with the speed of the network traffic as well as with the number and complexity of the regexes being matched. The current software-based NIDSes cannot perform the regex matching on networks beyond 1 Gbps [2,3], so they cannot handle the current speed of backbone networks ranging between tens and hundreds of Gbps. A promising approach to speed up NIDSes is to (partially)

© The Author(s) 2018
D. Beyer and M. Huisman (Eds.): TACAS 2018, LNCS 10806, pp. 155–175, 2018.
https://doi.org/10.1007/978-3-319-89963-3_9

offload regex matching into hardware [3–5]. The hardware then serves as a pre-filter of the network traffic, discarding the majority of the packets from further processing. Such pre-filtering can easily reduce the traffic the NIDS needs to handle by two or three orders of magnitude [3].

Field-programmable gate arrays (FPGAs) are the leading technology in high-throughput regex matching. Due to their inherent parallelism, FPGAs provide an efficient way of implementing *nondeterministic finite automata* (NFAs), which naturally arise from the input regexes. Although the amount of available resources in FPGAs is continually increasing, the speed of networks grows even faster. Working with multi-gigabit networks requires the hardware to use many parallel packet processing branches in a single FPGA [5]; each of them implementing a separate copy of the concerned NFA, and so reducing the size of the NFAs is of the utmost importance. Various language-preserving automata reduction approaches exist, mainly based on computing (bi)simulation relations on automata states (cf. the related work). The reductions they offer, however, do not satisfy the needs of high-speed hardware-accelerated NIDSes.

Our answer to the problem is *approximate reduction* of NFAs, allowing for a trade-off between the achieved reduction and the precision of the regex matching. To formalise the intuitive notion of precision, we propose a novel *probabilistic distance* of automata. It captures the probability that a packet of the input network traffic is incorrectly accepted or rejected by the approximated NFA. The distance assumes a *probabilistic model* of the network traffic (we show later how such a model can be obtained).

Having formalised the notion of precision, we specify the target of our reductions as two variants of an optimization problem: (1) minimizing the NFA size given the maximum allowed error (distance from the original), or (2) minimizing the error given the maximum allowed NFA size. Finding such optimal approximations is, however, computationally hard (**PSPACE**-complete, the same as precise NFA minimization).

Consequently, we sacrifice the optimality and, motivated by the typical structure of NFAs that emerge from a set of regexes used by NIDSes (a union of many long "tentacles" with occasional small strongly-connected components), we limit the space of possible reductions by restricting the set of operations they can apply to the original automaton. Namely, we consider two reduction operations: (i) collapsing the future of a state into a *self-loop* (this reduction over-approximates the language), or (ii) *removing states* (such a reduction is under-approximating).

The problem of identifying the optimal sets of states on which these operations should be applied is still **PSPACE**-complete. The restricted problem is, however, more amenable to an approximation by a *greedy algorithm*. The algorithm applies the reductions state-by-state in an order determined by a pre-computed *error labelling* of the states. The process is stopped once the given optimization goal in terms of the size or error is reached. The labelling is based on the probability of packets that may be accepted through a given state and hence over-approximates the error that may be caused by applying the reduction at a given state. As our experiments show, this approach can give us high-quality reductions while ensuring formal error bounds.

Finally, it turns out that even the pre-computation of the error labelling of the states is costly (again **PSPACE**-complete). Therefore, we propose several ways to cheaply over-approximate it such that the strong error bound guarantees are still preserved. Particularly, we are able to exploit the typical structure of the "union of tentacles" of the hardware NFA in an algorithm that is exponential in the size of the largest "tentacle" only, which is indeed much faster in practice.

We have implemented our approach and evaluated it on regexes used to classify malicious traffic in SNORT. We obtain quite encouraging experimental results demonstrating that our approach provides a much better reduction than language-preserving techniques with an almost negligible error. In particular, our experiments, going down to the level of an actual implementation of NFAs in FPGAs, confirm that we can squeeze into an up-to-date FPGA chip real-life regexes encoding malicious traffic, allowing them to be used with a negligible error for filtering at speeds of 100 Gbps (and even 400 Gbps). This is far beyond what one can achieve with current exact reduction approaches.

Related Work. Hardware acceleration for regex matching at the line rate is an intensively studied technology that uses general-purpose hardware [6–14] as well as FPGAs [3–5,15–20]. Most of the works focus on DFA implementation and optimization techniques. NFAs can be exponentially smaller than DFAs but need, in the worst case, $\mathcal{O}(n)$ memory accesses to process each byte of the payload where n is the number of states. In most cases, this incurs an unacceptable slowdown. Several works alleviate this disadvantage of NFAs by exploiting reconfigurability and fine-grained parallelism of FPGAs, allowing one to process one character per clock cycle (e.g. [3–5,15,16,19,20]).

In [14], which is probably the closest work to ours, the authors consider a set of regexes describing network attacks. They replace a potentially prohibitively large DFA by a tree of smaller DFAs, an alternative to using NFAs that minimizes the latency occurring in a non-FPGA-based implementation. The language of every DFA-node in the tree over-approximates the languages of its children. Packets are filtered through the tree from the root downwards until they belong to the language of the encountered nodes, and may be finally accepted at the leaves, or are rejected otherwise. The over-approximating DFAs are constructed using a similar notion of probability of an occurrence of a state as in our approach. The main differences from our work are that (1) the approach targets approximation of DFAs (not NFAs), (2) the over-approximation is based on a given traffic sample only (it cannot benefit from a probabilistic model), and (3) no probabilistic guarantees on the approximation error are provided.

Approximation of DFAs was considered in various other contexts. Hyper-minimization is an approach that is allowed to alter language membership of a finite set of words [21,22]. A DFA with a given maximum number of states is constructed in [23], minimizing the error defined either by (i) counting prefixes of misjudged words up to some length, or (ii) the sum of the probabilities of the misjudged words wrt the Poisson distribution over Σ^*. Neither of these approaches considers reduction of NFAs nor allows to control the expected error with respect to the real traffic.

In addition to the metrics mentioned above when discussing the works [21–23], the following metrics should also be mentioned. The Cesaro-Jaccard distance studied in [24] is, in spirit, similar to [23] and does also not reflect the probability of individual words. The edit distance of weighted automata from [25] depends on the minimum edit distance between pairs of words from the two compared languages, again regardless of their statistical significance. None of these notions is suitable for our needs.

Language-preserving minimization of NFAs is a **PSPACE**-complete problem [26,38]. More feasible (polynomial-time) is language-preserving size reduction of NFAs based on (bi)simulations [27–30], which does not aim for a truly minimal NFA. A number of advanced variants exist, based on multi-pebble or look-ahead simulations, or on combinations of forward and backward simulations [31–33]. The practical efficiency of these techniques is, however, often insufficient to allow them to handle the large NFAs that occur in practice and/or they do not manage to reduce the NFAs enough. Finally, even a minimal NFA for the given set of regexes is often too big to be implemented in the given FPGA operating on the required speed (as shown even in our experiments). Our approach is capable of a much better reduction for the price of a small change of the accepted language.

2   Preliminaries

We use $\langle a, b \rangle$ to denote the set $\{x \in \mathbb{R} \mid a \leq x \leq b\}$ and $\mathbb{N}$ to denote the set $\{0, 1, 2, \dots\}$. Given a pair of sets X_1 and X_2, we use $X_1 \triangle X_2$ to denote their *symmetric difference*, i.e., the set $\{x \mid \exists! i \in \{1, 2\} : x \in X_i\}$. We use the notation $[v_1, \dots, v_n]$ to denote a vector of n elements, $\mathbf{1}$ to denote the all 1's vector $[1, \dots, 1]$, $\boldsymbol{A}$ to denote a matrix, and $\boldsymbol{A}^\top$ for its transpose, and $\boldsymbol{I}$ for the identity matrix.

In the following, we fix a finite non-empty alphabet Σ. A *nondeterministic finite automaton* (NFA) is a quadruple $A = (Q, \delta, I, F)$ where Q is a finite set of states, $\delta : Q \times \Sigma \to 2^Q$ is a transition function, $I \subseteq Q$ is a set of initial states, and $F \subseteq Q$ is a set of accepting states. We use $Q[A], \delta[A], I[A]$, and $F[A]$ to denote Q, δ, I, and F, respectively, and $q \xrightarrow{a} q'$ to denote that $q' \in \delta(q, a)$. A sequence of states $\rho = q_0 \cdots q_n$ is a *run* of A over a word $w = a_1 \cdots a_n \in \Sigma^*$ from a state q to a state q', denoted as $q \overset{w,\rho}{\rightsquigarrow} q'$, if $\forall 1 \leq i \leq n : q_{i-1} \xrightarrow{a_i} q_i$, $q_0 = q$, and $q_n = q'$. Sometimes, we use ρ in set operations where it behaves as the set of states it contains. We also use $q \overset{w}{\rightsquigarrow} q'$ to denote that $\exists \rho \in Q^* : q \overset{w,\rho}{\rightsquigarrow} q'$ and $q \rightsquigarrow q'$ to denote that $\exists w : q \overset{w}{\rightsquigarrow} q'$. The *language* of a state q is defined as $L_A(q) = \{w \mid \exists q_F \in F : q \overset{w}{\rightsquigarrow} q_F\}$ and its *banguage* (back-language) is defined as $L_A^\flat(q) = \{w \mid \exists q_I \in I : q_I \overset{w}{\rightsquigarrow} q\}$. Both notions can be naturally extended to a set $S \subseteq Q$: $L_A(S) = \bigcup_{q \in S} L_A(q)$ and $L_A^\flat(S) = \bigcup_{q \in S} L_A^\flat(q)$. We drop the subscript A when the context is obvious. A accepts the language $L(A)$ defined as $L(A) = L_A(I)$. A is called *deterministic* (DFA) if $|I| = 1$ and $\forall q \in Q$ and $\forall a \in \Sigma : |\delta(q, a)| \leq 1$, and *unambiguous* (UFA) if $\forall w \in L(A) : \exists! q_I \in I, \rho \in Q^*, q_F \in F : q_I \overset{w,\rho}{\rightsquigarrow} q_F$.

The *restriction* of A to $S \subseteq Q$ is an NFA $A_{|S}$ given as $A_{|S} = (S, \delta \cap (S \times \Sigma \times 2^S), I \cap S, F \cap S)$. We define the *trim* operation as $trim(A) = A_{|C}$ where $C = \{q \mid \exists q_I \in I, q_F \in F : q_I \rightsquigarrow q \rightsquigarrow q_F\}$. For a set of states $R \subseteq Q$, we use $reach(R)$ to denote the set of states reachable from R, formally, $reach(R) = \{r' \mid \exists r \in R : r \rightsquigarrow r'\}$. We use the number of states as the measurement of the size of A, i.e., $|A| = |Q|$.

A (discrete probability) *distribution* over a set X is a mapping $\Pr : X \to \langle 0, 1 \rangle$ such that $\sum_{x \in X} \Pr(x) = 1$. An n-state *probabilistic automaton* (PA) over Σ is a triple $P = (\boldsymbol{\alpha}, \boldsymbol{\gamma}, \{\boldsymbol{\Delta}_a\}_{a \in \Sigma})$ where $\boldsymbol{\alpha} \in \langle 0, 1 \rangle^n$ is a vector of *initial weights*, $\boldsymbol{\gamma} \in \langle 0, 1 \rangle^n$ is a vector of *final weights*, and for every $a \in \Sigma$, $\boldsymbol{\Delta}_a \in \langle 0, 1 \rangle^{n \times n}$ is a *transition matrix* for symbol a. We abuse notation and use $Q[P]$ to denote the set of states $Q[P] = \{1, \ldots, n\}$. Moreover, the following two properties need to hold: (i) $\sum\{\boldsymbol{\alpha}[i] \mid i \in Q[P]\} = 1$ (the initial probability is 1) and (ii) for every state $i \in Q[P]$ it holds that $\sum\{\boldsymbol{\Delta}_a[i, j] \mid j \in Q[P], a \in \Sigma\} + \boldsymbol{\gamma}[i] = 1$ (the probability of accepting or leaving a state is 1). We define the *support* of P as the NFA $supp(P) = (Q[P], \delta[P], I[P], F[P])$ s.t.

$$\delta[P] = \{(i, a, j) \mid \boldsymbol{\Delta}_a[i, j] > 0\} \quad I[P] = \{i \mid \boldsymbol{\alpha}[i] > 0\} \quad F[P] = \{i \mid \boldsymbol{\gamma}[i] > 0\}.$$

Let us assume that every PA P is such that $supp(P) = trim(supp(P))$. For a word $w = a_1 \ldots a_k \in \Sigma^*$, we use $\boldsymbol{\Delta}_w$ to denote the matrix $\boldsymbol{\Delta}_{a_1} \cdots \boldsymbol{\Delta}_{a_k}$. It can be easily shown that P represents a distribution over words $w \in \Sigma^*$ defined as $\Pr_P(w) = \boldsymbol{\alpha}^\top \cdot \boldsymbol{\Delta}_w \cdot \boldsymbol{\gamma}$. We call $\Pr_P(w)$ the *probability* of w in P. Given a language $L \subseteq \Sigma^*$, we define the probability of L in P as $\Pr_P(L) = \sum_{w \in L} \Pr_P(w)$.

If Conditions (i) and (ii) from the definition of PAs are dropped, we speak about a *pseudo-probabilistic automaton (PPA)*, which may assign a word from its support a quantity that is not necessarily in the range $\langle 0, 1 \rangle$, denoted as the *significance* of the word below. PPAs may arise during some of our operations performed on PAs.

3   Approximate Reduction of NFAs

In this section, we first introduce the key notion of our approach: a *probabilistic distance* of a pair of finite automata wrt a given probabilistic automaton that, intuitively, represents the significance of particular words. We discuss the complexity of computing the probabilistic distance. Finally, we formulate two problems of *approximate automata reduction via probabilistic distance*. Proofs of the lemmas can be found in [43].

3.1   Probabilistic Distance

We start by defining our notion of a probabilistic distance of two NFAs. Assume NFAs A_1 and A_2 and a probabilistic automaton P specifying the distribution

$\Pr_P : \Sigma^* \to \langle 0, 1 \rangle$. The *probabilistic distance* $d_P(A_1, A_2)$ between A_1 and A_2 wrt $\Pr_P$ is defined as

$$d_P(A_1, A_2) = \Pr_P(L(A_1) \triangle L(A_2)).$$

Intuitively, the distance captures the significance of the words accepted by one of the automata only. We use the distance to drive the reduction process towards automata with small errors and to assess the quality of the resulting automata.

The value of $\Pr_P(L(A_1) \triangle L(A_2))$ can be computed as follows. Using the fact that (1) $L_1 \triangle L_2 = (L_1 \setminus L_2) \uplus (L_2 \setminus L_1)$ and (2) $L_1 \setminus L_2 = L_1 \setminus (L_1 \cap L_2)$, we get

$$
\begin{aligned}
d_P(A_1, A_2) &= \Pr_P(L(A_1) \setminus L(A_2)) + \Pr_P(L(A_2) \setminus L(A_1)) \\
&= \Pr_P(L(A_1) \setminus (L(A_1) \cap L(A_2))) + \Pr_P(L(A_2) \setminus (L(A_2) \cap L(A_1))) \\
&= \Pr_P(L(A_1)) + \Pr_P(L(A_2)) - 2 \cdot \Pr_P(L(A_1) \cap L(A_2)).
\end{aligned}
$$

Hence, the key step is to compute $\Pr_P(L(A))$ for an NFA A and a PA P. Problems similar to computing such a probability have been extensively studied in several contexts including verification of probabilistic systems [34–36]. The below lemma summarises the complexity of this step.

Lemma 1. *Let P be a PA and A an NFA. The problem of computing $\Pr_P(L(A))$ is **PSPACE**-complete. For a UFA A, $\Pr_P(L(A))$ can be computed in **PTIME**.*

In our approach, we apply the method of [36] and compute $\Pr_P(L(A))$ in the following way. We first check whether the NFA A is unambiguous. This can be done by using the standard product construction (denoted as $\cap$) for computing the intersection of the NFA A with itself and trimming the result, formally $B = trim(A \cap A)$, followed by a check whether there is some state $(p, q) \in Q[B]$ s.t. $p \neq q$ [37]. If A is ambiguous, we either determinise it or disambiguate it [37], leading to a DFA/UFA A', respectively.[1] Then, we construct the trimmed product of A' and P (this can be seen as computing $A' \cap supp(P)$ while keeping the probabilities from P on the edges of the result), yielding a PPA $R = (\alpha, \gamma, \{\Delta_a\}_{a \in \Sigma})$.[2] Intuitively, R represents not only the words of $L(A)$ but also their probability in P. Now, let $\Delta = \sum_{a \in \Sigma} \Delta_a$ be the matrix that expresses, for any $p, q \in Q[R]$, the significance of getting from p to q via any $a \in \Sigma$. Further, it can be shown (cf. the proof of Lemma 1 in [43]) that the matrix Δ^*, representing the significance of going from p to q via any $w \in \Sigma^*$, can be computed as $(I - \Delta)^{-1}$. Then, to get $\Pr_P(L(A))$, it suffices to take $\alpha^\top \cdot \Delta^* \cdot \gamma$. Note that, due to the determinisation/disambiguation step, the obtained value indeed is $\Pr_P(L(A))$ despite R being a PPA.

---

[1] In theory, disambiguation can produce smaller automata, but, in our experiments, determinisation proved to work better.

[2] R is not necessarily a PA since there might be transitions in P that are either removed or copied several times in the product construction.

3.2   Automata Reduction Using Probabilistic Distance

We now exploit the above introduced probabilistic distance to formulate the task of approximate reduction of NFAs as the following two optimisation problems. Given an NFA A and a PA P specifying the distribution $\Pr_P : \Sigma^* \to \langle 0, 1 \rangle$, we define

- **size-driven reduction:** for $n \in \mathbb{N}$, find an NFA A' such that $|A'| \leq n$ and the distance $d_P(A, A')$ is minimal,
- **error-driven reduction:** for $\epsilon \in \langle 0, 1 \rangle$, find an NFA A' such that $d_P(A, A') \leq \epsilon$ and the size $|A'|$ is minimal.

The following lemma shows that the natural decision problem underlying both of the above optimization problems is **PSPACE**-complete, which matches the complexity of computing the probabilistic distance as well as that of the *exact* reduction of NFAs [38].

Lemma 2. *Consider an NFA A, a PA P, a bound on the number of states $n \in \mathbb{N}$, and an error bound $\epsilon \in \langle 0, 1 \rangle$. It is **PSPACE**-complete to determine whether there exists an NFA A' with n states s.t. $d_P(A, A') \leq \epsilon$.*

The notions defined above do not distinguish between introducing a *false positive* (A' accepts a word $w \notin L(A)$) or a *false negative* (A' does not accept a word $w \in L(A)$) answers. To this end, we define *over-approximating* and *under-approximating* reductions as reductions for which the additional conditions $L(A) \subseteq L(A')$ and $L(A) \supseteq L(A')$ hold, respectively.

A naïve solution to the reductions would enumerate all NFAs A' of sizes from 0 up to k (resp. $|A|$), for each of them compute $d_P(A, A')$, and take an automaton with the smallest probabilistic distance (resp. a smallest one satisfying the restriction on $d_P(A, A')$). Obviously, this approach is computationally infeasible.

4   A Heuristic Approach to Approximate Reduction

In this section, we introduce two techniques for approximate reduction of NFAs that avoid the need to iterate over all automata of a certain size. The first approach under-approximates the automata by removing states—we call it the *pruning reduction*—while the second approach over-approximates the automata by adding self-loops to states and removing redundant states—we call it the *self-loop reduction*. Finding an optimal automaton using these reductions is also **PSPACE**-complete, but more amenable to heuristics like greedy algorithms. We start with introducing two high-level greedy algorithms, one for the size- and one for the error-driven reduction, and follow by showing their instantiations for the pruning and the self-loop reduction. A crucial role in the algorithms is played by a function that labels states of the automata by an estimate of the error that will be caused when some of the reductions is applied at a given state.

4.1   A General Algorithm for Size-Driven Reduction

Algorithm 1 shows a general greedy method for performing the size-driven reduction. In order to use the same high-level algorithm in both directions of reduction (over/under-approximating), it is parameterized with three functions: *label*, *reduce*, and *error*. The real intricacy of the procedure is hidden inside

---

Algorithm 1. A greedy size-driven reduction

Input   : NFA $A = (Q, \delta, I, F)$, PA P, $n \geq 1$
Output: NFA A', $\epsilon \in \mathbb{R}$ s.t. $|A| \leq n$ and
$\qquad\qquad d_P(A, A') \leq \epsilon$

1 $V \leftarrow \emptyset$;
2 **for** $q \in Q$ *in the order* $\preceq_{A, label(A,P)}$ **do**
3 $\quad$ $V \leftarrow V \cup \{q\}$; $A' \leftarrow reduce(A, V)$;
4 $\quad$ **if** $|A'| \leq n$ **then break** ;
5 **return** A', $\epsilon = error(A, V, label(A, P))$;

---

these three functions. Intuitively, *label*(A, P) assigns every state of an NFA A an approximation of the error that will be caused wrt the PA P when a reduction is applied at this state, while the purpose of *reduce*(A, V) is to create a new NFA A' obtained from A by introducing some error at states from V.[3] Further, *error*$(A, V, label(A, P))$ estimates the error introduced by the application of *reduce*(A, V), possibly in a more precise (and costly) way than by just summing the concerned error labels: Such a computation is possible outside of the main computation loop. We show instantiations of these functions later, when discussing the reductions used. Moreover, the algorithm is also parameterized with a total order $\preceq_{A, label(A, P)}$ that defines which states of A are processed first and which are processed later. The ordering may take into account the precomputed labelling. The algorithm accepts an NFA A, a PA P, and $n \in \mathbb{N}$ and outputs a pair consisting of an NFA A' of the size $|A'| \leq n$ and an error bound ϵ such that $d_P(A, A') \leq \epsilon$.

The main idea of the algorithm is that it creates a set V of states where an error is to be introduced. V is constructed by starting from an empty set and adding states to it in the order given by $\preceq_{A, label(A, P)}$, until the size of the result of *reduce*(A, V) has reached the desired bound n (in our setting, *reduce* is always antitone, i.e., for $V \subseteq V'$, it holds that $|reduce(A, V)| \geq |reduce(A, V')|$). We now define the necessary condition for *label*, *reduce*, and *error* that makes Algorithm 1 correct.

Condition C1 *holds if for every NFA A, PA P, and a set $V \subseteq Q[A]$, we have that (a) error$(A, V, label(A, P)) \geq d_P(A, reduce(A, V))$, (b) $|reduce(A, Q[A])| \leq 1$, and (c) reduce$(A, \emptyset) = A$.*

C1(a) ensures that the error computed by the reduction algorithm indeed over-approximates the exact probabilistic distance, **C1**(b) ensures that the algorithm can (in the worst case, by applying the reduction at every state of A) for any $n \geq 1$ output a result $|A'|$ of the size $|A'| \leq n$, and **C1**(c) ensures that when no error is to be introduced at any state, we obtain the original automaton.

Lemma 3. *Algorithm 1 is correct if C1 holds.*

---

[3] We emphasize that this does not mean that states from V will be simply removed from A—the performed operation depends on the particular reduction.

4.2   A General Algorithm for Error-Driven Reduction

In Algorithm 2, we provide a high-level method of computing the error-driven reduction. The algorithm is in many ways similar to Algorithm 1; It also computes a set of states V where an error is to be introduced, but an important difference is that we compute an approximation

---

Algorithm 2. A greedy error-driven reduction.

Input : NFA $A = (Q, \delta, I, F)$, PA P, $\epsilon \in \langle 0, 1 \rangle$
Output: NFA A' s.t. $d_P(A, A') \leq \epsilon$

1 $\ell \leftarrow label(A, P)$;
2 $V \leftarrow \emptyset$;
3 **for** $q \in Q$ *in the order* $\preceq_{A, label(A,P)}$ **do**
4     $e \leftarrow error(A, V \cup \{q\}, \ell)$;
5   **if** $e \leq \epsilon$ **then** $V \leftarrow V \cup \{q\}$;
6 **return** $A' = reduce(A, V)$;

---

of the error in each step and only add q to V if it does not raise the error over the threshold ϵ. Note that the *error* does not need to be monotone, so it may be advantageous to traverse all states from Q and not terminate as soon as the threshold is reached. The correctness of Algorithm 2 also depends on **C1**.

Lemma 4. *Algorithm 2 is correct if **C1** holds.*

4.3   Pruning Reduction

The pruning reduction is based on identifying a set of states to be removed from an NFA A, under-approximating the language of A. In particular, for $A = (Q, \delta, I, F)$, the pruning reduction finds a set $R \subseteq Q$ and restricts A to $Q \setminus R$, followed by removing useless states, to construct a reduced automaton $A' = trim(A_{|Q \setminus R})$. Note that the natural decision problem corresponding to this reduction is also **PSPACE** complete.

Lemma 5. *Consider an NFA A, a PA P, a bound on the number of states $n \in \mathbb{N}$, and an error bound $\epsilon \in \langle 0, 1 \rangle$. It is **PSPACE**-complete to determine whether there exists a subset of states $R \subseteq Q[A]$ of the size $|R| = n$ such that $d_P(A, A_{|R}) \leq \epsilon$.*

Although Lemma 5 shows that the pruning reduction is as hard as a general reduction (cf. Lemma 2), the pruning reduction is more amenable to the use of heuristics like the greedy algorithms from Sects. 4.1 and 4.2. We instantiate *reduce*, *error*, and *label* in these high-level algorithms in the following way (the subscript p means *pruning*):

$$reduce_p(A, V) = trim(A_{|Q \setminus V}), \quad error_p(A, V, \ell) = \min_{V' \in \lfloor V \rfloor_p} \sum \{\ell(q) \mid q \in V'\},$$

where $\lfloor V \rfloor_p$ is defined as follows. Because of the use of *trim* in *reduce_p*, for a pair of sets V, V' s.t. $V \subset V'$, it holds that $reduce_p(A, V)$ may, in general, yield the same automaton as $reduce_p(A, V')$. Hence, we define a partial order $\sqsubseteq_p$ on 2^Q as $V_1 \sqsubseteq_p V_2$ iff $reduce_p(A, V_1) = reduce_p(A, V_2)$ and $V_1 \subseteq V_2$, and use $\lfloor V \rfloor_p$ to denote the set of minimal elements wrt V and $\sqsubseteq_p$. The value of the approximation $error_p(A, V, \ell)$ is therefore the minimum of the sum of errors over all sets from $\lfloor V \rfloor_p$.

Note that the size of $\lfloor V \rfloor_p$ can again be exponential, and thus we employ a greedy approach for guessing an optimal V'. Clearly, this cannot affect the soundness of the algorithm, but only decreases the precision of the bound on the distance. Our experiments indicate that for automata appearing in NIDSes, this simplification has typically only a negligible impact on the precision of the bounds.

For computing the state labelling, we provide the following three functions, which differ in the precision they provide and the difficulty of their computation (naturally, more precise labellings are harder to compute): $label_p^1$, $label_p^2$, and $label_p^3$. Given an NFA A and a PA P, they generate the labellings ℓ_p^1, ℓ_p^2, and ℓ_p^3, respectively, defined as

$$\ell_p^1(q) = \sum \left\{ \mathrm{Pr}_P(L_A^\flat(q')) \mid q' \in reach(\{q\}) \cap F \right\},$$

$$\ell_p^2(q) = \mathrm{Pr}_P\left(L_A^\flat(F \cap reach(q)) \right), \qquad \ell_p^3(q) = \mathrm{Pr}_P\left(L_A^\flat(q).L_A(q) \right).$$

A state label $\ell(q)$ approximates the error of the words removed from $L(A)$ when q is removed. More concretely, $\ell_p^1(q)$ is a rough estimate saying that the error can be bounded by the sum of probabilities of the banguages of all final states reachable from q (in the worst case, all those final states might become unreachable). Note that $\ell_p^1(q)$ (1) counts the error of a word accepted in two different final states of $reach(q)$ twice, and (2) also considers words that are accepted in some final state in $reach(q)$ without going through q. The labelling ℓ_p^2 deals with (1) by computing the total probability of the banguage of the set of all final states reachable from q, and the labelling ℓ_p^3 in addition also deals with (2) by only considering words that traverse through q (they can still be accepted in some final state not in $reach(q)$ though, so even ℓ_p^3 is still imprecise). Note that if A is unambiguous then $\ell_p^1 = \ell_p^2$.

When computing the label of q, we first modify A to obtain A' accepting the language related to the particular labelling. Then, we compute the value of $\mathrm{Pr}_P(L(A'))$ using the algorithm from Sect. 3.1. Recall that this step is in general costly, due to the determinisation/disambiguation of A'. The key property of the labelling computation resides in the fact that if A is composed of several disjoint sub-automata, the automaton A' is typically much smaller than A and thus the computation of the label is considerable less demanding. Since the automata appearing in regex matching for NIDS are composed of the union of "tentacles", the particular A's are very small, which enables efficient component-wise computation of the labels.

The following lemma states the correctness of using the pruning reduction as an instantiation of Algorithms 1 and 2 and also the relation among ℓ_p^1, ℓ_p^2, and ℓ_p^3.

Lemma 6. *For every $x \in \{1,2,3\}$, the functions $reduce_p$, $error_p$, and $label_p^x$ satisfy **C1**. Moreover, consider an NFA A, a PA P, and let $\ell_p^x = label_p^x(A, P)$ for $x \in \{1,2,3\}$. Then, for each $q \in Q[A]$, we have $\ell_p^1(q) \geq \ell_p^2(q) \geq \ell_p^3(q)$.*

4.4   Self-loop Reduction

The main idea of the self-loop reduction is to over-approximate the language of A by adding self-loops over every symbol at selected states. This makes some states of A redundant, allowing them to be removed without introducing any more error. Given an NFA $A = (Q, \delta, I, F)$, the self-loop reduction searches for a set of states $R \subseteq Q$, which will have self-loops added, and removes other transitions leading out of these states, making some states unreachable. The unreachable states are then removed.

Formally, let $sl(A, R)$ be the NFA (Q, δ', I, F) whose transition function δ' is defined, for all $p \in Q$ and $a \in \Sigma$, as $\delta'(p, a) = \{p\}$ if $p \in R$ and $\delta'(p, a) = \delta(p, a)$ otherwise. As with the pruning reduction, the natural decision problem corresponding to the self-loop reduction is also **PSPACE**-complete.

Lemma 7. *Consider an NFA A, a PA P, a bound on the number of states $n \in \mathbb{N}$, and an error bound $\epsilon \in \langle 0, 1 \rangle$. It is **PSPACE**-complete to determine whether there exists a subset of states $R \subseteq Q[A]$ of the size $|R| = n$ such that $d_P(A, sl(A, R)) \leq \epsilon$.*

The required functions in the error- and size-driven reduction algorithms are instantiated in the following way (the subscript sl means *self-loop*):

$$reduce_{sl}(A, V) = trim(sl(A, V)), \quad error_{sl}(A, V, \ell) = \sum \{\ell(q) \mid q \in \min(\lfloor V \rfloor_{sl})\},$$

where $\lfloor V \rfloor_{sl}$ is defined in a similar manner as $\lfloor V \rfloor_p$ in the previous section (using a partial order $\sqsubseteq_{sl}$ defined similarly to $\sqsubseteq_p$; in this case, the order $\sqsubseteq_{sl}$ has a single minimal element, though).

The functions $label_{sl}^1$, $label_{sl}^2$, and $label_{sl}^3$ compute the state labellings ℓ_{sl}^1, ℓ_{sl}^2, and ℓ_{sl}^3 for an NFA A and a PA P defined as follows:

$$\ell_{sl}^1(q) = weight_P(L_A^b(q)), \qquad \ell_{sl}^2(q) = \Pr_P\left(L_A^b(q).\Sigma^*\right),$$

$$\ell_{sl}^3(q) = \ell_{sl}^2(q) - \Pr_P\left(L_A^b(q).L_A(q)\right).$$

Above, $weight_P(w)$ for a PA $P = (\alpha, \gamma, \{\Delta_a\}_{a \in \Sigma})$ and a word $w \in \Sigma^*$ is defined as $weight_P(w) = \alpha^\top \cdot \Delta_w \cdot 1$ (i.e., similarly as $\Pr_P(w)$ but with the final weights γ discarded), and $weight_P(L)$ for $L \subseteq \Sigma^*$ is defined as $weight_P(L) = \sum_{w \in L} weight_P(w)$.

Intuitively, the state labelling $\ell_{sl}^1(q)$ computes the probability that q is reached from an initial state, so if q is pumped up with all possible word endings, this is the maximum possible error introduced by the added word endings. This has the following sources of imprecision: (1) the probability of some words may be included twice, e.g., when $L_A^b(q) = \{a, ab\}$, the probabilities of all words from $\{ab\}.\Sigma^*$ are included twice in $\ell^1_{sl}(q)$ because $\{ab\}.\Sigma^* \subseteq \{a\}.\Sigma^*$, and (2) $\ell^1_{sl}(q)$ can also contain probabilities of words that are already accepted on a run traversing q. The state labelling ℓ^2_{sl} deals with (1) by considering the probability of the language $L^b_A(q).\Sigma^*$, and ℓ^3_{sl} deals also with (2) by subtracting from the result of ℓ^2_{sl} the probabilities of the words that pass through q and are accepted.

The computation of the state labellings for the self-loop reduction is done in a similar way as the computation of the state labellings for the pruning reduction (cf. Sect. 4.3). For a computation of $weight_P(L)$ one can use the same algorithm as for $\mathrm{Pr}_P(L)$, only the final vector for PA P is set to $\mathbf{1}$. The correctness of Algorithms 1 and 2 when instantiated using the self-loop reduction is stated in the following lemma.

Lemma 8. *For every* $x \in \{1,2,3\}$, *the functions* $reduce_{sl}$, $error_{sl}$, *and* $label^x_{sl}$ *satisfy* **C1**. *Moreover, consider an NFA* A, *a PA* P, *and let* $\ell^x_{sl} = label^x_{sl}(A,P)$ *for* $x \in \{1,2,3\}$. *Then, for each* $q \in Q[A]$, *we have* $\ell^1_{sl}(q) \geq \ell^2_{sl}(q) \geq \ell^3_{sl}(q)$.

5 Reduction of NFAs in Network Intrusion Detection Systems

We have implemented our approach in a Python prototype named APPREAL (APProximate REduction of Automata and Languages)[4] and evaluated it on the use case of network intrusion detection using SNORT [1], a popular open source NIDS. The version of APPREAL used for the evaluation in the current paper is available as an artifact [44] for the TACAS'18 artifact virtual machine [45].

5.1 Network Traffic Model

The reduction we describe in this paper is driven by a probabilistic model representing a distribution over Σ^*, and the formal guarantees are also wrt this model. We use *learning* to obtain a model of network traffic over the 8-bit ASCII alphabet at a given network point. Our model is created from several gigabytes of network traffic from a measuring point of the CESNET Internet provider connected to a 100 Gbps backbone link (unfortunately, we cannot provide the traffic dump since it may contain sensitive data).

Learning a PA representing the network traffic faithfully is hard. The PA cannot be too specific—although the number of different packets that can occur is finite, it is still extremely large (a conservative estimate assuming the most common scenario Ethernet/IPv4/TCP would still yield a number over $2^{10,000}$). If we assigned non-zero probabilities only to the packets from the dump (which are less than 2^{20}), the obtained model would completely ignore virtually all packets that might appear on the network, and, moreover, the model would also be very large (millions of states), making it difficult to use in our algorithms. A generalization of the obtained traffic is therefore needed.

---

[4] https://github.com/vhavlena/appreal/tree/tacas18.

A natural solution is to exploit results from the area of PA learning, such as [39,40]. Indeed, we experimented with the use of ALERGIA [39], a learning algorithm that constructs a PA from a prefix tree (where edges are labelled with multiplicities) by merging nodes that are "similar." The automata that we obtained were, however, *too* general. In particular, the constructed automata destroyed the structure of network protocols—the merging was too permissive and the generalization merged distant states, which introduced loops over a very large substructure in the automaton (such a case usually does not correspond to the design of network protocols). As a result, the obtained PA more or less represented the Poisson distribution, having essentially no value for us.

In Sect. 5.2, we focus on the detection of malicious traffic transmitted over HTTP. We take advantage of this fact and create a PA representing the traffic while taking into account the structure of HTTP. We start by manually creating a DFA that represents the high-level structure of HTTP. Then, we proceed by feeding 34,191 HTTP packets from our sample into the DFA, at the same time taking notes about how many times every state is reached and how many times every transition is taken. The resulting PA P_{HTTP} (of 52 states) is then obtained from the DFA and the labels in the obvious way.

The described method yields automata that are much better than those obtained using ALERGIA in our experiments. A disadvantage of the method is that it is only semi-automatic— the basic DFA needed to be provided by an expert. We have yet to find an algorithm that would suit our needs for learning more general network traffic.

5.2 Evaluation

We start this section by introducing the experimental setting, namely, the integration of our reduction techniques into the tool chain implementing efficient regex matching, the concrete settings of APPREAL, and the evaluation environment. Afterwards, we discuss the results evaluating the quality of the obtained approximate reductions as well as of the provided error bounds. Finally, we present the performance of our approach and discuss its key aspects. Due to the lack of space, we selected the most interesting results demonstrating the potential as well as the limitations of our approach.

General Setting. SNORT detects malicious network traffic based on *rules* that contain *conditions*. The conditions may take into consideration, among others, network addresses, ports, or Perl compatible regular expressions (PCREs) that the packet payload should match. In our evaluation, we always select a subset of SNORT rules, extract the PCREs from them, and use NETBENCH [20] to transform them into a single NFA A. Before applying APPREAL, we use the state-of-the-art NFA reduction tool REDUCE [41] to decrease the size of A. REDUCE performs a language-preserving reduction of A using advanced variants of simulation [31] (in the experiment reported in Table 3, we skip the use of REDUCE at this step as discussed in the performance evaluation). The automaton A^{RED} obtained as the result of REDUCE is the input of APPREAL, which performs one of the approximate reductions from Sect. 4 wrt the traffic model P_{HTTP}, yielding A^{APP}. After the approximate reduction, we, one more time, use REDUCE and obtain the result A'.

Settings of APPREAL. In the use case of NIDS pre-filtering, it may be important to never introduce a false negative, i.e., to never drop a malicious packet. Therefore, we focus our evaluation on the *self-loop reduction* (Sect. 4.4). In particular, we use the state labelling function $label_{sl}^2$, since it provides a good trade-off between the precision and the computational demands (recall that the computation of $label_{sl}^2$ can exploit the "tentacle" structure of the NFAs we work with). We give more attention to the *size-driven reduction* (Sect. 4.1) since, in our setting, a bound on the available FPGA resources is typically given and the task is to create an NFA with the smallest error that fits inside. The order $\preceq_{A,\ell_{sl}^2}$ over states used in Sects. 4.1 and 4.2 is defined as $s \preceq_{A,\ell_{sl}^2} s' \Leftrightarrow \ell_{sl}^2(s) \leq \ell_{sl}^2(s')$.

Evaluation Environment. All experiments run on a 64-bit LINUX DEBIAN workstation with the Intel Core(TM) i5-661 CPU running at 3.33 GHz with 16 GiB of RAM.

Description of Tables. In the caption of every table, we provide the name of the input file (in the directory `regexps/tacas18/` of the repository of APPREAL) with the selection of SNORT regexes used in the particular experiment, together with the type of the reduction (size- or error-driven). All reductions are over-approximating (self-loop reduction). We further provide the size of the input automaton $|A|$, the size after the initial processing by REDUCE ($|A^{\text{RED}}|$), and the time of this reduction ($time(\text{REDUCE})$). Finally, we list the times of computing the state labelling $label_{sl}^2$ on A^{RED} ($time(label_{sl}^2)$), the exact probabilistic distance ($time(\text{Exact})$), and also the number of *look-up tables* ($LUTs(A^{\text{RED}})$) consumed on the targeted FPGA (Xilinx Virtex 7 H580T) when A^{RED} was synthesized (more on this in Sect. 5.3). The meaning of the columns in the tables is the following:

k/ϵ is the parameter of the reduction. In particular, k is used for the size-driven reduction and denotes the desired reduction ration $k = \frac{n}{|A^{\text{RED}}|}$ for an input NFA A^{RED} and the desired size of the output n. On the other hand, ϵ is the desired maximum error on the output for the error-driven reduction.

$|A^{\text{APP}}|$ shows the number of states of the automaton A^{APP} after the reduction by APPREAL and the time the reduction took (we omit it when it is not interesting).

$|A'|$ contains the number of states of the NFA A' obtained after applying REDUCE on A^{APP} and the time used by REDUCE at this step (omitted when not interesting).

Table 1. Results for the `http-malicious` regex, $|A_{mal}| = 249$, $|A^{RED}_{mal}| = 98$, $time(\text{REDUCE}) = 3.5\,s$, $time(label^2_{sl}) = 38.7\,s$, $time(\text{Exact}) = 3.8\text{–}6.5\,s$, and $LUTs(A^{RED}_{mal}) = 382$.

(a) size-driven reduction

k	$\lvert A^{APP}_{mal}\rvert$	$\lvert A'_{mal}\rvert$	Error bound	Exact error	Traffic error	LUTs
0.1	9 (0.65 s)	9 (0.4 s)	0.0704	0.0704	0.0685	—
0.2	19 (0.66 s)	19 (0.5 s)	0.0677	0.0677	0.0648	—
0.3	29 (0.69 s)	26 (0.9 s)	0.0279	0.0278	0.0598	154
0.4	39 (0.68 s)	36 (1.1 s)	0.0032	0.0032	0.0008	—
0.5	49 (0.68 s)	44 (1.4 s)	2.8e-05	2.8e-05	4.1e-06	—
0.6	58 (0.69 s)	49 (1.7 s)	8.7e-08	8.7e-08	0.0	224
0.8	78 (0.69 s)	75 (2.7 s)	2.4e-17	2.4e-17	0.0	297

(b) error-driven reduction

ϵ	$\lvert A^{APP}_{mal}\rvert$	$\lvert A'_{mal}\rvert$	Error bound	Exact error	Traffic error
0.08	3	3	0.0724	0.0724	0.0720
0.07	4	4	0.0700	0.0700	0.0683
0.04	35	32	0.0267	0.0212	0.0036
0.02	36	33	0.0105	0.0096	0.0032
0.001	41	38	0.0005	0.0005	0.0003
1e-04	47	41	7.7e-05	7.7e-05	1.2e-05
1e-05	51	47	6.6e-06	6.6e-06	0.0

Error bound shows the estimation of the error of A' as determined by the reduction itself, i.e., it is the probabilistic distance computed by the function *error* in Sect. 4.

Exact error contains the values of $d_{P_{HTTP}}(A, A')$ that we computed *after* the reduction in order to evaluate the precision of the result given in **Error bound**. The computation of this value is very expensive ($time(Exact)$) since it inherently requires determinisation of the whole automaton A. We do not provide it in Table 3 (presenting the results for the automaton A_{bd} with 1,352 states) because the determinisation ran out of memory (the step is not required in the reduction process).

Traffic error shows the error that we obtained when compared A' with A on an HTTP traffic sample, in particular the ratio of packets misclassified by A' to the total number of packets in the sample (242,468). Comparing **Exact error** with **Traffic error** gives us a feedback about the fidelity of the traffic model P_{HTTP}. We note that there are no guarantees on the relationship between **Exact error** and **Traffic error**.

LUTs is the number of LUTs consumed by A' when synthesized into the FPGA. Hardware synthesis is a costly step so we provide this value only for selected NFAs.

Approximation Errors

Table 1 presents the results of the self-loop reduction for the NFA A_{mal} describing `http-malicious` regexes. We can observe that the differences between the upper bounds on the probabilistic distance and its real value are negligible (typically in the order of 10^{-4} or less). We can also see that the probabilistic distance agrees with the traffic error. This indicates a good quality of the traffic model employed in the reduction process. Further, we can see that our approach can provide useful trade-offs between the reduction error and the reduction factor. Finally, Table 1 shows that a significant reduction is obtained when the error threshold ϵ is increased from 0.04 to 0.07.

Table 2 presents the results of the size-driven self-loop reduction for NFA $A_{\mathtt{att}}$ describing http-attacks regexes. We can observe that the error bounds provide again a very good approximation of the real probabilistic distance. On the other hand, the difference between the probabilistic distance and the traffic error is larger than for $A_{\mathtt{mal}}$. Since all experiments use the same probabilistic automaton and the same traf-

Table 2. Results for the http-attacks regex, size-driven reduction, $|A_{\mathtt{att}}| = 142$, $|A_{\mathtt{att}}^{\mathrm{RED}}| = 112$, $time(\mathrm{REDUCE}) = 7.9\,\mathrm{s}$, $time(label_{sl}^2) = 28.3\,\mathrm{min}$, $time(\mathrm{Exact}) = 14.0\text{--}16.4\,\mathrm{min}$.

k	$|A_{\mathtt{att}}^{\mathrm{APP}}|$	$|A_{\mathtt{att}}'|$	Error bound	Exact error	Traffic error
0.1	11 (1.1 s)	5 (0.4 s)	1.0	0.9972	0.9957
0.2	22 (1.1 s)	14 (0.6 s)	1.0	0.8341	0.2313
0.3	33 (1.1 s)	24 (0.7 s)	0.081	0.0770	0.0067
0.4	44 (1.1 s)	37 (1.6 s)	0.0005	0.0005	0.0010
0.5	56 (1.1 s)	49 (1.2 s)	3.3e–06	3.3e–06	0.0010
0.6	67 (1.1 s)	61 (1.9 s)	1.2e–09	1.2e–09	8.7e–05
0.7	78 (1.1 s)	72 (2.4 s)	4.8e–12	4.8e–12	1.2e–05
0.9	100 (1.1 s)	93 (4.7 s)	3.7e–16	1.1e–15	0.0

fic, this discrepancy is accounted to the different set of packets that are incorrectly accepted by $A_{\mathtt{att}}^{\mathrm{RED}}$. If the probability of these packets is adequately captured in the traffic model, the difference between the distance and the traffic error is small and vice versa. This also explains an even larger difference in Table 3 (presenting the results for $A_{\mathtt{bd}}$ constructed from http-backdoor regexes) for $k \in \langle 0.2, 0.4 \rangle$. Here, the traffic error is very small and caused by a small set of packets (approx. 70), whose probability is not correctly captured in the traffic model. Despite this problem, the results clearly show that our approach still provides significant reductions while keeping the traffic error small: about a 5-fold reduction is obtained for the traffic error 0.03 % and a 10-fold reduction is obtained for the traffic error 6.3 %. We discuss the practical impact of such a reduction in Sect. 5.3.

Performance of the Approximate Reduction

In all our experiments (Tables 1, 2 and 3), we can observe that the most time-consuming step of the reduction process is the computation of state labellings (it takes at least 90 % of the total time). The crucial observation is that the structure of the NFAs fundamentally affects the performance of this step. Although after REDUCE, the size of $A_{\mathtt{mal}}$ is very similar to the size of $A_{\mathtt{att}}$,

Table 3. Results for http-backdoor, size-driven reduction, $|A_{\mathtt{bd}}| = 1,352$, $time(label_{sl}^2) = 19.9\,\mathrm{min}$, $LUTs(A_{\mathtt{bd}}^{\mathrm{RED}}) = 2,266$.

k	$|A_{\mathtt{bd}}^{\mathrm{APP}}|$	$|A_{\mathtt{bd}}'|$	Error bound	Traffic error	LUTs
0.1	135 (1.2 m)	8 (2.6 s)	1.0	0.997	202
0.2	270 (1.2 m)	111 (5.2 s)	0.0012	0.0631	579
0.3	405 (1.2 m)	233 (9.8 s)	3.4e–08	0.0003	894
0.4	540 (1.3 m)	351 (21.7 s)	1.0e–12	0.0003	1063
0.5	676 (1.3 m)	473 (41.8 s)	1.2e–17	0.0	1249
0.7	946 (1.4 m)	739 (2.1 m)	8.3e–30	0.0	1735
0.9	1216 (1.5 m)	983 (5.6 m)	1.3e–52	0.0	2033

computing $label_{sl}^2$ takes more time (28.3 min vs. 38.7 s). The key reason behind this slowdown is the determinisation (or alternatively disambiguation) process required by the product construction underlying the state labelling computation (cf. Sect. 4.4). For $A_{\mathtt{att}}$, the process results in a significantly larger product when compared to the product for $A_{\mathtt{mal}}$. The size of the product directly determines the time and space complexity of solving the linear equation system required for computing the state labelling.

As explained in Sect. 4, the computation of the state labelling $label_{sl}^2$ can exploit the "tentacle" structure of the NFAs appearing in NIDSes and thus can be done component-wise. On the other hand, our experiments reveal that the use of REDUCE typically breaks this structure and thus the component-wise computation cannot be effectively used. For the NFA A_{mal}, this behaviour does not have any major performance impact as the determinisation leads to a moderate-sized automaton and the state labelling computation takes less than 40 s. On the other hand, this behaviour has a dramatic effect for the NFA A_{att}. By disabling the initial application of REDUCE and thus preserving the original structure of A_{att}, we were able to speed up the state label computation from 28.3 min to 1.5 min. Note that other steps of the approximate reduction took a similar time as before disabling REDUCE and also that the trade-offs between the error and the reduction factor were similar. Surprisingly, disabling REDUCE caused that the computation of the exact probabilistic distance became computationally infeasible because the determinisation ran out of memory.

Due to the size of the NFA A_{bd}, the impact of disabling the initial application of REDUCE is even more fundamental. In particular, computing the state labelling took only 19.9 min, in contrast to running out of memory when the REDUCE is applied in the first step (therefore, the input automaton is not processed by REDUCE in Table 3; we still give the number of LUTs of its reduced version for comparison, though). Note that the size of A_{bd} also slows down other reduction steps (the greedy algorithm and the final REDUCE reduction). We can, however, clearly see that computing the state labelling is still the most time-consuming step.

5.3   The Real Impact in an FPGA-Accelerated NIDS

Further, we also evaluated some of the obtained automata in the setting of [5] implementing a high-speed NIDS pre-filter. In that setting, the amount of resources available for the regex matching engine is 15,000 LUTs[5] and the frequency of the engine is 200 MHz. We synthesized NFAs that use a 32-bit-wide data path, corresponding to processing 4 ASCII characters at once, which is— according to the analysis in [5]—the best trade-off between the utilization of the chip resources and the maximum achievable frequency. A simple analysis shows that the throughput of one automaton is 6.4 Gbps, so in order to reach the desired link speed of 100 Gbps, 16 units are required, and 63 units are needed to handle 400 Gbps. With the given amount of LUTs, we are therefore bounded by 937 LUTs for 100 Gbps and 238 LUTs for 400 Gbps.

We focused on the consumption of LUTs by an implementation of the regex matching engines for http-backdoor (A_{bd}^{RED}) and http-malicious (A_{mal}^{RED}).

- **100 Gbps:** For this speed, A_{mal}^{RED} can be used without any approximate reduction as it is small enough to fit in the available space. On the other hand, A_{bd}^{RED}

---

[5] We omit the analysis of flip-flop consumption because in our setting it is dominated by the LUT consumption.

without the approximate reduction is way too large to fit (at most 6 units fit inside the available space, yielding the throughput of only 38.4 Gbps, which is unacceptable). The column **LUTs** in Table 3 shows that using our framework, we are able to reduce $A_{\text{bd}}^{\text{RED}}$ such that it uses 894 LUTs (for $k = 0.3$), and so all the needed 16 units fit into the FPGA, yielding the throughput over 100 Gbps and the theoretical error bound of a false positive $\leq 3.4 \times 10^{-8}$ wrt the model P_{HTTP}.

– **400 Gbps:** Regex matching at this speed is extremely challenging. The only reduced version of $A_{\text{bd}}^{\text{RED}}$ that fits in the available space is the one for the value $k = 0.1$ with the error bound almost 1. The situation is better for $A_{\text{mal}}^{\text{RED}}$. In the exact version, at most 39 units can fit inside the FPGA with the maximum throughput of 249.6 Gbps. On the other hand, when using our approximate reduction framework, we are able to place 63 units into the FPGA, each of the size 224 LUTs ($k = 0.6$) with the throughput over 400 Gbps and the theoretical error bound of a false positive $\leq 8.7 \times 10^{-8}$ wrt the model P_{HTTP}.

6   Conclusion

We have proposed a novel approach for approximate reduction of NFAs used in network traffic filtering. Our approach is based on a proposal of a probabilistic distance of the original and reduced automaton using a probabilistic model of the input network traffic, which characterizes the significance of particular packets. We characterized the computational complexity of approximate reductions based on the described distance and proposed a sequence of heuristics allowing one to perform the approximate reduction in an efficient way. Our experimental results are quite encouraging and show that we can often achieve a very significant reduction for a negligible loss of precision. We showed that using our approach, FPGA-accelerated network filtering on large traffic speeds can be applied on regexes of malicious traffic where it could not be applied before.

In the future, we plan to investigate other approximate reductions of the NFAs, maybe using some variant of abstraction from abstract regular model checking [42], adapted for the given probabilistic setting. Another important issue for the future is to develop better ways of learning a suitable probabilistic model of the input traffic.

Data Availability Statement and Acknowledgements. The tool used for the experimental evaluation in the current study is available in the following figshare repository: https://doi.org/10.6084/m9.figshare.5907055.v1. We thank Jan Kořenek, Vlastimil Košař, and Denis Matoušek for their help with translating regexes into automata and synthesis of FPGA designs, and Martin Žádník for providing us with the backbone network traffic. We thank Stefan Kiefer for helping us proving the **PSPACE** part of Lemma 1 and Petr Peringer for testing our artifact. The work on this paper was supported by the Czech Science Foundation project 16-17538S, the IT4IXS: IT4Innovations Excellence in Science project (LQ1602), and the FIT BUT internal project FIT-S-17-4014.

References

1. The Snort Team: Snort. http://www.snort.org
2. Becchi, M., Wiseman, C., Crowley, P.: Evaluating regular expression matching engines on network and general purpose processors. In: Proceedings of ANCS 2009, pp. 30–39. ACM (2009)
3. Kořenek, J., Kobierský, P.: Intrusion detection system intended for multigigabit networks. In: Proceedings of DDECS 2007. IEEE (2007)
4. Kaštil, J., Kořenek, J., Lengál, O.: Methodology for fast pattern matching by deterministic finite automaton with perfect hashing. In: Proceedings of DSD 2007, pp. 823–829. IEEE (2009)
5. Matoušek, D., Kořenek, J., Puš, V.: High-speed regular expression matching with pipelined automata. In: Proceedings of FPT 2016, pp. 93–100. IEEE (2016)
6. Kumar, S., Dharmapurikar, S., Yu, F., Crowley, P., Turner, J.S.: Algorithms to accelerate multiple regular expressions matching for deep packet inspection. In: Proceedings of SIGCOMM 2006, pp. 339–350. ACM (2006)
7. Tan, L., Sherwood, T.: A high throughput string matching architecture for intrusion detection and prevention. In: Proceedings of ISCA 2005, pp. 112–122. IEEE (2005)
8. Kumar, S., Turner, J.S., Williams, J.: Advanced algorithms for fast and scalable deep packet inspection. In: Proceedings of ANCS 2006, pp. 81–92. ACM (2006)
9. Becchi, M., Crowley, P.: A hybrid finite automaton for practical deep packet inspection. In: Proceedings of CoNEXT 2007. ACM (2007)
10. Becchi, M., Crowley, P.: An improved algorithm to accelerate regular expression evaluation. In: Proceedings of ANCS 2007, pp. 145–154. ACM (2007)
11. Kumar, S., Chandrasekaran, B., Turner, J.S., Varghese, G.: Curing regular expressions matching algorithms from insomnia, amnesia, and acalculia. In: Proceedings of ANCS 2007, 155–164. ACM (2007)
12. Yu, F., Chen, Z., Diao, Y., Lakshman, T.V., Katz, R.H.: Fast and memory efficient regular expression matching for deep packet inspection. In: Proceedings of ANCS 2006, pp. 93–102. ACM (2006)
13. Liu, C., Wu, J.: Fast deep packet inspection with a dual finite automata. IEEE Trans. Comput. **62**(2), 310–321 (2013)
14. Luchaup, D., De Carli, L., Jha, S., Bach, E.: Deep packet inspection with DFA-trees and parametrized language overapproximation. In: Proceedings of INFOCOM 2014, pp. 531–539. IEEE (2014)
15. Mitra, A., Najjar, W.A., Bhuyan, L.N.: Compiling PCRE to FPGA for accelerating SNORT IDS. In: Proceedings of ANCS 2007. ACM (2007) 127–136
16. Brodie, B.C., Taylor, D.E., Cytron, R.K.: A scalable architecture for high-throughput regular-expression pattern matching. In: Proceedings of ISCA 2006, pp. 191–202. IEEE (2006)
17. Clark, C.R., Schimmel, D.E.: Efficient reconfigurable logic circuits for matching complex network intrusion detection patterns. In: Y. K. Cheung, P., Constantinides, G.A. (eds.) FPL 2003. LNCS, vol. 2778, pp. 956–959. Springer, Heidelberg (2003). https://doi.org/10.1007/978-3-540-45234-8_94
18. Hutchings, B.L., Franklin, R., Carver, D.: Assisting network intrusion detection with reconfigurable Hardware. In: Proceedings of FCCM 2002, pp. 111–120. IEEE (2002)
19. Sidhu, R.P.S., Prasanna, V.K.: Fast regular expression matching using FPGAs. In: Proceedings of FCCM 2001, pp. 227–238. IEEE (2001)

20. Puš, V., Tobola, J., Košař, V., Kaštil, J., Kořenek, J.: Netbench: framework for evaluation of packet processing algorithms. In: Proceedings of ANCS 2011, pp. 95–96. ACM/IEEE (2011)
21. Maletti, A., Quernheim, D.: Optimal Hyper-Minimization. CoRR abs/1104.3007 (2011)
22. Gawrychowski, P., Jeż, A.: Hyper-minimisation made efficient. In: Královič, R., Niwiński, D. (eds.) MFCS 2009. LNCS, vol. 5734, pp. 356–368. Springer, Heidelberg (2009). https://doi.org/10.1007/978-3-642-03816-7_31
23. Gange, G., Ganty, P., Stuckey, P.J.: Fixing the state budget: approximation of regular languages with small DFAs. In: D'Souza, D., Narayan Kumar, K. (eds.) ATVA 2017. LNCS, vol. 10482, pp. 67–83. Springer, Cham (2017). https://doi.org/10.1007/978-3-319-68167-2_5
24. Parker, A.J., Yancey, K.B., Yancey, M.P.: Regular Language Distance and Entropy. CoRR abs/1602.07715 (2016)
25. Mohri, M.: Edit-distance of weighted automata. In: Champarnaud, J.-M., Maurel, D. (eds.) CIAA 2002. LNCS, vol. 2608, pp. 1–23. Springer, Heidelberg (2003). https://doi.org/10.1007/3-540-44977-9_1
26. Malcher, A.: Minimizing finite automata is computationally hard. Theor. Comput. Sci. **327**(3), 375–390 (2004)
27. Hopcroft, J.E.: An $N.logN$ Algorithm for Minimizing States in a Finite Automaton. Technical report (1971)
28. Paige, R., Tarjan, R.E.: Three partition refinement algorithms. SIAM J. Comput. **16**(6), 973–989 (1987)
29. Bustan, D., Grumberg, O.: Simulation-based minimization. ACM Trans. Comput. Log. **4**(2), 181–206 (2003)
30. Champarnaud, J., Coulon, F.: NFA reduction algorithms by means of regular inequalities. Theor. Comput. Sci. **327**(3), 241–253 (2004)
31. Mayr, R., Clemente, L.: Advanced automata minimization. In: Proceedings of POPL 2013, pp. 63–74. ACM (2013)
32. Etessami, K.: A hierarchy of polynomial-time computable simulations for automata. In: Brim, L., Křetínský, M., Kučera, A., Jančar, P. (eds.) CONCUR 2002. LNCS, vol. 2421, pp. 131–144. Springer, Heidelberg (2002). https://doi.org/10.1007/3-540-45694-5_10
33. Clemente, L.: Büchi automata can have smaller quotients. In: Aceto, L., Henzinger, M., Sgall, J. (eds.) ICALP 2011. LNCS, vol. 6756, pp. 258–270. Springer, Heidelberg (2011). https://doi.org/10.1007/978-3-642-22012-8_20
34. Vardi, M.Y.: Automatic verification of probabilistic concurrent finite state programs. In: Proceedings of SFCS 1985, pp. 327–338. IEEE (1985)
35. Baier, C., Kiefer, S., Klein, J., Klüppelholz, S., Müller, D., Worrell, J.: Markov chains and unambiguous Büchi automata. In: Chaudhuri, S., Farzan, A. (eds.) CAV 2016. LNCS, vol. 9779, pp. 23–42. Springer, Cham (2016). https://doi.org/10.1007/978-3-319-41528-4_2
36. Baier, C., Kiefer, S., Klein, J., Klüppelholz, S., Müller, D., Worrell, J.: Markov Chains and Unambiguous Büchi Automata. CoRR abs/1605.00950 (2016)
37. Mohri, M.: A disambiguation algorithm for finite automata and functional transducers. In: Moreira, N., Reis, R. (eds.) CIAA 2012. LNCS, vol. 7381, pp. 265–277. Springer, Heidelberg (2012). https://doi.org/10.1007/978-3-642-31606-7_23
38. Jiang, T., Ravikumar, B.: Minimal NFA problems are hard. SIAM J. Comput. **22**(6), 1117–1141 (1993)

39. Carrasco, R.C., Oncina, J.: Learning stochastic regular grammars by means of a state merging method. In: Carrasco, R.C., Oncina, J. (eds.) ICCI 1994. LNCS, vol. 862, pp. 139–152. Springer, Heidelberg (1994). https://doi.org/10.1007/3-540-58473-0_144
40. Thollard, F., Clark, A.: Learning stochastic deterministic regular languages. In: Paliouras, G., Sakakibara, Y. (eds.) ICGI 2004. LNCS (LNAI), vol. 3264, pp. 248–259. Springer, Heidelberg (2004). https://doi.org/10.1007/978-3-540-30195-0_22
41. Mayr, R., et al.: Reduce: A Tool for Minimizing Nondeterministic Finite-Word and Büchi Automata. http://languageinclusion.org/doku.php?id=tools. Accessed 30 Sept 2017
42. Bouajjani, A., Habermehl, P., Rogalewicz, A., Vojnar, T.: Abstract regular (Tree) model checking. STTT 14(2), 167–191 (2012)
43. Češka, M., Havlena, V., Holík, L., Lengál, O., Vojnar, T.: Approximate Reduction of Finite Automata for High-Speed Network Intrusion Detection. Technical report. CoRR abs/1710.08647 (2017)
44. Češka, M., Havlena, V., Holík, L., Lengál, O., Vojnar, T.: Approximate Reduction of Finite Automata for High-Speed Network Intrusion Detection. Figshare (2018). https://doi.org/10.6084/m9.figshare.5907055.v1
45. Hartmanns, A., Wendler, P.: TACAS 2018 Artifact Evaluation VM. Figshare (2018). https://doi.org/10.6084/m9.figshare.5896615

Validity-Guided Synthesis of Reactive Systems from Assume-Guarantee Contracts

Andreas Katis[1]([⊠]) [iD], Grigory Fedyukovich[2] [iD], Huajun Guo[1], Andrew Gacek[3], John Backes[3], Arie Gurfinkel[4], and Michael W. Whalen[1]

[1] Department of Computer Science and Engineering,
University of Minnesota, Minneapolis, USA
{katis001,guoxx663}@umn.edu, whalen@cs.umn.edu
[2] Department of Computer Science, Princeton University,
Princeton, USA
grigoryf@cs.princeton.edu
[3] Rockwell Collins Advanced Technology Center,
Cedar Rapids, USA
{andrew.gacek,john.backes}@rockwellcollins.com
[4] Department of Electrical and Computer Engineering,
University of Waterloo, Waterloo, Canada
agurfinkel@uwaterloo.ca

Abstract. Automated synthesis of reactive systems from specifications has been a topic of research for decades. Recently, a variety of approaches have been proposed to extend synthesis of reactive systems from propositional specifications towards specifications over rich theories. We propose a novel, completely automated approach to program synthesis which reduces the problem to deciding the validity of a set of $\forall\exists$-formulas. In spirit of IC3/PDR, our problem space is recursively refined by blocking out regions of unsafe states, aiming to discover a fixpoint that describes safe reactions. If such a fixpoint is found, we construct a witness that is directly translated into an implementation. We implemented the algorithm on top of the JKIND model checker, and exercised it against contracts written using the Lustre specification language. Experimental results show how the new algorithm outperforms JKIND's already existing synthesis procedure based on k-induction and addresses soundness issues in the k-inductive approach with respect to unrealizable results.

1 Introduction

Program synthesis is one of the most challenging problems in computer science. The objective is to define a process to automatically derive implementations that are guaranteed to comply with specifications expressed in the form of logic formulas. The problem has seen increased popularity in the recent years, mainly due to the capabilities of modern symbolic solvers, including Satisfiability Modulo Theories (SMT) [1] tools, to compute compact and precise regions that describe

© The Author(s) 2018
D. Beyer and M. Huisman (Eds.): TACAS 2018, LNCS 10806, pp. 176–193, 2018.
https://doi.org/10.1007/978-3-319-89963-3_10

under which conditions an implementation exists for the given specification [25]. As a result, the problem has been well-studied for the area of propositional specifications (see Gulwani [15] for a survey), and approaches have been proposed to tackle challenges involving richer specifications. Template-based techniques focus on synthesizing programs that match a certain shape (the template) [28], while *inductive synthesis* uses the idea of refining the problem space using counterexamples, to converge to a solution [12]. A different category is that of *functional synthesis*, in which the goal is to construct functions from pre-defined input/output relations [22].

Our goal is to effectively synthesize programs from safety specifications written in the Lustre [18] language. These specifications are structured in the form of *Assume-Guarantee* contracts, similarly to approaches in Linear Temporal Logic [11]. In prior work, we developed a solution to the synthesis problem which is based on k-induction [14,19,21]. Despite showing good results, the approach suffers from soundness problems with respect to unrealizable results; a contract could be declared as unrealizable, while an actual implementation exists. In this work, we propose a novel approach that is a direct improvement over the k-inductive method in two important aspects: performance and generality. On all models that can be synthesized by k-induction, the new algorithm always outperforms in terms of synthesis time while yielding roughly approximate code sizes and execution times for the generated code. More importantly, the new algorithm can synthesize a strictly larger set of benchmark models, and comes with an improved termination guarantee: unlike in k-induction, if the algorithm terminates with an "unrealizable" result, then there is no possible realization of the contract.

The technique has been used to synthesize contracts involving linear real and integer arithmetic (LIRA), but remains generic enough to be extended into supporting additional theories in the future, as well as to liveness properties that can be reduced to safety properties (as in k-liveness [7]). Our approach is completely automated and requires no guidance to the tools in terms of user interaction (unlike [26,27]), and it is capable of providing solutions without requiring any templates, as in e.g., work by Beyene et al. [2]. We were able to automatically solve problems that were "hard" and required hand-written templates specialized to the problem in [2].

The main idea of the algorithm was inspired by induction-based model checking, and in particular by IC3/Property Directed Reachability (PDR) [4,9]. In PDR, the goal is to discover an inductive invariant for a property, by recursively blocking generalized regions describing unsafe states. Similarly, we attempt to reach a greatest fixpoint that contains states that react to arbitrary environment behavior and lead to states within the fixpoint that comply with all guarantees. Formally, the greatest fixpoint is sufficient to prove the validity of a $\forall\exists$-formula, which states that for any state and environment input, there exists a system reaction that complies with the specification. Starting from the entire problem space, we recursively block regions of states that violate the contract, using *regions of validity* that are generated by invalid $\forall\exists$-formulas. If the refined $\forall\exists$-formula is valid, we reach a fixpoint which can effectively be used by the specified transition relation to provide safe reactions to environment inputs. We then extract a witness for the formula's satisfiability, which can be directly transformed into the language intended for the system's implementation.

The algorithm was implemented as a feature in the JKIND model checker and is based on the general concept of extracting a witness that satisfies a $\forall\exists$-formula, using the AE-VAL Skolemizer [10,19]. While AE-VAL was mainly used as a tool for solving queries and extracting Skolems in our k-inductive approach, in this paper we also take advantage of its capability to generate *regions of validity* from invalid formulas to reach a fixpoint of satisfiable assignments to state variables.

The contributions of the paper are therefore:

- A novel approach to synthesis of contracts involving rich theories that is efficient, general, and completely automated (no reliance on templates or user guidance),
- an implementation of the approach in a branch of the JKIND model checker, and
- an experiment over a large suite of benchmark models demonstrating the effectiveness of the approach.

The rest of the paper is organized as follows. Section 2 briefly describes the Cinderella-Stepmother problem that we use as an example throughout the paper. In Sect. 3, we provide the necessary formal definitions to describe the synthesis algorithm, which is presented then in Sect. 4. We present an evaluation in Sect. 5 and comparison against a method based on k-induction that exists using the same input language. Finally, we discuss the differences of our work with closely related ideas in Sect. 6 and conclude in Sect. 7.

2   Overview: The Cinderella-Stepmother Game

We illustrate the flow of the validity guided-synthesis algorithm using a variation of the minimum-backlog problem, the two player game between Cinderella and her wicked Stepmother, first expressed by Bodlaender *et al.* [3].

The main objective for Cinderella (i.e. the reactive system) is to prevent a collection of buckets from overflowing with water. On the other hand, Cinderella's Stepmother (i.e. the system's environment) refills the buckets with a predefined amount of water that is distributed in a random fashion between the buckets. For the running example, we chose an instance of the game that has been previously used in template-based synthesis [2]. In this instance, the game is described using five buckets, where each bucket can contain up to two units of water. Cinderella has the option to empty two adjacent buckets at each of her turns, while the Stepmother distributes one unit of water over all five buckets. In the context of this paper we use this example to show how specification is expressed, as well as how we can synthesize an efficient implementation that describes reactions for Cinderella, such that a bucket overflow is always prevented.

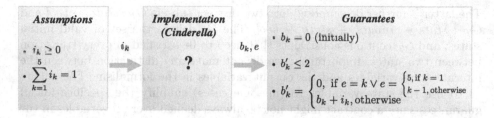

Fig. 1. An Assume-Guarantee contract.

We represent the system requirements using an *Assume-Guarantee Contract*. The *assumptions* of the contract restrict the possible inputs that the environment can provide to the system, while the *guarantees* describe safe reactions of the system to the outside world.

A (conceptually) simple example is shown in Fig. 1. The contract describes a possible set of requirements for a specific instance of the Cinderella-Stepmother game. Our goal is to synthesize an implementation that describes Cinderella's winning region of the game. Cinderella in this case is the implementation, as shown by the middle box in Fig. 1. Cinderella's inputs are five different values i_k, $1 \leq k \leq 5$, determined by a random distribution of one unit of water by the Stepmother. During each of her turns Cinderella has to make a choice denoted by the output variable e, such that the buckets b_k do not overflow during the next action of her Stepmother. We define the contract using the set of assumptions A (left box in Fig. 1) and the guarantee constraints G (right box in Fig. 1). For the particular example, it is possible to construct at least one implementation that satisfies G given A which is described in Sect. 4.3. The proof of existence of such an implementation is the main concept behind the *realizability* problem, while the automated construction of a witness implementation is the main focus of *program synthesis*.

Given a proof of realizability of the contract in Fig. 1, we are seeking for an efficient synthesis procedure that could provide an implementation. On the other hand, consider a variation of the example, where $A = true$. This is a practical case of an *unrealizable* contract, as there is no feasible Cinderella implementation that can correctly react to Stepmother's actions. An example counterexample allows the Stepmother to pour random amounts of water into the buckets, leading to overflow of at least one bucket during each of her turns.

3 Background

We use two disjoint sets, *state* and *inputs*, to describe a system. A straightforward and intuitive way to represent an *implementation* is by defining a *transition system*, composed of an initial state predicate $I(s)$ of type *state* $\rightarrow$ *bool*, as well as a transition relation $T(s, i, s')$ of type *state* $\rightarrow$ *inputs* $\rightarrow$ *state* $\rightarrow$ *bool*.

Combining the above, we represent an Assume-Guarantee (AG) contract using a set of *assumptions*, A : *state* $\rightarrow$ *inputs* $\rightarrow$ *bool*, and a set of *guarantees* G.

The latter is further decomposed into two distinct subsets $G_I : state \to bool$ and $G_T : state \to inputs \to state \to bool$. The G_I defines the set of valid initial states, and G_T contains constraints that need to be satisfied in every transition between two states. Importantly, we do not make any distinction between the internal state variables and the output variables in the formalism. This allows us to use the state variables to (in some cases) simplify the specification of guarantees since a contract might not be always defined over all variables in the transition system.

Consequently, we can formally define a realizable contract, as one for which any preceding state s can transition into a new state s' that satisfies the guarantees, assuming valid inputs. For a system to be ever-reactive, these new states s' should be further usable as preceding states in a future transition. States like s and s' are called *viable* if and only if:

$$\text{Viable}(s) = \forall i.(A(s,i) \Rightarrow \exists s'. \; G_T(s,i,s') \wedge \text{Viable}(s')) \tag{1}$$

This equation is recursive and we interpret it coinductively, i.e., as a greatest fixpoint. A necessary condition, finally, is that the intersection of sets of viable states and initial states is non-empty. As such, to conclude that a contract is realizable, we require that

$$\exists s.G_I(s) \wedge \text{Viable}(s) \tag{2}$$

The synthesis problem is therefore to determine an initial state s_i and function $f(s,i)$ such that $G_I(s_i)$ and $\forall s,i.\text{Viable}(s) \Rightarrow \text{Viable}(f(s,i))$.

The intuition behind our proposed algorithm in this paper relies on the discovery of a fixpoint F that only contains viable states. We can determine whether F is a fixpoint by proving the validity of the following formula:

$$\forall s,i. \; (F(s) \wedge A(s,i) \Rightarrow \exists s'.G_T(s,i,s') \wedge F(s'))$$

In the case where the greatest fixpoint F is non-empty, we check whether it satisfies G_I for some initial state. If so, we proceed by extracting a witnessing initial state and witnessing skolem function $f(s,i)$ to determine s' that is, by construction, guaranteed to satisfy the specification.

To achieve both the fixpoint generation and the witness extraction, we depend on AE-VAL, a solver for $\forall\exists$-formulas.

3.1 Skolem Functions and Regions of Validity

We rely on the already established algorithm to decide the validity of $\forall\exists$-formulas and extract Skolem functions, called AE-VAL [10]. It takes as input a formula $\forall x \,.\, \exists y \,.\, \Phi(x,y)$ where $\Phi(x,y)$ is quantifier-free. To decide its validity, AE-VAL first normalizes $\Phi(x,y)$ to the form $S(x) \Rightarrow T(x,y)$ and then attempts to extend all models of $S(x)$ to models of $T(x,y)$. If such an extension is possible, then the input formula is valid, and a relationship between x and y are gathered in a

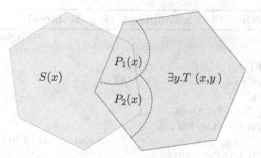

Fig. 2. Region of validity computed for an example requiring AE-VAL to iterate two times.

Skolem function. Otherwise the formula is invalid, and no Skolem function exists. We refer the reader to [19] for more details on the Skolem-function generation.

Our approach presented in this paper relies on the fact that during each run, AE-VAL iteratively creates a set of formulas $\{P_i(x)\}$, such that each $P_i(x)$ has a common model with $S(x)$ and $P_i(x) \Rightarrow \exists y \,.\, T(x,y)$. After n iterations, AE-VAL establishes a formula $R_n(x) \stackrel{\text{def}}{=} \bigvee_{i=1}^{n} P_i(x)$ which by construction implies $\exists y \,.\, T(x,y)$. If additionally $S(x) \Rightarrow R_n(x)$, the input formula is valid, and the algorithm terminates. Figure 2 shows a Venn diagram for an example of the opposite scenario: $R_2(x) = T_1(x) \vee T_2(x)$, but the input formula is invalid. However, models of each $S(x) \wedge P_i(x)$ can still be extended to a model of $T(x,y)$.

In general, if after n iterations $S(x) \wedge T(x,y) \wedge \neg R_n(x)$ is unsatisfiable, then AE-VAL terminates. Note that the formula $\forall x.\ S(x) \wedge R_n(x) \Rightarrow \exists y.\ T(x,y)$ is valid by construction at any iteration of the algorithm. We say that $R_n(x)$ is a *region of validity*, and in this work, we are interested in the *maximal* regions of validity, i.e., the ones produced by disjoining all $\{P_i(x)\}$ produced by AE-VAL before termination and by conjoining it with $S(x)$. Throughout the paper, we assume that all regions of validity are maximal.

Lemma 1. *Let $R_n(x)$ be the region of validity returned by AE-VAL for formula* $\forall s.\ S(x) \Rightarrow \exists y \,.\, T(x,y)$. *Then* $\forall x.\ S(x) \Rightarrow (R_n(x) \Leftrightarrow \exists y \,.\, T(x,y))$.

Proof. ($\Rightarrow$) By construction of $R_n(x)$.

($\Leftarrow$) Suppose towards contradiction that the formula does not hold. Then there exists x_0 such that $S(x_0) \wedge (\exists y.T(x_0,y)) \wedge \neg R_n(x_0)$ holds. But this is a direct contradiction for the termination condition for AE-VAL. Therefore the original formula does hold.

4   Validity-Guided Synthesis from Assume-Guarantee Contracts

Algorithm 1, named JSYN-VG (for *validity guided*), shows the validity-guided technique that we use towards the automatic synthesis of implementations.

Algorithm 1. JSYN-VG (A: assumptions, G: guarantees)

1: $F(s) \leftarrow true$;   ▷ Fixpoint of viable states
2: **while** *true* **do**
3:     $\phi \leftarrow \forall s, i. \ (F(s) \wedge A(s,i) \Rightarrow \exists s'.G_T(s,i,s') \wedge F(s'))$;
4:     $\langle valid, validRegion, Skolem \rangle \leftarrow \text{AE-VAL}(\phi)$;
5:     **if** *valid* **then**
6:         **if** $\exists s.G_I(s) \wedge F(s)$ **then**
7:             **return** $\langle \text{REALIZABLE}, Skolem, s, F \rangle$;
8:         **else**   ▷ Empty set of initial or viable states
9:             **return** UNREALIZABLE;
10:    **else**   ▷ Extract region of validity $Q(s,i)$
11:        $Q(s,i) \leftarrow validRegion$;
12:        $\phi' \leftarrow \forall s. \ (F(s) \Rightarrow \exists i.A(s,i) \wedge \neg Q(s,i))$;
13:        $\langle \_, violatingRegion, \_ \rangle \leftarrow \text{AE-VAL}(\phi')$;
14:        $W(s) \leftarrow violatingRegion$;
15:        $F(s) \leftarrow F(s) \wedge \neg W(s)$;   ▷ Refine set of viable states

The specification is written using the Assume-Guarantee convention that we described in Sect. 3 and is provided as an input. The algorithm relies on AE-VAL, for each call of which we write $\langle x, y, z \rangle \leftarrow \text{AE-VAL}(\ldots)$: x specifies if the given formula is *valid* or *invalid*, y identifies the region of validity (in both cases), and z – the Skolem function (only in case of the validity).

The algorithm maintains a formula $F(s)$ which is initially assigned *true* (line 1). It then attempts to strengthen $F(s)$ until it only contains viable states (recall Eqs. 1 and 2), i.e., a greatest fixpoint is reached. We first encode Eq. 1 in a formula ϕ and then provide it as input to AE-VAL (line 4) which determines its validity (line 5). If the formula is valid, then a witness *Skolem* is non-empty. By construction, it contains valid assignments to the existentially quantified variables of ϕ. In the context of viability, this witness is capable of providing viable states that can be used as a safe reaction, given an input that satisfies the assumptions.

With the valid formula ϕ in hand, it remains to check that the fixpoint intersects with the initial states, i.e., to find a model of formula in Eq. 2 by a simple satisfiability check. If a model exists, it is directly combined with the extracted witness and used towards an implementation of the system, and the algorithm terminates (line 7). Otherwise, the contract is unrealizable since either there are no states that satisfy the initial state guarantees G_I, or the set of viable states F is empty.

If ϕ is not true for every possible assignment of the universally quantified variables, AE-VAL provides a *region of validity* $Q(s,i)$ (line 11). At this point, one might assume that $Q(s,i)$ is sufficient to restrict F towards a solution. This is not the case since $Q(s,i)$ creates a subregion involving both state and input variables. As such, it may contain constraints over the contract's inputs above what are required by A, ultimately leading to implementations that only work correctly for a small part of the input domain.

Fortunately, we can again use AE-VAL's capability of providing regions of validity towards removing inputs from Q. Essentially, we want to remove those states from Q if even one input causes them to violate the formula on line 3. We denote by W the *violating region* of Q. To construct W, AE-VAL determines the validity of formula $\phi' \leftarrow \forall s.\ (F(s) \Rightarrow \exists i.A(s,i) \wedge \neg Q(s,i))$ (line 12) and computes a new region of validity.

If ϕ' is invalid, it indicates that there are still non-violating states (i.e., outside W) that may lead to a fixpoint. Thus, the algorithm removes the unsafe states from $F(s)$ in line 15, and iterates until a greatest fixpoint for $F(s)$ is reached. If ϕ' is valid, then every state in $F(s)$ is unsafe, under a specific input that satisfies the contract assumptions (since $\neg Q(s,i)$ holds in this case), and the specification is unrealizable (i.e., in the next iteration, the algorithm will reach line 9).

4.1   Soundness

Lemma 2. Viable $\Rightarrow F$ *is an invariant for Algorithm 1.*

Proof. It suffices to show this invariant holds each time F is assigned. On line 1, this is trivial. For line 15, we can assume that Viable $\Rightarrow F$ holds prior to this line. Suppose towards contradiction that the assignment on line 15 violates the invariant. Then there exists s_0 such that $F(s_0)$, $W(s_0)$, and Viable(s_0) all hold. Since W is the region of validity for ϕ' on line 12, we have $W(s_0) \wedge F(s_0) \Rightarrow \exists i.A(s_0,i) \wedge \neg Q(s_0,i)$ by Lemma 1. Given that $W(s_0)$ and $F(s_0)$ hold, let i_0 be such that $A(s_0,i_0)$ and $\neg Q(s_0,i_0)$ hold. Since Q is the region of validity for ϕ on line 3, we have $F(s_0) \wedge A(s_0,i_0) \wedge \exists s'.G_T(s_0,i_0,s') \wedge F(s') \Rightarrow Q(s_0,i_0)$ by Lemma 1. Since $F(s_0)$, $A(s_0,i_0)$ and $\neg Q(s_0,i_0)$ hold, we conclude that $\exists s'.G_T(s_0,i_0,s') \wedge F(s') \Rightarrow \perp$. We know that Viable $\Rightarrow F$ holds prior to line 15, thus $\exists s'.G_T(s_0,i_0,s') \wedge$ Viable$(s') \Rightarrow \perp$. But this is a contradiction since Viable(s_0) holds. Therefore the invariant holds on line 15.

Theorem 1. *The* REALIZABLE *and* UNREALIZABLE *results of Algorithm 1 are sound.*

Proof. If Algorithm 1 terminates, then the formula for ϕ on line 3 is valid. Rewritten, F satisfies the formula

$$\forall s.\ F(s) \Rightarrow (\forall i.\ A(s,i) \Rightarrow \exists s'.G_T(s,i,s') \wedge F(s')). \tag{3}$$

Let the function f be defined over state predicates as

$$f = \lambda V.\lambda s.\ \forall i.\ A(s,i) \Rightarrow \exists s'.G_T(s,i,s') \wedge V(s'). \tag{4}$$

State predicates are equivalent to subsets of the state space and form a lattice in the natural way. Moreover, f is monotone on this lattice. From Eq. 3 we have $F \Rightarrow f(F)$. Thus F is a post-fixed point of f. In Eq. 1, Viable is defined as the greatest fixed-point of f. Thus $f \Rightarrow$ Viable by the Knaster-Tarski theorem. Combining this with Lemma 2, we have $F =$ Viable. Therefore the check on line 7 is equivalent to the check in Eq. 2 for realizability.

```
const C = 2.0;

-- empty buckets e and e+1 each round
node game(i1,i2,i3,i4,i5: real; e: int) returns (guarantee: bool);
var
  b1, b2, b3, b4, b5 : real;
let
  assert i1 >= 0.0 and i2 >= 0.0 and i3 >= 0.0 and i4 >= 0.0 and i5 >= 0.0;
  assert i1 + i2 + i3 + i4 + i5 = 1.0;

  b1 = 0.0 -> (if (e = 5 or e = 1) then i1 else (pre(b1) + i1));
  b2 = 0.0 -> (if (e = 1 or e = 2) then i2 else (pre(b2) + i2));
  b3 = 0.0 -> (if (e = 2 or e = 3) then i3 else (pre(b3) + i3));
  b4 = 0.0 -> (if (e = 3 or e = 4) then i4 else (pre(b4) + i4));
  b5 = 0.0 -> (if (e = 4 or e = 5) then i5 else (pre(b5) + i5));

  guarantee = b1 <= C and b2 <= C and b3 <= C and b4 <= C and b5 <= C;

  --%REALIZABLE i1, i2, i3, i4, i5;
  --%PROPERTY guarantee;
tel;
```

Fig. 3. An Assume-Guarantee contract for the Cinderella-Stepmother game in Lustre.

4.2 Termination on Finite Models

Lemma 3. *Every loop iteration in Algorithm 1 either terminates or removes at least one state from F.*

Proof. It suffices to show that at least one state is removed from F on line 15. That is, we want to show that $F \cap W \neq \varnothing$ since this intersection is what is removed from F by line 15.

If the query on line 4 is valid, then the algorithm terminates. If not, then there exists a state s^* and input i^* such that $F(s^*)$ and $A(s^*, i^*)$ such that there is no state s' where both $G(s^*, i^*, s')$ and $F(s')$ hold. Thus, $\neg Q(s^*, i^*)$, and $s^* \in violatingRegion$, so $W \neq \varnothing$. Next, suppose towards contradiction that $F \cap W = \varnothing$ and $W \neq \varnothing$. Since W is the region of validity for ϕ' on line 12, we know that F lies completely outside the region of validity and therefore $\forall s. \neg \exists i. A(s, i) \wedge \neg Q(s, i)$ by Lemma 1. Rewritten, $\forall s, i. A(s, i) \Rightarrow Q(s, i)$. Note that Q is the region of validity for ϕ on line 3. Thus A is completely contained within the region of validity and formula ϕ is valid. This is a contradiction since if ϕ is valid then line 15 will not be executed in this iteration of the loop. Therefore $F \cap W \neq \varnothing$ and at least one state is removed from F on line 15.

Theorem 2. *For finite models, Algorithm 1 terminates.*

Proof. Immediately from Lemma 3 and the fact that AE-VAL terminates on finite models [10].

4.3 Applying JSyn-vg to the Cinderella-Stepmother Game

Figure 3 shows one possible interpretation of the contract designed for the instance of the Cinderella-Stepmother game that we introduced in Sect. 2. The contract is expressed in Lustre [18], a language that has been extensively used for specification as well as implementation of safety-critical systems, and is the kernel language in SCADE, a popular tool in model-based development. The contract is defined as a Lustre node game, with a global constant C denoting the bucket capacity. The node describes the game itself, through the problem's input and output variables. The main input is Stepmother's distribution of one unit of water over five different input variables, i1 to i5. While the node contains a sixth input argument, namely e, this is in fact used as the output of the system that we want to implement, representing Cinderella's choice at each of her turns.

We specify the system's inputs i1, . . . , i5 using the REALIZABLE statement and define the contract's assumptions over them: $A(i_1, \ldots, i_5) = (\bigwedge_{k=1}^{5} i_k >= 0.0) \wedge (\sum_{k=1}^{5} i_k = 1.0)$. The assignment to boolean variable guarantee (distinguished via the PROPERTY statement) imposes the guarantee constraints on the buckets' states through the entire duration of the game, using the local variables b1 to b5. Initially, each bucket is empty, and with each transition to a new state, the contents depend on whether Cinderella chose the specific bucket, or an adjacent one. If so, the value of each b_k at the next turn becomes equal to the value of the corresponding input variable i_k. Formally, for the initial state, $G_I(C, b_1, \ldots, b_5) = (\bigwedge_{k=1}^{5} b_k = 0.0) \wedge (\bigwedge_{k=1}^{5} b_k \leq C)$, while the transitional guarantee is $G_T([C, b_1, \ldots, b_5, e], i_1, \ldots, i_5, [C', b_1', \ldots, b_5', e']) = (\bigwedge_{k=1}^{5} b_k' = ite(e = k \vee e = k_{prev}, i_k, b_k + i_k) \wedge (\bigwedge_{k=1}^{5} b_k' \leq C')$, where $k_{prev} = 5$ if $k = 1$, and $k_{prev} = k - 1$ otherwise. Interestingly, the lack of explicit constraints over e, i.e. Cinderella's choice, permits the action of Cinderella skipping her current turn, i.e. she does not choose to empty any of the buckets. With the addition of the guarantee $(e = 1) \vee \ldots \vee (e = 5)$, the contract is still realizable, and the implementation is verifiable, but Cinderella is not allowed to skip her turn anymore.

If the bucket was not covered by Cinderella's choice, then its contents are updated by adding Stepmother's distribution to the volume of water that the bucket already had. The arrow (->) operator distinguishes the initial state (on the left) from subsequent states (on the right), and variable values in the previous state can be accessed using the pre operator. The contract should only be realizable if, assuming valid inputs given by the Stepmother (i.e. positive values to input variables that add up to one water unit), Cinderella can keep reacting indefinitely, by providing outputs that satisfy the guarantees (i.e. she empties buckets in order to prevent overflow in Stepmother's next turn). We provide the contract in Fig. 3 as input to Algorithm 1 which then iteratively attempts to construct a fixpoint of viable states, closed under the transition relation.

Initially $F = true$, and we query AE-VAL for the validity of formula $\forall i_1, \ldots, i_5, b_1, \ldots, b_5 . A(i_1, \ldots, i_5) \Rightarrow \exists b_1', \ldots, b_5', e . G_T(i_1, \ldots, i_5, b_1, \ldots, b_5, b_1', \ldots, b_5', e)$. Since F is empty, there are states satisfying A, for which there is no transition to G_T. In particular, one such counterexample identified by AE-VAL is represented by the set of assignments $cex = \{\ldots, b_4 = 3025, i_4 = 0.2, b_4' = 3025.2, \ldots\}$, where the already overflown bucket b_4 receives additional water during the transition to the next state, violating the contract guarantees. In addition,

AE-VAL provides us with a region of validity $Q(i_1, \ldots, i_5, b_1, \ldots, b_5)$, a formula for which $\forall i_1, \ldots, i_5, b_1, \ldots, b_5 . A(i_1, \ldots, i_5) \wedge Q(i_1, \ldots, i_5, b_1, \ldots, b_5) \Rightarrow \exists b_1', \ldots, b_5', e . G_T(i_1, \ldots, i_5, b_1, \ldots, b_5, b_1', \ldots, b_5', e)$ is valid. Precise encoding of Q is too large to be presented in the paper; intuitively it contains some constraints on $i_1, \ldots, i_5$ and $b_1, \ldots, b_k$ which are stronger than A and which block the inclusion of violating states such as the one described by *cex*.

Since Q is defined over both state and input variables, it might contain constraints over the inputs, which is an undesirable side-effect. In the next step, AE-VAL decides the validity of formula $\forall b_1, \ldots, b_5 . \exists i_1, \ldots, i_5 . A(i_1, \ldots, i_5) \wedge \neg Q(i_1, \ldots, i_5, b_1, \ldots, b_5)$ and extracts a violating region W over $b_1, \ldots, b_5$. Precise encoding of W is also too large to be presented in the paper; and intuitively it captures certain steps in which Cinderella may not take the optimal action. Blocking them leads us eventually to proving the contract's realizability.

From this point on, the algorithm continues following the steps explained above. In particular, it terminates after one more refinement, at depth 2. At that point, the refined version of ϕ is valid, and AE-VAL constructs a witness containing valid reactions to environment behavior. In general, the witness is described through the use of nested *if-then-else* blocks, where the conditions are subsets of the antecedent of the implication in formula ϕ, while the body contains valid assignments to state variables to the corresponding subset.

5   Implementation and Evaluation

The implementation of the algorithm has been added to a branch of the JKIND [13] model checker[1]. JKIND officially supports synthesis using a k-inductive approach, named JSYN [19]. For clarity, we named our validity-guided technique JSYN-VG (i.e., validity-guided synthesis). JKIND uses Lustre [18] as its specification and implementation language. JSYN-VG encodes Lustre specifications in the language of linear real and integer arithmetic (LIRA) and communicates them to AE-VAL[2]. Skolem functions returned by AE-VAL get then translated into an efficient and practical implementation. To compare the quality of implementations against JSYN, we use SMTLIB2C, a tool that has been specifically developed to translate Skolem functions to C implementations[3].

5.1   Experimental Results

We evaluated JSYN-VG by synthesizing implementations for 124 contracts [4] originated from a broad variety of contexts. Since we have been unable to find past work that contained benchmarks directly relevant to our approach, we propose a comprehensive collection of contracts that can be used by the research community for future advancements in reactive system synthesis for contracts that rely on infinite theories. Our benchmarks are split into three categories:

---

[1] The JKIND fork with JSYN-VG is available at https://goo.gl/WxupTe.
[2] The AE-VAL tool is available at https://goo.gl/CbNMVN.
[3] The SMTLIB2C tool is available at https://goo.gl/EvNrAU.
[4] All of the benchmark contracts can be found at https://goo.gl/2p4sT9.

- 59 contracts correspond to various industrial projects, such as a Quad-Redundant Flight Control System, a Generic Patient Controlled Analgesia infusion pump, as well as a collection of contracts for a Microwave model, written by graduate students as part of a software engineering class;
- 54 contracts were initially used for the verification of existing handwritten implementations [16];
- 11 models contain variations of the Cinderella-Stepmother game, as well as examples that we created.

All of the synthesized implementations were verified against the original contracts using JKIND.

The goal of this experiment was to determine the performance and generality of the JSYN-VG algorithm. We compared against the existing JSYN algorithm, and for the Cinderella model, we compared against [2] (this was the only synthesis problem in the paper). We examined the following aspects:

- time required to synthesize an implementation;
- size of generated implementations in lines of code (LoC);
- execution speed of generated C implementations derived from the synthesis procedure; and
- number of contracts that could be synthesized by each approach.

Since JKIND already supports synthesis through JSYN, we were able to directly compare JSYN-VG against JSYN's k-inductive approach. We ran the experiments using a computer with Intel Core i3-4010U 1.70 GHz CPU and 16 GB RAM.

A listing of the statistics that we tracked while running experiments is presented in Table 1. Fig. 4a shows the time allocated by JSYN and JSYN-VG to solve each problem, with JSYN-VG outperforming JSYN for the vast majority of the benchmark suite, often times by a margin greater than 50%. Fig. 4b on the other hand, depicts small differences in the overall size between the synthesized implementations. While it would be reasonable to conclude that there are no noticeable improvements, the big picture is different: solutions by JSYN-VG always require just a single Skolem function, but solutions by JSYN may require several ($k - 1$ to initialize the system, and one for the inductive step). In our evaluation, JSYN proved the realizability of the majority of benchmarks by constructing proofs of length $k = 0$, which essentially means that the entire space of states is an inductive invariant. However, several spikes in Fig. 4b refer to benchmarks, for which JSYN constructed a proof of length $k > 0$, which was significantly longer that the corresponding proof by JSYN-VG. Interestingly, we also noticed cases where JSYN implementations are (insignificantly) shorter. This provides us with another observation regarding the formulation of the problem for $k = 0$ proofs. In these cases, JSYN proves the existence of viable states, starting from a set of *pre-initial* states, where the contract does not need to hold. This has direct implications to the way that the $\forall\exists$-formulas are constructed in JSYN's underlying machinery, where the assumptions are "baked" into the transition relation, affecting thus the performance of AE-VAL.

188   A. Katis et al.

Table 1. Benchmark statistics.

	JSYN	JSYN-VG
Problems solved	113	**124**
Performance (avg - seconds)	5.72	**2.78**
Performance (max - seconds)	352.1	**167.55**
Implementation Size (avg - Lines of Code)	72.88	**70.66**
Implementation Size (max - Lines of Code)	2322	**2142**
Implementation Performance (avg - ms)	57.84	**56.32**
Implementation Performance (max - ms)	485.88	**459.95**

Table 2. Cinderella-Stepmother results.

Game	JSYN-VG			CONSYNTH [2]	
	Impl. Size (LoC)	Impl. Performance (ms)	Time	Time (Z3)	Time (Barcelogic)
Cind (C = 3)	204	128.09	4.5 s	3.2 s	1.2 s
Cind2 (C = 3)	2081	160.87	28.7 s		
Cind (C = 2)	202	133.04	4.7 s	1m 52 s	1m 52 s
Cind2 (C = 2)	1873	182.19	27.2 s		

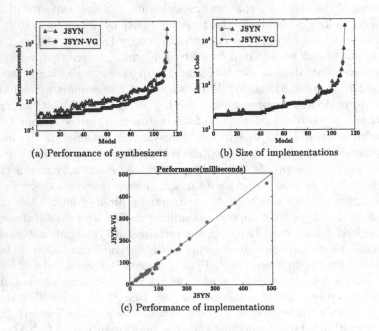

(a) Performance of synthesizers

(b) Size of implementations

(c) Performance of implementations

Fig. 4. Experimental results.

One last statistic that we tracked was the performance of the synthesized C implementations in terms of execution time, which can be seen in Fig. 4c. The performance was computed as the mean of 1000000 iterations of executing each implementation using random input values. According to the figure as well as Table 1, the differences are minuscule on average.

Figure 4 does not cover the entirety of the benchmark suite. From the original 124 problems, eleven of them cannot be solved by JSYN's k-inductive approach. Four of these files are variations of the Cinderella-Stepmother game using different representations of the game, as well as two different values for the bucket capacity (2 and 3). Using the variation in Fig. 3 as an input to JSYN, we receive an "unrealizable" answer, with the counterexample shown in Fig. 5. Reading through the feedback provided by JSYN, it is apparent that the underlying SMT solver is incapable of choosing the correct buckets to empty, leading eventually to a state where an overflow occurs for the third bucket. As we already discussed though, a winning strategy exists for the Cinderella game, as long as the bucket capacity C is between 1.5 and 3. This provides an excellent demonstration of the inherent weakness of JSYN for determining unrealizability. JSYN-VG's validity-guided approach, is able to prove the realizability for these contracts, as well as synthesize an implementation for each.

Table 2 shows how JSYN-VG performed on the four contracts describing the Cinderella-Stepmother game. We used two different interpretations for the game, and exercised both for the cases where the bucket capacity C is equal to 2 and 3. Regarding the synthesized implementations, their size is analogous to the complexity of the program (Cinderella2 contains more local variables and a helper function to empty buckets). Despite this, the implementation performance remains the same across all implementations. Finally for reference, the table contains the results from the template-based approach followed in CON-SYNTH [2]. From the results, it is apparent that providing templates yields better performance for the case of $C = 3$, but our approach overperforms CONSYNTH when it comes to solving the harder case of $C = 2$. Finally, the original paper for CONSYNTH also explores the synthesis of winning strategies for Stepmother using the liveness property that a bucket will eventually overflow. While JKIND does not natively support liveness properties, we successfully synthesized an implementation for Stepmother using a bounded notion of liveness with counters. We leave an evaluation of this category of specifications for future work.

Overall, JSYN-VG's validity-guided approach provides significant advantages over the k-inductive technique followed in JSYN, and effectively expands JKIND's solving capabilities regarding specification realizability. On top of that, it provides an efficient "hands-off" approach that is capable of solving complex games. The most significant contribution, however, is the applicability of this approach, as it is not tied to a specific environment since it can be extended to support more theories, as well as categories of specification.

```
++++++++++++++++++++++++++++++++++++++++++++++++++++++++++++++++++
    UNREALIZABLE || K = 6 || Time = 2.017s
              Step
    variable    0    1      2      3       4      5
    INPUTS
    i1          0    0      0 0.416* 0.944* 0.666*
    i2          1    0 0.083* 0.083*     0 0.055*
    i3          0    1 0.305*    0.5 0.027* 0.194*
    i4          0    0 0.611*     0      0 0.027*
    i5          0    0      0      0 0.027* 0.055*

    OUTPUTS
    e           1    3      1      5      4      5

    NODE OUTPUTS
    guarantee  true true   true   true   true  false

    NODE LOCALS
    b1          0    0      0 0.416* 1.361* 0.666*
    b2          0    0 0.083* 0.166* 0.166* 0.222*
    b3          0    1 1.305* 1.805* 1.833* 2.027*
    b4          0    0 0.611* 0.611*     0 0.027*
    b5          0    0      0      0 0.027* 0.055*

    * display value has been truncated
++++++++++++++++++++++++++++++++++++++++++++++++++++++++++++++++++
```

Fig. 5. Spurious counterexample for Cinderella-Stepmother example using JSYN

6   Related Work

The work presented in this paper is closely related to approaches that attempt to construct infinite-state implementations. Some focus on the continuous interaction of the user with the underlying machinery, either through the use of templates [2,28], or environments where the user attempts to guide the solver by choosing reactions from a collection of different interpretations [26]. In contrast, our approach is completely automatic and does not require human ingenuity to find a solution. Most importantly, the user does not need to be deeply familiar with the problem at hand.

Iterative strengthening of candidate formulas is also used in abductive inference [8] of loop invariants. Their approach generates candidate invariants as maximum universal subsets (MUS) of quantifier-free formulas of the form $\phi \Rightarrow \psi$. While a MUS may be sufficient to prove validity, it may also mislead the invariant search, so the authors use a backtracking procedure that discovers new subsets while avoiding spurious results. By comparison, in our approach the regions of validity are maximal and therefore backtracking is not required. More importantly, reactive synthesis requires mixed-quantifier formulas, and it requires that inputs are unconstrained (other than by the contract assumptions), so substantial modifications to the MUS algorithm would be necessary to apply the approach of [8] for reactive synthesis.

The concept of synthesizing implementations by discovering fixpoints was mostly inspired by the IC3/PDR [4,9], which was first introduced in the context of verification. Work from Cimatti *et al.* effectively applied this idea for the parameter synthesis in the HYCOMP model checker [5,6]. Discovering fixpoints to synthesize reactive designs was first extensively covered by Piterman *et al.* [23] who proved that the problem can be solved in cubic time for the class of GR(1) specifications. The algorithm requires the discovery of least fixpoints for the state variables, each one covering a greatest fixpoint of the input variables. If the specification is realizable, the entirety of the input space is covered by the greatest fixpoints. In contrast, our approach computes a single greatest fixpoint over the system's outputs and avoids the partitioning of the input space. As the tools use different notations and support different logical fragments, practical comparisons are not straightforward, and thus are left for the future.

More recently, Preiner *et al.* presented work on model synthesis [24], that employs a counterexample-guided refinement process [25] to construct and check candidate models. Internally, it relies on enumerative learning, a syntax-based technique that enumerates expressions, checks their validity against ground test cases, and proceeds to generalize the expressions by constructing larger ones. In contrast, our approach is syntax-insensitive in terms of generating regions of validity. In general, enumeration techniques such as the one used in CONSYNTH's underlying E-HSF engine [2] is not an optimal strategy for our class of problems, since the witnesses constructed for the most complex contracts are described by nested if-then-else expressions of depth (i.e. number of branches) 10–20, a point at which space explosion is difficult to handle since the number of candidate solutions is large.

7   Conclusion and Future Work

We presented a novel and elegant approach towards the synthesis of reactive systems, using only the knowledge provided by the system specification expressed in infinite theories. The main goal is to converge to a fixpoint by iteratively blocking subsets of unsafe states from the problem space. This is achieved through the continuous extraction of regions of validity which hint towards subsets of states that lead to a candidate implementation.

This is the first complete attempt, to the best of our knowledge, on handling valid subsets of a ∀∃-formula to construct a greatest fixpoint on specifications expressed using infinite theories. We were able to prove its effectiveness in practice, by comparing it to an already existing approach that focuses on constructing k-inductive proofs of realizability. We showed how the new algorithm performs better than the k-inductive approach, both in terms of performance as well as the soundness of results. In the future, we would like to extend the applicability of this algorithm to other areas in formal verification, such as invariant generation. Another interesting goal is to make the proposed benchmark collection available to competitions such as SYNTCOMP, by establishing a formal extension for the TLSF format to support infinite-state problems [17]. Finally, a particularly interesting challenge is that of mapping infinite theories to finite counterparts, enabling the synthesis of secure and safe implementations.

Data Availability Statement. The datasets generated during and/or analyzed during the current study are available in the figshare repository: https://doi.org/10.6084/m9.figshare.5904904.v1 [20].

References

1. Barrett, C., Fontaine, P., Tinelli, C.: The Satisfiability Modulo Theories Library (SMT-LIB) (2016). www.SMT-LIB.org
2. Beyene, T., Chaudhuri, S., Popeea, C., Rybalchenko, A.: A constraint-based approach to solving games on infinite graphs. In: POPL, pp. 221–233. ACM (2014)
3. Bodlaender, M.H.L., Hurkens, C.A.J., Kusters, V.J.J., Staals, F., Woeginger, G.J., Zantema, H.: Cinderella versus the wicked stepmother. In: Baeten, J.C.M., Ball, T., de Boer, F.S. (eds.) TCS 2012. LNCS, vol. 7604, pp. 57–71. Springer, Heidelberg (2012). https://doi.org/10.1007/978-3-642-33475-7_5
4. Bradley, A.R.: SAT-based model checking without unrolling. In: Jhala, R., Schmidt, D. (eds.) VMCAI 2011. LNCS, vol. 6538, pp. 70–87. Springer, Heidelberg (2011). https://doi.org/10.1007/978-3-642-18275-4_7
5. Cimatti, A., Griggio, A., Mover, S., Tonetta, S.: Parameter synthesis with IC3. In: FMCAD, pp. 165–168. IEEE (2013)
6. Cimatti, A., Griggio, A., Mover, S., Tonetta, S.: HyComp: an SMT-based model checker for hybrid systems. In: Baier, C., Tinelli, C. (eds.) TACAS 2015. LNCS, vol. 9035, pp. 52–67. Springer, Heidelberg (2015). https://doi.org/10.1007/978-3-662-46681-0_4
7. Claessen, K., Sörensson, N.: A liveness checking algorithm that counts. In: Formal Methods in Computer-Aided Design (FMCAD), 2012, pp. 52–59. IEEE (2012)
8. Dillig, I., Dillig, T., Li, B., McMillan, K.: Inductive invariant generation via abductive inference. In: OOPSLA, pp. 443–456. ACM (2013)
9. Een, N., Mishchenko, A., Brayton, R.: Efficient implementation of property directed reachability. In: FMCAD, pp. 125–134. IEEE (2011)
10. Fedyukovich, G., Gurfinkel, A., Sharygina, N.: Automated discovery of simulation between programs. In: Davis, M., Fehnker, A., McIver, A., Voronkov, A. (eds.) LPAR 2015. LNCS, vol. 9450, pp. 606–621. Springer, Heidelberg (2015). https://doi.org/10.1007/978-3-662-48899-7_42
11. Firman, E., Maoz, S., Ringert, J.O.: Performance heuristics for GR(1) synthesis and related algorithms. In: SYNT@CAV. EPTCS, vol. 260, pp. 62–80. Open Publishing Association (2017)
12. Flener, P., Partridge, D.: Inductive programming. Autom. Softw. Eng. 8(2), 131–137 (2001)
13. Gacek, A.: JKind - an infinite-state model checker for safety properties in Lustre (2016). http://loonwerks.com/tools/jkind.html
14. Gacek, A., Katis, A., Whalen, M.W., Backes, J., Cofer, D.: Towards realizability checking of contracts using theories. In: Havelund, K., Holzmann, G., Joshi, R. (eds.) NFM 2015. LNCS, vol. 9058, pp. 173–187. Springer, Cham (2015). https://doi.org/10.1007/978-3-319-17524-9_13
15. Gulwani, S.: Dimensions in program synthesis. In: PPDP, pp. 13–24. ACM (2010)
16. Hagen, G., Tinelli, C.: Scaling up the formal verification of Lustre programs with SMT-based techniques. In: FMCAD, pp. 1–9. IEEE (2008)
17. Jacobs, S., Klein, F., Schirmer, S.: A high-level LTL synthesis format: TLSF v1.1. In: SYNT@CAV. EPTCS, vol. 229, pp. 112–132 (2016)

18. Jahier, E., Raymond, P., Halbwachs, N.: The Lustre V6 reference manual. http://www-verimag.imag.fr/Lustre-V6.html
19. Katis, A., Fedyukovich, G., Gacek, A., Backes, J.D., Gurfinkel, A., Whalen, M.W.: Synthesis from assume-guarantee contracts using Skolemized Proofs of Realizability. CoRR abs/1610.05867 (2016). http://arxiv.org/abs/1610.05867
20. Katis, A., Fedyukovich, G., Guo, H., Gacek, A., Backes, J., Gurfinkel, A., Whalen, M.W.: Validity-guided synthesis of reactive systems from assume-guarantee contracts. Figshare (2018). https://doi.org/10.6084/m9.figshare.5904904.v1
21. Katis, A., Gacek, A., Whalen, M.W.: Towards synthesis from assume-guarantee contracts involving infinite theories: a preliminary report. In: FormaliSE, pp. 36–41. IEEE (2016)
22. Kuncak, V., Mayer, M., Piskac, R., Suter, P.: Functional synthesis for linear arithmetic and sets. STTT **15**(5–6), 455–474 (2013)
23. Piterman, N., Pnueli, A., Saŝar, Y.: Synthesis of reactive(1) designs. In: Emerson, E.A., Namjoshi, K.S. (eds.) VMCAI 2006. LNCS, vol. 3855, pp. 364–380. Springer, Heidelberg (2005). https://doi.org/10.1007/11609773_24
24. Preiner, M., Niemetz, A., Biere, A.: Counterexample-guided model synthesis. In: Legay, A., Margaria, T. (eds.) TACAS 2017. LNCS, vol. 10205, pp. 264–280. Springer, Heidelberg (2017). https://doi.org/10.1007/978-3-662-54577-5_15
25. Reynolds, A., Deters, M., Kuncak, V., Tinelli, C., Barrett, C.: Counterexample-guided quantifier instantiation for synthesis in SMT. In: Kroening, D., Păsareanu, C.S. (eds.) CAV 2015, Part II. LNCS, vol. 9207, pp. 198–216. Springer, Cham (2015). https://doi.org/10.1007/978-3-319-21668-3_12
26. Ryzhyk, L., Walker, A.: Developing a practical reactive synthesis tool: experience and lessons learned. arXiv preprint arXiv:1611.07624 (2016)
27. Ryzhyk, L., Walker, A., Keys, J., Legg, A., Raghunath, A., Stumm, M., Vij, M.: User-guided device driver synthesis. In: OSDI, pp. 661–676 (2014)
28. Srivastava, S., Gulwani, S., Foster, J.S.: Template-based program verification and program synthesis. STTT **15**(5–6), 497–518 (2013)

RVHyper: A Runtime Verification Tool for Temporal Hyperproperties

Bernd Finkbeiner, Christopher Hahn, Marvin Stenger(✉),
and Leander Tentrup

Reactive Systems Group, Saarland University,
Saarbrücken, Germany
{finkbeiner,hahn,stenger,
tentrup}@react.uni-saarland.de

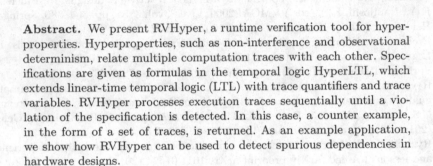

Abstract. We present RVHyper, a runtime verification tool for hyperproperties. Hyperproperties, such as non-interference and observational
determinism, relate multiple computation traces with each other. Specifications are given as formulas in the temporal logic HyperLTL, which
extends linear-time temporal logic (LTL) with trace quantifiers and trace
variables. RVHyper processes execution traces sequentially until a violation of the specification is detected. In this case, a counter example,
in the form of a set of traces, is returned. As an example application,
we show how RVHyper can be used to detect spurious dependencies in
hardware designs.

1 Introduction

Hyperproperties [4] generalize trace properties in that they not only check the
correctness of *individual* computation traces in isolation, but relate *multiple*
computation traces to each other. HyperLTL [3] is a logic for expressing temporal hyperproperties, by extending linear-time temporal logic with *explicit* trace
quantification. HyperLTL has been used to specify a variety of information-
flow and security properties. Examples include classical properties like non-
interference and observational determinism, as well as quantitative information-
flow properties, symmetries in hardware designs, and formally verified error
correcting codes [8]. While model checking and satisfiability checking tools for
HyperLTL already exist [5,8], the *runtime verification* of HyperLTL specifications has so far, despite recent theoretical progress [1,2,7], not been supported
by practical tool implementations.

Monitoring hyperproperties is difficult: in principle, the monitor not only
needs to process every observed trace, but must also *store* every trace observed
so far, so that future traces can be compared with the traces seen so far. On the

This work was partially supported by the German Research Foundation (DFG) as
part of the Collaborative Research Center "Methods and Tools for Understanding
and Controlling Privacy" (SFB 1223) and by the European Research Council (ERC)
Grant OSARES (No. 683300).

D. Beyer and M. Huisman (Eds.): TACAS 2018, LNCS 10806, pp. 194–200, 2018.
https://doi.org/10.1007/978-3-319-89963-3_11

other hand, a runtime verification tool for hyperproperties is certainly useful, in particular if the implementation of a security critical system is not available. Even without access to the source code, monitoring the observable execution traces still detects insecure information flow.

In this paper, we present RVHyper, a runtime verification tool for monitoring temporal hyperproperties. RVHyper tackles this challenging problem by implementing two major optimizations: (1) a *trace analysis*, which detects all redundant traces that can be omitted during the monitoring process and (2) a *specification analysis* to detect exploitable properties of a hyperproperty, such as *symmetry*.

We have applied RVHyper in classical information-flow security, such as checking for violations of observational determinism. HyperLTL is, however, not limited to security policies. As an example of such an application beyond security, we show how RVHyper can be used to detect spurious dependencies in hardware designs.

2 RVHyper

In this section we give an overview on the monitoring approach, including the input and output of the monitoring algorithm and the two major optimization techniques implemented in RVHyper.

Specification. The input to RVHyper is a HyperLTL specification. HyperLTL [3] is a temporal logic for specifying hyperproperties. The logic extends LTL with quantification over trace variables π and a method to link atomic propositions to specific traces. The set of trace variables is $\mathcal{V}$. Formulas in HyperLTL are given by the grammar

$$\varphi ::= \forall \pi. \varphi \mid \exists \pi. \varphi \mid \psi, \text{ and}$$

$$\psi ::= a_\pi \mid \neg \psi \mid \psi \vee \psi \mid \bigcirc \psi \mid \psi \, \mathcal{U} \, \psi,$$

where $a \in \text{AP}$ and $\pi \in \mathcal{V}$. The finite trace semantics [2] for HyperLTL is based on the finite trace semantics of LTL. In the following, when using $\mathcal{L}(\varphi)$ we refer to the finite trace semantics of a HyperLTL formula φ. Let t be a finite trace, ϵ denotes the empty trace, and $|t|$ denotes the length of a trace. Since we are in a finite trace setting, $t[i, \ldots]$ denotes the subsequence from position i to position $|t| - 1$. Let $\Pi_{fin} : \mathcal{V} \to \Sigma^*$ be a partial function mapping trace variables to finite traces. We define $\epsilon[0]$ as the empty set. $\Pi_{fin}[i, \ldots]$ denotes the trace assignment that is equal to $\Pi_{fin}(\pi)[i, \ldots]$ for all π. We define a subsequence of t as follows.

$$t[i, j] = \begin{cases} \epsilon & \text{if } i \geq |t| \\ t[i, min(j, |t| - 1)], & \text{otherwise} \end{cases}$$

$$
\begin{array}{ll}
\Pi_{fin} \vDash_T a_\pi & \text{if } a \in \Pi_{fin}(\pi)[0] \\
\Pi_{fin} \vDash_T \neg \varphi & \text{if } \Pi_{fin} \nvDash_T \varphi \\
\Pi_{fin} \vDash_T \varphi \vee \psi & \text{if } \Pi_{fin} \vDash_T \varphi \text{ or } \Pi_{fin} \vDash_T \psi \\
\Pi_{fin} \vDash_T \bigcirc \varphi & \text{if } \Pi_{fin}[1, \ldots] \vDash_T \varphi \\
\Pi_{fin} \vDash_T \varphi \, \mathcal{U} \, \psi & \text{if } \exists i \geq 0. \, \Pi_{fin}[i, \ldots] \vDash_T \psi \wedge \forall 0 \leq j < i. \, \Pi_{fin}[j, \ldots] \vDash_T \varphi \\
\Pi_{fin} \vDash_T \exists \pi. \varphi & \text{if there is some } t \in T \text{ such that } \Pi_{fin}[\pi \mapsto t] \vDash_T \varphi
\end{array}
$$

input : $\forall^n$ HyperLTL formula φ,
          set of traces T,
          fresh trace t
output: satisfied or n-ary tuple
          witnessing violation

$\mathcal{M}_\varphi = $ build_template(φ);

for *each tuple* $N \in (T \cup \{t\})^n$ **do**
    if $\mathcal{M}_\varphi$ *accepts* N **then**
      | proceed;
    else
      | **return** N;
    end
end
return satisfied;

Algorithm 1. A high-level sketch of the monitoring algorithm for $\forall^n$ HyperLTL formulas.

input : HyperLTL formula φ,
          redundancy free trace set
          T, fresh trace t
output: redundancy free set of
          traces $T_{min} \subseteq T \cup \{t\}$

$\mathcal{M}_\varphi = $ build_template(φ)

foreach $t' \in T$ **do**
    if t' *dominates* t **then**
      | **return** T
    end
end
foreach $t' \in T$ **do**
    if t *dominates* t' **then**
      | $T := T \setminus \{t'\}$
    end
end
return $T \cup \{t\}$

Algorithm 2. Trace analysis algorithm to minimize trace storage.

For example, above mentioned observational determinism can be formalized as the HyperLTL formula $\forall\pi.\forall\pi'.(O_\pi = O_{\pi'})\,\mathcal{W}\,(I_\pi \neq I_{\pi'})$, where $\mathcal{W}$ is the weak version of $\mathcal{U}$.

Input and Output. The input of RVHyper consists of a HyperLTL formula and the observed behavior of the system under consideration. The observed behavior is represented as a trace set T, where each $t \in T$ represents a previously observed execution of the system under consideration. If RVHyper detects that the system violates the hyperproperty, it outputs a counter example, i.e, a k-ary tuple of traces, where k is the number of quantifiers in the HyperLTL formula.

Monitoring Algorithm. Given a HyperLTL formula φ and a trace set T, RVHyper processes a fresh trace under consideration as depicted in Algorithm 1. The algorithm revolves around a *monitor-template* $\mathcal{M}_\varphi$, which is constructed from the HyperLTL formula φ. The basic idea of the monitor template is that it still contains every trace variables of φ, which can be initialized with explicit traces at runtime. This way, the automaton construction of the monitor template is constructed only once as a preprocessing step.

RVHyper initializes the monitor template for each k-ary combination of traces in $T \cup \{t\}$. If one tuple violates the hyperproperty, RVHyper returns that k-ary tuple of traces as a counter example, otherwise RVHyper returns *satisfied*.

Trace Analysis: Minimizing Trace Storage. The main obstacle in monitoring hyperproperties is the potentially unbounded space consumption. RVHyper uses a *trace analysis* to detect redundant traces, with respect to a given Hyper-LTL formula, i.e., traces that can be safely discarded without losing any information and without losing the ability to return a counter example.

RVHyper's trace analysis is based on the definition of trace redundancy: we say a fresh trace t is (T, φ)-redundant, if T is a model of φ if and only if $T \cup \{t\}$ is a model of φ. The idea, depicted in Algorithm 2, is to check if another trace t' contains at least as much informations as t: we say a t' dominates t if $\bigwedge_{\pi \in \mathcal{V}} \mathcal{L}(\mathcal{M}_\varphi[t'/\pi]) \subseteq \mathcal{L}(\mathcal{M}_\varphi[t/\pi])$. For a fresh incoming trace, RVHyper performs this language inclusion check in both directions in order to compute the minimal trace set that must be stored to monitor the hyperproperty under consideration.

Specification Analysis: Decreasing Running Time. RVHyper uses a *specification analysis*, which is a preprocessing step that analyzes the HyperLTL formula under consideration. RVHyper detects whether a formula is (1) *symmetric*, i.e., we halve the number of instantiated monitors, (2) *transitive*, i.e, we reduce the number of instantiated monitors to two, or (3) *reflexive*, i.e., we can omit the self comparison of traces [7].

Symmetry is especially interesting because many information flow policies satisfy this property. Consider, for example, observational determinism: $\forall \pi. \forall \pi'. (O_\pi = O_{\pi'}) \, W \, (I_\pi \neq I_{\pi'})$. RVHyper detects symmetry by translating this formula to a formula that is unsatisfiable if there exists no pair of traces which violates the symmetry condition: $\exists \pi. \exists \pi'. ((O_\pi = O_{\pi'}) \, W \, (I_\pi \neq I_{\pi'}))$ $((O_{\pi'} = O_\pi) W (I_{\pi'} \neq I_\pi))$. If the resulting formula turns out to be unsatisfiable, RVHyper omits the symmetric instantiations of the monitor automaton, which turns out to be, especially in combination with RVHypers *trace analysis*, a major optimization in practice [7].

Implementation. RVHyper[1] is written in C++. It uses *spot* for building the deterministic monitor automata and the *Buddy* BDD library for handling symbolic constraints. We use the HyperLTL satisfiability solver EAHyper [5,6] to determine whether the input formula is reflexive, symmetric, or transitive. Depending on those results, we omit redundant tuples in the monitoring algorithm.

3   Detecting Spurious Dependencies in Hardware Designs

While HyperLTL has been applied to a range of domains, including security and information flow properties, we focus in the following on a classical verification problem, the independence of signals in hardware designs. We demonstrate how RVHyper can automatically detect such dependencies from traces generated from hardware designs.

---

[1] The implementation is available at https://react.uni-saarland.de/tools/rvhyper/.

Input and Output. The input to RVHyper is a set of traces where the propositions match the atomic propositions of the HyperLTL formula. For the following experiments, we generate a set of traces from the Verilog description of several example circuits by random simulation. If a set of traces violates the specification, RVHyper returns a counter example.

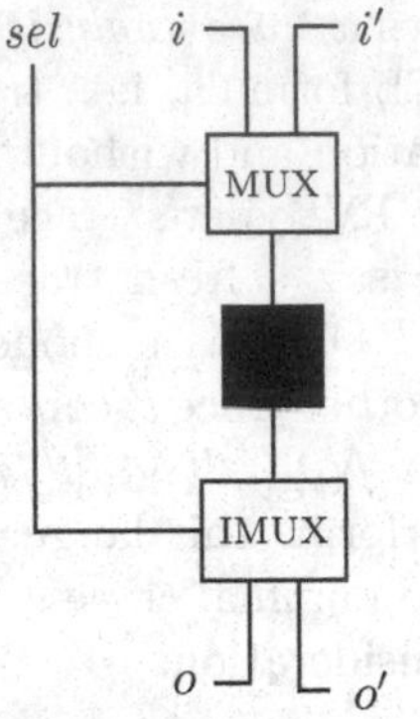

Specification. We consider the problem of detecting whether input signals influence output signals in hardware designs. We write $i \not\rightarrow o$ to denote that the inputs i do not influence the outputs o. Formally, we specify this property as the following HyperLTL formula:

$$\forall \pi_1 \forall \pi_2. (o_{\pi_1} = o_{\pi_2}) \, \mathcal{W} \, (\bar{i}_{\pi_1} \neq \bar{i}_{\pi_2}),$$

where $\bar{i}$ denotes all inputs except i. Intuitively, the formula asserts that for every two pairs of execution traces (π_1, π_2) the value of o has to be the same until there is a difference between π_1 and π_2 in the input vector $\bar{i}$, i.e., the inputs on which o may depend.

Fig. 1. MUX circuit with black box

Sample Hardware Designs. We apply RVHyper to traces generated from the following hardware designs. Note that, since RVHyper observes traces and treats the system that generates the traces as a black box, the performance of RVHyper does not depend on the size of the circuit.

Example 1 (XOR). As a first example, consider the XOR function $o = i \oplus i'$. In the corresponding circuit, every j-th output bit o_j is only influenced by the j-the input bits i_j and i'_j.

Example 2 (MUX). This example circuit is depicted in Fig. 1. There is a black box combinatorial circuit, guarded by a multiplexer that selects between the two input vectors i and i' and an inverse multiplexer that forwards the output of the black box either towards o or o'. Despite there being a syntactic dependency between o and i', there is no semantic dependency, i.e., the output o does solely depend on i and the selector signal.

When using the same example, but with a sequential circuit as black box, there may be information flow from the input vector i' to the output vector o because the state of the latches may depend on it. We construct such a circuit that leaks information about i' via its internal state.

Example 3 (counter). Our last example is a binary counter with two input control bits *incr* and *decr* that increments and decrements the counter. The corresponding Verilog design is shown in Fig. 2. The counter has a single output, namely a signal that is set to one when the counter value overflows. Both inputs influence the output, but timing of the overflow depends on the number of counter bits.

```
1  module counter(increase,        15  begin
2    decrease, overflow);          16    counter = 0;
3  input increase;                 17  end
4  input decrease;                 18  always @($global_clock)
5  output overflow;                19  begin
6                                   20  if (increase && !decrease)
7  reg[2:0] counter;               21    counter = counter + 1;
8                                   22  else if (!increase && decrease
9  assign overflow = (counter      23          && counter > 0)
10    == 3'b111 && increase        24    counter = counter - 1;
11    && !decrease);               25  else
12                                  26    counter = counter;
13                                  27  end
14 initial                         28  endmodule
```

Fig. 2. Verilog description of Example 3 (counter).

Table 1. Results of RVHyper on traces generated from circuit instances. Every instance was run 10 times with different seeds and the average is reported.

Instance	Property	Satisfied	# traces	Length	Time	# instances
XOR	$i_0 \not\leadsto o_0$	no	18	5	12 ms	222
XOR	$i_1 \not\leadsto o_0$	yes	1000	5	16913 ms	499500
counter	$incr \not\leadsto overflow$	no	1636	20	28677 ms	1659446
counter	$decr \not\leadsto overflow$	no	1142	20	15574 ms	887902
MUX	$i' \not\leadsto o$	yes	1000	5	14885 ms	499500
MUX2	$i' \not\leadsto o$	no	82	5	140 ms	3704

Results. The results of multiple random simulations are given in Table 1. Despite the high complexity of the monitoring problem, RVHyper is able to scale up to thousands of input traces with millions of monitor instantiations (cf. Algorithm 1). RVHyper's optimizations, i.e., keeping only a minimal set of traces and reducing the number of instances by the specification analysis, are a key factor to those results. For the two instances where the property is satisfied (XOR and MUX), RVHyper has not found a violation for any of the runs. For instances where the property is violated, RVHyper is able to find counter examples. While counter examples can be found quickly for XOR and MUX2, the counter instances need more traces since the chance of finding a violating pair of traces is lower.

4 Conclusion

RVHyper monitors a running system for violations of a HyperLTL specification. The functionality of RVHyper thus complements model checking tools for HyperLTL, like MCHyper [8], and tools for satisfiability checking, like EAHyper [6]. RVHyper is in particular useful during the development of a HyperLTL specification, where it can be used to check the HyperLTL formula on sample traces without the need for a complete model. Based on the feedback of the tool, the user can refine the HyperLTL formula until it captures the intended policy.

References

1. Agrawal, S., Bonakdarpour, B.: Runtime verification of k-safety hyperproperties in HyperLTL. In: Proceedings of CSF, pp. 239–252. IEEE Computer Society (2016)
2. Brett, N., Siddique, U., Bonakdarpour, B.: Rewriting-based runtime verification for alternation-free HyperLTL. In: Legay, A., Margaria, T. (eds.) TACAS 2017. LNCS, vol. 10206, pp. 77–93. Springer, Heidelberg (2017). https://doi.org/10.1007/978-3-662-54580-5_5
3. Clarkson, M.R., Finkbeiner, B., Koleini, M., Micinski, K.K., Rabe, M.N., Sánchez, C.: Temporal logics for hyperproperties. In: Abadi, M., Kremer, S. (eds.) POST 2014. LNCS, vol. 8414, pp. 265–284. Springer, Heidelberg (2014). https://doi.org/10.1007/978-3-642-54792-8_15
4. Clarkson, M.R., Schneider, F.B.: Hyperproperties. J. Comput. Secur. 18(6), 1157–1210 (2010)
5. Finkbeiner, B., Hahn, C.: Deciding hyperproperties. In: Proceedings of CONCUR, LIPIcs, vol. 59, pp. 13:1–13:14. Leibniz-Zentrum fuer Informatik (2016)
6. Finkbeiner, B., Hahn, C., Stenger, M.: EAHyper: satisfiability, implication, and equivalence checking of hyperproperties. In: Majumdar, R., Kunčak, V. (eds.) CAV 2017. LNCS, vol. 10427, pp. 564–570. Springer, Cham (2017). https://doi.org/10.1007/978-3-319-63390-9_29
7. Finkbeiner, B., Hahn, C., Stenger, M., Tentrup, L.: Monitoring hyperproperties. In: Lahiri, S., Reger, G. (eds.) RV 2017. LNCS, vol. 10548, pp. 190–207. Springer, Cham (2017). https://doi.org/10.1007/978-3-319-67531-2_12
8. Finkbeiner, B., Rabe, M.N., Sánchez, C.: Algorithms for model checking HyperLTL and HyperCTL*. In: Kroening, D., Păsăreanu, C.S. (eds.) CAV 2015. LNCS, vol. 9206, pp. 30–48. Springer, Cham (2015). https://doi.org/10.1007/978-3-319-21690-4_3

The Refinement Calculus of Reactive Systems Toolset

Iulia Dragomir[1](✉), Viorel Preoteasa[2](✉), and Stavros Tripakis[2,3](✉)

[1] Univ. Grenoble Alpes, CNRS,
Grenoble INP, VERIMAG, Grenoble, France
iulia.dragomir@univ-grenoble-alpes.fr
[2] Aalto University, Espoo, Finland
[3] University of California, Berkeley, USA

Abstract. We present the Refinement Calculus of Reactive Systems Toolset, an environment for compositional modeling and reasoning about reactive systems, built on top of Isabelle, Simulink, and Python.

1 Introduction

The *Refinement Calculus of Reactive Systems* (RCRS) is a compositional framework for modeling and reasoning about reactive systems. RCRS has been inspired by component-based frameworks such as interface automata [3] and has its origins in the theory of relational interfaces [14]. The theory of RCRS has been introduced in [13] and is thoroughly described in [11].

RCRS comes with a publicly available toolset, the *RCRS toolset* (Fig. 1), which consists of:

- A full implementation of RCRS in the Isabelle proof assistant [9].
- A set of analysis procedures for RCRS components, implemented on top of Isabelle and collectively called the *Analyzer*.
- A *Translator* of Simulink diagrams into RCRS code.
- A *library* of basic RCRS components, including a set of basic Simulink blocks modeled in RCRS.

An extended version of this paper contains an additional six-page appendix describing a demo of the RCRS toolset [6]. The extended paper can also be found in a figshare repository [7]. The figshare repository contains all data (code and models) required to reproduce all results of this paper as well as of [6]: see Section "Data Availability Statement" for more details. The RCRS toolset can be downloaded also from the RCRS web page: http://rcrs.cs.aalto.fi/.

This work has been supported by the Academy of Finland and the U.S. National Science Foundation (awards #1329759 and #1139138).
I. Dragomir—Partially supported by the H2020 Programme SRC ESROCOS and ERGO projects.
Grenoble INP—Institute of Engineering Univ. Grenoble Alpes.

D. Beyer and M. Huisman (Eds.): TACAS 2018, LNCS 10806, pp. 201–208, 2018.
https://doi.org/10.1007/978-3-319-89963-3_12

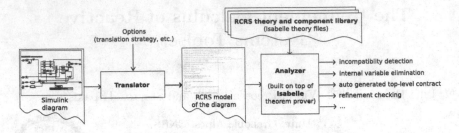

Fig. 1. The RCRS toolset.

2   Modeling Systems in RCRS

RCRS provides a language of *components* to model systems in a modular fashion. Components can be either *atomic* or *composite*. Here are some examples of atomic RCRS components:

```
definition "Id = [: x ⤳ y . y = x :]"
definition "Add = [: (x, y) ⤳ z . z = x + y :]"
definition "Constant c = [: x::unit ⤳ y . y = c :]"
definition "UnitDelay = [: (x,s) ⤳ (y,s') . y = s ∧ s' = x :]"
definition "SqrRoot = {. x . x ≥ 0 .} o [- x ⤳ √x -]"
definition "NonDetSqrt = {. x . x ≥ 0 .} o [: x ⤳ y . y ≥ 0 :]"
definition "ReceptiveSqrt = [: x ⤳ y . x ≥ 0 ⟶ y = √x :]"
definition "A = {. x . □◇x .} o [: x ⤳ y . □◇y :]"
```

Id models the identity function: it takes input x and returns y such that $y = x$. Add returns the sum of its two inputs. Constant is parameterized by c, takes no input (equivalent to saying that its input variable is of type unit), and returns an output which is always equal to c. UnitDelay is a *stateful* component: s is the current-state variable and s' is the next-state variable. SqrRoot is a *non-input-receptive* component: its input x is required to satisfy x≥0. (SqrRoot may be considered non-atomic as it is defined as the serial composition of two predicate transformers – see Sect. 3.) NonDetSqrt is a *non-deterministic* version of SqrRoot: it returns an arbitrary (but non-negative) y, and not necessarily the square-root of x. ReceptiveSqrt is an input-receptive version of SqrRoot: it accepts negative inputs, but may return an arbitrary output for such inputs. RCRS also allows to describe components using the temporal logic QLTL, an extension of LTL with quantifiers [11]. An example is component A above. A accepts an infinite input sequence of x's, provided x is infinitely often true, and returns a (non-deterministic) output sequence which satisfies the same property.

Composite components are formed by composing other (atomic or composite) components using three primitive composition operators, as illustrated in Fig. 2: $C \circ C'$ (in series) connects outputs of C to inputs of C'; C ** C' (in parallel) "stacks" C and C' "on top of each other"; and feedback(C) connects the first

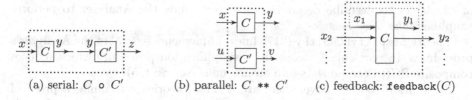

(a) serial: $C \circ C'$ (b) parallel: $C ** C'$ (c) feedback: feedback(C)

Fig. 2. The three composition operators of RCRS.

output of C to its first input. These operators are sufficient to express any block diagram, as described in Sect. 4.

3   The Implementation of RCRS in Isabelle

RCRS is fully implemented in the Isabelle theorem prover. The RCRS implementation currently consists of 22 Isabelle *theories* (.thy files), totalling 27588 lines of Isabelle code. Some of the main theories are described next.

Theory.Refinement.thy (1209 lines) contains a standard implementation of refinement calculus [1]. Systems are modeled as monotonic predicate transformers [4] with a weakest precondition interpretation. Within this theory we implemented non-deterministic and deterministic update statements, assert statements, parallel composition, refinement and other operations, and proved necessary properties of these.

Theory RefinementReactive.thy (1144 lines) extends Reactive.thy to reactive systems by introducing predicates over infinite traces in addition to predicates over values, and *property* transformers in addition to predicate transformers [11,13].

Theory Temporal.thy (788 lines) implements a semantic version of QLTL, where temporal operators are interpreted as predicate transformers. For example, the operator $\Box$, when applied to the predicate on infinite traces $(x > 0)$: (nat $\rightarrow$ real) $\rightarrow$ bool, returns another predicate on infinite traces $\Box(x > 0)$: (nat $\rightarrow$ real) $\rightarrow$ bool. Temporal operators have been implemented to be polymorphic in the sense that they apply to predicates over an arbitrary number of variables.

Theory Simulink.thy (873 lines) defines a subset of the basic blocks in the Simulink library as RCRS components (at the time of writing, 48 Simulink block types can be handled). In addition to discrete-time, we can handle continuous-time blocks with a fixed-step forward Euler integration scheme. For example, Simulink's integrator block can be defined in two equivalent ways as follows:

```
definition "Integrator dt = [- (x,s) ⤳ (s, s+x*dt) -]"
definition "Integrator dt = [: (x,s) ⤳ (y,s'). y=s ∧ s'=s+x*dt :]"
```

The syntax [- x⤳ f(x) -] assumes that f is a function, whereas [: :] can be used also for relations (i.e., non-deterministic systems). Using the former instead of the latter to describe deterministic systems aids the Analyzer to perform simplifications – see Sect. 5.

Theory `SimplifyRCRS.thy` (2175 lines) implements several of the Analyzer's procedures. In particular, it contains a simplification procedure which reduces composite RCRS components into atomic ones (see Sect. 5).

In addition to the above, there are several theories containing a proof of correctness of our block-diagram translation strategies (see Sect. 4 and [10]), dealing with Simulink types [12], generating Python simulation code, and many more. A detailed description of all these theories and graphs depicting their dependencies is included in the documentation of the toolset.

The syntax of RCRS components is implemented in Isabelle using a *shallow embedding* [2]. This has the advantage of all datatypes and other mechanisms of Isabelle (e.g., renaming) being available for component specification, but also the disadvantage of not being able to express properties and simplifications of the RCRS language within Isabelle, as discussed in [11]. A *deep embedding*, in which the syntax of components is defined as a datatype of Isabelle, is possible, and is left as an open future work direction.

4 The Translator

The Translator, called `simulink2isabelle`, translates *hierarchical block diagrams* (HBDs), and in particular Simulink models, into RCRS theories [5]. The Translator (implemented in about 7100 lines of Python code) takes as input a Simulink model (`.slx` file) and a list of options and generates as output an Isabelle theory (`.thy` file). The output file contains: (1) the definition of all instances of basic blocks in the Simulink diagram (e.g., all Adders, Integrators, Constants, etc.) as atomic RCRS components; (2) the bottom-up definition of all subdiagrams as composite RCRS components; (3) calls to simplification procedures; and (4) theorems stating that the resulting simplified components are equivalent to the original ones. The `.thy` file may also contain additional content depending on user options as explained below.

As shown in [5], there are many possible ways to translate a block diagram into an algebra of components with the three primitive composition operators of RCRS. This means that step (2) above is not unique. `simulink2isabelle` implements the several translation strategies proposed in [5] as user options.

For example, when run on the Simulink diagram of Fig. 3, the Translator produces a file similar to the one shown in Fig. 4. `IC_Model` and `FP_Model` are composite RCRS components generated automatically w.r.t. two different translation strategies, implemented by user options `-ic` and `-fp`. The `simplify_RCRS` construct is explained in Sect. 5 that follows.

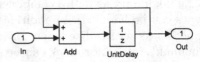

Fig. 3. A Simulink diagram.

Other user options to the Translator include: whether to flatten the input diagram, optional typing information for wires, and whether to generate in addition to the top-level STS component, a QLTL component representing the temporal behavior of the system. The user can also ask the Translator to generate: (1) components w.r.t. all translation strategies; (2) the corresponding theorems showing that these components are all semantically equivalent; and (3) Python simulation scripts for the top-level component.

```
theory Summation imports ...
begin
named_theorems basic_simps
lemmas basic_simps = simulink_simps
definition [basic_simps]: "Split = [- a ⤳ a, a -]"
definition [basic_simps]: "Add = [- f, g ⤳ f + g -]"
definition [basic_simps]: "UnitDelay = [- d, s ⤳ s, d -]"
simplify_RCRS "IC_Model = feedback([- f, g, s ⤳ (f, g), s -] o
    (Add ** Id) o UnitDelay o (Split ** Id) o
    [- (f, h), s' ⤳ f, h, s' -])"
    "(g, s)" "(h, s')"
simplify_RCRS "FP_Model = feedback (feedback (feedback ([- f, d, a, g, s
    ⤳ (f, g), (d, s), a -] o (Add ** UnitDelay ** Split) o
    [- d, (a, s'), (f, h) ⤳ f, d, a, h, s' -])))"
    "(g, s)" "(h, s')"
end
```

Fig. 4. Auto-generated Isabelle theory for the Simulink diagram of Fig. 3

5   The Analyzer

The Analyzer is a set of procedures implemented on top of Isabelle and ML, the programming language of Isabelle. These procedures implement a set of functionalities such as simplification, compatibility checking, refinement checking, etc. Here we describe the main functionalities, implemented by the simplify_RCRS construct. As illustrated in Fig. 4, the general usage of this construct is simplify_RCRS "Model = C" "in" "out", where C is a (generally composite) component and in, out are (tuples of) names for its input and output variables. When such a statement is executed in Isabelle, it performs the following steps: (1) It creates the definition Model = C. (2) It *expands* C, meaning that it replaces all atomic components and all composition operators in C with their definitions. This results in an Isabelle expression E. E is generally a complicated expression, containing formulas with quantifiers, case expressions for tuples, function compositions, and several other operators. (3) simplify_RCRS *simplifies* E, by eliminating quantifiers, renaming variables, and performing several other simplifications. The simplified expression, F, is of the form {.p.} o [:r:], where p is a predicate on input variables and r is a relation on input and output variables. That is, F is an atomic RCRS component. (4) simplify_RCRS generates a theorem stating that Model is semantically equivalent to F, and also the mechanized proof of this theorem (in Isabelle). Note that the execution by the Analyzer of the .thy file generated by the Translator is fully automatic, despite the fact that Isabelle generally requires human interaction. This is thanks to the fact that the theory generated by the Translator contains all declarations (equalities, rewriting rules, etc.) neccessary for the Analyzer to produce the simplifications and their mechanical proofs, without user interaction.

For example, when the theory in Fig. 4 is executed, the following theorem is generated and proved automatically:

$$\text{Model} = [- \; (g, \; s) \rightsquigarrow (s, \; s+g) \; -]$$

where Model is either IC_Model or FP_Model. The rightmost expression is the automatically generated simplification of the top-level system to an atomic RCRS component.

If the model contains *incompatibilities*, where for instance the input condition of a block like SqrRoot cannot be guaranteed by the upstream diagram, the top-level component automatically simplifies to $\perp$ (i.e., false). Thus, in this usage scenario, RCRS can be seen as a static analysis and behavioral type checking and inference tool for Simulink.

6 Case Study

We have used the RCRS toolset on several case studies, the most significant of which is a real-world benchmark provided by Toyota [8]. The benchmark consists of a set of Simulink diagrams modeling a Fuel Control System.[1] A typical diagram in the above suite contains 3 levels of hierarchy, 104 Simulink blocks in total (out of which 8 subsystems), and 101 wires (out of which 8 are feedbacks, the most complex composition operator in RCRS). Using the Translator on this diagram results in a .thy file of 1671 lines and 57037 characters. Translation time is negligible. The Analyzer simplifies this model to a top-level atomic STS component with no inputs, 7 (external) outputs and 14 state variables (note that all internal wires have been automatically eliminated in this top-level description). Simplification takes approximately 15 seconds and generates a formula which is 8337 characters long. The formula is consistent (not false), which proves statically that the original Simulink diagram has no incompatibilities. More details about the case study can be found in [5,6].

---

[1] We downloaded the Simulink models from https://cps-vo.org/group/ARCH/benchmarks. One of those models is made available in the figshare repository [7] – see also Section "Data Availability Statement".

7   Data Availability Statement

All results mentioned in this paper as well as in the extended version of this paper [6] are fully reproducible using the code, data, and instructions available in the figshare repository: https://doi.org/10.6084/m9.figshare.5900911.v1.

The figshare repository contains the full implementation of the RCRS toolset, including the formalization of RCRS in Isabelle, the Analyzer, the RCRS Simulink library, and the Translator. The figshare repository also contains sample Simulink models, including the Toyota model discussed in Sect. 6, a demo file named RCRS_Demo.thy, and detailed step-by-step instructions on how to conduct a demonstration and how to reproduce the results of this paper. Documentation on RCRS is also provided.

The figshare repository provides a snapshot of RCRS as of February 2018. Further developments of RCRS will be reflected on the RCRS web page: http://rcrs.cs.aalto.fi/.

References

1. Back, R.-J., von Wright, J.: Refinement Calculus. Springer, Heidelberg (1998)
2. Boulton, R.J., Gordon, A., Gordon, M.J.C., Harrison, J., Herbert, J., Tassel, J.V.: Experience with embedding hardware description languages in HOL. In: IFIP TC10/WG 10.2 International Conference on Theorem Provers in Circuit Design, pp. 129–156. North-Holland Publishing Co., Amsterdam (1992)
3. de Alfaro, L., Henzinger, T.: Interface automata. In: Foundations of Software Engineering (FSE). ACM Press, New York (2001)
4. Dijkstra, E.: Guarded commands, nondeterminacy and formal derivation of programs. Comm. ACM **18**(8), 453–457 (1975)
5. Dragomir, I., Preoteasa, V., Tripakis, S.: Compositional semantics and analysis of hierarchical block diagrams. In: Bošnački, D., Wijs, A. (eds.) SPIN 2016. LNCS, vol. 9641, pp. 38–56. Springer, Cham (2016). https://doi.org/10.1007/978-3-319-32582-8_3
6. Dragomir, I., Preoteasa, V., Tripakis, S.: The Refinement Calculus of Reactive Systems Toolset. CoRR, abs/1710.08195:1–12 (2017)
7. Dragomir, I., Preoteasa, V., Tripakis, S.: The Refinement Calculus of Reactive Systems Toolset, February 2018. figshare. https://doi.org/10.6084/m9.figshare.5900911.v1
8. Jin, X., Deshmukh, J.V., Kapinski, J., Ueda, K., Butts, K.: Powertrain control verification benchmark. In: Proceedings of the 17th International Conference on Hybrid Systems: Computation and Control, HSCC 2014, pp. 253–262. ACM (2014)
9. Nipkow, T., Wenzel, M., Paulson, L.C. (eds.): Isabelle/HOL. LNCS, vol. 2283. Springer, Heidelberg (2002). https://doi.org/10.1007/3-540-45949-9
10. Preoteasa, V., Dragomir, I., Tripakis, S.: A nondeterministic and abstract algorithm for translating hierarchical block diagrams. CoRR, abs/1611.01337 (2016)
11. Preoteasa, V., Dragomir, I., Tripakis, S.: The Refinement Calculus of Reactive Systems. CoRR, abs/1710.03979 (2017)
12. Preoteasa, V., Dragomir, I., Tripakis, S.: Type inference of Simulink hierarchical block diagrams in Isabelle. In: Bouajjani, A., Silva, A. (eds.) FORTE 2017. LNCS, vol. 10321, pp. 194–209. Springer, Cham (2017). https://doi.org/10.1007/978-3-319-60225-7_14

13. Preoteasa, V., Tripakis, S.: Refinement calculus of reactive systems. In: 2014 International Conference on Embedded Software (EMSOFT), pp. 1–10, October 2014
14. Tripakis, S., Lickly, B., Henzinger, T.A., Lee, E.A.: A theory of synchronous relational interfaces. ACM TOPLAS **33**(4), 14:1–14:41 (2011)

Static and Dynamic Program Analysis

TESTOR: A Modular Tool for On-the-Fly Conformance Test Case Generation

Lina Marsso[✉], Radu Mateescu, and Wendelin Serwe

Univ. Grenoble Alpes, Inria, CNRS, Grenoble INP*, LIG, 38000 Grenoble, France
Lina.Marsso@inria.fr

Abstract. We present TESTOR, a tool for on-the-fly conformance test case generation, guided by test purposes. Concretely, given a formal specification of a system and a test purpose, TESTOR automatically generates test cases, which assess using black box testing techniques the conformance to the specification of a system under test. In this context, a test purpose describes the goal states to be reached by the test and enables one to indicate parts of the specification that should be ignored during the testing process. Compared to the existing tool TGV, TESTOR has a more modular architecture, based on generic graph transformation components, is capable of extracting a test case completely on the fly, and enables a more flexible expression of test purposes, taking advantage of the multiway rendezvous. TESTOR has been implemented on top of the CADP verification toolbox, evaluated on three published case-studies and more than 10000 examples taken from the non-regression test suites of CADP.

1 Introduction

Model-Based Testing [7] is a validation technique taking advantage of a model of a system (both, requirements and behavior) to automate the generation of relevant test cases. This technique is suitable for complex industrial systems, such as embedded systems [45] and automotive software [35]. Using formal models for testing is required for certification of safety-critical systems [36]. Conformance testing aims at extracting from a formal model of a system a set of test cases to assess whether an actual implementation of the system under test (SUT) is conform to the model, using black-box testing techniques (i.e., without knowledge of the actual code of the SUT). This approach is particularly suited for nondeterministic concurrent systems, where the behavior of the SUT can be observed and controlled by a tester only via dedicated interfaces, named points of control and observation.

Often, the formal model is an IOLTS (Input/Output Labeled Transition System), where transitions between states of the system are labeled with an action classified as input, output, or internal (i.e., unobservable, usually denoted by τ).

---

* Institute of Engineering Univ. Grenoble Alpes.

© The Author(s) 2018
D. Beyer and M. Huisman (Eds.): TACAS 2018, LNCS 10806, pp. 211–228, 2018.
https://doi.org/10.1007/978-3-319-89963-3_13

In this setting, the most prominent conformance relation is input-output conformance (**ioco**) [39,41]. The theory underlying **ioco** is well established, implemented in several tools [1,2,22,25,28], and still actively used, as witnessed by a series of recent case studies [9,10,20,27,38].

As regards asynchronous systems, i.e., systems consisting of concurrent processes with message-passing communication, there exist two different approaches to model-based conformance testing: *coverage-oriented approaches* run the test(s) to stimulate the SUT until a coverage goal has been reached, whereas *test purpose guided approaches* use test suites, each test of which terminates with a verdict (passed, failed, or inconclusive). The generation of tests from the model can be carried out *offline*, before executing them against the SUT, or *online* [28] during their execution, by combining the exploration of the model and the interaction with the SUT.

In this paper, we present TESTOR, a tool for on-the-fly conformance test case generation guided by test purposes, which, following the approach of TGV [25], characterize some state(s) of the model as accepting. The generated test cases are automata that attempt to drive a SUT towards these states. TESTOR extends the algorithms of TGV to extract test cases completely on the fly (i.e., during test case execution against the SUT), making TESTOR suitable for online testing. TESTOR is constructed following a modular architecture based on generic, recent, and optimized graph manipulation components. This also makes the description of test purposes more convenient, by replacing the specific synchronous product of TGV and taking advantage of the multiway rendezvous [18,23], a powerful primitive to express communication and synchronization among a set of distributed processes. TESTOR was built on top of the OPEN/CAESAR [15] generic environment for on-the-fly graph manipulation provided by the CADP [16] verification toolbox.

The remainder of the paper is organized as follows. Section 2 recalls the essential notions of the underlying theory. Section 3 presents the architecture, main algorithms, and implementation of TESTOR, and gives some examples. Section 4 describes various experiments to validate TESTOR and compare it to TGV. Section 5 compares TESTOR to existing test generation approaches. Finally, Sect. 6 gives some concluding remarks and future work directions.

2   Background: Essential Definitions of [25]

Conformance testing checks that a SUT behaves according to a formal reference model (M), which is used as an oracle. We use Input-Output Labelled Transition Systems (IOLTS) [25] to represent the behavior of the model M. We assume that the behavior of the SUT can also be represented as an IOLTS, even if it is unknown (the so-called testing hypothesis [25]). An IOLTS (Q, A, T, q_0) consists of a set of states Q, a set of actions A, a transition relation $T \subseteq Q \times A \times Q$, and an initial state $q_0 \in Q$. The set of actions is partitioned in $A = A_I \cup A_O \cup \{\tau\}$, where A_I, A_O are the subsets of input and output actions, and τ is the internal (unobservable) action. A transition $(q_1, b, q_2) \in T$ (also noted $q_1 \xrightarrow{b} q_2$) indicates

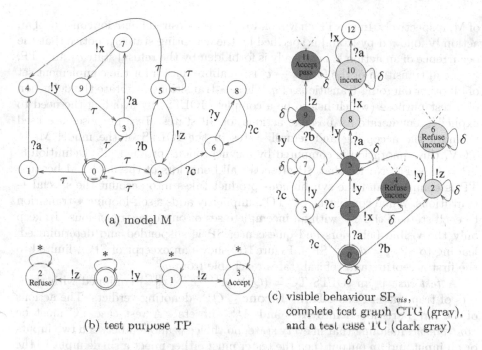

(a) model M

(b) test purpose TP

(c) visible behaviour SP$_{vis}$,
complete test graph CTG (gray),
and a test case TC (dark gray)

Fig. 1. Example of test case selection (taken from [25])

that the system can move from state q_1 to state q_2 by performing action b. Input (resp. output) actions are noted $?a$ (resp. $!a$). In the sequel, we consider the same running example as [25], whose IOLTS model M is shown on Fig. 1(a).

Input actions of the SUT are controllable by the environment, whereas output actions are only observable. Testing allows one to observe the execution traces of the SUT, and also to detect *quiescence*, i.e., the presence of deadlocks (states without successors), outputlocks (states without outgoing output actions), or livelocks (cycles of internal actions). The quiescence present in an IOLTS L (either the model M or the SUT) is modeled by a *suspension automaton* $\Delta(L)$, an IOLTS obtained from L by adding self-loops labeled by a special output action δ on the quiescent states. The SUT conforms to the model M modulo the **ioco** relation [40] if after executing each trace of $\Delta(M)$, the suspension automaton $\Delta(SUT)$ exhibits only those outputs and quiescences that are allowed by the model. Since two sequences having the same observable actions (including quiescence) cannot be distinguished, the suspension automaton $\Delta(M)$ must be determinized before generating tests.

The test generation technique of TGV is based upon *test purposes*, which allow one to guide the selection of test cases. A test purpose for a model $M = (Q^M, A^M, T^M, q_0^M)$ is a deterministic and complete (i.e., in each state all actions are accepted) IOLTS $TP = (Q^{TP}, A^{TP}, T^{TP}, q_0^{TP})$, with the same actions as the model $A^{TP} = A^M$. TP is equipped with two sets of trap states $Accept^{TP}$ and $Refuse^{TP}$, which are used to select desired behaviors and to cut the exploration of M, respectively. In the TP shown on Fig. 1b, the desired behavior consists of an action !y followed by !z and is specified by the accepting state q_3; notice that the occurrence of an action !z before a !y is forbidden by the refusal state q_2. In a TP, a special transition of the form $q \xrightarrow{*} q'$ is an abbreviation for the complement set of all other outgoing transitions of q. These *-transitions facilitate the definition of a test purpose (which has to be a complete IOLTS) by avoiding the need to explicitly enumerate all possible actions for all states. Test purposes are used to mark the accepting and refusal states in the IOLTS of the model M. In TGV, this annotation is computed by a synchronous product [25, Definition 8] $SP = M \times TP$. Notice that SP preserves all behaviors of the model M because TP is complete and the synchronous product takes into account the special *-transitions. When computing SP, TGV implicitly adds a self-looping *-transition to each state of the TP with an incomplete set of outgoing transitions. To keep only the visible behaviors and quiescence, SP is suspended and determinized, leading to $SP_{vis} = det(\Delta(SP))$. Figure 1(c) shows an excerpt of SP_{vis} limited to the first accepting and refusal states reachable from $q_0^{SP_{vis}}$.

A *test case* is an IOLTS $TC = (Q^{TC}, A^{TC}, T^{TC}, q_0^{TC})$ equipped with three sets of trap states **Pass** $\cup$ **Fail** $\cup$ **Inconc** $\subseteq Q^{TC}$ denoting verdicts. The actions of TC are partitioned into A_I^{TC} and A_O^{TC} subsets[1]. A test case TC must be *controllable*, meaning that in every state, no choice is allowed between two inputs or an input and an output (i.e., the tester must either inject a single input to the SUT, or accept all the outputs of the SUT). Intuitively, a TC denotes a set of traces containing visible actions and quiescence that should be executable by the SUT to assess its conformance with the model M and a test purpose TP.From every state of the TC, a verdict must be reachable: **Pass** indicates that TP has been fulfilled, **Fail** indicates that SUT does not conform to M, and **Inconc** indicates that correct behavior has been observed but TP cannot be fulfilled. An example of TC (dark gray states) is shown on Fig. 1(c). Pass verdicts correspond to accepting states (e.g., q_{11}). Inconclusive verdicts correspond either to refusal states (e.g., q_4 or q_6) or to states from which no accepting state is reachable (e.g., state q_{10}). Fail verdicts, not displayed on the figure, are reached from every state when the SUT exhibits an output action (or a quiescence) not specified in the TC (e.g., an action !z or a quiescence in state q_1).

In general, there are several test cases that can be generated from a given model and test purpose. The union of these test cases forms the Complete Test Graph (CTG), which is an IOLTS having the same characteristics as a TC except for controllability. Figure 1(c) shows the CTG (light and dark gray states) corresponding to M and TP, which is not controllable (e.g., in state q_5 the two input actions ?a and ?b are possible). Formally, a CTG is the subgraph of SP_{vis} induced by the states L2A (*lead to accept*) from which an accepting state

---

[1] In TGV [25], the actions of test cases are symmetric w.r.t. those of the model M and the SUT, i.e., $A_O^{TC} \subseteq A_I^M$ (TC emits only inputs of M) and $A_I^{TC} \subseteq A_O^{SUT} \cup \{\delta\}$ (TC captures outputs and quiescences of SUT). To avoid confusion, we consider here that inputs and outputs of TC are the same as those of M and SUT.

is reachable, decorated with pass and inconclusive verdicts. A controllable TC exists iff the CTG is not empty, i.e., $q_0^{SP_{vis}} \in$ L2A [25].

The execution of a TC against the SUT corresponds to a parallel composition TC || SUT with synchronization on common observable actions, verdicts being determined by the trap states reached by a maximal trace of TC || SUT, i.e., a trace leading to a verdict state. Quiescent livelock states (infinite sequences of internal actions in the SUT) are detected using timers, and lead to inconclusive verdicts. A TC may have cycles, in which case global timers are required to prevent infinite test executions.

3   TESTOR

We present the architecture and implementation of TESTOR, its on-the-fly algorithm for test-case extraction, and show several ways of specifying test purposes.

3.1   Architecture

TESTOR takes as input a formal model (M), a test purpose (TP), and a predicate specifying the input/output actions of M. Depending on the chosen options, it produces as output either a complete test graph (CTG), or a test case (TC) extracted on the fly. TESTOR has a modular component-based architecture consisting of several on-the-fly IOLTS transformation components, interconnected according to the architecture shown on Fig. 2. The boxes represent transformation components and the arrows between them denote the implicit representations (*post* functions) of IOLTSs.

The first component produces the synchronous product (SP) between the model M and the test purpose TP. Following the conventions of TGV [25], the synchronous product supports ∗-transitions and implements the implicit addition of self-looping ∗-transitions. The next four reduction components progressively transform SP into $SP_{vis} = det(\Delta(SP))$ as follows: (i) τ-compression produces the suspension automaton $\Delta(SP)$ by squeezing the strongly connected components of τ-transitions and replacing them with δ-loops representing quiescence; (ii) τ-confluence eliminates redundant interleavings by giving priority to confluent τ-transitions, i.e., whose neighbor transitions (going out from the same source state) do not bring new observational behavior; (iii) τ-closure computes the transitive reflexive closure on τ-transitions; (iv) the resulting τ-free IOLTS is determinized by applying the classical subset construction. The reduction by τ-compression is necessary for τ-confluence (which operates on IOLTSs without τ-cycles) and is also useful as a preprocessing step for τ-closure (whose algorithm is simpler in the absence of τ-cycles). Although τ-confluence is optional, it may reduce drastically the size of the IOLTS prior to τ-closure, therefore acting as an accelerator for the whole test selection procedure when SP contains large diamonds of τ-transitions produced by the interleavings of independent actions [31]. The first three reductions [31] are applied only if TESTOR detects the presence of τ-transitions in SP.

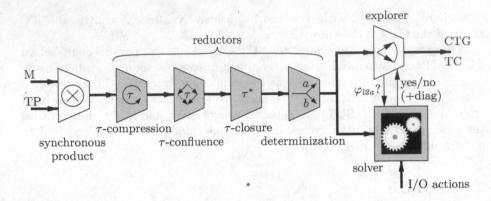

Fig. 2. Architecture of TESTOR

The determinization produces as output the post function of the IOLTS SP_{vis}, whose states correspond to sets of states of the τ-free IOLTS produced by τ-closure. SP_{vis} is processed by the explorer component, which builds the CTG or the TC by computing the corresponding subgraph whose states are contained in L2A. The reachability of accepting states is determined on the fly by evaluating the PDL [14] formula $\varphi_{l2a} = \langle\text{true}^*\rangle\, accept$ on the states visited by the explorer, where the atomic proposition $accept$ denotes the accepting states. This check is done by translating the verification problem into a Boolean equation system (BES) and solving it on the fly using a BES solver component [32]. The synchronous product and the explorer are the only components newly developed, all the other ones (represented in gray on Fig. 2) being already available in the libraries of the OPEN/CAESAR [15] environment of CADP.

3.2 On-the-Fly Test Selection Algorithm

We describe below the algorithm used by the explorer component to extract the CTG or a (controllable) TC from the SP_{vis} IOLTS on the fly.

Basically, the CTG is the subgraph of SP_{vis} containing all states in L2A, extended with some states denoting verdicts. The accepting states (which are by definition part of L2A) correspond to pass verdicts. For every state $q \in$ L2A, the output transitions $q \xrightarrow{!a} q'$ with $q' \notin$ L2A lead to inconclusive verdicts, and the output transitions other than those contained in SP_{vis} lead to fail verdicts. To compute the CTG, the explorer component performs a forward traversal of SP_{vis} and keeps the states $q \in$ L2A, which satisfy the formula φ_{l2a}. The check $q \models \varphi_{l2a}$ is done by solving the variable X_q of the minimal fixed point BES $\{X_q = (q \models accept) \vee \bigvee_{q \xrightarrow{b} q'} X_{q'}\}$ denoting the interpretation of φ_{l2a} on SP_{vis}. The resolution is carried out on the fly using the algorithm for disjunctive BESs proposed in [32]. If the CTG is not empty (i.e., $q_0^{SP_{vis}} \models \varphi_{l2a}$), then it contains at least one controllable TC [25].

The extraction of a TC uses a similar forward traversal as for generating the CTG, extended to ensure controllability, i.e., every state q of TC either has only one outgoing input transition $q \xrightarrow{?a} q'$ with $q' \in$ L2A, or has all output transitions $q \xrightarrow{!a} q''$ of SP_{vis} with $q'' \in$ L2A. The essential ingredient for selecting the input transitions on the fly is the diagnostic generation for BESs [30], which provides, in addition to the Boolean value of a variable, also the minimal fragment (w.r.t. inclusion) of the BES illustrating the value of that variable. For a variable X_q evaluated to true in the disjunctive BES underlying φ_{l2a}, the diagnostic (witness) is a sequence $X_q \xrightarrow{b_1} X_{q_1} \xrightarrow{b_2} \cdots \xrightarrow{b_k} X_{q_k}$ where $q_k \models$ accept. This induces a sequence of transitions $q \xrightarrow{b_1} q_1 \xrightarrow{b_2} \cdots \xrightarrow{b_k} q_k$ in SP_{vis} leading to an accepting state. Since all states $q, q_1, ..., q_k$ also belong to L2A, this diagnostic sequence is naturally part of the TC under construction.

More precisely, the TC extraction algorithm works as follows. If $q_0^{\text{SP}_{vis}} \models \varphi_{l2a}$, the diagnostic sequence for $q_0^{\text{SP}_{vis}}$ is inserted in the TC (otherwise the algorithm stops because the CTG is empty). For the TC illustrated on Fig. 1(c), this first diagnostic sequence is $q_0 \xrightarrow{?a} q_1 \xrightarrow{!y} q_5 \xrightarrow{?b} q_9 \xrightarrow{!z} q_{11}$. Then, the main loop consists in choosing an unexplored transition of the TC and processing it.

- If it is an input transition $q \xrightarrow{?a} q'$, nothing is done, since the target state $q' \in$ L2A by construction. Furthermore, the presence of this transition in the TC makes its source state q controllable. This is the case, e.g., for the transition $q_0 \xrightarrow{?a} q_1$ in the TC shown on Fig. 1(c).
- If it is an output transition $q \xrightarrow{!a} q'$, each of its neighboring output transitions $q \xrightarrow{!a'} q''$ is examined in turn. If the target state $q'' \notin$ L2A, the transition is inserted in TC and q'' is marked with an inconclusive verdict. This is the case, e.g., for the transition $q_1 \xrightarrow{!x} q_4$ in the TC on Fig. 1(c). If $q'' \in$ L2A, the transition in inserted in the TC, together with the diagnostic sequence produced for q''. This is the case, e.g., for the transition $q_9 \xrightarrow{!y} q_5$ in the TC on Fig. 1(c).

The insertion of a diagnostic sequence in the TC stops when it meets a state q that already belongs to the TC, since by construction the TC already contains a sequence starting at q and leading to an accepting state. This is the case, e.g., for the diagnostic sequence starting at state q_5 in the TC on Fig. 1(c). In this way, the TC is built progressively by inserting the diagnostic sequences produced for each of the encountered states in L2A.

During the forward traversal of SP_{vis}, the explorer component continuously interacts with the BES solver, which in turn triggers other forward explorations of SP_{vis} to evaluate φ_{l2a}. The repeated invocations of the solver have a cumulated linear complexity in the size of the BES (and hence, the size of SP_{vis}), because the BES solver keeps its context in memory and does not recompute already solved Boolean variables [32].

3.3 Implementation

TESTOR is built upon the generic libraries of the OPEN/CAESAR [15] environment, in particular the on-the-fly reductions by τ-compression, τ-confluence and τ-closure [31], and the on-the-fly BES resolution [32]. The tool (available at http://convecs.inria.fr/software/testor) consists of 5022 lines of C and 1106 lines of shell script.

3.4 Examples of Different Ways to Express a Test Purpose

Consider an asynchronous implementation of the DES (Data Encryption Standard) [37]. In a nutshell, the DES is a block-cipher taking three inputs: a Boolean indicating whether encryption or decryption is requested, a 64-bit key, and a 64-bit block of data. For each triple of inputs, the DES computes the 64-bit (de)crypted data, performing sixteen iterations of the same cipher function, each iteration with a different 48-bit subkey extracted from the 64-bit key.

A natural TP for the DES is to search for a sequence corresponding to the encryption of a single data block, for instance 0x0123456789abcdef with key 0x133457799bbcdff1, the expected result of which is 0x85e813540f0ab405. Using the LNT language [8,17], one would be tempted to write this TP as the process PURPOSE1, simply containing the desired sequence of three inputs (on gates CRYPT, KEY, and DATA) followed by an output (on gate OUTPUT):

```
process PURPOSE1 [CRYPT: CB, KEY, DATA, OUTPUT: C64, T_ACCEPT: none] is
   CRYPT (true); -- input
   KEY (C_13345779_9bbcdff1); -- input
   DATA (C_01234567_89abcdef); -- input
   OUTPUT (C_85e81354_0f0ab405); -- output
   loop T_ACCEPT end loop
end process
```

Following the conventions of TGV, we mark accepting (respectively, refusal) states by a self-loop labeled with T_ACCEPT (respectively, T_REFUSE).

However, PURPOSE1 is not complete: e.g., initially only one action out of the possible set {CRYPT (true), CRYPT (false), KEY (C_13345779_9bbcdff1), ...} is specified. Thus, when computing the synchronous product with the model, PURPOSE1 is implicitly completed by self-loops labeled with "*" (as in the TP shown on Fig. 1b), yielding a significantly more complex TC than expected. For instance, the implicit *-transition in the initial state allows the tester to perform the sequence "CRYPT (false); CRYPT (true)" rather than the expected first action "CRYPT (true)". To force the generation of a TC corresponding to the simple sequence, it is necessary to explicitly complete the TP with transitions to refusal states, as shown by the LNT process PURPOSE2, where gate OTHERWISE stands for the special label "*":

```
process PURPOSE2 [CRYPT: CB, KEY, DATA, OUTPUT: C64, SUBKEY: C48,
                  T_ACCEPT, T_REFUSE, OTHERWISE: none] is
   select -- refuse any rendezvous but "CRYPT (TRUE)"
      CRYPT (true)
   [] OTHERWISE; loop T_REFUSE end loop
   end select;
   select -- refuse any rendezvous but "KEY (C_13345779_9BBCDFF1)"
```

```
      KEY (C_13345779_9BBCDFF1)
   [] OTHERWISE; loop T_REFUSE end loop
   end select;
   loop L in
      select -- refuse any rendezvous but on gates DATA and SUBKEY
         DATA (C_01234567_89ABCDEF); break L
      [] SUBKEY (?any BIT48)
      [] OTHERWISE; loop T_REFUSE end loop
      end select
   end loop;
   loop -- refuse any rendezvous but on gates OUTPUT and SUBKEY
      select -- test target is reached by a rendezvous on OUTPUT
         OUTPUT (C_85E81354_0F0AB405); loop T_ACCEPT end loop
      [] SUBKEY (?any BIT48)
      [] OTHERWISE; loop T_REFUSE end loop
      end select
   end loop
end process
```

Instead of using the dedicated synchronous product, it is also possible to take advantage of the multiway rendezvous [18,23] to compositionally annotate the model, relying on the LNT operational semantics [8, Appendix B] to cut undesired branches. For instance, the same effect as the synchronous product with PURPOSE2 can be obtained by skipping the left-most component "synchronous product" of Fig. 2, i.e., feeding the τ-reduction steps with the IOLTS described by the following LNT parallel composition:

```
par CRYPT, KEY, DATA, OUTPUT in
   DES [CRYPT, KEY, DATA, OUTPUT, SUBKEY]
|| PURPOSE1 [CRYPT, KEY, DATA, OUTPUT, T_ACCEPT]
end par
```

This approach based on the multiway rendezvous even supports data handling. For instance, to observe the data (variable D), key (variable K), and whether an encryption or decryption is requested (variable C), and to verify the correctness of the result (in the rendezvous "OUTPUT (DES (C, K, D))", DES denotes a function implementing the DES algorithm), one has just to replace in the above parallel composition the call to PURPOSE1 by a call to the process PURPOSE3:

```
process PURPOSE3 [CRYPT: CB, KEY, DATA, OUTPUT: C64, T_ACCEPT: none] is
   var C: BOOL, D, K: BIT64 in
      CRYPT (?C);
      KEY (?K);
      DATA (?D);
      OUTPUT (DES (C, K, D));
      loop T_ACCEPT end loop
   end var
end process
```

4   Experimental Evaluation

TESTOR follows TGV's implementation of the **ioco**-based testing theory [39, 41], using the same IOLTS processing steps, adding only the τ-confluence reduction. For each step, TESTOR uses components developed, tested, and used in other tools for more than a decade. In this section, we focus on performance aspects and we compare TESTOR to TGV. For this purpose, we conducted several experiments with models and test purposes, both automatically generated and drawn from academic examples and realistic case studies.

For assessing the correctness of TESTOR, we checked that each TC is included in the CTG, and we compared the TCs and CTGs generated by TESTOR to those generated by TGV. The latter comparison required several additional steps, automated using shell scripts and a dedicated tool (about 300 lines of C code). First, we generated the LTS of each TP, applying appropriate renamings, because TGV expects the TP to be an explicit LTS, with accepting (resp. refusing) states marked by a self-looping transition labeled with ACCEPT (resp. REFUSE), and with the label "*". Then, we modified the TC and CTG generated by TESTOR so that each label includes the information whether the label is an input or output, and which verdict state (if any) is reached by the corresponding transition. Using this approach, we found that the CTGs generated by both tools were strongly bisimilar. The same does not hold for all the TCs, because the tools may ensure controllability in different ways, leading to non-bisimilar, but correct TCs.

For each pair of model and TP, we measured the runtime and peak memory usage of computing a TC or CTG (using TESTOR and TGV), excluding the fixed cost of compiling the LNT code (model and TP) and generating the executable. The experiments presented in this paper were carried out using the Grid'5000 testbed, supported by a scientific interest group hosted by Inria and including CNRS, RENATER and several Universities as well as other organizations (see https://www.grid5000.fr). Concretely, we used the `petitprince` cluster located in Luxembourg, consisting of sixteen machines, each equipped with 2 Intel Xeon E5-2630L CPUs, 32 GB RAM, and running 64-bit Debian GNU/Linux 8 and CADP 2017-i. Each measurement corresponds to the average of ten executions.

4.1   Test Purposes Taken from Case Studies

Table 1 summarizes the results for some selected examples. The first two have been kindly provided by Alexander Graf-Brill, and correspond to initial versions of TPs for his EnergyBus model [20]; both aim at exhibiting a particular boot sequence, the second one using REFUSE transitions. The next four examples have been used by STMicroelectronics to verify a cache-coherence protocol [27]. The last three correspond to the three TPs presented in Sect. 3.4 and check the

Table 1. Run-time performance for selected examples

example	TESTOR				TGV			
	test case		CTG		test case		CTG	
	time	mem.	time	mem.	time	mem.	time	mem.
EnergyBus	3	81	182	181	2	137	52	858
EnergyBus (with REFUSE)	1	67	1	66	0	66	0	43
ACE UniqueDirty	45	121	346	451	75	159	3047	643
ACE SharedDirty	384	510	342	529	3821	746	3920	746
ACE SharedClean	298	415	325	523	2820	628	3474	663
ACE Data Inconsistency	24	116	580	711	24	142	6701	894
DES (PURPOSE1)	22109	300	>1 week		>43 GB		>220 GB	
DES (PURPOSE2)	27344	332	27	86	24	6177	24	6176
DES (PURPOSE3)	2	74	4	100	not applicable			

Execution time is given in seconds and memory usage in MB.

correctness of a simplified[2] version of the asynchronous implementation of the DES (Data Encryption Standard) [37]. These examples cover a large spectrum of characteristics: from no τ-transitions (ACE) to huge confluent τ-components (DES), from few visible transitions (DES) to many outgoing visible transitions (EnergyBus), and a test selection more or less guided via refusal states.

We observe that TESTOR requires less memory than TGV for all examples, but most significantly for the DES. However, although TESTOR is several orders of magnitude slower than TGV for the DES when using the synchronous product (TPs PURPOSE1 and PURPOSE2), TESTOR requires only two seconds to generate a TC or CTG when using an LNT parallel composition with the TP with data handling PURPOSE3. This is because the LNT parallel composition, handled by the LNT compiler, enables more aggressive optimizations. Thus, using LNT parallel composition to annotate the model's accepting and refusal states is not only more convenient (thanks to the multiway rendezvous) and data aware, but also much more efficient — it is even possible to generate a TC for the original DES model (167 million states, 1.5 billion transitions) in less than 40 min.

For the ACE examples, TESTOR is both faster and requires less memory than TGV. This is partly due to an optimization of TESTOR, which deactivates the various reductions of τ-transitions. For a fair comparison, we also run experiments forcing the execution of these reductions. For the extraction of a TC, this increases the execution time by a factor of two and the memory requirements by a factor of three. For the computation of a CTG, this increases the memory requirements by a factor of one and a half, without modifying the execution time significantly.

---

[2] The S-boxes are executed sequentially rather than in parallel and the gate SUBKEY is left visible to separate the iterations of the DES algorithm and thus significantly reduce the size of τ-components. For the extraction of TC for PURPOSE2 from the full version of the DES, TESTOR would run for several weeks and TGV would require more than 700 GB of RAM.

4.2   Automatically Generated Test Purposes

To evaluate the performance, we used a collection of 9791 LTSs with up to 50 million transitions, taken from the non-regression test-base for CADP. For each LTS M of the collection, we automatically generated two TPs: one to test the reachability of an action and another to test the presence of an execution sequence. For the former TP, we sorted the actions of the LTS alphabetically, and checked the reachability of the first action, considering the second half of the action set as inputs. For the latter TP, we used the EXECUTOR tool[3] to extract a sequence of up to 1000 visible actions, which we transformed into a TP, considering all actions whose ranking is an odd number as inputs. Technically, this transformation consists in adding to each state of the sequence a self-loop labeled with τ and a *-transition to a refusal state.

From the generated pairs (M, TP) we eliminated those for which the automatic generation of a TP failed (for instance, due to special actions that would require particular treatment) and those for which the computation of a TC or CTG took too much time or required too much memory by either TESTOR or TGV. This led to a collection of 13,142 pairs (M, TP) for which both tools could extract a TC. For 12,654 of them, both tools also could compute the CTG. Figure 3 displays the results for each example, using logarithmic scales for both execution time and memory requirements, to make the differences for small values more visible.

As for the case studies, we observe that TESTOR and TGV choose different tradeoffs between computation time and memory requirements. On average, TESTOR requires 0.3 times less memory and runs 1.3 (respectively 0.5) times faster to compute a TC (respectively the CTG). When considering only the 1005 pairs with more than 500,000 transitions in the LTS, the average numbers show a larger difference. On average for these larger examples, to compute a CTG, TESTOR requires 1.4 times less memory, but runs 3.5 times longer; to compute a TC, TESTOR requires 2.7 times less memory and runs 0.7 times faster.

Also, while both tools required the exclusion of examples due to excessive runtime, we excluded several examples due to insufficient memory for TGV, but not for TESTOR. Given that TCs are usually much smaller than CTGs, the on-the-fly extraction of a TC by TESTOR is generally faster and consumes less memory than the generation of the CTG. We also observed that the CTGs produced by TESTOR are sometimes smaller than (although strongly bisimilar to) those produced by TGV.

While trying to understand these results in more detail, we found examples where each tool is one or two magnitudes faster or memory-efficient than the other. Indeed, the benefits of the different reductions applied in the tools depend heavily on the characteristics of the example, most notably the sizes of the various subgraphs explored (τ-components, L2A). For instance, when the model M does not contain any τ-transition, there is no point in applying the reductions (τ-compression, τ-confluence, and τ-closure).

---

[3] http://cadp.inria.fr/man/executor.html.

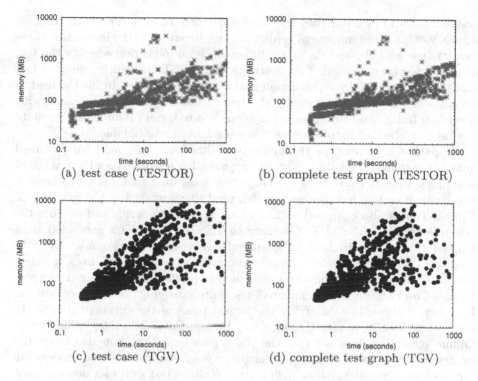

Fig. 3. Compared performance of TESTOR and TGV

The modular architecture of TESTOR enabled us to easily experiment with variants of the algorithm used for solving the BES underlying φ_{l2a}. By default, when extracting a TC on the fly, we use the depth-first search (DFS) algorithm, which for disjunctive BESs stores only variables and not their dependencies (and hence only the states, and not the transitions of the model). Using the breadth-first search (BFS) algorithm of the solver produces smaller TCs, because it generates the shortest diagnostic sequences for states in L2A. However, this comes at the price of an increased execution time and memory consumption, a known phenomenon regarding BFS versus DFS algorithms [32]. Thus, one can choose between BFS or DFS resolution if the size of the TC extracted on the fly is judged more important or not than the resources required to compute it.

5   Related Work

Although model-based conformance testing has been intensively studied, there are only a few tools that use variants of the **ioco** conformance relation and that are still actively developed [4]. Other model-based tools for combinatorial and statistical testing, or white box testing are described in [43]. In the following, we compare TESTOR to the most closely related tools.

TorX [42] and JTorX [2] are online test generation tools, equipped with a set of adapters to connect the tester to the SUT. The latest versions support test purposes (TPs), but they are used differently than in TESTOR. Indeed, JTorX yields a two-dimensional verdict [3]: one dimension is the **ioco** correctness verdict (pass or fail), and the other dimension is an indication whether the test objective has been reached. This contrasts with TESTOR, which generates test cases (TCs) ensuring by construction that the execution stays inside the lead to accept states (L2A), and stopping the test execution as soon as possible with a verdict: **fail** if non-conformance has been detected, **pass** if an accepting state has been reached, or **inconclusive** if leaving L2A is unavoidable.

Uppaal is a toolbox for the analysis of timed systems, modeled as timed automata extended with data. Three test generation tools exist for Uppaal timed automata. Uppaal-Tron [28] is an online test generation tool, taking as input a specification and an environment model, used to constrain the test generation. Uppaal-Tron is also equipped with a set of adapters to derive and execute the generated tests on the SUT. Contrary to TESTOR, the TCs generated from Uppaal-Tron can be irrelevant, because the generation is not guided by TPs. Uppaal-Cover [22] generates offline a comprehensive test suite from a deterministic Uppaal model and coverage criteria specified by observer automata. Uppaal-Cover attempts to build small test suite satisfying the coverage criteria, by selecting those TCs satisfying the largest parts of the coverage criteria. In contrast to TESTOR and Uppaal-Tron, Uppaal-Cover generates offline tests. Offline generation does not face the state-space explosion, but also limits the expressiveness of the specification language (e.g, nondeterministic models are not allowed). Uppaal-Yggdrasil [26] generates offline test suites for deterministic Uppaal models, using a three-step strategy to achieve good coverage: (i) a set of reachability formulas, (ii) random execution, and (iii) structural coverage of the transitions in the model. The guidance of the test generation by a temporal logic formula is similar to the use of a TP. However, the TPs supported by TESTOR (and TGV) can express more complex properties than reachability, and enable one to control the explored part of the model (using refusal states).

On-the-fly test generation tools also exist for the synchronous dataflow language Lustre [21], e.g., Lutess [12], Lurette [24], and Gatel [29]. Contrary to TESTOR, these tools do not check the **ioco** relation, but randomly select TCs, satisfying constraints of an environment description and an oracle.

In IOLTS, actions are monolithic, which does not fit for realistic models that involve data handling. STG (Symbolic Test Generator) [11] breaks the monolithic structure of actions, enabling access to the data values, and generates tests on the fly, handling data values symbolically. This enables more user-friendly TPs and more abstract TCs, because not all possible values have to be enumerated. However, the complexity of symbolic computation is not negligible in practice. When using the LNT parallel composition, TESTOR can handle data (see example in Sect. 3.4) without the cost of symbolic computation, but still has to enumerate data explicitly when generating the TC. T-Uppaal [34] uses symbolic reachability analysis to generate tests on the fly and then simultaneously executes them on the SUT. The complexity of symbolic algorithms turns out to be expensive for online testing.

When executing a generated TC against a SUT, it is necessary to refine it to take into account the asynchronous communication between the SUT and the tester. Actually, the SUT accepts every input at any time, whereas the TC is deterministic, i.e., there is no choice between an input and an output. An approach for connecting a TC (randomly selected) and an asynchronous SUT was defined in [44]. A similar approach using TPs to guide the test generation was proposed in [5] and subsequently extended to timed automata [6]. Recently, this kind of connection was automated by the MOTEST tool [19].

6 Conclusion

We presented TESTOR, a new tool for on-the-fly conformance test case generation for asynchronous concurrent systems. Like the existing tool TGV, TESTOR was developed on top of the CADP toolbox [16] and brings several enhancements: online testing by generating (controllable) test cases completely on the fly; a more versatile description of test purposes using the LNT language; and a modular architecture involving generic graph manipulation components from the OPEN/-CAESAR environment [15]. The modularity of TESTOR simplifies maintenance and fine-tuning of graph manipulation components, e.g., by adding or removing on-the-fly reductions, or by replacing the synchronous product. Besides the ability to perform online testing, the on-the-fly test selection algorithm sometimes makes possible the extraction of test cases even when the generation of the complete test graph (CTG) is infeasible.

The experiments we carried out on ten-thousands of benchmark examples and three industrial case studies show that TESTOR consumes less memory than TGV, which in turn is sometimes faster, for generating CTGs. We plan to experiment with state space caching techniques [33] and with other on-the-fly reductions to accelerate CTG generation in TESTOR. We also plan to investigate how to facilitate the description of test purposes, by deriving them from the action-based, branching-time temporal properties of the model (following the results of [13] in the state-based, linear-time setting) or by synthesizing them according to behavioral coverage criteria.

Acknowledgements. We are grateful to Alexander Graf-Brill and Holger Hermanns for providing us with the model and test purposes of their EnergyBus case study. We also thank Hubert Garavel for helpful remarks about the paper. This work was supported by the Région Auvergne-Rhône-Alpes within the program ARC 6.

References

1. Aichernig, B.K., Lorber, F., Tiran, S.: Integrating model-based testing and analysis tools via test case exchange. TASE **2012**, 119–126 (2012)
2. Belinfante, A.: JTorX: a tool for on-line model-driven test derivation and execution. In: Esparza, J., Majumdar, R. (eds.) TACAS 2010. LNCS, vol. 6015, pp. 266–270. Springer, Heidelberg (2010). https://doi.org/10.1007/978-3-642-12002-2_21

3. Belinfante, A.: JTorX: exploring model-based testing. Ph.D. thesis, University of Twente (2014)
4. Belinfante, A., Frantzen, L., Schallhart, C.: 14 tools for test case generation. In: [7], pp. 391–438
5. Bhateja, P.: A TGV-like approach for asynchronous testing. In: ISEC 2014, pp. 13:1–13:6. ACM (2014)
6. Bhateja, P.: Asynchronous testing of real-time systems. In: SCSS 2017, EPiC Series in Computing, vol. 45, pp. 42–48. EasyChair (2017)
7. Broy, M., Jonsson, B., Katoen, J.-P., Leucker, M., Pretschner, A. (eds.): Model-Based Testing of Reactive Systems. LNCS, vol. 3472. Springer, Heidelberg (2005). https://doi.org/10.1007/b137241
8. Champelovier, D., Clerc, X., Garavel, H., Guerte, Y., McKinty, C., Powazny, V., Lang, F., Serwe, W., Smeding, G.: Reference Manual of the LNT to LOTOS Translator (Version 6.7). INRIA (2017)
9. Chimisliu, V., Wotawa, F.: Improving test case generation from UML statecharts by using control, data and communication dependencies. In: QSIC, vol. 13, pp. 125–134 (2013)
10. Chimisliu, V., Wotawa, F.: Using dependency relations to improve test case generation from UML statecharts. In: COMPSAC, pp. 71–76. IEEE (2013)
11. Clarke, D., Jéron, T., Rusu, V., Zinovieva, E.: STG: a symbolic test generation tool. In: Katoen, J.-P., Stevens, P. (eds.) TACAS 2002. LNCS, vol. 2280, pp. 470–475. Springer, Heidelberg (2002). https://doi.org/10.1007/3-540-46002-0_34
12. du Bousquet, L., Ouabdesselam, F., Richier, J., Zuanon, N.: Lutess: a specification-driven testing environment for synchronous software. In: ICSE 1999, pp. 267–276. ACM (1999)
13. Falcone, Y., Fernandez, J.-C., Jéron, T., Marchand, H., Mounier, L.: More testable properties. STTT 14(4), 407–437 (2012)
14. Fischer, M.J., Ladner, R.E.: Propositional dynamic logic of regular programs. J. Comput. Syst. Sci. 18(2), 194–211 (1979)
15. Garavel, H.: OPEN/CÆSAR: an open software architecture for verification, simulation, and testing. In: Steffen, B. (ed.) TACAS 1998. LNCS, vol. 1384, pp. 68–84. Springer, Heidelberg (1998). https://doi.org/10.1007/BFb0054165
16. Garavel, H., Lang, F., Mateescu, R., Serwe, W.: CADP 2011: a toolbox for the construction and analysis of distributed processes. STTT 15(2), 89–107 (2013)
17. Garavel, H., Lang, F., Serwe, W.: From LOTOS to LNT. In: Katoen, J.-P., Langerak, R., Rensink, A. (eds.) ModelEd, TestEd, TrustEd. LNCS, vol. 10500, pp. 3–26. Springer, Cham (2017). https://doi.org/10.1007/978-3-319-68270-9_1
18. Garavel, H., Serwe, W.: The unheralded value of the multiway rendezvous: illustration with the production cell benchmark. In: MARS 2017, EPTCS, vol. 244, pp. 230–270 (2017)
19. Graf-Brill, A., Hermanns, H.: Model-based testing for asynchronous systems. In: Petrucci, L., Seceleanu, C., Cavalcanti, A. (eds.) FMICS/AVoCS-2017. LNCS, vol. 10471, pp. 66–82. Springer, Cham (2017). https://doi.org/10.1007/978-3-319-67113-0_5
20. Graf-Brill, A., Hermanns, H., Garavel, H.: A model-based certification framework for the energybus standard. In: Ábrahám, E., Palamidessi, C. (eds.) FORTE 2014. LNCS, vol. 8461, pp. 84–99. Springer, Heidelberg (2014). https://doi.org/10.1007/978-3-662-43613-4_6
21. Halbwachs, N., Caspi, P., Raymond, P., Pilaud, D.: The synchronous dataflow programming language LUSTRE. Proc. IEEE 79(9), 1305–1320 (1991)

22. Hessel, A., Pettersson, P.: Model-based testing of a WAP gateway: an industrial case-study. In: Brim, L., Haverkort, B., Leucker, M., van do Pol, J. (eds.) FMICS 2006. LNCS, vol. 4346, pp. 116–131. Springer, Heidelberg (2007). https://doi.org/10.1007/978-3-540-70952-7_8

23. Hoare, C.A.R.: Communicating sequential processes. Commun. ACM 21(8), 666–677 (1978)

24. Jahier, E., Raymond, P., Baufreton, P.: Case studies with Lurette V2. STTT 8(6), 517–530 (2006)

25. Jard, C., Jéron, T.: TGV: theory, principles and algorithms - a tool for the automatic synthesis of conformance test cases for non-deterministic reactive systems. STTT 7(4), 297–315 (2005)

26. Kim, J.H., Larsen, K.G., Nielsen, B., Mikučionis, M., Olsen, P.: Formal analysis and testing of real-time automotive systems using UPPAAL tools. In: Núñez, M., Güdemann, M. (eds.) FMICS 2015. LNCS, vol. 9128, pp. 47–61. Springer, Cham (2015). https://doi.org/10.1007/978-3-319-19458-5_4

27. Kriouile, A., Serwe, W.: Using a formal model to improve verification of a cache-coherent system-on-chip. In: Baier, C., Tinelli, C. (eds.) TACAS 2015. LNCS, vol. 9035, pp. 708–722. Springer, Heidelberg (2015). https://doi.org/10.1007/978-3-662-46681-0_62

28. Larsen, K.G., Mikucionis, M., Nielsen, B., Skou, A.: Testing real-time embedded software using UPPAAL-TRON: an industrial case study. In: EMSOFT 2005, pp. 299–306. ACM (2005)

29. Marre, B., Arnould, A.: Test sequences generation from LUSTRE descriptions: GATeL. In: ASE 2000, p. 229. IEEE (2000)

30. Mateescu, R.: Efficient diagnostic generation for Boolean equation systems. In: Graf, S., Schwartzbach, M. (eds.) TACAS 2000. LNCS, vol. 1785, pp. 251–265. Springer, Heidelberg (2000). https://doi.org/10.1007/3-540-46419-0_18

31. Mateescu, R.: On-the-fly state space reductions for weak equivalences. In: FMICS 2015, pp. 80–89. ACM (2005)

32. Mateescu, R.: CAESAR_SOLVE: a generic library for on-the-fly resolution of alternation-free boolean equation systems. STTT 8(1), 37–56 (2006)

33. Mateescu, R., Wijs, A.: Hierarchical adaptive state space caching based on level sampling. In: Kowalewski, S., Philippou, A. (eds.) TACAS 2009. LNCS, vol. 5505, pp. 215–229. Springer, Heidelberg (2009). https://doi.org/10.1007/978-3-642-00768-2_21

34. Mikucionis, M., Larsen, K.G., Nielsen, B.: T-UPPAAL: online model-based testing of real-time systems. In: ASE 2004, pp. 396–397. IEEE (2004)

35. Mjeda, A.: Standard-compliant testing for safety-related automotive software. Ph.D. thesis, University of Limerick (2013)

36. Moy, Y., Ledinot, E., Delseny, H., Wiels, V., Monate, B.: Testing or formal verification: DO-178C alternatives and industrial experience. IEEE Softw. 30(3), 50–57 (2013)

37. Serwe, W.: Formal specification and verification of fully asynchronous implementations of the data encryption standard. In: MARS 2015, EPTCS, vol. 196, pp. 61–147 (2015)

38. Sijtema, M., Belinfante, A., Stoelinga, M., Marinelli, L.: Experiences with formal engineering: model-based specification, implementation and testing of a software bus at neopost. Sci. Comput. Program. 80(Part A), 188–209 (2014)

39. Tretmans, J.: A Formal Approach to Conformance Testing. Twente University Press (1992)

40. Tretmans, J.: Conformance testing with labelled transition systems: implementation relations and test generation. Comput. Netw. ISDN Syst. **29**(1), 49–79 (1996)
41. Tretmans, J.: Model based testing with labelled transition systems. In: Hierons, R.M., Bowen, J.P., Harman, M. (eds.) Formal Methods and Testing. LNCS, vol. 4949, pp. 1–38. Springer, Heidelberg (2008). https://doi.org/10.1007/978-3-540-78917-8_1
42. Tretmans, J., Brinksma, H.: TorX: automated model-based testing. In: Model-Driven Software Engineering, pp. 32–43 (2003)
43. Utting, M., Pretschner, A., Legeard, B.: A taxonomy of model-based testing approaches. Softw. Test. Verif. Reliab. **22**(5), 297–312 (2012)
44. Weiglhofer, M., Wotawa, F.: Asynchronous input-output conformance testing. In: COMPSAC 2009, pp. 154–159. IEEE (2009)
45. Zander, J., Schieferdecker, I., Mosterman, P.J. (eds.): Model-Based Testing for Embedded Systems. CRC Press, Boca Raton (2017)

Optimal Dynamic Partial Order Reduction with Observers

Stavros Aronis[iD], Bengt Jonsson[iD], Magnus Lång$^{(\boxtimes)}$[iD],
and Konstantinos Sagonas[iD]

Department of Information Technology,
Uppsala University, Uppsala, Sweden
{stavros.aronis,bengt.jonsson,
magnus.lang,konstantinos.sagonas}@it.uu.se

Abstract. Dynamic partial order reduction (DPOR) algorithms are used in stateless model checking (SMC) to combat the combinatorial explosion in the number of schedulings that need to be explored to guarantee soundness. The most effective of them, the Optimal DPOR algorithm, is optimal in the sense that it explores only one scheduling per Mazurkiewicz trace. In this paper, we enhance DPOR with the notion of *observability*, which makes dependencies between operations conditional on the existence of future operations, called *observers*. Observers naturally lead to a lazy construction of dependencies. This requires significant changes in the core of POR algorithms (and Optimal DPOR in particular), but also makes the resulting algorithm, Optimal DPOR with Observers, super-optimal in the sense that it explores exponentially less schedulings than Mazurkiewicz traces in some cases. We argue that observers come naturally in many concurrency models, and demonstrate the performance benefits that Optimal DPOR with Observers achieves in both an SMC tool for shared memory concurrency and a tool for concurrency via message passing, using both synthetic and actual programs as benchmarks.

1 Introduction

Testing and verification of concurrent programs is hard, as it requires reasoning about all the ways in which operations executed by different processes (or threads) can interfere. *Stateless model checking (SMC)* [12] is a technique with low memory requirements that can be effective in finding concurrency errors or proving that a program cannot reach an error state by systematically exploring all the ways in which such operations can be interleaved. The technique requires taking control of the scheduler and subsequently executing the program multiple times, each time imposing a different scheduling of the processes. By considering every process at every execution step, however, the number of possible schedulings grows exponentially w.r.t. the total length of program execution. *Partial order reduction (POR)* techniques [9,11,20,22] address this problem by prescribing the exploration of only a subset of schedulings, albeit a subset that

© The Author(s) 2018
D. Beyer and M. Huisman (Eds.): TACAS 2018, LNCS 10806, pp. 229–248, 2018.
https://doi.org/10.1007/978-3-319-89963-3_14

is sufficient to cover all behaviours. POR techniques take advantage of the fact that most pairs of operations by different processes in typical concurrent programs are not interfering. As a result, a scheduling E that can be obtained from another scheduling E' by swapping adjacent but non-interfering (independent) execution steps will make the program behave in exactly the same way as E'; such schedulings have the same partial order of interfering operations and belong to the same equivalence class, called a *Mazurkiewicz trace* [19]. It is sufficient for SMC algorithms to explore only one scheduling in each such equivalence class.

POR algorithms operate by examining pairs of interfering operations. If it is possible to execute such operations in the reverse order, then their partial order will be different, and a scheduling from the relevant equivalence class must also be explored. For soundness, POR techniques need to be conservative, treating operations as interfering even in cases where they are not. Increasing the accuracy of interference detection can therefore significantly improve the effectiveness of any POR technique. In early POR techniques, interference was determined statically, leading to over-approximations and limiting the achievable reduction. The efficiency of POR was later increased using semantic information to decide which operations interfere [13]. *Dynamic Partial Order Reduction* (DPOR) [10] further improved the effectiveness of POR algorithms by allowing interference to be determined from data obtained during the program's execution.

In this paper, we introduce the notion of *observability* of operations, allowing *observer* operations that appear later in a scheduling to be used when deciding whether earlier operations are interfering. We start by explaining observers with a series of examples (Sect. 2), and continue by presenting key notions of DPOR and explaining why using observers in DPOR algorithms is challenging (Sect. 3). We then present a formal framework (Sect. 4) and describe an extension to the Optimal DPOR algorithm [2] that enables use of observers (Sect. 5). The extension is generic in the sense that it can be applied to several models of concurrency, such as shared memory and message passing. We demonstrate this claim by two implementations: one in an SMC tool for C/C++ programs with pthreads and one in an SMC tool for Erlang programs (Sect. 6). Finally, in Sect. 7 we evaluate our implementations and show that Optimal DPOR with Observers can achieve significantly better reduction in both synthetic and 'real' programs.

2 DPOR and Observers by Example

Consider the program shown in Fig. 1 in which a *main* process spawns two concurrent processes, p and q, which issue write operations on two different shared variables x and y. After p and q finish their execution, the *main* process reads the values of x and y and checks a correctness property. A DPOR algorithm will begin exploring this program by executing an arbitrary scheduling; see Fig. 1 (middle). Nodes show the values of the shared variables and each transition consists of an execution step. By inspecting the operations in this scheduling, the algorithm sees that if the second step of q is scheduled before the second step of p, the partial order of the writes to the y variable is different. It therefore

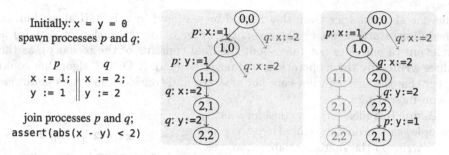

Fig. 1. Writers program (its correctness property as assertion) and two of its schedulings.

plans to execute a scheduling in which the second step of p happens after the one from q. The start of this scheduling can be denoted as $p.q$. Similarly, the order of the writes on x can be reversed, by executing q's first step before the first step of p. Therefore, a scheduling starting with q should also be explored. In Optimal DPOR [2], future explorations are added as partial schedulings, forming *wakeup trees* (shown in blue). These trees are quite trivial in this example, each consisting of a single path.

The algorithm continues exploration from the "deepest" point where a new scheduling should be tried; in the example, this is the (1,0) node. A second scheduling is explored with the intention to execute some operation before the second step of p. Without any other constraint, a non-optimal DPOR algorithm could execute p's second step immediately after the first step of q, ending up in a state identical with the previously explored (2,1) and then again in (2,2). The *sleep sets* technique [11] can be used to avoid or stop such redundant explorations. Sleep sets retain information from already explored earlier process steps that have not yet been 'overtaken' by some step in the current exploration. In our example, information about p's second step is retained in the sleep set until some other interfering operation (here q's second step) has been executed. Moreover, sleep sets can be used to infer that swapping (again) the second step of p and the second step of q (based on their interference in the second scheduling) is redundant. Any DPOR algorithm using sleep sets will explore four schedulings for this program (instead of the six ones possible). Each of these four schedulings leads to a different final state. Notice that two writes on the same variable were always deemed as interfering.

Consider now the program shown on the right. The shared variable x (whose initial value is 0) is accessed by processes

$$p \qquad\qquad q \qquad\qquad r$$
$$\texttt{x := 1} \ \| \ \texttt{x := 2} \ \| \ \texttt{assert(x < 3)}$$

p, q and r. Here, the correctness property is checked by process r. If interference is decided using the same criteria as a *data race* (i.e., two operations interfere if they access the same memory location and at least one of them is a write), then all three operations interfere with each other. As a result, each of the $3! = 6$ possible interleavings has a different partial order and therefore belongs to a different Mazurkiewicz trace that should be explored by a DPOR algorithm. In schedulings starting with r, however, the order of the execution of p and q is irrelevant (if one does not care about the final contents of the memory), as the values written by these operations will never be read. A DPOR algorithm could detect that the written values are *not observed* and consider the write operations as non-interfering.

Taking this idea further, consider a next example, shown on the right. Here, N processes write on the shared variable x, and as a result there exist $N!$ schedulings. In each such scheduling, however, only the last writ-

$$p_1 \qquad p_2 \qquad \ldots \qquad p_N$$
$$\mathtt{x := 1} \parallel \mathtt{x := 2} \parallel \ldots \parallel \mathtt{x := } N$$
$$\text{join processes } p_1, p_2, \ldots, p_N;$$
$$\mathtt{assert(x > 0)}$$

ten value will be read. A DPOR algorithm could consider write operations that are not subsequently observed as independent and therefore explore just N instead of $N!$ schedulings, thereby achieving an exponential reduction.

In the last two examples, better reduction could be obtained if the interference of write operations, which are conservatively considered as "always interfering", was characterized more accurately by looking at complete executions and taking observability by "future" operations into account. This idea is applicable not only in shared memory but also in other models of concurrency. In the next message passing program, processes p and q each send a different message to the mailbox of process r using the send operator "!". Process r uses a receive operation to retrieve a message and store it in a (local) variable x. If we assume that receive operations pick and return the oldest message in the mailbox or return null if no message exists, send opera-

$$p \qquad\quad q \qquad\qquad r$$
$$r \ ! \ \mathtt{M_1} \parallel r \ ! \ \mathtt{M_2} \parallel \mathtt{receive\ x}$$

tions can interfere (the order of delivery is significant) and so can send and receive operations (an empty mailbox can yield a different value). As a result, six schedulings are possible. However, only three schedulings need to really be explored: the receive operation interferes only with the earliest send operation and cannot be affected by a later send; moreover, if the receive operation is executed first, the order of the send operations is irrelevant.

If we instead assume that receive operations *block* if no matching message exists, only *two* schedulings need to be explored, as r can receive either M_1 or M_2. Again, if we generalize the example to N processes instead of just two, the behaviour is similar to the program with N writes: only N schedulings (instead of $N!$) are relevant, each determined by the first message delivered; the remaining message deliveries are not observable. Note that, in this concurrency model, we are interested in the observability of the *first* instead of the last operation in an execution sequence.

In some message-passing concurrency models (e.g., in Erlang programs [4]), it is further possible to use *selective* receive operations instead, which also block when no message can be selected. Using this feature, the previous program can be generalized and rewritten so that r is explicitly picking messages in order, using pattern matching. Such a program is shown on the right. Here r wants to pick up the N messages in order: first M_1, then M_2, etc.

Thus, the order of delivery of messages is irrelevant. A DPOR algorithm could take advantage of the additional information provided by the selective receive operations, notice that the messages from

p_1	p_2	$\ldots$	p_N	r
$r \; ! \; M_1$	$r \; ! \; M_2$	$\ldots$	$r \; ! \; M_N$	receive M_1;
				receive M_2;
				$\vdots$
				receive M_N

$p_{i+1} \ldots p_N$ cannot be selected before the message from p_i, and therefore determine that the N sends are independent. A *single* scheduling is enough to explore all behaviours of the program!

Having explained the concept of *observability* of operations by examples, let us see how it can be combined with the Optimal DPOR algorithm and achieve such reductions.

3   Using Observers in a DPOR Algorithm

Our objective is to construct a DPOR algorithm that *lazily* considers interferences based on the existence of *later* operations, called *observers*. In the simplest case, operations that would be conservatively considered interfering are treated as independent in the absence of an observer. Examples in Sect. 2 included write operations whose values were never read, or cases where the order of message deliveries does not affect the order in which the messages are received.

The intuition behind such an SMC approach comes from the fact that it is only operations that *observe* a value (e.g., assertions, receive statements, etc.) that can influence the control flow and lead to erroneous or generally unexpected behaviour. Other operations (e.g., writes, sends, etc.) cannot affect program behaviour if no future operation observes their effects. In such cases, interference between those other operations can be ignored.

3.1   POR Concepts and Optimal DPOR

The goal of POR techniques is the exploration of only a (small) subset of the possible schedulings of a concurrent program which is *sound*; that is, a subset that includes at least one scheduling from each Mazurkiewicz trace. DPOR algorithms perform a depth-first exploration of the tree of all possible schedulings. Reduction is achieved by exploring only a sound subset of all scheduling choices that are possible at each point in the tree. Such subsets are formed on the basis of two complementary techniques.

- Each point in the tree is associated with a *sleep set*, which contains a set of processes whose exploration would be redundant. More precisely, a process p is in the sleep set after a sequence of form $E.v$ if p has previously been explored after E, and furthermore p does not interfere with v. Thus, exploring $E.v.p$ is redundant, since it was previously explored after $E.p$ (as $E.p.v$).

- From each point in the tree, the set of explored processes must form a *source set* [2]. (Some DPOR algorithms employ persistent or stubborn sets, which are subsumed by source sets.) Source sets have the property that for any extension which forms a complete (aka *maximal*) scheduling, there is an equivalent extension in which the next step is taken by a process in the source set. A source set is constructed incrementally during the exploration by inspecting encountered races: whenever a scheduling of form $E.p.v$ is explored, in which the step of p is in a race with some step in v, then the reversal of that race will be explored in some other scheduling, where some process q in v is scheduled immediately after E: this is achieved by adding q to the source set after E.

Most existing DPOR algorithms prescribe that from each point in the tree (i) all processes in a source set should be explored, and (ii) no process in the sleep set should be explored. However, these principles are not sufficient to avoid redundant exploration [2]. The reason is that the reversal of a race in $E.p.v$ may happen only by exploring a particular subsequence of v; since a source set can only contain the first step in such a sequence, it can not prevent continued exploration beyond that first step from being redundant. Optimal DPOR improves on earlier techniques by using *wakeup trees* [2] in addition to sleep sets. Wakeup trees are composed of partial execution sequences (called *wakeup sequences*) that (a) reverse the order of the interfering operations, and (b) are provably non-redundant. Optimal DPOR, currently the state-of-the-art DPOR algorithm, always uses wakeup sequences to explore new schedulings. As a result, Optimal DPOR does not even initiate redundant exploration, and can achieve exponential reduction over e.g., the original [10] or the Source DPOR [2] algorithm.

3.2 Observers and Sleep Sets

The use of sleep sets is not trivial when using observers, because interference between events can often not be determined when they occur, but only later in the scheduling. Let us illustrate using an example. In the next program, three processes (p, q and s) send tagged messages (with tags A and B) to a receiver process r, which uses selective receive to read matching messages from its mailbox. Each message also contains the process identifier of the sender.

```
       p                q               s              r
   r ! {B,p};  ║  r ! {A,q};  ║  r ! {B,s};  ║  receive {A,x};
   r ! {A,p}   ║              ║               ║  if (x == p)
                                                 receive {B,y}
```

In standard DPOR, the sends are interfering, since the order of delivery can affect the values assigned to the x and y variables in r. Using observers, sends are interfering only if justified by an observing **receive** operation. Assume that the first explored scheduling is $p.p.q.s.r.r$. Here, the second send by p (sending the message tagged with A) interferes with the send by q, since their order is observed by the first receive of r (if the message from q had been delivered first, it would have been the one picked instead). Furthermore, the first send by p (sending the message tagged with B) interferes with the message send by s, since they have the second receive of r as observer. In order to explore the reversal of the race between the first send of p and that of s, the algorithm needs to explore a scheduling in which p's first send is executed after s. Such a scheduling must clearly start with s. The rules for sleep sets prescribe that p should be in the sleep set at the start of this exploration, and that p should be removed from the sleep set after executing s if p and s interfere. However, this interference is visible only later, making it unclear what to do. On the one hand, removing p from the sleep set on the grounds that it "might" interfere with s risks to explore redundant schedulings and defeats the purpose of observers. On the other hand, keeping p in the sleep set and "see what happens" prevents exploring the effects of the race reversal, since that requires the second send of p to be explored before q, which is forbidden if p remains in the sleep set. Thus, sleep sets are not a sufficiently precise mechanism for avoiding redundant exploration without missing non-redundant schedulings.

3.3 Introducing Observers to Optimal DPOR

We will now explain how Optimal DPOR can be adapted to work with observers. There are two main challenges: (1) we need to address the fact that, in the presence of observers, interference is conditional, and (2) we also need a suitable replacement for sleep sets, since we can no longer use them to guarantee that there is no redundant exploration.

In Optimal DPOR, it is assumed that operations that are interfering in some execution sequence remain interfering in any prefix of that sequence. This is no longer true when we determine interference by the existence of observing operations. If an observer is not included in a prefix of an execution sequence in which two operations were observably interfering, the same two operations will be independent. To address challenge 1 in Optimal DPOR with observers, we need to extend the wakeup sequences constructed for reversing the order of interfering operations that require an observer, with a suffix that includes the observer. It is allowed for this suffix to include operations happening after the interfering operations (even in program order); any such operations will behave identically in the reversal because in the original scheduling the observer was the first event that could be affected by the ordering of the interfering operations. To address challenge 2, we can build on the intuition behind sleep sets and assert that when our algorithm is done with a particular state, it has explored all schedulings that can start with the step that led to that state. When the algorithm considers a new scheduling (based on a wakeup sequence), information about observers in that scheduling needs to be recalculated from the operations in the sequence. The algorithm can then perform an exhaustive test, that ensures that each step previously explored from any point in the execution is overtaken by some other step in the wakeup sequence under consideration.

4   Framework

We consider a concurrent system composed of a finite set of *processes* (or threads). Each process executes a deterministic program, in which statements act on the global *state* of the system. Processes can interact via shared variables, messages, etc. We assume that the state space does not contain cycles, and that executions have bounded length. A step of a process may not disable another process.

Formally, let Σ be the set of states of a concurrent system and $s_0 \in \Sigma$ be the unique *initial state*. The partial function $execute_p : \Sigma \mapsto \Sigma$ describes execution, representing an atomic *execution step* of process p, which may depend on and affect the state. An *execution sequence* E of the system is a finite sequence of execution steps of its processes that is performed from the initial state. We use $\langle \rangle$ to denote the empty sequence and . to denote concatenation of sequences of process steps (e.g., $p.p.q$ denotes the execution sequence where first p performs two steps, followed by a step of q). The sequence of process steps in E also uniquely determine the state of the system after E, which is denoted $s_{[E]}$. For a state s, let $enabled(s)$ denote the set of processes p that are enabled in s (i.e., for which $execute_p(s)$ is defined). If $p \in enabled(s_{[E]})$, then $E.p$ is an execution sequence. A sequence E is *maximal* if $enabled(s_{[E]}) = \emptyset$, i.e., no process is enabled after E. An *event* $\langle p, i \rangle$ of E is a particular occurrence of a process in E, representing the i-th occurrence of process p in the execution sequence. We use $w, w', \ldots$ to range over sequences, $e, e', \ldots$ to range over events, as well as:

- $E \vdash w$ to denote that $E.w$ is an execution sequence.
- $w \setminus p$ to denote the sequence w with its first occurrence of p removed.
- $dom(E)$ to denote the set of events $\langle p, i \rangle$ which are in E.
- $dom_{[E]}(w)$ to denote $dom(E.w) \setminus dom(E)$, i.e., the events in $E.w$ which are in w.
- $next_{[E]}(p)$ to denote $dom_{[E]}(p)$ as a special case.
- $\widehat{e}$ to denote the process p of an event $e = \langle p, i \rangle$.
- $e <_E e'$ to denote that e occurs before e' in E, i.e., $<_E$ is the total order of events.
- $E' \leq E$ to denote that the sequence E' is a prefix of the sequence E.

We assume a function which assigns a *happens-before relation* [15] to any execution sequence E, denoted as $\rightarrow_E$.

We will keep the general approach of Optimal DPOR and require the happens-before relation to satisfy a set of properties, collected in Definition 1. These properties are the first point where we diverge from the underlying model for Optimal DPOR [2, Definition 3.2]. In that definition, Properties (3) and (5) need to be weakened, Property (6) needs to be replaced, whereas Property (7) was only required for Source DPOR and is thus dropped.

Definition 1 (Properties of valid happens-before relations). *A happens-before assignment, which assigns a unique happens-before relation $\rightarrow_E$ to any execution sequence E, is* valid *if it satisfies the following properties for all execution sequences E:*

1. $\to_E$ is an irreflexive partial order on $dom(E)$, which is included in $<_E$.
2. The execution steps of each process are totally ordered, i.e., $\langle p, i \rangle \to_E \langle p, i+1 \rangle$ whenever $\langle p, i+1 \rangle \in dom(E)$.
3. Given an execution sequence E and a process p s.t. $E \vdash p$, then for all events $e, e' \in dom(E)$, if $e \to_E e'$ then $e \to_{E.p} e'$.
4. Any linearization E' of $\to_E$ on $dom(E)$ is an execution sequence which has exactly the same "happens-before" relation $\to_{E'}$ as $\to_E$. This means that the relation $\to_E$ induces a set of equivalent execution sequences, all containing the same set of events, and with the same "happens-before" relation. We use.

   - $E \simeq E'$ to denote that $dom(E) = dom(E')$ and that E and E' are linearizations of the same "happens-before" relation, and
   - $[E]_\simeq$ to denote the equivalence class of E.

5. If $E \simeq E'$, then $enabled(s_{[E]}) = enabled(s_{[E']})$.

For the last property, we need to introduce a few definitions. Given $\to_E$, if $e, e' \in dom(E)$ and $e <_E e'$, define

- $e \lessdot_E e'$ (read as e is in a race with e') to denote that $e \to_E e'$ and $\hat{e} \neq \hat{e'}$ and there is no event $e'' \in dom(E)$, different from e' and e, such that $e \to_E e'' \to_E e'$.
- $e \precsim_E o'$ (read as e is in a reversible race with e') to denote that $e \lessdot_E e'$ and in any equivalent execution sequence $E' \simeq E$ where e occurs immediately before e', e' is not blocked before the occurrence of e.

Now we continue listing properties of valid happens-before relations.

6. Given an execution sequence E, then for all events $e, e' \in dom(E)$ where $e \lessdot_E e'$, there exists a set $O = observers(e, e', E) \subseteq dom(E)$ such that:

   (a) For all $o \in O$, it holds that $e \to_E o$, $o \neq e'$, and $o \not\to_E e'$.
   (b) For all $o, o' \in O$ it holds that $o \not\to_E o'$.
   (c) If $E' \simeq E$ then $O' = observers(e, e', E') = O$.
   (d) For every prefix $E' < E$ of E such that $e, e' \in dom(E')$:

   - If O is empty, then $e \to_{E'} e'$.
   - If O is nonempty, then $e \to_{E'} e'$ iff $dom(E') \cap O \neq \emptyset$.

   (e) If $e \precsim_E e'$, then for all sequences w such that $E \vdash w$ and all events $e'' \in dom(E)$:

   - If $e \not\to_E e''$, then $e \not\lessdot_{E.w} e''$.
   - If $e'' \not\to_E e'$, then $e'' \not\lessdot_{E.w} e'$.

   (f) For all $e'' \in dom(E)$ such that $e' \to_E e''$ it holds that $O \cap observers(e', e'', E) = \emptyset$.
   (g) If $O = \{o\}$ and $E = E'.\hat{o}$ for some o and E', then for any $E'' \simeq E'$, either $e \to_{E''.\hat{o}} e'$ or $e' \to_{E''.\hat{o}} e$.

We give some intuition for the changed properties. Property 3 requires the happens-before assignment to maintain edges in extensions, but allows having fewer edges in prefixes. Property 5 allows execution sequences that reach different states (due to unobserved races) to be considered equivalent. Property 6 summarizes properties for races that require observers. Most requirements are intuitive. Property 6.(d) clarifies Property 3: an "observed" race is included in a sequence only if some observers of the race are also included. Property 6.(e) prevents extensions to an execution sequence from adding edges to the events of a reversible race in such a way that the race can not be reversed. Property 6.(f) prohibits an observer from creating "dependency chains". Finally, Property 6.(g) requires that an observer observes a fixed set of pairs of events in each execution sequence; a consequence of this is that whether or not some particular race is observed never depends on the ordering of some other pair of events observed by the same observer. All these properties are satisfied by "natural" happens-before assignments for events in message passing programs and most shared memory programs. Limitations include e.g., models in which the written memory regions of two write operations may overlap without being equal; such pairs of operations need to be treated as unconditionally racing.

5   Optimal DPOR with Observers

We now present a DPOR algorithm with observers that achieves optimal reduction.

In Sect. 3.2 we explained why sleep sets are not suitable when observers are used. We instead introduce a notion of redundancy based solely on the set of explored steps from each state. We will base this notion on a concept defined in Optimal DPOR.

Definition 2 (Initials and Weak Initials [2]). *For an execution sequence* $E.w$, *the set* $I_{[E]}(w)$ *of processes that are initials and the set* $WI_{[E]}(w)$ *of processes that are weak initials are defined as follows:*

1. $p \in I_{[E]}(w)$ *iff there is a sequence* w' *such that* $E.w \simeq E.p.w'$
2. $p \in WI_{[E]}(w)$ *iff there are sequences* w' *and* v *such that* $E.w.v \simeq E.p.w'$

Definition 3 (Redundant Sequences). *For an execution sequence* E *and a function done from prefixes of* E *to sets of processes, the set of sequences* $redundant(E, done)$ *is defined such that* $v \in redundant(E, done)$ *iff* $E.v$ *is an execution sequence and there is a partitioning* $E = w.w'$ *of* E *such that some process* $p \in done(w)$ *is also in* $p \in WI_{[w]}(w'.v)$.

The intuition is that if $v \in redundant(E, done)$, then the execution sequence $E.v$ is equivalent to a previously explored execution sequence. In the special case where races do not need observers (i.e., the set of observers for each race is empty), we can define sleep sets in the classical sense by letting $p \in sleep(E)$ denote that E is of form $E'.v$ for some v such that $p \in done(E')$ and p and v

are independent. Then $sleep(E)$ will consists of all single-process sequences in $redundant(E, done)$, and $v \in redundant(E, done)$ is equivalent to $sleep(E) \cap WI_{[E]}(v) \neq \emptyset$.

If E is an execution sequence, and v and w are sequences of processes, let:

- $v \sqsubseteq_{[E]} w$ denote that there is a sequence v' such that $E.v.v'$ and $E.w$ are execution sequences with $E.v.v' \simeq E.w$. Intuitively, $v \sqsubseteq_{[E]} w$ if, after E, the sequence v is a possible way to start an execution that is equivalent to w.
- $v\sim_{[E]}w$ denote that there are sequences v' and w' such that $E.v.v'$ and $E.w.w'$ are execution sequences with $E.v.v' \simeq E.w.w'$. Intuitively, $v\sim_{[E]}w$ if, after E, the sequence v is a possible way to start an execution that is equivalent to an execution sequence of form $E.w.w'$, and vice versa.

Let us define an *ordered tree* as a pair $\langle B, \prec \rangle$, where B (the set of *nodes*) is a finite prefix-closed set of sequences of processes, with the empty sequence $\langle \rangle$ being the root. The children of a node w, of form $w.p$ for some set of processes p, are ordered by $\prec$. In $\langle B, \prec \rangle$, such an ordering between children has been extended to the total order $\prec$ on B by letting $\prec$ be the induced post-order relation between the nodes in B. This means that if the children $w.p_1$ and $w.p_2$ are ordered as $w.p_1 \prec w.p_2$, then $w.p_1 \prec w.p_2 \prec w$ in the induced post-order.

Definition 4 (Wakeup Tree). *Let E be an execution sequence, and done be a function from prefixes of E to sets of processes. A* wakeup tree *after $\langle E, done \rangle$ is an ordered tree $\langle B, \prec \rangle$, such that the following properties hold*

1. *No leaf w of B is redundant after E, i.e., $w \notin redundant(E, done)$;*
2. *whenever $u.p$ and $u.w$ are nodes in B with $u.p \prec u.w$, and $u.w$ is a leaf, then $p \notin WI_{[E.u]}(w)$.*

Property (2) is the same as Optimal DPOR; Property (1) has been modified.

Regarding inserting sequences in a wakeup tree, let $\langle B, \prec \rangle$ be a wakeup tree after $\langle E, done \rangle$. For any sequence w such that $w \notin redundant(E, done)$ we need an operation $insert_{[E]}(w, \langle B, \prec \rangle)$ that satisfies the following properties:

1. $insert_{[E]}(w, \langle B, \prec \rangle)$ is also a wakeup tree after $\langle E, done \rangle$,
2. any leaf of $\langle B, \prec \rangle$ remains a leaf of $insert_{[E]}(w, \langle B, \prec \rangle)$, and
3. $insert_{[E]}(w, \langle B, \prec \rangle)$ contains a leaf u with $u\sim_{[E]}w$.

The $insert_{[E]}(w, \langle B, \prec \rangle)$ operation can be implemented as follows. Let v be the smallest (w.r.t. to $\prec$) sequence in B such that $v\sim_{[E]}w$. If v is a leaf, $insert_{[E]}(w, \langle B, \prec \rangle)$ can leave the tree unmodified. Otherwise, let w' be a shortest sequence such that $w \sqsubseteq_{[E]} v.w'$, and add $v.w'$ as a new leaf, ordered after all already existing nodes in B of form $v.w''$.

5.1   Algorithm

Algorithm 1 is a modified and extended version of the plain Optimal DPOR algorithm [2], so that it supports observers. Since sleep sets is no longer an applicable mechanism for avoiding redundant exploration, the algorithm accepts only two arguments, E, the prefix to explore, and WuT, the initial wakeup tree after E. It keeps two global variables, wut, a mapping from execution sequences to wakeup trees, and $done$, a mapping from execution sequences to sets of processes. For a pair of events $e, e' \in dom(E)$ that are in a reversible race ($e \precsim_E e'$) in E, the algorithm employs the following notation:

- $pre(E, e)$ denotes the prefix of E up to, but not including, the event e,
- $notdep(e, E)$ denotes the sub-sequence of E consisting of the events that occur after e but do not "happen after" e (i.e., the events e' that occur after e such that $e \nrightarrow_E e'$).
- $notobs(e, e', E)$ denotes the sub-sequence of E containing the events that "happen after" e, but are not observers $o \in O = observers(e, e', E)$ of the race $e \rightarrow_E e'$, nor "happen after" any such o: $notobs(e, e', E) = \langle q \parallel q \in E, e \rightarrow_E q, q \notin O, \nexists o \in O.o \rightarrow_E q \rangle$.

Algorithm 1. Optimal DPOR with Observers.

Initial call: $Explore(\langle \rangle, \langle \{\langle \rangle\}, \emptyset \rangle)$

```
1  Explore(E, WuT)
2      done(E) := ∅;
3      if enabled(s[E]) = ∅ then                          // Race detection only at maximal execution sequences
4          foreach e, e' ∈ dom(E) such that (e ≾E e') do  // For each racing pair e, e'
5              let E' = pre(E, e);                         // Goto state before e
6              if observers(e, e', E) ≠ ∅ then             // Is e→E e' an observed race?
7                  choose o ∈ observers(e, e', E) ;        // Select an arbitrary observer as a witness
8                  let v = notdep(e, E).ê'.ê.(notobs(e, e', E) \ ê').ô;   // Find events that don't observe e→E e'
9              else                                        // If e→E e' are independently racing
10                 let v = notdep(e, E).ê';                // Find events independent with e
11             if v ∉ redundant(E', done) then             // Has no equivalent already been explored?
12                 wut(E') := insert[E'](v, wut(E'));      // If not, insert into the wakeup tree
13     else                                                // If not at a maximal execution sequence, explore...
14         if WuT ≠ ⟨{⟨⟩}, ∅⟩ then
15             wut(E) := WuT;                              // ... either using an existing wakeup tree
16         else
17             choose p ∈ enabled(s[E]);                   // ... or by selecting an arbitrary p...
18             wut(E) := ⟨{⟨⟩, p}, {(p, ⟨⟩)}⟩;            // ... and making a wakeup tree from it
19         while ∃p ∈ wut(E) do                            // While the wakeup tree is not empty...
20             let p = min≺{p ∈ wut(E)};                   // ... pick next branch, ...
21             let WuT' = subtree(wut(E), p);              // ... compute next wakeup tree (a subtree of the current),...
22             Explore(E.p, WuT');                         // ... and do a recursive call to Explore
23             remove all sequences of form p.w from wut(E);  // When done, cleanup...
24             add p to done(E);                           // ... and mark p as explored
```

The first change compared to Optimal DPOR is in lines 6 to 8 which describe how to construct a wakeup sequence for an observed race, including an observer operation. Second, the test $v \in redundant(E, done)$ on lines 11 replaces the test $sleep(E') \cap WI_{[E']}(v) \neq \emptyset$ at the corresponding place in Optimal DPOR. The rest of the algorithm is essentially the same, with initialization, update and propagation of sleep sets removed.

5.2   Correctness and Optimality

The correctness and optimality of Algorithm 1 are stated in the following theorems.

Theorem 1 (Correctness of Optimal DPOR with Observers). *When-ever a call to Explore(E, WuT) returns during Algorithm 1, then for all maximal execution sequences E.w, the algorithm has explored some execution sequence E' which is in $[E.w]_\simeq$.*

Since the initial call to the algorithm uses the arguments $Explore(\langle\rangle$, $\langle\{\langle\rangle\}, \emptyset\rangle)$, Theorem 1 implies that for all maximal execution sequences E the algorithm explores some execution sequence E' which is in $[E]_\simeq$.

Theorem 2 (Optimality of Optimal DPOR with Observers). *Algorithm 1 never explores two maximal execution sequences which are equivalent.*

If Algorithm 1 is not at the end of a maximal sequence, it will continue exploring the scheduling either by using information from a wakeup tree (line 15) or by choosing an arbitrary enabled process (line 18). Theorem 2 ensures that all maximal execution sequences reached are non redundant.

6   Implementations

We have implemented Algorithm 1 in two SMC tools: Nidhugg and Concuerror.

Observers in Nidhugg. Nidhugg [1] is a stateless model checking tool for shared-memory pthreads programs written in C or C++ that operates by inter-preting LLVM IR. Nidhugg can test programs also under relaxed memory models (TSO, PSO, and Power), but in this paper we will limit ourselves to testing pro-grams under Sequential Consistency.

In the context of shared memory, the observers extension was used to make races between writes to the same memory location conditional on the existence of a read of that memory location that "observes" those writes. In order to add the observers extension to Nidhugg, the tool was first extended to support Optimal DPOR, as it previously only implemented Source DPOR, which is not easily extended with observers, as discussed in Sect. 3.2. The tool now records symbolic representations of program events that contain enough information to reconstruct the happens-before relation induced by a particular execution. For Source DPOR, these symbolic events are unnecessary if the happens-before relation is stored in vector clocks [18], as it is in Nidhugg. For Optimal DPOR, symbolic events are the most reasonable way to implement tests that check whether a given process is a weak initial of some sequence, which is needed for both the redundancy check and wakeup tree insertion.

To extend this implementation with observers, symbolic events for writes were extended with an "observed"-flag, which is unset until a read that reads the value written by that write is executed. At the end of the execution, we compute the vector clocks of the happens-before relation, only considering two write events to the same memory location as interfering if at least one of them has the "observed"-flag set. Then, Optimal DPOR was modified as described in Sect. 5.1. The check whether a wakeup sequence is redundant on line 11 is implemented using sleep sets extended with processes conditionally sleeping unless an address is read, and a set of addresses that must be read, without intervening writes, before the end of the program.

Observers in Concuerror. Concuerror [8] is a stateless model checking tool for Erlang, a functional programming language based on the actor model of concurrency [4]. In Erlang, actors are realized by language-level processes implemented by the runtime system instead of being directly mapped to OS threads. Each Erlang process communicates with other processes via asynchronous message passing. Messages are placed in the mailbox of the receiving process in the order they are delivered. A process can consume messages using *selective* `receive`, which is a *blocking* operation when the mailbox does not contain any matching message, unless a timeout clause is specified. If multiple messages can match, the oldest message is picked from the mailbox.

Concuerror already implemented Optimal DPOR, but treated any two message deliveries to the same mailbox as interfering. With the extension, Concuerror uses `receives` as observers of `sends`. When examining a complete scheduling, an extra pass is performed, annotating each message delivery event with the patterns that were used in the `receive` that picked the message (if present) and the receive order. If the message of a later delivery matches any of the pattern annotations of an earlier delivery, the deliveries interfere. The *notobs* sequence is constructed from all the events that lead up to the corresponding `receive` (which is the observer), excluding events in the *notdep* sequence. Because the resulting wakeup sequence contains fewer events, observer information is recomputed, and then all the earlier *done* sets are checked for weak initials of the wakeup sequence, exactly as described in Algorithm 1.

7   Experimental Results

We report experimental results that compare the performance of two algorithms: Optimal DPOR (denoted in the tables as "optimal") and Optimal DPOR with Observers (denoted as "observers"). We ran all benchmarks on a desktop with an i7-3770 CPU (3.40 GHz) with 16 GB of RAM running Debian 4.12.0-2-amd64 and LLVM 3.8.1. The machine has four physical cores, but presently both tools use only one of them.

Observers in Nidhugg. Table 1 shows the effect of observers on shared memory C/pthread programs. We used two kinds of programs: (1) synthetic benchmarks similar to those of Sect. 2, and (2) programs from SV-COMP and/or from "similar" papers. We report the number of traces that the two algorithms explore, the time it takes to explore them, and the memory used (although this number is not interesting for an SMC tool).

Table 1. Performance of Optimal DPOR vs. Optimal DPOR with Observers in Nidhugg.

	Traces Explored		Time		Memory	
Benchmark	optimal	observers	optimal	observers	optimal	observers
lastwrite(2)	2	2	<0.1s	<0.1s	10MB	10MB
lastwrite(7)	5040	7	0.5s	<0.1s	10MB	10MB
lastwrite(8)	40320	8	5.2s	<0.1s	10MB	10MB
lastwrite(9)	362880	9	52.0s	<0.1s	10MB	10MB
floating_read(2)	6	5	<0.1s	<0.1s	10MB	10MB
floating_read(6)	5040	193	0.5s	<0.1s	11MB	10MB
floating_read(7)	40320	449	5.0s	<0.1s	11MB	11MB
floating_read(8)	362880	1025	53.3s	0.2s	11MB	11MB
apr_1	1145	1145	4.8s	5.0s	19MB	20MB
fib	218243	218243	18.9s	20.1s	11MB	11MB
lamport(2)	16+16	14+12	<0.1s	<0.1s	10MB	10MB
lamport(3)	9216+11525	5466+6132	4.0s	?.7s	11MB	11MB

lastwrite(n). A synthetic program where n threads write to a shared variable x and a single process first joins (awaits the termination of) the writing threads, and then reads that variable.

floating_read(n). A synthetic program where n threads write to a shared variable x and a single process reads that variable without waiting for the writing processes to exit.

apr_1. A benchmark adapted from the sources of the Apache Portable Runtime library version 1.5.1. Also used in [1], there called apr_1.c. (Here, no loop bounding was applied.)

fib. A benchmark from SV-COMP, also used in [1] where it was called fib_true.c.

lamport(n). This standard benchmark has n worker processes acquiring a mutex implemented by Lamport's second fast mutual exclusion protocol [16] and immediately releasing it. We show it for 2 and 3 processes which are the only sizes that are both non-trivial and tractable.

For lastwrite(n), we see a reduction in the number of interleavings explored from $n!$ to n, as explained in Sect. 2. For floating_read(n), optimal shows the predicted $(n + 1)!$ interleavings, and for $n = 2$, observers reduce the interleaving count from 6 to 5 as expected. In general, the benchmark has $n \times 2^{n-1} + 1$ interleavings with observers. Notice that any technique that differentiates equivalence classes by the partial order of program steps must explore at least as many interleavings or violate Property 4. The next two programs (apr_1 and fib) are examples of programs for which observers have no effect. We see that the extra overhead is very moderate for both programs.

In the last benchmark (lamport), we see that observers improve performance. As Nidhugg does not implement await statements (which are used by lamport), it emulates these with assumes. In such cases, Nidhugg might explore some traces in which these assumptions are violated. We list those traces separately, so for this benchmark the "Traces Explored" columns show $a + b$ entries, which means that Nidhugg explored $a + b$ traces but b of those times an `assume` statement was violated.

Observers in Concuerror. Table 2 shows the effect of observers in message passing programs; we omit memory used, as both algorithms have similar requirements.

Table 2. Comparison of Optimal DPOR vs. Optimal DPOR with Observers in Concuerror.

	Traces Explored		Time			Traces Explored		Time	
Benchmark	optimal	observers	optimal	observers	Benchmark	optimal	observers	optimal	observers
not_selective(2)	2	2	<1.0s	<1.0s	lock(3)	30	6	0.9s	0.9s
not_selective(6)	720	720	1.7s	1.8s	lock(4)	336	24	1.4s	0.9s
not_selective(7)	5040	5040	6.0s	6.8s	lock(5)	5040	120	9.0s	1.3s
not_selective(8)	40320	40320	48.0s	56.0s	lock(6)	95040	720	3m27s	2.6s
selective(2)	2	1	<1.0s	<1.0s	poolboy	746	265	6.6s	4.0s
selective(6)	720	1	1.8s	<1.0s	gproc	1168	784	12.7s	10.0s
selective(7)	5040	1	6.3s	<1.0s					
selective(8)	40320	1	51.0s	<1.0s	corfu-repair	92750496	3864604	1022h	52h

not_selective(n). n processes send messages to a process, that can receive any message sent to it.

selective(n). This is a generalized version of the last example of Sect. 2. A process uses pattern matching to choose between messages from n different senders.

lock(n). This is a program in which n workers acquire and release a lock simulated by an Erlang process. When using observers, it has $n!$ schedulings. Without observers the number of schedulings is higher.

poolboy. A benchmark created from a unit test of a worker pool library [2].

gproc. A benchmark created from a library implementing an extended process dictionary [2].

corfu-repair. A program that verifies the correctness of a repair protocol of CORFU, a distributed database using a variant of Chain Replication. From a paper [5] that motivated our work.

The two benchmarks on the left sub-table confirm the behaviour we expect. When `receives` are not selective, the number of traces explored by both algorithms is $n!$. With selective `receive` (selective benchmark) observers explore only one trace.

The first program on the right sub-table (lock) is originally a shared-memory program that when translated to Erlang simulate locks using message passing. To acquire the lock, a process sends a message with its identifier to the "lock process" and then waits for a reply. Upon receiving the `acquire` message, the lock process uses the identifier to reply and then waits for a `release` message. Other `acquire` messages become queued in the mailbox of the lock process. Upon receiving the `release` message, the lock process loops back to the start, retrieving the next `acquire` message and notifying the next process. Notice that, without observers, the delivery of the `release` message of a process interferes (redundantly) with the delivery of `acquire` messages of other processes, unlike acquire operations on true locks which cannot be executed before a release operation (such messages were treated exceptionally in the evaluation of Optimal DPOR). Observers remove the need for special handling: the receive statements are enough to precisely determine which pairs of send operations are interfering.

The next two table rows (`poolboy` and `gproc`) show results from "real" Erlang programs. We see that observers provide a moderate reduction in both the number of traces that need to be explored as well as in time.

Finally, the last program (`corfu-repair`) is the one that triggered this work. As can be seen in the table, observers allow Concuerror to complete SMC in a bit more than two days, while without observers the tool needs to explore exactly 24 times as many traces, taking more than 42 days to finish.

8 Related Work

POR techniques have been continuously evolving w.r.t. how they determine interference. Refining the conditions under which higher-level operations interfere has been shown to have significant impact, regardless of whether the states in which such operations are executed is also a parameter or not [13]. In this work, we have extended this idea, parameterizing the interference between operations using distinct observer operations.

DPOR techniques have also been extended to take advantage of special properties of the underlying concurrency model. For the actor model, the transitivity of the dependency relation for send operations has been exploited to defer early planning of interleavings [21]. This improvement is orthogonal with Optimal DPOR (and with our extension), as it reduces the number of wakeup sequences that are added "early" in an exploration. For event-driven systems, it has been shown [17] that two post operations to an event dispatch queue need not be considered dependent: reordering of such operations can be decided later, upon detection of interference between other operations within the respective event handlers. However, this treatment applies only under a specific interpretation of 'message passing' that exploits additional semantic structure of an actor's mailbox. Our technique is applicable to a wider spectrum of programs.

Context-Sensitive DPOR [3] uses an external procedure to decide whether alternative schedulings would lead to identical states and, like optimal DPOR with observer, is also able to achieve exponential reduction in certain cases. However, since it needs to compare states, it is an inherently stateful technique, in contrast to our technique that inspects only one trace at a time to lazily construct reversible races.

Data-Centric DPOR (DC-DPOR) [7] is an SMC technique that explores a related but different notion of observability. It defines two executions to be equivalent if each read reads from ("observes") the same write in both executions. In contrast, our notion of observability is based on observing *interference of operations*, not just individual writes. DC-DPOR's resulting equivalence relation is coarser than ours, which is based on Mazurkiewicz traces. However, DC-DPOR is optimal only for programs with acyclic communication graphs, while being non-optimal otherwise. Also, DC-DPOR models message passing using locks and shared memory, which at best gives as few traces as Optimal DPOR gives without the improvements presented in this paper.

9   Concluding Remarks

In this paper we presented an extension to the Optimal DPOR algorithm for SMC that uses observability to refine which operations are considered as interfering. We described the challenges and motivated the necessary modifications, gave a formal description of the algorithm and the theory behind it and reported on two implementations in SMC tools, demonstrating that Optimal DPOR with Observers can achieve significantly better reduction in both shared memory and message passing programs.

Acknowledgments. This work was carried out within the Linnaeus centre of excellence UPMARC (Uppsala Programming for Multicore Architectures Research Center), and was partly supported by grants from the Swedish Research Council.

Data Availability Statement. The versions of Nidhugg and Concuerror, as well as all the programs we used to obtain the experimental results of Tables 1 and 2 are available in the Figshare repository [6]. Also included in the artifact are instructions on how to use it to reproduce the results reported in this paper. As per the TACAS 2018 submission rules, the artifact is designed for use with the TACAS 2018 Artifact Evaluation Virtual Machine [14], although, as source code is included, it can probably be used on any Linux platform. We refer to the documentation of the respective tool on how to compile them from source code; the tools may of course evolve over time, but the way to build them will not change significantly.

References

1. Abdulla, P.A., Aronis, S., Atig, M.F., Jonsson, B., Leonardsson, C., Sagonas, K.: Stateless model checking for TSO and PSO. In: Baier, C., Tinelli, C. (eds.) TACAS 2015. LNCS, vol. 9035, pp. 353–367. Springer, Heidelberg (2015). https://doi.org/10.1007/978-3-662-46681-0_28
2. Abdulla, P.A., Aronis, S., Jonsson, B., Sagonas, K.: Source sets: a foundation for optimal dynamic partial order reduction. J. ACM **64**(4), 251–2549 (2017). http://doi.acm.org/10.1145/3073408
3. Albert, E., Arenas, P., de la Banda, M.G., Gómez-Zamalloa, M., Stuckey, P.J.: Context-sensitive dynamic partial order reduction. In: Majumdar, R., Kunčak, V. (eds.) CAV 2017. LNCS, vol. 10426, pp. 526–543. Springer, Cham (2017). https://doi.org/10.1007/978-3-319-63387-9_26
4. Armstrong, J.: Erlang. Commun. ACM **53**(9), 68–75 (2010). http://doi.acm.org/10.1145/1810891.1810910

5. Aronis, S., Fritchie, S.L., Sagonas, K.: Testing and verifying chain repair methods for CORFU using stateless model checking. In: Polikarpova, N., Schneider, S. (eds.) IFM 2017. LNCS, vol. 10510, pp. 227–242. Springer, Cham (2017). https://doi.org/10.1007/978-3-319-66845-1_15
6. Aronis, S., Jonsson, B., Lång, M., Sagonas, K.: Binary artifact for TACAS-2018 paper "Optimal DPOR with Observers". Figshare, February 2018. https://doi.org/10.6084/m9.figshare.5918701.v1
7. Chalupa, M., Chatterjee, K., Pavlogiannis, A., Sinha, N., Vaidya, K.: Data-centric dynamic partial order reduction. Proc. ACM Program. Lang. 2(POPL), 31:1–31:30 (2017). http://doi.acm.org/10.1145/3158119
8. Christakis, M., Gotovos, A., Sagonas, K.: Systematic testing for detecting concurrency errors in Erlang programs. In: Sixth IEEE International Conference on Software Testing, Verification and Validation, ICST 2013, pp. 154–163. IEEE Computer Society, Los Alamitos, CA, USA (2013). https://doi.org/10.1109/ICST.2013.50
9. Clarke, E.M., Grumberg, O., Minea, M., Peled, D.: State space reduction using partial order techniques. Int. J. Softw. Tools Technol. Transf. 2(3), 279–287 (1999). http://dx.doi.org/10.1007/s100090050035
10. Flanagan, C., Godefroid, P.: Dynamic partial-order reduction for model checking software. In: Proceedings of the 32nd ACM SIGPLAN-SIGACT Symposium on Principles of Programming Languages, POPL 2005, pp. 110–121. ACM, New York (2005). http://doi.acm.org/10.1145/1040305.1040315
11. Godefroid, P.: Partial-order methods for the verification of concurrent systems: an approach to the state-explosion problem. Ph.D. thesis, University of Liége (1996). http://www.springer.com/gp/book/9783540607618, also. LNCS, vol. 1032. Springer, Heidelberg
12. Godefroid, P.: Model checking for programming languages using VeriSoft. In: Proceedings of the 24th ACM SIGPLAN-SIGACT Symposium on Principles of Programming Languages, POPL 1997, pp. 174–186. ACM, New York (1997). http://doi.acm.org/10.1145/263699.263717
13. Godefroid, P., Pirottin, D.: Refining dependencies improves partial-order verification methods (extended abstract). In: Courcoubetis, C. (ed.) CAV 1993. LNCS, vol. 697, pp. 438–449. Springer, Heidelberg (1993). https://doi.org/10.1007/3-540-56922-7_36
14. Hartmanns, A., Wendler, P.: TACAS 2018 Artifact Evaluation VM. Figshare (2018). https://doi.org/10.6084/m9.figshare.5896615
15. Lamport, L.: Time, clocks and the ordering of events in a distributed system. Commun. ACM 21(7), 558–565 (1978). http://doi.acm.org/10.1145/359545.359563
16. Lamport, L.: A fast mutual exclusion algorithm. ACM Trans. Comput. Syst. 5(1), 1–11 (1987). http://doi.acm.org/10.1145/7351.7352
17. Maiya, P., Gupta, R., Kanade, A., Majumdar, R.: Partial order reduction for event-driven multi-threaded programs. In: Chechik, M., Raskin, J.-F. (eds.) TACAS 2016. LNCS, vol. 9636, pp. 680–697. Springer, Heidelberg (2016). https://doi.org/10.1007/978-3-662-49674-9_44
18. Mattern, F.: Virtual time and global states of distributed systems. In: Cosnard, M., et al. (eds.) Proceedings of the Workshop on Parallel and Distributed Algorithms, pp. 215–226. North-Holland/Elsevier (1989)
19. Mazurkiewicz, A.: Trace theory. In: Brauer, W., Reisig, W., Rozenberg, G. (eds.) ACPN 1986. LNCS, vol. 255, pp. 278–324. Springer, Heidelberg (1987). https://doi.org/10.1007/3-540-17906-2_30

248   S. Aronis et al.

20. Peled, D.: All from one, one for all: on model checking using representatives. In: Courcoubetis, C. (ed.) CAV 1993. LNCS, vol. 697, pp. 409–423. Springer, Heidelberg (1993). https://doi.org/10.1007/3-540-56922-7_34
21. Tasharofi, S., Karmani, R.K., Lauterburg, S., Legay, A., Marinov, D., Agha, G.: TransDPOR: a novel dynamic partial-order reduction technique for testing actor programs. In: Giese, H., Rosu, G. (eds.) FMOODS/FORTE -2012. LNCS, vol. 7273, pp. 219–234. Springer, Heidelberg (2012). https://doi.org/10.1007/978-3-642-30793-5_14
22. Valmari, A.: Stubborn sets for reduced state space generation. In: Rozenberg, G. (ed.) ICATPN 1989. LNCS, vol. 483, pp. 491–515. Springer, Heidelberg (1991). https://doi.org/10.1007/3-540-53863-1_36

Structurally Defined Conditional Data-Flow Static Analysis

Elena Sherman[1(✉)] and Matthew B. Dwyer[2]

[1] Boise State University, Boise, ID 83706, USA
elenasherman@boisestate.edu
[2] University of Nebraska - Lincoln, Lincoln, NE 68588, USA
matthewbdwyer@unl.edu

Abstract. Data flow analysis (DFA) is an important verification technique that computes the effect of data values propagating over program paths. While more precise than flow-insensitive analyses, such an analysis is time-consuming.

This paper investigates the acceleration of DFA by structural decomposition of the underlying control flow graph. Specifically, we explore the cost and effectiveness of dividing program paths into subsets by partitioning path suffixes at conditional statements, applying a DFA on each subset, and then combining the resulting invariants. This yields a family of independent DFA problems that are solved in parallel and where the partial results of each problem represent safe program invariants.

Empirical evaluations reveal that depending on the DFA type and its conditional implementation the invariants for a large fraction of program points can be computed in less time than traditional DFA. This work suggests a strategy for an "anytime DFA" algorithm: computing safe program invariants as the analysis proceeds.

1 Introduction

Software developers use static analyses as a supplement to traditional dynamic testing approaches. Tools such as AbsInt Astrée [1], Facebook Infer [2], and MathWorks Polyspace[1] are becoming standard parts of development workflows. Advances in program analysis and theorem proving have helped static program analysis become more feasible for verification of general-purpose software.

The power of static analysis to consider all program behaviors follows from its ability to safely over-approximate program behaviors by abstracting the concrete domain of program variables and the programming language semantics. But at the same time its over-approximating nature causes static analysis to identify some property violations as uncertain. The reason for this uncertainty is that a static analysis cannot tell if a violation happens on a feasible or an infeasible, i.e., strictly over-approximating, program behavior. This inconclusiveness is

---

[1] http://www.mathworks.com/products/polyspace.html

© The Author(s) 2018
D. Beyer and M. Huisman (Eds.): TACAS 2018, LNCS 10806, pp. 249–265, 2018.
https://doi.org/10.1007/978-3-319-89963-3_15

unacceptable since each potential violation must be examined further. An automatic solution to the elimination of false positive violations is to increase the precision of a static analysis, i.e., improve the analysis so it considers fewer infeasible behaviors.

However, improving analysis precision generally increases analysis cost in terms of running time and memory consumption. A common approach to address this problem is to decompose the program's state space into several subspaces and perform analysis on each separately. What distinguishes those techniques are the underlying decomposition methods.

One approach focuses on making a precise static analysis scalable by decomposing a large program into modules like procedures and classes, and allowing the analysis to examine each partition independently. Next, the analyzed information of each module is composed together to obtain the result of the whole program analysis. In the literature [3,4] this method is referred to as *partial static analysis*.

Another approach aims to improve the scalability of precise analysis by permitting the analysis to explore only those program states for which it is adequately precise, i.e., able to provide definitive result. In the literature [5–7] this approach is called *conditional static analysis* (CSA) since the permitted states are described by a condition θ expressed as a logical formula. In such a framework an analysis verifies a program under some assumptions, i.e., there are no null pointer exceptions or a pre-condition on input values is assumed to hold. Next, another analysis attempts to prove these assumptions by showing that the states, which do not satisfy θ are either not reachable or do not lead to property violations. In prior work the condition θ is either determined from the analysis design [5,6], where θ is applicable to all program states, or determined during program analysis execution [7], where θ is composed of the conditions assumed to hold for a certain set of states.

While previous work on CSA focuses on finding values of θ that ensure an increase in analysis precision, in this paper we explore the decomposition of the program's state space in order to improve the efficiency of the analysis. We decompose the program's state space based on the program's control flow graph (CFG), i.e., on the program's structural information. Each partition corresponds to a set of paths expressed as a set of CFG branches π. This permits a path, or π, defined CSA to compute invariants for each π independently and in parallel. While one can use a logical formula θ as a precondition to restrict program input values to those that follow a particular path, we conjecture two primary advantages of structural decomposition. First, π is expressed directly as a subset of CFG branches and computing an equivalent θ, expressing constraints on input values, would require complex value propagating analyses. Second, because π is structural its effect on the analysis is independent of the abstract domain, whereas even an equivalent θ may not be effective in preventing values from flowing along a branch due to over-approximation by the abstract domain.

The contributions of this paper are presentation of:

1. A formalization of the path-define CSA as a data-flow framework.
2. Two algorithms for implementing CSA in existing analysis frameworks.
3. An approach to efficiently partition CFG paths for path-defined CSA.

In the next section, we provide an overview of the structural CSA approach and pose our research questions. After that we formalize CSA in Sect. 3 and demonstrate in Sect. 4 two different ways of implementing CSA in an existing program analysis framework. In Sect. 5 we present our approach to partitioning a CFG. Then we present our experiments and discuss related work.

2   Overview

We begin with an example of a traditional data-flow analysis. Data-flow analysis calculates some information for each point in a program based on the program structure and the language semantics. The calculated facts, i.e., program invariants, are then later used to reason about program properties, usually safety properties, which must hold on all feasible program executions. Data-flow analyses that compute invariants that are satisfied by all paths are called *must* analyses. In our example we show how a data-flow analysis computes invariants for each program statement.

Consider a program and its corresponding CFG in Fig. 1(a). In this example x is an integer variable. The edges of the CFG are labeled with T for *true* branches and F for *false* branches of the conditional statement.

In order to calculate invariants *static analysis* (SA) works with abstract values of x, which are composed of the elements of an abstract domain. For example, the *signs* abstract domain has three elements $\{+, 0, -\}$. 0 denotes the singleton set $\{0\}$ of concrete values, $+$ denotes positive values, and $-$ denotes negative values. If SA employs the *signs* abstract domain then the values of x are expressed as a set containing any of those three elements, including special cases $\{\} \equiv \bot$ for no values and $\{+, 0, -\} \equiv \top$ for all values

SA starts by assigning x to $\top$ at the CFG's entry point, since x can have any concrete value. Upon encountering the conditional statement SA computes invariants for x along the true branch, then along the false branch, and then merges these values before the return statement. The left CFG in Fig. 1 shows the result of the analysis where the CFG's edges are annotated with computed invariants for x. Clearly, the computations along these two branches are independent of each other and could be done simultaneously, thus reducing the computational time. This observation is the main idea behind our approach.

In other parallel SA approaches that we discuss in Sect. 7, the parallel computation is done inside a full SA. During the computation a parallel SA waits at the merge point, where the analysis combines the results of the two branches, on the completion of each branch before proceeding further thereby reducing parallelism.

```
if (x >= 0){
    x = 0;
} else {
    x = -2*x;
}
return x;
```

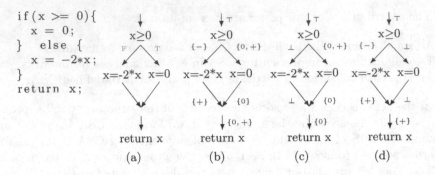

Fig. 1. Source code and its CFG (a); analysis examples: *signs* analysis result (b), CSA *sign* analysis result for set paths with *1t* prefix (c) and *1f* prefix (d)

Moreover, if we can analyze the true and the false branches independently then the invariants computed along the true branch could be accessed even sooner for a user to process. This observation is another inspiration for designing "anytime DFA", which provides a sound information about some program's invariants.

As mentioned, in general, it would be difficult to compute a precondition θ that restricts the input values of x to only those that would take the CSA computation to a particular set of branches. However, in path-defined CSA those branches can be stated explicitly. In our example we can have two set of paths: one defined by $\pi_1 = \{1t\}$, i.e., take the true branch of the first conditional statement only, and $\pi_2 = \{1f\}$, i.e., take the false branch of the first conditional statement. The results of these two path-defined CSA are in (c) and (d) in Fig. 1, respectively. We can see that the union of the abstract element sets for π_1 CSA and π_2 CSA on the corresponding edges results in the same invariants of the full analysis, that is CSA produces sound results. Section 3 formalizes the conditions under which soundness holds in CSA. Overall CSA can potentially provide two main benefits to a user: (1) the speedup of the analysis using parallelism *and* (2) delivering fast useful feedback to users.

One of the objectives of our work is to investigate the efficiency of two π-defined CSA implementations in an existing data-flow framework and its ability to compute sound invariants at intermediate points in the analysis.

To evaluate efficiency improvements we consider a traditional reaching definitions (RD) analysis and value-based data flow analysis (VB) for disjoint domains [8] similar to one used in the above example. Our approach automatically generates a set of π for each method based on heuristics discussed in Sect. 5. Then based on π it recombines CSA in the order of its completion and then compares the result of each combination step to the results of the full SA. Through our experiments we aim to answer the following research questions:

1. Does path-defined CSA compute sound invariants faster than SA?
2. At what rate does CSA compute sound invariants?
3. How efficient are the two implementations of CSA?

We answer these research questions through an extensive empirical evaluation on real-world programs.

3 Conditional Analysis

In this section we first present the traditional monotone framework for data flow analysis followed by the discussion of the necessary changes that extend it to a conditional data flow framework. This section also outlines the approach of composing the unconditional result from conditional ones.

We use the data flow analysis framework similar to one presented in [9] for an analysis $\mathcal{A}$, only we extended it to express branch-sensitive analysis, where the outgoing flow of a statement $l \in CFG_P$ is defined for each of its outgoing edges $(l, l') \in CFG_P$. Thus, the following parameters define $\mathcal{A}$.

- The complete lattice $D_\mathcal{A}$ that describes the abstract domain of $\mathcal{A}$.
- CFG_P for a program P.
- A set of monotone transfer functions $\mathcal{F}_\mathcal{A}$ for each statement $(l, l') \in CFG_P$ that maps an element of $D_\mathcal{A}$ to itself, i.e., $f_{ll'} \in \mathcal{F}_\mathcal{A} : D_\mathcal{A} \mapsto D_\mathcal{A}$.
- Entry statements E in CFG_P.
- An initial value $\iota \in D_\mathcal{A}$ for statements in E.

Then the set of equations for forward $\mathcal{A}$ is defined as follows on entry and exit of each statement $l \in CFG_P$:

$$A_{in}(l) = \bigsqcup \{A_{out}(l', l) \mid (l', l) \in CFG_P\} \sqcup \iota_E^l \qquad (1)$$

$$\text{where } \iota_E^l = \begin{cases} \iota & \text{if } l \in E \\ \bot & \text{if } l \notin E \end{cases}$$

$$A_{out}(l, l') = f_{ll'}(A_{in}(l)), (l, l') \in CFG_P$$

where $\sqcup$ is the least upper bound operator, $\bot$ is the bottom element of $D_\mathcal{A}$ for which $\forall d \in D_\mathcal{A} : \bot \sqcup d = d$ and $\forall (l, l') \in CFG_P : f_{ll'}(\bot) = \bot$. For safety, $\bot$ corresponds to the empty set of concrete values and $\top$ to the set containing all concrete values. The value of ι is assigned to $\top$, i.e., the analysis considers all possible input values for a program. The solution of the above set of equations provides the result of the analysis for P.

In our work we express a condition for DFA as a condition that identifies the set of paths to be analyzed π, which defines a CFG partition. We describe CSA as a special case of $\mathcal{A}$, which we denote as $\mathcal{A}^\pi$. Thus, a traditional data flow analysis $\mathcal{A} = \mathcal{A}^{(\emptyset)}$; unspecified branches in π are explored fully. For our formulation of CSA, the edges in π are not nested inside a loop.

We have chosen π to be represented by the set of branch edges in CFG_P, at most one for each conditional statement l, which the analysis must include while excluding their counterparts. If l has l' and l'' as its true and false targets, respectively, then π can contain the edge (l, l'), or the edge (l, l''), or none of them. To capture the relation between the opposite branches of l we designate

254   E. Sherman and M. B. Dwyer

$(l, l') = \neg(l, l'')$ and vice versa $(l, l'') = \neg(l, l')$. If $(l, l') \in \pi$ then the values of all variables x_i incoming to the target of its opposite edge l'', i.e., along edge $\neg(l, l')$, are set to $\bot$. For brevity, we denote such case, i.e., when $\forall i : x_i = \bot$, as $\bot$ state. Those $\bot$ values of the infeasible edges are propagated further to its children making them excluded from the analysis. The same principle applies when the opposite target $(l, l'') \in \pi$. When none of the edges are present in π then the analysis treats them in its usual manner, i.e., propagates the information through both branches.

With these path-based conditions we can now write the set of equations for conditional data flow framework for an analysis $\mathcal{A}^\pi$:

$$\mathcal{A}_{in}^\pi(l) = \bigsqcup \{\mathcal{A}_{out}^\pi(l', l) \mid (l', l) \in CFG_P\} \sqcup \iota_E^l \tag{2}$$

$$\text{where } \iota_E^l = \begin{cases} \top & \text{if } l \in E \\ \bot & \text{if } l \notin E \end{cases}$$

$$\mathcal{A}_{out}^\pi(l, l') = \begin{cases} f_{ll'}(\mathcal{A}_{in}^\pi(l)) & \text{if } (l, l') \in CFG_P \text{ and } \neg(l, l') \notin \pi \\ \bot & \text{if } (l, l') \in CFG_P \text{ and } \neg(l, l') \in \pi \end{cases}$$

Let Π be the set of path-based conditions for an analysis $\mathcal{A}$. Executing $\mathcal{A}$ with different conditions $\pi_j \in \Pi$ produces a set of conditional analysis $\mathcal{A}^{\pi_j}$. The solution for an $l \in CFG_P$ over Π can be expressed as the meet over all maximal fixed point computations (MFP) produced by each $\mathcal{A}^{\pi_j}$, which, when equal to the MFP for $\mathcal{A}$, means that SA and CSA produce the same results.

$$\bigsqcup_{\pi_j \in \Pi} MFP_{\mathcal{A}^{\pi_j}}(l) = MFP_{\mathcal{A}}(l) \tag{3}$$

Since SA performs the computation over all program execution paths then in order for CSA to be sound it must ensure the same. For example consider two conditions $\{(l, l')\}$ and $\{\neg(l, l')\}$. The conditional analysis $\mathcal{A}^{\{(l,l')\}}$ analyzes all possible input values for the set of paths containing the true branch of l while $\mathcal{A}^{\{\neg(l,l')\}}$ does it for the set of paths containing the false branch of l. Thus, together $\mathcal{A}^{\{(l,l')\}}$ and $\mathcal{A}^{\{\neg(l,l')\}}$ analyze all program paths. To formalize the soundness of CSA, we express π as a boolean function g_π as follows.

Each true edge in CFG_P is mapped to a boolean variable x_i and each false edge is mapped to $\neg x_i$. Then edges in π are mapped to a set of literals and g_π is expressed as a conjunction of those literals. In our example if (l, l') is mapped to x_1 then $g_{\{(l,l')\}} := x_1$ and $g_{\{\neg(l,l')\}} := \neg x_1$. The union of these two sets of paths is equivalent to the disjunction of $g_{(l,l')}$ and $g_{\neg(l,l')}$. Thus, the combination of arbitrary π_1 and π_2 is given as $g_{\pi_1} \vee g_{\pi_2} \equiv \pi_1 \cup \pi_2$.

Π yields a sound CSA if $\bigvee_{\pi_j \in \Pi} g_{\pi_j}$ is a tautology. To maximize efficiency of CSA π should be pairwise disjoint – thereby eliminating duplicate computation.

$$\forall \pi_i, \pi_j \in \Pi \text{ and } \pi_i \neq \pi_j : g_{\pi_i} \wedge g_{\pi_j} = false$$

Therefore in order for the analysis to be sound and efficient the partition algorithm should generate partitions of Π that satisfy these two constraints. We discuss our partitioning algorithm in Sect. 5.

Algorithm 1. A branch-sensitive work-list algorithm for a *CFG*

```
 1:  w ← quasiTopOrder(CFG)
 2:  while ¬w.isEmpty() do
 3:      l ← w.removeNext()
 4:      in = ⊥
 5:      for p ∈ pred(l) do
 6:          in ← merge(in, out[p][l])
 7:      end for
 8:      outNew = f(in, l)
 9:      for s ∈ succ(l) do
10:          if outNew[s] ≠ out[l][s] then
11:              out[l][s] = outNew[s]
12:              if ¬w.contains(s) then
13:                  w.insert(s)
14:              end if
15:          end if
16:      end for
17:  end while
```

Algorithm 2. A quasi-topological order for a *CFG*

```
 1:  quasiTopOrder(CFG)
 2:  N ← |CFG|
 3:  for i ∈ (1, ..., N) do
 4:      marked[i] ← false
 5:  end for
 6:  indx ← 0
 7:  DFS(CFG.entry())
 8:  return ordered
```

```
 1:  DFS(l)
 2:  if ¬mark[i] then
 3:      mark[i] ← true
 4:      for s ∈ succ(l) do
 5:          DFS(s)
 6:      end for
 7:      ordered[indx] ← l
 8:      indx ← indx + 1
 9:  end it
```

4 Implementations of Conditional Analysis

Static analysis developers commonly solve Eq. 1 using an iterative work-list algorithm that propagates the abstract values from the entry nodes $l \in E$, usually the single entry node of a program, to the rest of the nodes while computing $\mathcal{A}_{in}$ and $\mathcal{A}_{out}$ flow values. The algorithm terminates when for each node in the CFG its $\mathcal{A}_{in}$ and $\mathcal{A}_{out}$ are unchanged.

Algorithm 1 sketches a basic work-list algorithm for a branch-sensitive data-flow analysis where for brevity $\mathcal{A}_{in}$ and $\mathcal{A}_{out}$ are denoted as *in* and *out*, respectively. A work-list data structure w keeps track of CFG nodes for which *in* values are changed in the previous iteration and, thus, require recalculation. The computation reaches a fixed-point when no changes in *in* are detected which corresponds to w becoming empty. At each iteration a new node l is removed from work-list w, its incoming flows are calculated (lines 4 - 7), and its new outgoing flow is recalculated using the transfer function f (line 8) for each of its successors. That is *outNew* is an array where each element contains an outgoing flow to each of l's successors. For example, a conditional statement would have its first elements associated with the true branch and the second elements associated with the false branch. Lines 9 - 16 determine the changes in the outgoing flows for each of l's successors by comparing the new and old values of *out* and insert the affected successors back to w.

In order to further improve the efficiency of the work-list algorithm, an analysis framework takes into the consideration the ordering of nodes in the CFG. It ensures that the nodes in w appearing topologically before a given node are processed first. Since, the CFG can be a cyclic graph, the framework populates w

Algorithm 3. CFA_1 implementation of a CFA

1: $\mathtt{f}(in, l)$
2: **for** $s \in \mathrm{succ}(l)$ **do**
3:    **if** $in = \bot \vee \neg(l, s) \in \pi$ **then**
4:       $outNew[s] \leftarrow \bot$
5:    **else**
6:       $outNew[s] \leftarrow \mathtt{f}(in, l, s)$
7:    **end if**
8: **end for**
9: **return** $outNew$

Algorithm 4. CFA_2 implementation of CFA

1: $\mathrm{CDFS}(l)$
2: **if** $\neg mark[i]$ **then**
3:    $mark[i] \leftarrow true$
4:    **for** $s \in \mathrm{succ}(l)$ **do**
5:       **if** $\neg(l, s) \notin \pi$ **then**
6:          $\mathrm{DFS}(s)$
7:       **end if**
8:    **end for**
9:    $ordered[indx] \leftarrow l$
10:    $indx \leftarrow indx + 1$
11: **end if**

using a quasi-topological ordering algorithm similar to one presented in Algorithm 2. The node removal and insertion operations on w preserve the CFG's quasi-topological ordering.

A program analysis framework provides analysis developers with implementations of these work-list and ordering algorithms. The developers instantiate their analyses by providing implementations for `merge` and `f` functions, as well as an abstract domain and initial flow values. We present two approaches for implementing CSA in such analysis framework.

The first approach CSA_1 uses the transfer function `f` to set the outgoing flows to the infeasible branches and its successors to $\bot$. Algorithm 3 details that approach. Here π is a global variable which in line 3 determines whether the outgoing flow for a successor should be set to $\bot$, or computed using $\mathtt{f}(in, l, s)$ of the full SA. Extending an analysis framework to implement CSA in `f` is straightforward and does not require analysis developers to further understand the framework's implementation. However, CSA_1 does perform extra computations along infeasible program paths.

The second approach CSA_2 addresses this potential performance drawback by modifying the quasi-topological DFS search as shown in Algorithm 4. The algorithm does not traverse CFG down the paths of the excluded branches

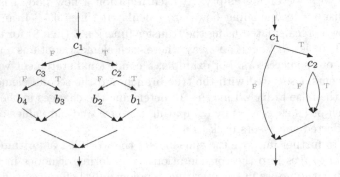

Fig. 2. Combining selected conditional statement c_2 and CFG (left) to produce an abstract graph (right) encoding $\Pi = \{c_1 f\}, \{c_1 t, c_2 f\}, \{c_1 t, c_2 t\}$

(line 5), thus assigning w only those nodes that are in π. When a node is inserted back to w (Algorithm 1 line 13) only the nodes in π are inserted in w at their proper positions. CSA_2 implementation requires that analysis developers an advanced understanding of the analysis framework, i.e., the algorithms and data-structures used in the quasi-topological ordering. However, this approach only iterates over the nodes that are defined in π. We have implemented two approaches and in Sect. 6 we empirically compare them. In the next section we present our approach on partitioning a CFG into a set of partitions Π.

5   Partitioning CFG

A program can have many branches and if we decide to use each of them to partition CFG then the size of Π could become prohibitively large, thus we need to determine which branches should be used to generate Π. The goal of our selection heuristic is to chose those branches that might reduce the computational time. We explore three main characteristics of a conditional statement: (a) whether it has non-empty blocks of code b_1 and b_2 on both $true$ and $false$ branches respectively, (b) the size of b_1 and b_2 in relation to the entire method and (c) the difference between the sizes of b_1 and b_2.

The first heuristic ensures that there is an opportunity for a parallel execution of two branches b_1 and b_2. The next two heuristics quantify that opportunity. Among b_1 and b_2, we select the one with the maximum block size and calculate its ratio to the number of statement in the method. We call this value r_t. Then we calculate another ratio r_d which is the ratio between the difference in block sizes to the number of statements in the method. If we use $|b_i|$ to denote the size of b_i block and $|m|$ the number of statements in method m, then

$$r_t = \frac{max(|b_1|, |b_2|)}{|m|}, r_d = \frac{abs(|b_1| - |b_2|)}{|m|}$$

The larger the r_t and the smaller the r_d, the higher the chances that CSA has better performance if those branches are used to partition CFG. After selecting a set of branches, we first ensure, for sound CSA analysis, that they do not appear inside loops. Next, we combine the selected conditional statements c_i with structural information about the CFG to generate an efficient set of Π.

For example, consider the CFG on the left of Fig. 2 where c_i are conditional statement and b_i are blocks of code. If the heuristic determines that the branches of c_2 are suitable for the CFG partition then simply expressing the set of partitions Π as $\{\{c_2f\}, \{c_2t\}\}$ would result in both CSA computing the invariants along c_1's false branch, that is performing the computation twice. In order to avoid this redundancy our partition algorithm traverses the CFG and finds all branches of the conditional statements through which the original conditional statements are reachable and store it as an "abstracted" graph similar to one shown on the left of Fig. 2. Next, using the abstracted graph we generate Π for CSA which in this case are $\{c_1f\}, \{c_1t, c_2f\}, \{c_1t, c_2t\}$.

Such post-processing also handles cases when both c_2 and c_3 are marked for partition. A simplistic approach is to create all possible combinations of their branches, but that results in identical partition that compute the same invariants, for example, $\{c_3t, c_4f\}$ and $\{c_3t, c_4f\}$ compute the true branch of c_3 both times. In contrast, our partition generation detects that c_3 and c_4 are independent. In our evaluation section we describe the threshold values we used for r_d and r_t parameters.

6 Evaluation

We evaluate our implementations of the path-defined conditional analysis using two distinct analyses: intra-procedural value-based analysis (VB) and an intra-procedural reaching definitions analysis (RD). For VB analysis we used implementation and abstract domains that we developed in our previous work [8]. For RD we used the implementation provided with Soot framework distribution. RD is a relatively fast analysis with an easily computable transfer function, while VA takes longer to complete due to its complex transfer function evaluations. For each of the analysis we performed experiments with their full versions SA, i.e., VB and RD, their CSA_1 versions implemented with Algorithm 3, which we name CVB_1 and CRD_1, and their CSA_2 versions implemented with Algorithm 4, which we name CVB_2 and CRD_2 respectively. The source code, program subjects and instructions on replicating the experiment are available on GitHub[2].

Program Subjects. In order to perform our evaluations we first analyzed 105 methods in 19 Java classes across 10 open-source projects that we used in our previous work [8] where we employed Boa [10] to mine methods of open-source programs from GitHub, count the number of operations in each method and then we randomly selected those methods that contain at least 180 of integer operations. Among those 105 methods we selected methods with conditional statements that meet the first requirement of our partitioning algorithm to have a non-trivial conditional statement where both true and false branches have non-empty blocks of code. This step reduced the number of methods to 68. Among them 53 methods have at least one non-trivial condition statement outside of loops, which allows for computing sound CSA. Those methods have on average 177 statements and 19 simple conditional statements.

Abstract Domain Subjects for VB Analysis. VB analysis uses atomic elements of its abstract domain to express the computed program invariants. To determine whether the size of the disjoint abstract domain influences the efficiency of VB analysis we used three disjoint abstract domains of small (8 atomic elements), medium (10 atomic elements) and large (12 atomic elements) sizes. We randomly chose those abstract domains among available disjoint domains with the same number of atomic elements. Our preliminary experiments have shown that there is no difference in the evaluation data between the domain sizes, so we present the data only for the medium size domain.

---

[2] https://github.com/BoiseState/Conditional-DFA.

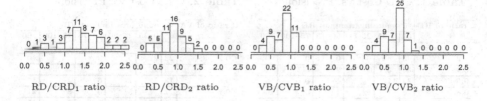

RD/CRD$_1$ ratio   RD/CRD$_2$ ratio   VB/CVB$_1$ ratio   VB/CVB$_2$ ratio

Fig. 3. Histograms of ratios between runtimes of full and conditional analyses.

6.1 Experiment Description

First we analyze 53 methods using full SA, recording its run time and computed invariants after each statement. The CSA evaluation consists of three main steps: (1) generating a set of partitions Π for each method, (2) running CSA$_1$ and CSA$_2$ analyses on the partitions and recoding run time and invariants, and (3) aggregating the computed invariants for partitions of the same method. We run experiments on a 2.9 GHz Intel Core i5 processor with 8 GB of memory running OS X operating system with the analysis running on Java RE 1.8.

Step 1. We implemented the partition algorithm from Sect. 5 in the Soot Java Optimization framework to take advantages Soot's CFG and other related data structures. The partition algorithm takes as input a class and its method to be partitioned, and parameters $r_{\bar{t}}$ that determine the minimum value for r_t, and $r_{\underline{d}}$ that determines the maximum value for r_d. In our evaluations we set $r_t = 3\%$ and $r_{\underline{d}} = 60\%$ for the majority of the methods and increased $r_{\bar{t}}$ and decreased $r_{\underline{d}}$ values when the number of partitions became greater than 45. This resulted in the increase of $r_{\bar{t}}$ to 15% for two methods and the following $(r_{\bar{t}}, r_{\underline{d}})$ values for three methods: $(15\%, 30\%)$, $(20\%, 15\%)$ and $(20\%, 30\%)$.

This step produced the total of 472 partitions for 53 methods, with the minimum of two partitions and maximum of 32 partitions per method. A partition π is encoded as a set of branches that CSA should take defined by the conditional statement id and the branch's outcomes: either true of false. As defined in our CSA framework, if a conditional statement is not present in π then CSA explores both of its branches.

Step 2. We implemented VB, CVB$_1$ and CVB$_2$ in the Soot Java Optimization framework and used Z3 version 4.3.2 as the constraint solver. CVB takes the following input parameters: a class name and its method to be analyzed, an abstract domain and a partition π. We executed VB$_1$ and VB$_2$, for each partition π and the full VB analysis. We implement RD, CRD$_1$ and CRD$_2$ also in the Soot framework. CRD takes three input parameters: a class name and its method to be analyzed and a partition π.

We recorded two sets of data that CSA produces: the running time of the analysis and the computed invariants for the corresponding analysis: set of reaching definition elements for CRD and abstract values for variables expressed as SMT constraints for CVB. We execute each experiment three times and use their

Table 1. CRD Cost vs. Precision

t, ratio of RD	% sound invariants of RD					
	0	0–25	25–50	50–75	75–100	100
CRD_1 analysis						
≤0.2	45	8	0	0	0	0
≤0.4	43	6	1	2	0	1
≤0.6	32	11	3	1	0	6
≤0.8	26	11	5	1	0	10
≤1.0	19	9	7	1	3	14
CRD_2 analysis						
≤0.2	31	18	1	2	0	1
≤0.4	21	16	4	4	2	6
≤0.6	13	10	9	3	5	13
≤0.8	10	8	5	2	5	23
≤1.0	1	2	2	2	6	40

Table 2. CVB Cost vs. Precision

t, ratio of VA	% sound invariants of VB					
	0	0–25	25–50	50–75	75–100	100
CVB_1 analysis						
≤0.2	23	21	5	3	1	0
≤0.4	15	18	7	5	4	4
≤0.6	13	11	7	6	3	13
≤0.8	7	7	5	5	8	21
≤1.0	1	0	2	0	5	45
CVB_2 analysis						
≤0.2	23	20	6	3	1	0
≤0.4	16	17	7	5	4	4
≤0.6	13	11	7	6	3	13
≤0.8	7	7	5	5	8	21
≤1.0	1	0	1	1	3	47

average to assess CSAs performances. We do not report the time for partitioning since the partitioning is performed once and its running time is negligible compared to the analysis time. For the same reason we do not report the time for combining the analysis described in the next step.

Step 3. In the last step we combine invariants of CSA in a way that allows us to answer our research questions. First we order the method partitions based on their average execution time. Then in order to determine all invariants computed at the point when a CSA completes, we combine all invariants from previously completed CSA with the current one. The result is aggregated invariants ordered based on the execution time of the partitions - from fastest to slowest. To compare SA and CSA invariants we use the logical equivalence relation for two invariants. To compare RD and CRD we compared their sets of reaching definition at each program location. To compare VB and CVB we evaluate implication relations between their SMT formulas, i.e, $(CVB \implies VB) \land (VB \implies CVB)$ at each program point. If the formula evaluates to true then we count it as a sound invariant for CVB. If the formula evaluates to false and the first implication evaluates to true, then CSA under-approximates the invariant of SA. All other evaluation of the formula to false indicate either a conceptual mistake in our CSA approach or a bug in our implementations. In all our experiments, we have not observed such cases.

6.2   Results

Performance. We used the ratio between runtimes of the slowest CSA partition and the full SA for each method to compare CSA and SA performances. Fig. 3 shows the histograms the ratios for each analysis implementation. The x-axes show the ratio values and the labels on top of the bars are the counts for that bar interval.

The histograms show that CRD_1 performed the worst since it has many executions with higher runtimes than RD. However, their average runtimes across 53 methods are comparable: CRD_1 is 148 ms and RD is 143 ms. This is because CRD_1 performed much better on larger methods than on smaller ones.

Even though CRD_2 has 16 method with ratios greater than 1, its average runtime is 108 ms, which makes this implementation 24% faster than RD.

Both CVB_1 and CVB_2 have few methods with ratios greater than 1.0, however those value are very close to 1.0. Among the 11 CVB_1 methods that underperformed, 6 have ratios of 1.01 and the rest have rations no greater than 1.05. For CVB_2's 8 underperforming methods, 5 of them have the ratios of 1.01, 2 have the ratios no greater than 1.05 and one has 1.28 ratio. The average runtimes across 53 methods are 6989 ms for CVB_1 and 7035 ms for CVB_2, which is 20% faster than VB's 8689 ms. Even though CVB_1 and CVB_2 have comparable performances, CVB_2 was able to compute more programs faster.

Invariants. The results for sound invariants computation are presented in Table 1 for CRD and in Table 2 for CVB. The column headers describe the two points "0", "100" and four ranges "(0,25)", "[25, 50)", "[50, 75)" and "[75, 100)" of the percentage of sound invariants of a full SA that CSA is able to compute. The row header shows the same ratios of running time of CSA to a full SA running time. The cell values represent the count of methods for which CSA is able to compute sound invariants within the given invariant range and within the given time interval. For example in Table 2 the first data row and the second data column contains value 21, which can be interpreted as such: for 21 methods CVB_1 is able to produce up to 25% of the sound invariants computed by a full VB in 20% of time of the full VB. The data in the second data row and in the last column tells us that within 40% of the full VB computational time CVB_1 is able to compute all invariants for 4 methods.

The data show that CSA can produce sound invariants faster for several methods and compute partial sound invariants for a majority of them. For example CVB computes all invariants for 21 methods within 80% of VB runtime and can produce partial sound invariants within 20% of VB runtime. Note that the histogram counts and the values in the last column might not equal. This is because CVB was able to produce the same invariant values as VB after computing only a few partitions, thus the rest of partitions compute redundant information.

The data shows that the efficiency of the CSA_1 and CSA_2 implementations depend on the analysis type. Thus, for CRD its CRD_2 performs better than CRD_1. However, for CVB analysis both implementation produce close results with CVB_2 performing slightly better than CVB_1. CRD is more sensitive to the implementation because it is a relatively fast analysis - it runs in a fraction of a second while CVB requires several minutes to complete. Overall, the second implementation of CSA that require modification of the underlying topological order algorithm is a better implementation choice.

6.3 Discussion

The results indicate that CSA allows for faster analysis, while requiring minimal modification in SA frameworks. However, the main contribution of CSA is its ability to provide partial invariants in a fraction of a time of SA. While a user waits for a completion of all partitions to complete she can use the invariants provided earlier to check the safety properties of the program. If such property does hold, then the user has more confidence about the program correctness. However, if the property does not hold for the computed invariants then she can start investigate the cause of it. Moreover, the partition information could accelerate this task since it narrows down the set of paths that causes property violation.

7   Related Work

Besides related work on conditional analysis described in the introduction our work relates the body of research that improve the performance of SA algorithms and the accuracy of SA using program's structural information. The body of work on designing parallel SA algorithms through partitioning the program's state space started back 1990's with the work of Lee at el., [11] that partitioned program CFG into strongly connected components applying fixed point computation inside those components and then using elimination algorithm [12] to combine the data from the external nodes of those components. Albarghouthi at el., [13] investigated parallel C interprocedural analysis, where based on the reachability in the call-graph multiple method analyzed intraprocedurally in parallel. Dewey at el., [14] explores parallel analysis of JavaScript by partitioning the state space of the program into regions that can be computed in parallel and those that require synchronizations of the parallel computations, i.e., merging points of the analysis.

Another body of work identifies partitions of CFG to improve the precision of the analysis by delaying the merge of abstract values from controls flows or adding new abstract elements that exactly describe the join of two abstract elements, i.e., computing disjunctive completion of the partially ordered set. However, disjunctive completion can lead to excessively large representation of abstract values, and at some point, at least some values should be joined in order for the computation to reach its fixed point. Prior research has explored what abstract values should be joined; computational traces [15] or some other heuristic based on the CFG, such as a trace partitioning domain method [16], can provide a basis for these determinations.

Another approach is to delay the join operation by conducting incremental analysis as guided analysis [17]. In this approach, each iteration of the fixed point computation is applied to an incrementally augmented subgraph of P's CFG. For instance on the first iteration, i.e., propagating abstract values through CFG, the analysis considers one true branch of a conditional statement, and on the second iteration it would add the false branch. This approach limits the loss of precision resulting from widening operators for numerical domains, such as polyhedra that have infinite ascending chains. This incremental approach also includes a disjunctive extension when the analysis first performs fixed point computation before extending the part of the CFG's to be analyzed, i.e., successively computing invariants. An orthogonal approach is the path focusing technique [18], which computes invariants separately for each path between two loop-free points in the CFG. Thus, each part of the CFG between entrance and exit of a loop is expanded into a set of paths. After the computation is done, then results of each path are joined.

The latest development has been in combining guided analysis and path focusing techniques [19]. Using this approach, analysis continues to evaluate paths between loop-free points encoded separately with the SMT formula. This approach allows the analysis to explore only those paths that have the potential to improve the precision of the invariants.

Our approach is complimentary to the above techniques, since a CSA for a single partition could use a parallel algorithm for computing its propagation to further improve CSA efficiency.

8   Conclusion and Future Work

In this work we introduce structurally defined conditional static analysis, formalize it in terms of standard data-flow frameworks, provide algorithms for CSA, and two distinct implementations. We evaluate the efficiency and precision of these techniques through extensive empirical study on real-world programs. The key insight is that CSA partitions a program's CFG into a subset of graphs at the conditional statements. These partitions induce a series of independent CSA executions that can run in parallel. The empirical evaluation suggest that CSA provides improvements over the full SA for a significant fraction of a program. In particular depending on the analysis around 24% of methods completed their analysis within 60% of run time required by the full SA. Moreover, CSA is able to produce partial safe invariant computations for a majority of the programs.

In the future we plan to further improve the efficiency of CSA and the confidence of the partial information that it produces. Currently CSA that follow the same path prefix compute identical information for the prefix, we plan to investigate an approach where only one analysis computes the prefix information and communicates to the rest of CSA with the common prefixes. In addition, we would like to qualify CSA's partially computed invariants into safe or underapproximating based on the partition that CSA analyzes. Thus, when a CSA computes an invariant that is marked as safe, the user should use it with the same amount of confidence as she would for the full SA.

Acknowledgment. The authors would like to thank Eric Keefe for working on CSA$_2$ implementation during his REU experience at Boise State University supported by the National Science Foundation under award CNS 1461133.

References

1. Cousot, P., Cousot, R., Feret, J., Mauborgne, L., Miné, A., Monniaux, D., Rival, X.: The ASTREÉ analyzer. In: Sagiv, M. (ed.) ESOP 2005. LNCS, vol. 3444, pp. 21–30. Springer, Heidelberg (2005). https://doi.org/10.1007/978-3-540-31987-0_3
2. Calcagno, C., Distefano, D.: Infer: an automatic program verifier for memory safety of C programs. In: Bobaru, M., Havelund, K., Holzmann, G.J., Joshi, R. (eds.) NFM 2011. LNCS, vol. 6617, pp. 459–465. Springer, Heidelberg (2011). https://doi.org/10.1007/978-3-642-20398-5_33
3. Cousot, P., Cousot, R.: Modular static program analysis. In: Horspool, R.N. (ed.) CC 2002. LNCS, vol. 2304, pp. 159–179. Springer, Heidelberg (2002). https://doi.org/10.1007/3-540-45937-5_13
4. Ballabriga, C., Cass, H., Sainrat, P.: WCET computation on software components by partial static analysis. In: Junior Researcher Workshop on Real-Time Computing, pp. 15–18 (2007)
5. Naik, M., Aiken, A.: Conditional must not aliasing for static race detection. In: Proceedings of the 34th Annual ACM SIGPLAN-SIGACT Symposium on Principles of Programming Languages, POPL 2007, pp. 327–338. ACM, New York (2007). https://doi.org/10.1145/1190216.1190265
6. Conway, C.L., Dams, D., Namjoshi, K.S., Barrett, C.: Pointer analysis, conditional soundness, and proving the absence of errors. In: Alpuente, M., Vidal, G. (eds.) SAS 2008. LNCS, vol. 5079, pp. 62–77. Springer, Heidelberg (2008). https://doi.org/10.1007/978-3-540-69166-2_5
7. Beyer, D., Henzinger, T.A., Keremoglu, M.E., Wendler, P.: Conditional model checking: a technique to pass information between verifiers. In: Proceedings of the ACM SIGSOFT 20th International Symposium on the Foundations of Software Engineering, FSE 2012, pp. 57:1–57:11. ACM, New York (2012). https://doi.org/10.1145/2393596.2393664
8. Sherman, E., Dwyer, M.B.: Exploiting domain and program structure to synthesize efficient and precise data flow analyses (T). In: 30th IEEE/ACM International Conference on Automated Software Engineering, ASE 2015, Lincoln, NE, USA, 9–13 November 2015, pp. 608–618 (2015). https://doi.org/10.1109/ASE.2015.41
9. Nielson, F., Nielson, H.R., Hankin, C.: Principles of Program Analysis. Springer, Heidelberg (1999). https://doi.org/10.1007/978-3-662-03811-6
10. Dyer, R., Nguyen, H.A., Rajan, H., Nguyen, T.N.: Boa: a language and infrastructure for analyzing ultra-large-scale software repositories. In: Proceedings of the 35th International Conference on Software Engineering, ICSE 2013, pp. 422–431, May 2013
11. Lee, Y.-F., Marlowe, T.J., Ryder, B.G.: Performing data flow analysis in parallel. In: Proceedings of the 1990 ACM/IEEE Conference on Supercomputing, Supercomputing 1990, pp. 942–951. IEEE Computer Society Press, Los Alamitos (1990). http://dl.acm.org/citation.cfm?id=110382.110625
12. Ryder, B.G., Paull, M.C.: Elimination algorithms for data flow analysis. ACM Comput. Surv. **18**(3), 277–316 (1986). https://doi.org/10.1145/27632.27649
13. Albarghouthi, A., Kumar, R., Nori, A.V., Rajamani, S.K.: Parallelizing top-down interprocedural analyses. In: Proceedings of the 33rd ACM SIGPLAN Conference on Programming Language Design and Implementation, PLDI 2012, pp. 217–228. ACM, New York (2012). https://doi.org/10.1145/2254064.2254091

14. Dewey, K., Kashyap, V., Hardekopf, B.: A parallel abstract interpreter for javascript. In: Proceedings of the 13th Annual IEEE/ACM International Symposium on Code Generation and Optimization, CGO 2015, pp. 34–45. IEEE Computer Society, Washington, DC (2015). http://dl.acm.org/citation.cfm?id=2738600.2738606

15. Holley, L.H., Rosen, B.K.: Qualified data flow problems. IEEE Trans. Softw. Eng. **7**(1), 60–78 (1981)

16. Rival, X., Mauborgne, L.: The trace partitioning abstract domain. ACM Trans. Program. Lang. Syst. **29**(5), 26 (2007)

17. Gopan, D., Reps, T.: Guided static analysis. In: Nielson, H.R., Filé, G. (eds.) SAS 2007. LNCS, vol. 4634, pp. 349–365. Springer, Heidelberg (2007). https://doi.org/10.1007/978-3-540-74061-2_22

18. Monniaux, D., Gonnord, L.: Using bounded model checking to focus fixpoint iterations. In: Yahav, E. (ed.) SAS 2011. LNCS, vol. 6887, pp. 369–385. Springer, Heidelberg (2011). https://doi.org/10.1007/978-3-642-23702-7_27

19. Henry, J., Monniaux, D., Moy, M.: Succinct representations for abstract interpretation. In: Miné, A., Schmidt, D. (eds.) SAS 2012. LNCS, vol. 7460, pp. 283–299. Springer, Heidelberg (2012). https://doi.org/10.1007/978-3-642-33125-1_20

Geometric Nontermination Arguments

Jan Leike[1] and Matthias Heizmann[2(✉)]

[1] Australian National University, Canberra, Australia
[2] University of Freiburg, Freiburg im Breisgau, Germany
`heizmann@informatik.uni-freiburg.de`

Abstract. We present a new kind of nontermination argument, called *geometric nontermination argument*. The geometric nontermination argument is a finite representation of an infinite execution that has the form of a sum of several geometric series. For so-called linear lasso programs we can decide the existence of a geometric nontermination argument using a nonlinear algebraic ∃-constraint. We show that a deterministic conjunctive loop program with nonnegative eigenvalues is nonterminating if an only if there exists a geometric nontermination argument. Furthermore, we present an evaluation that demonstrates that our method is feasible in practice.

1 Introduction

The problem whether a program is terminating is undecidable in general. One way to approach this problem in practice is to analyze the existence of termination arguments and nontermination arguments. The existence of a certain termination argument like, e.g, a linear ranking function, is decidable [4,31] and implies termination. However, if we cannot find a linear ranking function we cannot conclude nontermination. Vice versa, the existence of a certain nontermination argument like, e.g, a linear recurrence set [20], is decidable and implies nontermination however, if we cannot find such a recurrence set we cannot conclude termination.

In this paper[1] we present a new kind of termination argument which we call *geometric nontermination argument (GNTA)*. Unlike a recurrence set, a geometric nontermination argument does not only imply nontermination, it also explicitly represents an infinite program execution. Hence a user sees immediately if the counterexample to termination is a fixpoint or an unbounded diverging execution. An infinite program execution that is represented by a geometric nontermination argument can be written as a pointwise sum of several geometric series. We show that such an infinite execution exists for each deterministic conjunctive loop program that is nonterminating and whose transition matrix has only nonnegative eigenvalues.

---

[1] An extended version of this paper [29] contains more examples and further explanations.

© The Author(s) 2018
D. Beyer and M. Huisman (Eds.): TACAS 2018, LNCS 10806, pp. 266–283, 2018.
https://doi.org/10.1007/978-3-319-89963-3_16

```
  b := 1;                 b := 1;                 b := 1;
  while (a+b >= 3):       while (a+b >= 3):       while (a+b >= 4):
    a := 3*a + 1;           a := 3*a - 2;           a := 3*a + b;
    b := nondet();          b := 2*b;               b := 2*b;
```

(a)   (b)   (c)

Fig. 1. Three nonterminating linear lasso programs. Each has an infinite execution which is either a geometric series or a pointwise sum of geometric series. The first lasso program is nondeterministic because the variable b gets some nondeterministic value in each iteration.

We restrict ourselves to linear lasso programs. A lasso program consists of a single while loop that is preceded by straight-line code. The name refers to the lasso shaped form of the control flow graph. Usually, linear lasso programs do not occur as stand-alone programs. Instead, they are used as a finite representation of an infinite path in a control flow graph. For example, in (potentially spurious) counterexamples in termination analysis [6,16,21,22,24,25,32,33,37], stability analysis [11,34], cost analysis [1,19], or the verification of temporal properties [7, 13–15,18] for programs.

We present a constraint based approach that allow us to check whether a linear conjunctive lasso program has a geometric nontermination argument and to synthesize one if it exists.

Our analysis is motived by the probably simplest form of an infinite executions, namely infinite execution where the same state is always repeated. We call such a state a fixed point. For lasso programs we can reduce the check for the existence of a fixed point to a constraint solving problem as follows. Let us assume that the stem and the loop of the lasso program are given as a formulas over primed and unprimed variables $\text{STEM}(x, x')$ and $\text{LOOP}(x, x')$. The infinite sequence $s_0, \bar{s}, \bar{s}, \bar{s}, \ldots$ is an nonterminating execution of the lasso program iff the assignment $x_0 \mapsto s_0, \bar{x} \mapsto \bar{s}$ is a satisfying assignment for the constraint $\text{STEM}(x_0, \bar{x}) \wedge \text{LOOP}(\bar{x}, \bar{x})$. In this paper, we present a constraint that is not only satisfiable if the program has a fixed point, it is also satisfiable if the program has a nonterminating execution that can be written as a pointwise sum of geometric series.

Let us motivate the representation of infinite executions as sums of geometric series in three steps. The program depicted in Fig. 1a shows a lasso program which does not have a fixed point but the following infinite execution.

$$\begin{pmatrix} 2 \\ 0 \end{pmatrix}, \begin{pmatrix} 2 \\ 1 \end{pmatrix}, \begin{pmatrix} 7 \\ 1 \end{pmatrix}, \begin{pmatrix} 22 \\ 1 \end{pmatrix}, \begin{pmatrix} 67 \\ 1 \end{pmatrix}, \ldots$$

We can write this infinite execution as a a geometric series where for $t > 1$ the t-th state is the sum $x_1 + \sum_{i=0}^{t-2} \lambda^i y$, where we have $x_1 = \begin{pmatrix} 2 \\ 1 \end{pmatrix}$, $y = \begin{pmatrix} 5 \\ 0 \end{pmatrix}$, and $\lambda = 3$. The state x_1 is the state before the loop was executed before the first time and intuitively y is the direction in which the execution is moving initially and λ is the speed at which the execution continues to move in this direction.

Next, let us consider the lasso program depicted in Fig. 1b which has the following infinite execution.

$$\left(\begin{smallmatrix}2\\0\end{smallmatrix}\right), \left(\begin{smallmatrix}2\\1\end{smallmatrix}\right), \left(\begin{smallmatrix}4\\4\end{smallmatrix}\right), \left(\begin{smallmatrix}10\\8\end{smallmatrix}\right), \left(\begin{smallmatrix}28\\16\end{smallmatrix}\right), \ldots$$

We cannot write this execution as a geometric series as we did above. Intuitively, the reason is that the values of both variables are increasing at different speeds and hence this execution is not moving in a single direction. However, we can write this infinite execution as a sum of geometric series where for $t \in \mathbb{N}\backslash\{0\}$ the t-th state can be written as a sum $\boldsymbol{x_1} + \sum_{i=0}^{t-2} Y \left(\begin{smallmatrix}\lambda_1 & 0\\0 & \lambda_2\end{smallmatrix}\right)^i \boldsymbol{1}$, where we have $\boldsymbol{x_1} = \left(\begin{smallmatrix}2\\1\end{smallmatrix}\right)$, $\boldsymbol{Y} = \begin{pmatrix}2 & 0\\0 & 1\end{pmatrix}$, $\lambda_1 = 3, \lambda_2 = 2$ and $\boldsymbol{1}$ denotes the column vector of ones. Intuitively, our execution is moving in two different directions at different speeds. The directions are reflected by the column vectors of Y, the values of λ_1 and λ_2 reflect the respective speeds.

Let us next consider the lasso program in Fig. 1c which has the following infinite execution.

$$\left(\begin{smallmatrix}3\\0\end{smallmatrix}\right), \left(\begin{smallmatrix}3\\1\end{smallmatrix}\right), \left(\begin{smallmatrix}10\\2\end{smallmatrix}\right), \left(\begin{smallmatrix}32\\4\end{smallmatrix}\right), \left(\begin{smallmatrix}100\\8\end{smallmatrix}\right), \ldots$$

We cannot write this execution as a pointwise sum of geometric series in the form that we used above. Intuitively, the problem is that one of the initial directions contributes at two different speeds to the overall progress of the execution. However, we can write this infinite execution as a pointwise sum of geometric series where for $t \in \mathbb{N}\backslash\{0\}$ the t-th state can be written as a sum $\boldsymbol{x_1} + \sum_{i=0}^{t-2} Y \left(\begin{smallmatrix}\lambda_1 & \mu\\0 & \lambda_2\end{smallmatrix}\right)^i \boldsymbol{1}$, where we have $\boldsymbol{x_1} = \left(\begin{smallmatrix}3\\1\end{smallmatrix}\right)$, $\boldsymbol{Y} = \begin{pmatrix}4 & 3\\0 & 1\end{pmatrix}$, $\lambda_1 = 3, \lambda_2 = 2, \mu = 1$ and $\boldsymbol{1}$ denotes the column vector of ones. We call the tuple $(\boldsymbol{x_0}, \boldsymbol{x_1}, Y, \lambda_1, \lambda_2, \mu)$ which we use as a finite representation for the infinite execution a *geometric nontermination argument*.

In this paper, we formally introduce the notion of a geometric nontermination argument for linear lasso programs (Sect. 3) and we prove that each nonterminating deterministic conjunctive linear loop program whose transition matrix has only nonnegative real eigenvalues has a geometric nontermination argument, i.e., each such nonterminating linear loop program has an infinite execution which can be written as a sum of geometric series (Sect. 4).

2   Preliminaries

We denote vectors $\boldsymbol{x}$ with bold symbols and matrices with uppercase Latin letters. Vectors are always understood to be column vectors, $\boldsymbol{1}$ denotes a vector of ones, $\boldsymbol{0}$ denotes a vector of zeros (of the appropriate dimension), and $\boldsymbol{e_i}$ denotes the i-th unit vector.

2.1   Linear Lasso Programs

In this work, we consider linear lasso programs, programs that consist of a program step and a single loop. We use binary relations over the program's states to define the stem and the loop transition relation. Variables are assumed to be real-valued.

We denote by x the vector of n variables $(x_1, \ldots, x_n)^T \in \mathbb{R}^n$ corresponding to program states, and by $x' = (x'_1, \ldots, x'_n)^T \in \mathbb{R}^n$ the variables of the next state.

Definition 1 (Linear Lasso Program). *A (conjunctive) linear lasso program $L = (\text{STEM}, \text{LOOP})$ consists of two binary relations defined by formulas with the free variables x and x' of the form*

$$A \left({}^{x}_{x'} \right) \leq b$$

for some matrix $A \in \mathbb{R}^{n \times m}$ and some vector $b \in \mathbb{R}^m$.

A *linear loop program* is a linear lasso program L without stem, i.e., a linear lasso program such that the relation STEM is equivalent to *true*.

Definition 2 (Deterministic Linear Lasso Program). *A linear loop program L is called* deterministic *iff its loop transition LOOP can be written in the following form*

$$(x, x') \in \text{LOOP} \iff Gx \leq g \wedge x' = Mx + m$$

for some matrices $G \in \mathbb{R}^{n \times m}$, $M \in \mathbb{R}^{n \times n}$, and vectors $g \in \mathbb{R}^m$ and $m \in \mathbb{R}^n$.

Definition 3 (Nontermination). *A linear lasso program L is* nonterminating *iff there is an infinite sequence of states $x_0, x_1, \ldots$, called an* infinite execution *of L, such that $(x_0, x_1) \in \text{STEM}$ and $(x_t, x_{t+1}) \in \text{LOOP}$ for all $t \geq 1$.*

2.2   Jordan Normal Form

Let $M \in \mathbb{R}^{n \times n}$ be a real square matrix. If there is an invertible square matrix S and a diagonal matrix D such that $M = SDS^{-1}$, then M is called *diagonalizable*. The column vectors of S form the basis over which M has diagonal form. In general, real matrices are not diagonalizable. However, every real square matrix M with real eigenvalues has a representation which is almost diagonal, called *Jordan normal form*. This is a matrix that is zero except for the eigenvalues on the diagonal and one superdiagonal containing ones and zeros.

Formally, a Jordan normal form is a matrix $J = \text{diag}(J_{i_1}(\lambda_1), \ldots, J_{i_k}(\lambda_k))$ where $\lambda_1, \ldots, \lambda_k$ are the eigenvalues of M and the real square matrices $J_i(\lambda) \in \mathbb{R}^{i \times i}$ are *Jordan blocks*,

$$J_i(\lambda) := \begin{pmatrix} \lambda & 1 & 0 & \ldots & 0 & 0 \\ 0 & \lambda & 1 & \ldots & 0 & 0 \\ \vdots & & & \ddots & & \vdots \\ 0 & 0 & 0 & \ldots & \lambda & 1 \\ 0 & 0 & 0 & \ldots & 0 & \lambda \end{pmatrix}.$$

The subspace corresponding to each distinct eigenvalue is called *generalized eigenspace* and their basis vectors *generalized eigenvectors*.

Theorem 4 (Jordan Normal Form). *For each real square matrix $M \in \mathbb{R}^{n \times n}$ with real eigenvalues, there is an invertible real square matrix $V \in \mathbb{R}^{n \times n}$ and a Jordan normal form $J \in \mathbb{R}^{n \times n}$ such that $M = VJV^{-1}$.*

3   Geometric Nontermination Arguments

Fix a conjunctive linear lasso program $L = (\text{STEM}, \text{LOOP})$ and let $A \in \mathbb{R}^{n \times m}$ and $b \in \mathbb{R}^m$ define the loop transition such that

$$(\boldsymbol{x}, \boldsymbol{x}') \in \text{LOOP} \iff A \left(\begin{smallmatrix} x \\ x' \end{smallmatrix} \right) \leq b.$$

Definition 5 (Geometric Nontermination Argument). *A tuple $(\boldsymbol{x_0}, \boldsymbol{x_1}, \boldsymbol{y_1}, \dots, \boldsymbol{y_s}, \lambda_1, \dots, \lambda_s, \mu_1, \dots, \mu_{s-1})$ is called a* geometric nontermination argument *for the linear lasso program $L = (\text{STEM}, \text{LOOP})$ iff all of the following statements hold.*

(domain) $\boldsymbol{x_0}, \boldsymbol{x_1}, \boldsymbol{y_1}, \dots, \boldsymbol{y_s} \in \mathbb{R}^n$, *and* $\lambda_1, \dots, \lambda_s, \mu_1, \dots, \mu_{s-1} \geq 0$

(initiation) $(\boldsymbol{x_0}, \boldsymbol{x_1}) \in \text{STEM}$

(point) $A \left(\begin{smallmatrix} x_1 \\ x_1 + \sum_{k=1}^s y_k \end{smallmatrix} \right) \leq b$

(ray) $A \left(\begin{smallmatrix} y_1 \\ \lambda_1 y_1 \end{smallmatrix} \right) \leq 0$ *and* $A \left(\begin{smallmatrix} y_i \\ \lambda_i y_k + \mu_{k-1} y_{k-1} \end{smallmatrix} \right) \leq 0$ *for each* $k \in \{2 \dots s\}$.

The number $s \geq 0$ is the size *of the geometric nontermination argument.*

The existence of a geometric nontermination argument can be checked using an SMT solver. The constraints given by (domain), (init), (point), (ray) are nonlinear algebraic constraints and the satisfiability of these constraints is decidable.

Proposition 6 (Soundness). *If there is a geometric nontermination argument for a linear lasso program L, then L is nonterminating.*

Proof. We define $Y := (\boldsymbol{y_1} \dots \boldsymbol{y_k})$ as the matrix containing the vectors $\boldsymbol{y_i}$ as columns, and we define the following matrix.

$$U := \begin{pmatrix} \lambda_1 & \mu_1 & 0 & \dots & 0 & 0 \\ 0 & \lambda_2 & \mu_2 & \dots & 0 & 0 \\ \vdots & & & \ddots & & \vdots \\ 0 & 0 & 0 & \dots & \lambda_{n-1} & \mu_{n-1} \\ 0 & 0 & 0 & \dots & 0 & \lambda_n \end{pmatrix} \tag{1}$$

Following Definition 3 we show that the linear lasso program L has the infinite execution

$$\boldsymbol{x_0}, \quad \boldsymbol{x_1}, \quad \boldsymbol{x_1} + Y1, \quad \boldsymbol{x_1} + Y1 + YU1, \quad \boldsymbol{x_1} + Y1 + YU1 + YU^2 1, \quad \dots \tag{2}$$

From (init) we get $(\boldsymbol{x_0}, \boldsymbol{x_1}) \in \text{STEM}$. It remains to show that

$$\left(\boldsymbol{x_1} + \sum_{j=0}^{t-1} YU^j\mathbf{1}, \; \boldsymbol{x_1} + \sum_{j=0}^{t} YU^j\mathbf{1} \right) \in \text{LOOP for all } t \in \mathbb{N}. \tag{3}$$

According to (domain) the matrix U has only nonnegative entries, so the same holds for the matrix $Z := \sum_{j=0}^{t-1} U^j$. Hence $Z\mathbf{1}$ has only nonnegative entries and thus $YZ\mathbf{1}$ can be written as $\sum_{k=1}^{s} \alpha_k \boldsymbol{y_k}$ for some $\alpha_k \geq 0$. We multiply the inequality number k from (ray) with α_k and get

$$A \left(\begin{smallmatrix} \alpha_k \boldsymbol{y_k} \\ \alpha_k \lambda_k \boldsymbol{y_k} + \alpha_k \mu_{k-1} \boldsymbol{y_{k-1}} \end{smallmatrix} \right) \leq 0. \tag{4}$$

where we define for convenience $\boldsymbol{y_0} := 0$ and $\mu_0 := 0$. Now we sum (4) for all k and add (point) to get

$$A \left(\begin{smallmatrix} \boldsymbol{x_1} + \sum_k \alpha_k \boldsymbol{y_k} \\ \boldsymbol{x_1} + \sum_k \boldsymbol{y_k} + \sum_k (\alpha_k \lambda_k \boldsymbol{y_k} + \alpha_k \mu_{k-1} \boldsymbol{y_{k-1}}) \end{smallmatrix} \right) \leq \boldsymbol{b}. \tag{5}$$

By definition of α_k, we have

$$\boldsymbol{x_1} + \sum_{k=1}^{s} \alpha_k \boldsymbol{y_k} = \boldsymbol{x_1} + YZ\mathbf{1} = \boldsymbol{x_1} + \sum_{j=0}^{t-1} YU^j\mathbf{1}$$

and

$$\boldsymbol{x_1} + \sum_{k=1}^{s} \boldsymbol{y_k} + \sum_{k=1}^{s} (\alpha_k \lambda_k \boldsymbol{y_k} + \alpha_k \mu_{k-1} \boldsymbol{y_{k-1}}) = \boldsymbol{x_1} + Y\mathbf{1} + \sum_{k=1}^{s} \alpha_k YUe_k$$

$$= \boldsymbol{x_1} + Y\mathbf{1} + YUZ\mathbf{1}$$

$$= \boldsymbol{x_1} + \sum_{j=0}^{t} YU^j\mathbf{1}.$$

Therefore (3) and (5) are the same, which concludes this proof. □

Proposition 7 (Closed Form of the Infinite Execution). *For $t \geq 2$ the following is the closed form of the state $\boldsymbol{x_t} = \boldsymbol{x_1} + \sum_{j=0}^{t-2} YU^j\mathbf{1}$ in the infinite execution* (2). *Let $U =: N + D$ where N is a nilpotent matrix and D is a diagonal matrix.*

$$YU^j\mathbf{1} = Y \left(\sum_{i=0}^{j} \binom{j}{i} N^i D^{j-i} \right) \mathbf{1} = \sum_{k=1}^{s} \boldsymbol{y_k} \sum_{i=0}^{j-k+1} \binom{j}{i} \lambda_{n-k-i}^{j-i} \prod_{\ell=k}^{k+i-1} \mu_\ell \qquad \Diamond$$

4   Completeness Results

First we show that a linear loop program has a GNTA if it has is a bounded infinite execution. In the next section we use this to prove our completeness result.

4.1   Bounded Infinite Executions

Let $|\cdot| : \mathbb{R}^n \to \mathbb{R}$ denote some norm. We call an infinite execution $(\boldsymbol{x}_t)_{t \geq 0}$ *bounded* iff there is a real number $d \in \mathbb{R}$ such that the norm of each state is bounded by d, i.e., $|\boldsymbol{x}_t| \leq d$ for all t (in $\mathbb{R}^n$ the notion of boundedness is independent of the choice of the norm).

Lemma 8 (Fixed Point). *Let $L = (true, \text{LOOP})$ be a linear loop program. The linear loop program L has a bounded infinite execution if and only if there is a fixed point $\boldsymbol{x}^* \in \mathbb{R}^n$ such that $(\boldsymbol{x}^*, \boldsymbol{x}^*) \in \text{LOOP}$.*

Proof. If there is a fixed point $\boldsymbol{x}^*$, then the loop has the infinite bounded execution $\boldsymbol{x}^*, \boldsymbol{x}^*, \dots$. Conversely, let $(\boldsymbol{x}_t)_{t \geq 0}$ be an infinite bounded execution. Boundedness implies that there is an $d \in \mathbb{R}$ such that $|\boldsymbol{x}_t| \leq d$ for all t. Consider the sequence $\boldsymbol{z}_k := \frac{1}{k} \sum_{t=1}^{k} \boldsymbol{x}_t$.

$$
|\boldsymbol{z}_k - \boldsymbol{z}_{k+1}| = \left| \frac{1}{k} \sum_{t=1}^{k} \boldsymbol{x}_t - \frac{1}{k+1} \sum_{t=1}^{k+1} \boldsymbol{x}_t \right| = \frac{1}{k(k+1)} \left| (k+1) \sum_{t=1}^{k} \boldsymbol{x}_t - k \sum_{t=1}^{k+1} \boldsymbol{x}_t \right|
$$

$$
= \frac{1}{k(k+1)} \left| \sum_{t=1}^{k} \boldsymbol{x}_t - k \boldsymbol{x}_{k+1} \right| \leq \frac{1}{k(k+1)} \left(\sum_{t=1}^{k} |\boldsymbol{x}_t| + k |\boldsymbol{x}_{k+1}| \right)
$$

$$
\leq \frac{1}{k(k+1)} (k \cdot d + k \cdot d) = \frac{2d}{k+1} \longrightarrow 0 \text{ as } k \to \infty.
$$

Hence the sequence $(\boldsymbol{z}_k)_{k \geq 1}$ is a Cauchy sequence and thus converges to some $\boldsymbol{z}^* \in \mathbb{R}^n$. We will show that $\boldsymbol{z}^*$ is the desired fixed point.

For all t, the polyhedron $Q := \{ \left(\begin{smallmatrix} \boldsymbol{x} \\ \boldsymbol{x}' \end{smallmatrix} \right) \mid A \left(\begin{smallmatrix} \boldsymbol{x} \\ \boldsymbol{x}' \end{smallmatrix} \right) \leq b \}$ contains $\left(\begin{smallmatrix} \boldsymbol{x}_t \\ \boldsymbol{x}_{t+1} \end{smallmatrix} \right)$ and is convex. Therefore for all $k \geq 1$,

$$
\frac{1}{k} \sum_{t=1}^{k} \left(\begin{smallmatrix} \boldsymbol{x}_t \\ \boldsymbol{x}_{t+1} \end{smallmatrix} \right) \in Q.
$$

Together with

$$
\left(\begin{smallmatrix} \boldsymbol{z}_k \\ \frac{k+1}{k} \boldsymbol{z}_{k+1} \end{smallmatrix} \right) = \frac{1}{k} \left(\begin{smallmatrix} \boldsymbol{0} \\ \boldsymbol{x}_1 \end{smallmatrix} \right) + \frac{1}{k} \sum_{t=1}^{k} \left(\begin{smallmatrix} \boldsymbol{x}_t \\ \boldsymbol{x}_{t+1} \end{smallmatrix} \right)
$$

we infer

$$
\left(\left(\begin{smallmatrix} \boldsymbol{z}_k \\ \frac{k+1}{k} \boldsymbol{z}_{k+1} \end{smallmatrix} \right) - \frac{1}{k} \left(\begin{smallmatrix} \boldsymbol{0} \\ \boldsymbol{x}_1 \end{smallmatrix} \right) \right) \in Q,
$$

and since Q is topologically closed we have

$$
\left(\begin{smallmatrix} \boldsymbol{z}^* \\ \boldsymbol{z}^* \end{smallmatrix} \right) = \lim_{k \to \infty} \left(\left(\begin{smallmatrix} \boldsymbol{z}_k \\ \frac{k+1}{k} \boldsymbol{z}_{k+1} \end{smallmatrix} \right) - \frac{1}{k} \left(\begin{smallmatrix} \boldsymbol{0} \\ \boldsymbol{x}_1 \end{smallmatrix} \right) \right) \in Q.
$$

$\square$

Note that Lemma 8 does not transfer to lasso programs: there might only be one fixed point and the stem might exclude this point (e.g., $a = -0.5$ and $b = 3.5$ in example Fig. 1a).

Because fixed points give rise to trivial geometric nontermination arguments, we can derive a criterion for the existence of geometric nontermination arguments from Lemma 8.

Corollary 9 (Bounded Infinite Executions). *If the linear loop program $L = (\text{true}, \text{LOOP})$ has a bounded infinite execution, then it has a geometric nontermination argument of size 0.*

Proof. By Lemma 8 there is a fixed point x^* such that $(x^*, x^*) \in \text{LOOP}$. We choose $x_0 = x_1 = x^*$ which satisfies (point) and (ray) and thus is a geometric nontermination argument for L. □

Example 10. Note that according to our definition of a linear lasso program, the relation LOOP is a topologically closed set. If we allowed the formula defining LOOP to also contain strict inequalities, Lemma 8 no longer holds: the following program is nonterminating and has a bounded infinite execution, but it does not have a fixed point. However, the topological closure of the relation LOOP contains the fixed point $a = 0$.

$$\textbf{while } (a > 0):$$
$$a := a / 2;$$

Nevertheless, this example has a geometric nontermination argument, namely $x_1 = 1$, $y_1 = -0.5$, $\lambda_1 = 0.5$. ◇

4.2 Nonnegative Eigenvalues

This section is dedicated to the proof of the following completeness result for deterministic linear loop programs.

Theorem 11 (Completeness). *If a deterministic linear loop program L of the form while $(Gx \leq g)$ do $x := Mx + m$ with n variables is nonterminating and M has only nonnegative real eigenvalues, then there is a geometric nontermination argument for L of size at most n.*

To prove this completeness theorem, we need to construct a GNTA from a given infinite execution. The following lemma shows that we can restrict our construction to exclude all linear subspaces that have a bounded execution.

Lemma 12 (Loop Disassembly). *Let $L = (\text{true}, \text{LOOP})$ be a linear loop program over $\mathbb{R}^n = \mathcal{U} \oplus \mathcal{V}$ where $\mathcal{U}$ and $\mathcal{V}$ are linear subspaces of $\mathbb{R}^n$. Suppose L is nonterminating and there is an infinite execution that is bounded when projected to the subspace $\mathcal{U}$. Let $x^{\mathcal{U}}$ be the fixed point in $\mathcal{U}$ that exists according to Lemma 8. Then the linear loop program $L^{\mathcal{V}}$ that we get by projecting to the subspace $\mathcal{V} + x^{\mathcal{U}}$ is nonterminating. Moreover, if $L^{\mathcal{V}}$ has a GNTA of size s, then L has a GNTA of size s.*

Proof. Without loss of generality, we are in the basis of $\mathcal{U}$ and $\mathcal{V}$ so that these spaces are nicely separated by the use of different variables. Using the infinite execution of L that is bounded on $\mathcal{U}$ we can do the construction from the proof of Lemma 8 to get an infinite execution $z_0, z_1, \ldots$ that yields the fixed point $x^{\mathcal{U}}$ when projected to $\mathcal{U}$. We fix $x^{\mathcal{U}}$ in the loop transition by replacing all variables from $\mathcal{U}$ with the values from $x^{\mathcal{U}}$ and get the linear loop program $L^{\mathcal{V}}$ (this is the projection to $\mathcal{V} + x^{\mathcal{U}}$). Importantly, the projection of $z_0, z_1, \ldots$ to $\mathcal{V} + x^{\mathcal{U}}$ is still an infinite execution, hence the loop $L^{\mathcal{V}}$ is nonterminating. Given a GNTA for $L^{\mathcal{V}}$ we can construct a GNTA for L by adding the vector $x^{\mathcal{U}}$ to x_0 and x_1. $\square$

Proof (of Theorem 11). The polyhedron corresponding to loop transition of the deterministic linear loop program L is

$$\begin{pmatrix} G & 0 \\ M & -I \\ -M & I \end{pmatrix} \begin{pmatrix} x \\ x' \end{pmatrix} \leq \begin{pmatrix} g \\ -m \\ m \end{pmatrix}. \tag{6}$$

Define $\mathcal{Y}$ to be the convex cone spanned by the rays of the guard polyhedron:

$$\mathcal{Y} := \{y \in \mathbb{R}^n \mid Gy \leq 0\}$$

Let $\overline{\mathcal{Y}}$ be the smallest linear subspace of $\mathbb{R}^n$ that contains $\mathcal{Y}$, i.e., $\overline{\mathcal{Y}} = \mathcal{Y} - \mathcal{Y}$ using pointwise subtraction, and let $\overline{\mathcal{Y}}^\perp$ be the linear subspace of $\mathbb{R}^n$ orthogonal to $\overline{\mathcal{Y}}$; hence $\mathbb{R}^n = \overline{\mathcal{Y}} \oplus \overline{\mathcal{Y}}^\perp$.

Let $P := \{x \in \mathbb{R}^n \mid Gx \leq g\}$ denote the guard polyhedron. Its projection $P^{\overline{\mathcal{Y}}^\perp}$ to the subspace $\overline{\mathcal{Y}}^\perp$ is again a polyhedron. By the decomposition theorem for polyhedra [36, Corollary 7.1b], $P^{\overline{\mathcal{Y}}^\perp} = Q + C$ for some polytope Q and some convex cone C. However, by definition of the subspace $\overline{\mathcal{Y}}^\perp$, the convex cone C must be equal to $\{0\}$: for any $y \in C \subseteq \overline{\mathcal{Y}}^\perp$, we have $Gy \leq 0$, thus $y \in \mathcal{Y}$, and therefore y is orthogonal to itself, i.e., $y = 0$. We conclude that $P^{\overline{\mathcal{Y}}^\perp}$ must be a polytope, and thus it is bounded. By assumption L is nonterminating, so $L^{\overline{\mathcal{Y}}^\perp}$ is nonterminating, and since $P^{\overline{\mathcal{Y}}^\perp}$ is bounded, any infinite execution of $L^{\overline{\mathcal{Y}}^\perp}$ must be bounded.

Let $\mathcal{U}$ denote the direct sum of the generalized eigenspaces for the eigenvalues $0 \leq \lambda < 1$. Any infinite execution is necessarily bounded on the subspace $\mathcal{U}$ since on this space the map $x \mapsto Mx + m$ is a contraction. Let $\mathcal{U}^\perp$ denote the subspace of $\mathbb{R}^n$ orthogonal to $\mathcal{U}$. The space $\overline{\mathcal{Y}} \cap \mathcal{U}^\perp$ is a linear subspace of $\mathbb{R}^n$ and any infinite execution in its complement is bounded. Hence we can turn our analysis to the subspace $\overline{\mathcal{Y}} \cap \mathcal{U}^\perp + x$ for some $x \in \overline{\mathcal{Y}}^\perp \oplus \mathcal{U}$ for the rest of the proof according to Lemma 12. From now on, we implicitly assume that we are in this space without changing any of the notation.

Part 1. In this part we show that there is a basis $y_1, \ldots, y_s \in \mathcal{Y}$ such that M turns into a matrix U of the form given in (1) with $\lambda_1, \ldots, \lambda_s, \mu_1, \ldots, \mu_{s-1} \geq 0$. Since we allow μ_k to be positive between different eigenvalues (Example 14 illustrates why), this is not necessarily a Jordan normal form and the vectors y_i are not necessarily generalized eigenvectors.

We choose a basis $v_1, \ldots, v_s$ such that M is in Jordan normal form with the eigenvalues ordered by size such that the largest eigenvalues come first. Define $\mathcal{V}_1 := \overline{\mathcal{Y}} \cap \mathcal{U}^\perp$ and let $\mathcal{V}_1 \supset \ldots \supset \mathcal{V}_s$ be a strictly descending chain of linear subspaces where $\mathcal{V}_i$ is spanned by $v_k, \ldots, v_s$.

We define a basis $w_1, \ldots, w_s$ by doing the following for each Jordan block of M, starting with $k = 1$. Let $M^{(k)}$ be the projection of M to the linear subspace $\mathcal{V}_k$ and let λ be the largest eigenvalues of $M^{(k)}$. The m-fold iteration of a Jordan block $J_\ell(\lambda)$ for $m \geq \ell$ is given by

$$
J_\ell(\lambda)^m = \begin{pmatrix} \lambda^m & \binom{m}{1}\lambda^{m-1} & \cdots & \binom{m}{\ell}\lambda^{m-\ell} \\ & \lambda^m & \cdots & \binom{m}{\ell-1}\lambda^{m-\ell+1} \\ & & \ddots & \vdots \\ 0 & & & \lambda^m \end{pmatrix} \in \mathbb{R}^{\ell \times \ell}. \tag{7}
$$

Let $z_0, z_1, z_2, \ldots$ be an infinite execution of the loop L in the basis $v_k, \ldots, v_s$ projected to the space $\mathcal{V}_k$. Since by Lemma 12 we can assume that there are no fixed points on this space, $|z_t| \to \infty$ as $t \to \infty$ in each of the top ℓ components. Asymptotically, the largest eigenvalue λ dominates and in each row of $J_k(\lambda_k)^m$ (7), the entries $\binom{m}{j}\lambda^{m-j}$ in the rightmost column grow the fastest with an asymptotic rate of $\Theta(m^j \exp(m))$. Therefore the sign of the component corresponding to basis vector $v_{k+\ell}$ determines whether the top ℓ entries tend to $+\infty$ or $-\infty$, but the top ℓ entries of z_t corresponding to the top Jordan block will all have the same sign eventually. Because no state can violate the guard condition we have that the guard cannot constraint the infinite execution in the direction of v_j or $-v_j$, i.e., $G^{\mathcal{V}_k} v_j \leq 0$ for each $j \in \{k, \ldots, k+\ell\}$ or $G^{\mathcal{V}_k} v_j \geq 0$ for each $j \in \{k, \ldots, k+\ell\}$, where $G^{\mathcal{V}_k}$ is the projection of G to the subspace $\mathcal{V}_k$. So without loss of generality the former holds (otherwise we use $-v_j$ instead of v_j for $j \in \{k, \ldots, k+\ell\}$) and for $j \in \{k, \ldots, k+\ell\}$ we get $v_j \in \mathcal{Y} + \mathcal{V}_k^\perp$ where $\mathcal{V}_k^\perp$ is the space spanned by $v_1, \ldots, v_{k-1}$. Hence there is a $u_j \in \mathcal{V}_k^\perp$ such that $w_j := v_j + u_j$ is an element of $\mathcal{Y}$. Now we move on to the subspace $\mathcal{V}_{k+\ell+1}$, discarding the top Jordan block.

Let T be the matrix M written in the basis $w_1, \ldots, w_k$. Then T is of upper triangular form: whenever we apply $M w_k$ we get $\lambda_k w_k + u_k$ (w_k was an eigenvector in the space $\mathcal{V}_k$) where $u_k \in \mathcal{V}_k^\perp$, the space spanned by $v_1, \ldots, v_{k-1}$ (which is identical with the space spanned by $w_1, \ldots, w_{k-1}$). Moreover, since we processed every Jordan block entirely, we have that for w_k and w_j from the same generalized eigenspace ($T_{k,k} = T_{j,j}$) that for $k > j$

$$
T_{j,k} \in \{0, 1\} \text{ and } T_{j,k} = 1 \text{ implies } k = j + 1. \tag{8}
$$

In other words, when projected to any generalized eigenspace T consists only of Jordan blocks.

Now we change basis again in order to get the upper triangular matrix U defined in (1) from T. For this we define the vectors

$$y_k := \beta_k \sum_{j=1}^{k} \alpha_{k,j} w_j.$$

with nonnegative real numbers $\alpha_{k,j} \geq 0$, $\alpha_{k,k} > 0$, and $\beta > 0$ to be determined later. Define the matrices $W := (w_1 \ldots w_s)$, $Y := (y_1 \ldots y_s)$, and $\alpha := (\alpha_{k,j})_{1 \leq j \leq k \leq s}$. So α is a nonnegative lower triangular matrix with a positive diagonal and hence invertible. Since α and W are invertible, the matrix $Y = \mathrm{diag}(\beta)\alpha W$ is invertible as well and thus the vectors $y_1, \ldots, y_s$ form a basis. Moreover, we have $y_k \in \mathcal{Y}$ for each k since $\alpha \geq 0$, $\beta > 0$, and $\mathcal{Y}$ is a convex cone. Therefore we get

$$GY \leq 0. \tag{9}$$

We will first choose α. Define $T =: D + N$ where $D = \mathrm{diag}(\lambda_1, \ldots, \lambda_s)$ is a diagonal matrix and N is nilpotent. Since w_1 is an eigenvector of M we have $My_1 = M\beta_1\alpha_{1,1}w_1 = \lambda_1\beta_1\alpha_{1,1}w_1 = \lambda_1 y_1$. To get the form in (1), we need for all $k > 1$

$$My_k = \lambda_k y_k + \mu_{k-1} y_{k-1}. \tag{10}$$

Written in the basis $w_1, \ldots, w_s$ (i.e., multiplied with W^{-1}),

$$(D+N)\beta_k \sum_{j \leq k} \alpha_{k,j} e_j = \lambda_k \beta_k \sum_{j \leq k} \alpha_{k,j} e_j + \mu_{k-1}\beta_{k-1} \sum_{j < k} \alpha_{k-1,j} e_j.$$

Hence we want to pick α such that

$$\sum_{j \leq k} \alpha_{k,j}(\lambda_j - \lambda_k) e_j + N \sum_{j \leq k} \alpha_{k,j} e_j - \mu_{k-1}\beta_{k-1} \sum_{j < k} \alpha_{k-1,j} e_j = 0. \tag{11}$$

First note that these constraints are independent of β if we set $\mu_{k-1} := \beta_{k-1}^{-1} > 0$, so we can leave assigning a value to β to a later part of the proof.

We distinguish two cases. First, if $\lambda_{k-1} \neq \lambda_k$, then $\lambda_j - \lambda_k$ is positive for all $j < k$ because larger eigenvalues come first. Since N is nilpotent and upper triangular, $N \sum_{j \leq k} \alpha_{k,j} e_j$ is a linear combination of $e_1, \ldots, e_{k-1}$ (i.e., only the first $k - 1$ entries are nonzero). Whatever values this vector assumes, we can increase the parameters $\alpha_{k,j}$ for $j < k$ to make (11) larger and increase the parameters $\alpha_{k-1,j}$ for $j < k$ to make (11) smaller.

Second, let ℓ be minimal such that $\lambda_\ell = \lambda_k$ wkth $\ell \neq k$, then $w_\ell, \ldots, w_j$ are from the same generalized eigenspace. For the rows $1, \ldots, \ell - 1$ we can proceed as we did in the first case and for the rows $\ell, \ldots, k - 1$ we note that by (8) $Ne_j = T_{j-1,j} e_{j-1}$. Hence the remaining constraints (11) are

$$\sum_{\ell < j \leq k} \alpha_{k,j} T_{j-1,j} e_{j-1} - \mu_{k-1} \sum_{\ell \leq j < k} \alpha_{k-1,j} e_j = 0,$$

which is solved by $\alpha_{k,j+1} T_{j,j+1} = \alpha_{k-1,j}$ for $\ell \leq j < k$. This is only a problem if there is a j such that $T_{j-1,j} = 0$, i.e., if there are multiple Jordan blocks for the same eigenvalue. In this case, we can reduce the dimension of the generalized eigenspace to the dimension of the largest Jordan block by combining all Jordan blocks: if $My_k = \lambda y_k + y_{k-1}$, and $My_j = \lambda y_j + y_{j-1}$, then $M(y_k + y_j) = \lambda(y_k + y_j) + (y_{k-1} + y_{j-1})$ and if $My_k = \lambda y_k + y_{k-1}$, and $My_j = \lambda y_j$, then $M(y_k + y_j) = \lambda(y_k + y_j) + y_{k-1}$. In both cases we can replace the basis vector y_k with $y_k + y_j$ without reducing the expressiveness of the GNTA.

Importantly, there are no cyclic dependencies in the values of α because neither one of the coefficients α can be made too large. Therefore we can choose $\alpha \geq 0$ such that (10) is satisfied for all $k > 1$ and hence the basis $y_1, \ldots, y_s$ brings M into the desired form (1).

Part 2. In this part we construct the geometric nontermination argument and check the constraints from Definition 5. Since L has an infinite execution, there is a point x that fulfills the guard, i.e., $Gx \leq g$. We choose $x_1 := x + Y\gamma$ with $\gamma \geq 0$ to be determined later. Moreover, we choose $\lambda_1, \ldots, \lambda_s$ and $\mu_1, \ldots, \mu_{s-1}$ from the entries of U given in (1). The size of our GNTA is s, the number of vectors $y_1, \ldots, y_s$. These vectors form a basis of $\overline{\mathcal{Y}} \cap \mathcal{U}^\perp$, which is a subspace of $\mathbb{R}^n$; thus $s \leq n$, as required.

The constraint (domain) is satisfied by construction and the constraint (init) is vacuous since L is a loop program. For (ray) note that from (9) and (10) we get

$$\begin{pmatrix} G & 0 \\ M & -I \\ -M & I \end{pmatrix} \begin{pmatrix} y_k \\ \lambda_k y_k + \mu_{k-1} y_{k-1} \end{pmatrix} \leq \begin{pmatrix} 0 \\ 0 \\ 0 \end{pmatrix}.$$

The remainder of this proof shows that we can choose β and γ such that (point) is satisfied, i.e., that

$$Gx_1 \leq g \text{ and } Mx_1 + m = x_1 + Y1. \tag{12}$$

The vector x_1 satisfies the guard since $Gx_1 = Gx + GY\gamma \leq g + 0$ according to (9), which yields the first part of (12). For the second part we observe the following.

$$Mx_1 + m = x_1 + Y1$$
$$\Longleftrightarrow \quad (M - I)(x + Y\gamma) + m = Y1$$
$$\Longleftrightarrow \quad (M - I)x + m = Y1 - (M - I)Y\gamma$$

Since Y is a basis, it is invertible, so

$$\Longleftrightarrow \quad Y^{-1}(M - I)x + Y^{-1}m = 1 - Y^{-1}(M - I)Y\gamma$$
$$\Longleftrightarrow \quad (U - I)Y^{-1}x + Y^{-1}m = 1 - (U - I)\gamma$$
$$\Longleftrightarrow \quad (U - I)\tilde{x} + \tilde{m} = 1 - (U - I)\gamma \tag{13}$$

with $\tilde{x} := Y^{-1}x = W^{-1}\alpha^{-1}\text{diag}(\beta)^{-1}x$ and $\tilde{m} := Y^{-1}m = W^{-1}\alpha^{-1}\text{diag}(\beta)^{-1}m$. Equation (13) is now conveniently in the basis $y_1, \ldots, y_s$ and all that remains to show is that we can choose $\gamma \geq 0$ and $\beta > 0$ such that (13) is satisfied.

We proceed for each (not quite Jordan) block of U separately, i.e., we assume that we are looking at the subspace $y_j, \ldots, y_k$ with $\mu_k = \mu_{j-1} = 0$ and $\mu_\ell > 0$ for all $\ell \in \{j, \ldots, k-1\}$. If this space only contains eigenvalues that are larger than 1, then $U - I$ is invertible and has only nonnegative entries. By using large enough values for β, we can make $\tilde{x}$ and $\tilde{m}$ small enough, such that $1 \geq (U-I)\tilde{x} + \tilde{m}$. Then we just need to pick γ appropriately.

If there is at least one eigenvalue 1, then $U - I$ is not invertible, so (13) could be overconstraint. Notice that $\mu_\ell > 0$ for all $\ell \in \{j, \ldots, k-1\}$, so only the bottom entry in the vector Eq. (13) is not covered by γ. Moreover, since eigenvalues are ordered in decreasing order and all eigenvalues in our current subspace are ≥ 1, we conclude that the eigenvalue for the bottom entry is 1. (Furthermore, k is the highest index since each eigenvalue occurs only in one block). Thus we get the equation $\tilde{m}_k = 1$. If $\tilde{m}_k$ is positive, this equation has a solution since we can adjust β_k accordingly. If it is zero, then the execution on the space spanned by y_k is bounded, which we can rule out by Lemma 12.

It remains to rule out that $\tilde{m}_k$ is negative. Let $\mathcal{U}$ be the generalized eigenspace to the eigenvector 1 and use Lemma 13 below to conclude that $o := N^{s-1}m + u \in \mathcal{Y}$ for some $u \in \mathcal{U}^\perp$. We have that $Mo = M(N^{s-1}m + u) = Mu \in \mathcal{U}^\perp$, so o is a candidate to pick for the vector w_k. Therefore without loss of generality we did so in part 1 of this proof and since y_k is in the convex cone spanned by the basis $w_1, \ldots, w_s$ we get $\tilde{m}_k > 0$. □

Lemma 13 (Deterministic Loops with Eigenvalue 1). *Let $M = I + N$ and let N be nilpotent with nilpotence index k ($k := \min\{i \mid N^i = 0\}$). If $GN^{k-1}m \not\leq 0$, then L is terminating.*

Proof. We show termination by providing an k-nested ranking function [28, Definition 4.7]. By [28, Lemma 3.3] and [28, Theorem 4.10], this implies that L is terminating.

According to the premise, $GN^{k-1}m \not\leq 0$, hence there is at least one positive entry in the vector $GN^{k-1}m$. Let h be a row vector of G such that $h^T N^{k-1}m =: \delta > 0$, and let $h_0 \in \mathbb{R}$ be the corresponding entry in g. Let x be any state and let x' be a next state after the loop transition, i.e., $x' = Mx + m$. Define the affine-linear functions $f_j(x) := -h^T N^{k-j}x + c_j$ for $1 \leq j \leq k$ with constants $c_j \in \mathbb{R}$ to be determined later. Since every state x satisfies the guard we have $h^T x \leq h_0$, hence $f_k(x) = -h^T x + c_k \geq -h_0 + c_k > 0$ for $c_k := h_0 + 1$.

$$f_1(x') = f_1(x + Nx + m) = -h^T N^{k-1}(x + Nx + m) + c_1$$
$$= f_1(x) - h^T N^k x - h^T N^{k-1}m$$
$$< f_1(x) - 0 - \delta$$

For $1 < j \leq k$,

$$f_j(x') = f_j(x + Nx + m) = -h^{T} N^{k-j}(x + Nx + m) + c_j$$
$$= f_j(x) + f_{j-1}(x) - h^T N^{k-j} m - c_{j-1}$$
$$< f_j(x) + f_{j-1}(x)$$

for $c_{j-1} := -h^T N^{k-j} m - 1$. □

Example 14 (U is not in Jordan Form). The matrix U defined in (1) and used in the completeness proof is generally *not* the Jordan normal form of the loop's transition matrix M. Consider the following linear loop program.

$$\textbf{while} \quad (a - b \geq 0 \wedge b \geq 0):$$
$$a := 3a;$$
$$b := b + 1;$$

This program is nonterminating because a grows exponentially and hence faster than b. It has the geometric nontermination argument

$$x_0 = \begin{pmatrix} 0 \\ 1 \end{pmatrix}, \quad x_1 = \begin{pmatrix} 0 \\ 1 \end{pmatrix}, \quad y_1 = \begin{pmatrix} 12 \\ 0 \end{pmatrix}, \quad y_2 = \begin{pmatrix} 6 \\ 1 \end{pmatrix}, \quad \lambda_1 = 3, \quad \lambda_2 = 1, \quad \mu_1 = 1.$$

The matrix corresponding to the linear loop update is

$$M = \begin{pmatrix} 3 & 0 \\ 0 & 1 \end{pmatrix}$$

which is diagonal (hence diagonalizable). Therefore M is already in Jordan normal form. The matrix U defined according to (1) is

$$U = \begin{pmatrix} 3 & 1 \\ 0 & 1 \end{pmatrix}.$$

The nilpotent component $\mu_1 = 1$ is important and there is no GTNA for this loop program where $\mu_1 = 0$ since the eigenspace to the eigenvalue 1 is spanned by $(0\ 1)^T$ which is in $\overline{\mathcal{Y}}$, but not in $\mathcal{Y}$. ◊

5 Experiments

We implemented our method in a tool that is specialized for the analysis of lasso programs and called ULTIMATE LASSORANKER[2]. LASSORANKER is used by ULTIMATE BÜCHI AUTOMIZER [22] which analyzes termination of (general) C programs. BÜCHI AUTOMIZER iteratively picks lasso shaped paths in the control flow graph converts them to lasso programs and lets LASSORANKER analyze them. In case LASSORANKER was able to prove nontermination a real counterexample to termination was found, in case LASSORANKER was able to provide a

---

[2] http://ultimate.informatik.uni-freiburg.de/lasso_ranker/.

termination argument (e.g., a linear ranking function), Büchi Automizer continues the analysis, but only on lasso shaped paths for which the termination arguments obtained in former iterations are not applicable.

We applied BÜCHI AUTOMIZER to the 803 C programs from the Termination Competition 2017[3] Our constraints for the existence of a geometric nontermination arguments (GNTA) were stated over the integers and we used the SMT solver Z3 [23] with a timeout of 12 s to solve these constraints. The overall timeout for the termination analysis was 60s. In our implementation, LASSORANKER first tries to find a fixpoint for a lasso and only if not fixpoint exists, it tries to find a GNTA that can also represent an unbounded execution. The tool was able to identify 143 nonterminating programs. For 82 of these a fixpoint was detected. For the other 61 programs the counterexample had only an unbounded execution but not fixpoint.

This experiment demonstrates that despite the nonlinear integer constraint the synthesis of GNTA is feasible in practice and that furthermore GNTAs which can also represent unbounded executions improved BÜCHI AUTOMIZER significantly.

6   Related Work

One line of related work is focused on decidability questions for deterministic lasso programs. Tiwari [38] considered linear loop programs over the reals where only strict inequalities are used in the guard and proved that termination is decidable. Braverman [5] generalized this result to loop programs that use strict and non-strict inequalities in the guard. Furthermore, he proved that termination is also decidable for homogeneous deterministic loop programs over the integers. Rebiha et al. [35] generalized the result to integer loops where the update matrix has only real eigenvalues. Ouaknine et al. [30] generalized the result to integer lassos where the update matrix of the loop is diagonalizable.

Another line of related work is also applicable to nondeterministic programs and uses a constraint-based synthesis of recurrence sets. The recurrence sets are defined by templates [20,39] or the constraint is given in a second order theory for bit vectors [17]. These approaches can be used to find nonterminating lassos that do not have a geometric nontermination argument; however, this comes at the price that for nondeterministic programs an $\exists\forall\exists$-constraint has to be solved.

Furthermore, there is a long line of research [2,3,8–10,12,17,26,27] that addresses programs that are more general than lasso programs.

7   Conclusion

We presented a new approach to nontermination analysis for (nondeterministic) linear lasso programs. This approach is based on geometric nontermination arguments, which are an explicit representation of an infinite execution. Unlike,

---

[3] http://termination-portal.org/wiki/Termination_Competition_2017.

e.g., a recurrence set which encodes a set of nonterminating executions, a user can immediate see if our nonterminating proof encodes a fixpoint or a diverging unbounded execution. Our nontermination arguments can be found by solving a set of nonlinear constraints. In Sect. 4 we showed that the class of nonterminating linear lasso programs that have a geometric nontermination argument is quite large: it contains at least every deterministic linear loop program whose eigenvalues are nonnegative. We expect that this statement can be extended to encompass also negative and complex eigenvalues.

References

1. Albert, E., Arenas, P., Genaim, S., Puebla, G.: Closed-form upper bounds in static cost analysis. J. Autom. Reasoning **46**(2), 161–203 (2011)
2. Atig, M.F., Bouajjani, A., Emmi, M., Lal, A.: Detecting fair non-termination in multithreaded programs. In: Madhusudan, P., Seshia, S.A. (eds.) CAV 2012. LNCS, vol. 7358, pp. 210–226. Springer, Heidelberg (2012). https://doi.org/10.1007/978-3-642-31424-7_19
3. Bakhirkin, A., Piterman, N.: Finding recurrent sets with backward analysis and trace partitioning. In: Chechik, M., Raskin, J.-F. (eds.) TACAS 2016. LNCS, vol 9636, pp. 17–35. Springer, Heidelberg (2016). https://doi.org/10.1007/978-3-662-49674-9_2
4. Ben-Amram, A.M., Genaim, S.: Ranking functions for linear-constraint loops. In: POPL (2013)
5. Braverman, M.: Termination of integer linear programs. In: Ball, T., Jones, R.B. (eds.) CAV 2006. LNCS, vol. 4144, pp. 372–385. Springer, Heidelberg (2006). https://doi.org/10.1007/11817963_34
6. Brockschmidt, M., Cook, B., Fuhs, C.: Better termination proving through cooperation. In: Sharygina, N., Veith, H. (eds.) CAV 2013. LNCS, vol. 8044, pp. 413–429. Springer, Heidelberg (2013). https://doi.org/10.1007/978-3-642-39799-8_28
7. Brockschmidt, M., Cook, B., Ishtiaq, S., Khlaaf, H., Piterman, N.: T2: temporal property verification. In: Chechik, M., Raskin, J.-F. (eds.) TACAS 2016. LNCS, vol. 9636, pp. 387–393. Springer, Heidelberg (2016). https://doi.org/10.1007/978-3-662-49674-9_22
8. Brockschmidt, M., Ströder, T., Otto, C., Giesl, J.: Automated detection of non-termination and nullpointerexceptions for Java Bytecode. In: Beckert, B., Damiani, F., Gurov, D. (eds.) FoVeOOS 2011. LNCS, vol. 7421, pp. 123–141. Springer, Heidelberg (2012). https://doi.org/10.1007/978-3-642-31762-0_9
9. Urban, C., Gurfinkel, A., Kahsai, T.: Synthesizing ranking functions from bits and pieces. In: Chechik, M., Raskin, J.-F. (eds.) TACAS 2016. LNCS, vol. 9636, pp. 54–70. Springer, Heidelberg (2016). https://doi.org/10.1007/978-3-662-49674-9_4
10. Chen, H.-Y., Cook, B., Fuhs, C., Nimkar, K., O'Hearn, P.: Proving nontermination via safety. In: Ábrahám, E., Havelund, K. (eds.) TACAS 2014. LNCS, vol. 8413, pp. 156–171. Springer, Heidelberg (2014). https://doi.org/10.1007/978-3-642-54862-8_11
11. Cook, B., Fisher, J., Krepska, E., Piterman, N.: Proving stabilization of biological systems. In: Jhala, R., Schmidt, D. (eds.) VMCAI 2011. LNCS, vol. 6538, pp. 134–149. Springer, Heidelberg (2011). https://doi.org/10.1007/978-3-642-18275-4_11
12. Cook, B., Fuhs, C., Nimkar, K., O'Hearn, P.W.: Disproving termination with over-approximation. In: FMCAD 2014, pp. 67–74. IEEE (2014)

13. Cook, B., Khlaaf, H., Piterman, N.: On automation of CTL* verification for infinite-state systems. In: Kroening, D., Păsăreanu, C.S. (eds.) CAV 2015, Part I. LNCS, vol. 9206, pp. 13–29. Springer, Cham (2015). https://doi.org/10.1007/978-3-319-21690-4_2

14. Cook, B., Khlaaf, H., Piterman, N.: Verifying increasingly expressive temporal logics for infinite-state systems. J. ACM **64**(2), 15:1–15:39 (2017)

15. Cook, B., Koskinen, E., Vardi, M.: Temporal property verification as a program analysis task. In: Gopalakrishnan, G., Qadeer, S. (eds.) CAV 2011. LNCS, vol. 6806, pp. 333–348. Springer, Heidelberg (2011). https://doi.org/10.1007/978-3-642-22110-1_26

16. Cook, B., Podelski, A., Rybalchenko, A.: TERMINATOR: beyond safety. In: Ball, T., Jones, R.B. (eds.) CAV 2006. LNCS, vol. 4144, pp. 415–418. Springer, Heidelberg (2006). https://doi.org/10.1007/11817963_37

17. David, C., Kroening, D., Lewis, M.: Unrestricted termination and non-termination arguments for bit-vector programs. In: Vitek, J. (ed.) ESOP 2015. LNCS, vol. 9032, pp. 183–204. Springer, Heidelberg (2015). https://doi.org/10.1007/978-3-662-46669-8_8

18. Dietsch, D., Heizmann, M., Langenfeld, V., Podelski, A.: Fairness modulo theory: a new approach to LTL software model checking. In: Kroening, D., Păsăreanu, C.S. (eds.) CAV 2015, Part I. LNCS, vol. 9206, pp. 49–66. Springer, Cham (2015). https://doi.org/10.1007/978-3-319-21690-4_4

19. Gulwani, S., Zuleger, F.: The reachability-bound problem. In: PLDI, pp. 292–304 (2010)

20. Gupta, A., Henzinger, T.A., Majumdar, R., Rybalchenko, A., Xu, R.-G.: Proving non-termination. In: POPL, pp. 147–158 (2008)

21. Harris, W.R., Lal, A., Nori, A.V., Rajamani, S.K.: Alternation for termination. In: Cousot, R., Martel, M. (eds.) SAS 2010. LNCS, vol. 6337, pp. 304–319. Springer, Heidelberg (2010). https://doi.org/10.1007/978-3-642-15769-1_19

22. Heizmann, M., Hoenicke, J., Podelski, A.: Termination analysis by learning terminating programs. In: Biere, A., Bloem, R. (eds.) CAV 2014. LNCS, vol. 8559, pp. 797–813. Springer, Cham (2014). https://doi.org/10.1007/978-3-319-08867-9_53

23. Jovanović, D., de Moura, L.: Solving non-linear arithmetic. In: Gramlich, B., Miller, D., Sattler, U. (eds.) IJCAR 2012. LNCS (LNAI), vol. 7364, pp. 339–354. Springer, Heidelberg (2012). https://doi.org/10.1007/978-3-642-31365-3_27

24. Kroening, D., Sharygina, N., Tonetta, S., Tsitovich, A., Wintersteiger, C.M.: Loop summarization using abstract transformers. In: Cha, S.S., Choi, J.-Y., Kim, M., Lee, I., Viswanathan, M. (eds.) ATVA 2008. LNCS, vol. 5311, pp. 111–125. Springer, Heidelberg (2008). https://doi.org/10.1007/978-3-540-88387-6_10

25. Kroening, D., Sharygina, N., Tsitovich, A., Wintersteiger, C.M.: Termination analysis with compositional transition invariants. In: Touili, T., Cook, B., Jackson, P. (eds.) CAV 2010. LNCS, vol. 6174, pp. 89–103. Springer, Heidelberg (2010). https://doi.org/10.1007/978-3-642-14295-6_9

26. Larraz, D., Nimkar, K., Oliveras, A., Rodríguez-Carbonell, E., Rubio, A.: Proving non-termination using max-SMT. In: Biere, A., Bloem, R. (eds.) CAV 2014. LNCS, vol. 8559, pp. 779–796. Springer, Cham (2014). https://doi.org/10.1007/978-3-319-08867-9_52

27. Le, T.C., Qin, S., Chin, W.: Termination and non-termination specification inference. In: PLDI, pp. 489–498. ACM (2015)

28. Leike, J., Heizmann, M.: Ranking templates for linear loops. Log. Methods Comput. Sci. **11**(1), 1–27 (2015)

29. Leike, J.M., Heizmann, M.: Geometric nontermination arguments. CoRR, abs/1609.05207 (2016)
30. Ouaknine, J., Pinto, J.S., Worrell, J.: On termination of integer linear loops. In: Symposium on Discrete Algorithms, pp. 957–969 (2015)
31. Podelski, A., Rybalchenko, A.: A complete method for the synthesis of linear ranking functions. In: Steffen, B., Levi, G. (eds.) VMCAI 2004. LNCS, vol. 2937, pp. 239–251. Springer, Heidelberg (2004). https://doi.org/10.1007/978-3-540-24622-0_20
32. Podelski, A., Rybalchenko, A.: Transition invariants. In LICS, pp. 32–41 (2004)
33. Podelski, A., Rybalchenko, A.: Transition predicate abstraction and fair termination. In: POPL, pp. 132–144 (2005)
34. Podelski, A., Wagner, S.: A sound and complete proof rule for region stability of hybrid systems. In: Bemporad, A., Bicchi, A., Buttazzo, G. (eds.) HSCC 2007. LNCS, vol. 4416, pp. 750–753. Springer, Heidelberg (2007). https://doi.org/10.1007/978-3-540-71493-4_76
35. Rebiha, R., Matringe, N., Moura, A.V.: Characterization of termination for linear homogeneous programs. Technical report, Institute of Computing, University of Campinas, March 2014
36. Schrijver, A.: Theory of Linear and Integer Programming. Wiley, Hoboken (1999)
37. Ströder, T., Giesl, J., Brockschmidt, M., Frohn, F., Fuhs, C., Hensel, J., Schneider-Kamp, P., Aschermann, C.: Automatically proving termination and memory safety for programs with pointer arithmetic. J. Autom. Reason. **58**(1), 33–65 (2017)
38. Tiwari, A.: Termination of linear programs. In: Alur, R., Peled, D.A. (eds.) CAV 2004. LNCS, vol. 3114, pp. 70–82. Springer, Heidelberg (2004). https://doi.org/10.1007/978-3-540-27813-9_6
39. Velroyen, H., Rümmer, P.: Non-termination checking for imperative programs. In: Beckert, B., Hähnle, R. (eds.) TAP 2008. LNCS, vol. 4966, pp. 154–170. Springer, Heidelberg (2008). https://doi.org/10.1007/978-3-540-79124-9_11

Hybrid and Stochastic Systems

Efficient Dynamic Error Reduction
for Hybrid Systems Reachability Analysis

Stefan Schupp[✉] and Erika Ábrahám

RWTH Aachen University, Aachen, Germany
stefan.schupp@cs.rwth-aachen.de

Abstract. To decide whether a set of states is reachable in a hybrid system, over-approximative symbolic successor computations can be used, where the symbolic representation of state sets as well as the successor computations have several parameters which determine the efficiency and the precision of the computations. Naturally, faster computations come with less precision and more spurious counterexamples. To remove a spurious counterexample, the only possibility offered by current tools is to reduce the error by re-starting the complete search with different parameters. In this paper we propose a CEGAR approach that takes as input a user-defined ordered list of search configurations, which are used to dynamically refine the search tree along potentially spurious counterexamples. Dedicated datastructures allow to extract as much useful information as possible from previous computations in order to reduce the refinement overhead.

1 Introduction

As the correct behavior of *hybrid systems* with mixed discrete-continuous behavior is often safety critical, a lot of effort was put into the development and implementation of techniques for their analysis. In this paper we focus on techniques for proving unreachability of a given set of unsafe states. Besides methods based on theorem proving [11,21,25], logical encoding [13,15,22,26] and validated simulation [12,28], *flowpipe-construction-based methods* [2,7,9,17–20,27] show increasing performance and usability. These methods over-approximate the set of states that are reachable in a hybrid system from a given set of initial states by executing an iterative forward reachability analysis algorithm. The result is a sequence of state sets whose union contains all system paths starting in any initial state (usually for bounded time duration and a bounded number of discrete steps, unless a fixedpoint could be detected).

If the resulting over-approximation does not intersect with the unsafe state set then the verification task is successfully completed. However, if the intersection is not empty, due to the over-approximation the results are not conclusive. In this case the only possibility for achieving a conclusive answer is to change

This work was supported by the German research council (DFG) in the context of the HyPro project and the DFG Research Training Group 2236 UnRAVeL.

D. Beyer and M. Huisman (Eds.): TACAS 2018, LNCS 10806, pp. 287–302, 2018.
https://doi.org/10.1007/978-3-319-89963-3_17

some analysis parameters to reduce the approximation error. As a smaller error typically comes with a higher computational effort, the choice of suitable parameters by the user can be a tedious task.

Most tools do not support the dynamic change of those parameters, thus after the modification of the parameters the user has to re-start the whole computation. One of the few tools implementing some hard-coded dynamic parameter adaptations is the STC mode [16] of SpaceEx [17], which dynamically adapts the time-step size during reachability analysis to detect the enabledness of discrete events more precisely. Another parameter (the degree of Taylor approximations) is dynamically adapted in the Flow* tool [9]. The method [5], also implemented in SpaceEx, uses cheap (but stronger over-approximating) computations to detect potentially unsafe paths and use this information to guide more precise (and more time-consuming) computations. In [6] the authors present a method to automatically derive template directions when using template polyhedra as a state set representation in a CEGAR refinement fashion during analysis. As a last example, in [24] the authors use model abstraction to hide model details and apply model refinement if potential counterexamples are detected; after each refinement, the approach makes use of previous reachability analysis results and adapts them for the refined model, instead of a complete restart.

However, none of the available tools supports the dynamic adjustments of several parameters by a more elaborate strategy, which is either defined by the user or chosen from a pre-defined set. In this paper we propose such an approach, provide an implementation based on the HyPro [27] programming library, present some use cases to demonstrate its applicability and advantages, and discuss ideas for further extensions and improvements. Our main contributions are:

- the definition of *search strategies* to specify the dynamic adjustment of parameter configurations;
- the formalization of a general *reachability analysis algorithm with dynamic configuration adjustment* following a search strategy, where *dynamic* means that adjustments are triggered during the analysis process in a fully automated manner only for parts of the search where they are needed to achieve conclusive analysis results;
- the identification of information, collected during reachability analysis, which can be *re-used* after a parameter adjustment to reduce the computational effort of forthcoming analysis steps;
- a *datatype* to store information about previously completed analysis steps, including information about re-usability, and supporting dynamic parameter adjustments according to a given strategy;
- the *implementation* of the reachability analysis algorithm using dynamic parameter adjustment and supporting information re-usage;
- the *evaluation* of our method on some case studies.

Outline. In Sect. 2 we recall some preliminaries on flowpipe-construction-based reachability analysis, before presenting our algorithm for the dynamic adjustment of parameter configurations in Sect. 3. In Sect. 4 we provide some experimental results and conclude the paper in Sect. 5.

2 Preliminaries

In this work we develop a method to dynamically adjust the parameters of a verification method for *autonomous linear hybrid systems* whose continuous dynamics can be described by *ordinary differential equations (ODEs)* of the form $\dot{x}(t) = A \cdot x(t)$, but our approach can be naturally extended to methods for non-autonomous hybrid systems with external input or non-linear dynamics.

Hybrid automata [3] are one of the modeling formalisms for hybrid systems. Similarly to discrete transition systems, nodes (called *locations* or *control modi*) model the discrete part of the state space (e.g. the states of a discrete controller) and transitions between the nodes (called *jumps*) labeled with guards and reset functions model discrete state changes. To model the continuous dynamics between discrete state changes, *flows* in the form of ordinary differential equation (ODE) systems, and *invariants* in the form of predicates over the model variables are attached to the locations. The ODEs specify the evolution of the continuous quantities over time (called the *flowpipe*), where the control is forced to leave the current location before its invariant gets violated. Initial predicates attached to the locations specify the initial states.

A *state* $\sigma = (\ell, \nu)$ of a hybrid automaton consists of a location l and a variable valuation ν. A *region* is a set of states $(\ell, P) = \{\ell\} \times P$. A *path* π of a hybrid automaton is a sequence $\pi = \sigma_0 \xrightarrow{t_0} \sigma_1 \xrightarrow{e_1} \sigma_2 \xrightarrow{t_2} \ldots$ of time steps $\sigma_i \xrightarrow{t_i} \sigma_{i+1}$ of duration t_i and discrete steps $\sigma_k \xrightarrow{e_k} \sigma_{k+1}$ following a jump, where $\sigma_0 = (\ell_0, \nu_0)$ is an initial state. A state is called *reachable* if there exists a path leading to it.

Flowpipe-construction-based reachability analysis aims at determining the states that are reachable in (a model of) a hybrid system, in order to show that certain unsafe states cannot be reached. Since the reachability problem for hybrid systems is in general undecidable, these methods usually *over-approximate* the set of states that are reachable along paths with a bounded number of jumps (called the *jump depth*) J and a bounded time duration T (called the *time horizon*) between two jumps. We explain the basic ideas needed to understand our contributions; for further reading we refer to, e.g., [8,23].

Starting from an initial region (ℓ_0, V_0), the analysis over-approximates flowpipes and jump successors iteratively. Due to non-determinism, this generates a *tree*, whose nodes n_i are either *unprocessed* leafs storing a tuple $(\pi_i; \ell_i, V_i; \bot)$, or *processed* inner nodes storing $(\pi_i; \ell_i, V_i; V_{i,0}, \ldots, V_{i,k_i})$.

The pair (ℓ_i, V_i) is the node's *initial region*, which is (ℓ_0, V_0) for the *root*. By $\pi_i = I_{i,0}, e_{i,0}, \ldots, I_{i,d_i}, e_{i,d_i}$, with $I_{i,l}$ being intervals and $e_{i,l}$ being jumps, we encode a set $\{\sigma_0 \xrightarrow{t_0} \sigma_0' \xrightarrow{e_{i,0}} \sigma_1 \ldots \xrightarrow{e_{i,d_i}} \sigma_{d_i+1} \mid \sigma_0 \in (\ell_0, V_0), t_l \in I_{i,l}\}$ of paths along which (ℓ_i, V_i) is reachable.

To process a node $(\pi_i; \ell_i, V_i; \bot)$, we divide the time horizon $[0, T]$ into segments $[t_{i,0}, t_{i,1}], \ldots, [t_{i,k_i}, t_{i,k_i+1}]$ with $t_{i,0} = 0$ and $t_{i,k_i+1} = T$, and for each segment $[t_{i,j}, t_{i,j+1}]$ we compute an over-approximation $V_{i,j}$ of the states reachable from V_i in ℓ_i within time $[t_{i,j}, t_{i,j+1}]$. I.e., $R_i = \cup_{j=0}^{k_i} V_{i,j}$ contains all valuations reachable in location ℓ_i from V_i within time T. The segmentation is usually homogeneous, meaning that the *time-step size* $t_{i,j+1} - t_{i,j}$ is constant, but there are also approaches for dynamic adaptations.

The processing is completed by computing for each *flowpipe segment* $V_{i,j}$ and each jump e from ℓ_i to some ℓ_i' an over-approximation $V_{i,j}^e$ of the valuations reachable from $V_{i,j}$ by executing e. To store the jump successors, either we add a child node $(\pi_i, [t_{i,j}, t_{i,j+1}], e; \ell_i', V_{i,j}^e; \perp)$ to n_i for each $V_{i,j}^e \neq \emptyset$, or we *aggregate* successors along a jump e into a single child node $(\pi_i, [t_{i,j}, t_{i,j'}], e; \ell_i', R_i^e; \perp)$ with $V_{i,l}^e = \emptyset$ for all $l \notin [j, j'-1]$ and $\cup_e \cup_{j'' \in [j,j'-1]} V_{i,j''}^e \subseteq R_i^e$, or we *cluster* successors along a jump into a fixed number of child nodes (see Fig. 3).

For illustration purposes, above we stored all flowpipe segments $V_{i,j}$ in the nodes. In practice they are too numerous and if they contain no unsafe states then they are deleted. In the following, we assume that each node stores a tuple $(\pi_i; \ell_i, V_i; p)$, where the flag p is 1 for processed nodes and 0 otherwise. (For a simple reachability analysis, we need to store neither the path nor the processed flag, but we will make use of the information stored in them later on. Furthermore, we could even delete the initial regions of processed nodes, however, besides counterexample and further output generation, they might be also useful for fixedpoint detection.)

State set representations are one of the core components in the above analysis procedure. Additionally to the storage of state sets, these datatypes need to provide certain (over-approximative) operations (union, intersection, linear transformation, Minkowski sum etc.) on states sets. Besides geometric representations (e.g., boxes/hyperrectangles, oriented rectangular hulls, convex polyhedra, template polyhedra, orthogonal polyhedra, zonotopes, ellipsoids) also symbolic representations (e.g., support functions or Taylor models) can be used for this purpose. The variety of representations is rooted in the general problem of deciding between computational effort and precision. Generally, faster computations often come at the cost of precision loss and vice versa, more precise computations need higher computational effort. The representations might differ in their size, i.e., the required memory consumption, which has a further influence on the computational costs for operations on these representations.

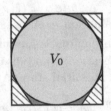

Fig. 1. Polytope (green) and box (hatched) approx. of state set V_0. (Color figure online)

3   CEGAR-Based Reachability Analysis

If potential reachability of an unsafe state is detected by over-approximative computations, in order to achieve a conclusive verification result, we need to *reduce the over-approximation error* to an extent that allows to determine that the counterexample is spurious.

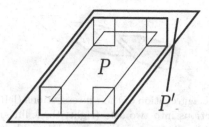

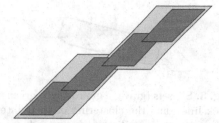

(a) Over-approximating the Minkowksi sum of a polytope P and a box by a less complex polytope. P'.

(b) Smaller time steps typically lead to more precise computations (dark blue) than larger time steps (light blue).

Fig. 2. Reduction and time-step size influence the flowpipe over-approximation error. (Color figure online)

Search parameters, parameter configurations and search strategies. The size of the over-approximation error depends on various search parameters, which influence besides the precision also the computational effort of the performed analysis:

1. *State set representation*: The choice of the state set representation has a very strong influence on both the error and the running time of the computations. For example, boxes are very efficient but introduce large over-approximations, whereas convex polyhedra are in general more precise but computationally much more expensive (see Fig. 1).
2. *Reductions*: Some of the state set representations can grow in the representation size during the computations. For example, during the analysis we need to compute the Minkowski sum $A \oplus B = \{a + b \mid a \in A \wedge b \in B\}$ of two state sets A and B. Figure 2(a) shows a 2-dimensional example to illustrate how the representation size of a polytope P in the vertex representation (storing the vertices of the polytope) increases from 4 to 6 when building the Minkowski sum with a box. Another source of growing representation sizes are large enumerators and/or denominators when using rationals to describe for instance coefficients of vectors. When the size of a representation gets too large we can try to reduce it on the cost of additional over-approximation. Thus the precision/cost is dependent also on the fact whether such reductions take place.
3. *Time-step size*: The time-step size for the flowpipe construction can be constant or dynamically adapted. In the constant case it directly determines the number of flowpipe segments that need to be over-approximated and for which jump successors need to be computed. In the case of dynamic adaptation, the adaptation heuristics determines the number of segments and thus the computational effort. In both cases, smaller time-step sizes often lead to more precise computations on the cost of higher computational effort as more segments are computed (see Fig. 2(b)).
4. *Aggregation and clustering*: The precision is higher if no aggregation takes place or if the number of clusters increases (see Fig. 3). However, completely

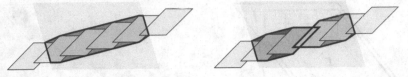

Fig. 3. Six sets (gray), a guard (light green), the aggregation of their intersections (left, thick line), and the clustering of their intersections into two sets (right, thick lines); both aggregation and clustering introduces additional error (dark green and dark blue). (Color figure online)

switching off both aggregation and clustering often leads to practically intractable computational costs. Increasing the precision by allowing a larger number of clusters can improve the precision by managable increase in the running times, but the number of clusters should be carefully chosen considering also the size of the time steps (as they determine the number of flowpipe segments and thus the number of state sets to be clustered).

5. *Splitting initial sets*: Large initial state sets might be challenging for the reachability analysis. If the algorithm cannot find a conclusive answer, we can split the initial set into several subsets and apply reachability analysis to each of the subsets. Besides the enabling/disabling of initial state set splitting, also the splitting heuristics is relevant for the precision. In general, a fewer number of initial state sets is less precise but more cheap to compute with. Furthermore, it might be also relevant where the splitting takes place.

Most flowpipe-construction-based tools allow the user to define a *search parameter configuration*, fixing values for the above-listed search parameters. Aside from a few exceptions mentioned in the introduction, this configuration remains constant during the whole analysis. Whenever an unsafe state is detected to be potentially reachable, the user can re-start the analysis with a different parameter configuration to reduce the over-approximation error.

As the executions with different parameter configurations are completely independent, potentially useful information from previous search processes gets lost. To enable the exploitation of such information, we propose an approach to build a connection between executions with different parameter configurations.

Instead of a single configuration, we propose to define an ordered sequence $c_0, \ldots, c_n$ of search parameter configurations, which we call a *search strategy*, whereas the position of a parameter configuration within a search strategy is called its *refinement level*. Configurations at higher refinement levels should typically lead to more precise computations, but this is not a soundness requirement.

Dynamic configuration adaptation. We start the analysis with the first configuration in the search strategy, i.e. the one at refinement level 0. If the analysis with this configuration can prove safety then the process is completed.

Otherwise, if the reachability computation detects a (potentially spurious) counterexample then the search with the current configuration is paused; note that at this point there might be unprocessed nodes whose successors were not yet computed. Now, our goal is to exclude the detected counterexample by doing as few computations as possible using configurations at higher refinement levels and, if we succeed, process those yet unprocessed nodes further at refinement level 0. For the first counterexample this means intuitively re-computing reachability only along the counterexample path with the configuration at refinement level 1; we say that we *refine the path*. Note that the result of a path refinement can be a tree, e.g. if the refinement switched off aggregation. If the counterexample could be excluded by the path refinement, then we switch back to the previous refinement level to process the remaining, yet unprocessed nodes. Otherwise, if the counterexample could not be excluded then we get another, refined counterexample; in this case we recursively try to exclude this counterexample by switching to the configuration at the second refinement level etc.

Let us first clarify what we mean by *refining a counterexample path*. We define a counterexample to be a path in the search tree. If the configuration, which created the counterexample, used aggregation then it means determining the flowpipes and the jump successors for the given sequence of locations (as stored in the nodes on the path) and jumps (as stored on the edges) with the configuration at the next-higher refinement level. However, if the previous configuration did not aggregate then we need to determine only a subset of the jump successors, namely those whose time point is covered by the counterexample.

Now let us discuss what it means to refine a path *by doing as few computations as possible*. If we find a counterexample at a refinement level i then we need a refinement for the whole path at level $i + 1$. However, another counterexample detected previously at level i might share a prefix with the current one; if the previous counterexample has already been refined then we need to refine only the not-yet-refined postfix of the current counterexample.

The analysis at refinement level 0 and each path refinement computation generates a search tree. To reduce the computational effort as much as possible, we have to exchange information between these search trees. For example, for a given counterexample found at refinement level i we need to know whether a prefix of it was already refined at level $i + 1$. To allow such information exchange, we could store each search tree separately and extract information from the trees when needed by traversing them. This option requires the least management overhead during reachability computations but it has major drawbacks from the point of computational costs for tree traversal. Alternatively, we could store each search tree separately but store in addition refinement relations between their nodes, allowing to relate paths and retrieve information more easily. However, we would have high costs for setting up and storing all node relations. Instead, we decided to collect all information in a single *refinement tree*. Tree updates require a careful management of the refinement nodes and their successors, but the advantage is that information about previous searches is easier accessible.

Next we first discuss how nodes of the refinement tree are processed, how paths in the refinement tree are refined, and finally we explain our dynamical parameter refinement algorithm.

The algorithm. Each refinement tree node n_i is a kind of "meta-node" that contains an ordered sequence $(n_i^0, \ldots, n_i^{u_i})$ with $0 \leq u_i \leq n$, where $n + 1$ is the size of the search strategy, and each entry n_i^j has the form $(\pi; \ell, V; p)$ as explained in Sect. 2.

Assume for simplicity that the model has a single initial region (ℓ_0, X_0), and let $V_{0,i}$ represent X_0 according to the state set representation of refinement level i. The refinement tree is initialized with a root node $n_0 = (n_0^0, \ldots, n_0^n)$ with $n_0^i = (\epsilon; \ell_0, V_{0,i}; 0)$.

We additionally introduce a *task list* which is initialized to contain $(n_0; 0; \epsilon)$ only. Elements $(n_i; j; \pi)$ in the task list store the fact that we need to compute successors for the jth element of the refinement node n_i at level j. If $\pi = \epsilon$ then we are not refining and we need to consider all the successors for further computations, otherwise we are at a refinement level $j > 0$ and only the successors along the counterexample-path π need to be considered.

We remove and process elements from the task list one by one. Assume we consider the task list element $(n_i; j; \pi')$ with $n_i^j = (\pi; \ell, V; p)$.

If $p = 0$ then we over-approximate the flowpipe starting from V in ℓ for the time horizon T, using the configuration at level j in the search strategy.

If the computed flowpipe segments contain no bad states and the jump depth J is not yet reached then we compute also the jump successors. Depending on the clustering/aggregation settings at level j, this yields a set of jump successor regions $R_1, \ldots, R_m$ with $R_k = (\ell_k, V_k)$ over time intervals $I_1, \ldots, I_m$ along jumps $e_1, \ldots, e_m$. If the number of children m' of n_i is less than m then we add $m - m'$ new children; if $m' > 0$ then we add to the newly created children as many dummy entries (containing empty sets) as the other children have, in order to bring all children to the same refinement level. After that, we select for each $k = 1, \ldots, m$ a different child $\hat{n}_k$ of n_i and append $(\pi, I_k, e_k; \ell_k, V_k; 0)$ to the child's entry sequence (see Fig. 4). If $m' > m$ then we add to all not selected children (to which no new entry was added) a dummy entry. Finally, we set p to 1.

If the node could be processed without discovering any bad states (or if p was already 1 and thus processing was not needed) then we update the task list as follows:

– If $\pi' = \epsilon$ then we have to process all successor nodes at the level j' determined by the number of entries E in each of the nodes $\hat{n}_k$. We add $(\hat{n}_k; E; \epsilon)$ to the task list for all $k = 1, \ldots, m$.
– Otherwise, if $\pi' = I, e, \pi''$ then we add $(\hat{n}_k; j; \pi'')$ for all $k = 1, \ldots, m$ for which $I_k \cap I \neq \emptyset$ and $e_k = e$.

Note that if $\pi' = \epsilon$ but $j > 0$ then we just succeeded to refine a spurious counterexample from level $j - 1$ to a safe path at level j and can continue further successor computations using a lower level configuration. This switch to a lower level happens because the children $\hat{n}_k$ of n_i have less then j entries in their queues. Now the processing is completed and the next element from the task list can be approached.

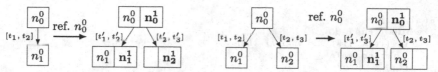

(a) Node refinement adds child nodes.   (b) Node refinement removes child nodes.

Fig. 4. Tree update after node refinement with changing number of child nodes and transition timing refinement.

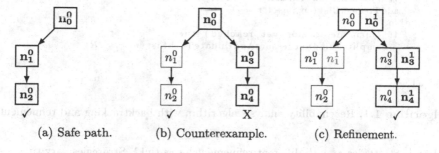

(a) Safe path.   (b) Counterexample.   (c) Refinement.

Fig. 5. Partial tree refinement to remove a spurious counterexample.

If during processing $(n_i; j; \pi')$ with $n_i^j = (\pi; \ell, V; p)$ the computed flowpipe had a non-empty intersection with the set of unsafe states then we have found a counterexample at level j. If $j = n$ then the highest refinement level has been reached and the algorithmus terminates without any conclusive answer. Otherwise, if $j < n$, we repeat the computations along the counterexample path with a higher-level configuration (see Fig. 5). This is implemented by adding $(n_0; j + 1; \pi, \pi')$ to the task list.

The main structure of the algorithm is shown in Algorithm 1.1.

3.1   Incrementality

The efficiency of the presented approach can be further improved by implementing *incrementality*: already available book-keeping and additional information gained throughout the computation can be exploited to speed up later refinements.

For example, the presented approach already keeps track of time intervals where jumps were enabled, i.e. the time intervals during which the intersection of a state set and the guard condition was non-empty. Assume we process $(n; i; \pi')$ at level i with $n_i = (\pi; \ell, V; p)$ being the ith entry in n. Let I be the union of all the time intervals for all flowpipe segments for which a non-empty jump successor was computed along a jump e. Later, when processing $(\hat{n}; j; \hat{\pi}')$ at level $j > i$ with $\hat{n}_j = (\hat{\pi}; \ell, \hat{V}; \hat{p})$ being the jth entry in $\hat{n}$, if the path set encoded by $\hat{\pi}$ is included in the path set encoded by π then we need to compute jump successors along e only for flowpipe segments over time intervals that have a non-empty intersection with I.

```
1  analyze(){
2    while (true) do
3      if (task list is empty) then
4        return safe
5      fi;
6      take an element (n_i; j; π') with n_i^j = (π; ℓ, V; p) from task list;
7      if (p = 0) then
8        R := computeFlowpipeSegments(ℓ, V, j)
9      fi;
10     if (p = 0 and R contains unsafe states) then
11       if (j = n) then return unknown;
12       addToTaskList((n_0; j + 1; π, π'))
13     else
14       if (jump depth not yet reached) then
15         computeJumpSuccessorsAndUpdateTaskList (n_i, j, π', R)
16       fi
17     fi
18   od
19 }
```

Algorithm 1.1. Reachability analysis algorithm with backtracking and refinement.

Table 1. Strategies s_i with different refinement levels (lvl.). Strategies vary time step size (δ) and state set representation (box, sf = support function). Strategy s_5 changes aggregation and clustering (n = no aggregation, c:max. number of successor nodes).

Strategies																	
s_0			s_1				s_2				s_3		s_4		s_5		
lvl. 0	1	2	0	1	2	3	0	1	2	3	0	1	0	1	0	1	2
δ .01	.001	.0001	.01	.001	.01	.001	.01	.001	.01	.0001	.1	.001	.1	.001	.1	.001	.001
rep. box	box	sf	box	box	sf	sf	box	box	sf	sf	box	sf	box	poly	box	box	sf
agg. y	y	y	y	y	y	y	y	y	y	y	y	y	y	y	n	c:3	c:3

Similarly, if (ℓ, V) contains no unsafe states but $(\ell, \hat{V})$ does then we know that the latter counterexample is spurious if the path set encoded by $\hat{\pi}$ is included in the path set encoded by π.

A similar observation holds for flowpipe segments: if a segment in the flowpipe of $(\ell, \hat{V})$ is empty, what happens if the invariant is violated, then we know that the same segment of the flowpipe from $(\ell, \hat{V})$ will also be empty.

4   Experimental Results

In order to show the general applicability of our approach we have conducted several experiments on an implementation of the method presented in Sect. 3. We have used our implementation to verify safety of several well-known benchmarks using different strategies (see Table 1). All experiments were carried on an Intel Core i7 (4×4 GHz) CPU with 16 GB RAM. Results for the used strategies can be found in Table 2.

Benchmarks. Different benchmarks from the area of hybrid systems verification are selected: The well-known bouncing ball benchmark models the height and velocity of a falling ball bouncing off the ground. The added set of bad states constrains the height of the ball after the first of 4 bounces. This benchmark already exhibits most properties more challenging benchmarks cover while being simple enough to be a sanity check for our method.

The 5-D switching system [10] is an artificially created model with 5 locations and 5 variables which shows more complex dynamic and is well-suited to show the differences in over-approximation error between the used state set representations. We added a set of bad states in the last location where the system's trajectories converge to a certain point.

The navigation benchmark [14] models the velocity and position of a point mass moving through cells on a two-dimensional plane (we used variations of instances 9 and 11). Each cell (location) exhibits different dynamic influencing the acceleration of the mass. The goal is to show that a set of good states can potentially be reached while a set of bad states will always be avoided (see Fig. 6(b)). The initial position of the mass is chosen from a set, such that this benchmark demonstrates non-determinism for the discrete transitions which results in a more complex search tree.

The platoon benchmark [1,4] models a vehicle platoon of three cars where two controlled cars follow the first one while keeping the distance e_i between each other within a certain threshold (see Fig. 6(a)). This benchmark was chosen, as it unifies a higher dimension of the state space with a more complex dynamic.

Strategies. During the development of our approach we tested several strategies with varying parameters (a) the state set representation, (b) the time step size and (c) aggregation settings. In general, other parameters (e.g. initial set splitting) could be also considered but our prototype currently does not yet support these. For this evaluation we selected six strategies $s_0, \ldots, s_5$ which mostly vary (a) and (b) (see Table 1). Changing aggregation settings has shown to be challenging for the tree update mechanism but the exponential blow-up of the number of tree nodes did not render this method effective in practice. Furthermore for disabled aggregation settings, the largest precision gain can be observed for boxes while for all other tested state set representations the effect can be neglected. Note that our prototype implements the general case where time step sizes are not necessarily monotonically decreasing and multiples of each other which implies refinement starting from the root node.

Comparison. We compare our refinement algorithm (1) with a classic approach where no refinement is performed. To achieve this, we specify only a single strategy element for our algorithm. We give results for (2) the fasted successful setting (of the respective strategy), an experienced user would choose and for (3) the setting with the highest precision level, a conservative user would select. The three entries per cell in Table 2 show the running times for our dynamical approach (gray), the fastest successful setting and the conservative approach. The numbers in brackets show the number of nodes in the search tree; for refinement strategies we give the number of nodes for each refinement level.

Table 2. Experimental results in seconds for different strategies. Timeout (TO) was set to 10 min, memout (MO) to 4 GB, (err) marks numerical errors. Three results per cell: (1) dynamic refinement (gray), (2) fastest successful setting only, (3) most precise setting. In brackets: Number of nodes in the search tree, refinement runs give the number of nodes on each level.

Bm.	Strategy					
	s_0	s_1	s_2	s_3	s_4	s_5
BBl	**0.15** (5|2|0)	**0.15** (5|2|0|0)	**0.15** (5|2|0|0)	0.46 (5|2)	1.58 (5|2)	0.21 (29|4|0)
	0.22 (5)	0.18 (5)	0.18 (5)	0.97 (5)	3.45 (5)	1.71 (121)
	11.93 (5)	0.97 (5)	9.90 (5)	0.97 (5)	3.45 (5)	9.47 (63)
Na09	TO	5.76 (279|6|4|0)	**5.09** (317|17|6|0)	549	err	TO
	TO	118 (244)	118 (244)	TO	TO	MO
	TO	TO	TO	TO	TO	TO
Na11	TO	7.15 (45|8|7|0)	7.61 (75|16|7|0)	63.4 (73|11)	err	120 (75|4168|0)
	TO	**6.4** (24)	**6.4** (24)	395 (24)	TO	130 (4170)
	TO	395 (24)	TO	395 (24)	TO	TO
5DS.	2.27 (5|5|5)	0.49(5|5|5|5)	2.3 (5|5|5|5)	0.39 (5|5)	15.31(5|5)	0.45(5|64|5)
	2.35 (5)	0.38 (5)	2.36 (5)	0.38 (5)	TO (5)	**0.37** (5)
	2.35 (5)	0.38 (5)	2.36 (5)	0.38 (5)	TO (5)	**0.37** (5)
Plat.	173 (5|4|4)	3.67 (5|4|4|0)	3.6 (5|4|4|5)	18.7 (5|4)	TO	19.16 (5|4|4)
	TO	**3.48** (5)	**3.48** (5)	18.9 (5)	TO	18.8 (5)
	TO	18.9 (5)	TO	18.9 (5)	TO	18.8 (5)

Observations. The results in Table 2 show that our method in general is competitive to classical approaches, as the running times are in the same orders of magnitude as the fastest setting when using dynamic refinement and in some cases our method is even faster. From the results we can infer manifold:

- Our implementation currently supports re-using information of guard intersection timings (see Sect. 3.1) while other information such as time intervals where a state set is fully contained in the set defined by the invariant of a location are not used. Keeping track of this reduced information already noticeably influences the running times as costly intersection operations for transition guards can be avoided for most computed segments and the running times can compete with the optimal setting. This shows that the additional cost of pre-computing parts of the search tree can be compensated in terms of running time when information is properly re-used.
- The length of the counterexample plays a significant role — in the bouncing ball benchmark the set of bad states is reachable after one discrete transition and from then on never again while in the 5-D switching system the set of bad states is reached in the last reachable location which causes a refinement of the whole tree and a recovery to a lower refinement level is not possible. In the platoon benchmark, stepping back to a lower refinement level does not provide any advantages, as an intersection with the set of bad states occurs before transition timings can be recorded (see Fig. 6(a)). To overcome this problem a future implementation should allow for additional entry points for refinement in order to reduce the length of the refinement path (see Sect. 5).
- The shape of the search tree influences the effectiveness of our approach. As the navigation benchmark is the only benchmark in our set where the resulting search tree naturally branches due to multiple outgoing transitions

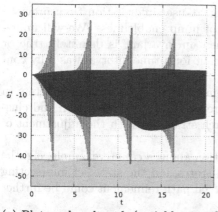

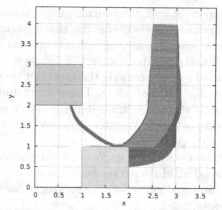

(a) Platoon benchmark (variables t and e_1) for strategy s_3. Refinements (blue) increase in saturation. Discrete jumps occur at multiples of $5t$, Bad states are $e_1 \leq 42$ (bottom, red).

(b) Navigation benchmark (instance 9) with strategy s_1. The set of bad states (left box, red); the set of good states (bottom box, green); Refinements of strategy s_1 (blue, orange).

Fig. 6. Result plots for the platoon and the navigation benchmarks with refinement. (Color figure online)

per location, the effect of partial refinement can especially be observed for this benchmark. Whole subtrees can be cut off and are shown to be unreachable on higher refinement levels such that the number of nodes is reduced. The presented method renders most effectively for systems exhibiting nondeterminism, which is reflected in a strongly branching search tree.

- Coarse analysis allows for fast discovery of the search tree, possibly requiring more nodes to be computed. We can observe that for models with nondeterminism the number of nodes at the highest required level is lower than when using the classical approach. Together with the running times this confirms our assumption that putting effort in selective, partial refinement of single branches pays off in terms of computational effort.

In conclusion we expect a strategy where a coarse analysis precedes a fine-grained setting (e.g. strategy s_3) which allows to detect enabled transitions quickly and to recover fast after the removal of a spurious counterexample shows good results on average.

5   Conclusion

We presented a reachability analysis algorithm with dynamic configuration adjustment, which allows to refine search configurations to obtain conclusive results, but exploits as much information as possible from previous computations in order to keep the computational effort as low as possible. We plan to continue our work in several directions:

Incrementality. Our current implementation re-uses information from previous refinement levels about the time intervals of jump enabledness. We will implement also the re-usage of information when an invariant is definitely true or definitely violated (when the flowpipe segment for a time interval was fully contained or fully outside the invariant set).

Additional parameters. The current implementation supports 3 parameters in search strategies: time-step size, state set representation, aggregation and clustering settings. We aim at extend our search strategies with the adjustment of further parameters.

Dynamic strategy synthesis. Using information about a counterexample, e.g. the Hausdorff distance between the set of bad states and the state set intersecting it, automatically deriving strategies for partial path refinement could be further investigated.

Parameter synthesis. With little modification we can use our approach also to synthesize the coarsest parameter setting which still allows to verify safety. This can be achieved by strategies, where the parameter settings decrease in precision and the analysis stops when a bad state is potentially reachable.

Partial path refinement. Partial refinement of counterexamples, for example restricted to a suffix, could possibly improve the effectiveness of the approach (if the refinement of the suffix renders a bad state unreachable).

Conditional strategies. We defined search strategies to be ordered sequences of parameter configurations, which are used one after the other for refinements. Introducing *trees* of configurations with conditional branching would allow even more powerful strategies where the characteristics of the system or runtime information (like previous refinement times, state set sizes, number of sets aggregated etc.) can be used to determine which branch to take for the next refinement.

References

1. Althoff, M., Bak, S., Cattaruzza, D., Chen, X., Frehse, G., Ray, R., Schupp, S.: ARCH-COMP17 category report: continuous and hybrid systems with linear continuous dynamics. In: Proceedings of ARCH 2017, pp. 143–159 (2017)
2. Althoff, M., Dolan, J.M.: Online verification of automated road vehicles using reachability analysis. IEEE Trans. Robot. **30**(4), 903–918 (2014)
3. Alur, R., Courcoubetis, C., Halbwachs, N., Henzinger, T., Ho, P.H., Nicollin, X., Olivero, A., Sifakis, J., Yovine, S.: The algorithmic analysis of hybrid systems. Theoret. Comput. Sci. **138**(1), 3–34 (1995)
4. Ben Makhlouf, I., Kowalewski, S., Chávez Grunewald, M., Abel, D.: Safety assessment of networked vehicle platoon controllers- practical experiences with available tools. In: Proceedings of ADHS 2009 (2009)
5. Bogomolov, S., Donzé, A., Frehse, G., Grosu, R., Johnson, T.T., Ladan, H., Podelski, A., Wehrle, M.: Guided search for hybrid systems based on coarse-grained space abstractions. STTT **18**(4), 449–467 (2016)
6. Bogomolov, S., Frehse, G., Giacobbe, M., Henzinger, T.A.: Counterexample-guided refinement of template polyhedra. In: Legay, A., Margaria, T. (eds.) TACAS 2017. LNCS, vol. 10205, pp. 589–606. Springer, Heidelberg (2017). https://doi.org/10.1007/978-3-662-54577-5_34

7. Bouissou, O., Chapoutot, A., Mimram, S.: Computing flowpipe of nonlinear hybrid systems with numerical methods. CoRR abs/1306.2305 (2013)
8. Chen, X.: Reachability Analysis of Non-Linear Hybrid Systems Using Taylor Models. Ph.D. thesis, RWTH Aachen University, Germany (2015)
9. Chen, X., Ábrahám, E., Sankaranarayanan, S.: Flow*: an analyzer for non-linear hybrid systems. In: Sharygina, N., Veith, H. (eds.) CAV 2013. LNCS, vol. 8044, pp. 258–263. Springer, Heidelberg (2013). https://doi.org/10.1007/978-3-642-39799-8_18
10. Chen, X., Schupp, S., Makhlouf, I.B., Ábrahám, E., Frehse, G., Kowalewski, S.: A benchmark suite for hybrid systems reachability analysis. In: Havelund, K., Holzmann, G., Joshi, R. (eds.) NFM 2015. LNCS, vol. 9058, pp. 408–414. Springer, Cham (2015). https://doi.org/10.1007/978-3-319-17524-9_29
11. Collins, P., Bresolin, D., Geretti, L., Villa, T.: Computing the evolution of hybrid systems using rigorous function calculus. In: Proceedings of ADHS 2012, pp. 284–290. IFAC-PapersOnLine (2012)
12. Duggirala, P.S., Mitra, S., Viswanathan, M., Potok, M.: C2E2: a verification tool for stateflow models. In: Baier, C., Tinelli, C. (eds.) TACAS 2015. LNCS, vol. 9035, pp. 68–82. Springer, Heidelberg (2015). https://doi.org/10.1007/978-3-662-46681-0_5
13. Eggers, A.: Direct handling of ordinary differential equations in constraint-solving-based analysis of hybrid systems. Ph.D. thesis, Universität Oldenburg, Germany (2014)
14. Fehnker, A., Ivančić, F.: Benchmarks for hybrid systems verification. In: Alur, R., Pappas, G.J. (eds.) HSCC 2004. LNCS, vol. 2993, pp. 326–341. Springer, Heidelberg (2004). https://doi.org/10.1007/978-3-540-24743-2_22
15. Fränzle, M., Herde, C., Ratschan, S., Schubert, T., Teige, T.: Efficient solving of large non-linear arithmetic constraint systems with complex Boolean structure. J. Satisf. Boolean Model. Comput. 1, 209–236 (2007)
16. Frehse, G., Kateja, R., Le Guernic, C.: Flowpipe approximation and clustering in space-time. In: Proceedings of HSCC 2013, pp. 203–212. ACM (2013)
17. Frehse, G., Le Guernic, C., Donzé, A., Cotton, S., Ray, R., Lebeltel, O., Ripado, R., Girard, A., Dang, T., Maler, O.: SpaceEx: scalable verification of hybrid systems. In: Gopalakrishnan, G., Qadeer, S. (eds.) CAV 2011. LNCS, vol. 6806, pp. 379–395. Springer, Heidelberg (2011). https://doi.org/10.1007/978-3-642-22110-1_30
18. Hagemann, W., Möhlmann, E., Rakow, A.: Verifying a PI controller using SoapBox and Stabhyli: experiences on establishing properties for a steering controller. In: Proceedings of ARCH 2014. EPiC Series in Computer Science, vol. 34, pp. 115–125. EasyChair (2014)
19. HyCreate. http://stanleybak.com/projects/hycreate/hycreate.html
20. HyREACH. https://embedded.rwth-aachen.de/doku.php?id=en:tools:hyreach
21. Immler, F.: Tool presentation: Isabelle/hol for reachability analysis of continuous systems. In: Frehse, G., Althoff, M. (eds.) ARCH14-15. 1st and 2nd International Workshop on Applied veRification for Continuous and Hybrid Systems. EPiC Series in Computer Science, vol. 34, pp. 180–187. EasyChair (2015)
22. Kong, S., Gao, S., Chen, W., Clarke, E.: dReach: δ-reachability analysis for hybrid systems. In: Baier, C., Tinelli, C. (eds.) TACAS 2015. LNCS, vol. 9035, pp. 200–205. Springer, Heidelberg (2015). https://doi.org/10.1007/978-3-662-46681-0_15
23. Le Guernic, C.: Reachability analysis of hybrid systems with linear continuous dynamics. Ph.D. thesis, Université Joseph-Fourier-Grenoble I, France (2009)

24. Nellen, J., Driessen, K., Neuhäußer, M., Ábrahám, E., Wolters, B.: Two CEGAR-based approaches for the safety verification of PLC-controlled plants. Inf. Syst. Front. **18**(5), 927–952 (2016)
25. Platzer, A., Quesel, J.-D.: KeYmaera: a hybrid theorem prover for hybrid systems (system description). In: Armando, A., Baumgartner, P., Dowek, G. (eds.) IJCAR 2008. LNCS (LNAI), vol. 5195, pp. 171–178. Springer, Heidelberg (2008). https://doi.org/10.1007/978-3-540-71070-7_15
26. Ratschan, S., She, Z.: Safety verification of hybrid systems by constraint propagation based abstraction refinement. In: Morari, M., Thiele, L. (eds.) HSCC 2005. LNCS, vol. 3414, pp. 573–589. Springer, Heidelberg (2005). https://doi.org/10.1007/978-3-540-31954-2_37
27. Schupp, S., Ábrahám, E., Makhlouf, I.B., Kowalewski, S.: HyPro: A C++ library of state set representations for hybrid systems reachability analysis. In: Barrett, C., Davies, M., Kahsai, T. (eds.) NFM 2017. LNCS, vol. 10227, pp. 288–294. Springer, Cham (2017). https://doi.org/10.1007/978-3-319-57288-8_20
28. Taha, W., et al.: Acumen: an open-source testbed for cyber-physical systems research. In: Mandler, B., et al. (eds.) IoT360 2015. LNICST, vol. 169, pp. 118–130. Springer, Cham (2016). https://doi.org/10.1007/978-3-319-47063-4_11

AMT 2.0: Qualitative and Quantitative Trace Analysis with Extended Signal Temporal Logic

Dejan Ničković[1]([✉]), Olivier Lebeltel[2], Oded Maler[2], Thomas Ferrère[3], and Dogan Ulus[2]

[1] Austrian Institute of Technology GmbH,
Vienna, Austria
dejan.nickovic@ait.ac.at

[2] Verimag, CNRS/University of Grenoble-Alpes,
Grenoble, France

[3] IST Austria, Klosterneuburg, Austria

Abstract. We introduce in this paper AMT 2.0, a tool for qualitative and quantitative analysis of hybrid continuous and Boolean signals that combine numerical values and discrete events. The evaluation of the signals is based on rich temporal specifications expressed in *extended Signal Temporal Logic* (xSTL), which integrates Timed Regular Expressions (TRE) within Signal Temporal Logic (STL). The tool features qualitative monitoring (property satisfaction checking), trace diagnostics for explaining and justifying property violations and specification-driven measurement of quantitative features of the signal.

1 Introduction

Cyber-physical systems, such as automotive embedded controllers, medical devices or autonomous vehicles, are often modeled and analyzed by simulation. Simulators generate traces admitting real values often interpreted as continuous-time signals. To evaluate the system under design, these traces are inspected for satisfying some correctness requirements and are often subject to quantitative analysis based on recording some values in certain segments of the signal and performing some computation (summation, minimum) on them.

Over the past decade an extensive framework has been developed whose goal was to bring automated support for this tedious and error-prone task, centered around Signal Temporal Logic (STL) [18,19]. STL extends the classical LTL in two directions: it uses predicates over real-valued variables in addition to atomic propositions, and it is defined over dense continuous time accessed symbolically with timed modalities as in Metric Temporal Logic (MTL) [17]. This framework, which was initially accompanied by a rudimentary prototype tool [20], had a lot of reported applications in domains such as automotive, robotics, analog circuits, systems biology. It can be viewed as an extension of *runtime verification* toward cyber-physical hybrid systems. Interested readers may consult the survey in [7].

© The Author(s) 2018
D. Beyer and M. Huisman (Eds.): TACAS 2018, LNCS 10806, pp. 303–319, 2018.
https://doi.org/10.1007/978-3-319-89963-3_18

In this article we present AMT 2.0, a new version of the tool. The new version is much more mature in terms of software engineering aspects such as rigorous typing of signals and properties, introducing programming language features that include *declarations* and *aliases*, improvement of the graphical editors, systematic software testing, etc. Furthermore, its functionality has been extended significantly by incorporating several new research results obtained over the last years:

1. We combine STL with a fragment of Timed Regular Expressions (TRE) [4,5], as a complementary formalism to express temporal patterns. The monitoring algorithm for our specification language xSTL thus obtained integrates the recent TRE pattern matching algorithm reported in [22].
2. We use the TRE formalism to define segments of the signal to which quantitative measurements should be applied. Thus we obtain a declarative measurement language that does for the quantitative domain what formal specification languages do for correctness checking. The results, first reported in [14], are fully incorporated into the tool.
3. We implement the error diagnostics algorithm of [13] which accompanies the report on a property violation with a justification: a small sub-signal (temporal implicant) which is sufficient to imply the property violation and to convince the user of this fact.

With all these features we progress in easing the task of designers who seek to analyze a complex system based on simulations, providing them with an alternative to manual inspection or explicit programming of observers.

The rest of the paper is organized as follows. In Sect. 2 we present the xSTL specification language. Section 3 gives an overview of the tool and its main features. We illustrate the usage of AMT 2.0 in Sect. 4 with two examples. We present the related work in Sect. 5 and give concluding remarks in Sect. 6.

2   Extended Signal Temporal Logic

Extended Signal Temporal Logix (xSTL) essentially combines STL with a variant of TRE. In this section, we provide the mathematical definitions of the specification language.

We denote by P and X finite sets of *propositional* and *data* variables, such that $|P| = m$ and $|X| = n$. Data variables are defined over an arbitrary domain $\mathbb{D}$, typically the reals or the integers. We use the notation $w : \mathbb{T} \to \mathbb{D}^n \times \mathbb{B}^m$ to represent a multi-dimensional *signal* with $\mathbb{T} = [0, d) \subseteq \mathbb{R}$ and $\mathbb{B} = \{\text{true}, \text{false}\}$. We denote by w_p the *projection* of w on its component p. We denote by $\theta : \mathbb{D}^n \to \mathbb{B}$ a *predicate* that maps valuations of variables in X into $\{\text{true}, \text{false}\}$.

The syntax of an STL formula φ with both *future* and *past* temporal operators and interpreted over $X \cup P$ is defined by the grammar

$$\varphi := p \mid \theta(x_1, \ldots, x_n) \mid \neg\varphi \mid \varphi_1 \vee \varphi_2 \mid \varphi_1 \mathcal{U}_I \varphi_2 \mid \varphi_1 \mathcal{S}_I \varphi_2$$

where $p \in P$, $x_1, \ldots, x_n \in X$ and $I \subseteq \mathbb{R}^+$ is an interval. We denote by $\mathcal{U}$ the until operator that is decorated with an unbounded interval $\mathcal{U}_{(0,\infty)}$. We use the *strict* semantics [2] for *until* and *since* temporal operators that allows us to define (continuous-time) *next* $\bigcirc \varphi \equiv \varphi \mathcal{U} \varphi$ and (continuous-time) *previous* $\ominus \varphi \equiv \varphi \mathcal{S} \varphi$. The instantaneous *rise* and *fall* events can be derived using the rules $\uparrow \varphi \equiv \ominus \neg \varphi \wedge \bigcirc \varphi$ and $\downarrow \varphi \equiv \ominus \varphi \wedge \bigcirc \neg \varphi$. We derive other standard operators as follows: $\mathsf{true} \equiv p \vee \neg p$, $\mathsf{false} \equiv \neg \mathsf{true}$, $\varphi_1 \wedge \varphi_2 \equiv \neg(\neg \varphi_1 \vee \neg \varphi_2)$, $\varphi_1 \rightarrow \varphi_2 \equiv \neg \varphi_1 \vee \varphi_2$, $\Diamond_I \varphi \equiv \mathsf{true}\ \mathcal{U}_I\ \varphi$, $\Diamond_I \varphi \equiv \mathsf{true}\ \mathcal{S}_I\ \varphi$, $\Box_I \varphi \equiv \neg \Diamond_I \neg \varphi$, and $\boxminus_I \varphi \equiv \neg \Diamond_I \neg \varphi$.

The semantics of an STL formula with respect to a signal w is described via the satisfiability relation $(w,t) \models \varphi$, indicating that the signal w satisfies φ at time point t, according to the following definition.

$$
\begin{aligned}
(w,t) &\models p & &\leftrightarrow w_p[t] = \mathsf{true} \\
(w,t) &\models \theta(x_1, \ldots, x_n) & &\leftrightarrow \theta(w_{x_1}[t], \ldots, w_{x_n}[t]) = \mathsf{true} \\
(w,t) &\models \neg \varphi & &\leftrightarrow (w,t) \not\models \varphi \\
(w,t) &\models \varphi_1 \vee \varphi_2 & &\leftrightarrow (w,t) \models \varphi_1 \text{ or } (w,t) \models \varphi_2 \\
(w,t) &\models \varphi_1 \mathcal{U}_I \varphi_2 & &\leftrightarrow \exists t' \in (t+I) \cap \mathbb{T} : (w,t') \models \varphi_2 \text{ and} \\
& & & \quad \forall t < t'' < t'\ (w,t'') \models \varphi_1 \\
(w,t) &\models \varphi_1 \mathcal{S}_I \varphi_2 & &\leftrightarrow \exists t' \subset (t-I) \cap \mathbb{T} : (w,t') \models \varphi_2 \text{ and} \\
& & & \quad \forall t' < t'' < t\ (w,t'') \models \varphi_1
\end{aligned}
$$

We now define a variant of TRE according to the following grammar:

$$
r := \epsilon \mid p \mid \theta(x_1, \ldots, x_n) \mid r_1 \cdot r_2 \mid r_1 \cup r_2 \mid r_1 \cap r_2 \mid r^* \mid \langle r \rangle_I \mid r_1 ? r_2 \mid r_2 ! r_2
$$

where I is an interval of $\mathbb{R}_+$. The semantics of a timed regular expression r with respect to a signal w and times $t \leq t'$ in $[0, d]$ is given in terms of a *match* relation $(w, t, t') \models r$, which indicates that the segment of w between t and t' matches the expression. This relation is defined inductively as follows:

$$
\begin{aligned}
(w,t,t') &\equiv \epsilon & &\leftrightarrow t = t' \\
(w,t,t') &\equiv p & &\leftrightarrow t < t' \text{ and } \forall t'' \in (t,t'),\ w_p[t] = \mathsf{true} \\
(w,t,t') &\equiv \theta(x_1, \ldots, x_n) & &\leftrightarrow t < t' \text{ and } \forall t'' \in (t,t'),\ \theta(w_{x_1}[t''], \ldots, w_{x_n}[t'']) = \mathsf{true} \\
(w,t,t') &\equiv r_1 \cdot r_2 & &\leftrightarrow \exists t''\ t \leq t'' \leq t',\ (w,t,t'') \equiv r_1 \text{ and } (w,t'',t') \equiv r_2 \\
(w,t,t') &\equiv r_1 \cup r_2 & &\leftrightarrow (w,t,t') \equiv r_1 \text{ or } (w,t,t') \equiv r_2 \\
(w,t,t') &\equiv r_1 \cap r_2 & &\leftrightarrow (w,t,t') \equiv r_1 \text{ and } (w,t,t') \equiv r_2 \\
(w,t,t') &\equiv r^* & &\leftrightarrow \exists k \geq 0,\ (w,t,t') \equiv r^k \\
(w,t,t') &\equiv \langle r \rangle_I & &\leftrightarrow (w,t,t') \equiv r \text{ and } t' - t \in I \\
(w,t,t') &\equiv r_1 ? r_2 & &\leftrightarrow (w,t,t') \equiv r_2 \text{ and } \exists t'' \leq t,\ (w,t'',t) \equiv r_1 \\
(w,t,t') &\equiv r_1 ! r_2 & &\leftrightarrow (w,t,t') \equiv r_1 \text{ and } \exists t'' \geq t',\ (w,t',t'') \equiv r_2
\end{aligned}
$$

The last two operations associate a pre-condition (resp. post-condition) to the expression. We note that with the pre- and post-condition, we can also syntactically define rise and fall operators by using the rules $\uparrow p \equiv \neg p \,?\, \epsilon \,!\, p$ and $\downarrow p \equiv p \,?\, \epsilon \,!\, \neg p$. Extended STL specifications require regular expressions to be embedded into STL formulas. We define two operators, *begin match* ($@(r)$) and *end match* ($(r)@$) that intuitively project any signal segment (t, t') that matches the expression r to its beginning t and its end t', respectively. Thus, xSTL simply extends STL with these two operators:

$$\varphi := p \mid \theta(x_1, \ldots, x_n) \mid \neg\varphi \mid \varphi_1 \vee \varphi_2 \mid \varphi_1 \mathcal{U}_I \varphi_2 \mid \varphi_1 \mathcal{S}_I \varphi_2 \mid @(r) \mid (r)@$$

and with the following semantics

$$(w, t) \models @(r) \leftrightarrow \exists t' \geq t \,\, (w, t, t') \equiv r$$
$$(w, t) \models (r)@ \leftrightarrow \exists t' \leq t \,\, (w, t', t) \equiv r$$

3 Tool Presentation

The AMT 2.0 tool provides for qualitative and quantitative analysis of simulation/measurement traces. Its input consists of two major ingredients. The first is typically a formula or a collection of formulas in xSTL specifying the desired properties (and later measurements) of a continuous signal. The second is a finite representation of the continuous signal. Input signals obtained from simulators or measurement devices are given as finite sequences of time-stamped values of the form $(t_i, w[t_i])$. The tool supports two commonly-used formats: Value Change Dump (vcd) and Comma Separated Values (csv) files. To obtain continuous-time signals, values between sampling points are interpolated inside the tool to yield either piecewise-constant or piecewise-linear signals.

The tool can work either interactively via its graphical user interface (GUI) or, alternatively, in batch mode when we want to monitor against many signals or incorporate monitoring in a more sophisticated analysis procedure that may iterate over behavior-generating models and/or properties in an outer loop. Figure 1 shows the main evaluation window of the GUI which provides two main functionalities: (1) editing xSTL specifications; and (2) launching the monitoring procedure by selecting properties and signals and presenting the outcome graphically. The AMT 2.0 tool is entirely implemented in Java to facilitate its usage across different platforms and operating systems.

The tool supports three main functionalities: (1) qualitative offline monitoring of extended STL specifications; (2) localization and explanation of property violations; and (3) measurements of quantitative features of signals driven by temporal pattern expressed using TRE. In the remainder of the section we present these functionalities in more detail.

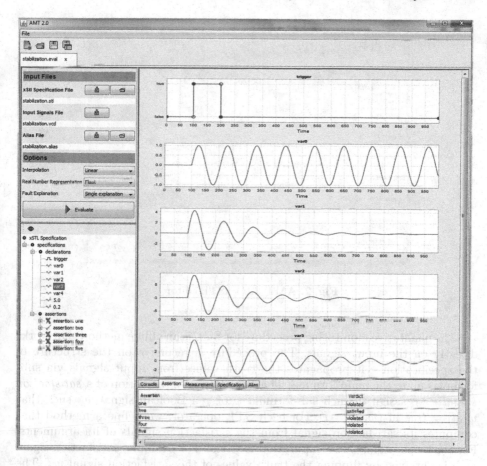

Fig. 1. AMT 2.0 - an overview of the graphical user interface.

3.1 Specifications in AMT 2.0

The tool facilitates specification of xSTL properties in several ways. The GUI provides an xSTL editor, depicted in Fig. 2, with syntax highlighting and line numbering. In addition, the xSTL parser implements a number of features borrowed from programming languages. This includes (1) declaration of variables and constants, (2) parameterized property templates, (3) support for Boolean, real and integer variables and (4) type checking with extensive error reporting.

3.2 Qualitative Monitoring of xSTL

In this section, we sketch the algorithm for the major functionality of the tool, qualitative monitoring of xSTL specifications. The procedure is based on two main methods that we describe in the sequel: the offline marking procedure for STL [19] and the pattern matching procedure for TRE [22].

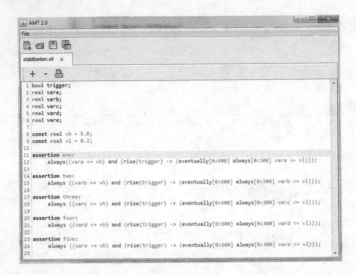

Fig. 2. AMT 2.0 - xSTL editor.

The qualitative monitoring procedure for STL is an offline method that works directly on the input signals. The procedure is recursive on the structure of the specification – it propagates the truth values from input signals via sub-formulas up to the main formula. The algorithm uses the notion of a *satisfaction signal* – we assign to each sub-formula ψ of φ a Boolean signal w_ψ such that $w_\psi[t] = $ true iff $(w,t) \models \psi$. For each STL operator, we define a method that computes its satisfaction signal from the satisfaction signals of its arguments. For some operators, this computation is trivial. For example, satisfaction signal $w_{\neg\varphi}$ is obtained by flipping the truth values of the satisfaction signal w_φ. The computation of satisfaction signals for temporal operators is more involved. We give an intuition on the computation of w_ψ where $\psi = \Diamond_I \varphi$ and refer the reader to [19] for the technical description of the complete procedure. The computation is based on the following observation: whenever φ holds throughout an interval J, ψ holds throughout $(J \ominus I) \cap \mathbb{T}$, where $J \ominus I = \{t - t' \mid t \in J \text{ and } t' \in I\}$ is the Minkowski difference. Hence, the essence of the procedure is to back-shift (Minkowski difference restricted to $\mathbb{T}$) all the positive intervals in w_φ and thus obtain the set of time points where $\Diamond_I \varphi$ holds. This method is illustrated in Fig. 3.

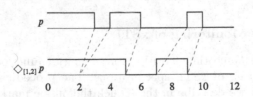

Fig. 3. Example of satisfaction signal computation for $\Diamond_{[1,2]} p$ using back-shifting.

The integration of TRE into the monitoring procedure of xSTL is done in two steps. First, we define the *match-set* $\mathcal{M}(r, w)$ of a TRE over a signal w as the set of all segments of w that match r, i.e. $\mathcal{M}(r, w) = \{(t, t') \mid (w, t, t') \models r\}$, and use the algorithm of [22] to compute the match-set. We then use the match begin ($@(r)$) and match end ($(r)@$) operators to project the match-sets to satisfaction signals that are then directly integrated into the STL monitoring procedure described above.

The algorithm proposed in [22] computes the set of segments of a signal w that match a TRE φ. Since we are dealing with continuous-time signals, the number of segments is non-countable and so is potentially the number of matches. The algorithm is based on the observation that all those segments can be can be embedded in two-dimensional space, inside the triangle $0 \leq t \leq t' \leq |w|$, where a point (t, t') represents the segment starting at t and ending in t'. The matching algorithm uses a symbolic representation of the matches as a finite union of two-dimensional *zones*. Zones are special class of convex polytopes which are defined as the conjunction of inequalities of the form $x_i \prec b_i$ and $x_i - x_j \prec c_{i,j}$, where $\prec \in \{<, \leq\}$. For instance, the match set $\mathcal{M}(\epsilon, w)$ for the empty word ϵ is the diagonal zone $\{(t, t') \in \mathbb{T} \times \mathbb{T} \mid t = t'\}$, while the match for a literal p or $\neg p$ is a disjoint union of triangles touching the diagonal whose number depends on the number of switching points in w_p. The match set of the time restriction operator is obtained by intersecting the match set with the corresponding diagonal band, hence $\mathcal{M}(\langle \varphi \rangle_I, w) = \mathcal{M}(\varphi) \cap \{(t, t') \mid t' - t \in I\}$. The match sets for p and $\langle p \rangle_{[1,2]}$

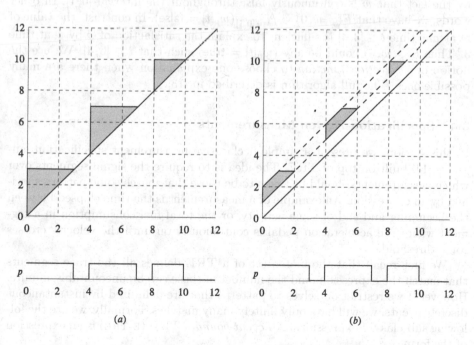

Fig. 4. Example of a match set - (a) p; and (b) $\langle p \rangle_{[1,2]}$.

are depicted in Fig. 4. We point the reader to [22] for a complete description of the procedure. The satisfaction signals $w_{@(r)}$ and $w_{(r)@}$ for the match-begin and match-end operators are computed from the match set of r by projecting every $(t, t') \in \mathcal{M}(r)$ on t and t', respectively.

3.3 Trace Diagnostics for STL

The trace diagnostics procedure implements the algorithm presented in [13]. Given an STL formula φ and a trace w that violates φ, the procedure gives an explanation of the fault in the form of a *temporal implicant*, which is a small sub-signal w' of w which is sufficient to imply violation. In other words, any possible completion of w' into a full signal will violate the property. The diagnostics procedure uses the satisfaction signals computed by the monitoring algorithm from Sect. 3.2 to explain the faults. The method uses the *satisfaction explanation* operator E (and its dual *violation explanation* operator F) that for a given formula φ returns an implicant of φ (respectively of $\neg\varphi$) which is satisfied by w. The explanation operators are defined inductively on the structure of the formula φ and on the times t at which explanation of its sub-formulas are required.

We illustrate the idea behind the procedure with the following example. Consider the STL specification $\varphi = \Diamond_{[0,1]} p$, a signal w in which p does not hold during $[0, 3)$ and then holds during $[3, 5)$. It is clear, for instance, that $(w, 0) \not\models \varphi$ and $(w, 3) \models \varphi$. The violation of φ by w at time 0 can be explained by the fact that w is continuously false throughout the interval $[0, 1]$. In other words, we have that $F(\varphi, w, 0) = \bigwedge_{t \in [0,1]} (w_p[t] = \mathsf{false})$. In contrast, the value of w at *any* time $t \in [3, 4]$ is sufficient to explain the satisfaction of φ by w at time 3. Thus $E(\varphi, w, 3)$ could be any $(w_p[t] = \mathsf{true})$ such that $t \in [3, 4]$. We use the notion of a *selection function* to choose one explanation when there are many possible ones. The full algorithm is described in [13].

3.4 Specification-Driven Measurements

In this section, we present a simple declarative measurement specification language [14] built on top of TRE. The idea is to require the signal segments over which measurements should be taken to be those that match some pattern specified by an expression. An example of a measurement is the time elapsed between the beginning and end of some activity, or the total fuel consumption in a segment where the acceleration pedal is continuously on until the velocity crosses some threshold.

We first recall that the match set of a TRE defines all the trace segments that match the expression, and the number of those can be uncountably infinite. However if we restrict ourselves to patterns that are delimited by instantaneous discrete events, we will have only finitely many matches. Formally, we use the following sub-class of expressions. An *event-bounded* TRE (E-TRE) is an expression of the form

$$\hat{r} := \uparrow p \mid \downarrow p \mid \hat{r}_1 \cdot r \cdot \hat{r}_2 \mid \hat{r}_1 \cup \hat{r}_2 \mid \hat{r}_1 \cap r$$

with p a proposition, and $\hat{r}_1, \hat{r}_2$ event-bounded TREs.

The *measure patterns* defining the segments to be measured are of the form $\alpha\,?\,\psi\,!\,\beta$, where ψ is the *main* pattern, and α and β are, respectively, pre- and post-conditions. The main pattern ψ specifies the portion of the signal over which the measure is taken. To guarantee a finite number of matching segments, ψ is restricted to be an E-TRE while α and β, which can be used to define additional constraints, are TREs.

Given a measure pattern φ and a signal w, we first compute all the segments of w that match φ. We then apply a measuring operator that collects specific signal values over the matched segments. A measure is written with the syntax $\mathsf{op}(\varphi)$ with $\mathsf{op} \in \{\mathsf{time}, \mathsf{value}_x, \mathsf{duration}, \mathsf{inf}_x, \mathsf{sup}_x, \mathsf{integral}_x, \mathsf{average}_x\}$. We finally aggregate the specific measures and provide to the user the minimum, maximum and average measured value, as well as a histogram that summarizes the measurements.

We illustrate specification-driven measurement with an example from the DSI3 automotive communication protocol [16]. The micro-controller and the sensors that use the protocol, communicate by sending *analog pulses* during the protocol initialization phase. The standard describes the acceptable shapes and duration of such pulses. Figure 5 depicts the specification of a *discovery response pulse* from the DSI3 standard. In particular, the standard defines the relevant thresholds ($2IResp$ and $IResp$) which are used to describe the shape, as well as the acceptable duration of the pulse's ramp (t_1) and its total duration (t_2).

To define the pulse pattern we first define the following predicates:

$$i_h \equiv i \geq 2IResp \qquad i_b \equiv IResp \leq i < 2IResp \qquad i_l \equiv i < IResp$$

and then let

$$\varphi = i_l\,?\,\uparrow(i_b) \cdot i_b \cdot i_h \cdot i_b \cdot \downarrow(i_b)\,!\,i_l.$$

We finally apply the measure operation $\mathsf{duration}(\varphi)$ to extract the duration of the segments that match the pulse pattern.

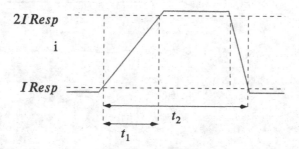

Fig. 5. Discovery response pulse from DSI3.

312   D. Ničković et al.

4   Examples

In this section, we introduce two running examples that we use to illustrate the features and the functionalities of AMT 2.0. The first example is concerned with a mixed-signal bounded stabilization property and is used to illustrate the qualitative monitoring and trace diagnostics functionalities. The second example demonstrates the measurement functionality as applied to jitter in a digital clock.

4.1   Mixed-Signal Bounded Stabilization

Informal Requirements. This requirement states that after every rising edge of the Boolean *trigger*, the usually-stable analog signal *var* is allowed to oscillate under the following conditions:

1. *var* must always remain below 5 V; and
2. *var* must within 600 s go below 0.2 V, and continuously remain under that threshold for at least 600 s.

Simulation Traces. We evaluate this requirement on 5 different simulation traces. Figure 6 depicts the Boolean *trigger* signal, as well as the 5 traces named *var0* to *var4*. We can already reason informally about the satisfaction of the bounded stabilization property by these traces:

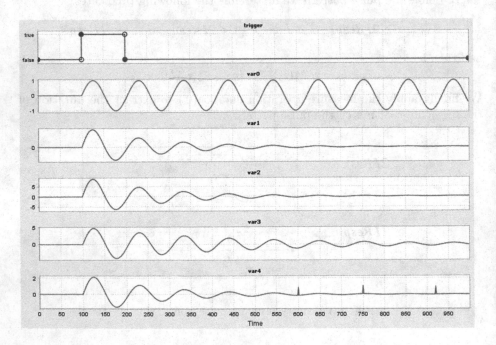

Fig. 6. Bounded stabilization - input signals.

1. Trace *var0* **violates** the specification because the signal never stabilizes, i.e. it continues oscillating until the end of simulation;
2. Trace *var1* **satisfies** the specification - the signal always remains smaller then 5 V, and it goes below 0.2 V within 600 s, continuously remaining below that threshold until the end of the simulation;
3. Trace *var2* **violates** the specification because the signal exceeds 5 V;
4. Trace *var3* **violates** the specification because the signal does not stabilize below 0.2 V within the specified period; and
5. Trace *var4* **violates** the specification because of the 3 glitches that occur towards the end of the simulation.

Formal Specification in xSTL. To define the property we first declare the Boolean variable *trigger*, as well as the real variables *var0* to *var4*. We also declare two constants *vh* and *vl*, representing the 5 V and 0.2 V thresholds, respectively. We note that we are evaluating the same formula over different signals. Hence, we define a generic property template *stab* for the bounded stabilization formula, which is the conjunction of conditions (1) and (2) of the informal requirements. The first conjunct says that the real-valued signal must be smaller than $5V$. The second conjunct is a conditional formula that uses logical implication. It says that whenever the *trigger* signal is on its rising edge, the x signal must go below 0.2 V within 600 s and continuously remain below that threshold for at least 300 s. Then each assertion is an instantiation of the template with one of the signals *var0* to *var4*.

```
1   bool trigger;
2   real vara;
3   ...
4   real vare;
5   const real vh = 5;
6   const real vl = 0.2;
7
8   template bool stabilization (bool tg, real x, real vhigh,
        real vlow) {
9     bool result = ((x <= vhigh) and (rise(tg) -> (eventually
        [0:600] always[0:300] x <= vlow)));
10    return result;
11  }
12
13  assertion one:
14    always(stabilization(trigger, vara, vh, vl));
15  ...
16  assertion five:
17    always(stabilization(trigger, vare, vh, vl));
```

Qualitative Monitoring of the Specification. We illustrate the qualitative monitoring of the property applied to the traces as done using the GUI of the tool. In the evaluation configuration window, we first specify the xSTL specification, the simulation traces and an optional alias file. In addition to setting up the inputs, we also select the Float representation of the real numbers, the Linear interpolation and the Single Explanation feature of the diagnostics module.

After evaluating the specification on the traces, we can visually depict the results, as shown in Fig. 1. The nodes in the xSTL parse tree view are expandable via a double click. By expanding the assertions node of the specification, we can see that assertion *two* is satisfied, while assertions *one*, *three*, *four* and *five* are violated. We note that we can visualize the satisfaction signals for any sub-property of the specification.

Fault Explanation. The fault explanation is given in the form of temporal implicants which are (small) sub-segments of the input signals which are sufficient to imply the property violation. Figure 7 illustrates the visual output of the diagnostics procedure in AMT 2.0 for the bounded stabilization specification. The first two figures show the trace diagnostics report for the third assertion. We can see that the *trigger* signal does not contribute to the fault, but *var3* does at a single point in time within the interval [100, 150]. At that time, *var3* is greater than the invariant threshold 5 V which explains the property violation. The last two figures show that same report, but for the fifth assertion. In this case, the fault is explained by the fact that signal *trigger* gets high at time 100 and by the values of signal *var4* at times 350, 600 and 750. We can see that the last two times coincide with the glitches, thus witnessing that *var4* never continuously holds below 0.2 V for at least 300 time units.

We note that the tool computes the fault explanations in a hierarchical manner, following the parse tree of the formula. This additional and complementary information can be quite useful in understanding the fault. We finally note that the trace diagnostics can be made hierarchic.

4.2 Digital Clock Jitter

Informal Requirements. Given a continuous-time Boolean-valued signal *clock*, a clock period is defined as a segment that starts with the rising edge of the *clock* and ends with its consecutive rising edge. The measurement specification is to measure the duration of all the clock periods matched within the *clock* signal in order to assess the clock jitter.

Simulation Trace. We apply the specifications to a Boolean *clock* signal, see Fig. 8.

Formal Specification in xSTL. We now formalize the measurement specification for the digital clock jitter analysis in xSTL. We first declare the Boolean variable *clock*, as well as its negation *nclock*. We then specify the pattern

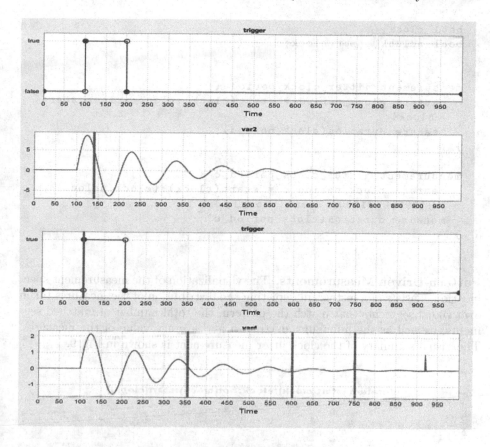

Fig. 7. Bounded stabilization - fault explanation.

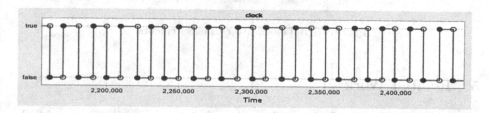

Fig. 8. Digital clock jitter - a segment of the input signal.

clock_period that consists of concatenations that starts with the rising edge of *clock* (*startclock*), followed by an interval of positive duration where *clock* holds, followed by another interval of positive duration where *nclock* holds, and ending with the next rising edge of *clock*. Finally, we declare the actual measurement to be taken as *duration(clock_period)* which extracts the durations of all signal segments that match the *clock_pattern* pattern.

```
1  bool clock;
2  bool nclock = not clock;
3
4
5  measurement jitter_clock_period {
6    pattern clock_period = start(clock):clock:nclock:start(
       clock);
7    measure duration(clock_period);
8  }
9
10 measurement jitter_clock_period_c {
11   pattern clock_period_c = start(clock):{clock:nclock
       }[19000:21000]:start(clock);
12   measure duration(clock_period_c);
13 }
```

Pattern-Driven Measurements. The visualization of the measurement specification consists of a histogram depicting the distribution of the measures taken
over signal segments that match the pattern, the total number of matched segments, as well as the minimum, maximum and average value of the measures.
The visual summary of the clock jitter measurement is shown in Fig. 9.

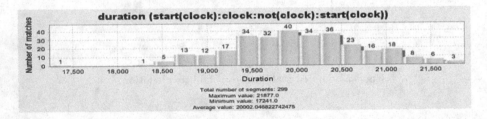

Fig. 9. Digital clock jitter - measurements.

5   Related Work

Breach [11] is a MATLAB/Simulink toolbox that enables various types of STL
specification analysis. In particular, Breach supports falsification-based testing,
parameter synthesis and requirement mining of STL properties. S-TaLiRo [3] is
another Simulink/MATLAB toolbox for different robustness analysis of MTL
specifications. It provides support for falsification-based testing, parameter mining, runtime verification, conformance testing, computing the worst expected
robustness for stochastic systems and debugging of formal requirements. The
ViSpec [15] tool, associated with S-TaLiRo, allows visual specification of MTL
requirements. BIOCHAM [10] is a tool for inferring unknown (biological) model
parameters from temporal logic constraints. The authors in [9] extend STL with

freeze quantifiers that allow them to express oscillatory properties. Similar oscillatory properties of the heart behavior are studied using quantitative regular expressions (QRE) in [1].

Montre [21] is a prototype tool for TRE pattern matching. It provides support for both offline and online matching. AMT 2.0 implements the offline matching algorithms used by Montre and adds a specification measurement language on top of it. Montre does not provide support for STL, monitoring and trace diagnostics.

The combination of STL and TRE was inspired by the Property Specification Language (PSL) [12] and SystemVerilog Assertions (SVA) [23] standards used in the digital hardware verification. Both PSL and SVA use the *suffix implication* operator to combine temporal logic with regular expressions. In contrast, we define *match begin* and *end* operators that give us more freedom to decide whether the begin or the end of an expression match is relevant for the property. The only other work that combines temporal logic and the regular expressions in the context of continuous-time applications is presented in [8], where the authors propose the *metric dynamic logic* as the specification language for reasoning about time-event sequences.

6 Conclusion

We introduced in this paper the AMT 2.0 tool for qualitative and quantitative analysis of traces coming from cyber-physical systems applications. The tool uses an expressive specification language based on a combination of STL and TRE and admits qualitative monitoring, trace diagnostics and property-driven measurements as its main functionalities. The development of the tool is a continuous work in progress and there is a number of features which are planned to be developed in the near future, in particular solving the inverse problem of finding parameters in a formula template the lead to satisfaction by a given signal or a set of signals [6].

Acknowledgments. This work was partially supported by project ANR-13-CESA-0008 CADMIDIA and the Productive 4.0 project (ECSEL 737459). The ECSEL Joint Undertaking receives support from the European Union's Horizon 2020 research and innovation programme and Austria, Denmark, Germany, Finland, Czech Republic, Italy, Spain, Portugal, Poland, Ireland, Belgium, France, Netherlands, United Kingdom, Slovakia, Norway.

References

1. Abbas, H., Rodionova, A., Bartocci, E., Smolka, S.A., Grosu, R.: Quantitative regular expressions for arrhythmia detection algorithms. In: Feret, J., Koeppl, H. (eds.) CMSB 2017. LNCS, vol. 10545, pp. 23–39. Springer, Cham (2017). https://doi.org/10.1007/978-3-319-67471-1_2
2. Alur, R., Feder, T., Henzinger, T.A.: The benefits of relaxing punctuality. J. ACM **43**(1), 116–146 (1996)

3. Annpureddy, Y., Liu, C., Fainekos, G., Sankaranarayanan, S.: S-TALiRo: a tool for temporal logic falsification for hybrid systems. In: Abdulla, P.A., Leino, K.R.M. (eds.) TACAS 2011. LNCS, vol. 6605, pp. 254–257. Springer, Heidelberg (2011). https://doi.org/10.1007/978-3-642-19835-9_21

4. Asarin, E., Caspi, P., Maler, O.: A Kleene theorem for timed automata. In: Logic in Computer Science (LICS), pp. 160–171 (1997)

5. Asarin, E., Caspi, P., Maler, O.: Timed regular expressions. J. ACM 49(2), 172–206 (2002)

6. Asarin, E., Donzé, A., Maler, O., Nickovic, D.: Parametric identification of temporal properties. In: Khurshid, S., Sen, K. (eds.) RV 2011. LNCS, vol. 7186, pp. 147–160. Springer, Heidelberg (2012). https://doi.org/10.1007/978-3-642-29860-8_12

7. Bartocci, E., Deshmukh, J., Donzé, A., Fainekos, G., Maler, O., Nickovic, D., Sankaranarayanan, S.: Specification-based monitoring of cyber-physical systems: a survey on theory, tools and applications. In: The Handbook of Runtime Verification (2018)

8. Basin, D., Krstić, S., Traytel, D.: Almost event-rate independent monitoring of metric dynamic logic. In: Lahiri, S., Reger, G. (eds.) RV 2017. LNCS, vol. 10548, pp. 85–102. Springer, Cham (2017). https://doi.org/10.1007/978-3-319-67531-2_6

9. Brim, L., Dluhos, P., Safránek, D., Vejpustek, T.: STL*: Extending Signal Temporal Logic with signal-value freezing operator. Inf. Comput. 236, 52–67 (2014)

10. Calzone, L., Fages, F., Soliman, S.: BIOCHAM: an environment for modeling biological systems and formalizing experimental knowledge. Bioinformatics 22(14), 1805–1807 (2006)

11. Donzé, A.: Breach, a toolbox for verification and parameter synthesis of hybrid systems. In: Touili, T., Cook, B., Jackson, P. (eds.) CAV 2010. LNCS, vol. 6174, pp. 167–170. Springer, Heidelberg (2010). https://doi.org/10.1007/978-3-642-14295-6_17

12. Eisner, C., Fisman, D.: A Practical Introduction to PSL. Springer, Boston (2006). https://doi.org/10.1007/978-0-387-36123-9

13. Ferrère, T., Maler, O., Ničković, D.: Trace diagnostics using temporal implicants. In: Finkbeiner, B., Pu, G., Zhang, L. (eds.) ATVA 2015. LNCS, vol. 9364, pp. 241–258. Springer, Cham (2015). https://doi.org/10.1007/978-3-319-24953-7_20

14. Ferrère, T., Maler, O., Ničković, D., Ulus, D.: Measuring with timed patterns. In: Kroening, D., Păsăreanu, C.S. (eds.) CAV 2015, Part II. LNCS, vol. 9207, pp. 322–337. Springer, Cham (2015). https://doi.org/10.1007/978-3-319-21668-3_19

15. Hoxha, B., Bach, H., Abbas, H., Dokhanci, A., Kobayashi, Y., Fainekos, G.: Towards formal specification visualization for testing and monitoring of cyber-physical systems. In: International Workshop on Design and Implementation of Formal Tools and Systems, DIFTS 2014 (2014)

16. Distributed System Interface. DSI3 Bus Standard. DSI Consortium

17. Koymans, R.: Specifying real-time properties with metric temporal logic. Real-Time Syst. 2(4), 255–299 (1990)

18. Maler, O., Nickovic, D.: Monitoring temporal properties of continuous signals. In: Lakhnech, Y., Yovine, S. (eds.) FORMATS/FTRTFT 2004. LNCS, vol. 3253, pp. 152–166. Springer, Heidelberg (2004). https://doi.org/10.1007/978-3-540-30206-3_12

19. Maler, O., Nickovic, D.: Monitoring properties of analog and mixed-signal circuits. STTT 15(3), 247–268 (2013)

20. Nickovic, D., Maler, O.: AMT: a property-based monitoring tool for analog systems. In: Raskin, J.-F., Thiagarajan, P.S. (eds.) FORMATS 2007. LNCS, vol. 4763, pp. 304–319. Springer, Heidelberg (2007). https://doi.org/10.1007/978-3-540-75454-1_22

21. Ulus, D.: MONTRE: a tool for monitoring timed regular expressions. In: Majumdar, R., Kunčak, V. (eds.) CAV 2017, Part I. LNCS, vol. 10426, pp. 329–335. Springer, Cham (2017). https://doi.org/10.1007/978-3-319-63387-9_16

22. Ulus, D., Ferrère, T., Asarin, E., Maler, O.: Timed pattern matching. In: Legay, A., Bozga, M. (eds.) FORMATS 2014. LNCS, vol. 8711, pp. 222–236. Springer, Cham (2014). https://doi.org/10.1007/978-3-319-10512-3_16

23. Vijayaraghavan, S., Ramanathan, M.: A Practical Guide for SystemVerilog Assertions. Springer, Boston (2006). https://doi.org/10.1007/b137011

Multi-cost Bounded Reachability in MDP

Arnd Hartmanns[1] , Sebastian Junges[2] , Joost-Pieter Katoen[1,2] ,
and Tim Quatmann[2(✉)]

[1] University of Twente, Enschede, The Netherlands
[2] RWTH Aachen University, Aachen, Germany
tim.quatmann@cs.rwth-aachen.de

Abstract. We provide an efficient algorithm for multi-objective model-checking problems on Markov decision processes (MDPs) with multiple cost structures. The key problem at hand is to check whether there exists a scheduler for a given MDP such that all objectives over cost vectors are fulfilled. Reachability and expected cost objectives are covered and can be mixed. Empirical evaluation shows the algorithm's scalability. We discuss the need for output beyond Pareto curves and exploit the available information from the algorithm to support decision makers.

1 Introduction

Markov decision processes [41] (MDPs) with *rewards* or *costs* are a popular model to describe planning problems under uncertainty. Planning algorithms aim to find strategies which perform well (or even optimally) for a given objective. These algorithms typically assume *that a goal is reached eventually* [41,45]. This however is unrealistic in many scenarios, e.g. due to insufficient resources or the possibility of failing actions. Furthermore, these policies often admit single runs which perform far below the user's expectation, which is unsuitable in many scenarios with high stakes. Examples range from deliveries reaching an airport after the plane's departure to more serious scenarios in e.g. wildfire management [1]. In particular, many scenarios call for minimising the probability to run out of resources before reaching the goal: while it is *beneficial* for a plane to reach its destination with low *expected* fuel consumption, it is *essential* to reach its destination with the *fixed* available amount of fuel.

Policies that optimise solely for the probability to reach a goal are mostly very expensive. Even in the presence of just a single cost structure, decision makers have to trade the success probability against the costs. This makes many planning problems inherently multi-objective [12,17]. In particular, safety properties cannot be averaged out by good performance [21]. Planning scenarios in various application areas [44] have different resource constraints. Typical examples are energy consumption and time [11], or optimal expected revenue and time [38] in robotics, and monetary cost and available capacity in logistics [17].

This work is supported by the 3TU project "Big Software on the Run", CDZ project CAP, and DFG RTG 2236 "UnRAVeL".

D. Beyer and M. Huisman (Eds.): TACAS 2018, LNCS 10806, pp. 320–339, 2018.
https://doi.org/10.1007/978-3-319-89963-3_19

task	time	energy consumption	scientific value	prob.
1	high	{low, medium}	medium	$1/2$
2	low	{medium, high}	medium	$3/5$
3	low	low	low	$4/5$
4	high	high	high	$1/10$

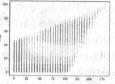

(a) Different possible tasks for a Mars rover   (b) Tradeoffs in costs

Fig. 1. Science on Mars: planning under several resource-constraints

Illustrative Example. Consider a simplified (discretised) version of the Mars rover task scheduling problem [11]. The task is to plan a variety of experiments for a day on Mars. The experiments vary in their success probability, time, energy consumption and their scientific value upon success. The time, energy consumption, and scientific value are uncertain and modelled by probability distributions, cf. Fig. 1(a). The objective is to achieve a minimum of daily scientific progress while limiting the risk of running out of time or out of energy. As the rover is expected to work for a longer period, we prefer a high expected scientific value.

Contributions and approach. This paper focuses on multi-objective cost-bounded reachability queries on MDPs, a natural setting for the aforementioned planning problems. The input is an MDP with multiple cost structures (e.g. energy, utility or time) and multiple objectives of the form "maximise/minimise the probability to reach a state in G_i such that the cumulative cost for the i-th cost structure is below/above a threshold b_i". This multi-objective variant of cost-bounded reachability is PSPACE-hard [43]. The focus of this paper is on the practical side: we aim at finding a practically efficient algorithm to obtain (an approximation of) the Pareto-optimal points. To accomplish this, we adapt and generalise recent approaches for the single-objective case [27,34] towards the multi-objective setting. The basic idea of [27,34] is to *implicitly* unfold the MDP along cost epochs, and exploit the regularities of the epoch-MDPs. PRISM [37] and the MODEST TOOLSET [29] have been updated with such methods for the single-objective case and significantly outperform the explicit unfolding approach of [2,40]. This paper presents an algorithm that lifts this principle to multiple cost objectives and determines approximation errors when using value iteration. Extensions towards quantiles and expected costs are considered too. Evaluation using a prototypical implementation in STORM [20] shows promising results. In addition, we equip our algorithm with means to visualise (inspired by the recent techniques in [39]) the trade-offs between various objectives that go beyond Pareto curves; we believe that this is key to obtain better insights into multi-objective decision making. An example is given in Fig. 1(b): it depicts the probability to satisfy an objective based on the remaining energy (y-axis) and time (x-axis).

Related work. The analysis of single-objective (cost-bounded) reachability in MDPs is an active area of research in both AI and formal method communities, and referred to in, e.g., [18,35,48]. Various model checking approaches for single objectives exist. In [32], the topology of the unfolded MDP is exploited to speed up the value iteration. In [27], three different model checking approaches are explored and compared. A survey for heuristic approaches is given in [45]. A Q-learning based approach is described in [13]. An extension of this problem in the partially observable setting was considered in [14], and for probabilistic timed automata in [27]. The method from [4] computes optimal expected values under e.g. the *condition* that the goal is reached, and is thus applicable in settings where a goal is not *necessarily* reached. A similar problem is considered in [46]. For multi-objective analysis, the model checking community typically focuses on probabilities and expected costs as in the seminal works [15,22]. Implementations are typically based on a value iteration approach in [24], and have been extended to stochastic games [16], Markov automata [42], and interval MDPs [28]. Other considered cases include e.g. multi-objective mean-payoff objectives [8], objectives over instantaneous costs [10], and parity objectives [7]. Multi-objective problems for MDPs with an unknown cost-function are considered in [33]. Surveys on multi-objective decision making in AI and machine learning can be found in [44] and [47], respectively.

2   Preliminaries

We write 2^S for the powerset of S. The i-th component of a tuple $t = \langle v_1, \ldots, v_n \rangle$ is $t[i] \stackrel{\text{def}}{=} v_i$. A (discrete) *probability distribution* over a set Ω is a function $\mu \in \Omega \to [0,1]$ such that $\text{support}(\mu) \stackrel{\text{def}}{=} \{ \omega \in \Omega \mid \mu(\omega) > 0 \}$ is countable and $\sum_{\omega \in \text{support}(\mu)} \mu(\omega) = 1$. $\text{Dist}(\Omega)$ is the set of all probability distributions over Ω. $\mathcal{D}(s)$ is the *Dirac distribution* for s, defined by $\mathcal{D}(s)(s) = 1$.

Definition 1. *A* Markov decision process *(MDP) with* m *cost structures is a triple* $M = \langle S, T, s_{init} \rangle$ *where* S *is a finite set of states,* $T \in S \to 2^{\text{Dist}(\mathbb{N}^m \times S)}$ *is the transition function, and* $s_{init} \in S$ *is the initial state. For all* $s \in S$, *we require that* $T(s)$ *is finite and non-empty.*

We write $s \to_T \mu$ for $\exists \mu \in T(s)$ and call it a *transition*. We write $s \xrightarrow{c}_T s'$ if additionally $\langle c, s' \rangle \in \text{support}(\mu)$. $\langle c, s' \rangle$ is a *branch* with cost vector c. If T is clear from the context, we just write $\to$. Graphically, transitions are lines to a node from which branches labelled with their probability and costs lead to successor states. We may omit the node and probability for transitions into Dirac distributions.

Example 1. Figure 2 shows an MDP M_{ex}. From the initial state s_0, the choice of going towards s_1 or s_2 is nondeterministic. Either way, the probability to return to s_0 is 0.5, otherwise we move to s_1 (or s_2). M_{ex} has two cost structures: Failing to move to s_1 has a cost of 1 for the first, and 2 for the second structure. Moving to s_2 yields cost 2 for the first and no cost for the second structure.

In the remainder of this paper, we fix a given MDP $M = \langle S, T, s_{init} \rangle$. Its semantics is captured by the notion of paths. A *path* in M represents the infinite concrete resolution of both nondeterministic and probabilistic choices: $\pi = s_0\,\mu_0\,c_0\,s_1\,\mu_1\,c_1\ldots$ where $s_i \in S$, $s_i \to \mu_i$, and $\langle c_i, s_{i+1}\rangle \in \mathrm{support}(\mu_i)$ for all $i \in \mathbb{N}$. A *finite path* $\pi_{\mathrm{fin}} = s_0\,\mu_0\,c_0\,s_1\,\mu_1\,c_1\,s_2\ldots\mu_{n-1}\,c_{n-1}\,s_n$ is a finite prefix of a path with $\mathrm{last}(\pi_{\mathrm{fin}}) \stackrel{\mathrm{def}}{=} s_n \in S$. Let $\mathrm{cost}_i(\pi_{\mathrm{fin}}) \stackrel{\mathrm{def}}{=} \sum_{j=0}^{n-1} c_j[i]$. $\mathrm{Paths}_{\mathrm{fin}}(M)$ ($\mathrm{Paths}(M)$) are the set of all (in)finite finite paths starting in s_{init}. A scheduler (*adversary*, *policy* or *strategy*) resolves nondeterministic choices:

Definition 2. $\mathfrak{S} \in \mathrm{Paths}_{\mathrm{fin}}(M) \to \mathrm{Dist}(\mathrm{Dist}(\mathbb{N}^m \times S))$ *is a scheduler for M if* $\forall\,\pi_{\mathrm{fin}}\colon \mu \in \mathrm{support}(\mathfrak{S}(\pi_{\mathrm{fin}})) \Rightarrow \mathrm{last}(\pi_{\mathrm{fin}}) \to_T \mu$. *The set of all schedulers of M is* $\mathrm{Sched}(M)$. $\mathfrak{S}$ *is deterministic if* $|\mathrm{support}(\mathfrak{S}(\pi))| = 1$ *for all finite paths* π.

Via the standard cylinder set construction [25], a scheduler $\mathfrak{S}$ induces a probability measure $\mathcal{P}_M^{\mathfrak{S}}$ on measurable sets of paths starting from s_{init}. We define the *extremal* values $\mathcal{P}_M^{\max}(\Pi) = \sup_{\mathfrak{S}\in\mathrm{Sched}(M)} \mathcal{P}_M^{\mathfrak{S}}(\Pi)$ and $\mathcal{P}_M^{\min}(\Pi) = \inf_{\mathfrak{S}\in\mathrm{Sched}(M)} \mathcal{P}_M^{\mathfrak{S}}(\Pi)$ for measurable $\Pi \subseteq \mathrm{Paths}(M)$. For clarity, we focus on probabilities in this paper, but note that expected accumulated costs can be defined analogously [25] and our methods apply to them with only minor changes.

Cost-Bounded Reachability. We are interested in the probabilities of sets of paths that reach certain goal states within multiple cost bounds:

Definition 3. *A* cost bound *is given by* $\langle C_j\rangle_{\sim b}\, G$ *where* $j \in \{1,\ldots,m\}$ *identifies a cost structure,* $\sim\, \in \{<,\le,>,\ge\}$, $b \in \mathbb{N}$ *is a bound value, and* $G \subseteq S$ *is a set of goal states. A* cost-bounded reachability formula *is a conjunction* $\bigwedge_{i=1}^{n\in\mathbb{N}}(\langle C_{j_i}\rangle_{\sim_i b_i}\, G_i)$ *of cost bounds. It characterises the measurable set of paths* Π *where, for every* i, *every* $\pi \in \Pi$ *has a prefix* π_{fin}^i *with* $\mathrm{last}(\pi_{\mathrm{fin}}^i) \in G_i$ *and* $\mathrm{cost}_{j_i}(\pi_{\mathrm{fin}}^i) \sim_i b_i$.

A (single-objective) multi-cost bounded reachability query asks for $\mathcal{P}_M^{opt}(e)$ where $opt \in \{\max,\min\}$ and e is a cost-bounded reachability formula. Unbounded and step-bounded reachability are special cases of cost-bounded reachability. A single-objective query may contain multiple bounds, but asks for a *single* scheduler that optimises the probability of satisfying them all.

We also consider multi-objective *tradeoffs*, i.e. sets of single-objective queries written as $\Phi = multi\big(\mathcal{P}_M^{opt_1}(e_1),\ldots,\mathcal{P}_M^{opt_\ell}(e_\ell)\big)$. We call the e_k *objectives*. For tradeoffs, we are interested in the *Pareto curve* $Pareto(M,\Phi)$ which consists of all achievable probability vectors $\boldsymbol{p}_{\mathfrak{S}} = \langle \mathcal{P}_M^{\mathfrak{S}}(e_1),\ldots,\mathcal{P}_M^{\mathfrak{S}}(e_\ell)\rangle$ for $\mathfrak{S} \in \mathrm{Sched}(M)$ that are not *dominated* by another achievable vector $\boldsymbol{p}_{\mathfrak{S}'}$. More precisely, $\boldsymbol{p}_{\mathfrak{S}} \in Pareto(M,\Phi)$ iff for all $\mathfrak{S}' \in \mathrm{Sched}(M)$ either $\boldsymbol{p}_{\mathfrak{S}} = \boldsymbol{p}_{\mathfrak{S}'}$ or for some $i \in \{1,\ldots,\ell\}$ we have $(opt_i = \max \wedge \boldsymbol{p}_{\mathfrak{S}}[i] > \boldsymbol{p}_{\mathfrak{S}'}[i]) \vee (opt_i = \min \wedge \boldsymbol{p}_{\mathfrak{S}}[i] < \boldsymbol{p}_{\mathfrak{S}'}[i])$.

Example 2. We consider $\Phi = multi\big(\mathcal{P}_{M_{ex}}^{\max}(\langle C_1\rangle_{\le 1}\{s_1\}), \mathcal{P}_{M_{ex}}^{\max}(\langle C_2\rangle_{\le 3}\{s_2\})\big)$ for M_{ex} of Fig. 2. Let $\mathfrak{S}_j$ be the scheduler that tries to move to s_1 for at most j attempts and afterwards moves to s_2. The induced probability vectors $\boldsymbol{p}_{\mathfrak{S}_1} = \langle 0.5, 1\rangle$ and $\boldsymbol{p}_{\mathfrak{S}_2} = \langle 0.75, 0.75\rangle$ both lie on the Pareto curve since no

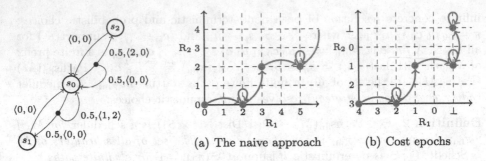

Fig. 2. Example MDP M_{ex} **Fig. 3.** An illustration of epochs

(a) The naive approach   (b) Cost epochs

$\mathfrak{S} \in \mathrm{Sched}(M_{ex})$ induces (strictly) larger probabilities $\boldsymbol{p}_{\mathfrak{S}}$. By also considering schedulers that randomise between the choices of $\mathfrak{S}_1$ and $\mathfrak{S}_2$ we obtain
$Pareto(M_{ex}, \Phi) = \{w \cdot \boldsymbol{p}_{\mathfrak{S}_1} + (1-w) \cdot \boldsymbol{p}_{\mathfrak{S}_2} \mid w \in [0, 1]\}$.

For clarity of presentation, we restrict to tradeoffs Φ where every cost structure
occurs exactly once, i.e., the number m of cost structures of M matches the
number of cost bounds occurring in Φ. Furthermore, we require that none of the
sets of goal states contains the initial state. Both assumptions are w.l.o.g. by
copying cost structures as needed and adding a new initial state with zero-cost
transition to the old initial state.

3   Multi-dimensional Sequential Value Iteration

We present a practically efficient approach to compute (an approximation of)
the Pareto curve for MDP M with m cost structures and tradeoff Φ. We
merge the ideas of [24] to approximate a Pareto curve for an (unbounded)
multi-objective tradeoff with those of [27,34] to efficiently compute (single-
objective) cost-bounded reachability probabilities. For clarity of presentation
we start with the upper-bounded maximum case and assume a tradeoff of the
form $\Phi = multi\big(\mathcal{P}_M^{\max}(e_1), \ldots, \mathcal{P}_M^{\max}(e_\ell)\big)$ with $e_k = \bigwedge_{i=n_{k-1}}^{n_k - 1}(\langle C_i \rangle_{\leq b_i} G_i)$ and
$0 = n_0 < n_1 < \cdots < n_\ell = m$. Other variants are discussed in Sect. 3.3.

Cost epochs and goal satisfaction. Central to our approach is the concept of
cost epochs. Consider the path $\pi = (s_0 \langle 2, 0 \rangle s_2 \langle 0, 0 \rangle s_0 \langle 1, 2 \rangle)^\omega$ through M_{ex} of
Fig. 2. We plot the accumulated cost in both dimensions along this path in
Fig. 3(a). Starting from $\langle 0, 0 \rangle$, the first transition yields cost 2 for the first cost
structure: we jump to coordinate $\langle 2, 0 \rangle$. The next transition, back to s_0, has
no cost, so we stay at $\langle 2, 0 \rangle$. Finally, the failed attempt to move to s_1 incurs
costs $\langle 1, 2 \rangle$. Consequently, for an infinite path, infinitely many points in this grid
may be reached. However, a tradeoff specifies bound values for the costs, e.g.,
for $\Phi_{ex} = multi\big(\mathcal{P}_{M_{ex}}^{\max}(\langle C_1 \rangle_{\leq 4}\{s_1\}), \mathcal{P}_{M_{ex}}^{\max}(\langle C_2 \rangle_{\leq 3}\{s_2\})\big)$ we get bound values 4
and 3. Once the bound value for a bound is reached, accumulating further costs
in this dimension does not impact the satisfaction of its formula. It thus suffices

to keep track, for each bound, of the *remaining* costs before reaching the bound value. This leads to a finite grid as depicted in Fig. 3(b). We refer to each of its coordinates as a *cost epoch*:

Definition 4. *An m-dimensional* cost epoch *is a tuple in $\boldsymbol{E}_m \stackrel{\text{def}}{=} (\mathbb{N} \cup \{\bot\})^m$. For $\boldsymbol{e} \in \boldsymbol{E}_m$, $\boldsymbol{c} \in \mathbb{N}^m$, the* successor epoch *is $succ(\boldsymbol{e}, \boldsymbol{c})[i] \stackrel{\text{def}}{=} \boldsymbol{e}[i] - \boldsymbol{c}[i]$ if that value is non-negative and $\bot$ otherwise.*

If the entry for a bound is $\bot$, it cannot be satisfied any more: too much costs have already been incurred. To check whether an objective $e_k = \bigwedge_{i=n_{k-1}}^{n_k - 1} (\langle C_i \rangle_{\leq b_i} G_i)$ is satisfied, we memorise whether each individual bound already holds. This is also used to ensure that satisfying a bound more than once has no effect.

Definition 5. *A* goal satisfaction *$\boldsymbol{g} \in \boldsymbol{G}_m \stackrel{\text{def}}{=} \{0, 1\}^m$ represents the cost structure indices i for which bound $\langle C_i \rangle_{\leq b_i} G_i$ already holds, i.e. G_i was reached before the bound value b_i. For $\boldsymbol{g} \in \boldsymbol{G}_m$, $\boldsymbol{e} \in \boldsymbol{E}_m$ and $s \in S$, let $succ(\boldsymbol{g}, s, \boldsymbol{e}) \in \boldsymbol{G}_m$ define the update upon reaching s: $succ(\boldsymbol{g}, s, \boldsymbol{e})[i] = 1$ if $s \in G_i \wedge \boldsymbol{e}[i] \neq \bot$ and $succ(\boldsymbol{g}, s, \boldsymbol{e})[i] = \boldsymbol{g}[i]$ otherwise.*

3.1 The Unfolding Approach

$Pareto(M, \Phi)$ can be computed by reducing Φ to a multi-objective *unbounded* reachability problem on the *unfolded* MDP Its states are the Cartesian product of the original MDP's states, the epochs, and the goal satisfactions:

Definition 6. *The* unfolding *for M as in Definition 1 and upper-bounded maximum tradeoff Φ is the MDP $M_{unf} = \langle S' \stackrel{\text{def}}{=} S \times \boldsymbol{E}_m \times \boldsymbol{G}_m, T', \langle s_{init}, \langle b_1, \ldots, b_m \rangle, \boldsymbol{0} \rangle \rangle$ with no cost structures, $T'(\langle s, \boldsymbol{e}, \boldsymbol{g} \rangle) \stackrel{\text{def}}{=} \{ unf(\mu) \in \text{Dist}(\mathbb{N}^0 \times S') \mid \mu \in T(s) \}$ and the unfolding of probability distribution μ defined by $unf(\mu)(\langle \langle s', \boldsymbol{e}', \boldsymbol{g}' \rangle \rangle) = \mu(\langle \boldsymbol{c}, s' \rangle)$ if $\boldsymbol{e}' = succ(\boldsymbol{e}, \boldsymbol{c}) \wedge \boldsymbol{g}' = succ(\boldsymbol{g}, s', \boldsymbol{e}')$ and 0 otherwise.*

Costs are now encoded in the state space, so it suffices to consider the unbounded tradeoff $\Phi' = multi(\mathcal{P}_{M_{unf}}^{\max}(e_1'), \ldots, \mathcal{P}_{M_{unf}}^{\max}(e_\ell'))$ with $e_k' = \langle \cdot \rangle_{\geq 0} G_k'$ and $G_k' = \{\langle s, \boldsymbol{e}, \boldsymbol{g} \rangle \mid \bigwedge_{i=n_{k-1}}^{n_k - 1} \boldsymbol{g}[i] = 1\}$.

Lemma 1. *There is a bijection $f \colon \text{Sched}(M) \to \text{Sched}(M_{unf})$ with $\mathcal{P}_M^{\mathfrak{S}}(e_k) = \mathcal{P}_{M_{unf}}^{f(\mathfrak{S})}(e_k')$ for all $\mathfrak{S} \in \text{Sched}(M)$ and $k \in \{1, \ldots, \ell\}$. Consequently, we have that $Pareto(M, \Phi) = Pareto(M_{unf}, \Phi')$.*

$Pareto(M_{unf}, \Phi')$ can be computed with existing multi-objective model checking algorithms for unbounded reachability. We build on the one of [24]. It iteratively chooses weight vectors $\boldsymbol{w} = \langle w_1, \ldots, w_\ell \rangle \in [0, 1]^\ell \setminus \{\boldsymbol{0}\}$ and computes points

$$p_{\boldsymbol{w}} = \langle \mathcal{P}_{M_{unf}}^{\mathfrak{S}}(e_1'), \ldots, \mathcal{P}_{M_{unf}}^{\mathfrak{S}}(e_\ell') \rangle \text{ with } \mathfrak{S} \in \arg\max_{\mathfrak{S}'} \left(\sum_{k=1}^{\ell} w_k \cdot \mathcal{P}_{M_{unf}}^{\mathfrak{S}'}(e_k') \right).$$

(1)

The Pareto curve P is convex, $p_w \in P$ for all w, and $q \in P$ implies $q \cdot w \leq p_w \cdot w$. These observations allow us to approximate the Pareto curve with arbitrary precision; see [24] for details. [24] characterises p_w via weighted expected costs: M_{unf} is equipped with ℓ cost structures used to calculate the probability of each of the ℓ objectives. This is achieved by setting the value of the k-th cost structure on each branch to 1 iff the objective e'_k is satisfied in the target state of the branch but was *not* satisfied in the transition's source state. On a path π through the resulting model M_{unf}^+, we collect exactly one cost w.r.t. cost structure k iff π satisfies objective e_k.

Definition 7. *For* $\mathfrak{S} \in \mathrm{Sched}(M_{unf}^+)$ *and* $w \in [0,1]^\ell$, *the* weighted expected cost *is* $\mathcal{E}^{\mathfrak{S}}_{M_{unf}^+}(w) = \sum_{k=1}^\ell w[k] \cdot \int_{\pi \in \mathrm{Paths}(M)} \mathrm{cost}_k(\pi) \mathrm{d}\mathcal{P}^{\mathfrak{S}}_{M_{unf}^+}(\pi)$, *i.e. the expected value of the weighted sum of the costs accumulated on paths in* M_{unf}^+.

The following characterisation of p_w is equivalent to Eq. 1:

$$p_w = \langle \mathcal{E}^{\mathfrak{S}}_{M_{unf}^+}(\mathbf{1}_1), \ldots, \mathcal{E}^{\mathfrak{S}}_{M_{unf}^+}(\mathbf{1}_\ell) \rangle \quad \text{where} \quad \mathfrak{S} \in \arg\max_{\mathfrak{S}'} \mathcal{E}^{\mathfrak{S}'}_{M_{unf}^+}(w) \quad (2)$$

and $\mathbf{1}_k \in \{0,1\}^\ell$ is the weight vector defined by $\mathbf{1}_k[j] = 1$ iff $j = k$. Standard MDP model checking algorithms [41] can be applied to compute an optimal (deterministic and memoryless) scheduler $\mathfrak{S}$ and the induced costs $\mathcal{E}^{\mathfrak{S}}_{M_{unf}^+}(\mathbf{1}_k)$.

3.2   An Epoch Model Approach Without Unfolding

The unfolding approach does not scale well: If the original MDP has n states, the unfolding will have on the order of $n \cdot \prod_{i=1}^m (b_i + 2)$ states. This makes it infeasible for larger bound values b_i over multiple bounds. The bottleneck lies in computing the points p_w as in Eqs. 1 and 2. We now show how to do so efficiently, i.e. given a weight vector $w = \langle w_1, \ldots, w_\ell \rangle \in [0,1]^\ell \setminus \{\mathbf{0}\}$, compute

$$p_w = \langle \mathcal{P}^{\mathfrak{S}}_M(e_1), \ldots, \mathcal{P}^{\mathfrak{S}}_M(e_\ell) \rangle \text{ with } \mathfrak{S} \in \arg\max_{\mathfrak{S}'}\left(\sum_{k=1}^\ell w_i \cdot \mathcal{P}^{\mathfrak{S}'}_M(\langle \cdot \rangle_{\geq 0} e_k)\right) \quad (3)$$

without unfolding. The characterisations of p_w given in Eqs. 1 and 3 are equivalent due to Lemma 1.

The efficient analysis of single-objective queries with a single bound $\Phi_1 = \mathcal{P}^{\max}_M(\langle \mathrm{C} \rangle_{\leq b} G)$ has recently been addressed in e.g. [27,34]. The key observation is that the unfolding M_{unf} can be decomposed into $b + 2$ *epoch model* MDPs $M^b, \ldots, M^0, M^\perp$ corresponding to the cost epochs. The epoch models are copies of M with only slight adaptations. Reachability probabilities in copies corresponding to epoch i only depend on the copies $\{ M^j \mid j \leq i \vee j = \perp \}$. It is thus possible to analyse $M^\perp, \ldots, M^b$ sequentially instead of considering all copies at once. In particular, it is not necessary to construct the full unfolding.

We lift this idea to multi-objective tradeoffs. The single-objective case is notably simpler in that reaching a goal state for the first time or exceeding the cost bound immediately suffices to determine whether the one property is

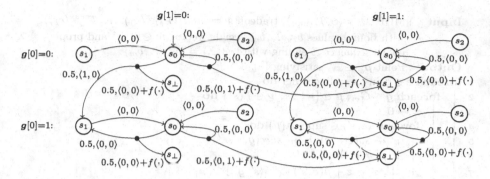

Fig. 4. An epoch model of M_{ex}

satisfied. In particular, while $M^\perp$ is just one sink state in the single-objective case, its structure is more involved here.

We first formalise the notion of *epoch models* for multiple bounds. The aim is to build an MDP for each epoch $e \in E_m$ that can be analysed via standard model checking techniques using the weighted expected cost encoding of objective probabilities. The state space of an epoch model consists of up to one copy of each original state for each goal satisfaction vector $g \in G_m$. Additional sink states $\langle s_\perp, g \rangle$ encode the target for a jump to *any* other cost epoch $e' \neq e$. We consider ℓ cost structures to encode the objective probabilities. Let function $satObj_\Phi : G_m \times G_m \to \{0,1\}^\ell$ assign value 1 in entry k iff a reachability property e_k is satisfied according to the second goal vector but was not satisfied in the first. For the transitions' branches, we distinguish two cases: (1) If the successor epoch $e' = succ(e, c)$ with respect to the *original* cost $c \in \mathbb{N}^m$ is the same as the current epoch e, we jump to the successor state as before, and update the goal satisfaction. We collect the *new* costs for the *objectives* if updating the goal satisfaction newly satisfies an objective as given by $satObj_\Phi$ (2). If the successor epoch $e' = succ(e, c)$ is different from the current epoch e, the probability is rerouted to the sink state with the corresponding goal state satisfaction vector. The collected costs contains the part of the goal satisfaction as in (1), but also the results obtained by analysing the reached epoch e', given by a function f.

Definition 8. *The epoch model of MDP M as in Definition 1 for $e \in E_m$ and a function $f : G_m \times \mathrm{Dist}(\mathbb{N}^m \times S) \to [0,1]^\ell$ is the MDP $M_f^e = \langle S^e, T_f^e, \langle s_{init}, \mathbf{0} \rangle \rangle$ with ℓ cost structures, $S^e \overset{def}{=} (S \uplus s_\perp) \times G_m$, $T_f^e(\langle s_\perp, g \rangle) = \{ \mathcal{D}(\langle 0, \langle s_\perp, g \rangle \rangle) \}$, and for every $\tilde{s} = \langle s, g \rangle \in S^e$ and $\mu \in T(s)$, there is some $\nu \in T_f^e(\tilde{s})$ defined by:*

1. $\nu(\langle satObj_\Phi(g, g'), \langle s', g' \rangle \rangle) = \mu(c, s')$ *if* $succ(e, c) = e \wedge g' = succ(g, s', e)$, *and*

2. $\nu(\langle f(g, \mu) + satObj_\Phi(g, g'), \langle s_\perp, g' \rangle \rangle) = \sum_{c \in C} \sum_{s' \in S_c'} \mu(c, s')$ *where* $C = \{ c \mid succ(e, c) \neq e \}$ *and* $S_c' = \{ s' \mid succ(g, s', succ(e, c)) = g' \}$.

Figure 4 shows an epoch model M_f^e of the MDP M_{ex} in Fig. 2 with respect to tradeoff Φ as in Example 2 and any epoch $e \in E_2$ with $e[1] \neq \perp$ and $e[2] \neq \perp$.

Input   : MDP $M = \langle S, T, s_{init} \rangle$, tradeoff $\Phi = multi(\mathcal{P}_M^{\max}(e_1), \ldots, \mathcal{P}_M^{\max}(e_\ell))$
with bound values $b_1, \ldots, b_m$, weight vector $\boldsymbol{w} \in [0,1]^\ell$ and proper
epoch sequence $\mathbb{E}$ ending with $\mathrm{last}(\mathbb{E}) = \langle b_1, \ldots, b_m \rangle$

Output : Point $\boldsymbol{p_w} \in \mathbb{R}^\ell$ satisfying Eq. 3

1 **foreach** $e \in \mathbb{E}$ in ascending order **do**

2 $\quad$ **foreach** $g \in G_m, \mu \in \{\nu \mid \exists s \colon \nu \in T(s)\}$ **do**

3 $\quad\quad$ $z \leftarrow 0$

4 $\quad\quad$ **foreach** $\langle c, s' \rangle \in \mathrm{support}(\mu)$ **do**

5 $\quad\quad\quad$ $e' \leftarrow succ(e, c);\ g' \leftarrow succ(g, s', e')$

6 $\quad\quad\quad$ **if** $e' \neq e$ **then**

7 $\quad\quad\quad\quad$ $z \leftarrow z + \mu(c, s') \cdot x^{e'}[\langle s', g' \rangle]$

8 $\quad\quad$ $f(g, \mu) \leftarrow z$

9 $\quad$ build epoch model $M_f^e = \langle S^e, T_f^e, s_{init}^e \rangle$

10 $\quad$ $\mathfrak{S} \leftarrow \arg\max_{\mathfrak{S}'} \mathcal{E}_{M_f^e}^{\mathfrak{S}'}(\boldsymbol{w})$

11 $\quad$ **foreach** $k \in \{1, \ldots, \ell\}, \tilde{s} \in S^e$ **do**

12 $\quad\quad$ $x^e[\tilde{s}][k] \leftarrow \mathcal{E}_{M_f^e}^{\mathfrak{S}}(\mathbf{1}_k)[\tilde{s}]$

13 **return** $x^{\mathrm{last}(\mathbb{E})}[s_{init}^{\mathrm{last}(\mathbb{E})}]$

Algorithm 1. Sequential multi-cost bounded analysis

Remark 1. The structure of M_f^e differs only slightly between epochs. In particular consider epochs e, e' with $e[i] = \bot$ iff $e'[i] = \bot$. To construct epoch model $M_f^{e'}$ from M_f^e, only transitions to the bottom states $\langle s_\bot, g \rangle$ need to be adapted.

To analyse an epoch model M_f^e, any successor epoch e' of e needs to be analysed before. Since costs are non-negative, we can ensure this by analysing the epochs in a specific order. In the single dimensional case the order is uniquely given by $\bot, 0, 1, \ldots, b$. For multiple cost bounds any linearisation of the partial order $\preceq \subseteq \boldsymbol{E}_m \times \boldsymbol{E}_m$ with $e' \preceq e$ iff $e'[i] \leq e[i] \vee e'[i] = \bot$ for all i can be considered. We call such a linearisation a *proper epoch sequence*.

We compute the points $\boldsymbol{p_w}$ by analysing the different epoch models (i.e. the coordinates of Fig. 3(b)) sequentially. The main procedure is outlined in Algorithm 1. The costs of the model for the current epoch are computed in lines 2-8. These costs comprise the results from previously analysed epochs e'. In lines 9-12, the current epoch model M_f^e is built and analysed: We compute weighted expected costs on M_f^e where $\mathcal{E}_{M_f^e}^{\mathfrak{S}}(\boldsymbol{w})[s]$ denotes the expected costs for M_f^e when changing the initial state to s. In line 10 a (deterministic and memoryless) scheduler $\mathfrak{S}$ that induces the maximal weighted expected costs (i.e. $\mathcal{E}_{M_f^e}^{\mathfrak{S}}(\boldsymbol{w})[s] = \max_{\mathfrak{S}'} \mathcal{E}_{M_f^e}^{\mathfrak{S}'}(\boldsymbol{w})[s]$ for all states s) is computed. In line 12 we then compute the expected costs induced by $\mathfrak{S}$ for the individual objectives.

Theorem 1. *The output of Algorithm 1 satisfies Eq. 3.*

Proof (sketch). Let e be the currently analysed epoch. Since $\mathbb{E}$ is assumed to be a *proper* epoch sequence, we already processed any reachable successor epoch e'

of e, i.e., line 7 is only executed for epochs e' for which $x^{e'}$ has already been computed. One can show that the values $x^e[\langle s, g \rangle][k]$ computed by the algorithm coincide with the probability to satisfy e'_k from state $\langle s, e, g \rangle$ in the unfolding M_{unf} under a scheduler $\mathfrak{S}$ that maximises the weighted sum.

Error propagation. So far, we assumed that (weighted) expected costs $\mathcal{E}_M^{\mathfrak{S}}(\boldsymbol{w})$ are computed exactly. Practical implementations, however, are often based on numerical methods that only approximate the correct solution. In fact, methods based on value iteration—the de-facto standard in MDP model checking—do not give any guarantee on the accuracy of the obtained result [26]. We therefore consider interval iteration [5,9] which for a predefined precision $\varepsilon > 0$ guarantees that the obtained result x_s is ε-precise, i.e. we have $|x_s - \mathcal{E}_M^{\mathfrak{S}}(\boldsymbol{w})[s]| \leq \varepsilon$.

For the single-cost bounded variant of Algorithm 1, [27] discusses that in order to compute $\mathcal{P}_M^{\max}(\langle C \rangle_{\leq b} G)$ with precision ε, each epoch model needs to be analysed with precision $\frac{\varepsilon}{b+1}$. We generalise this result to multi-dimensional tradeoffs. Assume the results of previously analysed epochs (given by f) are ε-precise and that M_f^e is analysed with precision δ. As in the single-dimensional case, the total error for M_f^e can accumulate to $\delta + \varepsilon$. Since a path through the MDP M can visit at most $\sum_{i=1}^m (b_i + 1)$ cost epochs whose analysis introduces error δ, the overall error can be upper bounded by $\delta \cdot \sum_{i=1}^m (b_i + 1)$.

Theorem 2. *If the values $x^e[\tilde{s}][k]$ at line 12 of Algorithm 1 are computed with precision $\varepsilon/\sum_{i=1}^m (b_i + 1)$ for some $\varepsilon > 0$, the output $\boldsymbol{p}'_w$ of the algorithm satisfies $|\boldsymbol{p}_w - \boldsymbol{p}'_w| \cdot \boldsymbol{w} \leq \varepsilon$ where $\boldsymbol{p}_w$ is as in Eq. 3.*

Remark 2. Alternatively, epochs can be analysed with the desired overall precision ε by lifting the results from topological interval iteration [5]. However, that requires to store the obtained bounds for the results of already analysed epochs.

3.3   Extensions

Minimising objectives. Objectives $\mathcal{P}_M^{\min}(e_k)$ can be handled by extending the function $satObj_\phi$ in Definition 8 such that it assigns cost -1 to branches that lead to the satisfaction of e_k. To obtain the desired probabilities we then maximise negative costs and multiply the result by -1 afterwards. As interval iteration supports mixtures of positive and negative costs [5], arbitrary combinations of minimising and maximising objectives can be considered[1].

Beyond upper bounds. Our approach also supports bounds of the form $\langle C_j \rangle_{\sim b} G$ for $\sim \in \{<, \leq, >, \geq\}$, i.e., we allow *combinations* of lower and upper cost-bounds. For strict upper bounds $< b$ and non-strict lower bounds $\geq b$ we consider $\leq b + 1$ and $> b - 1$ instead. For bound $\langle C_i \rangle_{>b_i} G_i$ we adapt the update of goal satisfactions such that $succ(g, s, e)[i] = 1$ if either $g[i] = 1$ or $s \in G_i \wedge e[i] = \bot$. Similarly, we support multi-bounded-single-goal queries of the form $\langle C_{(j_1,...,j_n)} \rangle_{(\sim_1 b_1,...,\sim_n b_n)} G$ which characterises the paths π with a single prefix π_{fin} satisfying $last(\pi_{\text{fin}}) \in G$ and *all* cost bounds, i.e., $cost_{j_i}(\pi_{\text{fin}}) \sim_i b_i$.

---

[1] This supersedes a restriction of the algorithm of [24].

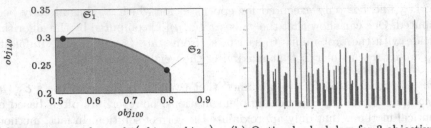

(a) Pareto curve for $multi(obj_{100}, obj_{140})$ (b) Optimal schedulers for 3 objectives

Fig. 5. Pareto curves

Example 3. The formula $e = \langle C_{(1,1)} \rangle_{(\leq 1, \geq 1)} G$ expresses the paths that reach G while collecting exactly one cost w.r.t. the first cost structure. This formula is not equivalent to $e' = \langle C_1 \rangle_{\leq 1} G \wedge \langle C_1 \rangle_{\geq 1} G$ since, e.g., for $G = \{ s_0 \}$ the path $\pi = s_0 \langle 2 \rangle s_0$ satisfies e' but not e.

Expected cost objectives. We can consider cost-bounded expected cost objectives $\mathcal{E}_M^{opt}(R_{j_1}, \langle C_{j_2} \rangle_{\leq b})$ with $opt \in \{ \max, \min \}$ which refer to the expected cost accumulated for cost structure j_1 within a given cost bound $\langle C_{j_2} \rangle_{\leq b}$. Similar to cost-bounded reachability queries, we compute cost-bounded expected costs via computing (weighted) expected costs within epoch models.

Quantiles. A (multi-dimensional) quantile has the form $Qu(\mathcal{P}_M^{opt}(e) \sim p)$ for $opt \in \{ \min, \max \}$, $\sim \in \{ <, \leq, >, \geq \}$, $e = \bigwedge_{i=1}^{n \in \mathbb{N}} (\langle C_{j_i} \rangle_{\sim_i b_i} G_i)$ and a fixed probability threshold $p \in [0, 1]$. The quantile asks for the set of bound values $\mathcal{B}$ that satisfy the probability threshold, i.e., $\mathcal{B} = \{ \langle b_1 \dots, b_n \rangle \mid \mathcal{P}_M^{opt}(e) \sim p \}$. The computation of quantiles for single-cost bounded reachability has been discussed in [3,34], where multiple cost bounds are supported via unfolding. Unfolding requires to fix bound values $b_2, \dots, b_n$ a priori, and one can only ask for all b_1 that satisfy the property. Our approach provides the basis for lifting the ideas of [3,34] to multi-bounded queries. Roughly, one extends the epoch sequence $\mathbb{E}$ in Algorithm 1 dynamically until the epochs in which the bounded reachability probability passes the threshold p are explored. Additional steps such as detecting the case where $\mathcal{B} = \emptyset$ are left for future work.

4   Visualisations

The results of a multi-objective model checking analysis are typically presented as a single (approximation of a) Pareto curve. For more than two objectives, the performance of the Pareto-optimal scheduler can be displayed in a bar chart as in Fig. 4, where the colours reflect different objectives and the groups different schedulers. The aim is to visualise the tradeoffs between the different objectives such that the user can make an informed decision about the system design or pick a scheduler for implementation. However, Pareto set visualisations alone

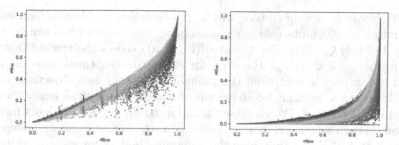

(a) Remaining scientific value requirement and the probabilities of the two objectives

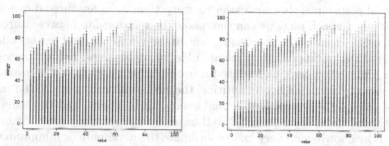

(b) obj_{100} depending on value and energy, worst- (left)/best-case (right) time budget

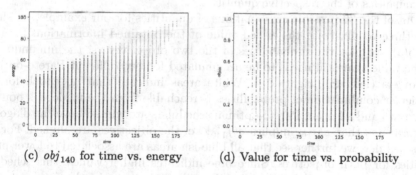

(c) obj_{140} for time vs. energy   (d) Value for time vs. probability

Fig. 6. Two-dimensional plots of Pareto-optimal schedulers for different quantities (Color figure online)

may not provide sufficient information, about, e.g., which objectives are aligned or conflicting (see e.g. [39] for a discussion in the non-probabilistic case). Cost bounds furthermore add an extra dimension for each cost structure. Consider the Mars rover MDP M_r and tradeoff $multi(obj_{100}, obj_{140})$ with

$$obj_v = \mathcal{P}_{M_r}^{\max}(\langle C_{time}\rangle_{\leq 175} B \wedge \langle C_{energy}\rangle_{\leq 100} B \wedge \langle C_{value}\rangle_{\geq v} B)$$

where B is the set of states where the rover has safely returned to its base. We ask for the tradeoff between performing experiments of scientific value at least 100 before returning to base within 175 time units and maximum energy consumption of 100 units (obj_{100}) vs. achieving the same with scientific value at least 140 (obj_{140}). The Pareto curve (Fig. 5(a)) shows the tradeoff between achieving obj_{100} and obj_{140}. However, for each Pareto-optimal scheduler, our method has implicitly computed the probabilities of the two objectives for all reachable epochs as well, i.e. for all bounds on the three quantities below the ones required in the tradeoff. We visualise this information for deep insights into the behaviour of each scheduler, its robustness w.r.t. the bounds, and its preferences for certain objectives depending on the remaining budget for each quantity.

We use plots as shown in Fig. 6. They can be generated in no extra runtime or memory since all required data is already computed implicitly. We restrict to two-dimensional plots since they are easier to grasp than complex three-dimensional visualisations. In each plot, we can thus show the relationship between three different quantities: one on the x-axis (x), one on the y-axis (y), and one encoded as the colour of the points (z, where we use blue for high values, red for low values, black for probability zero, and white for unreachable epochs). Yet our example tradeoff already contains five quantities: the probability for obj_{100}, the probability for obj_{140}, the available time and energy to be spent, and the remaining scientific value to be accumulated. We thus need to project out some quantities. We do this by showing at every $\langle x, y \rangle$ coordinate the maximum or minimum value of the z quantity when ranging over *all* reachable values of the hidden *costs* at this coordinate. That is, we show a best- or worst-case situation, depending on the semantics of the respective quantities.

Out of the 30 possible combinations of quantities for our example, we showcase three to illustrate the added value of the obtained information. First, in Fig. 6(a), we plot the probabilities of the two objectives vs. the minimum scientific value that still needs to be accumulated for two different Pareto-optimal schedulers (left: $\mathfrak{S}_1$, right: $\mathfrak{S}_2$). White areas indicate that no epoch for the particular combination of probabilities is reachable from the tradeoff's bounds. These two and all other Pareto-optimal schedulers are white above the diagonal, which means that obj_{100} implies obj_{140}, i.e. the objectives are aligned. For the left scheduler, we further see that all blue-ish areas are associated to lower probabilities for both objectives. Since blue indicates higher values, this scheduler achieves only low probabilities when it still needs to make the rover accumulate a high amount of value. However, it overall achieves higher probabilities for obj_{140} at medium value requirements, whereas the right scheduler is "safer" and focuses on satisfying obj_{100}. The erratic spikes on the left occur because some probabilities are only reached after very unlikely paths.

In Fig. 6(b), we show for $\mathfrak{S}_1$ the probability to achieve obj_{100} depending on the remaining energy to be spent vs. the remaining scientific value to be accumulated. We see a white vertical line for every odd x-value; this is because, over all branches in the model, the gcd of all value costs is 2. The left plot shows the minimum probabilities over the hidden costs, i.e. we see the probability for the worst-case remaining time; the right plot shows the best-case scenario. Not surprisingly, when time is low, only a lot of energy makes it possible to reach the objective with non-zero probability.

Table 1. Runtime comparison for multi-cost single-objective queries

Benchmark instance							Interval It			Policy It.	
Case Study		$|S|$	$|T|$	$r\text{-}m$	$|\mathbb{E}|$	$|S_{unf}|$	UNF-dd	UNF-sp	SEQ	UNF-sp	SEQ
Service	[38]	$8{\cdot}10^4$	$2{\cdot}10^5$	1-1	162	$6{\cdot}10^6$	47	136	**10**	1945	**48**
JobSched2	[34]	349	660	2-2	503	$2{\cdot}10^4$	<1	<1	<1	1	<1
JobSched3		4584	$1{\cdot}10^5$	2-2	922	$3{\cdot}10^6$	4	10	4	26	**13**
JobSched5		$1{\cdot}10^6$	$4{\cdot}10^6$	2-2	2114	$4{\cdot}10^8$	**2944**	TO	3220	TO	TO
FireWire	[36]	776	1411	2-2	6024	$7{\cdot}10^5$	7	8	**2**	274	**144**
FireWire		776	1411	2-2	$1{\cdot}10^5$	$1{\cdot}10^7$	165	147	**45**	TO	**2803**
Resources	[6]	94	326	3-3	$2{\cdot}10^4$	$6{\cdot}10^5$	<1	18	5	46	9
Resources		94	326	3-3	$1{\cdot}10^7$	$6{\cdot}10^8$	TO	TO	**2693**	TO	TO
Rover		16	30	3-3	$9{\cdot}10^4$	$1{\cdot}10^6$	38	24	**4**	704	**106**
Rover		16	30	3-3	$1{\cdot}10^7$	$2{\cdot}10^8$	TO	6040	**713**	TO	TO
UAV	[23]	$1{\cdot}10^5$	$6{\cdot}10^4$	1-1	52	$4{\cdot}10^4$	1	**1**	1	4	27
UAV		$1{\cdot}10^5$	$6{\cdot}10^4$	1-1	102	$4{\cdot}10^5$	7	16	2	72	**46**
Wlan3	[36]	$1{\cdot}10^5$	$2{\cdot}10^5$	1-1	82	$3{\cdot}10^6$	9	63	8	**126**	800
Wlan3		$1{\cdot}10^5$	$2{\cdot}10^5$	1-1	202	$1{\cdot}10^7$	820	293	**14**	**848**	2155
Wlan6		$5{\cdot}10^6$	$1{\cdot}10^7$	1-1	82	$2{\cdot}10^7$	**12**	363	989	**643**	TO
Wlan6		$5\,10^6$	$1{\cdot}10^7$	1-1	202	$6{\cdot}10^8$	2292	TO	**1399**	TO	TO

Table 2. Runtime comparison for multi-cost multi-objective queries

Benchmark instance							Interval It		Policy It.	
Case Study	$|S|$	$|T|$	$\ell\text{-}r\text{-}m$	$|\mathbb{E}|$	$\#w$	$|S_{unf}|$	UNF-sp	SEQ	UNF-sp	SEQ
Service	$8{\cdot}10^4$	$2{\cdot}10^5$	2-1-2	162	34	$6{\cdot}10^6$	1918	**543**	TO	**4679**
JobSched2	349	660	2-4-4	$4{\cdot}10^4$	2	$1{\cdot}10^5$	**3**	54	**15**	183
JobSched3	4584	$1{\cdot}10^5$	2-4-4	$1{\cdot}10^6$	35	$2{\cdot}10^6$	**96**	TO	**6239**	TO
JobSched5	$1{\cdot}10^6$	$4{\cdot}10^6$	2-4-4	$3{\cdot}10^5$	?	?	TO	TO	TO	TO
FireWire	776	1411	2-2-2	6024	3	$7{\cdot}10^5$	32	**17**	TO	**1159**
FireWire	776	1411	2-2-2	$1{\cdot}10^5$	2	$1{\cdot}10^7$	863	**225**	TO	TO
Resources	94	326	2-3-4	$2{\cdot}10^5$	3	$6{\cdot}10^5$	25	**16**	2047	**52**
Resources	94	326	2-3-4	$1{\cdot}10^8$	?	?	TO	TO	TO	TO
Rover	16	30	2-3-3	$9{\cdot}10^5$	7	$1{\cdot}10^6$	177	**39**	5817	**3328**
Rover	16	30	2-3-3	$1{\cdot}10^8$	7	$2{\cdot}10^8$	TO	**5785**	TO	TO
UAV	$1{\cdot}10^5$	$6{\cdot}10^4$	2-1-2	52	18	$4{\cdot}10^4$	**2**	24	**102**	1098
UAV	$1{\cdot}10^5$	$6{\cdot}10^4$	2-1-2	102	22	$4{\cdot}10^5$	70	**39**	**2282**	3062
Wlan3	$1{\cdot}10^5$	$2{\cdot}10^5$	3-1-2	82	68	$3{\cdot}10^6$	5239	**2231**	TO	TO
Wlan3	$1{\cdot}10^5$	$2{\cdot}10^5$	3-1-2	202	4	$1{\cdot}10^7$	1769	**185**	TO	TO
Wlan6	$5{\cdot}10^6$	$1{\cdot}10^7$	3-1-2	82	?	$2{\cdot}10^7$	TO	TO	TO	TO

Finally, Fig. 6(c) shows the probability for obj_{140} depending on available time and energy for $\mathfrak{S}_2$. We plot the minimum probability over the hidden scientific value requirement, i.e. a worst-case view. The plot shows that time is of little use in case of low remaining energy, but it helps significantly when there is sufficient energy, too. In Fig. 6(d), we depict for the same scheduler the minimum remaining scientific value (z) under which a certain probability for obj_{100} can be achieved (y), given a certain remaining time budget (x). The upper left corner shows that a high probability in little time is only achievable if we need to collect little more value; the value requirement gradually relaxes as we aim for lower probabilities or have more time.

5   Experiments

Implementation. We implemented the presented approach into STORM [20] v1.2, and available via [19]. The implementation computes extremal probabilities for single-objective multi-cost bounded queries, as well as Pareto curves for the multi-objective case. We consider the *sparse* engine of STORM, i.e., explicit data structures such as sparse matrices. For single-cost bounded properties, this has already been addressed in [34]. For the computation of expected cost (Lines 10 to 12 of Algorithm 1) we employ interval iteration with finite precision floats as well as policy iteration with infinite precision rationals. The expected costs (lines 10 to 12 of Algorithm 1) are computed either numerically (via interval iteration over finite precision floats) or exactly (via policy iteration over infinite precision rationals). To reduce the memory consumption, the analysis result of an epoch model M_f^e is erased as soon as possible.

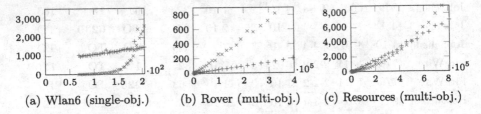

(a) Wlan6 (single-obj.)   (b) Rover (multi-obj.)   (c) Resources (multi-obj.)

Fig. 7. Runtime (y-axis) of SEQ $(+)$ and UNF $(\times)$ for increasing cost bounds (x-axis)

Set-up & reproduction. We evaluate the approach on wide range of case studies, available in the artefact [30]. The models are given in PRISM's [37] guarded command language. For each case study we consider single- and multi-objective queries that yield non-trivial results, i.e., probabilities strictly between zero and one. We compare the naive unfolding approach (UNF) as in Sect. 3.1 with the sequential approach (SEQ) as in Sect. 3.2. The unfolding of the model is applied on the PRISM language level, by considering a parallel composition with cost counting structures. On the unfolded model we apply the algorithms for unbounded reachability as available in STORM. We considered precision $\eta = 10^{-4}$ for the Pareto curve approximation and precision $\varepsilon = 10^{-6}$ for interval iteration. We increased the precision for single epoch models as in Theorem 2.

We ran our experiments on a single core (2 GHz) of a HP BL685C G7 system with 192 GB of memory. We stopped each experiment after a time limit of 2 hours. For experiments that completed within the time limit, we observed a memory consumption of up to 36 GB for UNF and up to 5 GB for SEQ.

A binary equivalent to the binary we used for the experiments is available in the artefact [30]. The binary has been tested in the artefact evaluation VM [31]. For other configurations, STORM should be recompiled using the sources [19].

Details on reproduction of the tables, as well as details on how to analyse multi-cost bounded properties using STORM in general can be found in the readme, enclosed in the artefact.

Experimental Results. Tables 1 and 2 show results for single- and multi-objective queries, respectively. The first columns yield the number of states and transitions of the original MDP, then for the query, the number of bounds m, the number of *different* cost structures r, and the number of reachable cost epochs (reflecting the magnitude of the bound values), $|S_{unf}|$ denotes the number of reachable states in the unfolding. For multi-objective queries, we additionally give the number of objectives and the number of analysed weight vectors w. The remaining columns depict the runtimes of the different approaches in seconds. For UNF, we considered both the sparse (sp) and symbolic (dd) engine of STORM. The symbolic engine neither supports multi-objective model checking nor exact policy iteration.

On the majority of benchmarks, SEQ performs better than UNF. Typically, SEQ is less sensitive to increases in the magnitude of the cost bounds, as illustrated in Fig. 7. For three benchmark and query instances, we plot the runtime of both approaches against different numbers $|\mathbb{E}|$ of reachable epochs. While for small cost bounds, UNF is sometimes even faster compared to SEQ, SEQ scales better with increasing $|\mathbb{E}|$. It is not surprising that SEQ scales better, ultimately, the increased state space and the accompanying memory consumption in UNF is a bottleneck. The most important reason that UNF performs better for some (smaller) cost bounds is the induced overhead of checking the full epoch. In particular, the epoch contains (often many) states that are not reachable from the initial state (in the unfolding).

6   Conclusion

Many real-world planning problems consider several limited resources and contain tradeoffs. This paper present a practically efficient approach to analyse these problems. It has been implemented in the STORM model checker and shows significant performance benefits. The algorithm implicitly computes a large amount of information that is hidden in the standard plots of Pareto curves shown to visualise the results of a multi-objective analysis. We have developed a new set of visualisations that exploit all the available data to provide new and clear insights to decision makers even for problems with many objectives and cost dimensions.

Data Availability Statement. The datasets analysed during the current study, and the binary used for the analysis, are available in the figshare repository [30]. Source code matching the binary is available in [19].

References

1. The International Probabilistic Planning Competition, http://www.icaps-conference.org/index.php/Main/Competitions
2. Andova, S., Hermanns, H., Katoen, J.-P.: Discrete-time rewards model-checked. In: Larsen, K.G., Niebert, P. (eds.) FORMATS 2003. LNCS, vol. 2791, pp. 88–104. Springer, Heidelberg (2004). https://doi.org/10.1007/978-3-540-40903-8_8
3. Baier, C., Daum, M., Dubslaff, C., Klein, J., Klüppelholz, S.: Energy-utility quantiles. In: Badger, J.M., Rozier, K.Y. (eds.) NFM 2014. LNCS, vol. 8430, pp. 285–299. Springer, Cham (2014). https://doi.org/10.1007/978-3-319-06200-6_24
4. Baier, C., Klein, J., Klüppelholz, S., Wunderlich, S.: Maximizing the conditional expected reward for reaching the goal. In: Legay, A., Margaria, T. (eds.) TACAS 2017. LNCS, vol. 10206, pp. 269–285. Springer, Heidelberg (2017). https://doi.org/10.1007/978-3-662-54580-5_16
5. Baier, C., Klein, J., Leuschner, L., Parker, D., Wunderlich, S.: Ensuring the reliability of your model checker: interval iteration for Markov decision processes. In: Majumdar, R., Kunčak, V. (eds.) CAV 2017, Part I. LNCS, vol. 10426, pp. 160–180. Springer, Cham (2017). https://doi.org/10.1007/978-3-319-63387-9_8
6. Barrett, L., Narayanan, S.: Learning all optimal policies with multiple criteria. In: ICML. AICPS, vol. 307, pp. 41–47. ACM (2008)
7. Berthon, R., Randour, M., Raskin, J.F.: Threshold constraints with guarantees for parity objectives in Markov decision processes. In: ICALP. LIPIcs, vol. 80, pp. 121:1–121:15. Schloss Dagstuhl - Leibniz-Zentrum fuer Informatik (2017)
8. Brázdil, T., Brozek, V., Chatterjee, K., Forejt, V., Kucera, A.: Two views on multiple mean-payoff objectives in Markov decision processes. LMCS **10**(1) (2014)
9. Brázdil, T., Chatterjee, K., Chmelík, M., Forejt, V., Křetínský, J., Kwiatkowska, M., Parker, D., Ujma, M.: Verification of Markov decision processes using learning algorithms. In: Cassez, F., Raskin, J.-F. (eds.) ATVA 2014. LNCS, vol. 8837, pp. 98–114. Springer, Cham (2014). https://doi.org/10.1007/978-3-319-11936-6_8
10. Brázdil, T., Chatterjee, K., Forejt, V., Kucera, A.: Trading performance for stability in Markov decision processes. J. Comput. Syst. Sci. **84**, 144–170 (2017)
11. Bresina, J.L., Jónsson, A.K., Morris, P.H., Rajan, K.: Activity planning for the mars exploration rovers. In: ICAPS, pp. 40–49. AAAI (2005)
12. Bryce, D., Cushing, W., Kambhampati, S.: Probabilistic planning is multi-objective. Technical report, Arizona State Univ., CSE (2007)
13. Cao, Z., Guo, H., Zhang, J., Oliehoek, F.A., Fastenrath, U.: Maximizing the probability of arriving on time: a practical q-learning method. In: AAAI, pp. 4481–4487. AAAI Press (2017)
14. Chatterjee, K., Chmelik, M., Gupta, R., Kanodia, A.: Optimal cost almost-sure reachability in POMDPs. Artif. Intell. **234**, 26–48 (2016)

15. Chatterjee, K., Majumdar, R., Henzinger, T.A.: Markov decision processes with multiple objectives. In: Durand, B., Thomas, W. (eds.) STACS 2006. LNCS, vol. 3884, pp. 325–336. Springer, Heidelberg (2006). https://doi.org/10.1007/11672142_26

16. Chen, T., Forejt, V., Kwiatkowska, M., Simaitis, A., Wiltsche, C.: On stochastic games with multiple objectives. In: Chatterjee, K., Sgall, J. (eds.) MFCS 2013. LNCS, vol. 8087, pp. 266–277. Springer, Heidelberg (2013). https://doi.org/10.1007/978-3-642-40313-2_25

17. Cheng, L., Subrahmanian, E., Westerberg, A.W.: Multiobjective decision processes under uncertainty: applications, problem formulations, and solution strategies. Ind. Eng. Chem. Res. 44(8), 2405–2415 (2005)

18. Christman, A., Cassamano, J.: Maximizing the probability of arriving on time. In: Dudin, A., De Turck, K. (eds.) ASMTA 2013. LNCS, vol. 7984, pp. 142–157. Springer, Heidelberg (2013). https://doi.org/10.1007/978-3-642-39408-9_11

19. Dehnert, C., Junges, S., Katoen, J.P., Quatmann, T., Volk, M.: Storm source files. zenodo (2018), https://doi.org/10.5281/zenodo.1181896

20. Dehnert, C., Junges, S., Katoen, J.-P., Volk, M.: A STORM is coming: a modern probabilistic model checker. In: Majumdar, R., Kunčak, V. (eds.) CAV 2017, Part II. LNCS, vol. 10427, pp. 592–600. Springer, Cham (2017). https://doi.org/10.1007/978-3-319-63390-9_31

21. Eastwood, R., Alexander, R., Kelly, T.: Safe multi-objective planning with a posteriori preferences. In: HASE, pp. 78–85. IEEE Computer Society (2016)

22. Etessami, K., Kwiatkowska, M., Vardi, M.Y., Yannakakis, M.: Multi-objective model checking of Markov decision processes. LMCS 4(4) (2008)

23. Feng, L., Wiltsche, C., Humphrey, L., Topcu, U.: Controller synthesis for autonomous systems interacting with human operators. In: ICCPS, pp. 70–79. ACM (2015)

24. Forejt, V., Kwiatkowska, M., Parker, D.: Pareto curves for probabilistic model checking. In: Chakraborty, S., Mukund, M. (eds.) ATVA 2012. LNCS, pp. 317–332. Springer, Heidelberg (2012). https://doi.org/10.1007/978-3-642-33386-6_25

25. Forejt, V., Kwiatkowska, M., Norman, G., Parker, D.: Automated verification techniques for probabilistic systems. In: Bernardo, M., Issarny, V. (eds.) SFM 2011. LNCS, vol. 6659, pp. 53–113. Springer, Heidelberg (2011). https://doi.org/10.1007/978-3-642-21455-4_3

26. Haddad, S., Monmege, B.: Reachability in MDPs: refining convergence of value iteration. In: Ouaknine, J., Potapov, I., Worrell, J. (eds.) RP 2014. LNCS, vol. 8762, pp. 125–137. Springer, Cham (2014). https://doi.org/10.1007/978-3-319-11439-2_10

27. Hahn, E.M., Hartmanns, A.: A comparison of time- and reward-bounded probabilistic model checking techniques. In: Fränzle, M., Kapur, D., Zhan, N. (eds.) SETTA 2016. LNCS, vol. 9984, pp. 85–100. Springer, Cham (2016). https://doi.org/10.1007/978-3-319-47677-3_6

28. Hahn, E.M., Hashemi, V., Hermanns, H., Lahijanian, M., Turrini, A.: Multi-objective robust strategy synthesis for interval Markov decision processes. In: Bertrand, N., Bortolussi, L. (eds.) QEST 2017. LNCS, vol. 10503, pp. 207–223. Springer, Cham (2017). https://doi.org/10.1007/978-3-319-66335-7_13

29. Hartmanns, A., Hermanns, H.: The Modest Toolset: an integrated environment for quantitative modelling and verification. In: Ábrahám, E., Havelund, K. (eds.) TACAS 2014. LNCS, vol. 8413, pp. 593–598. Springer, Heidelberg (2014). https://doi.org/10.1007/978-3-642-54862-8_51

30. Hartmanns, A., Junges, S., Katoen, J.P., Quatmann, T.: Evaluated artefact for this paper. figshare (2018), https://doi.org/10.6084/m9.figshare.5907349.v1
31. Hartmanns, A., Wendler, P.: Artefact vm. figshare (2018), https://doi.org/10.6084/m9.figshare.5896615
32. Hou, P., Yeoh, W., Varakantham, P.: Revisiting risk-sensitive MDPs: new algorithms and results. In: ICAPS. AAAI (2014)
33. Junges, S., Jansen, N., Dehnert, C., Topcu, U., Katoen, J.-P.: Safety-constrained reinforcement learning for MDPs. In: Chechik, M., Raskin, J.-F. (eds.) TACAS 2016. LNCS, vol. 9636, pp. 130–146. Springer, Heidelberg (2016). https://doi.org/10.1007/978-3-662-49674-9_8
34. Klein, J., Baier, C., Chrszon, P., Daum, M., Dubslaff, C., Klüppelholz, S., Märcker, S., Müller, D.: Advances in probabilistic model checking with PRISM: variable reordering, quantiles and weak deterministic Büchi automata. In: STTT, pp. 1–16 (2017)
35. Kolobov, A., Mausam, Weld, D.S.: A theory of goal-oriented MDPs with dead ends. In: UAI, pp. 438–447. AUAI Press (2012)
36. Kwiatkowska, M., Norman, G., Parker, D.: The PRISM benchmark suite. In: QEST, pp. 203–204. IEEE CS Press (2012)
37. Kwiatkowska, M., Norman, G., Parker, D.: PRISM 4.0: verification of probabilistic real-time systems. In: Gopalakrishnan, G., Qadeer, S. (eds.) CAV 2011. LNCS, vol. 6806, pp. 585–591. Springer, Heidelberg (2011). https://doi.org/10.1007/978-3-642-22110-1_47
38. Lacerda, B., Parker, D., Hawes, N.: Multi-objective policy generation for mobile robots under probabilistic time-bounded guarantees. In: ICAPS, pp. 504–512. AAAI Press (2017)
39. Lankaites Pinheiro, R., Landa-Silva, D., Atkin, J.: A technique based on trade-off maps to visualise and analyse relationships between objectives in optimisation problems. J. Multi-Criteria Decis. Anal. **24**(1–2), 37–56 (2017)
40. Laroussinie, F., Sproston, J.: Model checking durational probabilistic systems. In: Sassone, V. (ed.) FoSSaCS 2005. LNCS, vol. 3441, pp. 140–154. Springer, Heidelberg (2005). https://doi.org/10.1007/978-3-540-31982-5_9
41. Puterman, M.L.: Markov Decision Processes. Wiley, New York (1994)
42. Quatmann, T., Junges, S., Katoen, J.-P.: Markov automata with multiple objectives. In: Majumdar, R., Kunčak, V. (eds.) CAV 2017, Part I. LNCS, vol. 10426, pp. 140–159. Springer, Cham (2017). https://doi.org/10.1007/978-3-319-63387-9_7
43. Randour, M., Raskin, J.F., Sankur, O.: Percentile queries in multi-dimensional Markov decision processes. FMSD **50**(2–3), 207–248 (2017)
44. Roijers, D.M., Vamplew, P., Whiteson, S., Dazeley, R.: A survey of multi-objective sequential decision-making. J. Artif. Intell. Res. **48**, 67–113 (2013)
45. Steinmetz, M., Hoffmann, J., Buffet, O.: Goal probability analysis in probabilistic planning: exploring and enhancing the state of the art. J. Artif. Intell. Res. **57**, 229–271 (2016)
46. Teichteil-Königsbuch, F.: Stochastic safest and shortest path problems. In: AAAI. AAAI Press (2012)
47. Vamplew, P., Dazeley, R., Berry, A., Issabekov, R., Dekker, E.: Empirical evaluation methods for multiobjective reinforcement learning algorithms. Mach. Learn. **84**(1–2), 51–80 (2011)
48. Yu, S.X., Lin, Y., Yan, P.: Optimization models for the first arrival target distribution function in discrete time. J. Math. Anal. Appl. **225**(1), 193–223 (1998)

A Statistical Model Checker
for Nondeterminism and Rare Events

Carlos E. Budde[1], Pedro R. D'Argenio[2,3,4], Arnd Hartmanns[1(✉)],
and Sean Sedwards[5]

[1] University of Twente,
Enschede, The Netherlands
{c.e.budde,a.hartmanns}@utwente.nl
[2] Universidad Nacional de Córdoba,
Córdoba, Argentina
dargenio@famaf.unc.edu.ar
[3] CONICET, Córdoba, Argentina
[4] Saarland University, Saarbrücken, Germany
[5] University of Waterloo, Waterloo, Canada
sean.sedwards@uwaterloo.ca

Abstract. Statistical model checking avoids the state space explosion problem in verification and naturally supports complex non-Markovian formalisms. Yet as a simulation-based approach, its runtime becomes excessive in the presence of rare events, and it cannot soundly analyse nondeterministic models. In this tool paper, we present modes: a statistical model checker that combines fully automated importance splitting to efficiently estimate the probabilities of rare events with smart lightweight scheduler sampling to approximate optimal schedulers in nondeterministic models. As part of the MODEST TOOLSET, it supports a variety of input formalisms natively and via the JANI exchange format. A modular software architecture allows its various features to be flexibly combined. We highlight its capabilities with an experimental evaluation across multi-core and distributed setups on three exemplary case studies.

1 Introduction

Statistical model checking (SMC [30,49]) is a formal verification technique for stochastic systems. Using a formal stochastic model, specified as e.g. a continuous-time Markov chain (CTMC) or a stochastic Petri net (SPN), SMC can answer questions such as "what is the probability of system failure between two inspections" or "what is the expected time to complete a given workload". It is gaining popularity for complex applications where traditional exhaustive probabilistic model checking is limited by the state space explosion problem and by its inability to efficiently handle non-Markovian formalisms or complex continuous dynamics. At its core, SMC

This work is supported by the 3TU.BSR project, ERC grant 695614 (POWVER), the JST ERATO HASUO Metamathematics for Systems Design project (JPMJER1603), the NWO SEQUOIA project, and SeCyT-UNC projects 05/BP12 and 05/B497.

D. Beyer and M. Huisman (Eds.): TACAS 2018, LNCS 10806, pp. 340–358, 2018.
https://doi.org/10.1007/978-3-319-89963-3_20

is the integration of classical Monte Carlo simulation with formal models. By only sampling concrete traces of the model's behaviour, its memory usage is effectively constant in the size of the state space, and it is applicable to any behaviour that can effectively be simulated.

The result of an SMC analysis is an *estimate* $\hat{q}$ of the actual quantity q together with a statistical statement on the potential error. A typical guarantee is that, with probability δ, any $\hat{q}$ will be within $\pm \epsilon$ of q. To strengthen such a guarantee, i.e. increase δ or decrease ϵ, more samples (that is, simulation runs) are needed. Compared to exhaustive model checking, SMC thus trades memory usage for accuracy or runtime. A particular challenge lies in *rare events*, i.e. behaviours of very low probability. Meaningful estimates need a small *relative* error: for a probability on the order of 10^{-19}, for example, ϵ should reasonably be on the order of 10^{-20}. In a standard Monte Carlo approach, this would require infeasibly many simulation runs.

SMC naturally works for formalisms with non-Markovian behaviour and complex continuous dynamics, such as generalised semi-Markov processes (GSMP) and stochastic hybrid Petri nets with many generally distributed transitions [42], for which the exact model checking problem is intractable or undecidable. As a simulation-based approach, however, SMC is incompatible with nondeterminism. Yet (continuous and discrete) nondeterministic choices are desirable in formal modelling for concurrency, abstraction, and to represent absence of knowledge. They occur in many formalisms such as Markov decision processes (MDP) or probabilistic timed automata (PTA [38]). In the presence of nondeterminism, quantities of interest are defined w.r.t. optimal *schedulers* (also called *policies*, *adversaries* or *strategies*) that resolve all nondeterministic choices: the verification result is the *maximum* or *minimum* probability or expected value ranging over *all* schedulers. Many SMC tools that appear to support nondeterministic models as input, e.g. PRISM [37] and UPPAAL SMC [14], implicitly use a single hidden scheduler by resolving all choices randomly. Results are thus only guaranteed to lie *somewhere* between minimum and maximum. Such implicit resolutions are a known problem affecting the trustworthiness of simulation studies [36].

In this paper, we present a statistical model checker, modes, that addresses both of the above challenges: It implements *importance splitting* [45] to efficiently estimate the probabilities of rare events and *lightweight scheduler sampling* [39] to statistically approximate optimal schedulers. Both methods can be combined to perform rare event simulation for nondeterministic models.

Rare Event Simulation. The key challenge in rare event simulation (RES) is to achieve a high degree of automation for a general class of models. Current approaches to automatically derive the importance function for importance splitting, which is critical for the method's performance, are mostly limited to restricted classes of models and properties, e.g. [7,18]. modes combines several importance splitting techniques with the compositional importance function construction of Budde et al. [5] and two different methods to derive levels and splitting factors [4]. These method combinations apply to arbitrary stochastic models with a partly discrete state space. We have shown them to work well across different Markovian and non-Markovian automata- and dataflow-based formalisms [4]. We present details on modes' support for RES in Sect. 3. Alongside PLASMA LAB [40], which implements automatic *importance sampling* [33] and semi-automatic importance splitting [32,34] for Markov chains (with APIs allowing for extensions to other models), modes is one of the most automated tools for RES on formal models today. In particular, we are not aware of any other tool that provides fully automated RES on general stochastic models.

Nondeterminism. Sound SMC for nondeterministic models is a hard problem. For MDP, Brázdil et al. [3] proposed a sound machine learning technique to incrementally improve a partial scheduler. UPPAAL STRATEGO [13] explicitly synthesises a "good" scheduler before using it for a standard SMC analysis. Both approaches suffer from worst-case memory usage linear in the number of states as all scheduler decisions must be stored explicitly. Classic memory-efficient sampling approaches like the one of Kearns et al. [35] address discounted models only. modes implements the lightweight scheduler sampling (LSS) approach introduced by Legay et al. [39]. It is currently the only technique that applies to reachability probabilities and undiscounted expected rewards—as typically considered in formal verification— that also keeps memory usage effectively constant in the number of states. Its efficiency depends only on the likelihood of sampling near-optimal schedulers. modes implements the existing LSS approaches for MDP [39] and PTA [10,26] and supports unbounded properties on Markov automata (MA [16]). We describe modes' LSS implementation in Sect. 4.

The modes Tool. modes is part of the MODEST TOOLSET [24], which also includes the explicit-state model checker mcsta and the model-based tester motest [21]. It inherits the toolset's support for a variety of input formalisms, including the high-level process algebra-based MODEST language [22] and xSADF [25], an extension of scenario-aware dataflow. Many other formalisms are supported via the JANI interchange format [6]. As simulation is easily and efficiently parallelisable, modes fully exploits multi-core systems, but can also be run in a distributed fashion across homogeneous or heterogeneous clusters of networked systems. We describe the various methods implemented to make modes a correct and scalable statistical model checker that supports classes of models ranging from CTMC to stochastic hybrid automata in Sect. 2. We focus on its software architecture in Sect. 5. Finally, Sect. 6 uses three very different case studies to highlight the varied kinds of models and analyses that modes can handle.

Previous Publications. modes was first described in a tool demonstration paper in 2012 [2]. Its focus was on the use of partial order and confluence reduction-based techniques [27] to decide on-the-fly if the nondeterminism in a model is spurious, i.e. whether maximum and minimum values are the same and an implicit randomised scheduler can safely be used. modes was again mentioned as a part of the MODEST TOOLSET in 2014 [24]. Since then, modes has been completely redesigned. The partial order and confluence-based methods have been replaced by LSS, enabling the simulation of non-spurious nondeterminism; automated importance splitting has been implemented for rare event simulation; support for MA and a subset of stochastic hybrid automata (SHA [22]) has been added; and the statistical evaluation methods have been extended and improved. Concurrently, advances in the shared infrastructure of the MODEST TOOLSET, now at version 3, provide access to new modelling features and formalisms as well as support for the JANI specification.

2   Ingredients of a Statistical Model Checker

A statistical model checker performs a number of tasks to analyse a given formal model w.r.t. to a property of interest. In this section, we describe these tasks, their challenges, and how modes implements them. All random selections in an SMC tool are typically resolved by a *pseudo*-random number generator (PRNG). For brevity, we write "random" to mean "pseudo-random" in this section.

Simulating Different Model Types. The most basic task is *simulation*: the generation of random samples—*simulation runs*—from the probability distribution over behaviours defined by the model. modes contains simulation algorithms specifically optimised for the following types of models:

- For deterministic **MDP** (Markov decision processes), i.e. DTMC (discrete-time Markov chains), simulation is simple and efficient: Obtain the current state's probability distribution over successors, randomly select one of them (using the distribution's probabilities), and continue from that state.
- Deterministic **MA** (Markov automata [16]) are CTMC. Here, the situation is similar: Obtain the set of enabled outgoing transitions, randomly select a delay from the exponential distribution parameterised by the sum of their rates, then make a random selection of one transition weighted by the transitions' rates.
- **PTA** (probabilistic timed automata [38]) extend MDP with clock variables, transition guards and location invariants as in timed automata. Like MA, they are a continuous-time model, but explicitly keep a memory of elapsed times in the clocks. They admit finite-state abstractions that preserve reachability probabilities and allow them to essentially be simulated as MDP. modes implements region graph- and zone-based simulation of PTA as MDP [10, 26]. With fewer restrictions, they can also be treated as SHA:
- **SHA** extend PTA with general continuous probability distributions and continuous variables with dynamics governed by differential equations and inclusions. modes supports deterministic SHA where all differential equations are of the form $\dot{v} = e$ for a continuous variable v and an expression e over *discrete* variables. This subset can be simulated without the need for approximations; it corresponds to deterministic rectangular hybrid automata [29]. For each transition, the SHA simulator needs to compute the set of time points at which it is enabled. These sets can be unions of several disjoint intervals, which results in relatively higher computational effort for SHA simulation.

Properties and Termination. SMC computes a value for the property on every simulation run. A run is a finite trace; consequently, standard SMC only works for linear-time properties that can be decided on finite traces. modes supports

- **transient (reachability)** queries of the form $\mathbb{P}(\neg avoid \, \mathsf{U} \, goal)$ for the probability of reaching a set of states characterised by the state formula *goal* before entering the set of states characterised by state formula *avoid*, and
- **expected reward** queries of the form $\mathbb{E}(reward \mid goal)$ for the expected accumulated reward (or cost) over the reward structure *reward* when reaching a location in the set of states characterised by *goal* for the first time.

Transient queries may be time- and reward-bounded. A state formula is an expression over the (discrete and continuous) variables of the model without any temporal operators. A reward structure assigns a rate reward $r(s) \in \mathbb{R}$ to every state s and a branch reward $r(b) \in \mathbb{R}$ to every probabilistic branch b of every transition. An example transient query is "what is the probability to reach a destination (*goal*) within an energy budget (a reward bound) while avoiding collisions (*avoid*)". Expected reward queries allow asking for e.g. the expected number of retransmissions (the reward) until a message is successfully transmitted (*goal*) in a wireless network protocol. Every query q can be turned into a *requirement* $q \sim c$ by adding a comparison $\sim \in \{\leq, \geq\}$ to a constant value $c \in \mathbb{R}$.

A simulation run ends when the value of a property is decided. For transient properties, this is the case when reaching an *avoid* state or a deadlock (value 0), or a *goal* state (value 1). To ensure termination, the probability of eventually encountering one of these events must be 1. modes additionally implements cycle detection: it keeps track of a configurable number n of previous visited states. When a run returns to a previous state without intermediate steps of probability <1, it will loop forever on this cycle and the run has value 0. modes uses $n = 1$ by default for good performance while still allowing models built for model checking, which avoid deadlocks but often contain terminal states with self-loops, to be simulated. For expected rewards, when entering a *goal* state, the property is decided with the value being the sum of the rewards along the run.

Statistical Evaluation of Samples. n simulation runs provide a sequence of independent values $v_1, \ldots, v_n$ for the property. $\hat{v}_n = \frac{1}{n} \sum_{i=1}^{n} v_i$ is an unbiased estimator of the actual probability or expected reward v. An SMC tool must stop generating runs at some point, and quantify the statistical properties of the estimate $\hat{v} = \hat{v}_n$ returned to the user. modes implements the following methods:

– For a given half-width w and confidence δ, the **CI** method returns a confidence interval $[x, y]$ that contains $\hat{v}$, with $y - x = 2 \cdot w$. Its guarantee is that, if the SMC analysis is repeated many times, $100 \cdot \delta \%$ of the confidence intervals will contain v. For transient properties, where the v_i are sampled from a Bernoulli distribution, modes constructs a binomial proportion confidence interval. For expected rewards, the underlying distribution is unknown, and modes uses the standard normal (or Gaussian) confidence interval. This relies on the central limit theorem for means, assuming a "large enough" n. modes requires $n \geq 50$ as a heuristic. modes requires the user to specify δ plus either of w and n. If n is not specified, the CI method becomes a sequential procedure: generate runs until the with of the interval for confidence δ is below $2 \cdot w$. The CI method can be turned into a hypothesis test for requirements $q \sim c$ by checking whether $\hat{v} \geq y$ or $\hat{v} \leq x$, and returning undecided if $\hat{v}$ is inside the interval. When n is unspecified, this is the Chow-Robbins sequential test [44]. Finally, modes can be instructed to interpret the value of w as a relative half-width, i.e. the final interval will have width $\hat{v} \cdot 2 \cdot w$. This is useful for rare events.
– The **APMC** [30] method, based on the Okamoto bound [41], guarantees for error ϵ and confidence δ that $\mathbb{P}(|\hat{v} - v| > \epsilon) < \delta$. It only applies to the Bernoulli-distributed samples for transient properties here. modes requires the user to

specify any two of ϵ, δ and n, out of which the missing value can be computed. The APMC method can be used as a hypothesis test for $\mathbb{P}(\cdot) \sim c$ by checking whether $\hat{v} \geq c + \epsilon$ or $\hat{v} \leq c - \epsilon$, and returning undecided if neither is true.

- modes also implements Wald's **SPRT**, the sequential probability ratio test [47]. As a sequential hypothesis test, it has no predetermined n, but decides on-the-fly whether more samples are needed as they come in. It is a test for Bernoulli-distributed quantities, i.e. it only applies to transient requirements of the form $\mathbb{P}(\cdot) \sim c$. For indifference level ϵ and error α, it stops when the collected samples so far provide sufficient evidence to decide between $\mathbb{P}(\cdot) \geq c + \epsilon$ or $\mathbb{P}(\cdot) \leq c - \epsilon$ with probability $\leq \alpha$ of wrongly accepting either hypothesis.

For a more detailed description of these and other statistical methods and especially hypothesis tests for SMC, we refer the interested reader to [44].

Distributed Sample Generation. Simulation is easily and efficiently parallelisable. Yet a naïve implementation of the statistical evaluation—processing the values from the runs in the order they flow in—risks introducing a bias in a parallel setting. Consider estimating the probability of system failure when simulation runs that encounter failure states are shorter than other runs, and thus quicker. In parallel simulation, failure runs will tend to arrive earlier and more frequently, thus overestimating the probability of failure. To avoid such bias, modes uses the adaptive schedule first implemented in YMER [48]. It adapts to differences in the speed of nodes by scheduling to process more future results from fast nodes when current results come in quickly. It always commits to a schedule *a priori* before the actual results arrive, ensuring the absence of bias. It is thus well-suited for heterogeneous clusters of machines with significant performance differences.

3 Automated Rare Event Simulation

With the standard confidence of $\delta = 0.95$, we have $n \approx 0.37/\epsilon^2$ in the APMC method: for every decimal digit of precision, the number of runs increases by a factor of 100. If we attempt to estimate probabilities on the order of 10^{-4}, i.e. $\epsilon \approx 10^{-5}$, we need billions of runs and days or weeks of simulation time. This is the problem tackled by rare event simulation (RES) techniques [45]. modes implements RES for transient properties via *importance splitting*, which iteratively increases the simulation effort for states "closer" to the goal set. Closeness is represented by an *importance function* $f_I \colon S \to \mathbb{N}$ that maps each state in S to its importance in $\{0, \dots, \max f_I\}$. The performance, but not the correctness, of all splitting methods hinges on the quality of the importance function.

Deriving Importance Functions. Traditionally, the importance function is specified ad hoc by a RES expert. Striving for usability by *domain* experts, modes implements the compositional importance function generation method of [5] that is applicable to any compositional stochastic model $M = M_1 \parallel \dots \parallel M_n$ with a partly discrete state space. We write $s|_i$ for the projection of state s of M to the discrete local variables of component M_i. The method works as follows [4]:

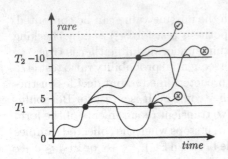

Fig. 1. Illustration of RESTART [4]   **Fig. 2.** Illustration of fixed effort [4]

1. Convert the goal set formula *goal* to negation normal form (NNF) and associate each literal $goal^j$ with the component $\mathrm{M}(goal^j)$ whose local state variables it refers to. Literals must not refer to multiple components.
2. Explore the *discrete part* of the state space of each component M_i. For each $goal^j$ with $\mathrm{M}_i = \mathrm{M}(goal^j)$, use reverse breadth-first search to compute the local minimum distance $f_i^j(s|_i)$ of each state $s|_i$ to a state satisfying $goal^j$.
3. In the syntax of the NNF of *goal*, replace every occurrence of $goal^j$ by $f_i^j(s|_i)$ with i such that $\mathrm{M}_i = \mathrm{M}(goal^j)$, and every Boolean operator $\wedge$ or $\vee$ by $+$. Use the resulting formula as the importance function $f_I(s)$.

The method takes into account both the structure of the goal set formula and the structure of the state space. This is in contrast to the approach of Jégourel et al. [32], implemented in a semi-automated fashion in PLASMA LAB [34, 40], that only considers the structure of the (more complex linear-time) logical property. The memory usage of the compositional method is determined by the number of discrete local states (required to be finite) over all components. Typically, component state spaces are small even when the composed state space explodes.

Levels and Splitting Factors. We also need to specify *when* and *how much* to "split", i.e. increase the simulation effort. For this purpose, the values of the importance function are partitioned into *levels* and a *splitting factor* is chosen for each level. Splitting too much too often will degrade performance (oversplitting), while splitting too little will cause starvation, i.e. few runs that reach the rare event. It is thus critical to choose good levels and splitting factors. Again, to avoid the user having to make these choices ad hoc, modes implements two methods to compute them automatically. One is based on the sequential Monte Carlo splitting technique [8], while the other method, named *expected success* [4], has been newly developed for modes. It strives to find levels and factors that lead to one run moving up from one level to the next in the expectation.

Importance Splitting Runs. The derivation of importance function, levels and splitting factors is a preprocessing step. Importance splitting then replaces the simulation algorithm by a variant that takes this information into account to more often encounter the rare event. modes implements three importance splitting techniques: RESTART, fixed effort and fixed success.

RESTART [46] is illustrated in Fig. 1: As soon as a RESTART run crosses the threshold into a higher level, $n_\ell - 1$ new child runs are started from the first state in the new level, where n_ℓ is the splitting factor of level ℓ. When a run moves below its creation level, it ends. It also ends on reaching an *avoid* or *goal* state. The result of a RESTART run—consisting of a main and several child runs—is the number of runs that reach *goal* times $1/\prod_\ell n_\ell$, i.e. a rational number ≥ 0.

Runs of the *fixed effort* method [17,19], illustrated in Fig. 2, are rather different. They consist of a fixed number of partial runs on each level, each of which ends when it crosses into the next higher level or encounters a *goal* or *avoid* state. When all partial runs for a level have ended, the next round starts from the previously encountered initial states of the next higher level. When a fixed effort run ends, the fraction of partial runs started in a level that moved up approximates the conditional probability of reaching the next level given that the current level was reached. If *goal* states exist only on the highest level, the overall result is the product of all of these fractions, i.e. a rational number in $[0,1]$.

Fixed success [1] is a variant of fixed effort that generates partial runs until a fixed number of them have reached the next higher level. For all three methods, the average of the result of many runs is again an unbiased estimator for the probability of the transient property [19]. However, each run is no longer a Bernoulli trial. Of the statistical evaluation methods offered by modes, only CI with normal confidence intervals is thus applicable. For a deeper discussion of the challenges in the statistical evaluation of rare event simulation results, we refer the interested reader to [43]. To the best of our knowledge, modes is today the most automated rare event simulator for general stochastic models. In particular, it defaults to the combination of RESTART with the expected success method for level calculation, which has shown consistently good performance [4].

4   Scheduler Sampling for Nondeterminism

Resolving nondeterminism in a randomised way leads to estimates that only lie *somewhere* between the desired extremal values. In addition to computing probabilities or expected rewards, we also need to find a (near-)optimal scheduler.

Lightweight Scheduler Sampling. modes implements the lightweight scheduler sampling (LSS) approach for MDP of [39] that identifies a scheduler by a single integer (typically of 32 bits). This allows to randomly select a large number m of schedulers (i.e. integers), perform standard or rare event simulation for each, and report the maximum and minimum estimates over all sampled schedulers as approximations of the actual extremal values. We show the core of the lightweight approach—performing a simulation run for a given scheduler identifier σ—for MDP and transient properties as Algorithm 1. An MDP consists of a countable set of states S, a transition function T that maps each state to a finite *set* of probability distributions over successor states, and an initial state

Input: MDP $\langle S, T, s_0 \rangle$, transient property ϕ, scheduler id $\sigma \in \mathbb{Z}$

```
1  s := s_0, π := s_0
2  while φ(π) = undecided do
3      U_nd.initialise(H(σ.s))          // use hash of σ and s as seed for U_nd
4      if T(s) = ∅ then return false    // end of run due to deadlock
5      μ := ⌈U_nd · |T(s)|⌉-th element of T(s)   // use U_nd to select transition
6      s' := μ ∘ U_pr.next()            // use U_pr to select successor state according to μ
7      π := π.s', s := s'               // append s' to π and continue from s'
8  return φ(π)
```

Algorithm 1. Simulation for an MDP and a fixed scheduler id [10]

s_0. The algorithm uses two PRNG: U_{pr} to simulate the probabilistic choices (line 6), and U_{nd} to resolve the nondeterministic ones (line 5). We want σ to represent a deterministic memoryless scheduler: within one simulation run as well as in different runs for the same value of σ, U_{nd} must always make the same choice for the same state s. To achieve this, U_{nd} is re-initialised with a seed based on σ and s in every step (line 3). The overall effectiveness of the lightweight approach only depends on the likelihood of selecting a σ that represents a (near-)optimal scheduler. We want to sample "uniformly" from the space of all schedulers to avoid actively biasing against "good" schedulers. Algorithm 1 achieves this naturally for MDP.

Beyond MDP. LSS can be adapted to any model and type of property where the class of optimal schedulers only uses *discrete* input to make its decision for every state [26]. This is obviously the case for discrete-space discrete-time models like MDP. It means that LSS can directly be applied to MA and *time-unbounded* properties, too. In addition to MDP and MA, modes also supports two LSS methods for PTA, based on a variant of forwards reachability with zones [10] and the region graph abstraction [26], respectively. While the former includes zone operations with worst-case runtime exponential in the number of clocks, the latter implements all operations in linear time. It exploits a novel data structure for regions based on representative valuations that performs very well in practice [26]. Extending LSS to models with general continuous probability distributions such as stochastic automata [11] is hindered by optimal schedulers requiring non-discrete information (the values and expiration times of all clocks [9]). modes currently provides prototypical LSS support for SA encoded in a particular form and various restricted classes of schedulers as described in [9].

Bounds and Error Accumulation. The results of an SMC analysis with LSS are lower bounds for maximum and upper bounds for minimum values up to the specified statistical error and confidence. They can thus be used to e.g. *disprove* safety (the maximum probability to reach an unsafe state is above a threshold) or *prove* schedulability (there is a scheduler that makes it likely to complete the workload in time), but not the opposite. The accumulation of statistical error introduced by the repeated simulation experiments over multiple schedulers must also be accounted for. [12] shows how to modify the APMC method accordingly and turn the SPRT into a correct sequential test *over schedulers*. In addition to these, modes allows the CI method to be used with LSS by applying the standard Šidák correction for multiple comparisons. This enables LSS for expected rewards and RES. All the adjustments essentially increase the required confidence depending on the (maximum) number of schedulers to be sampled.

Two-Phase and Smart Sampling. If an SMC analysis for fixed statistical parameters would need n runs on a deterministic model, it will need significantly more than $m \cdot n$ runs for a nondeterministic model when m schedulers are sampled due to the increase in the required confidence. modes implements a two-phase approach and smart sampling [12] to reduce this overhead. The former's first phase consists of performing n simulation runs for each of the m schedulers. The scheduler that resulted in the maximum (or minimum) value is selected, and independently evaluated once more with n runs to produce the final estimate. The first phase is a heuristic to find a near-optimal scheduler before the second phase estimates the value under this scheduler according to the required statistical parameters. Smart sampling generalises this principle to multiple phases, dropping only the "worst" *half* of the evaluated schedulers between phases. It starts with an informed guess of good initial values for n and m. For details, see [12]. Smart sampling tends to find more extremal schedulers faster while the two-phase approach has predictable performance as it always needs $(m + 1) \cdot n$ runs. We thus use the two-phase approach for our experiments in Sect. 6.

5   Architecture and Implementation

modes is implemented in C# and works on Linux, Mac OS X and Windows systems. It builds on a solid foundation of shared infrastructure with other tools of the MODEST TOOLSET. This includes input language parsers that map MODEST, xSADF and JANI input into a common internal metamodel for networks of stochastic hybrid automata with rewards and discrete variables. Before simulation, every model is compiled to bytecode, making the metamodel executable. The same compilation engine is also used by the mcsta and motest tools.

The architecture of the SMC-specific part of modes is shown as a class diagram in Fig. 3. Boxes represent classes, with rounded rectangles for abstract classes and invisible boxes for interfaces. Solid lines are inheritance relations. Dotted lines are associations, with double arrows for collection associations. The architecture mirrors the three distinct tasks of a statistical model checker: the generation of individual simulation runs and per-run evaluation of properties, implemented in modes by *RunGenerator* and *RunEvaluator*, respectively; the coordination of simulation over multiple threads across CPU cores and networked machines, implemented by classes derived from *Worker* and *IWorkerHost*; and the statistical evaluation of simulation runs, implemented by *PropertyEvaluator*.

The central component of modes' architecture is the *Master*. It compiles the model, derives the importance function, sends both to the workers (on the same

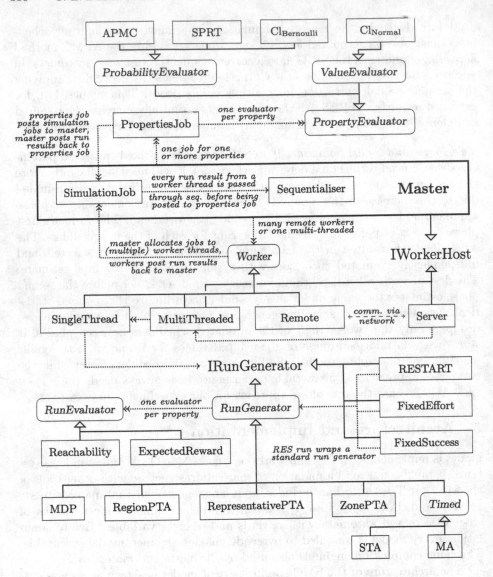

Fig. 3. The software architecture of the modes statistical model checker

or different machines), and instantiates a *PropertiesJob* for every partition of the
properties to be analysed that can share simulation runs.[1] Each *PropertiesJob*
then posts simulation jobs back to the master in parallel or in sequence. A simulation job is a description of how to generate and evaluate runs: which run type
(i.e. *RunGenerator* derived class) to use, whether to wrap it in an importance

---

[1] Using the same set of runs for multiple properties is an optimisation at the cost of
statistical independence. modes can also generate independent runs for each property.

splitting method, whether to simulate for a specific scheduler id, which compiled expressions to evaluate to determine termination and the values of the runs, etc. The master allocates posted jobs to available simulation threads offered by the workers, and notifies workers when a job is scheduled for one of their threads. As the result for an individual run is handed from the *RunEvaluator* by the *RunGenerator* via the workers to the master, it is fed into a *Sequentialiser* that implements the adaptive schedule for bias avoidance. Only after that, possibly at a later point, is it handed on to the *PropertiesJob* for statistical evaluation.

For illustration, consider a *PropertiesJob* for LSS with 10 schedulers, RES with RESTART, and the expected success method for level calculation. It is given the importance function by the master, and its first task is to compute the levels. It posts a simulation job for fixed effort runs with level information collection to the master. Depending on the current workload from other *PropertiesJobs*, the master will allocate many threads to this job. Once enough results have come in, the *PropertiesJob* terminates the simulation job, computes the levels and splitting factors, and starts with the actual simulations: It selects 10 random scheduler identifiers and concurrently posts for each of them a simulation job for RESTART runs. The master will try to allocate available threads evenly over these jobs. As results come in, the evaluation may finish early for some schedulers, at which point the master will be instructed to stop the corresponding simulation job. It can then allocate the newly free threads to other jobs. This scheme results in a maximal exploitation of the available parallelism across workers and threads.

Due to the modularity of this architecture, it is easy to extend modes in different ways. For example, to support a new type of model (say, non-linear hybrid automata) or a new RES method, only a new *(1)RunGenerator* needs to be implemented. Adding another statistical evaluation method from [44] means adding a new *PropertyEvaluator*, and so on.

In distributed simulation, an instance of modes is started on each node with the --server parameter. This results in the creation of an instance of the *Server* class instead of a *Master*, which listens for incoming connections. Once all servers are running, a master can be started with a list of hosts to connect to. modes comes with a template script to automate this task on SLURM-based clusters.

6   Experiments

We present three case studies in this section. They have been chosen to highlight modes' capabilities in terms of the diverse types of models it supports, its ability to distribute work across compute clusters, and the new analyses possible with RES and LSS. None of them has been studied before with modes or the combinations of methods that we apply here. Our experiments ran on an Intel Core i7-4790 workstation (3.6–4.0 GHz, 4 cores), a homogeneous cluster of 40 AMD Opteron 4386 nodes (3.1–3.8 GHz, 8 cores), and an inhomogeneous cluster of 15 nodes with different Intel Xeon processors. All systems run 64-bit Linux. We use 1, 2 or 4 simulation threads on the workstation (denoted "1", "2" and "4" in our tables), and n nodes with t simulation threads each on the clusters (denoted

Table 1. Performance and scalability on the electric vehicle charging case study

	$n_{fail} = 2$		$n_{fail} = 3$		$n_{fail} = 4$		$n_{fail} = 5$	
	MC	RES	MC	RES	MC	RES	MC	RES
conf. interval	[6.4E−2, 7.8E−2]		[5.2E−3, 6.4E−3]		[2.7E−4, 3.2E−4]		[8.3E−6, 1.0E−5]	
1	2 s	4 s	30 s	19 s	585 s	206 s		
2	1 s	2 s	15 s	11 s	315 s	101 s	—	
4	1 s	1 s	8 s	5 s	163 s	69 s		
5 × 4	1 s	1 s	4 s	4 s	69 s	23 s	2241 s	496 s
5 × 8	1 s	2 s	2 s	3 s	40 s	16 s	1238 s	328 s
40 × 2	0 s	1 s	1 s	2 s	16 s	8 s	483 s	135 s
20 × 8	0 s	2 s	1 s	2 s	10 s	6 s	314 s	105 s
40 × 8	0 s	2 s	1 s	3 s	5 s	6 s	159 s	64 s

"$n \times t$"). We used a one-hour timeout, marked "—" in the tables. Note that runtimes cannot directly be compared between the workstation and the clusters.

Electric Vehicle Charging. We first consider a model of an electric vehicle charging station. It is a MODEST model adapted from the "extended" case study of [42]: a stochastic hybrid Petri net with general transitions, which in turn is based on the work in [31]. The scenario we model is of an electric vehicle being connected to the charger every evening in order to be recharged the next morning. The charging process may be delayed due to high load on the power grid, and the exact time at which the vehicle is needed in the morning follows a normal distribution. We consider one week of operation and compute the probability that the desired level of charge is not reached on any $n_{fail} \in \{2, \dots, 5\}$ of the seven mornings.

This model is not amenable to exhaustive model checking due to the non-Markovian continuous probability distributions and the hybrid dynamics modelling the charging process. However, it is deterministic. We thus applied modes with standard Monte Carlo simulation (MC) as well as with RES using RESTART. We performed the same analysis on different configurations of the workstation and the homogeneous cluster. To compare MC and RES, we use CI with $\delta = 0.95$ and a relative half-with of 10 % for both. All other parameters of modes are set to default values, which implies an automatic compositional importance function and the expected success method to determine levels and splitting factors. The results are shown in Table 1. Row "conf. interval" gives the average confidence intervals that we obtained over all experiments.

RES starts to noticeably pay off as soon as probabilities are on the order of 10^{-4}. The runtime of RESTART is known to heavily depend on the levels and splitting factors, and we indeed noticed large variations in runtime for RES over several repetitions of the experiments. The runtimes for RES should thus not be used to judge the speedup w.r.t. parallelisation. However, when looking at the MC runtimes, we see good speedups as we increase the number of threads per node, and near-ideal speedups as we increase the total number of nodes, as long as there is a sufficient amount of work.

Table 2. Performance and results for the low-latency wireless network case study

		time	$\mathbb{P}(i < 4\,\mathbf{U}\,failed)$	$\mathbb{P}(i < 4\,\mathbf{U}\,offline_{\{1\}})$	$\mathbb{P}(i < 4\,\mathbf{U}\,offline_{\{2\}})$
optimal			$[0.028, 0.472]$	$[0.026, 0.269]$	$[0\quad\,, 0.424]$
1	100	3523 s			
2	100	2045 s	$[0.041, 0.363]$	$[0.030, 0.189]$	$[0.000, 0.309]$
4	100	1205 s			
20×8	1000	607 s			
40×8	1000	308 s	$[0.033, 0.383]$	$[0.028, 0.242]$	$[0.000, 0.327]$

Although this model was not designed with RES in mind and has only moderately rare events, the fully automated methods of modes could be applied directly, and they significantly improved performance. For a detailed experimental comparison of the RES methods implemented in modes on a larger set of examples, including events with probabilities as low as $4.8 \cdot 10^{-23}$, we refer the reader to [4].

Low-latency Wireless Networks. We now turn to the PTA model of a low-latency wireless networking protocol being used among three stations, originally presented in [15]. We take the original model, increase the probability of message loss, and make one of the communication links nondeterministically drop messages. This allows us to study the influence of the message loss probabilities and the protocol's robustness to adversarial interference. The model *is* amenable to model checking, as demonstrated in [15]. It allows us to show that modes can be applied to such models originally built for traditional verification, and since we can calculate the precise maximum and minimum values of all properties via model checking, we have a reference to evaluate the results of LSS.

We show the results of using modes with LSS on this model in Table 2. Row "optimal" lists the maximum and minimum probabilities computed via model checking for three properties: the probability that the protocol fails within four iterations, and that either the first or the second station goes offline. We used the two-phase LSS method with $m = 100$ schedulers on the workstation, and with $m = 1000$ schedulers on the homogeneous cluster. The intervals are the averages of the min. and max. values returned by all analyses. The statistical evaluation is APMC with $\delta = 0.95$ and $\epsilon = 0.0025$, which means that 59556 simulation runs are needed per scheduler.

Near-optimal schedulers for the minimum probabilities do not appear to be rare: we find good bounds for the minima even with 100 schedulers. However, for maximum probabilities, sampling more schedulers pays off in terms of better approximations. In all cases, the results are conservative approximations of the actual optima (as expected), and they are clearly more useful than the single value that would be obtained by other tools via a (hidden) randomised scheduler. Performance scales ideally with parallelism on the cluster, and still linearly on the workstation. For a deeper evaluation of the characteristics of LSS, including experiments on models too large for model checking, we refer the reader to the description of the original approach [12,39] and its extensions to PTA [10,26].

Table 3. Performance and results for the reliable database system case study

R	uniform scheduler			lightweight scheduler sampling (20)			
	MC	RES	conf. interval	MC	RES	min. conf. int.	max. conf. int.
2	1 s	4 s	[1.5E–2, 1.8E–2]	4 s	31 s	[1.4E–2, 1.7E–2]	[1.5E–2, 1.9E–2]
3	8 s	3 s	[1.0E–4, 1.3E–4]	181 s	26 s	[7.9E–5, 9.6E–5]	[1.3E–4, 1.6E–4]
4	816 s	13 s	[9.3E–7, 1.1E–6]	—	221 s	[6.3E–7, 7.6E–7]	[1.3E–6, 1.6E–6]
5	—	229 s	[1.1E–8, 1.3E–8]	—	3072 s	[6.2E–9, 7.6E–9]	[1.6E–8, 2.0E–8]

Redundant Database System. The redundant database system [20] is a classic RES case study. It models a system consisting of six disk clusters of $R + 2$ disks each plus two types of processors and disk controllers with R copies of each type. Component lifetimes are exponentially distributed. Components fail in one of two modes with equal probability, each mode having a different repair rate. The system is operational as long as fewer than R processors of each type, R controllers of each type, and R disks in each cluster are currently failed. The model is a CTMC with a state space too large and a transition matrix too dense for it to be amenable to model checking with symbolic tools like PRISM [37].

In the original model, any number of failed components can be repaired in parallel. We consider this unrealistic, and extend the model by a *repairman* that can repair a single component at a time. If more than one component fails during a repair, then as soon as the current repair is finished, the repairman has to decide which to repair next. Instead of enforcing a particular repair policy, we leave this decision as nondeterministic. The model thus becomes an MA. We use LSS in combination with RES to investigate the impact of the repair policy. We study the scenario where one *component* of each kind (one disk, one processor, one controller) is in failed state, and estimate the probability for *system* failure before these components are repaired. The minimum probability is achieved by a perfect repair strategy, while the maximum results from the worst possible one.

Table 3 shows the results of our LSS-plus-RES analysis with modes using default RES parameters and sampling $m = 20$ schedulers. Due to the complexity of the model, we ran this experiment on the inhomogeneous cluster only, using 16 cores on each node for 240 concurrent simulation threads in total. We see that RES needs a somewhat rare event to improve performance. We also compare LSS to the uniform randomised scheduler (as implemented in many other SMC tools). It results in a single confidence interval for the probability of failure. With LSS, we get two intervals. They do not overlap when $R \geq 3$, i.e. the repair strategy matters: a bad strategy makes failure approximately twice as likely as a good strategy! Since the results of LSS are conservative, the difference between the worst and the best strategy may be even larger.

Experiment Replication. To enable independent replication of our experimental results, we have created a publicly available evaluation artifact [23]. It contains the version of modes and the model files used for our experiments, the raw experimental results, summarising tabular views of those results (from which we derived Tables 1, 2 and 3), and a Linux shell script to automatically replicate a subset of the experiments. Since the complete experiments take several hours to complete and require powerful hardware and computer clusters, we have selected a subset for the replication script. Using the virtual machine of the TACAS 2018 Artifact Evaluation [28] on typical workstation hardware of 2017, it runs to completion in less than one hour while still substantiating our main results.

7 Conclusion

We presented modes, the MODEST TOOLSET's distributed statistical model checker. It provides methods to tackle both of the prominent challenges in simulation: nondeterminism and rare events. Its modular software architecture allows its various features to be easily combined and extended. For the first time, we used lightweight scheduler sampling with Markov automata, and combined it with rare event simulation to gain insights into a challenging case study that, currently, cannot be analysed for the same aspects with any other tool that we are aware of. modes is available for download at www.modestchecker.net.

Acknowledgments. The authors thank Carina Pilch and Sebastian Junges for their support with the *vehicle charging* and *wireless networks* case studies.

Data Availability. The data generated in our experimental evaluation is archived and available at DOI 10.4121/uuid:64cd25f4-4192-46d1-a951-9f99b452b48f [23].

References

1. Amrein, M., Künsch, H.R.: A variant of importance splitting for rare event estimation: fixed number of successes. ACM Trans. Model. Comput. Simul. **21**(2), 13:1–13:20 (2011)
2. Bogdoll, J., Hartmanns, A., Hermanns, H.: Simulation and statistical model checking for Modestly nondeterministic models. In: Schmitt, J.B. (ed.) MMB&DFT 2012. LNCS, vol. 7201, pp. 249–252. Springer, Heidelberg (2012). https://doi.org/10.1007/978-3-642-28540-0_20
3. Brázdil, T., Chatterjee, K., Chmelík, M., Forejt, V., Křetínský, J., Kwiatkowska, M., Parker, D., Ujma, M.: Verification of Markov decision processes using learning algorithms. In: Cassez, F., Raskin, J.-F. (eds.) ATVA 2014. LNCS, vol. 8837, pp. 98–114. Springer, Cham (2014). https://doi.org/10.1007/978-3-319-11936-6_8
4. Budde, C.E., D'Argenio, P.R., Hartmanns, A.: Better automated importance splitting for transient rare events. In: Larsen, K.G., Sokolsky, O., Wang, J. (eds.) SETTA 2017. LNCS, vol. 10606, pp. 42–58. Springer, Cham (2017). https://doi.org/10.1007/978-3-319-69483-2_3
5. Budde, C.E., D'Argenio, P.R., Monti, R.E.: Compositional construction of importance functions in fully automated importance splitting. In: VALUETOOLS. ICST (2016)
6. Budde, C.E., Dehnert, C., Hahn, E.M., Hartmanns, A., Junges, S., Turrini, A.: JANI: quantitative model and tool interaction. In: Legay, A., Margaria, T. (eds.) TACAS 2017. LNCS, vol. 10206, pp. 151–168. Springer, Heidelberg (2017). https://doi.org/10.1007/978-3-662-54580-5_9

7. Cérou, F., Guyader, A.: Adaptive multilevel splitting for rare event analysis. Stochast. Anal. Appl. **25**(2), 417–443 (2007)
8. Cérou, F., Moral, P.D., Furon, T., Guyader, A.: Sequential Monte Carlo for rare event estimation. Stat. Comput. **22**(3), 795–808 (2012)
9. D'Argenio, P.R., Gerhold, M., Hartmanns, A., Sedwards, S.: A hierarchy of scheduler classes for stochastic automata. In: FoSSaCS. LNCS, vol. 10803. Springer (2018, to appear)
10. D'Argenio, P.R., Hartmanns, A., Legay, A., Sedwards, S.: Statistical approximation of optimal schedulers for probabilistic timed automata. In: Ábrahám, E., Huisman, M. (eds.) IFM 2016. LNCS, vol. 9681, pp. 99–114. Springer, Cham (2016). https://doi.org/10.1007/978-3-319-33693-0_7
11. D'Argenio, P.R., Katoen, J.P.: A theory of stochastic systems part I: stochastic automata. Inf. Comput. **203**(1), 1–38 (2005)
12. D'Argenio, P.R., Legay, A., Sedwards, S., Traonouez, L.M.: Smart sampling for lightweight verification of Markov decision processes. STTT **17**(4), 469–484 (2015)
13. David, A., Jensen, P.G., Larsen, K.G., Mikučionis, M., Taankvist, J.H.: UPPAAL STRATEGO. In: Baier, C., Tinelli, C. (eds.) TACAS 2015. LNCS, vol. 9035, pp. 206–211. Springer, Heidelberg (2015). https://doi.org/10.1007/978-3-662-46681-0_16
14. David, A., Larsen, K.G., Legay, A., Mikučionis, M., Wang, Z.: Time for statistical model checking of real-time systems. In: Gopalakrishnan, G., Qadeer, S. (eds.) CAV 2011. LNCS, vol. 6806, pp. 349–355. Springer, Heidelberg (2011). https://doi.org/10.1007/978-3-642-22110-1_27
15. Dombrowski, C., Junges, S., Katoen, J.P., Gross, J.: Model-checking assisted protocol design for ultra-reliable low-latency wireless networks. In: SRDS, pp. 307–316. IEEE (2016)
16. Eisentraut, C., Hermanns, H., Zhang, L.: On probabilistic automata in continuous time. In: LICS, pp. 342–351. IEEE Computer Society (2010)
17. Garvels, M.J.J., Kroese, D.P.: A comparison of RESTART implementations. In: Winter Simulation Conference, pp. 601–608 (1998)
18. Garvels, M.J.J., van Ommeren, J.C.W., Kroese, D.P.: On the importance function in splitting simulation. Eur. Trans. Telecommun. **13**(4), 363–371 (2002)
19. Garvels, M.J.J.: The splitting method in rare event simulation. Ph.D. thesis, University of Twente, Enschede, The Netherlands (2000)
20. Goyal, A., Shahabuddin, P., Heidelberger, P., Nicola, V.F., Glynn, P.W.: A unified framework for simulating Markovian models of highly dependable systems. IEEE Trans. Comput. **41**(1), 36–51 (1992)
21. Graf-Brill, A., Hartmanns, A., Hermanns, H., Rose, S.: Modelling and certification for electric mobility. In: Industrial Informatics (INDIN). IEEE (2017)
22. Hahn, E.M., Hartmanns, A., Hermanns, H., Katoen, J.: A compositional modelling and analysis framework for stochastic hybrid systems. Formal Methods Syst. Des. **43**(2), 191–232 (2013)
23. Hartmanns, A.: A Statistical Model Checker for Nondeterminism and Rare Events (artifact). 4TU.Centre for Research Data (2018). http://doi.org/10.4121/uuid:64cd25f4-4192-46d1-a951-9f99b452b48f
24. Hartmanns, A., Hermanns, H.: The Modest Toolset: an integrated environment for quantitative modelling and verification. In: Ábrahám, E., Havelund, K. (eds.) TACAS 2014. LNCS, vol. 8413, pp. 593–598. Springer, Heidelberg (2014). https://doi.org/10.1007/978-3-642-54862-8_51
25. Hartmanns, A., Hermanns, H., Bungert, M.: Flexible support for time and costs in scenario-aware dataflow. In: EMSOFT. ACM (2016)

26. Hartmanns, A., Sedwards, S., D'Argenio, P.R.: Efficient simulation-based verification of probabilistic timed automata. In: Winter Simulation Conference (2017)
27. Hartmanns, A., Timmer, M.: Sound statistical model checking for MDP using partial order and confluence reduction. STTT 17(4), 429–456 (2015)
28. Hartmanns, A., Wendler, P.: TACAS 2018 Artifact Evaluation VM. Figshare (2018). https://doi.org/10.6084/m9.figshare.5896615
29. Henzinger, T.A., Kopke, P.W., Puri, A., Varaiya, P.: What's decidable about hybrid automata? J. Comput. Syst. Sci. 57(1), 94–124 (1998)
30. Hérault, T., Lassaigne, R., Magniette, F., Peyronnet, S.: Approximate probabilistic model checking. In: Steffen, B., Levi, G. (eds.) VMCAI 2004. LNCS, vol. 2937, pp. 73–84. Springer, Heidelberg (2004). https://doi.org/10.1007/978-3-540-24622-0_8
31. Huls, J., Remke, A.: Coordinated charging strategies for plug-in electric vehicles to ensure a robust charging process. In: VALUETOOLS. ICST (2016)
32. Jégourel, C., Legay, A., Sedwards, S.: Importance splitting for statistical model checking rare properties. In: Sharygina, N., Veith, H. (eds.) CAV 2013. LNCS, vol. 8044, pp. 576–591. Springer, Heidelberg (2013). https://doi.org/10.1007/978-3-642-39799-8_38
33. Jégourel, C., Legay, A., Sedwards, S.: Command-based importance sampling for statistical model checking. Theor. Comput. Sci. 649, 1–24 (2016)
34. Jégourel, C., Legay, A., Sedwards, S., Traonouez, L.M.: Distributed verification of rare properties using importance splitting observers. In: ECEASST, vol. 72 (2015)
35. Kearns, M.J., Mansour, Y., Ng, A.Y.: A sparse sampling algorithm for near-optimal planning in large Markov decision processes. Machine Learn. 49(2–3), 193–208 (2002)
36. Kurkowski, S., Camp, T., Colagrosso, M.: MANET simulation studies: the incredibles. Mob. Comput. Commun. Rev. 9(4), 50–61 (2005)
37. Kwiatkowska, M., Norman, G., Parker, D.: PRISM 4.0: verification of probabilistic real-time systems. In: Gopalakrishnan, G., Qadeer, S. (eds.) CAV 2011. LNCS, vol. 6806, pp. 585–591. Springer, Heidelberg (2011). https://doi.org/10.1007/978-3-642-22110-1_47
38. Kwiatkowska, M.Z., Norman, G., Segala, R., Sproston, J.: Automatic verification of real-time systems with discrete probability distributions. Theor. Comput. Sci. 282(1), 101–150 (2002)
39. Legay, A., Sedwards, S., Traonouez, L.-M.: Scalable verification of Markov decision processes. In: Canal, C., Idani, A. (eds.) SEFM 2014. LNCS, vol. 8938, pp. 350–362. Springer, Cham (2015). https://doi.org/10.1007/978-3-319-15201-1_23
40. Legay, A., Sedwards, S., Traonouez, L.-M.: Plasma Lab: a modular statistical model checking platform. In: Margaria, T., Steffen, B. (eds.) ISoLA 2016. LNCS, vol. 9952, pp. 77–93. Springer, Cham (2016). https://doi.org/10.1007/978-3-319-47166-2_6
41. Okamoto, M.: Some inequalities relating to the partial sum of binomial probabilities. Ann. Inst. Stat. Math. 10(1), 29–35 (1959)
42. Pilch, C., Remke, A.: Statistical model checking for hybrid Petri nets with multiple general transitions. In: DSN, pp. 475–486. IEEE Computer Society (2017)
43. Reijsbergen, D., de Boer, P.-T., Scheinhardt, W.: Hypothesis testing for rare-event simulation: limitations and possibilities. In: Margaria, T., Steffen, B. (eds.) ISoLA 2016. LNCS, vol. 9952, pp. 16–26. Springer, Cham (2016). https://doi.org/10.1007/978-3-319-47166-2_2
44. Reijsbergen, D., de Boer, P., Scheinhardt, W.R.W., Haverkort, B.R.: On hypothesis testing for statistical model checking. STTT 17(4), 377–395 (2015)
45. Rubino, G., Tuffin, B. (eds.): Rare Event Simulation Using Monte Carlo Methods. Wiley, New York (2009)

358   C. E. Budde et al.

46. Villén-Altamirano, M., Villén-Altamirano, J.: RESTART: a method for accelerating rare event simulations. In: Queueing, Performance and Control in ATM (ITC-13), pp. 71–76. Elsevier (1991)
47. Wald, A.: Sequential tests of statistical hypotheses. Ann. Math. Stat. **16**(2), 117–186 (1945)
48. Younes, H.L.S.: Ymer: a statistical model checker. In: Etessami, K., Rajamani, S.K. (eds.) CAV 2005. LNCS, vol. 3576, pp. 429–433. Springer, Heidelberg (2005). https://doi.org/10.1007/11513988_43
49. Younes, H.L.S., Simmons, R.G.: Probabilistic verification of discrete event systems using acceptance sampling. In: Brinksma, E., Larsen, K.G. (eds.) CAV 2002. LNCS, vol. 2404, pp. 223–235. Springer, Heidelberg (2002). https://doi.org/10.1007/3-540-45657-0_17

Temporal Logic and Mu-calculus

Permutation Games for the Weakly Aconjunctive μ-Calculus

Daniel Hausmann$^{(\boxtimes)}$, Lutz Schröder$^{(\boxtimes)}$, and Hans-Peter Deifel

Friedrich-Alexander-Universität Erlangen-Nürnberg,
Erlangen, Germany
{daniel.hausmann,lutz.schroeder}@fau.de

Abstract. We introduce a natural notion of limit-deterministic parity automata and present a method that uses such automata to construct satisfiability games for the weakly aconjunctive fragment of the μ-calculus. To this end we devise a method that determinizes limit-deterministic parity automata of size n with k priorities through limit-deterministic Büchi automata to deterministic parity automata of size $\mathcal{O}((nk)!)$ and with $\mathcal{O}(nk)$ priorities. The construction relies on limit-determinism to avoid the full complexity of the Safra/Piterman-construction by using partial permutations of states in place of Safra-Trees. By showing that limit-deterministic parity automata can be used to recognize unsuccessful branches in pre-tableaux for the weakly aconjunctive μ-calculus, we obtain satisfiability games of size $\mathcal{O}((nk)!)$ with $\mathcal{O}(nk)$ priorities for weakly aconjunctive input formulas of size n and alternation-depth k. A prototypical implementation that employs a tableau-based global caching algorithm to solve games on-the-fly shows promising initial results.

1 Introduction

The modal μ-calculus [15] is an expressive logic for reasoning about concurrent systems. Its satisfiability problem is ExpTime-complete [5]. Due to nesting of fixpoints, the semantic structure of the μ-calculus is quite involved, which is reflected in the high degree of sophistication of reasoning algorithms for the μ-calculus. One convenient modular approach is the definition of suitable *satisfiability games* (e.g. [10]); solving such games (i.e. computing their winning regions) then amounts to deciding the satisfiability of the input formulas. A standard method for obtaining satisfiability games is to first construct a *tracking automaton* that accepts the *bad branches* in a pre-tableau for the input formula, i.e. those that infinitely defer satisfaction of a least fixpoint; this automaton then is determinized and complemented, and the satisfiability game is built over the carrier set of the resulting automaton. The moves in the game are those transitions from the automaton that correspond to applications of tableau-rules; the existence of a winning strategy in this game ensures the existence of a model,

© The Author(s) 2018
D. Beyer and M. Huisman (Eds.): TACAS 2018, LNCS 10806, pp. 361–378, 2018.
https://doi.org/10.1007/978-3-319-89963-3_21

i.e. a locally coherent structure that does not contain bad branches. As they typically incur exponential blowup, good determinization procedures for automata on infinite words play a crucial role in standard decision procedures for the satisfiability problem of the μ-calculus and its fragments; in particular, better determinization procedures lead to smaller satisfiability games which are easier to solve.

The *weakly aconjunctive* μ-calculus [15,24] restricts occurrences of recursion variables in conjunctions but is still quite expressive, e.g. can define winning regions in parity games with bounded number of priorities [4]. The key observation for the present paper is that in the weakly aconjunctive case, pre-tableau branches are made 'bad' by a single formula; this implies that the tracking automaton for such formulas is *limit-deterministic*, i.e. that it is sufficient to deterministically track a single formula from some point on. This motivates a notion of *limit-deterministic parity automata* in which all accepting runs are deterministic from some point on. Because the nondeterminism is restricted to finite prefixes of accepting runs in such automata, they can be determinized in a simpler way than unrestricted parity automata. We present a reformulation of a recent determinization method for limit-deterministic *Büchi* automata [6]. The method is inspired by, but significantly less involved than the more general Safra/Piterman construction [19,20], essentially due to the fact that the tree structure of Safra trees collapses, leaving only the permutation structure. The resulting parity automaton can thus be described as a *permutation automaton*. The method yields deterministic parity automata with $\mathcal{O}(n!)$ states, compared to $\mathcal{O}((n!)^2)$ in the Safra/Piterman construction. Crucially, we show that we obtain a similarly simplified determinization for limit-deterministic *parity* automata by translating into Büchi automata.

As indicated above, limit-deterministic parity automata are able to recognize bad branches in pre-tableaux for weakly aconjunctive μ-calculus formulas. Employing them in the standard construction of satisfiability games, we obtain *permutation games* in which nodes from the pre-tableau are annotated with a partial permutation (i.e. a non-repetitive list) of (levelled) formulas. A parity condition is used to detect indices in the permutation that are active infinitely often without ever being removed from the permutation. The resulting parity games are of size $\mathcal{O}((nk)!)$ and have $\mathcal{O}(nk)$ priorities; as a side result, we thus obtain a new bound $\mathcal{O}((nk)!)$ on model size for weakly aconjunctive formulas.

The resulting decision procedure generalizes to the weakly aconjunctive *coalgebraic* μ-calculus, thus covering also, e.g., probabilistic and alternating-time versions of the μ-calculus. The generic algorithm has been implemented as an extension of the *Coalgebraic Ontology Logic Reasoner* (COOL) [11,13]. Our implementation constructs and solves the presented permutation games *on-the-fly*, possibly finishing satisfiability proofs early, and shows promising initial results. The content of the paper is structured as follows: We describe the determinization of limit-deterministic automata in Sect. 2 and the construction of permutation games in Sect. 3, and discuss implementation and evaluation in Sect. 4.

Related Work.   Liu and Wang [17] give a tighter estimate $\mathcal{O}((n!)^2)$ for the num
ber of states in Piterman's determinization [19]. Schewe [21] simplifies Piterman's
construction (establishing the same bound as Liu and Wang). Tian and Duan [23]
further improve Schewe's construction. Fisman and Lustig [7] present a modular-
ization of Büchi determinization that is aimed mainly at easing understanding
of the construction. Parity automata can be determinized by first converting
them to Büchi automata and then applying Büchi determinization. Schewe and
Varghese [22] address the direct determinization of parity automata (via Rabin
automata), and prove optimality within a small constant factor, and even abso-
lute optimality for the Büchi subcase. All these constructions and estimates
concern unrestricted Büchi or parity automata. Recently, Safra-less determinization of limit-deterministic Büchi automata has been described in the context of
controller synthesis for LTL [6]; the determinization method that we present
in Sect. 2.2. has been devised independently from [6] but employs a very similar construction (yielding essentially the same results on the complexity of the
construction).

The use of games in μ-calculus satisfiability checking goes back to Niwiński
and Walukiewicz [18] and has since been extended to the unguarded μ-
calculus [10] and the coalgebraic μ-calculus [2]. Game-based procedures for
the relational μ-calculus have been implemented in MLSolver [9], and for the
alternation-free coalgebraic μ-calculus in COOL [13].

2   Determinizing Limit-Deterministic Automata

2.1   Limit-Deterministic Automata

We recall the basics of parity automata: A *parity automaton* is a tuple $\mathcal{A} =
(V, \Sigma, \delta, u_0, \alpha)$ where V is a set of *states*, Σ is an *alphabet*, $\delta \subseteq V \times \Sigma \times V$ is a *tran-
sition relation*, $u_0 \in V$ is an *initial state*, and $\alpha : \delta \to \mathbb{N}$ is a *priority function* that
assigns natural numbers to *transitions* (assigning priorities to transitions rather
than states yields a slightly more succinct notion of automata while retaining the
computational properties of standard parity automata [22]). For $(v, a) \in V \times \Sigma$,
we write $\delta(v, a) = \{u \mid (v, a, u) \in \delta\}$. The *index* $\mathsf{idx}(\mathcal{A}) = \max\{\alpha(t) \mid t \in \delta\}$
of a parity automaton $\mathcal{A}$ is its maximal priority. A *run* $\rho = v_0 v_1 \ldots$ of $\mathcal{A}$ on
an infinite word $w = a_0 a_1 \ldots \in \Sigma^\omega$ starting at $v \in V$ is a (possibly infinite)
sequence of states v_i such that $v_0 = v$ and for all $i \geq 0$, $v_{i+1} \in \delta(v_i, a_i)$. We see
runs ρ or words w as functions from natural numbers to states $\rho(i) = v_i \in V$ or
letters $w(i) = a_i \in \Sigma$. For a run ρ on a word w, we define the according sequence
$\mathsf{trans}(\rho)$ of transitions by $\mathsf{trans}(\rho)(i) = (\rho(i), w(i), \rho(i+1))$. We denote the set of
all runs of $\mathcal{A}$ on a word w starting at v by $\mathsf{run}(\mathcal{A}, v, w)$, or just by $\mathsf{run}(\mathcal{A}, w)$ if
$v = u_0$. A run ρ of $\mathcal{A}$ on a word w is *accepting* if the highest priority that occurs
infinitely often in it (notation: $\max(\mathsf{Inf}(\alpha \circ \mathsf{trans}(\rho)))$; we generally write $\mathsf{Inf}(s)$
for the set of elements occurring infinitely often in a sequence s) is even. A parity
automaton $\mathcal{A}$ *accepts* an infinite word w if $\mathsf{run}(\mathcal{A}, w)$ contains an accepting run,
and we denote by $L(\mathcal{A}) \subseteq \Sigma^\omega$ the set of all words that are accepted by $\mathcal{A}$.

Given a state $v \in V$ and a letter $a \in \Sigma$, we define $\delta|_{v,a} = \{(v, a, u) \mid u \in \delta(v, a)\}$. Given a set $\gamma \subseteq \delta$ of transitions, a state $v \in V$, a set of states $U \subseteq V$ and a letter $a \in \Sigma$, we put $\gamma(U, a) = \bigcup\{\gamma(v, a) \mid v \in U\}$; given a finite word $w = a_0 \ldots a_n$, we then recursively define $\gamma(v, w) = \gamma(\gamma(v, a_0), a_1 \ldots a_n)$, obtaining the set of all states reachable from v when reading w while only using transitions from γ. For $U \subseteq V$, $\gamma \subseteq \delta$ and $w \in \Sigma^*$, we put $\gamma(U, w) = \bigcup\{\gamma(u, w) \mid u \in U\}$. Furthermore, we define the set of states that are *reachable* from a node $v \in V$ using transitions from γ as $\mathsf{reach}_\gamma(v) = \bigcup\{\gamma(v, w) \mid w \in \Sigma^*\}$; we extend this notation to sets of nodes, putting $\mathsf{reach}_\gamma(U) = \bigcup\{\mathsf{reach}_\gamma(u) \mid u \in U\}$ for $U \subseteq V$. If $\gamma = \delta$, then we omit the subscripts. A state $v \in V$ is said to be *deterministic* (in $\gamma \subseteq \delta$) if it has at most one (γ-)successor for each letter $a \in \Sigma$. A set $U \subseteq V$ is deterministic (in $\gamma \subseteq \delta$) if every state $v \in U$ is deterministic (in γ). The automaton $\mathcal{A}$ is said to be *deterministic* if V is deterministic; the transition relation in deterministic automata hence is a partial function (since such automata can be transformed to equivalent automata with total transition function, this definition suffices for purposes of determinization). We put $\alpha(i) = \{t \in \delta \mid \alpha(t) = i\}$ and $\alpha_\le(i) = \{t \in \delta \mid \alpha(t) \le i\}$.

A *Büchi automaton* is a parity automaton with only the priorities 1 and 2; the set of *accepting transitions* then is $F = \alpha(2)$ and a run is accepting if it passes infinitely many accepting transitions. For Büchi automata, we assume w.l.o.g. that every transition $t \in F$ is part of a cycle. We use the abbreviations (N/D)PA, (N/D)BA to denote the different types of automata.

Our notion of limit-determinism of automata is defined as a semantic property:

Definition 1 (Limit-deterministic parity automata). A PA $\mathcal{A} = (V, \Sigma, \delta, u_0, \alpha)$ is *limit-deterministic* if there is, for each word w and each accepting run $\rho \in \mathrm{run}(\mathcal{A}, w)$, a number i such that for all $j \ge i$, $\delta|_{\rho(j),w(j)} \cap \alpha_\le(l) = \{\mathsf{trans}(\rho)(j)\}$, where $l = \max(\mathsf{Inf}(\alpha \circ \mathsf{trans}(\rho)))$.

If $\mathcal{A}$ is a BA, then we have $\max(\mathsf{Inf}(\alpha \circ \mathsf{trans}(\rho))) = 2$ for every accepting run ρ; as $\alpha_\le(2) = \delta$, the above definition instantiates to requiring the existence of a number i such that for all $j \ge i$, $\delta(\rho(j), w(j)) = \{\rho(j + 1)\}$.

Definition 2 (Compartments). Given a PA $\mathcal{A} = (V, \Sigma, \delta, u_0, \alpha)$ with k priorities, and an even number $l \le k$, the *l-compartment* $C_l(t)$ of a transition $t \in \alpha(l)$ is the set $\mathsf{reach}_{\alpha_\le(l)}(\pi_3(t))$ where π_3 projects transitions $t = (v, a, u)$ to their target nodes u. If l is irrelevant, then we refer to l-compartments just as compartments. The *size* of a compartment C is just $|C|$. A compartment C is *internally deterministic* if for each $v \in C$ and all $a \in \Sigma$, $|\delta(v, a) \cap C| \le 1$.

Note that the union of all l-compartments is $\mathsf{reach}_{\alpha_\le(l)}(\pi_3[\alpha(l)])$. Compartments allow for a syntactic characterization of limit-determinism:

Lemma 3. *A PA is limit-deterministic if and only if all its compartments are internally deterministic.*

Corollary 4. *It is decidable in polynomial time whether a given automaton is limit-deterministic.*

Lemma 3 specializes to BA as follows: we have $\alpha(0) = \emptyset$, $\alpha_{\leq}(2) = \delta$ and $\alpha(2) = F$, so that the union of all 0-compartments is empty and that of all 2-compartments is $\mathsf{reach}(\pi_3[F])$; thus a BA is limit-deterministic if and only if $\mathsf{reach}(\pi_3[F])$ is deterministic. Such Büchi automata are also called *semi-deterministic* [3].

2.2   Determinizing Limit-Deterministic Büchi Automata

The Safra/Piterman construction [19,20] determinizes Büchi automata by means of so-called Safra trees, i.e. trees whose nodes are labelled with sets of states of the input automaton such that the label of a node is a proper superset of the union of all its children's labels. Additionally, the nodes are ordered by their age and upon each transition between Safra trees, the ages of the oldest nodes that are active and/or removed during this transition determine the priority of the new Safra tree. In its original formulation, the Safra/Piterman construction adds new child nodes to the graph that are labelled with the accepting states in their parent's label. We observe that this step can be modified slightly – without affecting the correctness of the construction – by letting every accepting state from the parent's label receive its own separate child node; then the labels of newly created nodes are always singletons. Limit-determinism of the input automaton then implies that the node labels also *remain* singletons. Since singleton nodes do not have children in Safra trees, this leads to the collapse of their tree structure; the resulting data structure is essentially a partial permutation, i.e. a non-repetitive list, of states (ordered by their age). The arising modified Safra/Piterman construction for the limit-deterministic case boils down to the following method, which (a) has a relatively short presentation and a simpler correctness proof than the full Safra/Piterman construction, and (b) results in asymptotically smaller automata; the underlying idea of the construction has first been described in the context of controller synthesis for LTL [6].

Definition 5 (Partial permutations). Given a set U of states, let $\mathsf{pperm}(U)$ denote the set of *partial permutations* over U, i.e. the set of non-repetitive lists $l = [v_1, \ldots, v_n]$ with $v_i \neq v_j$ for $i \neq j$ and $v_i \in U$, for all $1 \leq i \leq n$. We denote the i-th element in l by $l(i) = v_i$, the empty partial permutation by $[\,]$ and the length of a partial permutation l by $|l|$.

Definition 6 (Determinization of limit-deterministic BA). Fix a limit-deterministic BA $\mathcal{A} = (V, \Sigma, \delta, u_0, F)$, and put $Q = \mathsf{reach}(\pi_3[F])$, $\overline{Q} = V \setminus Q$, $q = |Q|$. Define the DPA $\mathcal{B} = (W, \Sigma, \delta', w_0, \alpha)$ by putting $W = \mathcal{P}(\overline{Q}) \times \mathsf{pperm}(Q)$, $w_0 = (\{u_0\}, [\,])$ if $u_0 \in \overline{Q}$, $w_0 = (\emptyset, [u_0])$ if $u_0 \in Q$ and for $g = (U, l) \in W$ and $a \in \Sigma$, $\delta'(g, a) = h$, where $h = (\delta(U, a) \cap \overline{Q}, l')$ and where l' is constructed from $l = [v_1, \ldots, v_m]$ as follows:

1. Define a list t of length m over $Q \cup \{*\}$ (with $*$ representing undefinedness) in which $t(i) = w$ if $\delta(v_i, a) = \{w\}$, and $t(i) = *$ if $\delta(v_i, a) = \emptyset$.

2. For $j < k$ and $t(j) = t(k)$, put $t(k) = *$.
3. Remove undefined entries in t, formally: for each $1 \leq i \leq |t|$, if $t(i) = *$, then iteratively put $t(j) = t(j+1)$ for each $i \leq j \leq |t|$, starting at i.
4. For any $w \in \delta(U, a) \cap Q$ that does not occur in t, add w to the end of t. If there are several such w, the order in which they are added to t is irrelevant.
5. Put $l' = t$.

Temporarily, t may contain duplicate or undefined entries, but Steps 2. and 3. ensure that in the end, t is a partial permutation of length at most q. Let r (for 'removed') denote the lowest index i such that $t(i) = *$ after Step 2. Let a (for 'active') denote the lowest index i such that $(l(i), a, l'(i)) \in F$. If $r > |l'|$ and there is no i with $(l(i), a, l'(i)) \in F$, then put $\alpha(g, a, h) = 1$. Otherwise, put

$$\alpha(g, a, h) = \begin{cases} 2(q-r)+3 & \text{if } r \leq a \\ 2(q-a)+2 & \text{if } r > a. \end{cases}$$

Theorem 7. *We have $L(\mathcal{A}) = L(\mathcal{B})$, and $\mathcal{B}$ has at most $2n+1$ priorities; for $n \geq 4$, we have $|W| \leq n!e$.*

Corollary 8. *Limit-deterministic Büchi automata of size n can be determinized to deterministic parity automata of size $\mathcal{O}(n!)$ and with $\mathcal{O}(n)$ priorities.*

Example 9. Consider the limit-deterministic BA $\mathcal{A}$ depicted below and the determinized DPA $\mathcal{B}$ that is constructed from it by applying the method. We see by Lemma 3 that $\mathcal{A}$ is really limit-deterministic: we have $F = \{(1, b, 3)\}$, i.e. the b-transition from state 1 to state 3 (depicted with a boxed transition label) is the only accepting transition; thus we have $Q = \text{reach}(\pi_3[F]) = \{1, 3\}$ (so $\overline{Q} = \{0, 2\}$), and the states 1 and 3 are deterministic. Moreover, $L(\mathcal{A}) = L(\mathcal{B}) = a(a|b)^+(a^+b)^\omega$.

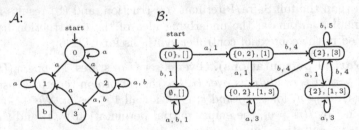

Notice that in $\mathcal{B}$, there is a b-transition with priority 1 from the initial state to the sink state $(\emptyset, [])$ and an a-transition to $(\{0, 2\}, [1])$; as $1 \in Q$ but $1 \notin F$, this transition has priority 1. A further b-transition leads from 1 to 3 in $\mathcal{A}$; in $\mathcal{B}$, we have a b-transition from $(\{0, 2\}, [1])$ to $(\{2\}, [3])$ and since $(1, b, 3) \in F$, the first position in the permutation component is active during this transition so that the transition has priority 4. Yet another b-transition loops from $(\{2\}, [3])$ to $(\{2\}, [3])$. Since there is no b-transition starting at state 3, the first element in the permutation is removed in Step 1. of the construction. Since there is a b-transition from 2 to 3, it is added to the permutation again in Step 4. of the construction. Crucially, however, the priority of the transition is 5, since the first item of the permutation has been (temporarily) removed. The intuition is that the trace of 3 ends when the letter b is read; even though a new trace of 3 immediately starts, we do not consider it to be the same trace as the previous one. Thus the transition obtains priority 5 so that it may be used only finitely often in an accepting run of $\mathcal{B}$, i.e. accepting runs contain an uninterrupted trace that visits state 3 infinitely often. Thus two or more consecutive b's can only occur finitely often in any accepted word.

2.3   Determinizing Limit-Deterministic Parity Automata

To determinize limit-deterministic PA, it suffices to transform them to equivalent limit-deterministic BA and determinize the BA. This transformation from PA to BA is achieved by a construction which is inspired by Theorems 2 and 3 in [14]; we add the observation that the construction preserves limit-determinism.

Definition 10. Given a limit-deterministic PA $\mathcal{C} = (V, \Sigma, \delta, u_0, \alpha)$ with $n = |V|$ and $k > 2$ priorities, we define the limit-deterministic BA $\mathcal{D} = (W, \Sigma, \delta', u_0, F)$ by putting $W = V \cup (V \times \{0, \ldots, \lceil \frac{k-1}{2} \rceil\})$, and for $w \in W$ and $a \in \Sigma$,

$$\delta'(v, a) = \begin{cases} \{(w, m) \mid (v, a, w) \in \alpha(2m)\} \cup \delta(v, a) & \text{if } v \in V \\ \{(w, l) \mid (v', a, w) \in \alpha_{\leq}(2l)\} & \text{if } v = (v', l) \notin V \end{cases}$$

Finally, we put $F = \{((v, l), a, (w, l)) \in \delta' \mid \alpha(v, a, w) = 2l\}$. To see that $\mathcal{D}$ is limit-deterministic, it suffices by Lemma 3 to show that $\mathrm{reach}(\pi_3[F])$ is deterministic. We observe that for each state $(w, l) \in \mathrm{reach}(\pi_3[F])$, (w, l) is deterministic by definition of δ' since w is contained in a (by Lemma 3, internally deterministic) $2l$-compartment of $\mathcal{C}$.

Lemma 11. We have $L(\mathcal{C}) = L(\mathcal{D})$ and $|W| \leq n(\lceil \frac{k}{2} \rceil + 1) \leq nk$.

By Theorem 7, $\mathcal{D}$ can be determinized to a DPA $\mathcal{E}$ of size at most $(nk)!e$, with at most $nk + 2$ priorities and with $L(\mathcal{D}) = L(\mathcal{E})$.

Corollary 12. *Limit-deterministic parity automata of size n with k priorities can be determinized to deterministic parity automata of size $\mathcal{O}((nk)!)$ and with $\mathcal{O}(nk)$ priorities.*

3   Permutation Games for the Aconjunctive μ-Calculus

3.1   The μ-Calculus

We briefly recall the definition of the μ-calculus. We fix a set P of *propositions*, a set A of *actions*, and a set $\mathfrak{V}$ of fixpoint variables. The set L_μ of μ-calculus formulas is the set of all formulas ϕ, ψ that can be constructed by the grammar

$$\psi, \phi ::= \bot \mid \top \mid p \mid \neg p \mid X \mid \psi \wedge \phi \mid \psi \vee \phi \mid \langle a \rangle \psi \mid [a]\psi \mid \mu X. \psi \mid \nu X. \psi$$

where $p \in P$, $a \in A$, and $X \in \mathfrak{V}$; we write $|\psi|$ for the size of a formula ψ. Throughout the paper, we use η to denote one of the fixpoint operators μ or ν. We refer to formulas of the form $\eta X. \psi$ as *fixpoint literals*, to formulas of the form $\langle a \rangle \psi$ or $[a]\psi$ as *modal literals*, and to p, $\neg p$ as *propositional literals*. The operators μ and ν *bind* their variables, inducing a standard notion of *free variables* in formulas. We denote the set of free variables of a formula ψ by $\mathsf{FV}(\psi)$. A formula ψ is *closed* if $\mathsf{FV}(\psi) = \emptyset$, and *open* otherwise. We write $\psi \leq \phi$ ($\psi < \phi$) to indicate that ψ is a (proper) subformula of ϕ. We say that ϕ *occurs free* in ψ if ϕ occurs in ψ as a subformula that is not in the scope of any fixpoint operator. Throughout, we *restrict to formulas that are guarded*, i.e. have at least one modal operator between any occurrence of a variable X and an enclosing binder ηX. (This is standard although possibly not without loss of generality [10].) Moreover we assume w.l.o.g. that input formulas are *clean*, i.e. all fixpoint variables are mutually distinct and distinct from all free variables, and *irredundant*, i.e. $X \in \mathsf{FV}(\psi)$ for all subformulas $\eta X. \psi$. We refer to a variable X that is bound by a least (greatest) fixpoint operator $\mu X.\chi$ ($\nu X.\chi$) in a formula ϕ as a μ-*variable* (ν-*variable*) of ϕ, and to the process of substituting such an X with its binding fixpoint literal ($\mu X.\chi$ or $\nu X.\chi$, respectively) as *unfolding*. An occurrence of a subformula ψ of a formula ϕ *contains an active μ-variable* [15] if ψ can be converted into a formula containing a free occurrence of a μ-variable of ϕ by repeatedly unfolding ν-variables of ϕ.

Formulas are evaluated over *Kripke structures* $\mathcal{K} = (W, (R_a)_{a \in A}, \pi)$, consisting of a set W of *states*, a family $(R_a)_{a \in A}$ of relations $R_a \subseteq W \times W$, and a valuation $\pi : P \to \mathcal{P}(W)$ of the propositions. Given an *interpretation* $i : \mathfrak{V} \to \mathcal{P}(W)$ of the fixpoint variables, define $[\![\psi]\!]_i \subseteq W$ by the obvious clauses for Boolean operators and propositions, $[\![X]\!]_i = i(X)$, $[\![\langle a \rangle \psi]\!]_i = \{v \in W \mid \exists w \in R_a(v).w \in [\![\psi]\!]_i\}$, $[\![[a]\psi]\!]_i = \{v \in W \mid \forall w \in R_a(v).w \in [\![\psi]\!]_i\}$, $[\![\mu X. \psi]\!]_i = \mu[\![\psi]\!]_i^X$ and $[\![\nu X. \psi]\!]_i = \nu[\![\psi]\!]_i^X$, where $R_a(v) = \{w \in W \mid (v, w) \in R_a\}$, $[\![\psi]\!]_i^X(G) = [\![\psi]\!]_{i[X \mapsto G]}$, and μ, ν take least and greatest fixpoints of monotone functions, respectively. If ψ is closed, then $[\![\psi]\!]_i$ does not depend on i, so we just write $[\![\psi]\!]$. We denote the *Fischer-Ladner closure* [16] of a formula ϕ by $\mathbf{F}(\phi)$, or just by $\mathbf{F}$, if no confusion arises; intuitively, $\mathbf{F}$ is the set of formulas that can arise as subformulas when unfolding each fixpoint operator in ϕ at most once. We note $\mathbf{F} \leq |\phi|$ [16].

The *aconjunctive fragment* [15] of the μ-calculus is obtained by requiring that for all conjunctions that occur as a subformula, at most one of the conjuncts contains an active μ-variable. In the *weakly aconjunctive fragment* [24], this requirement is loosened to the constraint that all conjunctions that occur as a subformula and contain an active μ-variable are of the shape $\psi \wedge \Diamond \psi_1 \wedge \ldots \wedge \Diamond \psi_n \wedge \Box(\psi_1 \vee \ldots \vee \psi_n)$, where ψ does not contain active μ-variables. For instance, for all n, the formula $\eta X_n \ldots \mu X_1.\nu X_0. \bigvee_{0 \leq i \leq n}(q_i \wedge \Diamond X_i)$ is aconjunctive (and equivalent to the weakly aconjunctive formula obtained by replacing $\Diamond X_i$ with $\Diamond X_i \wedge \Diamond \top \wedge \Box(X_i \vee \top)$). The permutation satisfiability games that we introduce work for the more expressive weakly aconjunctive fragment.

We will make use of the standard *tableau rules* [10] (each consisting of one *premise* and a possibly empty set of *conclusions*):

$$(\bot) \quad \frac{\Gamma, \bot}{} \qquad (\notz) \quad \frac{\Gamma, p, \neg p}{} \qquad (\wedge) \quad \frac{\Gamma, \psi \wedge \phi}{\Gamma, \psi, \phi}$$

$$(\vee) \quad \frac{\Gamma, \psi \vee \phi}{\Gamma, \psi \quad \Gamma, \phi} \qquad (\langle a \rangle) \quad \frac{\Gamma, [a]\psi_1, \ldots, [a]\psi_n, \langle a \rangle \phi}{\psi_1, \ldots, \psi_n, \phi} \qquad (\eta) \quad \frac{\Gamma, \eta X. \psi}{\Gamma, \psi[X \mapsto \eta X. \psi]}$$

(for $a \in A$, $p \in P$); we refer to the tableau rules by $\mathcal{R}$ and usually write rule applications with premise Γ and conclusion $\Sigma = \Gamma_1, \ldots, \Gamma_n$ sequentially: (Γ/Σ).

To track fixpoint formulas through pre-tableaux, we will use deferrals, that is, the decomposed form of formulas that are obtained by unfolding fixpoint literals.

Definition 13 (Deferrals). Given fixpoint literals $\chi_i = \eta X_i . \psi_i$, $i = 1, \ldots, n$, we say that a substitution $\sigma = [X_1 \mapsto \chi_1]; \ldots; [X_n \mapsto \chi_n]$ *sequentially unfolds* χ_n if $\chi_i <_f \chi_{i+1}$ for all $1 \le i < n$, where we write $\psi <_f \eta X. \phi$ if $\psi \le \phi$ and ψ is open and occurs free in ϕ (i.e. σ unfolds a nested sequence of fixpoints in χ_n innermost-first). We say that a formula χ is *irreducible* if for every substitution $[X_1 \mapsto \chi_1]; \ldots; [X_n \mapsto \chi_n]$ that sequentially unfolds χ_n, we have that $\chi = \chi_1([X_2 \mapsto \chi_2]; \ldots; [X_n \mapsto \chi_n])$ implies $n = 1$ (i.e. $\chi = \chi_1$). A formula ψ *belongs* to an irreducible closed fixpoint literal θ_n, or is a θ_n-*deferral*, if $\psi = \alpha\sigma$ for some substitution $\sigma = [X_1 \mapsto \theta_1]; \ldots; [X_n \mapsto \theta_n]$ that sequentially unfolds θ_n and some $\alpha <_f \theta_1$. We denote the set of θ_n-deferrals by $\mathsf{dfr}(\theta_n)$.

E.g. the substitution $\sigma = [Y \mapsto \mu Y. (\Box X \wedge \Diamond\Diamond Y)]; [X \mapsto 0]$ sequentially unfolds the irreducible closed formula $\theta = \nu X. \mu Y. (\Box X \wedge \Diamond\Diamond Y)$, and $(\Diamond Y)\sigma = \Diamond\mu Y. (\Box \theta \wedge \Diamond\Diamond Y)$ is a θ-deferral. A fixpoint literal is irreducible if it is not an unfolding $\psi[X \mapsto \eta X. \psi]$ of a fixpoint literal $\eta X. \psi$; in particular, every clean irredundant fixpoint literal is irreducible.

As a technical tool, we define a measure for the depth of alternation at which a deferral resides inside the fixpoint to which it belongs:

Definition 14 (Alternation level and alternation depth). The *alternation level* $\mathsf{al}(\phi\sigma) := \mathsf{al}(\sigma)$ of a deferral $\phi\sigma$ is defined inductively over $|\sigma|$, where $\mathsf{al}(\epsilon) = \mathsf{al}(\epsilon)_\mu = \mathsf{al}(\epsilon)_\nu = 0$, for the empty substitution ϵ, $\mathsf{al}(\sigma; [X \mapsto \eta X. \psi]) = \mathsf{al}(\sigma)_\mu + 1$ if $\eta = \mu$ and $\mathsf{al}(\sigma; [X \mapsto \eta X. \psi]) = \mathsf{al}(\sigma)_\nu$ otherwise, and

$$\mathsf{al}(\sigma; [X \mapsto \eta X. \psi])_\mu = \begin{cases} \mathsf{al}(\sigma)_\mu & \text{if } \eta = \mu \\ \mathsf{al}(\sigma)_\nu + 1 & \text{otherwise} \end{cases}$$

$$\mathsf{al}(\sigma; [X \mapsto \eta X. \psi])_\nu = \begin{cases} \mathsf{al}(\sigma)_\nu & \text{if } \eta = \nu \\ \mathsf{al}(\sigma)_\mu + 1 & \text{otherwise} \end{cases}$$

This definition assigns greater numbers to inner fixpoint literals, i.e. to deferrals which occur at higher nesting depth, i.e. with more alternation inside their sequence σ. Given a formula ψ, its *alternation depth* $\mathsf{ad}(\phi)$ is defined as $\mathsf{ad}(\phi) = \max\{\mathsf{al}(\delta) \mid \delta \in \mathbf{F}, \exists \theta. \delta \in \mathsf{dfr}(\theta)\}$.

3.2 Limit-Deterministic Tracking Automata

As a first step towards deciding the satisfiability of a weakly aconjunctive μ-calculus formula ϕ, we now construct a tracking automaton that takes branches of (that is, infinite paths through) standard pre-tableaux for ϕ as input and accepts a branch if and only if it contains a least fixpoint formula whose satisfaction is deferred indefinitely on that branch. To this end, we import the following notions of threads and tableaux from [10]:

Definition 15. A *pre-tableau* for a formula ϕ is a graph the nodes of which are labelled with subsets of the Fischer-Ladner closure $\mathbf{F}$; the graph structure L of a pre-tableau is constructed by applying tableau rules from $\mathcal{R}$ to the labels of nodes with the requirement that for each rule application (Γ/Σ) to the label Γ of a node v, there is a w with $(v, w) \in L$ such that the label of w is contained in Σ. Nodes whose labels are *saturated* (i.e. do not contain propositional or fixpoint operators) are called *states*. Formulas are tracked through rule applications by the *connectedness relation* $\leadsto \subseteq (\mathcal{P}(\mathbf{F}) \times \mathbf{F})^2$ that is defined by putting $\Phi, \phi \leadsto \Psi, \psi$ if and only if Ψ is a conclusion of an application of a rule from $\mathcal{R}$ to Φ such that $\phi \in \Phi$, $\psi \in \Psi$, and the rule application transforms ϕ to ψ; if the rule application does not change ϕ, then $\phi = \psi$. E.g. we have $\Phi, \psi_1 \wedge \psi_2 \leadsto \Psi, \psi_i$, where $i \in \{1, 2\}$ and Ψ is obtained from Φ by applying the rule $(\wedge)$ to $\psi_1 \wedge \psi_2$. A *branch* $\Psi_0, \Psi_1 \ldots$ in a pre-tableau is a sequence of labels such that for all $i > 0$, Ψ_{i+1} is an L-successor of Ψ_i. A *thread* on an infinite branch $\Psi_0, \Psi_1, \ldots$ is an infinite sequence $t = \psi_0, \psi_1 \ldots$ of formulas with $\Psi_0, \psi_0 \leadsto \Psi_1, \psi_1 \leadsto \ldots$. A μ-*thread* is a thread t such that $\min(\mathsf{Inf}(\mathsf{al} \circ t))$ is odd, i.e. the outermost fixpoint literal that is unfolded infinitely often in t is a least fixpoint literal. A *bad branch* is an infinite branch that contains a μ-thread. A *tableau* for ϕ is a pre-tableau for ϕ that does not contain bad branches.

We import from [10] the well-known fact that the existence of tableaux in the sense defined above characterizes satisfiability. In [10], the result is shown for the more general *unguarded* μ-calculus; we note that the restriction to guarded formulas does not invalidate the theorem.

Theorem 16 ([10]). *A μ-calculus formula ψ is satisfiable if and only if there is a tableau for ψ.*

Given a formula ϕ, we define the alphabet Σ_ϕ to consist of letters that each identify a rule $R \in \mathcal{R}$, a principal formula from $\mathbf{F}$ and one of the conclusions of R. E.g. the letter $((\vee), 0, p \vee \Diamond q)$ identifies the application of the disjunction rule to a principal formula $p \vee \Diamond q$ and the choice of the left conclusion; thus this letter identifies the transition from $p \vee \Diamond q$ to p by use of rule $(\vee)$. We note $|\Sigma_\phi| \in \mathcal{O}(|\phi|)$. Further, we denote the set of all words that encode some branch and some bad branch in some pre-tableau for ϕ by $\mathsf{Branch}(\phi)$ and $\mathsf{BadBranch}(\phi)$, respectively.

  As a crucial result, we now show that limit-deterministic automata are expressive enough to exactly recognize the bad branches in pre-tableaux for weakly aconjunctive formulas.

Lemma 17. *Let ϕ be a weakly aconjunctive formula. Then there is a* limit deterministic *PA $\mathcal{A} = (V, \Sigma_\phi, \delta, \phi, \alpha)$ with $|V| \leq |\psi|$ and $\mathrm{idx}(\mathcal{A}) \leq \mathrm{ad}(\phi) + 1$ such that $L(\mathcal{A}) \cap \mathsf{Branch}(\phi) = \mathsf{BadBranch}(\phi)$.*

Proof (Sketch). The automaton nondeterministically guesses formulas to be tracked, one at a time; the set of states of the automaton is the Fischer-Ladner closure of ϕ. The priorities of the transitions in the automaton are derived from the alternation level of the target formula of the respective transition; then every word $w \in L(\mathcal{A})$ that encodes some branch encodes a bad branch. Once a deferral is tracked, weak aconjunctivity implies that all compartments to which the tracked formula belongs are internally deterministic; this is the case since for conjunctions $\psi = \psi_0 \wedge \Diamond\psi_1 \wedge \ldots \wedge \Diamond\psi_n \wedge \Box(\psi_1 \vee \ldots \vee \psi_n)$ – the only case that can introduce nondeterminism – each next modal step determines just one of the formulas ψ_i that has to be tracked; the conjunct ψ_0 does not contain active μ-variables, so tracking it causes the automaton to leave all compartments to which ψ belongs. Thus the automaton is limit-deterministic. $\square$

Example 18. We consider the aconjunctive formula

$$\phi = \mu X.(\, p \wedge \nu Y.\, (\Diamond(Y \wedge p) \vee \Diamond X))$$

which expresses the existence of a finite or infinite path on which p holds everywhere. We have the ϕ-deferrals ϕ_ϵ, $\psi := (p \wedge \nu Y.\, (\Diamond(Y \wedge p) \vee \Diamond X))\sigma_1$, $\theta := (\nu Y.\, (\Diamond(Y \wedge p) \vee \Diamond X))\sigma_1$, $\chi := (\Diamond(Y \wedge p) \vee \Diamond X)\sigma_2$, $(\Diamond(Y \wedge p))\sigma_2$, $\tau := (Y \wedge p)\sigma_2$, $Y\sigma_2$, $\Diamond X \sigma_2$ and $X\sigma_2$, where $\sigma_1 = [X \mapsto \phi]$ and $\sigma_2 = [Y \mapsto \psi]; \sigma_1$. We consider a pre-tableau P_ϕ for ϕ and like in the proof of Lemma 17, we construct the limit-deterministic tracking automaton $\mathcal{A}_\phi$, depicted below:

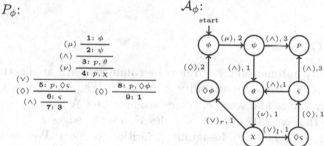

The priorities in $\mathcal{A}_\phi$ are derived as follows: As $\mathrm{ad}(\phi) = 2$ is even, we put $k = \mathrm{ad}(\phi) + 1 = 3$; since $\mathrm{al}(\phi) = \mathrm{al}(\psi) = 1$, $\alpha(\phi, (\mu), \psi) = \alpha(\Diamond\phi, (\Diamond), \phi) = k - \mathrm{al}(\phi) = 2$ and since $\mathrm{al}(p) = 0$, $\alpha(\psi, (\wedge), p) = \alpha(\varsigma, (\wedge), p) = k - \mathrm{al}(p) = 3$. All other formulas have alternation level 2 and transitions to them obtain priority 1. The tracking automaton accepts exactly those branches in P_ϕ that start at node **1** and take the loop through node **9** infinitely often; in these branches, ϕ can be tracked forever and evolves to ϕ infinitely often, i.e. their dominating formula is the least fixpoint formula ϕ. All other branches loop through node **7** without passing node **9** from some point on; their dominating fixpoint formula is θ, a greatest fixpoint formula. We observe that due to the aconjunctivity of ϕ, $\mathcal{A}_\phi$ is limit-deterministic since the only two nondeterministic states ψ and ς each have only one outgoing $(\wedge)$-transition with priority less than $k = 3$.

Given a weakly aconjunctive formula ϕ, we use Lemma 17 to construct a limit-deterministic tracking automaton $\mathcal{A}_\phi$ with $L(\mathcal{A}_\phi) \cap \mathsf{Branch}(\phi) = \mathsf{BadBranch}(\phi)$. Then we put Lemma 11 to use to obtain an equivalent BA in which all states from $Q = \mathsf{reach}(\pi_3[F])$ are *levelled deferrals*, i.e. pairs (ψ, q) consisting of a deferral ψ and a number $q \leq \lceil \frac{k}{2} \rceil$, the *level* of the pair (ψ, q); the level q encodes the odd alternation level $2q - 1$. A levelled deferral (ψ, q) is *active* if $\mathsf{al}(\psi) = 2q - 1$ and the automaton accepts branches which contain a levelled deferral that is active infinitely often without being finished. The set $\overline{Q}$ is just a subset of $\mathbf{F}$. Next we use Theorem 7 to transform this BA to a DPA $\mathcal{B}_\phi$ with $L(\mathcal{A}_\phi) = L(\mathcal{B}_\phi)$. We complement $\mathcal{B}_\phi$ to a DPA $\mathcal{C}_\phi = (W, \Sigma_\phi, \delta, \phi, \alpha)$ by decreasing the priority of each state in $\mathcal{B}_\phi$ by one; we have $L(\mathcal{C}_\phi) = \overline{L(\mathcal{B}_\phi)}$, that is, $\mathcal{C}_\phi$ accepts exactly those words that encode only 'good' branches, if they encode some branch in some pre-tableau for ϕ. By construction, $|W| \in \mathcal{O}((nk)!)$ and $\mathcal{C}_\phi$ has at most $nk + 1$ priorities, and (recalling Definitions 6 and 10) the states in the carrier W of $\mathcal{C}_\phi$ are of the shape (U, l), where U is a subset of $\mathbf{F}$ and l is a partial permutation of levelled deferrals. For a transition $t = ((U, l), r, (V, l'))$ with $(U, l), (V, l') \in W$, $r \in \Sigma_\phi$, if $\alpha(t) = 2(n-a)+1$, then a is the lowest number such that $\mathsf{al}(\phi) = 2q-1$, where $l'(a) = (\phi, q)$ and the a-th element of l is not removed by the transition t (i.e. $\alpha(t)$ references the oldest levelled deferral in l' that is active but not removed by the transition t) and if $\alpha(t) = 2(n-r)+2$, then $\alpha(t)$ is the index of the oldest levelled deferral $(\phi, 2q-1)$ that is finished (i.e. removed from l) in the transition t of the automaton $\mathcal{C}_\phi$, which means that the according r-transition in $\mathcal{A}_\phi$ makes ϕ leave its $2q - 1$-compartment. For a state $v = (U, l)$, we define the *label* $\Gamma(v)$ of v as $\Gamma(v) = U$.

3.3   Permutation Games

The deterministic parity automaton $\mathcal{C}_\phi$ can now be combined with applications of tableau rules from $\mathcal{R}$ to form a satisfiability game for ϕ. We proceed to recall the definition of parity games and some ensuing basic notions. A *parity game* is a graph $\mathcal{G} = (V, E, \alpha)$ that consists of a set of nodes V, a set of edges $E \subseteq V \times V$ and a priority function $\alpha : E \rightarrow \mathbb{N}$, assigning priorities to *edges*. We assume $V = V_\exists \uplus V_\forall$, that is, every node in V either belongs to player Eloise $(V_\exists)$ or to player Abelard $(V_\forall)$. A *play* ρ of $\mathcal{G}$ is a (possibly infinite) sequence $v_0 v_1 \ldots$ such that for all $i \geq 0$, $v_i \in V$ and $(v_i, v_{i+1}) \in E$. A play ρ of $\mathcal{G}$ is won by Eloise if and only if ρ is finite and ends in a node that belongs to Abelard or ρ is infinite and $\max(\mathsf{Inf}(\alpha \circ \mathsf{trans}(\rho)))$ is even (where $\mathsf{trans}(\rho)$ is defined by $\mathsf{trans}(\rho)(i) = (\rho(i), \rho(i + 1))$); Abelard wins a play ρ if and only if Eloise does not win ρ. A (memoryless) strategy $s : V \twoheadrightarrow V$ assigns moves to states. A play ρ *conforms* to a strategy s if for all $\rho(i) \in \mathsf{dom}(s)$, $\rho(i + 1) = s(\rho(i))$. Eloise has a winning strategy for a node v if there is a strategy $s : V_\exists \rightarrow V$ such that every play of $\mathcal{G}$ that starts at v and conforms to s is won by Eloise; we have a dual notion of winning strategies for Abelard. The winning regions $\mathsf{win}_\exists(\mathcal{G})$ and

$\text{win}_\forall(\mathcal{G})$ are the sets of those nodes for which Eloise and Abelard have winning strategies, respectively. *Solving* a parity game $\mathcal{G}$ (locally) for a particular node $v \in V$ amounts to computing the winner of v.

Now we are ready to define permutation games for weakly aconjunctive formulas ϕ, using the DPA $\mathcal{C}_\phi = (W, \Sigma_\phi, \delta, \phi, \alpha)$ from the previous section.

Definition 19 (Permutation games). Let ϕ be a weakly aconjunctive formula. We define the *permutation game* $\mathcal{G}(\phi) = (W, E, \beta)$ to be a parity game that has the carrier of $\mathcal{C}_\phi$ as set of nodes. For every node $v \in W$ for which $\Gamma(v)$ is not a state, we fix a single rule that is to be applied to $\Gamma(v)$ and a single principal formula $\psi_v \in \Gamma(v)$ to which the rule is to be applied. If $(\vee)$ is to be applied to $\Gamma(v)$, then we put $v \in W_\exists$; otherwise, $v \in W_\forall$. In particular, all state nodes are contained in $W_\forall$. For $v \in W$, we put $E(v) = \bigcup\{\delta(v, a) \mid a \in \Sigma_v\}$, where $\Sigma_v \subseteq \Sigma_\phi$ consists of all letters a that encode the application of some rule to $\Gamma(v)$ with the condition that the principal formula of the rule application must be ψ_v if v is not a state node. Finally, we put $\beta(v, w) = \alpha(v, a, w)$ for $(v, w) \in E$, where $a \in \Sigma_v$ encodes the rule application that leads from v to w.

Theorem 20. *Let ϕ be a closed, irreducible and weakly aconjunctive formula. Then we have $(\{\phi\}, []) \in \text{win}_\exists(\mathcal{G}(\phi))$ if and only if ϕ is satisfiable.*

Proof. By construction, Eloise wins $(\{\phi\}, [])$ if and only if there is a tableau for ϕ (labelled by the labelling function Γ); we are done by Theorem 16.   □

Due to the relatively simple structure and the asymptotically smaller size of the determinized automata $\mathcal{C}_\phi$, the resulting permutation games are somewhat easier to construct and can be solved asymptotically faster than the structures created by standard satisfiability decision procedures for the full μ-calculus (e.g. [5,10]) which employ the full Safra/Piterman-construction; note however, that our method is restricted to the weakly aconjunctive fragment.

Corollary 21. *The satisfiability of weakly aconjunctive μ-calculus formulas can be decided by solving parity games of size $\mathcal{O}((nk)!)$ and $\mathcal{O}(nk)$ priorities.*

The winning strategies for Eloise or Abelard in these games define models for or refutations of the respective formulas, so that we have

Corollary 22. *Satisfiable weakly aconjunctive μ-calculus formulas have models of size $\mathcal{O}((nk)!)$.*

4 Implementation and Benchmarking

We have implemented the permutation satisfiability games as an extension of the *Coalgebraic Ontology Logic Reasoner* (COOL) [11], a generic reasoner for coalgebraic modal logics[1]. COOL achieves its genericity by instantiating an abstract reasoner that works for all coalgebraic logics to concrete instances of logics.

---

[1] Available at https://www8.cs.fau.de/research:software:cool.

To incorporate support for the aconjunctive coalgebraic μ-calculus, we have extended the global caching algorithm that forms the core of COOL to generate and solve the corresponding permutation games, with optional *on-the-fly* solving; games are solved using either our own implementation of the fixpoint iteration algorithm for parity games (as in [1]) or PGSolver [8], which supports a range of game solving algorithms. Instance logics implemented in COOL currently include linear-time, relational, monotone, and alternating-time logics, as well as any logics that arise as combinations thereof. In particular, this makes COOL, to our knowledge, the only implemented reasoner for the aconjunctive fragments of the alternating-time μ-calculus and Parikh's game logic.

Although our tool supports the aconjunctive coalgebraic μ-calculus, we concentrate on the standard relational aconjunctive μ-calculus for experiments, as this allows us to compare our implementation with the reasoner MLSolver [9], which constructs satisfiability games using the Safra/Piterman-construction and hence supports the full relational μ-calculus; MLSolver uses PGSolver for game solving.

To test the implementations, we devise two series of hard aconjunctive formulas with deep alternating nesting of fixpoints. The following formulas encode that each reachable state in a Kripke structure has one of n priorities (encoded by atoms q_i for $1 \leq i \leq n$) and belongs to either Eloise (q_e) or Abelard (q_a):

$$\phi_{\text{aut}}(n) = \text{AG}(\bigvee_{1 \leq i \leq n} (q_i \wedge \bigwedge_{j \neq i} \neg q_j)) \quad \phi_{\text{game}}(n) = \phi_{\text{aut}}(n) \wedge \text{AG}((q_e \wedge \neg q_a) \vee (\neg q_e \wedge q_a))$$

Here we use AG ψ to abbreviate $\nu X.(\psi \wedge \Box X)$. Then the non-emptiness regions in parity automata and Eloise's winning region in parity games can be specified by the following *aconjunctive* formulas (where $\heartsuit \in \{\Diamond, \Box\}$):

$$\phi_{\text{ne}}(n) = \eta X_n.\ldots.\nu X_2.\mu X_1.\psi_\Diamond \qquad\qquad \psi_\heartsuit = \bigvee_{1 \leq i \leq n}(q_i \wedge \heartsuit X_i)$$
$$\phi_{\text{win}}(n) = \eta X_n.\ldots.\nu X_2.\mu X_1.\phi_{\text{strat}}(\psi_\heartsuit) \qquad \phi_{\text{strat}}(\psi_\heartsuit) = (q_e \wedge \psi_\Diamond) \vee (q_a \wedge \psi_\Box)$$

Furthermore, we define (for $\heartsuit \in \{\Diamond, \Box\}$)

$$\theta_\heartsuit(i) = (q_i \wedge \heartsuit Y) \vee \bigvee_{i < j \leq n}(q_j \wedge \heartsuit X) \vee \bigvee_{1 \leq j \leq i}(q_j \wedge \heartsuit Z)$$

The following series of valid formulas states that parity automata with n priorities can be transformed to nondeterministic parity automata with three priorities without affecting the non-emptiness region:

$$\theta_1(n) := \phi_{\text{aut}}(n) \rightarrow (\phi_{\text{ne}}(n) \leftrightarrow \bigvee_{i \text{ even}} \mu X.\nu Y.\mu Z.\, \theta_\Diamond(i))$$

Similarly, if Eloise wins a parity game with n priorities, then she can ensure that in each play, each odd priority $1 \leq i \leq n$ is visited only finitely often, unless a priority greater than i is visited infinitely often (the converse does not hold in general [4]):

$$\theta_2(n) := \phi_{\text{game}}(n) \rightarrow (\phi_{\text{win}}(n) \rightarrow \bigwedge_{i \text{ odd}} \nu X.\mu Y.\nu Z.\, \phi_{\text{strat}}(\theta_\heartsuit(i)))$$

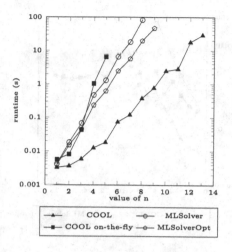

Fig. 1. Times for $\neg\theta_1(n)$ (unsatisfiable)

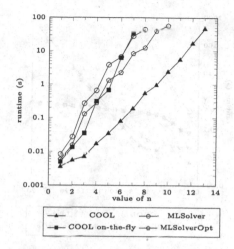

Fig. 2. Times for $\neg\theta_2(n)$ (unsatisfiable)

Additionally, we devise two series of unsatisfiable formulas that exhibit the advantages of COOL's global caching and on-the-fly-solving capabilities. These formulas are inspired by the CTL-formula series $\mathsf{early}(n, j, k)$ and $\mathsf{early}_{\mathsf{gc}}(n, j, k)$ from [13] but contain fixpoint-alternation of depth 2^k inside the subformula θ:

$$\mathsf{early\text{-}ac}(n, j, k) = start_p \wedge \mathsf{init}(p, n) \wedge \mathsf{init}(r, k) \wedge \mathsf{AG} ((r \to \mathsf{c}(r, k)) \wedge (p \to \mathsf{c}(p, n))) \wedge$$
$$\mathsf{AG} ((\textstyle\bigwedge_{0 \leq i \leq j} p_i \to \Diamond(start_r \wedge \theta)) \wedge \neg(p \wedge r) \wedge (r \to \Box \, r))$$
$$\mathsf{early\text{-}ac}_{\mathsf{gc}}(n, j, k) = \mathsf{early\text{-}ac}(n, j, k) \wedge b \wedge \mathsf{init}(q, n) \wedge \mathsf{AG} (\neg(p \wedge q) \wedge \neg(q \wedge r)) \wedge$$
$$\mathsf{AG} ((q \to \mathsf{c}(q, n)) \wedge \mathsf{AF} \, b \wedge (b \to (\Diamond \, p \wedge \Diamond \, start_q \wedge \Box \, \neg b)))$$
$$\mathsf{init}(x, m) = \mathsf{AG} ((start_x \to (x \wedge \textstyle\bigwedge_{0 \leq i < m} \neg x_i)) \wedge (x \to \Diamond \, x))$$
$$\theta = \eta X_{(2^k)}.\ldots.\nu X_2.\mu X_1.\textstyle\bigvee_{1 \leq i \leq 2^k} (\mathsf{bin}(r, i-1) \wedge \Diamond X_i),$$

where $\mathsf{c}(x, m)$ encodes an m-bit counter using atoms $x_0, \ldots, x_{m-1}$ and $\mathsf{bin}(r, i)$ denotes the binary encoding of the number i using atoms $r_0, \ldots, r_{k-1}$. The formulas $\mathsf{early\text{-}ac}(n, j, k)$ specify a loop p of length 2^n that branches after j steps to a second loop r of length 2^k on which the highest value of the counter (which counts from 0 to $2^k - 1$ and then restarts at 0) is required to be an even number. For constant k, the contradiction on loop r yields a small refutation which can be found early, using on-the-fly solving. The formulas $\mathsf{early\text{-}ac}_{\mathsf{gc}}(n, j, k)$ extend this specification by stating that a third loop q of length 2^n is started from loop p infinitely often. Procedures with sufficient caching capabilities will have to (partially) explore this loop at most once.

We compare the runtimes of MLSolver and COOL on the formulas described above; we let COOL and MLSolver solve games using the local strategy improvement algorithm `stratimprloc2` provided by PGSolver. To solve games *on-the-fly* with COOL however, we use our own implementation of the fixpoint iteration

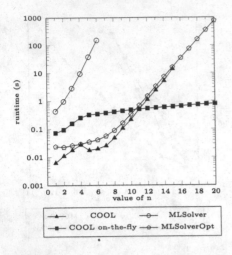

Fig. 3. early-ac$(n, 4, 2)$ (unsatisfiable)   **Fig. 4.** early-ac$_{gc}(n, 4, 2)$ (unsatisfiable)

algorithm, which in general is slower than PGSolver but has the advantage that it enables on-the-fly solving. With this option enabled, COOL constructs and solves the satisfiability games step by step and finishes as soon as one of the players has a winning strategy in the partial game. For COOL, we have conducted all experiments with and without on-the-fly solving. For MLSolver, we also enabled the optimizations -opt litpro and -opt comp (and refer to the resulting prover configuration as MLSolverOpt). Tests have been run on a system with Intel Core i7 3.60 GHz CPU with 16 GB RAM. A more detailed description of the results of the experiments as well as binaries of a formula generator, the prover COOL and scripts that benchmark the various configurations of the provers are available in a figshare repository at [12].

We observe that COOL without on-the-fly solving generally finishes faster than both MLSolver and MLSolverOpt throughout all tested series of formulas (see Figs. 1–4); the reason for this appears to be that the permutation games solved by COOL are of size $\mathcal{O}((nk)!)$, where $n \leq k$, and hence asymptotically smaller than the Safra/Piterman games solved by MLSolver which are of size $\mathcal{O}(((nk)!)^2)$. The size of the refutations for the formulas $\theta_1(n)$ and $\theta_2(n)$ is exponential in n so that on-the-fly solving does in fact *increase* the runtimes of COOL (see Figs. 1 and 2); basically, these formulas cannot be decided early, and therefore any (necessarily unsuccessful) attempt to do so just consumes additional computation time. The formulas early-ac$(n, 4, 2)$ and early-ac$_{gc}(n, 4, 2)$, on the other hand, have refutations of size polynomial in n, and COOL appears to benefit from on-the-fly solving for these formulas as it is able to decide them early (see Figs. 3 and 4). As mentioned above, COOL uses our own unoptimized implementation of the fixpoint iteration algorithm [1] for on-the-fly solving; while this implementation is slower than PGSolver's stratimprloc2 algorithm, the on-the-fly abilities of COOL seem to compensate this disadvantage for the early-ac$(n, 4, 2)$ and early-ac$_{gc}(n, 4, 2)$ formulas from $n = 11$ and $n = 8$ on, respectively.

5   Conclusion

We have presented a method to obtain satisfiability games for the *weakly aconjunctive* μ-calculus. The game construction uses determinization of *limit-deterministic* parity automata, avoiding the full complexity of the Safra/Piterman construction a) in the presentation of the procedure and its correctness proof and b) in the size of the obtained DPA (which comes from $\mathcal{O}((nk)!^2)$ to $\mathcal{O}((nk)!)$). The resulting permutation satisfiability games for the weakly aconjunctive μ-calculus are of size $\mathcal{O}((nk)!)$, have $\mathcal{O}(nk)$ priorities, and yield a new bound of $\mathcal{O}((nk)!)$ on the model size for this fragment. We have implemented this decision procedure in coalgebraic generality and with support for on-the-fly solving as part of the coalgebraic satisfiability solver COOL; initial experiments show favourable results.

The datasets generated and analyzed during the current study are available in the figshare repository: https://doi.org/10.6084/m9.figshare.5919451.v1.

References

1. Bruse, F., Falk, M., Lange, M · The fixpoint-iteration algorithm for parity games. In: Games, Automata, Logics and Formal Verification, GandALF 2014, EPTCS, vol. 161, pp. 116–130 (2014)
2. Cîrstea, C., Kupke, C., Pattinson, D.: EXPTIME tableaux for the coalgebraic μ-calculus. In: Grädel, E., Kahle, R. (eds.) CSL 2009. LNCS, vol. 5771, pp. 179–193. Springer, Heidelberg (2009). https://doi.org/10.1007/978-3-642-04027-6_15
3. Courcoubetis, C., Yannakakis, M.: The complexity of probabilistic verification. J. ACM 42(4), 857–907 (1995)
4. Dawar, A., Grädel, E.: The descriptive complexity of parity games. In: Kaminski, M., Martini, S. (eds.) CSL 2008. LNCS, vol. 5213, pp. 354–368. Springer, Heidelberg (2008). https://doi.org/10.1007/978-3-540-87531-4_26
5. Emerson, E.A., Jutla, C.: The complexity of tree automata and logics of programs. SIAM J. Comput. 29(1), 132–158 (1999)
6. Esparza, J., Křetínský, J., Raskin, J.-F., Sickert, S.: From LTL and limit-deterministic Büchi automata to deterministic parity automata. In: Legay, A., Margaria, T. (eds.) TACAS 2017. LNCS, vol. 10205, pp. 426–442. Springer, Heidelberg (2017). https://doi.org/10.1007/978-3-662-54577-5_25
7. Fisman, D., Lustig, Y.: A modular approach for Büchi determinization. In: Concurrency Theory, CONCUR 2015, LIPIcs, vol. 42, pp. 368–382. Schloss Dagstuhl - Leibniz-Zentrum für Informatik (2015)
8. Friedmann, O., Lange, M.: The PGSolver collection of parity game solvers. Technical report, LMU Munich (2009)
9. Friedmann, O., Lange, M.: A solver for modal fixpoint logics. In: Methods for Modalities, M4M-6 2009, ENTCS, vol. 262, pp. 99–111 (2010)
10. Friedmann, O., Lange, M.: Deciding the unguarded modal μ-calculus. J. Appl. Non-Classical Log. 23, 353–371 (2013)
11. Gorín, D., Pattinson, D., Schröder, L., Widmann, F., Wißmann, T.: COOL – a generic reasoner for coalgebraic hybrid logics (system description). In: Demri, S., Kapur, D., Weidenbach, C. (eds.) IJCAR 2014. LNCS (LNAI), vol. 8562, pp. 396–402. Springer, Cham (2014). https://doi.org/10.1007/978-3-319-08587-6_31

12. Hausmann, D., Schröder, L., Deifel, H.-P.: Permutation games for the weakly aconjunctive μ-calculus (artifact). Figshare (2018). https://doi.org/10.6084/m9.figshare.5919451.v1
13. Hausmann, D., Schröder, L., Egger, C.: Global caching for the alternation-free coalgebraic μ-calculus. In: Concurrency Theory, CONCUR 2016, LIPIcs, vol. 59, pp. 34:1–34:15 (2016). Schloss Dagstuhl - Leibniz-Zentrum für Informatik
14. King, V., Kupferman, O., Vardi, M.Y.: On the complexity of parity word automata. In: Honsell, F., Miculan, M. (eds.) FoSSaCS 2001. LNCS, vol. 2030, pp. 276–286. Springer, Heidelberg (2001). https://doi.org/10.1007/3-540-45315-6_18
15. Kozen, D.: Results on the propositional μ-calculus. Theor. Comput. Sci. **27**, 333–354 (1983)
16. Kozen, D.: A finite model theorem for the propositional μ-calculus. Stud. Log. **47**, 233–241 (1988)
17. Liu, W., Wang, J.: A tighter analysis of Piterman's Büchi determinization. Inf. Process. Lett. **109**, 941–945 (2009)
18. Niwinski, D., Walukiewicz, I.: Games for the μ-calculus. Theor. Comput. Sci. **163**, 99–116 (1996)
19. Piterman, N.: From nondeterministic Büchi and Streett automata to deterministic parity automata. Log. Methods Comput. Sci. **3** (2007)
20. Safra, S.: On the complexity of omega-automata. In: Foundations of Computer Science, FOCS 1988, pp. 319–327. IEEE Computer Society (1988)
21. Schewe, S.: Tighter bounds for the determinisation of Büchi automata. In: de Alfaro, L. (ed.) FoSSaCS 2009. LNCS, vol. 5504, pp. 167–181. Springer, Heidelberg (2009). https://doi.org/10.1007/978-3-642-00596-1_13
22. Schewe, S., Varghese, T.: Determinising parity automata. In: Csuhaj-Varjú, E., Dietzfelbinger, M., Ésik, Z. (eds.) MFCS 2014. LNCS, vol. 8634, pp. 486–498. Springer, Heidelberg (2014). https://doi.org/10.1007/978-3-662-44522-8_41
23. Tian, C., Duan, Z.: Büchi determinization made tighter. CoRR, abs/1404.1436 (2014)
24. Walukiewicz, I.: Completeness of Kozen's axiomatisation of the propositional μ-calculus. Inf. Comput. **157**, 142–182 (2000)

Symmetry Reduction for the Local Mu-Calculus

Kedar S. Namjoshi[1(✉)] and Richard J. Trefler[2(✉)]

[1] Bell Labs, Nokia, Murray Hill, USA
kedar.namjoshi@nokia-bell-labs.com
[2] University of Waterloo, Waterloo, Canada
trefler@uwaterloo.ca

Abstract. Model checking large networks of processes is challenging due
to state explosion. In many cases, individual processes are isomorphic,
but there is insufficient global symmetry to simplify model checking. This
work considers the verification of local properties, those defined over the
neighborhood of a process. Considerably generalizing earlier results on
invariance, it is shown that all local mu-calculus properties, including
safety and liveness properties, are preserved by neighborhood symmetries. Hence, it suffices to check them locally over a set of representative
process neighborhoods. In general, local verification approximates verification over the global state space; however, if process interactions are
outward-facing, the relationship is shown to be exact. For many network
topologies, even those with little global symmetry, analysis with representatives provides a significant, even exponential, reduction in the cost
of verification. Moreover, it is shown that for network families generated
from building-block patterns, neighborhood symmetries are easily determined, and verification over the entire family reduces to verification over
a finite set of representative process neighborhoods.

1 Introduction

Networks of communicating processes are a model for distributed systems, cloud
computing environments, routing protocols, many-core hardware processors, and
other such systems. Often, networks are described parametrically, that is, a process template is instantiated at each node of a network graph. The expectation
then is that basic correctness properties should hold regardless of the size and
the shape of the network.

Model checkers can determine, fully automatically, whether a fixed instance
of a process network satisfies a correctness property. However, model checking
suffers from exponential state explosion as the size of the analyzed network
increases. Thus, one may aim for parameteric analysis of a network family, "in
one fell swoop"; however, the parametric model checking problem (PMCP) is
undecidable in general [2]. Limiting to *compositional* proofs makes parametrized
verification more tractable; as shown in [20], the PCMCP (Parameterized Compositional Model Checking problem) can be solved efficiently for standard

D. Beyer and M. Huisman (Eds.): TACAS 2018, LNCS 10806, pp. 379–395, 2018.
https://doi.org/10.1007/978-3-319-89963-3_22

network families (rings, tori, wrap-around mesh, etc.) where the PMCP is undecidable even for invariance properties.

In this work, we generalize these results considerably, from invariance to mu-calculus properties. We formulate a local version of the mu-calculus to describe behaviors of a single process and its immediate neighborhood. The logic allows specification of safety and liveness properties, each property being limited to assertions over a fixed process neighborhood – e.g., "A hungry philosopher eventually acquires all adjacent forks". The goal of this work is a method to prove such properties for all processes in a network and, moreover, to prove properties parametrically, i.e., for all networks in a family.

Our analysis is based on a grouping of processes by local symmetry, where "balanced" processes have (recursively) similar neighborhoods [17,18,20]. Such symmetries are common in parametric network structures, for example [18,19], c.f. [17,20]. We establish that the local state spaces of balanced processes are sufficiently bisimilar that they satisfy the same local mu-calculus properties. It is, therefore, enough to model-check a representative process from each balance class, while paying particular attention to 'interference' transitions from neighboring processes.

We show that any *universal* local mu-calculus property established locally also holds on the global state space. Thus, a universal property can be established globally for all processes by checking it on the local state spaces of a few representatives.

Many communication protocols are designed in such a way that a typical process must offer a given set of input/output services to its communication environment, irrespective of its internal state. We show that under such outward-facing interactions, the correspondence is exact: a local mu-calculus property holds globally if, and only if, it holds locally.

We also detail the implications for entire families of networks that are defined by 'symmetry patterns.' For instance, a network family with a transitive global symmetry group can be analyzed by examining a single representative node. Such dramatic reductions in complexity are generally not possible for non-local properties.

None of the symmetry reduction results rely in any essential manner on the processes being finite-state. To summarize the main results:

- The local state spaces of balanced processes (the spaces incorporate interference from neighbors) are bisimilar. Hence, it suffices to model-check properties on representative processes of the balance equivalence classes,
- The local state space simulates the global space up to stuttering. Thus, a universal local mu-calculus property holds on the global space if it holds on a representative local space,
- With 'outward-facing' interaction, the local and global spaces are stuttering-bisimilar. A local mu-calculus property holds on the global space if, and only if, it holds on a representative local space.

We also explore the implications of these results and, in particular, show that in several settings, local symmetries can be determined easily from process syntax. We show that for isomorphic 'normal' processes operating in a network whose communication graph has at least transitive symmetry, a balance relation with a single representative process can be generated from the syntactic description of the network. In another direction, we show that for networks formed from 'building block' patterns, the pattern instances serve as balance representatives. These direct, syntactic constructions avoid having to build global symmetry reduced structures, can lead to exponential reductions in the cost of model checking, and apply to many networks where global symmetry reduction techniques are ineffective. Moreover, entire network families can be model-checked via the analysis of a small number of representative processes, so that the savings in the cost of analysis are unbounded.

2   Preliminaries

Processes and Networks: Syntax. A *network* is a directed graph, defined by a set of *nodes*, N, a set of *edges*, E, and two connection relations: $Out \subseteq N \times E$ and $In \subseteq N \times E$. Connections are directed from node n to the edges in $Out(n)$, and directed inwards from the edges in $In(n)$ to n. Nodes m and n are neighbors, denoted $nbr(n, m)$, if they have a common connected edge. Node m *points to* node n if there is an edge o in $Out(m) \cap In(n)$.

A *process* is defined by a tuple (V, I, T), where V is a set of variables which defines its local state space; $I(V)$ is a Boolean predicate defining the initial states; and $T(V, V')$ is a Boolean predicate defining the state transitions, using a copy V' to denote the next state. Variables are partitioned into *internal* and *external* variables. External variables are labeled as *read*, or *write*, or both. The transition relation is required to preserve the value of read-only variables and its enabledness cannot depend on the values of write-only variables.

A *process network* P is defined by a network graph, a set of processes, and an assignment, ξ. Every node n is assigned a process $\xi(n)$, which we denote for convenience by $P_n = (V_n, I_n, T_n)$. Each edge e is assigned a variable $\xi(e)$ in $V = (\bigcup n : V_n)$. The assignment ξ must assign $In(n)$ to the read variables in V_n, $Out(n)$ to the write variables of V_n, and the internal variables of V_n to no network edge. The *shared* variables of processes P_m and P_n are those assigned to common connected edges of m and n.

Processes and Networks: Semantics. Semantically, the behavior of a process network P is defined as the process $P = (I, V, T)$, where $V = (\bigcup n : V_n), I = (\bigwedge n : I_n)$, and $T = (\bigvee n : T_n \wedge \mathsf{unchanged}(V \setminus V_n))$. This defines an interleaving semantics, with $\mathsf{unchanged}(W)$ denoting that the values of variables in W are unchanged.

A *global* state is a function mapping variables in V to values in their domain. A *local* state of P_n is a function mapping the variables in V_n to values in their domain. An *internal* state of P_n is a function mapping the internal variables of P_n to values in their domains.

For neighbors m, n, a *joint state* is a pair $x = (x_m, x_n)$, where x_m and x_n are local states of processes P_m and P_n, respectively, such that x_m and x_n have the same value for all shared variables. The transition relation T_n is extended to joint states as $T_n(x, y)$, which holds iff $T_n(x_n, y_n)$ holds and the values of variables in P_m that are not shared with P_n are unchanged.

Invariants: Global and Compositional. Invariance is central to reasoning about dynamic system behavior. For a process network P as defined above, a *global assertion*, θ, is a set of global states of P. It is an *inductive invariant* for P if all initial states are in θ, i.e., $[I(x) \rightarrow \theta(x)]$, and θ is closed under transitions, i.e., $[\theta(x) \wedge T(x, y) \rightarrow \theta(y)]$.[1]

In place of a single invariance assertion, compositional reasoning postulates a set of *local assertions*, $\{\theta_n\}$, where θ_n is a set of local states of P_n, for each n. This set is a *compositional inductive invariant* if, for all n:

(Init) The initial states of P_n are included in θ_n. That is, $[I_n(x_n) \rightarrow \theta_n(x_n)]$

(Step) Transitions of P_n preserve θ_n. That is, $[\theta_n(x_n) \wedge T_n(x_n, y_n) \rightarrow \theta_n(y_n)]$

(Non-Interference) Assertion θ_n is preserved by transitions of neighbors P_m, from every joint state satisfying both θ_m and θ_n. I.e., For all m such that $nbr(n, m)$ and all joint states $x = (x_n, x_m), y = (y_n, y_m) : [\theta_n(x_n) \wedge \theta_m(x_m) \wedge T_m(x, y) \rightarrow \theta_n(y_n)]$

These constraints are in a simultaneous pre-fixpoint form over $\{\theta_n\}$. The least fixpoint is the strongest compositional invariant. For finite-state processes, this computation is polynomial-time in the size of the local state spaces.

Theorem 1 [17]. *If $\{\theta_n\}$ is a compositional inductive invariant then $\bigwedge_i \theta_i$ is a global inductive invariant.*

Symmetry Between Neighborhoods. A neighborhood symmetry between nodes m and n is witnessed by a bijection, β, which maps edges in $In(m)$ to those in $In(n)$ and edges in $Out(m)$ to those in $Out(n)$; we call (m, β, n) a similarity. The set of similarities (m, β, n) is a groupoid[2].

A *balance* relation ([17], *c.f.* [11]) links symmetries throughout a network: balanced nodes m, n have isomorphic neighborhoods, nodes connected to corresponding edges of m, n are themselves balanced, and so on. Formally, a balance relation, B, is a set of triples (m, β, n), such that (m, β, n) is a similarity; (n, β^{-1}, m) is in B; and for any node k that points to m, there is a node l which points to n and a bijection γ such that (k, γ, l) is in B, and $\gamma(e) = \beta(e)$ for every edge e that is connected to both m and k.

The structure of this condition is similar to that of bisimulation (it is coinductive); thus, there is a greatest fixpoint, which is the largest balance relation. Nodes m, n are *balanced* if (m, β, n) is in the largest balance relation for some β.

---

[1] The notation, $[\varphi]$, from Dijkstra and Scholten [7], means that φ is valid.

[2] I.e., (n, ι, n) is a similarity for the identity map ι; if (m, β, n) is a similarity, so is (n, β^{-1}, m); and if (m, β, q) and (q, γ, n) are similarities, so is $(m, (\gamma\beta), n)$.

A process network P *respects* balance relation B if balanced nodes are assigned processes with isomorphic initial states and transition relations: i.e., for all $(m, \beta, n) \in B$, it is the case that $[I_n(\beta(s)) \equiv I_m(s)]$ for all s, and $[T_n(\beta(s), \beta(t)) \equiv T_m(s, t)]$ for all s, t. Similarly, we say that local assertions $\{\phi_i\}$ respect B if $[\phi_n(\beta(s)) \equiv \phi_m(s)]$ for all $(m, \beta, n) \in B$. We abbreviate these conditions as $[I_n \equiv \beta(I_m)], [T_n \equiv \beta(T_m)]$ and $[\phi_n \equiv \beta(\phi_m)]$, respectively. Here, β is overloaded to permute local states of P_m. For local state s of node m, the local state $\beta(s)$ at node n is defined as follows: the internal states of m in s and n in $\beta(s)$ are identical and, for every edge e connected to m, the value on e in s is identical to the value of $\beta(e)$ in $\beta(s)$. A key result is that balanced nodes have isomorphic compositional invariants.

Theorem 2 ([17]). *If a process network respects balance relation B, its strongest compositional invariant also respects B.*

This theorem implies that it suffices to compute the strongest compositional invariant only for representative nodes[3], as the invariants for all other nodes are isomorphic to those of their representatives.

3   The Local Mu-Calculus

Intuitively, a local property is one that refers to the local state of a node, e.g., "the process at node n is in its critical section", or "the philosopher at node n holds all adjacent forks". We are interested in establishing a local property $f(n)$, parameterized by node n, and so isomorphic between nodes, for *all* nodes of a process network. We represent such a property by a mu-calculus formula. This has two interpretations: one in the global state space, the other in a compositionally constructed local state space. Their connections are discussed in the next section.

3.1   Syntax

The local mu-calculus syntax and semantics is largely identical to that of the standard *mu*-calculus [15]. The only difference is the use of the $\mathsf{E}[\,\mathsf{U}\,]$ operator in place of EX, this is given a stuttering-insensitive semantics.

Let Σ be a set of atomic propositions, Γ be a set of propositional variables, and Δ a set of transition labels; these sets are mutually disjoint. Local mu-calculus formulas are defined by the following grammar. A formula is one of

- An atomic proposition from Σ,
- A propositional variable from Γ,
- $\neg \varphi$, for a formula φ,

---

[3] A balance relation B induces the equivalence relation $m \simeq_B n$ if $(m, \beta, n) \in B$ for some β. The compositional fixpoint is calculated for a representative of each class of $\simeq_B$. In the fixpoint calculation, the assertion θ_n is replaced by $\gamma(\theta_r)$, where r is the representative for n, and γ is a chosen isomorphism such that (r, γ, n) is in B.

- $\varphi \wedge \psi$, the conjunction of formulae φ and ψ,
- $\mathsf{E}[\varphi \, \mathsf{U}_a \, \psi]$, where φ, ψ are formulas, and a is a transition label from Δ,
- $\mu Z.\varphi(Z)$, where $\varphi(Z)$ is a formula syntactically monotone in Z (i.e., all occurrences of Z fall under an even number of negations).

Operators $\mathsf{A}[\varphi \, \mathsf{W}_a \, \psi] = \neg \mathsf{E}[\neg \varphi \, \mathsf{U}_a \, \neg \psi]$ and $\nu Z.\varphi(Z) = \neg \mu Z.(\neg \varphi(\neg Z))$ are the negation duals of $\mathsf{E}[\, \mathsf{U} \,]$ and μ, respectively, with Boolean operations $\vee$ and $\rightarrow$ defined as usual.

3.2   Semantics

A state space has the form (S, S_0, R, L), where S is a set of states, S_0 is the set of initial states, $R \subseteq S \times \Delta \cup \{\tau\} \times S$ is a left-total transition relation, and $L : S \rightarrow 2^\Sigma$ labels states with atomic propositions. A path is a sequence $s_0, a_0, s_1, a_1, \ldots$ such that $(s_i, a_i, s_{i+1}) \in R$ for all i, where the sub-sequence $a_0, a_1, \ldots$ is the label sequence of the path.

The state set S generates a complete lattice of all subsets of S, ordered by set inclusion. A functional $\Pi : 2^S \rightarrow 2^S$ is monotone if for all A, B such that $A \subseteq B$ it is the case that $\Pi(A) \subseteq \Pi(B)$. By the Knaster-Tarski theorem, every monotone functional has a least and a greatest fixpoint. Consider a formula $\varphi(Z_1, \ldots, Z_d)$ with free variables $Z_1, \ldots, Z_d$. Given an assignment λ mapping each free variable to a subset of S, the interpretation of φ under λ is defined inductively as follows. We write $M, s \models \varphi$ to mean that state s in space M satisfies a closed formula φ, i.e., s is in $\mathsf{interp}(\varphi, \epsilon)$ where ϵ is the empty interpretation.

- $\mathsf{interp}(p, \lambda) = \{s \in S \mid p \in L(s)\}$, for proposition $p \in \Sigma$,
- $\mathsf{interp}(Z, \lambda) = \lambda(Z)$,
- $\mathsf{interp}(\varphi \wedge \psi, \lambda) = \mathsf{interp}(\varphi, \lambda) \cap \mathsf{interp}(\psi, \lambda)$,
- $\mathsf{interp}(\neg \varphi, \lambda) = S \setminus \mathsf{interp}(\varphi, \lambda)$,
- State s is in $\mathsf{interp}(\mathsf{E}[\varphi \, \mathsf{U}_a \, \psi], \lambda)$ if, and only if, there is a finite path π from s to state t with label sequence $\tau^*; a$, where t is in $\mathsf{interp}(\psi, \lambda)$ and every other state s' on π is in $\mathsf{interp}(\varphi, \lambda)$. Informally, φ holds until the first a-action, after which ψ is true,
- $\mathsf{interp}(\mu Z.\varphi(Z), \lambda)$ is the least fixpoint of functional $\Pi(X) = \mathsf{interp}(\varphi(Z), \lambda')$ where λ' extends λ with the assignment of X to Z.

3.3   Local and Global Interpretations

Let θ be a compositional invariant respecting a balance relation B. For any node n of the network, define H_n^θ as the following transition system:

- The states are the local states of P_n that satisfy θ_n,
- A transition (s, s') is either
  - A transition (labeled with n) by P_n from state s, or
  - An interference transition (labeled with m) by a neighbor P_m from a joint state (s, u) where $\theta_n(s)$ and $\theta_m(u)$ hold, to a joint state (s', u').

By the properties of a compositional invariant, s' is in θ_n in both cases.

The only missing ingredient is a labeling of the states with atomic propositions. Given such a labeling, L, a closed formula evaluates to a set of local states.

The global transition system G defines the semantics of the process network. For a given n, let G_n be G with transitions by P_n labeled with n, transitions by neighbors m of n labeled with m, and all other transitions (which cannot change the local state of P_n) labeled with τ. A local labeling L of P_n is extended to G_n by labeling a global state s with proposition p if p labels the local state of P_n in s. Formulas local to node n are evaluated over G_n. A closed formula evaluates to a set of global states.

3.4   Simulation and Bisimulation

For processes without τ actions, a simulation relation α from process P to process Q is a relation from the state space of P to that of Q, satisfying:

- Every initial state of P is related to an initial state of Q by α, and
- If $s\alpha t$ holds, then s and t satisfy the same atomic propositions, and
- If $s\alpha t$ holds and s' is a successor state of s in P, there is a successor state t' of t in Q such that $s'\alpha t'$ holds.

If a simulation relation exists from P to Q, we say that Q simulates P. It is well known that if Q simulates P, then any standard universal mu-calculus formula that holds for all initial states of Q also holds for all initial states of P. A universal local mu-calculus formula is one where its negation normal form does not contain $\mathsf{E}[\,\mathsf{U}\,]$. Relation α is a bisimulation from P to Q if α is a simulation from P to Q and α^{-1} is a simulation from Q to P. It is well known that bisimilar processes satisfy the same standard mu-calculus properties.

For processes with τ transitions, one can relax the third condition to allow the possibility of stuttering (cf. [4]): if $s\alpha t$ holds, then for any state s' reachable from s by a finite path π with label sequence $\tau^*; a$ (for a non-τ letter a), there is a state t' reachable from t by a finite path δ labeled $\tau^*; a$ such that s' and t' are related by α, and every other pair of states u on π and v on δ is related by α. Relation α is a stuttering bisimulation if α and α^{-1} are stuttering simulations.

Theorem 3. *Stuttering simulation preserves universal local mu-calculus properties. Stuttering bisimulation preserves all local mu-calculus properties.*

4   Connecting Local Mu-Calculus Interpretations

We explore relationships between the local and global interpretation of formulas, and show the following:

- The local state spaces of balanced nodes are bisimilar. It follows from Theorem 3 that balanced nodes satisfy the same local mu-calculus formulas. From this result, to model check a property of the form $(\bigwedge i :: f(i))$, it suffices to check $f(i)$ for the representatives of the balance equivalence classes.

- The local state space of node m stuttering-simulates the global state space up to the local state of m. It follows from Theorem 3 that a universal local mu-calculus formula on m holds globally if it holds locally.
- If processes exhibit 'outward-facing' interaction, i.e., (roughly) the effect of interfering transitions is independent of the internal state of the interfering process, then the local and global state spaces are stuttering-bisimilar up to the local state of m. It follows that the two spaces satisfy precisely the same local mu-calculus formulas over m.

Notation. In the proofs below, for a local state s of node n, the notation $s[n]$ refers to the internal state of P_n in s, and for an edge e that is connected to n, the notation $s[e]$ refers to the value in s of the variable assigned to e.

4.1   Bisimilarity Between Local State Spaces

Theorem 4. *Let B be a balance relation on a process network P, and θ a compositional invariant for the network. If P and θ respect B, then for every (m, β, n) in B, H_m^θ and H_n^θ are bisimilar up to β.*

Proof: The bisimulation relation R relates a local state s of node m to a local state t of node n if $\beta(s) = t$. Before getting to the details of the proof, which is technical, we sketch the main reasoning. First, local transitions are easily matched by symmetry. For an interfering transition from a neighbor k of m, by balance, there is a matching neighbor l of n with a symmetric interference transition. Crucially, the preservation of the compositional invariant under balance lets us transfer the joint state from which the interference transition occurs in H_m^θ to a joint state with a matching interference transition in H_n^θ.

Suppose that s, t are states of m and n in the local state spaces H_m^θ and H_n^θ, respectively, such that sRt holds, that is $\beta(s) = t$. By construction of H_m^θ and H_n^θ, $\theta_m(s)$ and $\theta_n(t)$ hold.

Consider a step transition $T_m(s, s')$. Since T_m and T_n respect the balance relation, B, by the local symmetry between the transition relations, $T_n(\beta(s), \beta(s'))$ holds as well. Thus, for $t' = \beta(s')$, we have that there is a step transition $T_n(t, t')$ such that $s'Rt'$. By construction, s' and t' are successors of s and t, respectively, in the local state spaces.

Now consider an interference transition in H_m^θ from a joint state (s, u) where u is a local state of a neighbor k of m. The transition $T_k(u, u')$ creates a joint state (s', u'). From the definition of balance, there is a neighbor l of n such that for some γ, we have (k, γ, l) in the balance relation. As θ respects B by assumption, we have that $\theta_l = \gamma(\theta_k)$. As $\theta_k(u)$ holds by the definition of the interference transition, the state $v = \gamma(u)$ is in θ_l. We claim that there is a matching transition from the joint state (t, v).

First, we show that the pair (t, v) forms a joint state. Consider any edge f that is shared between n and l. By balance, shared edges are mapped identically by β and γ; hence, $e = \beta^{-1}(f) = \gamma^{-1}(f)$ is shared by m and k. By the definition of $t = \beta(s)$ and $v = \gamma(u)$, we have that $t[f] = s[e]$ and $v[f] = u[e]$. As (s, u) is a joint state, we have $s[e] = u[e]$; hence, $t[f] = v[f]$. As f was chosen arbitrarily, it follows that t and v agree on the values of all shared edges, so (t, v) is a joint state. Moreover, the state t is in θ_n by assumption, and v is in θ_l by construction.

By the similarity between P_k and P_l, there is a transition $T_l(\gamma(u), \gamma(u'))$; letting $v' = \gamma(u')$, this can be expressed as $T_l(v, v')$. That induces an interference transition in H_n^θ from the joint state (t, v) to a joint state (t', v').

Finally, we show that $t' = \beta(s')$. Let e be an edge connected to node m and let $f = \beta(e)$. Note that f is shared between n and l if, and only if, e is shared between m and k. Now if f is not shared between n and l, then $t'[f] = t[f]$ by definition of interference; $t[f] = s[e]$ as $t = \beta(s)$; and $s'[e] = s[e]$ by definition of interference. By transitivity, $t'[f] = s'[e]$, as required. If f is a shared edge, then $t'[f] = v'[f]$ by joint state; $v'[f] = u'[e]$ as $v' = \gamma(u')$; and $u'[e] = s'[e]$ by joint state. By transitivity, $t'[f] = s'[e]$. The internal states of t, t' and s, s' are (respectively) identical, as they are unaffected by interference. Hence, $t' = \beta(s')$.

The proof so far shows that R is a simulation if (m, β, n) is in the balance relation. From the same argument applied to (n, β^{-1}, m), which must also be in the balance relation, the inverse of R is also a simulation. Hence, R is a bisimulation between H_m^θ and H_n^θ. **EndProof.**

We say that per-process propositional labelings *respect* balance if for every (m, β, n) in the balance relation, every atomic proposition p, and every local state s: $[p \in L_n(\beta(s)) \equiv p \in L_m(s)]$. From Theorems 3 and 4, we obtain:

Corollary 1. *Let $f(i)$ be a local mu-calculus formula parameterized by i. If the compositional invariant θ and the interpretation of the atomic propositions in f respect balance relation B, then for any (m, β, n) in B and any local state s: $H_m^\theta, s \models f(m)$ if, and only if, $H_n^\theta, \beta(s) \models f(n)$.*

4.2   Local-Global Simulation

From the point of view of a process P_m, a transition in the global state space is either a transition of P_m, or an interference transition by one of the neighbors of m, or a transition by a "far away" process that has no immediate effect on the local space of m. Thus, global transitions can be simulated by step or interference transitions in the local space, with far-away transitions exhibiting stuttering. The converse need not be true, as interference transitions appear in the local space without the constraining context of the entire global state.

Theorem 5. *Let the scheduling of transitions in the global system be unconditionally fair. For every m and any compositional inductive invariant θ, H_m^θ simulates the global transition system G_m up to stuttering.*

Proof: For a global state s, let $s[m]$ refer to the local state of node m in s. Define the relation R from global states to those of H_m^θ by $(s, t) \in R$ iff $\theta(s)$ and $s[m] = t$. We show that R is a simulation, up to stuttering. The proof is by cases on the kinds of transitions from global state s to a successor state, s'. As θ is a global *inductive* invariant by Theorem 1, it is the case that $\theta(s')$ holds.

Suppose the transition is by process m. Thus, $T_m(s[m], s'[m])$ should hold. As $\theta_m(s[m])$ holds, this transition is in the local state space as well. Letting $t' = s'[m]$, we have $s'Rt'$.

Suppose the transition is by a neighbor k of m, so that $T_k(s[k], s'[k])$ holds, and for all edges e that are not connected to k, $s'[e] = s[e]$. By definition, $\theta_m(s[m])$ and $\theta_k(s[k])$ hold, so this is a valid interference transition in the local state space H_m^θ. Denoting $s[k]$ by u, this can be re-expressed as a joint transition from state (t, u) to (t', u'), where $u' = s'[k]$. Consider an edge e that is connected to m but not to k. Then $t'[e] =$ (by non-adjacency) $t[e] =$ (by R) $s[m][e] =$ (by non-adjacency) $s'[m][e]$. Now consider an edge e that is shared by nodes m and k; then $t'[e] =$ (by shared edge) $u'[e] =$ (by definition) $s'[k][e] =$ (by shared edge) $s'[m][e]$. The internal state of m is unchanged on either transition. Thus, $t' = s'[m]$, so that $s'Rt'$, as desired.

Finally, suppose the transition is by a process that is not a neighbor of m. Then $s'[m] = s[m]$, so that $s'Rt$ holds. This is the stuttering step. As transitions are scheduled in an unconditionally fair manner, on any infinite computation from s, process m or one of its neighbors must eventually make a move. Hence, all stuttering is bounded. This establishes (fair) stuttering simulation between the two spaces. **EndProof.**

From the preservation of universal local mu-calculus properties under stuttering simulation, we have:

Corollary 2. *If $f(m)$ is a universal local mu-calculus formula, then for any t, s such that $s[m] = t$: $H_m^\theta, t \models f(m)$ implies that $G_m, s \models f(m)$ under fairness.*

4.3 Outward-Facing Interactions and Local-Global Bisimulation

The obstacle to establishing bisimilarity in the proof of Theorem 5 is that an interference transition from local state t may not have a corresponding transition from a related global state s, as the internal state of the interfering neighbor in s may be different from the internal state of the interfering neighbor of t. In some protocols, however, we see that interference depends only on the shared state. For instance, in a form of the dining philosophers' protocol where a process may give up a fork if it is not eating, the interference transition (passing a fork to a neighbor) is dependent only on possession of the fork. In this setting, one can indeed show that the two spaces are bisimilar.

We express the independence from internal state as a stuttering bisimulation within the interfering process. Define a relation $B_{m,n}$ on the local state space of P_n by $(u, v) \in B_{m,n}$ if u and v are both in θ_n, and $u[e] = v[e]$ for every edge e shared between m and n. We say that process n is *outward-facing* in interactions with its neighbor m if the relation $B_{m,n}$ is a stuttering bisimulation on H_n^θ.

Theorem 6. *With outward-facing interaction, the local state space of process m is stuttering bisimilar to the global state space in terms of the local state of m.*

Proof: Define the relation R from global states to those of H_m^θ as in the proof of Theorem 5 by $(s, t) \in R$ iff $\theta(s)$ and $s[m] = t$.

Consider a transition from t to t'. If the move is by process m, it is enabled in s as well, and the resulting states are related by R. Now suppose the move is an interference transition by a neighbor, n. Hence there is some joint state (t, u) of (m, n) such that the move is by n from (t, u) to (t', u'). As $u \in \theta_n$ (by joint state) and $s[n] \in \theta_n$ (by definition of R), and the two are connected to the same local state of m, the pair $(s[n], u)$ is in $B_{m,n}$. As $B_{m,n}$ is a stuttering bisimulation, there is a sequence, say σ, of transitions by P_n alone from $s[n]$ to a state v' such that $(v', u') \in B_{m,n}$, and all intermediate states on σ from $s[n]$ to v' are related by $B_{m,n}$ to u. Hence, the value of the shared edges between m and n is unchanged on σ until the final step, where it matches u'. Therefore, for the global computation induced by σ from s, the final state s' is such that $s'Rt'$, and for all intermediate global states x on that path, xRt holds. This shows that R^{-1} is a stuttering simulation from the local to the global space. By Theorem 5, the relation R is a simulation from the global to the local space. Hence, R is a stuttering bisimulation between the spaces. **EndProof.**

Corollary 3. *With outward-facing interaction and unconditionally fair scheduling, the local state space of a process m satisfies the same local mu-calculus properties as the global state space.*

5   Syntactic Determination of Local Symmetries

We show how to recognize local symmetry from syntactic structure. This also applies to network families, with corresponding unbounded savings in local verification. First, we use relations between structure and global symmetry, and between global and local symmetries. Next, we show how local symmetries may be directly derived if network families are induced by a finite set of tilings. We note that when local symmetry is derived syntactically, either through the use of normal process descriptions, or through building block tiles, the computation of the compositional invariant can be done symbolically, and in the case of tilings, directly on each tile, unlike the case of global symmetry reduction, where the symbolic (BDD-based) orbit relation is difficult to compute even for fully symmetric networks [5].

5.1   Program Symmetries

Let $P = \|_{i \in [0..k-1]} P_i, k \geq 1$ be a fixed network where each component P_i is an implementation of a process template W. Network topology is restricted so that all edges are bidirectional and connect only two nodes. Each P_m is described by a finite transition graph where if there is an arc from the internal node g to the internal node h then the arc is labeled by a guarded command $\rho \rightarrow A$. Transitions are given by $g : \rho \rightarrow A : h$ where A is the local update function and ρ is a predicate over the neighborhood of P_m. The action A is given by a list of simultaneous updates to the shared variables, $v_1, \ldots, v_d$, where v_i is the variable across the edge (m, n_i).

We name the variables associated with a process, depending on the specific topology, the left variable, the right variable, the forward variable of P_m, etc. This modeling tactic is used (see [8]) to stipulate that the update functions for the variables be process-index independent.

Two transitions $g : \rho \to A : h$ and $g' : \rho' \to A' : h'$ are equivalent if $g = g', h = h', \rho$ is semantically equivalent to ρ' and A and A' are semantically equivalent (c.f. [8]). Processes P_m and P_n are equivalent if there is a bijective mapping between equivalent transitions of P_m and P_n. A permutation π of process indices is an automorphism of P if P_m is equivalent to $P_{\pi(m)}$ for all $m \in [0..k-1]$.

As shown in [8] the global symmetries of the program P, essentially the permutations of $[0..k-1]$ that leave P unchanged, are a subset of the global symmetries of the global state space G. From P, one defines an undirected graph, the *communication relation*, CR [8]. The nodes of CR are the nodes of N of the topology (N, E) and there is an edge from m to n in CR iff the nodes are connected to a common edge.

P is *normal* [8] if the transitions of P are given in the following form:

$$g : (\wedge_{n \in CR(m)} \rho(m, n)) \to (\wedge_{n \in CR(m)} A(m, n)) : h$$

where each $\rho(m, n)$ is a boolean expression over the internal state of P_m and the neighborhood variables of P_m, or equality tests between the variables local to the neighborhood of P_m, and the assignments of $A(m, n)$ are concurrent assignments to the neighborhood variables of P_m, where variable values may be swapped with each other or assigned constant values. When P is a normal process network [8] showed that global symmetries of CR are symmetries of P and are automorphisms of G.

This setting substantially simplifies the application of local symmetry. First, the balance relation can be "read off" directly from the relation CR, as by results in [17], the global symmetries of CR define a balance relation over (N, E), which includes (m, β, n) if there is a symmetry π of CR such that $\pi(m) = n$. Secondly, if CR induces a transitive symmetry group, then local symmetry reduction reduces to analysis of a single representative process and its neighborhood. This may result in an exponential reduction in the cost of model checking, compared with an analysis of the entire state space. (The global symmetry used in [8] provides an exponential reduction only when CR is fully symmetric.) The check is in general over-approximate (cf. Corollary 2) but is exact under outward-facing interaction. In the parametric setting, the reduction is unbounded.

5.2   Tilings

Rings, tori, and other 'regular' network patterns have considerable local symmetry but little global symmetry. Here we show how to enforce local symmetry across network families by generating them from a finite set of *tiles*. The tiles directly induce local symmetries and balance.

Consider a fixed, finite set of process types where each process type has a fixed, finite set of edge directions, which are given unique names. The initial condition and the transition relation of a process type may refer to the values on edges in the given direction. Each type is associated with a tile describing a fixed neighborhood pattern around a node of that type. The pattern specifies for each edge connected to the central node its direction from the center and the type and direction of the other process connected to it. The tiles induce a family of networks, typically of unbounded size, as follows. A network is in the family if (1) each node is assigned an instance of a process type, and (2) the neighborhood of a node matches the tile for that node type. For instance, a tile for a torus shape would have 4 neighbors, labeled north, south, east and west.

A network family constructed in this manner has an induced balance relation, B, defined as follows. Let m, n be nodes of a network in the family. Let (m, β, n) belong to B if (a) both nodes are instances of the same type and (b) β is the mapping which, for each direction a, relates the edge reachable in direction a from m to the edge reachable in the same direction from n. (E.g., it maps the north edge of m to the north edge of n.)

Theorem 7. B *is a balance relation for the induced family, with finitely many equivalence classes.*

Proof: We show that B is a balance relation, and that it is respected by the process assignment. The mapping β is an isomorphism of the edges connected to m and n, as both have the same type. Moreover, as their initial conditions and transition relations are derived from those of the type and are independent of node identities, they are isomorphic up to β.

We now establish that B meets the balance relation. Consider a direction a. Let m' (n') be the node connected to m (n) in that direction. As m and n have the same tiling pattern, m' and n' have the same type, so the tuple (m', γ, n') is in B, for the isomorphism γ between the edges of m' and n' as given in the definition of B. Consider the edge e reached from m in direction a, and let b be the direction that this edge is reached from m'. Let f be the edge in direction a from n. As m and n follow the same tiling pattern, f must be reached from direction b from n'. Therefore, β and γ agree on this edge. As the edge was chosen arbitrarily, this establishes the balance condition. The number of equivalence classes induced by the greatest balance relation is, then, at most the number of tiles, which equals the number of process types. **EndProof.**

Theorem 7 implies that the compositional analysis of all instances of the network family can be reduced to the analysis of a finite set of representatives. This contrasts with global symmetry reduction for network families, where parameterized collapse is not as simple, nor as general. Moreover, the required representatives are just the tiles. The easy syntactic symmetry reduction contrasts with the difficulty of computing global symmetry groups for network families.

6   Applications

Example 1. Consider a non-deterministic token-ring system $P = ||_i P_i$. The internal states of P_i range over $\{T, H, E\}$ with shared variables x_i and x_{i+1} ranging over $\{\perp, tok\}$. Initially, each process is in internal state T and either owns 0 tokens or owns 1 token. The initial condition specifies that a single process owns the token. Processes cycle through states in the order T, H and E. A process in H can move to E only if it owns the token. When exiting E the process puts the token on its right and enters T. If a process is in T and has the token, then it either enters H or passes the token to the right. It can be shown that the process interactions are outward-facing. Verification of the mutual exclusion property *for all* i: $\mathsf{AG}(E_i \rightarrow (x_i = tok))$ can then be performed on a model with 3 processes that suffices to see all reachable local states.

In addition, a liveness property, *for all* i : $\mathsf{AG}(H_i \rightarrow \mathsf{AF}E_i)$, can also be verified using a combination of local arguments. The proof is constructed as follows: first, show that the system satisfies the invariant that there is exactly 1 token in the system. Then show every process that has the token eventually passes the token to the neighbor on the right. Using the global system fairness assumption that each process executes infinitely often we can chain these proofs together to conclude that for any particular process P_n: $\mathsf{AG}(H_n \rightarrow \mathsf{AF}E_n)$ holds which by local symmetry implies: *for all* i : $\mathsf{AG}(H_i \rightarrow \mathsf{AF}E_i)$.

Example 2. Interestingly, the results about a single token ring network can be extended to a ring with 2 tokens. However, the minimal model requires 4 processes. Similar reasoning holds for 3 tokens and we hypothesize can be generalized to any fixed number of tokens. A related example is a ring with 2 types of processes, one labeled *red* and one labeled *black*. For rings with even numbers of processes, half of them *red* and half of them *black*, there are 2 equivalence classes. Local symmetry reduction can be used to verify behavior of the two equivalence classes for any even number of processes, though the networks have little global symmetry and do not have transitive symmetry.

Example 3. Several works including [3,9,10,14] have considered using counting arguments as a way of implementing full symmetry reduction. Given an n process system, with isomorphic processes having local state spaces of size m, and full global symmetry on $[1..n]$ the idea is to replace the global symmetry-reduced model with a set of m counters, where the counter values record the number of components in each of the different local states. A combinatorial argument [22] shows that the number of combinations of n isomorphic process each with m local states, is $(m + n - 1)!/(n!(m - 1)!)$. If $n > 2m$, this is more than 2^m. On the other hand, if each component has b neighbors, the local representative (full global symmetry implies a single balance class) has a local state space of size approximately m^b. Over a parametric analysis m^b is a constant and b, the number of neighbors, is likely to be small in comparison with m.

7   Discussion and Related Work

We studied the relationship between the satisfaction of temporal properties on the global state space of a process network and on individual local state spaces. We show that "balanced" processes have bisimilar local spaces and therefore satisfy the same local mu-calculus formulas. Hence, for a local formula $f(n)$ that is universal in nature, the satisfaction of $f(n)$ on the local space of node n implies that $f(n)$ holds of the global state space. Thus, if universal formulas $\{f(n)\}$ hold for all nodes n, then $(\bigwedge i : f(i))$ holds for the global state space. This provides an approximate way to establish quantified mu-calculus properties. Moreover, as balanced nodes satisfy the same formulas, it is only necessary to model-check representatives of the balance equivalence relation. For a fixed process network, the restriction to local state spaces can result in exponential savings (in the number of nodes), and the further restriction to representative spaces results in a further linear cost saving. More dramatically, we show that network families constructed from building-block "tiles" have a finite set of representative nodes, so the cost saving is unbounded for parametric analysis. When network processes communicate with their neighbors in an outward-facing manner, these results carry over to the entire local mu-calculus, not just to universal properties.

The results build on our earlier work on balance relations and local symmetry [17,18,20]. That work focused on compositional invariants [21] the central result being that the strongest compositional invariants for balanced nodes are isomorphic. The current paper shows that the isomorphism applies to all local mu-calculus properties. The local state spaces on which the mu-calculus properties are evaluated are built using compositional invariants. An elegant methodology using 3-valued logic to compositionally verify mu-calculus properties is developed in [23]; however, it applies to pairs of processes, and thus does not consider symmetries in larger networks. The definition of network families through tilings has similarities to the network grammars used in [24,26]; however, the verification techniques are different.

The framework of this paper considers the neighborhood of a single node. Compositional invariants have been generalized to apply to groups of processes, to accommodate properties stated over all pairs i, j, or over all neighbors i, j; see for example [1,6,12,13,16]. Construction of a comprehensive theory of neighborhood symmetry for groups of processes is still an open question.

Global symmetry reduction, developed in [5,8,14], is based on a beautiful mathematical theory of automorphisms in graphs. However, in practice, symmetry reduction runs into difficulties, usually because there is not enough global symmetry in a process network, but also because for even highly symmetric networks, symbolic manipulation of symmetry reduced structures is difficult. In fact [5] shows that any BDD-based representation of the global symmetry group for any network with only transitive symmetry would likely incur a prohibitive cost. By focusing on local similarities, a strict generalization of global symmetries [17,20], we can avoid these problems and obtain exponential improvements. The theory of local symmetries is based on network groupoids, and we note that any network automorphism group induces a balance relation.

We also consider parameterized verification. For network families built from building-block tiles, there is a finite set of representative neighborhoods, and it suffices to prove a parameterized local mu-calculus property for each of those representatives to show that it holds for the entire family. This is an approximate method for parameterized verification. In prior work [20], we had introduced the local PCMCP (parameterized compositional model-checking) question as a decision problem that is, in many cases, more tractable than the global PMCP (parameterized model-checking) problem. Deciding PCMCP for local mu-calculus properties is a challenging open question.

Acknowledgements. Kedar Namjoshi was supported, in part, by grant CCF-1563393 from the National Science Foundation. Richard Trefler was supported, in part, by an Individual Discovery Grant from the Natural Sciences and Engineering Research Council of Canada. Both authors thank E. Allen Emerson for inspiring discussions on the topic.

References

1. Abdulla, P.A., Haziza, F., Holík, L.: All for the price of few. In: Giacobazzi, R., Berdine, J., Mastroeni, I. (eds.) VMCAI 2013. LNCS, vol. 7737, pp. 476–495. Springer, Heidelberg (2013). https://doi.org/10.1007/978-3-642-35873-9_28
2. Apt, K.R., Kozen, D.: Limits for automatic verification of finite-state concurrent systems. Inf. Process. Lett. **22**(6), 307–309 (1986)
3. Basler, G., Mazzucchi, M., Wahl, T., Kroening, D.: Symbolic counter abstraction for concurrent software. In: Bouajjani, A., Maler, O. (eds.) CAV 2009. LNCS, vol. 5643, pp. 64–78. Springer, Heidelberg (2009). https://doi.org/10.1007/978-3-642-02658-4_9
4. Browne, M.C., Clarke, E.M., Grumberg, O.: Reasoning about networks with many identical finite state processes. Inf. Comput. **81**(1), 13–31 (1989)
5. Clarke, E.M., Enders, R., Filkorn, T., Jha, S.: Exploiting symmetry in temporal logic model checking. Form. Methods Syst. Des. **9**(1–2), 77–104 (1996)
6. Cohen, A., Namjoshi, K.S.: Local proofs for global safety properties. In: Damm, W., Hermanns, H. (eds.) CAV 2007. LNCS, vol. 4590, pp. 55–67. Springer, Heidelberg (2007). https://doi.org/10.1007/978-3-540-73368-3_9
7. Dijkstra, E., Scholten, C.: Predicate Calculus and Program Semantics. Springer, New York (1990). https://doi.org/10.1007/978-1-4612-3228-5
8. Emerson, E., Sistla, A.: Symmetry and model checking. Formal Methods Syst. Des. **9**(1–2), 105–131 (1996)
9. Emerson, E.A., Havlicek, J., Trefler, R.J.: Virtual symmetry reduction. In: LICS, pp. 121–131. IEEE Computer Society (2000)
10. Emerson, E.A., Trefler, R.J.: From asymmetry to full symmetry: new techniques for symmetry reduction in model checking. In: Pierre, L., Kropf, T. (eds.) CHARME 1999. LNCS, vol. 1703, pp. 142–157. Springer, Heidelberg (1999). https://doi.org/10.1007/3-540-48153-2_12
11. Golubitsky, M., Stewart, I.: Nonlinear dynamics of networks: the groupoid formalism. Bull. Am. Math. Soc. **43**, 305–364 (2006)
12. Gurfinkel, A., Shoham, S., Meshman, Y.: SMT-based verification of parameterized systems. In: Proceedings of the 2016 24th ACM SIGSOFT International Symposium on Foundations of Software Engineering, FSE 2016, New York, NY, USA, pp. 338–348 (2016)
13. Hoenicke, J., Majumdar, R., Podelski, A.: Thread modularity at many levels: a pearl in compositional verification. In: Castagna, G., Gordon, A.D. (eds.) Proceedings of the 44th ACM SIGPLAN Symposium on Principles of Programming Languages, POPL 2017, Paris, France, 18–20 January 2017, pp. 473–485. ACM (2017)
14. Ip, C., Dill, D.: Better verification through symmetry. Formal Methods Syst. Des. **9**(1/2), 41–75 (1996)

15. Kozen, D.: Results on the propositional μ-calculus. In: Nielsen, M., Schmidt, E.M. (eds.) ICALP 1982. LNCS, vol. 140, pp. 348–359. Springer, Heidelberg (1982). https://doi.org/10.1007/BFb0012782
16. Namjoshi, K.S.: Symmetry and completeness in the analysis of parameterized systems. In: Cook, B., Podelski, A. (eds.) VMCAI 2007. LNCS, vol. 4349, pp. 299–313. Springer, Heidelberg (2007). https://doi.org/10.1007/978-3-540-69738-1_22
17. Namjoshi, K.S., Trefler, R.J.: Local symmetry and compositional verification. In: Kuncak, V., Rybalchenko, A. (eds.) VMCAI 2012. LNCS, vol. 7148, pp. 348–362. Springer, Heidelberg (2012). https://doi.org/10.1007/978-3-642-27940-9_23
18. Namjoshi, K.S., Trefler, R.J.: Analysis of dynamic process networks. In: Baier, C., Tinelli, C. (eds.) TACAS 2015. LNCS, vol. 9035, pp. 164–178. Springer, Heidelberg (2015). https://doi.org/10.1007/978-3-662-46681-0_11
19. Namjoshi, K.S., Trefler, R.J.: Loop freedom in AODVv2. In: Graf, S., Viswanathan, M. (eds.) FORTE 2015. LNCS, vol. 9039, pp. 98–112. Springer, Cham (2015). https://doi.org/10.1007/978-3-319-19195-9_7
20. Namjoshi, K.S., Trefler, R.J.: Parameterized compositional model checking. In: Chechik, M., Raskin, J.-F. (eds.) TACAS 2016. LNCS, vol. 9636, pp. 589–606. Springer, Heidelberg (2016). https://doi.org/10.1007/978-3-662-49674-9_39
21. Owicki, S.S., Gries, D.: Verifying properties of parallel programs: an axiomatic approach. Commun. ACM **19**(5), 279–285 (1976)
22. Roberts, F.: Applied Combinatorics Prentice-Hall, Upper Saddle River (1984). ISBN 0 13-039313-4
23. Shoham, S., Grumberg, O.: Compositional verification and 3-valued abstractions join forces. In: Nielson, H.R., Filé, G. (eds.) SAS 2007. LNCS, vol. 4634, pp. 69–86. Springer, Heidelberg (2007). https://doi.org/10.1007/978-3-540-74061-2_5
24. Shtadler, Z., Grumberg, O.: Network grammars, communication behaviors and automatic verification. In: Sifakis [25], pp. 151–165
25. Sifakis, J. (ed.): CAV 1989. LNCS, vol. 407. Springer, Heidelberg (1990). https://doi.org/10.1007/3-540-52148-8
26. Wolper, P., Lovinfosse, V.: Verifying properties of large sets of processes with network invariants. In: Sifakis [25], pp. 68–80

Bayesian Statistical Parameter Synthesis for Linear Temporal Properties of Stochastic Models

Luca Bortolussi[1] and Simone Silvetti[2,3]([✉]) [iD]

[1] University of Trieste, Trieste, Italy
lbortolussi@units.it
[2] University of Udine, Udine, Italy
simone.silvetti@gmail.com
[3] Esteco S.p.A., Trieste, Italy

Abstract. Parameterized verification of temporal properties is an active research area, being extremely relevant for model-based design of complex systems. In this paper, we focus on parameter synthesis for stochastic models, looking for regions of the parameter space where the model satisfies a linear time specification with probability greater (or less) than a given threshold. We propose a statistical approach relying on simulation and leveraging a machine learning method based on Gaussian Processes for statistical parametric verification, namely Smoothed Model Checking. By injecting active learning ideas, we obtain an efficient synthesis routine which is able to identify the target regions with statistical guarantees. Our approach, which is implemented in Python, scales better than existing ones with respect to state space of the model and number of parameters. It is applicable to linear time specifications with time constraints and to more complex stochastic models than Markov Chains.

Keywords: Parameter synthesis · Parametric verification
Smoothed model checking · Gaussian Processes

1 Introduction

Overview. Stochastic models are commonly used in many areas to describe and reason about complex systems, from molecular and systems biology to performance evaluation of computer networks. In all these cases, the system dynamics is usually described by high-level languages as Chemical Reaction Networks [1], population models [2] or Stochastic Petri Nets [3], which generate an underlying *Continuous Time Markov Chain* (CTMC). Formal reasoning about these models often amounts to the computation of reachability probabilities. This is the basic tool behind successful *Stochastic Model Checking* tools like PRISM [4] or the more recent STORM [5]. These tools implement numerical algorithms that compute probabilities up to a given precision, suffering though from state space

© The Author(s) 2018
D. Beyer and M. Huisman (Eds.): TACAS 2018, LNCS 10806, pp. 396–413, 2018.
https://doi.org/10.1007/978-3-319-89963-3_23

explosion, as well as simulation engines that allow statistical estimation when models are too large.

All classic quantitative verification tools assume that a model is fully specified, which is typically a strong assumption, particularly in application domains like system biology, where many model parameters are estimated from data or are only known to belong to a given range. An alternative approach is that of parameterised verification, which tries to verify properties for a whole set of models, indexed by some parameters. In case of stochastic models, this typically requires us to compute how reachability probabilities change as a function of model parameters, which is a much harder task [6]. A related problem is that of synthesis [7], where one looks for a subset of the parameter space where a given property (or multiple properties [8]) is guaranteed to be satisfied. Alternatively, one can try to design a system by finding a value that maximises the probability of satisfying a specification.

Problem Statement. In this paper, we focus on parameter synthesis for CTMC models described by chemical reaction networks, benchmarking against the approach of [7].

More specifically, we consider the following problem. We have a collection of CTMCs, indexed by a parameter vector $\theta \in \Theta$, taking values in a bounded and compact hyperrectangle $\Theta \subset \mathbb{R}^k$. We assume that the CTMCs depends on θ through their rates, and that this dependency is smooth. We consider a linear time specifications ϕ described by Metric Interval Temporal Logic [9], with bounded time operators. For each ϕ and θ, we can in principle compute the probability that a random trajectory, generated by that specific CTMC, satisfies it, i.e. $P_\phi(\theta)$.

Our goal is to find a partition of the parameter space Θ composed by three classes. The positive class $\mathcal{P}_\alpha$ which is composed by parameters where the probability of satisfying ϕ is higher than a threshold value α, the negative class $\mathcal{N}_\alpha$ composed by parameters where this probability is lower than α and the undefined class $\mathcal{U}_\alpha$ which collects all the other parameters. Following [7], we will look for a partition where the volume of the undefined class is lower a fraction of the volume of Θ. This is the *threshold synthesis problem*.

Our approach will be statistic: we assume that models are too complex to numerically compute bounds on the reachability probability, and we only rely on the possibility of simulating the model. As a consequence, our solution to the parameter synthesis problem will have only statistical guarantees of being correct. For example, if a parameter belongs to $\mathcal{P}_\alpha$, the confidence of this point satisfying $P_\phi(\theta) \geq \alpha$ will be larger than a prescribed probability (typically 95% or 99%), though for most points this probability will be essentially one, and similarly for $\mathcal{N}_\alpha$. The challenge of such an approach is that estimating the satisfaction probability at many different points in the parameter space by simulation is very expensive and inefficient, unless we are able to share the information carried by simulation runs at neighbouring points in the parameter space.

Contributions. We propose a Bayesian statistical approach for parameter synthesis, which leverages a statistical parameterised verification method known as Smoothed Model Checking [6] and the nice theoretical approximation properties of Gaussian Process [10]. Being based on a Bayesian inference engine, this naturally gives statistical error bounds for the estimated probabilities. Our algorithm uses active learning strategies to steer the exploration of the parameter space only where the satisfaction probability is close to the threshold. We also provide a prototype implementation of the approach in Python.

Despite being implemented in Python, our approach turns to be remarkably efficient, being slightly faster than [7] for small models, and outperforming it for more complex and large models or when the number of parameters is increased, at the price of a weaker form of correctness. Compared to [7], we also have an additional advantage: the method treats the simulation engine and the routine to verify of the linear time specification on individual trajectories as black boxes. This means that we can not only treat arbitrary MTL properties (while in [7] they is an essential restriction to non-nested CSL properties, i.e. reachability), but also other more complex linear time specifications (e.g. using hybrid automata, provided that the satisfaction probability is a smooth function of model parameters), and we can also apply the same approach to more complex stochastic models for which efficient simulation routines exist, like stochastic differential equations.

Related Work. Parameter synthesis of CTMC is an active field of research. In [7,11] the authors use Continuous Stochastic Logic (CSL) and uniformization methods for computing exact probability bounds for parameteric models of CTMCs obtained from chemical reaction networks. In [12] the same authors extend their algorithm to GPU architecture to improve the scalability. Authors in these two papers solve two problems: one is the threshold synthesis, the other is the identification of a parameter configuration maximising the satisfaction probability. In this paper we focus on the former, as we already presented a statistical approach to deal the latter problem in [13] for the single objective case and in [8] for the multi-objective case. An alternative statistical approach for multi-objective optimisation is that of [14], where authors use ANOVA test to estimate the dominance relation. Another approach to parameter synthesis for CTMC is [15], where the authors rely on a combination of discretisation of parameters with a refinement technique.

In this work we use a statistical approach to approximate the satisfaction probability function, building on Smoothed Model Checking [6]. This approach is applicable to CTMC with rate functions that are smooth with respect to parameters, and leverages statistical tools based on Gaussian Process regression [10] to learn an approximation of the satisfaction function from few observations. Moreover, this approach allows us to deal with a richer class of linear time properties than reachability, like those described by Metric Temporal Logic [9,16], for which numerical verification routines are heavily suffering from state space explosion [17]. Another statistical approach is that of [18], which combines sensitivity analysis, statistical model checking and uniform continuity to approximate the satisfaction probability function, but it is restricted to cases when the satisfaction probability is monotonic in the parameters. In contrast, Gaussian Process-based methods have no restriction (as Gaussian Processes are universal approximators), and have also the advantage of requiring much less simulations than pointwise statistical model checking, as information is shared between neighbouring points (see [6] for a discussion in this sense). Parametric verification and synthesis approaches are more consolidated for Discrete Time Markov Chains [19], where mature tools like PROPhESY exist [20], which rely on an symbolic representation of the reachability probability, which does not generalise to the continuous time setting.

Paper Structure. The paper is organized as follows. In Sect. 2 we discuss background material, including Parametric CTMCs, MITL, and Smoothed Model Checking and Gaussian Processes. In Sect. 3 we present our method in detail. In Sect. 4 we discuss experimental results, comparing with [7]. Conclusions and future work are discussed in Sect. 5.

2   Background

In this section we introduce the relevant background material: a formalism to describe the systems of interest, i.e. Parametric Chemical Reaction Networks, and one to describe linear time properties, i.e. Signal Temporal Logic. We then present smoothed model checking [21] and Gaussian Processes [10], which form the underlying statistical backbone of the parameter synthesis.

2.1   Parametric Chemical Reaction Networks

Chemical Reaction Networks [1] are a standard model of population processes, known in literature also as Population Continuous Time Markov Chains [2] or Markov Population Models [22]. We consider a variant with an explicit representation of kinetic parameters.

Definition 1. *A Parametric Chemical Reaction Network (PCRN) $\mathcal{M}$ is a tuple $(S, \mathbf{X}, D, \mathbf{x_0}, \mathcal{R}, \Theta)$ where*

- *$S = \{s_1, \ldots, s_n\}$ is the set of species;*
- *$\mathbf{X} = (X_1, \ldots, X_n)$ is the vector of variables counting the amount of each species, with values $\mathbf{X} \in D$, with $D \subseteq \mathbb{N}^n$ the state space;*
- *$\mathbf{x_0} \in D$ is the initial state;*
- *$\mathcal{R} = \{r_1, \ldots, r_m\}$ is the set of chemical reactions, each of the form $r_j = (\mathbf{v_j}, \alpha_j)$, with $\mathbf{v_j}$ the stoichiometry or update vector and $\alpha_j = \alpha_j(\mathbf{X}, \boldsymbol{\theta})$ the propensity or rate function. Each reaction can be represented as*

$$r_j : u_{j,1}s_1 + \ldots + u_{j,n}s_n \xrightarrow{\alpha_j} w_{j,1}s_1 + \ldots + w_{j,n}s_n,$$

where $u_{j,i}$ ($w_{j,i}$) is the amount of elements of species s_i consumed (produced) by reaction r_j. With $\mathbf{u}_j = (u_{j,1}, \ldots, u_{j,n})$ (and similarly $\mathbf{w}_j$), $\mathbf{v}_j = \mathbf{w}_j - \mathbf{u}_j$.

– $\boldsymbol{\theta} = (\theta_1, \ldots, \theta_k)$ *is the vector of (kinetic) parameters, taking values in a compact hyperrectangle* $\Theta \subset \mathbb{R}^k$.

To stress the dependency of $\mathcal{M}$ on the parameters $\boldsymbol{\theta} \in \Theta$, we will often write $\mathcal{M}_\theta$. A PCRN $\mathcal{M}_\theta$ defines a Continuous Time Markov Chain [2,23] on D, with infinitesimal generator Q, where $Q_{\boldsymbol{x},\boldsymbol{y}} = \sum_{r_j \in \mathcal{R}} \{\alpha_j(\boldsymbol{x}, \boldsymbol{\theta}) \mid \boldsymbol{y} = \boldsymbol{x} + \boldsymbol{v}_j\}$, $\boldsymbol{x} \neq \boldsymbol{y}$. We denote by P_θ the probability over the paths $Path^{\mathcal{M}_\theta}$ of $\mathcal{M}_\theta$ of such a CTMC.

2.2 Metric Interval Temporal Logic

Metric Interval Temporal Logic (MITL [16]) is a discrete linear time temporal logic used to reason about the future evolution of a path in continuous time. Generally this formalism is used to qualitatively describe the behaviors of trajectories of differential equations or stochastic models. The temporal operators we consider are all time-bounded, like in Signal Temporal Logic [9], a signal-based version of MITL. This implies that time-bounded trajectories are sufficient to verify every formula. The atomic predicates of MITL are inequalities on a set of real-valued variables, i.e. of the form $\mu(\boldsymbol{X}) := [g(\boldsymbol{X}) \geq 0]$, where $g : \mathbb{R}^n \to \mathbb{R}$ is a continuous function and consequently $\mu : \mathbb{R}^n \to \{\top, \bot\}$.

Definition 2. *A formula* $\phi \in \mathcal{F}$ *of MITL is defined by the following syntax:*

$$\phi := \bot \mid \top \mid \mu \mid \neg\phi \mid \phi \vee \phi \mid \phi \mathbf{U}_{[T_1,T_2]}\phi, \tag{1}$$

where μ *are atomic predicates as defined above, and* $T_1 < T_2 < +\infty$.

Eventually and globally modal operators are defined as customary as $\mathbf{F}_{[T_1,T_2]}\phi \equiv \top \mathbf{U}_{[T_1,T_2]}\phi$ and $\mathbf{G}_{[T_1,T_2]}\phi \equiv \neg\mathbf{F}_{[T_1,T_2]}\neg\phi$. MITL formulae are interpreted over the paths $\boldsymbol{x}(t)$ of a PCRN $\mathcal{M}_\theta$. We will consider here the Boolean semantics of [9], which given a trajectory $\boldsymbol{x}(t)$, returns either true or false, referring the reader to [9] for its definition and for a description of monitoring algorithms. Combining this with the probability distribution P_θ over trajectories induced by a PCRN model $\mathcal{M}_\theta$, we obtain the satisfaction probability of a formula ϕ as

$$P_\phi(\boldsymbol{\theta}) \equiv P(\phi \mid \mathcal{M}_\theta) := P_\theta(\{\boldsymbol{x}(t) \in Path^{\mathcal{M}_\theta} \mid (\boldsymbol{x}, 0) \models \phi\})$$

2.3 Parametric Verification and Smoothed Model Checking

Given an MITL formula ϕ and a CTMC $\mathcal{M}_\theta$, we consider two verification tasks:

– (Classic) Verification: compute or estimate the satisfaction probability $P_\phi(\boldsymbol{\theta})$ for a fixed $\boldsymbol{\theta}$.
– Parametric verification: compute or estimate the satisfaction probability $P_\phi(\boldsymbol{\theta})$ as a function of $\boldsymbol{\theta} \in \Theta$.

The classic verification task can be solved with specialised numerical algo-rithms [17,24]. These methods calculate $P_\phi(\boldsymbol{\theta})$ by a clever numerical integration of the Kolmogorov equations of the CTMC. This approach, however, suffers from the curse of state space explosion, becoming inefficient for big or complex models. A viable alternative is rooted in statistics. The key idea is to estimate the satis-faction probability by combining simulation and monitoring of MITL formulas. In practice, for each trajectory $\boldsymbol{x}$ generated by a simulation of the CTMC $\mathcal{M}_\theta$, we verify if $\boldsymbol{x} \models \phi$. This produces observations of a Bernoulli random variable Z_ϕ, which is equal to 1 if and only if the trajectory satisfies the property, and 0 otherwise. By definition, the probability of observing 1 is exactly $P_\phi(\boldsymbol{\theta})$, which can thus be estimated by frequentist or Bayesian statistical inference [25,26].

Parametric verification brings additional challenges. For PCRN, the numeri-cal approach of [27] provides upper and lower bounds on the satisfaction function. By decomposing the parameter space in small regions, one can provide a tight approximation of the satisfaction function, at the price of a polynomial cost in the dimension of the state space and of an exponential cost in the dimension of the parameter space [27].

The statistical counterpart for parametric verification is known as Smoothed Model Checking [6]. This method combines simulations in few points of the parameter space with state-of-the-art generalised regression methods from statis-tics and machine learning to infer an analytic approximation of the satisfaction function, mapping each $\boldsymbol{\theta}$ to the corresponding value of $P_\phi(\boldsymbol{\theta})$. The basic idea is to cast the estimation of the satisfaction function as a learning problem: from the observation of few simulation runs at some points of the parameter space, we wish to learn an approximation of the satisfaction function, with statistical error guarantees. Smoothed Model Checking solves this problem relying on Gaussian Process (generalised) regression, a Bayesian non-parametric method that returns in each point an estimate of the value of the satisfaction function together with confidence bounds, defining the region containing the true value of the function with a prescribed probability. The only substantial requirement for Smoothed Model Checking is that the satisfaction probability is smooth with respect to the parameters. This holds for MITL properties interpreted over PCTMCs [6]. Smoothed Model Checking will be the key tool for our synthesis problem, hence we will introduce it in more detail, after a brief introduction of its underlying inference engine, i.e. Gaussian Processes.

Gaussian Processes. Gaussian Processes (GPs) are a family of distributions over function spaces, used mostly for Bayesian non-parametric classification or regression. More specifically, a GP is a collection of random variables $f(\boldsymbol{x}) \in \mathbb{R}$ ($\boldsymbol{x} \in E$, a compact subset of $\mathbb{R}^h$) of which any finite subset defines a multivariate normal distribution. A GP is uniquely determined by its mean and covariance functions (called also kernels) denoted respectively with $m : E \to \mathbb{R}$ and $k : E \times E \to \mathbb{R}$ such that for every finite set of points $(\boldsymbol{x}_1, \boldsymbol{x}_2, \ldots, \boldsymbol{x}_n)$:

$$f \sim \mathcal{GP}(m, k) \iff (f(\boldsymbol{x}_1), f(\boldsymbol{x}_2), \ldots, f(\boldsymbol{x}_n)) \sim \mathcal{N}(\mathbf{m}, K) \qquad (2)$$

where $\mathbf{m} = (m(t_1), m(t_2), \ldots, m(t_n))$ is the vector mean and $K \in \mathbb{R}^{n \times n}$ is the covariance matrix, such that $K_{ij} = k(\boldsymbol{x}_i, \boldsymbol{x}_j)$. From a functional point of view, GP is a probability distribution on the set of functions $g : E \to \mathbb{R}$. The choice of the covariance function is important from a modeling perspective because it determines which functions will be sampled with higher probability from a GP, see [10].

GP are popular as they provide a Bayesian non-parametric framework for regression and classification. Starting from a training set $\{(\boldsymbol{x}_i, y_i)\}_{i=1,\ldots,n}$ of input $\boldsymbol{x}_i$ and output y_i pairs, and a prior GP, typically with zero mean and a given covariance function, GP regression computes a posterior distribution given the observations, which is another GP, whose mean and covariance depend on the prior kernel and the observation points. In particular, for real valued y_i and Gaussian observation noise, the posterior mean at a point $\boldsymbol{x}^*$ is a linear combination of the prior kernel $k(\boldsymbol{x}^*, \boldsymbol{x}_i)$ evaluated at $\boldsymbol{x}^*$ and observation points $\boldsymbol{x}_i$ with coefficients depending on the observations y_i. The prior kernel thus plays a central role, and it sometimes depends on hyperparameters, that can be set automatically by optimising the marginal likelihood, as traditionally happens in Bayesian methods [10].

In this work we use the Gaussian Radial Basis Function (GRBF) kernel [10], as samples from a GP defined by it can approximate arbitrarily well any continuous function on a compact set E. The kernel is defined as

$$k(\boldsymbol{x}_1, \boldsymbol{x}_2) = \exp(-\|\boldsymbol{x}_1 - \boldsymbol{x}_2\|^2 / l^2),$$

where l is the lengthscale hyperparameter, which roughly governs how far away observations are contributing to predictions in a point (as if $\boldsymbol{x}^*$ and $\boldsymbol{x}_i$ are much more distant than l, then $k(\boldsymbol{x}^*, \boldsymbol{x}_i)$ is approximately zero). Moreover, l determines the Lipschitz constant of the GRBF kernel, which is $\frac{\sqrt{2/e}}{l}$, and a *fortiori* of the prediction itself (being a linear combination of kernel functions).

Smoothed Model Checking. Smoothed Model Checking is a statistical method to estimate the function $P_\phi(\boldsymbol{\theta})$, casting it into a learning problem taking as input the truth value of ϕ for several simulations at different parameter values $\boldsymbol{\theta}_1, \ldots, \boldsymbol{\theta}_n$, with few simulation runs ($M \ll +\infty$) per parameter point. The method tries to reconstruct a real-valued latent function $f(\boldsymbol{\theta})$, which is squeezed to $[0, 1]$ via the Probit transform[1] Ψ to give the satisfaction probability at $\boldsymbol{\theta}$: $P_\phi(\boldsymbol{\theta}) = \Psi(f(\boldsymbol{\theta}))$. Let us denote with $\mathcal{O} = [\mathbf{o}_1, \mathbf{o}_2, \ldots, \mathbf{o}_n]$ the matrix whose rows $\mathbf{o}_i$ are the Boolean m-vectors of the evaluations in $\boldsymbol{\theta}_j$. Hence, we have that each observation $\mathbf{o}_i$ is an independent draw from a $Binomial(M, P_\phi(\boldsymbol{\theta}_j)))$.

Smoothed Model Checking plugs these observations into a Bayesian inference scheme, assuming a prior $p(f)$ for the latent variable f. As f is a random function, one can take as a prior a GP, specifying its mean and kernel function,

---

[1] The Probit $\Psi(x) = p(Z \leq x)$ is the cumulative distribution function of a standard normal distribution $Z \sim \mathcal{N}(0, 1)$, evaluated at the point x.

and then invoke Bayes theorem to compute the joint posterior distribution of f at a prediction point $\boldsymbol{\theta}^*$ and at the observation points $\boldsymbol{\theta}_1, \ldots, \boldsymbol{\theta}_n$ as

$$p(f(\boldsymbol{\theta}^*), f(\boldsymbol{\theta}_1), \ldots, f(\boldsymbol{\theta}_n) \mid \mathbf{o}) = \frac{1}{Z} p(f(\boldsymbol{\theta}^*), f(\boldsymbol{\theta}_1), \ldots, f(\boldsymbol{\theta}_n)) \prod_{j=1}^{n} p(\mathbf{o}_j \mid f(\boldsymbol{\theta}_j)).$$

In the previous expression, on the right hand side, Z is a normalisation constant, while $p(f(\boldsymbol{\theta}^*), f(\boldsymbol{\theta}_1), \ldots, f(\boldsymbol{\theta}_n))$ is the prior, which is Gaussian distribution with mean and covariance matrix computed according to the GP. $p(\mathbf{o}_j \mid f(\boldsymbol{\theta}_j))$, instead, is the noise model, which in our case is given by a Binomial density. By integrating out the value of the latent function at observations points in the previous expression, one gets the predictive distribution

$$p(f(\boldsymbol{\theta}^*) \mid \mathcal{O}) = \int \prod_{j=1}^{n} d(f(\boldsymbol{\theta}_j)) p(f(\boldsymbol{\theta}^*), f(\boldsymbol{\theta}_1), \ldots, f(\boldsymbol{\theta}_n) \mid \mathcal{O}).$$

The presence of a Binomial observation model makes this integral analytically intractable, and forces us to resort to an efficient variational approximation known as Expectation Propagation [6,10]. The result is a Gaussian form for the predictive distribution for $p(f(\boldsymbol{\theta}^*) \mid \mathcal{O})$, whose mean and δ-confidence region are then Probit transformed into $[0, 1]$.

It is important to stress that the prediction of Smoothed Model Checking, being a Bayesian method, depends on the choice of the prior. In case of Gaussian Processes, choosing the prior means fixing a covariance function, which makes assumptions on the smoothness and density of the functions that can be sampled by the GP. The Gaussian Radial Basis Function is dense in the space of continuous functions over a compact set [28], hence it can approximate arbitrarily well the satisfaction probability function. By setting its lengthscale via marginal likelihood optimization, we are picking the best prior for the observed data.

3   Methodology

3.1   Problem Definition

We start by rephrasing the parameter synthesis problem defined in [7] in the context of Bayesian statistics, where truths are quantified probabilistically. The basic idea is that we will exhibit a set of parameters that satisfy the specification with high confidence, which in the Bayesian world means with high posterior probability. To recall and fix the notation, let $\mathcal{M}_\theta$ be a PCRN defined over a parameter space Θ, ϕ a MITL formula and $\tilde{P}_\phi(\boldsymbol{\theta})$ be a statistical approximate model of the satisfaction probability of ϕ at each point $\boldsymbol{\theta}$. In the Bayesian setting, $\tilde{P}_\phi(\boldsymbol{\theta})$ is in fact a posterior probability distribution over $[0, 1]$, hence we can compute for each measurable set $B \subseteq [0, 1]$ the probability $p(\tilde{P}_\phi(\boldsymbol{\theta}) \in B)$.

Problem (Bayesian Threshold Synthesis): Let $\mathcal{M}_\theta$, Θ, ϕ, and $\tilde{P}_\phi(\boldsymbol{\theta})$ as before. Fix a threshold α and consider the threshold inequality $P_\phi(\boldsymbol{\theta}) > \alpha$, for the true satisfaction probability $P_\phi(\theta)$. Fix $\epsilon > 0$ a volume tolerance, and $\delta \in (0.5, 1]$ a confidence threshold. The *Bayesian threshold synthesis problem* consists in partitioning the parameter space Θ in three classes $\mathcal{P}_\alpha$ (positive), $\mathcal{N}_\alpha$ (negative) and $\mathcal{U}_\alpha$ (undefined) as follows:

- for each $\theta \in \mathcal{P}_\alpha$, $p(\tilde{P}_\phi(\theta) > \alpha) > \delta$
- for each $\theta \in \mathcal{N}_\alpha$, $p(\tilde{P}_\phi(\theta) < \alpha) > \delta$
- $\mathcal{U}_\alpha = \Theta \setminus (\mathcal{P}_\alpha \cup \mathcal{N}_\alpha)$, and $\frac{vol(U)}{vol(\Theta)} < \epsilon$, where *vol* is the volume of the set.

Note that the set $\mathcal{P}_\alpha$ solves the threshold synthesis problem defined above, while $\mathcal{N}_\alpha$ solves the threshold synthesis problem $P_\phi(\theta) < \alpha$.

3.2   Bayesian Parameter Synthesis: The Algorithm

Our Bayesian synthesis algorithm essentially combines smoothed Model Checking (smMC) with an active learning step to adaptively refine the sets $\mathcal{P}_\alpha, \mathcal{N}_\alpha, \mathcal{U}_\alpha$, trying to keep the number of simulations of the PCRN $\mathcal{M}_\theta$ to a minimum. smMC is used to compute a Bayesian estimate of the satisfaction probability, given the samples of the truth of ϕ accumulated up to a certain point. More specifically, we use the posterior distribution $p(\tilde{P}_\phi(\theta))$ of the satisfaction probability at each θ returned by smMC to compute the following two functions of θ:

- $\lambda^+(\theta, \delta)$ is such that $p\left(\tilde{P}_\phi(\theta) < \lambda^+(\theta, \delta)\right) > \delta$
- $\lambda^-(\theta, \delta)$ is such that $p\left(\tilde{P}_\phi(\theta) > \lambda^-(\theta, \delta)\right) > \delta$

Essentially, at each point θ, $\lambda^+(\theta, \delta)$ is the upper bound for the estimate $\tilde{P}_\phi(\theta)$ at confidence δ (i.e. with probability at least δ, the true value $P_\phi(\theta)$ is less than λ^+), while $\lambda^-(\theta, \delta)$ is the lower bound. These two values will be used to split the parameter space into the three regions $\mathcal{P}_\alpha, \mathcal{N}_\alpha, \mathcal{U}_\alpha$ as follows:

- $\theta \in \mathcal{P}_\alpha$ iff $\lambda^-(\theta, \delta) > \alpha$
- $\theta \in \mathcal{N}_\alpha$ iff $\lambda^+(\theta, \delta) < \alpha$
- $\mathcal{U}_\alpha = \Theta \setminus (\mathcal{P}_\alpha \cup \mathcal{N}_\alpha)$, $\frac{vol(U)}{vol(\Theta)} < \epsilon$

To dig into how λ^+ and λ^- are computed, recall that smMC computes a real-valued Gaussian process $f_\phi(\theta)$, with mean function μ and covariance function k, from which the pointwise standard deviation can be obtained as $\sigma(\theta) = \sqrt{k(\theta, \theta)}$. At each θ, the function $f_\phi(\theta)$ is Gaussian distributed, hence we can compute the upper and lower confidence bounds for the Gaussian, and then squeeze them into $[0, 1]$ by the Probit transform Ψ. Letting $\beta_\delta = \Psi^{-1}(\frac{\delta+1}{2})$, as customary while working with Normal distributions, we get:

- $\lambda^+(\theta, \delta) = \Psi(\mu(\tilde{f}_\phi(\theta)) + \beta_\delta \sigma(\tilde{f}_\phi(\theta)))$
- $\lambda^-(\theta, \delta) = \Psi(\mu(\tilde{f}_\phi(\theta)) - \beta_\delta \sigma(\tilde{f}_\phi(\theta)))$

Algorithm 1. Bayesian Parameter Synthesis.

Input: Θ parameter space, $\mathcal{M}$ PCRN, ϕ MTL formula, α threshold, ϵ volume precision, δ confidence

```
 1: S ← initial_samples(Θ, M, φ)
 2: P_α ← ∅, N_α ← ∅, U_α ← Θ
 3: while true do
 4:    λ⁺, λ⁻ ← smoothed_MC(Θ, S)
 5:    P_α, N_α, U_α ← update_regions( λ⁺, λ⁻, P_α, N_α, U_α )
 6:    if vol(U_α)/vol(Θ) < ε then
 7:       return P_α, N_α, U_α
 8:    else
 9:       S ← refine_samples( S, U_α )
10:    end if
11: end while
```

The Bayesian synthesis procedure is described in Algorithm 1, which after initialisation enters the main loop, in which the computation of the positive, negative, and uncertain sets are carried out adaptively until convergence. Before proceeding further, we introduce some notation to describe regular grids, as they are used in the current implementation of the method. Let us consider the hyper-rectangular parameter space $\Theta = \bigtimes_{i=1}^{n}[w_i^-, w_i^+] \subset \mathbb{R}^n$, where w_i^- and w_i^+ are respectively the lower and the upper bound of the domain of the parameter θ_i. An h-grid of Θ is the set h-grid $= \cup_{m \in M}\{w^- + m * h\}$ where $h = \{h_1, \ldots, h_n\}$, $M = \bigtimes_{i=1}^{n}\{0, \ldots, \frac{w_i^+ - w_i^-}{h_i}\}$, $w^- = (w_1^-, \ldots, w_n^-)$ and $*$ is the elementwise multiplication. Given a grid, we define as *basic cell* a small hyperrectangle of size h whose vertices are points of the grid.

Initialisation. The initialisation phase consists in running some simulations of the PCRN at some points of the parameter space, to have a first reconstruction of the satisfaction function. As we do not need to be very precise in every part of the parameter space, but only for points θ whose satisfaction probability $P_\phi(\theta)$ is close to the threshold α, we start by simulating the model on all parameters of a coarse grid h_0-grid, with h_0 chosen such that the total number of parameters θ explored is reasonably small for smMC to be fast. The actual choice will depend on the number of dimensions of the parameter space, as grids depend exponentially on it. Once the grid h_0-grid is fixed, we simulate N runs of the model per each point and pass them to a monitoring algorithm for MITL, obtaining N observations of the truth value of the property ϕ at each point of h_0-grid, collected in the set S. We also initialise the sets P_α, N_α, and U_α.

Computation of P_α, N_α, and U_α Regions. The algorithm then enters the main loop, first running smMC with the current set of sample points S to compute the two functions λ^+ and λ^-. These are then used to update the regions P_α, N_α, and U_α. Here we discuss several possible approaches.

Approach 1: Fixed Grid. The simplest approach is to partition the parameter space in small cells, i.e. using a *h*-grid with *h* small, and then assign each cell to one of the sets. The assignment will be discussed later, but it involves evaluating the functions λ^+ and λ^- in each point of the grid. The method is accurate if each basic cell contains only a fraction of the volume much smaller than ϵ. However, this requires to work with fine grids, whose size blows up quickly with the number of parameters. Practically, this approach is feasible up to dimension 3 or 4 of the parameter space.

Approach 2: Adaptive Grid. To scale better with the dimension of the parameter space, we can start evaluating the $\lambda^{+/-}$ functions on a coarse grid, and refine the grid iteratively only for cells that are assigned to the uncertain set, until a minimum grid size is reached.

Central in both approaches is how to guarantee that all points of a basic cell are all belonging to one set, inspecting only a finite number of them. In particular, we will limit the evaluation of the $\lambda^{+/-}$ functions to the vertices of each cell c, i.e. to the points in the grid *h*-grid. Intuitively, this will work if the cell has a small edge size compared to the rate of growth of the satisfaction function, and the values of the satisfaction function in its vertices are all (sufficiently) above or below the threshold. However, we need to precisely quantify this "sufficient". We sketch here two exact methods and an heuristic one, which performs well in practice. We discuss here how to check that a cell belongs to the positive set, the negative one being symmetric.

Method 1: Global Lipschitz bound. This approach relies on computing the Lipschitz constant L of the satisfaction function. This can be obtained by estimating its derivatives (e.g. by finite difference or better by learning it using methods discussed in [10]), and performing a global optimization of the modulus of the gradient after each call to smMC. Let $d(\boldsymbol{h})$ be the length of the largest diagonal of a basic cell c in a *h*-grid. Consider the smallest value of the satisfaction function in one of the vertices of c, and call it $\hat{p}$. Then the value of the satisfaction function in the cell is surely greater than $\hat{p} - Ld(\boldsymbol{h})/2$ (after decreasing for half the diagonal, we need to increase again to reach the value of another vertex). The test then is $\hat{p} - Ld(\boldsymbol{h})/2 \geq \alpha$.

Method 2: Local Lipschitz bound. The previous method will suffer if the slope of the satisfaction function is large in some small region, as this will result in a large Lipschitz constant everywhere. To improve it, we can split the parameter space is subregions (for instance, by using a coarse grid), and compute the Lipschitz constant in each subregion. An alternative we are investigating is to compute in each cell of the grid a lower bound of the function $f(\theta)$ learned from the GP from its analytic expression.

Heuristic Method. In order to speed up computation and avoid computing Lipschitz constants, we can make the function λ^- more strict. Specifically, we can use a larger β_δ than the one required by our confidence level δ. For instance for a 95% confidence, $\beta_\delta = 1.96$, while we can use instead $\beta_\delta = 3$, corresponding roughly to a confidence of 99%. Coupling this with a choice of the grid step h at least one order of magnitude smaller than the lenghtscale of the kernel learned from the data (which is proportional to the Lipschitz constant of the kernel and of the satisfaction function), which guarantees that the satisfaction function will vary very little in each cell, we can be confident that if the strict λ^- is above the threshold in all vertices of the cell, then the same will hold for all points inside c for the less strict λ^-.

Refinement Step. After having build the sets $\mathcal{P}_\alpha$, $\mathcal{N}_\alpha$, and $\mathcal{U}_\alpha$, we check if the volume of $\mathcal{U}_\alpha$ is below the tolerance threshold. If so, we stop and return these sets. Otherwise, we need to increase the precision of the satisfaction function near the uncertain region. This means essentially reducing the variance inside $\mathcal{U}_\alpha$, which can be obtained by increasing the number of observations in this region. Hence, the refinement step samples points from the undefined regions $\mathcal{U}$, simulates the model few times in each of these points, computes the truth of ϕ for each trace, and add these points to the training set $\mathcal{S}$ of the smoothed model checking process. This refinement will reduce the uncertainty bound in the undefined regions which leads some part of this region to be classified as Positive $\mathcal{P}$ or Negative $\mathcal{N}$. We iterate this process until the exit condition $\frac{vol(U)}{vol(\Theta)} <$ ϵ is satisfied. The convergence of the algorithm is rooted in the properties of smoothed Model Checking, which is guaranteed to converge to the true function with vanishing variance as the number of observation points goes to infinity. In practice, the method converges quite fast, unless the problem is very hard (the true satisfaction function is close to the threshold for a large fraction of the parameter space).

4   Results

Implementation. We have implemented our algorithm in Python 3.6. The code is available at http://simonesilvetti.com/pycheck/. To improve the scalability of our algorithm, we profiled it to identify the most computationally expensive steps, among simulating the PCRN, checking the MITL formulae at each step, running smMC and partitioning the state space. The most expensive part in our test turned out to be the simulation step, which we performed using Gillespie SSA algorithm [1]. To speed up simulations, we ran them in parallel leveraging the Numba [29] package of Python which is optimal to execute array-oriented and math-heavy Python code. The smoothed model checking step, instead, is substantially independent with respect the number of repetitions. Its execution time depends on the cardinality of the training points. This is why, compared with [6], we increased the number of simulations per parameter point and reduced their number. We ran all the experiments on a Dell XPS, Intel Core i7-7700HQ 2.8 GHz, 8 GB 1600 MHz memory, equipped with Windows 10 Pro.

SIR Epidemic Model. We consider the popular SIR epidemic model [30], which is widely used to simulate the spreading of a disease among a population. The population of N individuals is divided in three classes:

– *susceptible* S individuals that are healthy and vulnerable to the infection;
– *infected* I individuals that are actively spreading the disease;
– *recovered* R individuals, which gained immunity to the disease.

The version of SIR model we consider is defined by the following two chemical reactions:

$$r_1 : S + I \xrightarrow{\alpha_1} 2I \qquad \alpha_1 = k_i \cdot \frac{X_s \cdot X_i}{N}$$
$$r_2 : I \xrightarrow{\alpha_2} R \qquad \alpha_2 = k_r \cdot X_i$$

Here, r_1 describes the possibility that an healthy individual gets the disease and becomes infected and the reaction r_2 models the recovery of an infected agent. We described the model as a PCRN where $k_i \in [0.005, 0.3]$, $k_r \in [0.005, 0.2]$ and initial population $(S, I, R) = (95, 5, 0)$ and we consider the following MITL formula:

$$\phi = (I > 0)\,\mathcal{U}_{[100,120]}\,(I = 0) \tag{3}$$

This formula expresses that the disease becomes extinct (i.e.; $I = 0$) between 100 and 120 time units. Note that for this model extinction will eventually happen with probability one, but the time of extinction depends on he parameters $\theta = (k_i, k_r)$. In the following, we report experiments to synthetise the parameter region such that $P_\phi(\theta) > \alpha$, with $\alpha = 0.1$, volume tolerance $\epsilon = 0.1$, and confidence $\delta = 95\%$. We consider all possible combinations of free parameters to explore (i.e. k_i alone, k_r alone, and k_i and k_r). The initial train set of the smoothed model checking approach has been obtained by sampling the truth value on the parameters disposed in a grid as described in Sect. 3, of size 40 points for 1D case and 400 points for the 2D case. The satisfaction probability of each parameter vector which compose the training set, as well as, the parameter vectors sampled by the refinement process have been obtained by simulating the PCRN and evaluating the MITL formula 3 with 1000 repetitions per parameter point.

Efficiency, Accuracy, and Scalability. The execution times of the experiments are reported in Table 1 (left). The results shows a good performance of our statistical algorithms, despite being implemented in Python rather then in a more efficient language like C. The execution time (in percentage) with respect to the results of the exact method reported in [7] are 42%, 18% and 7% for Case 1, Case 2 and Case 3. Our results are reported using the heuristic method to compute the sets and a fixed grid of small stepsize h.

In Case 1, we also compare the three methods to classify the regions, computing the derivative of the satisfaction probability function by finite differences and (i) optimising it globally to obtain the Lipschitz constant (equal to 4.31), (ii) optimising it in every cell of the fine prediction grid to compute a local Lipschitz constant (in each cell). As for the heuristic method, we use $\beta'_\delta = 3$ instead of $\beta_\delta = 1.96$, and a grid step of order 10^{-4}, three orders of magnitude less than the lengthscale of the kernel, set by marginal likelihood optimization equal to 0.1. All three methods gave the same results for the grid size we used. More specifically, the maximum displacement of the approximated satisfaction probability inside the cell is estimated to be 0.003

As a statistical accuracy test, we computed the "true" value of the satisfaction probability (by deep statistical model checking, using 10000 runs) for points in the positive and negative set close to the undefined set, and counted how many times these points were misclassified. More specifically, in Case 1 we consider 300 equally-spaced points between 0.1 and 0.07 (consider that a portion of the undefined region is located in a neighborhood of 0.05, see Fig. 1). All points turned to be classified correctly, pointing out to the accuracy of the smMC prediction.

We performed also a scalability test with respect to the size of the state space of the PCRN model, increasing the initial population size N of the SIR model (case 1). The results are reported in Table 1 (right). We increase the initial population size maintaining the original proportion $\frac{I}{S} = \frac{1}{19}$. Moreover we consider different thresholds α and volume tolerance ϵ in order to force the algorithm to execute at least one refinement step, as the shape of the satisfaction function changes with N. The execution time increase moderately, following a linear trend.

Table 1. (LEFT) Results for the Statistical Parameter Synthesis for the SIR model with $N = 100$ individuals and the formula $\phi = (I > 0)\mathcal{U}_{[100,120]}(I = 0)$. We report the mean and standard deviation of the execution time of the algorithm. The volume tolerance is set to 10% and the threshold α is set to 0.1. The h-grid column shows the size h of the grid used to compute the positive, negative, and uncertain sets. (RIGHT) Scalability of the method w.r.t. the size of the state space of the SIR model, increasing initial population N. α and δ are the threshold and volume tolerance used in the experiments.

Case	$k_i \times k_r$	h-grid	Time (sec)
1	$[0.005, 0.3] \times 0.05$	0.0007	17.92 ± 2.61
2	$0.12 \times [0.005, 0.2]$	0.0005	4.87 ± 0.01
3	$[0.005, 0.3] \times [0.005, 0.2]$	(0.003,0.002)	116.4 ± 4.06

Pop. Size	α	δ	Time (sec)
200	0.13	10%	$13,05 \pm 3,22$
400	0.08	10%	$13,86 \pm 5,99$
800	0.2	4%	$15,02 \pm 0,05$
1000	0.23	4%	$17,44 \pm 0,23$
2000	0.3	4%	$28,81 \pm 0,07$

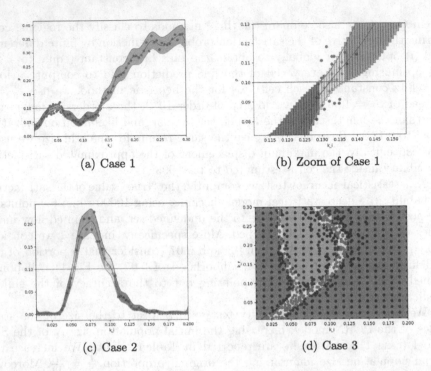

(a) Case 1   (b) Zoom of Case 1

(c) Case 2   (d) Case 3

Fig. 1. (a),(c) and (d) show the partition of the parameter space for Cases 1, 2, and 3 respectively. The positive area $\mathcal{P}_\alpha$ is depicted in red, the negative area $\mathcal{N}_\alpha$ is in blue and the undefined region $\mathcal{U}_\alpha$ is in yellow. (a) and (c) are one dimensional case: in the x-axis we report the parameter explored (respectively k_i and k_r), on the y-axis we show the value of the satisfaction function and the confidence bounds (for $\beta_\delta = 3$). The green horizontal line is the threshold $\alpha = 0.1$ (d) shows a two dimensional parameter space, hence no confidence bound has been represented. The circle dot represent the training set. In (b) we have zoomed a portion of the parameter space of (a) to visualize the cells with base length equals to h and height equal to the span of the confidence bounds. (Color figure online)

5   Conclusions

We presented an efficient statistical algorithm for parameter synthesis, to iden- tify parameters satisfying MITL specifications with a probability greater than a certain threshold. The algorithm is based on Bayesian statistics and leverages the powerful parametric verification framework of Smoothed Model Checking, inte- grating it into an active learning refinement loop which drives the computational effort of simulations near the critical region concentrated around the threshold α. The developed approach shows good performance in terms of execution time and outperforms the exact algorithm developed in [7], retaining good accuracy at the price of having only statistical guarantees.

Note that we compared with the performance of [7] and not of their GPU implementation [12], as our method uses only CPU computing power at the moment. However, it can be implemented on a GPU, leveraging e.g. [31]. We expect a substantial increase of the performance. Fully distributing on CPU the computations of the algorithm, beyond only stochastic simulation, is also feasible, the hard part being to parallelise GP inference [32].

Other directions for future work include the implementation of the adaptive grid strategy to construct the $\mathcal{P}_\alpha$, $\mathcal{N}_\alpha$, and $\mathcal{U}_\alpha$ regions, given the output of the smMC, and a divide and conquer strategy to split the parameter space (and the uncertain set $\mathcal{U}_\alpha$) in subregions, to reduce the complexity of the smMC. These two extensions are mandatory to scale the method in higher dimensions, up to 6–8 parameters. To scale even further, we plan to integrate techniques to speed up GP reconstruction: more classical sparsity approximation techniques [10] and more recent methods for GPs tailored to work on grids [33,34]. This techniques have a computational cost of $O(n)$ instead of standard implementation which costs $O(n^3)$. Finally, we aim to combine our approach with the exact algorithm developed in [7]. The idea is to use our approach for a rough exploration of the parameter space to cut out the region with higher statistical confidence to be higher or lower than the considered threshold, applying the exact approach in the remain area, when feasible.

References

1. Gillespie, D.T.: Exact stochastic simulation of coupled chemical reactions. J. Phys. Chem. **81**(25), 2340–2361 (1977)
2. Bortolussi, L., Hillston, J., Latella, D., Massink, M.: Continuous approximation of collective systems behaviour: a tutorial. Perform. Eval. **70**(5), 317–349 (2013)
3. Haas, P.J.: Stochastic Petri nets for modelling and simulation. In: Winter Simulation Conference, vol. 1 (2004)
4. Kwiatkowska, M., Norman, G., Parker, D.: PRISM 4.0: verification of probabilistic real-time systems. In: Gopalakrishnan, G., Qadeer, S. (eds.) CAV 2011. LNCS, vol. 6806, pp. 585–591. Springer, Heidelberg (2011). https://doi.org/10.1007/978-3-642-22110-1_47
5. Dehnert, C., Junges, S., Katoen, J.P., Volk, M.: A storm is coming: a modern probabilistic model checker. arXiv preprint (2017). arXiv:1702.04311
6. Bortolussi, L., Milios, D., Sanguinetti, G.: Smoothed model checking for uncertain continuous-time markov chains. Inf. Comput. **247**, 235–253 (2016)
7. Češka, M., Dannenberg, F., Paoletti, N., Kwiatkowska, M., Brim, L.: Precise parameter synthesis for stochastic biochemical systems. Acta Informatica **54**(6), 589–623 (2017)
8. Bortolussi, L., Policriti, A., Silvetti, S.: Logic-based multi-objective design of chemical reaction networks. In: Cinquemani, E., Donzé, A. (eds.) HSB 2016. LNCS, vol. 9957, pp. 164–178. Springer, Cham (2016). https://doi.org/10.1007/978-3-319-47151-8_11
9. Maler, O., Nickovic, D.: Monitoring temporal properties of continuous signals. In: Lakhnech, Y., Yovine, S. (eds.) FORMATS/FTRTFT 2004. LNCS, vol. 3253, pp. 152–166. Springer, Heidelberg (2004). https://doi.org/10.1007/978-3-540-30206-3_12
10. Rasmussen, C.E., Williams, C.K.I.: Gaussian Processes for Machine Learning. MIT Press, Cambridge (2006)

11. Češka, M., Dannenberg, F., Kwiatkowska, M., Paoletti, N.: Precise parameter synthesis for stochastic biochemical systems. In: Mendes, P., Dada, J.O., Smallbone, K. (eds.) CMSB 2014. LNCS, vol. 8859, pp. 86–98. Springer, Cham (2014). https://doi.org/10.1007/978-3-319-12982-2_7

12. Češka, M., Pilař, P., Paoletti, N., Brim, L., Kwiatkowska, M.: PRISM-PSY: precise GPU-accelerated parameter synthesis for stochastic systems. In: Chechik, M., Raskin, J.-F. (eds.) TACAS 2016. LNCS, vol. 9636, pp. 367–384. Springer, Heidelberg (2016). https://doi.org/10.1007/978-3-662-49674-9_21

13. Bartocci, E., Bortolussi, L., Nenzi, L., Sanguinetti, G.: System design of stochastic models using robustness of temporal properties. Theoret. Comput. Sci. **587**, 3–25 (2015)

14. David, A., Du, D., Guldstrand Larsen, K., Legay, A., Mikučionis, M.: Optimizing control strategy using statistical model checking. In: Brat, G., Rungta, N., Venet, A. (eds.) NFM 2013. LNCS, vol. 7871, pp. 352–367. Springer, Heidelberg (2013). https://doi.org/10.1007/978-3-642-38088-4_24

15. Han, T., Katoen, J.P., Mereacre, A.: Approximate parameter synthesis for probabilistic time-bounded reachability. In: Proceedings of Real-Time Systems Symposium, pp. 173–182 (2008)

16. Alur, R., Feder, T., Henzinger, T.A.: The benefits of relaxing punctuality. J. ACM **43**(1), 116–146 (1996)

17. Barbot, B., Chen, T., Han, T., Katoen, J.-P., Mereacre, A.: Efficient CTMC model checking of linear real-time objectives. In: Abdulla, P.A., Leino, K.R.M. (eds.) TACAS 2011. LNCS, vol. 6605, pp. 128–142. Springer, Heidelberg (2011). https://doi.org/10.1007/978-3-642-19835-9_12

18. Jha, S.K., Langmead, C.J.: Synthesis and infeasibility analysis for stochastic models of biochemical systems using statistical model checking and abstraction refinement. Theoret. Comput. Sci. **412**(21), 2162–2187 (2011)

19. Katoen, J.P.: The probabilistic model checking landscape. In: LICS, pp. 31–45 (2016)

20. Dehnert, C., Junges, S., Jansen, N., Corzilius, F., Volk, M., Bruintjes, H., Katoen, J.-P., Ábrahám, E.: PROPhESY: a probabilistic parameter synthesis tool. In: Kroening, D., Păsăreanu, C.S. (eds.) CAV 2015. LNCS, vol. 9206, pp. 214–231. Springer, Cham (2015). https://doi.org/10.1007/978-3-319-21690-4_13

21. Bortolussi, L., Sanguinetti, G.: Smoothed model checking for uncertain continuous time Markov chains. arXiv preprint. arXiv:1402.1450 (2014)

22. Henzinger, T.A., Jobstmann, B., Wolf, V.: Formalisms for specifying markovian population models. In: Bournez, O., Potapov, I. (eds.) RP 2009. LNCS, vol. 5797, pp. 3–23. Springer, Heidelberg (2009). https://doi.org/10.1007/978-3-642-04420-5_2

23. Norris, J.R.: Markov Chains. Number 2008. Cambridge University Press, Cambridge (1998)

24. Baier, C., Haverkort, B., Hermanns, H., Katoen, J.P.: Model-checking algorithms for continuous-time Markov chains. IEEE Trans. Softw. Eng. **29**(6), 524–541 (2003)

25. Younes, H.L., Simmons, R.G.: Statistical probabilistic model checking with a focus on time-bounded properties. Inf. Comput. **204**(9), 1368–1409 (2006)

26. Jha, S.K., Clarke, E.M., Langmead, C.J., Legay, A., Platzer, A., Zuliani, P.: A bayesian approach to model checking biological systems. In: Degano, P., Gorrieri, R. (eds.) CMSB 2009. LNCS, vol. 5688, pp. 218–234. Springer, Heidelberg (2009). https://doi.org/10.1007/978-3-642-03845-7_15

27. Brim, L., Češka, M., Dražan, S., Šafránek, D.: Exploring parameter space of stochastic biochemical systems using quantitative model checking. In: Sharygina, N., Veith, H. (eds.) CAV 2013. LNCS, vol. 8044, pp. 107–123. Springer, Heidelberg (2013). https://doi.org/10.1007/978-3-642-39799-8_7

28. Steinwart, I.: On the influence of the kernel on the consistency of support vector machines. J. Mach. Learn. Res. **2**, 67–93 (2002)

29. Lam, S.K., Pitrou, A., Seibert, S.: Numba: a LLVM-based Python JIT compiler. In: Proceedings of the Second Workshop on the LLVM Compiler Infrastructure in HPC, p. 7. ACM (2015)

30. Gardner, T.S., Cantor, C.R., Collins, J.J.: Construction of a genetic toggle switch in escherichia coli. Nature **403**(6767), 339–342 (2000)

31. Dai, Z., Damianou, A., Hensman, J., Lawrence, N.: Gaussian process models with parallelization and GPU acceleration. arXiv:1410.4984 (2014). [cs, stat]

32. Zhang, M.M., Williamson, S.A.: Embarrassingly parallel inference for Gaussian processes. arXiv:1702.08420 (2017). [stat]

33. Wilson, A., Nickisch, H.: Kernel interpolation for scalable structured Gaussian processes (KISS-GP). In: International Conference on Machine Learning, pp. 1775–1784 (2015)

34. Wilson, A.G., Hu, Z., Salakhutdinov, R., Xing, E.P.: Deep kernel learning. In: Artificial Intelligence and Statistics, pp. 370–378 (2016)

7th Competition on Software Verification (SV-COMP)

2LS: Memory Safety and Non-termination
(Competition Contribution)

Viktor Malík[1,3], Štefan Martiček[1,3], Peter Schrammel[1,2(✉)],
Mandayam Srivas[4], Tomáš Vojnar[3], and Johanan Wahlang[4]

[1] Diffblue Ltd., Oxford, UK
[2] University of Sussex, Brighton, UK
p.schrammel@sussex.ac.uk
[3] FIT BUT, IT4Innovations Centre of Excellence, Brno, Czech Republic
[4] Chennai Mathematical Institute, Chennai, India

Abstract. 2LS is a C program analyser built upon the CPROVER infrastructure. 2LS is bit-precise and it can verify and refute program assertions and termination. 2LS implements template-based synthesis techniques, e.g. to find invariants and ranking functions, and incremental loop unwinding techniques to find counterexamples and k induction proofs. New features in this year's version are improved handling of heap-allocated data structures using a template domain for shape analysis and two approaches to prove program non-termination.

1 Overview

2LS is a static analysis and verification tool for sequential C programs that is based on an algorithm called kIkI (k-invariants and k-induction) [1], which combines bounded model checking, k-induction, and abstract interpretation into a single, scalable framework. 2LS relies on incremental SAT solving to employ all these techniques simultaneously in order to find proofs and refutations of assertions, as well as to perform termination analysis [2].

This year's competition version introduces a new *abstract shape domain* allowing 2LS to reason about properties of programs manipulating heap and dynamic data structures, and a *non-termination analysis*, which serves as a counterpart to the existing termination analysis and allows 2LS to prove non-termination of a program.

Architecture. 2LS is built upon the CPROVER infrastructure [3] and thus uses *GOTO programs* as the internal program representation. It first performs various static analyses and transformations of the program, including resolution of function pointers, points-to analysis, and insertion of assertions guarding against

The Czech authors were supported by the Czech Science Foundation project 17-12465S, the IT4IXS: IT4Innovations Excellence in Science project (LQ1602), and the FIT BUT internal project FIT-S-17-4014.

P. Schrammel—Jury member.

D. Beyer and M. Huisman (Eds.): TACAS 2018, LNCS 10806, pp. 417–421, 2018.
https://doi.org/10.1007/978-3-319-89963-3_24

invalid pointer and memory operations. The analysed program is then translated into an acyclic, over-approximate single static assignment (SSA) form, in which loops are cut at the edges returning to the loop head. Subsequently, 2LS refines this over-approximation by computing inductive invariants in various abstract domains represented by parametrised logical formulae, so-called templates [1]. The competition version uses the interval domain for numerical variables and the new shape domain for pointer-typed variables described below.

The kIkI algorithm [1] operates on the SSA form, which is translated into a CNF formula over a bitvector representation of program configurations and given to a SAT solver. This formula is incrementally extended and amended to perform loop unwindings and abstract domain operations. The model returned by the solver is then used either to refine the predicates representing abstract values or to find a counterexample refuting the property to be checked. A more detailed description of the 2LS architecture can be found in the tool paper [7].

2   New Features

For SV-COMP'18, apart from various bug fixes and minor improvements, two major improvements of 2LS have been implemented: namely, a support for dealing with inductive list-like data structures and a support for proving program non-termination. Although 2LS supports certain interprocedural analyses, the competition version performs both analyses in a monolithic way, i.e. after inlining function calls. These improvements tackle weaknesses observed in previous years in the heap and memory safety categories, as well as they give a boost to 2LS' capabilities in non-termination analysis.

2.1   Memory Safety and Heap Invariants

To support shape analysis of dynamic data structures, a new abstract domain has been added to 2LS to express invariants describing heap configurations in the context of the bitvector logic used by 2LS [4]. The domain is based on recording (1) information about

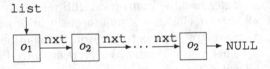

Fig. 1. A singly-linked list with nodes allocated at two different program locations.

abstract heap objects pointed to by pointer variables and (2) information about reachability of abstract objects using *pointer access paths* [6]. Here, an abstract heap object represents all objects allocated at a given program location. The access paths then record which target abstract objects can be reached from a given source abstract object while going through some set of intermediary objects. For instance, the list in Fig. 1 would be encoded as $\text{list} = \&o_1 \wedge path(o_1, \text{nxt}, \{o_1, o_2\}, \text{NULL})$, meaning that list points to an object o_1 and there is a path from o_1 via nxt fields of abstract objects o_1 and o_2 to NULL. This representation is integrated as a template over pointer-typed variables and fields of dynamic objects into $kIkI$. The template is a parametrised logical formula. The parameters encode sets of memory objects that can be pointed by each pointer-typed variable as well as the set of paths that can lead from each dynamic object to other objects. 2LS computes these sets using an incremental SAT solver. This allows 2LS to prove or to refute assertions related to manipulation of dynamically linked data structures. The supported properties include null-pointer dereferencing, double-free, or memory leaks, for instance. Assertions for these properties are automatically instrumented into the code.

2.2   Proving Non-termination

Last year's version of 2LS provided a technique for proving termination based on linear lexicographic ranking functions synthesised using templates over bitvectors [2], but the tool was unable to prove non-termination except for trivial cases. For SV-COMP'18, two techniques for *proving non-termination* have been added [5]. Both of the approaches are relatively simple, yet appear to be reasonably efficient on the SV-COMP benchmarks.

The first approach is based on finding *singleton recurrence sets*. All loops are unfolded k times (with k being incrementally increased), followed by a check whether there is some loop L and a program configuration that can be reached at the head of L after both k' and k unwindings for some $k' < k$. Such a check can be easily formulated in 2LS as a formula over the SSA representation of programs with loops unfolded k times. This technique is able to find lasso-shaped executions in which a loop returns to the same program configuration every $k - k'$ iterations after k' initial iterations.

The second approach tries to reduce the number of unwindings by looking for loops that generate an *arithmetic progression* over every integer variable. More precisely, it looks for loops L for which each integer variable x can be associated with a constant c_x such that every iteration of L changes the value of x to $x + c_x$, keeping non-integer variables unchanged. Two queries are used to detect such loops: the first one asks whether there is a configuration $\bar{x}$ and a constant vector $\bar{c}$ (with the vectors ranging over all integer variables modified in the loop and constants from their associated bitvector domains) such that one iteration of L ends in the configuration $\bar{x} + \bar{c}$, while the second makes sure that there is no configuration $\bar{x}'$ over which one iteration of L would terminate in a configuration other than $\bar{x}' + \bar{c}$. If such a loop L and a constant vector $\bar{c}$ are found, non-termination of L can be proved as follows: First, we gradually exclude each configuration $\bar{x}$ reachable at the head of L for which there is some k such that L cannot be executed from $\bar{x} + k.\bar{c}$ (intuitively meaning that L cannot be executed $k + 1$ times from $\bar{x}$). Second, we check whether there remains some non-excluded configuration reachable at the head of L.

The termination and non-termination analyses are run in parallel, and the first definite answer is used. Among the new non-termination analyses, several rounds of unwinding are first tried with the singleton recurrence set approach. If that is not sufficient, the arithmetic progression approach is tried. If that does not succeed either, further rounds of unwinding with the former approach are run.

3   Strengths and Weaknesses

2LS' core algorithm, kIkI, is designed to be efficient for simultaneously finding proofs as well as refutations. Our SSA encoding allows us to introduce abstractions only at certain program points where these are necessary to infer the predicates required to construct proofs (e.g. invariants, ranking functions, recurrence sets). The remaining program is represented in a bit-precise large-block encoding.

Compared to the previous editions of the competition, 2LS is now able to reason about dynamic linked data structures. The approach used is currently able to handle various forms of linked lists (singly- or doubly-linked, a subset of nested or circular lists). However, more elaborate template domains will be required to handle other dynamic data structures such as trees and more general graph structures.

2LS' template-based approach to abstract interpretation allows easy combination of domains. We combine the heap domain with intervals over bitvectors, which is sufficient for many benchmarks. However, some benchmarks, e.g. those requiring reasoning about arrays contents, demand stronger invariants than we are currently able to infer.

The termination analysis scales well, but is currently limited to rather simple termination conditions (lexicographic linear). The newly implemented non-termination analyses are surprisingly effective on many SV-COMP termination benchmarks (638 out of 657 non-termination benchmarks proved). However, if a larger number of unwindings is needed the approach becomes quite inefficient. kIkI does not yet support recursion, which is another limitation, in particular w.r.t. the SV-COMP termination benchmark set, which contains a large number of recursive programs. The output of witnesses in the new categories (memory safety and termination) is still lacking (more than 550 points have been lost there).

4   Tool Setup

The competition submission is based on 2LS version 0.6.[1] Installation instructions are given in the file COMPILING. The executable 2ls is in the directory src/2ls. See the 2ls wrapper script (contained in the tarball) for the relevant command line options given to 2LS. The BenchExec script is called two_ls.py and the benchmark definition file 2ls.xml. As a back end, the competition submission of 2LS uses Glucose 4.0. 2LS competes in all categories except Concurrency.

5   Software Project

2LS is maintained by Peter Schrammel with pull requests contributed by the community. It is publicly available under a BSD-style license. The source code is available at http://www.github.com/diffblue/2ls.

---

[1] Executable available at https://gitlab.com/sosy-lab/sv-comp/archives/tags/svcomp18.

References

1. Brain, M., Joshi, S., Kroening, D., Schrammel, P.: Safety verification and refutation by k-invariants and k-induction. In: Blazy, S., Jensen, T. (eds.) SAS 2015. LNCS, vol. 9291, pp. 145–161. Springer, Heidelberg (2015). https://doi.org/10.1007/978-3-662-48288-9_9
2. Chen, H.Y., David, C., Kroening, D., Schrammel, P., Wachter, B.: Bit-precise procedure-modular termination proofs. TOPLAS, **40** (2017)
3. Clarke, E., Kroening, D., Lerda, F.: A tool for checking ANSI-C programs. In: Jensen, K., Podelski, A. (eds.) TACAS 2004. LNCS, vol. 2988, pp. 168–176. Springer, Heidelberg (2004). https://doi.org/10.1007/978-3-540-24730-2_15
4. Malík, V.: Template-based synthesis of heap abstractions. Master's thesis, Brno University of Technology, Brno (2017)
5. Martiček, Š.: Synthesizing non-termination proofs from templates. Master's thesis, Brno University of Technology, Brno (2017)
6. Rinetzky, N., Bauer, J., Reps, T., Sagiv, M., Wilhelm, R.: A semantics for procedure local heaps and its abstractions. In: POPL. pp. 296–309. ACM (2005)
7. Schrammel, P., Kroening, D.: 2LS for program analysis (competition contribution). In: Chechik, M., Raskin, J.-F. (eds.) TACAS 2016. LNCS, vol. 9636, pp. 905–907. Springer, Heidelberg (2016). https://doi.org/10.1007/978-3-662-49674-0_56

YOGAR-CBMC: CBMC with Scheduling Constraint Based Abstraction Refinement
(Competition Contribution)

Liangze Yin[1], Wei Dong[1]([✉]), Wanwei Liu[1], Yunchou Li[2], and Ji Wang[1]

[1] National University of Defense Technology, Changsha, China
yinliangze@163.com, wdong@nudt.edu.cn
[2] Beijing Institution of Tracking and Telecommunication Technology, Beijing, China

Abstract. This paper presents the YOGAR-CBMC tool for verification of multi-threaded C programs. It employs a scheduling constraint based abstraction refinement method for bounded model checking of concurrent programs. To obtain effective refinement constraints, we have proposed the notion of *Event Order Graph (EOG)*, and have devised two graph-based algorithms over EOG for counterexample validation and refinement generation. The experiments in SV-COMP 2017 show the promising results of our tool.

1 Verification Approach and Software Architecture

Bounded model checking (BMC) is among the most efficient techniques for concurrent program verification [1]. However, due to non-deterministic interleavings, a huge encoding is required for an exact description of the thread interaction.

YOGAR-CBMC is a verification tool for multi-threaded C programs based on shared variables under *sequential consistency (SC)*. For these programs, we have observed that the *scheduling constraint*, which defines that "for any pair $\langle w, r \rangle$ s.t. r reads the value of a variable v written by w, there should be no other write of v between them", significantly contributes to the complexity of the behavior encoding. In the existing work of BMC, the scheduling constraint is encoded into a complicated logic formula, the size of which is cubic in the number of shared memory accesses [2].

To avoid the huge encoding of scheduling constraint, YOGAR-CBMC performs abstraction refinement by weakening and strengthening the scheduling constraint [3]. Figure 1 demonstrates the high-level overview of its architecture. We initially ignore the scheduling constraint and then obtain an over-approximation abstraction φ_0 of the original program (w.r.t. the given loop

This work was supported by the National key R&D program of China (No. 2017YFB1001802); the 973 National Program on Key Basic Research Project of China (No. 2014CB340703); and the National Nature Science Foundation of China (No. 61690203, No. 61532007).

D. Beyer and M. Huisman (Eds.): TACAS 2018, LNCS 10806, pp. 422–426, 2018.
https://doi.org/10.1007/978-3-319-89963-3_25

unwinding depth). If the property is safe on the abstraction, then it also holds on the original bounded program. Otherwise, an abstraction counterexample is obtained and the abstraction will be refined if the counterexample is infeasible.

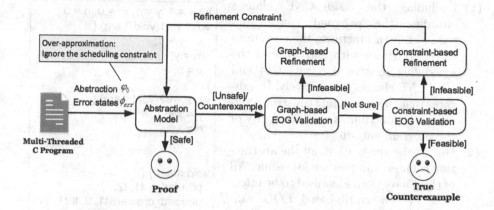

Fig. 1. High-level overview of YOGAR-CBMC architecture.

The performance of this method significantly depends on the generated refinement constraints. Ideally, a refinement constraint should have a small size yet a large amount of space should be reduced during each iteration. To achieve this goal, we have proposed the notion of *Event Order Graph (EOG)*, and have devised two graph-based algorithms over EOG for counterexample validation and refinement generation. Given an abstraction counterexample π, the corresponding EOG G_π captures all the event order requirements of π defined in the scheduling constraint. The counterexample π is feasible iff the EOG G_π is feasible. To validate the feasibility of G_π, we have proposed several deduction rules to deduce those implicit order requirements of G_π. If any cycle exists in G_π, then both π and G_π are infeasible. A graph-based refinement algorithm is then employed to analyze all the possible "kernel reasons" of all cycles. By eliminating those "redundant" kernel reasons, we can usually obtain a small set of "core kernel reasons", which can usually be encoded into a small refinement constraint. The experimental results show that: (1) Our graph-based EOG validation method is powerful enough in practice. Given an infeasible EOG, it can usually identify the infeasibility with rare exceptions. (2) Our graph-based refinement method is effective. If some cycle exists in G_π, it can usually obtain a small refinement constraint which reduces a large amount of search space.

If no cycle exists in G_π, we are not sure whether the EOG is feasible or not. We employ a constraint-based EOG validation process to further validate its feasibility by constraint solving. If an infeasibility is determined, a constraint-based refinement generation process is performed to refine the abstraction, which obtains only one kernel reason of the infeasibility. Enhanced by these two constraint-based processes, we have proved that our method is sound and complete w.r.t the given loop unwinding depth.

Consider the example shown in Fig. 2. We attempt to verify that it is impossible for both m and n to be 1 after the exit of threads thr1 and thr2, which has a modular proof in this program. In this example, we have observed that:

(1) Excluding the 3049 CNF clauses encoding the pthread_create and pthread_join functions, the encodings of this program with and without the scheduling constraint have 10214 and 1018 CNF clauses, respectively. It indicates that the scheduling constraint significantly contributes the complexity of the program encoding.

(2) During the verification, all the abstraction counterexamples are infeasible. All of them have been identified to be infeasible by our graph-based EOG validation method. It indicates that our graph-based EOG validation method is powerful enough in practice.

(3) The property is verified through only three refinements, and only 7 simple CNF clauses are added during the refinement processes. It indicates that the refinement constraints usually have small sizes yet reduce large amount of the search space, and our graph-based refinement method is effective.

```
int x = 1, y = 1, m = 0, n = 0;
void* thr1(void * arg) {
  x = y + 1;
  m = y;
  x = 0;
}
void* thr2(void * arg) {
  y = x + 1;
  n = x;
  y = 0;
}
void main() {
  pthread_t t1, t2;
  pthread_create(&t1, 0, thr1, 0);
  pthread_create(&t2, 0, thr2, 0);
  pthread_join(t1, 0);
  pthread_join(t2, 0);
  assert (!(m == 1 && n == 1));
}
```

Fig. 2. An illustration example.

2   Strengths and Weaknesses

The strengths of our tool include: (1) Our approach is a general purpose technique for multi-threaded C program verification, not assuming any special characteristics of the programs. Our tool supports nearly all features of C and PThreads. (2) Our approach is efficient in practice. Without the scheduling constraint, the size of the encoding can be dramatically reduced. Moreover, it can usually verify the property with a small number of refinements, while the refinement constraints usually have small sizes. (3) Enhanced by the constraint-based counterexample validation and refinement generation processes, our approach is sound and complete w.r.t. the given loop unwinding depth. It provides both proofs and refutations for the property. If the property is found to be false, a counterexample will be provided. (4) As the abstractions usually have small sizes, our tool generally consumes less memory than those tools giving an exact description of the scheduling constraint. In this sense, our tool is more scalable.

We have applied YOGAR-CBMC to the benchmarks in the concurrency track of SV-COMP 2017. Our tool has successfully verified all these examples within

1550 s and 43 GB of memory. It has won the gold medal in the Concurrency Safety category of SV-COMP 2017 [4].

However, for those programs where the scheduling constraint is not the major part of the encoding, our method may still need dozens of refinements. Given that the abstractions may have similar size with the monolithic encoding, our tool may run worse than those monolithic encoding tools. Moreover, for those real-world programs with a large number of read/write accesses and complex data structures, how to reduce the number of refinements and how to deal with the shared structure members more efficiently, are still challenging problems.

3   Tool Setup and Configuration

The binary file of YOGAR-CBMC for Ubuntu 16.04 (x86_64-linux) is available at https://gitlab.com/sosy-lab/sv-comp/archives. It is implemented on top of CBMC-4.9[1]. Its setup and configuration are same as that of CBMC. The tool-info module and benchmark definition of our tool is "yogar-cbmc.py" and "yogar-cbmc.xml" respectively.

Our tool needs two parameters of CBMC: --no-unwinding-assertions and --32. The unwind bound of YOGAR-CBMC is dynamically determined through a syntax analysis. Particularly, the bound is set to 2 for programs with arrays, and n if some of the program's for loops are upper bounded by a constant n, which is the same as for MU-CSEQ [5]. To run YOGAR-CBMC for a program ⟨file⟩, just use the following command:

./yogar-cbmc --no-unwinding-assertions --32 ⟨file⟩

Participation/Opt Out. YOGAR-CBMC competes only in the *concurrency category.*

4   Software Project and Contributors

YOGAR-CBMC is developed at HPCL, School of Computers, National University of Defense Technology, and includes contributions by the authors of this paper. Its source code is available at https://github.com/yinliangze/yogar-cbmc. For more information, contact Liangze Yin.

References

1. Beyer, D.: Software verification with validation of results - (Report on SV-COMP 2017). In: Legay, A., Margaria, T. (eds.) TACAS 2017. LNCS, vol. 10206, pp. 331–349. Springer, Heidelberg (2017). https://doi.org/10.1007/978-3-662-54580-5_20
2. Alglave, J., Kroening, D., Tautschnig, M.: Partial orders for efficient bounded model checking of concurrent software. In: Sharygina, N., Veith, H. (eds.) CAV 2013. LNCS, vol. 8044, pp. 141–157. Springer, Heidelberg (2013). https://doi.org/10.1007/978-3-642-39799-8_9

---

[1] Download from https://github.com/diffblue/cbmc/releases on Nov 20, 2015.

3. Yin, L., Dong, W., Liu, W., Wang, J.: Scheduling constraint based abstraction refinement for multi-threaded program verification (2017). https://arxiv.org/abs/1708.08323
4. SV-COMP: 2017 software verification competition (2017). http://sv-comp.sosy-lab.org/2017/
5. Tomasco, E., Nguyen, T.L., Inverso, O., Fischer, B., La Torre, S., Parlato, G.: MU-CSeq 0.4: individual memory location unwindings (competition contribution). In: Chechik, M., Raskin, J.-F. (eds.) TACAS 2016. LNCS, vol. 9636, pp. 938–941. Springer, Heidelberg (2016). https://doi.org/10.1007/978-3-662-49674-9_65

CPA-BAM-Slicing: Block-Abstraction Memoization and Slicing with Region-Based Dependency Analysis
(Competition Contribution)

Pavel Andrianov, Vadim Mutilin, Mikhail Mandrykin[✉], and Anton Vasilyev

Ivannikov Institute for System Programming of the Russian Academy of Sciences, Moscow, Russia
{andrianov,mutilin,mandrykin,vasilyev}@ispras.ru

Abstract. Our submission to SV-COMP'18 is a composite tool based on software verification framework CPACHECKER and static analysis platform FRAMA-C. The base verifier uses a combination of predicate and explicit value analysis with block-abstraction memoization as the CPA-BAM-BnB tool presented at SV-COMP'17. In this submission we augment the verifier on reachability verification tasks with a slicer that is able to remove those statements that are irrelevant to the reachability of error locations in the analysed program. The slicer is based on context-sensitive flow-insensitive separation analysis with typed polymorphic regions and simple dependency analysis with transitive closures. The resulting analysis preserves reachability modulo possible non-termination while removing enough irrelevant code to achieve considerable speedup of the main analysis. The slicer is implemented as a FRAMA-C plugin.

1 Verification Approach

The submission presents a composite setting comprised of a mature static verification tool CPACHECKER [1] and an experimental reachability slicer (a FRAMA-C [2] plugin) intended to speed up verification by pruning the verification scope prior the application of the main analysis. By verification scope we understand the code to be analyzed rather than the search space explored by the main analysis since the slicer doesn't prune the search space as it is, but rather removes statements (including function calls) that can be proved to not influence the verification outcome. The slicer included in this submission is currently only applicable to reachability verification tasks, though the underline algorithm is not generally limited to reachability of a small number of error locations and so can be potentially extended to support e.g. memory safety properties.

The slicer is based on a relatively simple mark-and-sweep algorithm, where the relevant statements are first identified by computing transitive closure of

---

M. Mandrykin—Jury member.

The research was supported by RFBR grant 18-01-00426.

D. Beyer and M. Huisman (Eds.): TACAS 2018, LNCS 10806, pp. 427–431, 2018.
https://doi.org/10.1007/978-3-319-89963-3_26

the dependency relation, then marked, and finally the remaining statements are removed to produce a sliced verification task. The mark-and-sweep slicing is performed on top of preliminary region analysis, which allows to handle abstract memory locations ascribed to the corresponding disjoint memory regions essentially similar to usual unaliased program variables.

The region analysis implemented in the current submission is a conservative over-approximation of context-sensitive flow-insensitive separation analysis with polymorphic regions for deductive verification. It was first described in [3] and later substantially extended in [4]. The conservative approximation is needed because the original analysis generally requires user annotations. The over-approximation is expressed in the form of additional dependencies introduced on the marking stage rather than in the region analysis itself. The dependencies allow to approximate reinterpretations of memory regions (corresponding to the use of unions and arbitrary pointer type casts), but not some corner cases of pointer arithmetic (mostly arithmetic dependent on a particular layout of structure fields), so the resulting analysis remains unsound in the general case. However, the results of analysis benchmarking using CPACHECKER as reachability verifier on the tasks in SV-COMP SoftwareSystems category showed no cases of unsoundness caused by the region analysis. This may be explained by the fact that most of the cases where the analysis is unsound with respect to a low-level C memory model are also regarded as undefined behavior by the C standard, so are probably quite rarely used in practice.

2   Software Architecture

The main CPACHECKER verification framework is included in the submission without any considerable changes. The combined tool is implemented as a wrapper script that encapsulates the main verifier invocation and does the following:

- extracts the property specification and verification task from the arguments;
- runs the slicer with timeout of 400 s (the sliced program is written to an intermediate C file);
- runs CPACHECKER configuration ldv-bam-svcomp on the sliced program;
- post-processes the witness produced by CPACHECKER.

The slicer (named CRUDE_SLICER) is implemented as a plugin to FRAMA-C [2], an extensible platform for source-code analysis of C software. The plugin implementation does not interact with other FRAMA-C plugins and only makes use of the FRAMA-C kernel. The plugin also uses OCAMLGRAPH [5] library. Both the FRAMA-C platform and the CRUDE_SLICER plugin are implemented in OCaml.

The witness post-processing stage currently simply removes the character offsets from the resulting witness (the line numbers are preserved using line directives supported by CPACHECKER) and substitutes checksum of the original program source.

Since the SoftwareSystems category of the competition also contains memory safety (and overflow) verification tasks, the submission also includes memory safety configuration smg-ldv based on shape analysis presented in [6].

3 Evaluation of the Approach

The slicer is currently able to handle only reachability verification tasks. It was evaluated on 2734 tasks from the `Systems_DeviceDriversLinux64_ReachSafety` subcategory of the SV-COMP'18 benchmarks on Intel Xeon E3-1230 v5 (3.4 GHz) machines in the competition setting. The submitted configuration with slicing was compared to baseline CPA-BAM-BnB [7,8] configuration (`-ldv-bam-svcomp`) without slicing that was also submitted to this year's competition. The results are presented in the following table:

TRUE verdicts			FALSE verdicts			Speedup		
New (+)	Lost (−)	Total	New (+)	Lost (−)	Total	Min	Max	Average
151	10	2252	97	11	267	0.03 ×	18.59 ×	1.17 ×

The table presents the results for correct verdicts only and does not take witness checking into account.

There are two significant limitations of the approach. First, the slicing is performed under assumption that all possible execution paths in the verified program are finite. This does not lead to unsoundness, since reachability (as a safety property) can be assumed to be violated only on finite paths. However, there is 3 wrong FALSE verdicts reported on the benchmarks where an error location is spuriously reached after passing through an infinite loop removed by the slicer. Another limitation is that the resulting tool can not produce precise witnesses both due to imprecision in source code locations and (more importantly) due to unavailability of either invariants or error paths in the sliced out parts of the code. The caused 1090 TRUE verdicts and all FALSE verdicts to fail to be confirmed by the witness checkers on the competition.

The time required for slicing varies from 0.08 to 1905.47 s with an average of 14.82 s. So in the submission the slicer is run with a timeout of 400 s and the remaining tasks (17 out of 2734 in the evaluation) are passed to the main verifier without slicing.

4 Tool Setup and Configuration

The submission is available for download as a ZIP archive named `cpa-bam-slicing.zip` from the SV-COMP repository by following URL: https://gitlab.com/sosy-lab/sv-comp/archives/tree/master/2018. The submission includes CPACHECKER version 1.6.1 and a statically linked version of FRAMA-C Sulfur-20171101-beta with CRUDE_SLICER plugin. The version of the plugin corresponds to commit `fcd3b927`. CPACHECKER requires Java 8 runtime environment. The invocation of the slicer is embedded in the CPACHECKER wrapper script, so the whole tool has to be executed with the following command line:

```
scripts/cpa.sh -ldv-bam-svcomp -disable-java-assertions
              -heap 10000m -spec prop.prp program.c
```
The tool participates in SoftwareSystems category, the corresponding benchmark definition is cpa-bam-slicing.xml.

Acknowledgements. The CPACHECKER project is open-source and developed by an international research group from Ludwig-Maximilian University of Munich, University of Passau, Ivannikov Institute for System Programming of the Russian Academy of Sciences and several other universities and institutions. More information about the project can be accessed at https://cpachecker.sosy-lab.org. The slicer is developed as part of the Linux Driver Verification project [9] (http://linuxtesting.org/ldv), the slicer project page is https://forge.ispras.ru/projects/crude_slicer. Both the CPACHECKER tool and the CRUDE_SLICER plugin are distributed under the terms of the Apache License, Version 2.0. The FRAMA-C platform (http://frama-c.com/) is co-developed at two French public institutions: CEA LIST and INRIA Saclay – Île-de-France, and licensed under GNU LGPL v2. We thank all contributors of the projects for their work.

References

1. Beyer, D., Keremoglu, M.E.: CPACHECKER: a tool for configurable software verification. In: Gopalakrishnan, G., Qadeer, S. (eds.) CAV 2011. LNCS, vol. 6806, pp. 184–190. Springer, Heidelberg (2011). https://doi.org/10.1007/978-3-642-22110-1_16

2. Cuoq, P., Kirchner, F., Kosmatov, N., Prevosto, V., Signoles, J., Yakobowski, B.: Frama-C: a software analysis perspective. In: Eleftherakis, G., Hinchey, M., Holcombe, M. (eds.) SEFM 2012. LNCS, vol. 7504, pp. 233–247. Springer, Heidelberg (2012). https://doi.org/10.1007/978-3-642-33826-7_16

3. Hubert, T., Marché, C.: Separation analysis for deductive verification. In: Heap Analysis and Verification (HAV 2007), Braga, Portugal, pp. 81–93, March 2007

4. Mandrykin, M.U., Khoroshilov, A.V.: Region analysis for deductive verification of C programs. Program. Comput. Softw. **42**(5), 257–278 (2016)

5. Conchon, S., Filliâtre, J.C., Signoles, J.: Designing a generic graph library using ML functors. In: Morazán, M.T. (ed.) Trends in Functional Programming, vol. 8, Selected Papers of the 8th International Symposium on Trends in Functional Programming (TFP 2007), New York, USA. Intellect (2008)

6. Muller, P., Vojnar, T.: CPALIEN: shape analyzer for CPAChecker. In: Ábrahám, E., Havelund, K. (eds.) TACAS 2014. LNCS, vol. 8413, pp. 395–397. Springer, Heidelberg (2014). https://doi.org/10.1007/978-3-642-54862-8_28

7. Andrianov, P., Friedberger, K., Mandrykin, M., Mutilin, V., Volkov, A.: CPA-BAM-BnB: block-abstraction memoization and region-based memory models for predicate abstractions. In: Legay, A., Margaria, T. (eds.) TACAS 2017. LNCS, vol. 10206, pp. 355–359. Springer, Heidelberg (2017). https://doi.org/10.1007/978-3-662-54580-5_22

8. Volkov, A., Mandrykin, M.: Predicate abstractions memory modeling method with separation into disjoint regions. Proc. Inst. Syst. Program. **29**, 203–216 (2017)

9. Zakharov, I.S., Mandrykin, M.U., Mutilin, V.S., Novikov, E.M., Petrenko, A.K., Khoroshilov, A.V.: Configurable toolset for static verification of operating systems kernel modules. Program. Comput. Softw. **41**(1), 49–64 (2015)

InterpChecker: Reducing State Space
via Interpolations
(Competition Contribution)

Zhao Duan[1], Cong Tian[1(✉)], Zhenhua Duan[1], and C.-H. Luke Ong[2]

[1] ICTT and ISN Lab, Xidian University, Xi'an 710071, People's Republic of China
ctian@mail.xidian.edu.cn
[2] Department of Computer Science, University of Oxford, Oxford, UK

Abstract. InterpChecker is a tool for verifying safety properties of C programs. It reduces the state space of programs throughout the verification via two new kinds of interpolations and associated optimization strategies. The implementation builds on the open-source, configurable software verification tool, CPAChecker.

1 Verification Approach

Our approach to scalable CEGAR-based model checking is to exploit Craig interpolation [3] to learn abstractions that can systematically reduce the program state space which must be explored for a given safety verification problem. In addition to the interpolants for parsimonious abstraction [4] (called *reachability interpolants* (*R-Interp*) here for clarity), we introduce two new kinds of interpolants, called *universal safety interpolants* and *existential error interpolants*.

- A *universal safety interpolant* (or *S-Interp*) is useful for determining whether all the paths emanating from a state are safe, without exploring all the possible branches from it.
- An *existential error interpolant* (or *E-Interp*) is useful for determining whether there exists an unsafe path emanating from a state, without exploring all the possible branches from it.

The *S-Interp* at a location of a control flow graph (CFG) collects predicates that are relevant to a yes-instance of the safety verification, so that whenever the *S-Interp* is implied by the current path, all paths emanating from this location are guaranteed to be safe. Dually, whenever the *E-Interp* at a location of a CFG is implied by the current path, there is an unsafe branch from it, and so, one can immediately conclude that the program is unsafe. We learn *S-Interp* and

This research is supported by the NSFC grant No. 61420106004, 61732013, and 61751207. The work was done partially while Duan and Ong were visiting the Institute for Mathematical Sciences, National University of Singapore in 2016. The visit was partially supported by the Institute.

D. Beyer and M. Huisman (Eds.): TACAS 2018, LNCS 10806, pp. 432–436, 2018.
https://doi.org/10.1007/978-3-319-89963-3_27

E-Interp from spurious error traces and apply them to reduce the state space of programs throughout the CEGAR-based program verification process. For convenience, we denote a CFG as a tuple $G = (L, T, l_0, f)$, where L is the set of program locations, $l_0 \in L$ is the initial location, $f \in L$ is the final location, $T \subseteq L \times Ops \times L$ is the transition relation, and Ops is the set of instructions.

When verifying a programs, we first unwind the CFG to generate an Abstract Reachability Tree (ART). An ART $A = (S_A, E_A)$, obtained from a CFG $G = (L, T, l_0, f)$, consists of a set S_A of abstract states and a set E_A of edges. An *abstract state* $s \in S_A$ is a triple $s = (l, c, p)$ where l is a location in the CFG, c is the current call stack, and p is an abstract predicate indicating the reachable region of the current state which is determined by the reachable interpolant, *R-Interp*. Given two states s and s', we say s is *covered* by s' just if $s[0] = s'[0]$, $s[1] = s'[1]$, and $s[2] \rightarrow s'[2]$. (Notation: for a tuple e, we write $e[i]$ for the i-th component of e.) Further, if s is covered by s' and all the future of s' (i.e. all abstract states reachable from s') has been explored, then it is safe to not explore the future of s. A branch (path) Π of an ART, denoting a possible execution of the program, is a finite alternating sequence of states and edges, $\Pi = \langle s_0, e_0, \cdots, e_{n-1}, s_n \rangle$, such that for all $0 \leq i < n$, $e_i[0] = s_i$ and $e_i[2] = s_{i+1}$. Given a path Π of an ART, we write $P_f(\Pi)$ for the path formula $\text{SSA}(e_0[1]) \land \cdots \land \text{SSA}(e_{n-1}[1])$ obtained from Π. Here $\text{SSA}(op)$ is the static single assignment (SSA) of an operation op where every variable occurring in Π is assigned a value at most once.

Given a CFG whose locations are enriched with default values of *R-Interp*, *S-Interp*, and *E-Interp*, we construct the ART for exploring a real counterexample by starting from the root, i.e. $s_0 : (l_0, -, true)$. The flowchart in Fig. 1 gives a bird's eye view of our approach to safety verification with reachability, safety and error interpolations. When a state $s : (l, c, p)$ is being explored and l is not an error location:

(1) Reversely traverse the current path for other possibilities if one of the following three conditions holds:
   - $p = false$;
   - $p \neq false$, $F(l) = f$, and $P_f(s_0, \cdots, s) \rightarrow I_s(l)$;
   - $p \neq false$ and s is covered by a visited state s'.
(2) Report the program is unsafe, if $p \neq false$ and $P_f(s_0, \cdots, s) \rightarrow E\text{-}Interp(l)$.
(3) Explore the succeeding state $s'' : (suc(l), c, p')$, otherwise.

When l of the current state $s : (l, c, p)$ is an error location, we first check whether the current path $\Pi = \langle s_0, \cdots, s \rangle$ is spurious. If Π is not spurious, we conclude that the program is unsafe. Otherwise, by *update S-Interp*, *update E-Interp*, and *update R-Interp* [5], the *S-Interp*, *E-Interp*, and *R-Interp* of locations involved in Π are updated, respectively. Subsequently, we reversely track the current path for other possibilities and treat a new current state $s : (l, c, p)$ in the same way until the program is reported as unsafe or there are no more states to be explored.

To maximise the effect of the proposed interpolations, we also present two kinds of optimizing strategies: *pruning CFG* and *weight-guided search*. In real-world

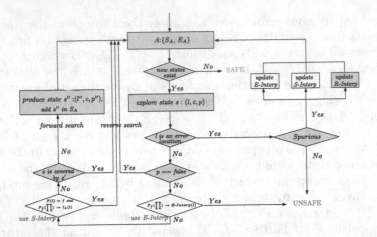

Fig. 1. Interpolation aided CEGAR approach for program verification

programs, there may exist some locations in a CFG which can never reach any error location. To avoid exploring these locations when verifying the program, the first strategy is to prune the CFG by removing these locations and the relative control flow edges in advance. A safety interpolant works only when it is full. Hence, the earlier full safety-interpolants are formed, the more effective the performance will be. To form full interpolants, the second strategy is to explore one side of a branch as early as possible if the other side has been explored. The goal is achieved by introducing an attribute *weight* to transitions of a CFG. Throughout the verification, the branch with the largest weight will be explored first.

2   Software Architecture

Our implementation of InterpChecker builds on the open-source, configurable software verification tool, CPAChecker [1]. Like CPAChecker, InterpChecker can verify safety properties of C program via reachability checking of the instrumented error labels. All extra functions are implemented in Java, using the existing libraries provided by CPAChecker. In Fig. 1, the white parts are new, while the grey parts are original CPAChecker functions. We set up the InterpChecker interpolants and optimizations as an option of CPAChecker, organised as a refinement-selection configuration, in the sense of [2].

3   Strengths and Weakness

The new interpolants implemented in InterpChecker do not affect the existing configurations of CPAChecker. InterpChecker supports the verification of safety properties of C program via reachability checking of the instrumented error labels. The power of InterpChecker is best illustrated when analysing large-scale programs because it can avoid exploring more paths. The current version does not support the verification of the properties written as temporal logic formulas. Like CPAChecker, we skip recursive functions and treat them as pure functions. Thus, false negatives may occur for programs with recursive functions.

4   Tool Setup and Configuration

A zipped file containing `InterpChecker 1.0` is available at http://github.com/ duanzhao-dz/interpchecker. It contains all the required libraries: no installation of external tools is required. To run InterpChecker, first download the code from the website, then run the following command to install the package in Ubuntu 16.04: `sudo apt-get install openjdk-8-jdk`.

To process a benchmark example test.c, invoke the script by the following command: `./scripts/cpa.sh -sv-comp18-interpcpachecker test.c`. The output of InterpChecker is written to the file `output/Statistics.txt`. When using BenchExec, the output can be translated by the `interpchecker.py` tool-info module. The categories verified by the competition candidate are listed in the file `interpchecker.xml`. The two files are contained in the zipped file. If the checked property does not hold, a human readable counterexample is written to `output/ErrorPath.txt` and an error witness is written to the zipped file `witness.graphml.gz`. Note that Java Runtime Environment is required, which should be at least Java 8 compatible.

5   Software Project and Contributors

Based on the open source tool CPAChecker, InterpChecker is developed by Xidian University, China, and the University of Oxford, UK. We thank Dirk Beyer and his team for their original contributions to CPAChecker.

References

1. Beyer, D., Keremoglu, M.E.: CPACHECKER: a tool for configurable software verification. In: Gopalakrishnan, G., Qadeer, S. (eds.) CAV 2011. LNCS, vol. 6806, pp. 184–190. Springer, Heidelberg (2011). https://doi.org/10.1007/978-3-642-22110-1_16
2. Beyer, D., Löwe, S., Wendler, P.: Refinement selection. In: Fischer, B., Geldenhuys, J. (eds.) SPIN 2015. LNCS, vol. 9232, pp. 20–38. Springer, Cham (2015). https://doi.org/10.1007/978-3-319-23404-5_3
3. Albarghouthi, A., Gurfinkel, A., Chechik, M.: Craig interpretation. In: Miné, A., Schmidt, D. (eds.) SAS 2012. LNCS, vol. 7460, pp. 300–316. Springer, Heidelberg (2012). https://doi.org/10.1007/978-3-642-33125-1_21
4. Henzinger, T.A., Jhala, R., Majumdar, R., McMillan, K.L.: Abstractions from proofs. In: Proceedings of POPL, pp. 232–244 (2004)
5. Tian, C., Duan, Z., Duan, Z.H., Ong, L.: More effective interpolations in software model checking. In: The 32nd IEEE/ACM International Conference on Automated Software Engineering, ASE 2017, pp. 183–193. IEEE (2017)

Map2Check Using LLVM and KLEE
(Competition Contribution)

Rafael Menezes[1], Herbert Rocha[1(✉)], Lucas Cordeiro[2],
and Raimundo Barreto[3]

[1] Department of Computer Science, Federal University of Roraima, Boa Vista, Brazil
herberthb12@gmail.com
[2] Department of Computer Science, University of Oxford, Oxford, UK
[3] Institute of Computing, Federal University of Amazonas, Manaus, Brazil

Abstract. Map2Check is a bug hunting tool that automatically checks safety properties in C programs. It tracks memory pointers and variable assignments to check user-specified assertions, overflow, and pointer safety. Here, we extend Map2Check to: (i) simplify the program using Clang/LLVM; (ii) perform a path-based symbolic execution using the KLEE tool; and (iii) transform and instrument the code using the LLVM dynamic information flow. The SVCOMP'18 results show that Map2Check can be effective in generating and checking test cases related to memory management of C programs.

1 Overview

Map2Check v7.1 uses source code instrumentation based on dynamic information flow, to monitor data from different program executions. Map2Check automatically produces concrete inputs to the program via symbolic execution, in order to execute different program paths and to detect failures related to arithmetic overflow, invalid deallocation, invalid pointers, and memory leaks. Map2Check uses Clang [5] as a front-end, which supports the main C standard, e.g., C99 according to the standard ISO/IEC 9899:1990. In its previous version [7], Map2Check was able to automatically generate test cases to check memory management using bounded model checkers (e.g., ESBMC [4]). The main original contributions of Map2Check v7.1 are: (i) added Clang [5] as a front-end to improve the symbolic execution of C programs; (ii) adopted the LLVM [6] framework as a code transformation engine; and (iii) integrated the KLEE [1] tool as a symbolic execution engine to automatically explore different program paths.

2 Verification Approach

The Map2Check tool is inspired by LEAKPOINT [3] and Symbiotic 4 [2], which use compiler techniques to analyze C programs using code instrumentation. The

---

H. Rocha—Jury member.

D. Beyer and M. Huisman (Eds.): TACAS 2018, LNCS 10806, pp. 437–441, 2018.
https://doi.org/10.1007/978-3-319-89963-3_28

main novelty of Map2Check v7.1 is the integration of the LLVM Intermediate
Representation (IR) to analyze and verify C programs. This LLVM IR is based
on the static single assignment representation and provides type safety, low-
level operations, and the capability of representing high-level languages. If we
compare Map2Check to other related tools, e.g., Symbiotic 4, it does not perform static program slicing and does not use the symbolic execution of KLEE to
directly explore the program state space. Map2Check applies source code instrumentation to monitor and gather areas of data memory from different concrete
program executions; this code instrumentation focuses on exploring dynamic
information flow to avoid the need for an approximate static analysis. Similarly
to LEAKPOINT, Map2Check taints program data (e.g., variables or memory
locations) with a taint mark metadata and then propagates the taint marks over
the concrete program executions. Fig. 1 shows an overview of the Map2Check
verification flow. The tool input is a C program and a safety property (e.g., overflow and pointer safety); it returns *TRUE* (if there is no path that violates the
safety property), *FALSE* (if there exists a path that violates the safety property),
or *UNKNOWN* otherwise.

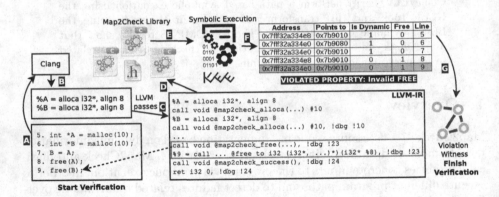

Fig. 1. Map2Check verification flow.

The Map2Check verification flow has the following main steps: (A) convert
the C code into the LLVM IR using Clang [5]; (B) apply specific code optimizations, e.g., dead code elimination and constant propagation; (C) add Map2Check
library functions to track pointers, and add assertions into the LLVM bitcode;
(D) connect the code instrumented by Map2Check to support the execution of
its functions; (E) apply further Clang optimizations to improve the symbolic
execution (e.g., canonicalize natural loops and promote memory to register);
(F) generate concrete inputs for the Map2Check instrumented functions by performing symbolic execution of the analyzed code in LLVM IR using KLEE; and
(G) generate witnesses: if a safety property is violated, then a "violation witness"
is produced using the KLEE output to trace the error location; if there is no
path that violates the safety property, then a "correctness witness" is produced,

which identifies each basic block executed in the control flow graph of the LLVM IR using the concrete inputs produced by KLEE (LLVM syntactically enforces some of those basic blocks as invariants from its assignments).

Map2Check v7.1 tracks important data of the analyzed C code to identify functions and operations over pointers. Then, it checks the respective assertions via symbolic execution, which produces inputs to concretely execute the program. In particular, Map2Check tracks the heap memory used by the analyzed code using the following data log lists: **Heap log** tracks the allocated memory address (i.e., arguments of functions, functions, and variables) and its memory size in the heap memory; **Malloc log** tracks the addresses that are dynamically allocated/deallocated, their size and pointer actions (allocation and deallocation), executed at the current program location; and **List log** stores data about operations over pointers, e.g., the code line number for each operation, program scope, variable name, memory addresses, and addresses pointed to by program variables.

Map2Check v7.1 implements a function map2check_non_det_x with x in the supported C data types (e.g., char, int, and float), which is interpreted by KLEE to model non-deterministic values. In this respect, Map2Check v7.1 differs from its previous version, which implements for non deterministic values, a function that returns a random number based on a probabilistic distribution. To check the unreachability of an error location, Map2Check identifies a given target function (e.g., __VERIFIER_error) and then replaces that by an error assertion, where the target function is called. To check overflow, Map2Check adds an assertion before all arithmetic instructions over integers to analyze the results over the signed operations and the maximum and minimum integer values. To check pointer safety, Map2Check checks whether a given address to be deallocated is tracked in the Malloc log list and then identifies whether the deallocation of memory was already performed for that program location (invalid deallocation); Map2Check also identifies whether allocated memory was not released at the end of the program execution (memory leak); Additionally, Map2Check analyzes the memory addresses in the Malloc log and Heap log lists to identify if those addresses point to a valid address (invalid pointer). Map2Check does not distinguish between the usual "valid-memtrack" and "valid-memclean" properties in SV-COMP.

3 Proposed Architecture

Map2Check v7.1 is implemented as a source-to-source transformation tool in C/C++ using LLVM (v3.8.1). It uses Clang (v3.8.1) as a front-end to parse a C program and to generate the respective LLVM bitcode to be used in the code transformation to track pointers to areas of memory and variable assignments (Fig. 2). It uses KLEE (v1.2.0) as a path-based symbolic execution engine; STP[1] (v2.1.2) is used as the SMT solver by KLEE to check constraints over bit-vectors and arrays. The Boost[2] C++ library is used as a helper library,

---

[1] http://stp.github.io.

[2] http://www.boost.org.

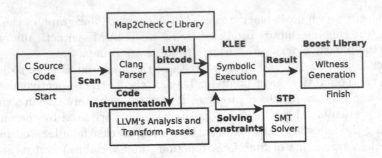

Fig. 2. Map2Check architecture flow.

e.g., to generate the witness in the GraphML format. Map2Check participates in SVCOMP'18 (as in the map2check.xml benchmark definition) in the following categories: ReachSafety-Arrays, ReachSafety-BitVectors, ReachSafety-Heap, ReachSafety-Loops, ReachSafety-Recursive, MemSafety, and NoOverflows.

3.1 Availability and Installation

Map2Check v7.1 (for 64-bit Linux) is available[3] under the GPL license. The Clang, LLVM, KLEE, and STP tools are included in the Map2Check distribution. Map2Check is invoked via a command-line (as in the map2check.py module for BenchExec) as:

```
./map2check-wrapper.py -p propertyFile.prp file.i
```

Map2Check accepts the property file and the verification task and provides as result: *TRUE + Witness, FALSE + Witness, or UNKNOWN*. For each error-path or correctness witness, a file (called witness.graphml) with the witness proof is generated in the Map2Check root-path folder.

4   Strengths and Weaknesses of the Approach

Map2Check exploits dynamic information flow by tainting program data. It uses Clang/LLVM as an industrial-strength compiler to simplify and instrument the code; and also employs KLEE to produce concrete inputs for different program executions. The integration between LLVM and KLEE opens up several possibilities to implement new testing and verification techniques in Map2Check. Particularly, we intend to improve our symbolic execution by synthesizing inductive invariants to prove properties of loops and recursive programs and also to prune the search-space, given that Map2Check bounds the loops and recursion up to a given depth k. The SVCOMP'18 results show that Map2Check can be effective in generating and checking test cases of memory management for C programs. Map2Check achieved a score of 228 in the MemSafety category with no single

---

[3] https://github.com/hbgit/Map2Check/archive/map2check_v7.1_svcomp18d.zip.

incorrect result; in particular, Map2Check produced the highest score (i.e., 106) in the MemSafety-Arrays subcategory. In the NoOverflows category, Map2Check achieved a score of −263; some incorrect results are due to our imprecise overflow check. In the ReachSafety category, we noted that Map2Check claims 312 correct results; however, it reported 16 incorrect true and 1 incorrect false. Some of these incorrect results are related to Map2Check limitation to handle loops and recursion.

Acknowledgments. We thank C. Cadar, D. Poetzl, and the anonymous reviewers for their comments, which helped us to improve the draft version of this paper.

References

1. Cadar, C., Dunbar, D., Engler, D.: KLEE: unassisted and automatic generation of high-coverage tests for complex systems programs. In: OSDI, pp. 209–224. USENIX (2008)
2. Chalupa, M., Vitovská, M., Jonáš, M., Slaby, J., Strejček, J.: Symbiotic 4: beyond reachability. In: Legay, A., Margaria, T. (eds.) TACAS 2017. LNCS, vol. 10206, pp. 385–389. Springer, Heidelberg (2017). https://doi.org/10.1007/978-3-662-54580-5_28
3. Clause, J., Orso, A.: LEAKPOINT: pinpointing the causes of memory leaks. In: ICSE, pp. 515–524. ACM (2010)
4. Cordeiro, L., Fischer, B., Marques-Silva, J.: SMT-based bounded model checking for embedded ANSI-C software. In: TSE, pp. 957–974. IEEE (2012)
5. Fandrey, D.: Clang/LLVM maturity report. In: Computer Science Department, University of Applied Sciences Karlsruhe (2010). http://www.iwi.hs-karlsruhe.de
6. Lattner, C., Adve, V.: LLVM: a compilation framework for lifelong program analysis & transformation. In: CGO, pp. 75–88. IEEE (2004)
7. Rocha, H.O., Barreto, R.S., Cordeiro, L.C.: Hunting memory bugs in C programs with Map2Check. In: Chechik, M., Raskin, J.-F. (eds.) TACAS 2016. LNCS, vol. 9636, pp. 934–937. Springer, Heidelberg (2016). https://doi.org/10.1007/978-3-662-49674-9_64

Symbiotic 5: Boosted Instrumentation
(Competition Contribution)

Marek Chalupa$^{(\boxtimes)}$, Martina Vitovská, and Jan Strejček

Masaryk University, Brno, Czech Republic
xchalup4@fi.muni.cz

Abstract. The fifth version of SYMBIOTIC significantly improves instrumentation capabilities that the tool uses to participate in the category *MemSafety*. It leverages an extended pointer analysis re-designed for instrumenting programs with memory safety errors, and staged instrumentation reducing the number of inserted function calls that track or check the memory state. Apart from various bugfixes, we have ported SYMBIOTIC (including the external symbolic executor KLEE) to LLVM 3.9 and improved the generation of violation witnesses by providing values of some variables.

1 Verification Approach

The basic approach of SYMBIOTIC remains unchanged [7]: it uses instrumentation to reduce checking of specific properties (e.g. *no-overflow* or *memory safety*) to checking reachability of error locations. Then we apply slicing which removes the code that has no influence on reachability of these locations. Finally, we symbolically execute the sliced code using KLEE [1] to refute or confirm that an error location is reachable.

For many years, our attention has been focused mainly on slicing [2,6,8]. Only in 2016, we implemented a configurable instrumentation that enabled SYMBIOTIC to check memory safety or, in general, any safety property. Consequently, SYMBIOTIC 4 [4] participated for the first time in the category *MemSafety* where it won the bronze medal.

The instrumentation used in SYMBIOTIC 4 to check memory safety inserts calls to functions that *track* every block of allocated memory and calls to functions that *check* validity of dereferences using the tracked information. A check is not inserted if a static pointer analysis guarantees that the dereferenced pointer points to a memory block that was allocated before. Later we have recognized a flaw of this optimization: a standard pointer analysis ignores memory deallocations and, hence, it can tell that a pointer can point to memory blocks allocated by specific program lines, but it does not tell whether these memory blocks are

---

The research is supported by the Czech Science Foundation grant GBP202/12/G061.
M. Chalupa—Jury member.

D. Beyer and M. Huisman (Eds.): TACAS 2018, LNCS 10806, pp. 442–446, 2018.
https://doi.org/10.1007/978-3-319-89963-3_29

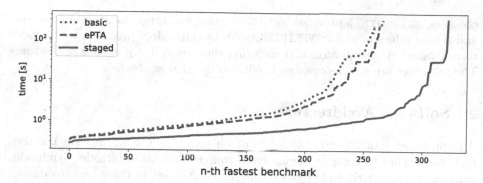

Fig. 1. Quantile plot of running times of the three considered configurations of SYMBIOTIC 5. On the x-axis are the benchmarks sorted according to the corresponding running times and on the logarithmic y-axis are the times.

still allocated. As a result, SYMBIOTIC 4 sometimes does not insert a check even if the dereference may be invalid and thus it may miss some bugs.

In SYMBIOTIC 5, we have fixed and significantly boosted the instrumentation part. First, we have extended the above mentioned pointer analysis such that it takes into account deallocations as well. Second, the instrumentation now works in two stages. The first stage inserts the checks where extended pointer analysis cannot guarantee the dereference safety. Moreover, compared to SYMBIOTIC 4, we use simpler checks if possible. For example, if a pointer analysis says that a given pointer points into a known fixed-size memory block, we just insert a check that the pointer's offset is within the size of the block (without searching the tracked information about the block). The second stage inserts calls to memory tracking functions only to allocations of the memory blocks that can be accessed by some dereference instrumented in the first stage. Hence, we track only the information that may be possibly used in the checks.

To evaluate the boosted instrumentation, we run the following three configurations of SYMBIOTIC on 393 benchmarks of the SV-COMP 2017 meta category *MemSafety* and of the category *MemSafety-TerminCrafted*:

- **basic** uses instrumentation without any pointer analysis,
- **ePTA** uses extended pointer analysis (i.e. it is a fixed version of the instrumentation in SYMBIOTIC 4),
- **staged** uses extended pointer analysis and staged instrumentation.

Figure 1 clearly shows that the performance improvement brought by the extended pointer analysis itself is negligible compared to the performance improvement delivered by the extended pointer analysis in combination with staged instrumentation. For a precise description of the boosted instrumentation, experimental setup and results, we refer to [3].

SYMBIOTIC 5 also changed the approach to error witness generation. SYMBIOTIC 4 describes an erroneous run by a sequence of passed program locations. The sequence is often very long and it turned out to be too restrictive for witness checkers. SYMBIOTIC 5 provides only the starting and target locations of the run and return values of some __VERIFIER_nondet* calls. More precisely, we provide return values of calls in main and such that they are called just once in the run. The witnesses are now more often confirmed by witness checkers.

2   Software Architecture

All components of SYMBIOTIC are built on top of LLVM 3.9 [9]. We use the CLANG compiler to compile the analyzed sources into LLVM bitcode. Symbiotic consists of scripts written in Python that distribute work to three basic modules, all written in C++:

Instrumentation module. This module inserts function calls to instructions according to a given configuration in JSON. The instrumented functions are implemented in C and compiled to LLVM automatically by SYMBIOTIC before the instrumentation process. We use this configurable instrumentation for instrumenting the *memory safety* property only. For instrumenting the *no-overflow* property, we use CLANG's sanitizer as it works sufficiently well in this case.

Slicing module. This module implements an interprocedural version of the slicing algorithm based on dependence graphs [5] altogether with analyses that are needed to compute dependencies between instructions, i.e. pointer analyses (including the extended pointer analysis as described in Sect. 1 that is used by the instrumentation) and analyses of reaching definitions.

Verification backend. For deciding reachability of error locations, we currently use our clone of the open-source symbolic executor KLEE [1], that was ported to LLVM 3.9 and modified to support error witness generation.

Before and after slicing, we optimize the code using available LLVM's optimizations. The rest of bitcode transformations that we use and whose nature is mostly technical (e.g. replacement of calls inserted by CLANG's sanitizer to __VERIFIER_error calls) are implemented as LLVM passes. All the components that transform bitcode take a bitcode as an input and give a valid bitcode as an output. This makes SYMBIOTIC highly modular: any part (module) can be easily replaced or used as a stand-alone tool.

3   Strengths and Weaknesses

The main strength of the approach is its universality and modularity. The instrumentation can reduce any safety property to reachability checks and therefore no special monitors need to be incorporated into the verification backend. Indeed, any tool that can decide reachability of error locations can be plugged-in.

The main disadvantage of the current configuration is that symbolic execution does not satisfactory handle programs with unbounded loops. Moreover, KLEE cannot generate invariants for loops.

4   Tool Setup and Configuration

- *Download:*   https://github.com/staticafi/symbiotic/releases/download/5.0.1/ symbiotic-5.0.1.zip.
- *Installation:* Unpack the archive.
- *Participation Statement:* SYMBIOTIC 5 participates in all categories.
- *Execution:* Run `bin/symbiotic OPTS <source>`, where available `OPTS` include:
  - `--prp=file`, which sets the property specification file to use,
  - `--witness=file`, which sets the output file for the witness,
  - `--32`, which sets the 32-bit environment,
  - `--help`, which shows the full list of possible options.

5   Software Project and Contributors

SYMBIOTIC 5 has been developed by M. Chalupa and M. Vitovská under supervision of J. Strejček. The tool and its components are available under Apache-2.0 and MIT Licenses. The project is hosted by the Faculty of Informatics, Masaryk University. LLVM and KLEE are also available under open-source licenses. The project web page is: https://github.com/staticafi/symbiotic.

References

1. Cadar, C., Dunbar, D., Engler, D.: KLEE: unassisted and automatic generation of high-coverage tests for complex systems programs. In: OSDI, pp. 209–224. USENIX Association (2008)
2. Chalupa, M., Jonáš, M., Slaby, J., Strejček, J., Vitovská, M.: Symbiotic 3: new slicer and error-witness generation - (competition contribution). In: Chechik, M., Raskin, J.-F. (eds.) TACAS 2016. LNCS, vol. 9636, pp. 946–949. Springer, Heidelberg (2016). https://doi.org/10.1007/978-3-662-49674-9_67
3. Chalupa, M., Strejček, J., Vitovská, M.: Joint forces for memory safety checking. Submitted to SPIN 2018
4. Chalupa, M., Vitovská, M., Jonáš, M., Slaby, J., Strejček, J.: Symbiotic 4: beyond reachability - (competition contribution). In: Legay, A., Margaria, T. (eds.) TACAS 2017. LNCS, vol. 10206, pp. 385–389. Springer, Heidelberg (2017). https://doi.org/ 10.1007/978-3-662-54580-5_28
5. Ferrante, J., Ottenstein, K.J., Warren, J.D.: The program dependence graph and its use in optimization. In: Paul, M., Robinet, B. (eds.) Programming 1984. LNCS, vol. 167, pp. 125–132. Springer, Heidelberg (1984). https://doi.org/10.1007/3-540-12925-1_33
6. Slaby, J., Strejček, J.: Symbiotic 2: more precise slicing (competition contribution). In: Ábrahám, E., Havelund, K. (eds.) TACAS 2014. LNCS, vol. 8413, pp. 415–417. Springer, Heidelberg (2014). https://doi.org/10.1007/978-3-642-54862-8_34
7. Slabý, J., Strejček, J., Trtík, M.: Checking properties described by state machines: on synergy of instrumentation, slicing, and symbolic execution. In: Stoelinga, M., Pinger, R. (eds.) FMICS 2012. LNCS, vol. 7437, pp. 207–221. Springer, Heidelberg (2012). https://doi.org/10.1007/978-3-642-32469-7_14

8. Slaby, J., Strejček, J., Trtík, M.: Symbiotic: synergy of instrumentation, slicing, and symbolic execution (competition contribution). In: Piterman, N., Smolka, S.A. (eds.) TACAS 2013. LNCS, vol. 7795, pp. 630–632. Springer, Heidelberg (2013). https://doi.org/10.1007/978-3-642-36742-7_50
9. LLVM. http://llvm.org/

Ultimate Automizer and the Search for Perfect Interpolants
(Competition Contribution)

Matthias Heizmann[✉], Yu-Fang Chen, Daniel Dietsch, Marius Greitschus,
Jochen Hoenicke, Yong Li, Alexander Nutz, Betim Musa,
Christian Schilling, Tanja Schindler, and Andreas Podelski

University of Freiburg, Freiburg im Breisgau, Germany
heizmann@informatik.uni-freiburg.de

Abstract. ULTIMATE AUTOMIZER is a software verifier that generalizes
proofs for traces to proofs for larger parts for the program. In recent
years the portfolio of proof producers that are available to ULTIMATE
has grown continuously. This is not only because more trace analysis
algorithms have been implemented in ULTIMATE but also due to the
continuous progress in the SMT community. In this paper we explain how
ULTIMATE AUTOMIZER dynamically selects trace analysis algorithms and
how the tool decides when proofs for traces are "good" enough for using
them in the abstraction refinement.

1 Verification Approach

ULTIMATE AUTOMIZER (in the following called AUTOMIZER) is a software verifier that is able to check safety and liveness properties. The tool implements an
automata-based [6] instance of the CEGAR scheme. In each iteration, we pick a
trace (which is a sequence of statements) that leads from the initial location to
the error location and check whether the trace is *feasible* (i.e., corresponds to an
execution) or *infeasible*. If the trace is feasible, we report an error to the user;
otherwise we compute a sequence of predicates along the trace as a proof of the
trace's infeasibility. We call such a sequence of predicates a sequence of *interpolants* since each predicate "interpolates" between the set of reachable states
and the set of states from which we cannot reach the error. In the refinement step
of the CEGAR loop, we try to find all traces whose infeasibility can be shown
with the given predicates and subtract these traces from the set of (potentially
spurious) error traces that have not yet been analyzed. We use automata to
represent sets of traces; hence the subtraction is implemented as an automata
operation. The major difference to a classical CEGAR-based predicate abstraction is that we never have to do any logical reasoning (e.g., SMT solver calls)
that involves predicates of different CEGAR iterations.

We use this paper to explain how our tool obtains the interpolants that
are used in the refinement step. The ULTIMATE program analysis framework

D. Beyer and M. Huisman (Eds.): TACAS 2018, LNCS 10806, pp. 447–451, 2018.
https://doi.org/10.1007/978-3-319-89963-3_30

provides a number of techniques to compute interpolants for an infeasible trace. We group them into the following two categories.

Path program focused techniques (*abstract interpretation* [5], *constraint-based invariant synthesis*). These techniques do not consider the trace in isolation but in the context of the analyzed program. The program is projected to the statements that occur in the trace; this projection is considered as a standalone program called *path program*. The techniques try to find a Floyd-Hoare style proof for the path program, which shows the infeasibility of all the path program's traces. If such a proof is found, the respective predicates are used as a sequence of interpolants. These interpolants are "good enough" to ensure that in the refinement step all (spurious) error traces of the path program are ruled out.

Trace focused techniques (*Craig interpolation, symbolic execution with unsatisfiable cores* [4]). These techniques consider only the trace. Typically they are significantly less expensive and more often successful than techniques from the first category. However, we do not have any guarantee that their interpolants help to prove the infeasibility of more than one trace.

Recent improvements of AUTOMIZER were devoted to techniques that fall into the second category. Our basic paradigms are: (1) use different techniques to compute many sequences of interpolants, (2) evaluate the "quality" of each sequence, (3) prefer "good" sequences in the abstraction refinement.

In contrast to related work [3] we have only one measure for the quality of a sequence of interpolants: We check if the interpolants constitute a Floyd-Hoare annotation of the path program for the trace. If this is the case, we call the sequence a *perfect sequence of interpolants*. If the sequence is perfect, we use it for the abstraction refinement. If the sequence is not perfect, we only use it if no better sequence is available. Our portfolio of *trace focused techniques* is quite large for three reasons.

1. We use different algorithms for interpolation. Several SMT solvers have implemented algorithms for Craig interpolation and we use these as a black box. Furthermore, ULTIMATE provides an algorithm [4] to construct an abstraction of the trace from an unsatisfiable core provided by an SMT solver. Afterwards, two sequences of predicates, one with the sp predicate transformer, the other with the wp predicate transformer, are constructed via symbolic execution.
2. We use different SMT solvers. Typically, different SMT solvers implement different algorithms and hence the resulting Craig interpolants or unsatisfiable cores are different.
3. We have several algorithms that produce an abstraction of a trace but preserve the infeasibility of the trace. We can apply these as a preprocessing of the interpolant computation.

   All our algorithms follow the same scheme: We replace all statements of the trace by skip statements. Then we incrementally check feasibility of the trace and undo replacements as long as the trace is feasible. Examples for the undo order of our algorithms are: (1) Apply the undo first to statements that occur outside of loops, follow the nesting structure of loops for further undo operations. (2) Do the very same as the first algorithm but start inside loops. (3) Apply the undo to statements with large constants later. (4) Apply the undo to statements whose SMT representation is less expensive first (e.g., postpone floating point arithmetic).

At first glance it looks like a good idea to apply different techniques to a given trace for as long as no perfect sequence of interpolants was found. This has however turned out to be a bad idea for the following reasons.

1. The path program might be unsafe and we just have to unwind a loop a few times until we find a feasible counterexample.
2. The path program might be so intricate that we are unable to find a loop invariant. However, there are cases where the loop can only be taken for a small number of times and our tool can prove correctness by proving infeasibility of each trace individually.
3. The path program might be so intricate that we are unable to find a loop invariant immediately. But if we consider certain unwindings of the loop (e.g., the loop is taken an even number of times) our interpolants will form a loop invariant.

We conclude that per iteration of the CEGAR loop (resp. per trace) we only want to apply a fixed number of techniques. According to our experiments there are some techniques that are on average more successful than others; however, no technique is strictly superior to another. Hence it is neither a good idea to always apply the n typically most successful techniques nor to take n random techniques in each iteration.

We follow an approach that we call *path program-based modulation*. We have a preferred sequence in which we apply our techniques. Whenever we see a *new* trace we start at the beginning of this sequence. Whenever we see a trace that is *similar* to a trace we have already seen, we continue in the sequence of techniques at the point where we stopped for the similar trace. Our notion of similarity is: Two traces are similar if they have the same path program.

Hence we make sure that for every path program every technique is eventually applied to some trace of the path program.

2 Project, Setup and Configuration

AUTOMIZER is developed on top of the open-source program analysis framework ULTIMATE[1]. ULTIMATE is mainly developed at the University of Freiburg and received contributions from more than 50 people. The framework and AUTOMIZER are written in Java, licensed under LGPLv3, and their source code is available on Github[2].

---

[1] https://ultimate.informatik.uni-freiburg.de.
[2] https://github.com/ultimate-pa/ultimate.

AUTOMIZER's competition submission is available as a zip archive[3]. It requires a current Java installation ($\geq$JRE 1.8) and a working Python 2.7 installation. The archive contains Linux binaries for AUTOMIZER and the required SMT solvers Z3[4], CVC4[5], and MATHSAT[6], as well as a Python script, `Ultimate.py`. The Python script translates command line parameters and results between ULTIMATE and SV-COMP conventions, and ensures that ULTIMATE is correctly configured to run AUTOMIZER. AUTOMIZER is invoked through `Ultimate.py` by calling

```
./Ultimate.py --spec prop.prp --file input.c --architecture
    32bit|64bit --full-output [--validate witness.graphml]
```

where `prop.prp` is the SV-COMP property file, `input.c` is the C file that should be analyzed, `32bit` or `64bit` is the architecture of the input file, and `--full-output` enables writing all output instead of just the status of the property to `stdout`. The option `--validate witness.graphml` is only used during witness validation and allows the specification of a file containing a violation [2] or correctness witness [1].

Depending on the status of the property, a violation or correctness witness may be written to the file `witness.graphml`. AUTOMIZER is not only able to generate witnesses, but also to validate them[7]. In any case, the complete output of AUTOMIZER is written to the file `Ultimate.log`.

The benchmarking tool BENCHEXEC[8] contains a tool-info module that provides support for AUTOMIZER (`ultimateautomizer.py`). AUTOMIZER participates in all categories, which is also specified in its SV-COMP benchmark definition[9] file `uautomizer.xml`. In its role as witness validator, AUTOMIZER supports all categories except `ConcurrencySafety`, which is specified in the corresponding SV-COMP benchmark definition files `uautomizer-validate-*-witnesses.xml`.

References

1. Beyer, D., Dangl, M., Dietsch, D., Heizmann, M.: Correctness witnesses: exchanging verification results between verifiers. In: FSE 2016, pp. 326–337 (2016)
2. Beyer, D., Dangl, M., Dietsch, D., Heizmann, M., Stahlbauer, A.: Witness validation and stepwise testification across software verifiers. In: ESEC/FSE 2015, pp. 721–733, (2015)

---

[3] https://ultimate.informatik.uni-freiburg.de/downloads/svcomp2018/
UltimateAutomizer-linux.zip.
[4] https://github.com/Z3Prover/z3.
[5] https://cvc4.cs.nyu.edu/.
[6] http://mathsat.fbk.eu/.
[7] https://github.com/sosy-lab/sv-witnesses.
[8] https://github.com/sosy-lab/benchexec.
[9] https://github.com/sosy-lab/sv-comp.

3. Beyer, D., Löwe, S., Wendler, P.: Refinement selection. In: Fischer, B., Geldenhuys, J. (eds.) SPIN 2015. LNCS, vol. 9232, pp. 20–38. Springer, Cham (2015). https://doi.org/10.1007/978-3-319-23404-5_3

4. Dietsch, D., Heizmann, V., Musa, B., Nutz, A., Podelski. A.: Craig vs. Newton in software model checking. In: ESEC/SIGSOFT FSE, pp. 487–497. ACM (2017)

5. Greitschus, M., Dietsch, D., Podelski, A.: Loop invariants from counterexamples. In: Ranzato, F. (ed.) SAS 2017. LNCS, vol. 10422, pp. 128–147. Springer, Cham (2017). https://doi.org/10.1007/978-3-319-66706-5_7

6. Heizmann, M., Hoenicke, J., Podelski, A.: Software model checking for people who love automata. In: Sharygina, N., Veith, H. (eds.) CAV 2013. LNCS, vol. 8044, pp. 36–52. Springer, Heidelberg (2013). https://doi.org/10.1007/978-3-642-39799-8_2

Ultimate Taipan with Dynamic Block Encoding
(Competition Contribution)

Daniel Dietsch[(✉)], Marius Greitschus[(✉)], Matthias Heizmann,
Jochen Hoenicke, Alexander Nutz, Andreas Podelski, Christian Schilling,
and Tanja Schindler

University of Freiburg, Freiburg im Breisgau, Germany
{dietsch,greitsch}@informatik.uni-freiburg.de

Abstract. ULTIMATE TAIPAN is a software model checker that uses trace
abstraction and abstract interpretation to prove correctness of programs.
In contrast to previous versions, ULTIMATE TAIPAN now uses dynamic
block encoding to obtain the best precision possible when evaluating
transition formulas of large block encoded programs.

1 Verification Approach

ULTIMATE TAIPAN (or TAIPAN for brevity) is a software model checker which
combines trace abstraction [9,10] and abstract interpretation [5]. The algorithm
of TAIPAN [8] iteratively refines an abstraction of a input program by analyzing
counterexamples (cf. CEGAR [4]).

The initial abstraction of the program is an automaton with the same graph
structure as the program's control flow graph, where program locations are states,
transitions are labeled with program statements, and error locations are accepting. Thus, the language of the automaton consists of all traces, i.e., sequences of
statements, that, if executable, lead to an error. In each iteration, the algorithm
chooses a trace from the language of the current automaton and constructs a path
program from it. A path program is a projection of the (abstraction of the) program
to the trace. The algorithm then uses abstract interpretation to compute fixpoints
for the path program. If the fixpoints of the path program are sufficient to prove
correctness, i.e., the error location is unreachable, at least the chosen trace and all
other traces that are covered by the path program are infeasible. The computed
fixpoints constitute a proof of correctness for the path program and can be represented as a set of state assertions. From this set of state assertions, the abstraction
is refined by constructing a new automaton whose language only consists of infeasible traces and then subtracting it from the current abstraction using an automata-
theoretic difference operation. If abstract interpretation was unable to prove correctness of the path program, the algorithm obtains a proof of infeasibility of the
trace using either interpolating SMT solvers or a combination of unsatisfiable cores
and strongest post or weakest pre [6]. If the currently analyzed trace is feasible,

© The Author(s) 2018
D. Beyer and M. Huisman (Eds.): TACAS 2018, LNCS 10806, pp. 452–456, 2018.
https://doi.org/10.1007/978-3-319-89963-3_31

```
1  procedure foo() {
2     var a, b : int;
3     assume a <= 5;
4     assume b == a;
5     assert b <= 5;
6  }
```

(a) Program in Boogie.   (b) No block encoding.   (c) Large block encoding.

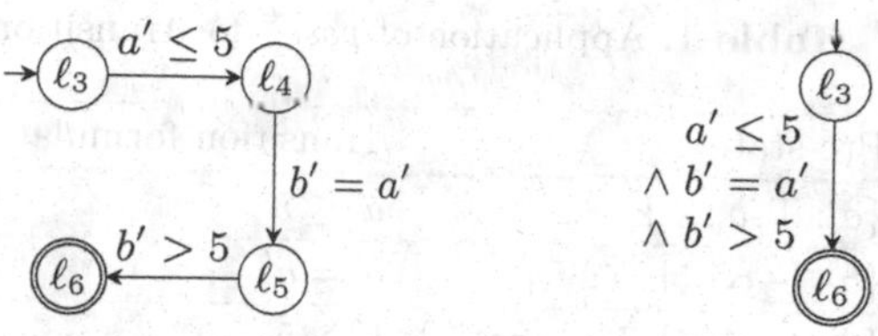

Fig. 1. Example program.

the trace represents a program execution that can reach the error. If the current automaton becomes empty after a difference operation, all potential error traces have been proven to be infeasible.

Dynamic Block Encoding. Large block encoding [1] is a technique to reduce the number of locations in a control flow graph. As TAIPAN relies on trace abstraction, the number of locations determines the performance of the automata operations, which impact the overall performance significantly. It is therefore beneficial to use a strong block encoding that removes as many locations as possible. Unfortunately, the resulting transitions can lead to a loss of precision during the application of an abstract post operator. Consider the example program and its control flow graph with different block encodings shown in Fig. 1. Each control flow graph consists of a set of program locations LOC, an initial location (ℓ_3 in Fig. 1), a set of error locations ($\{\ell_6\}$ in Fig. 1), and a transition relation $\rightarrow \subseteq LOC \times TF \times LOC$ which defines the transitions between the locations and labels each transition with a *transition formula* from the set of transition formulas TF. Transition formulas encode the semantics of the program as first-order logic formulas over various SMT theories. In ULTIMATE, a transition formula ψ is a tuple $(\varphi, IN, OUT, AUX, pv)$ where φ is a closed formula over the three disjoined sets of input (IN), output (OUT), and auxiliary (AUX) variables, and $pv : IN \cup OUT \rightarrow \mathcal{V}$ is an injective function that maps variables occurring in φ to program variables. We write output variables as primed variables and input variables as unprimed variables.

TAIPAN computes a fixpoint for each location of a control flow graph by (repeatedly) applying an abstract post operator $post^\#$ to these transition formulas. To this end, an abstract domain $\mathcal{D} = (A, \alpha, \gamma, \sqcup, \sqcap, \nabla, post^\#)$ is used, where A is a complete lattice representing all possible abstract states containing the designated abstract states $\top$ and $\bot$, α is an abstraction function, γ is a concretization function, $\sqcup$ is a join operator, $\sqcap$ is a meet operator, ∇ is a widening operator, and $post^\# : A \times TF \rightarrow A$ is an abstract transformer which computes an abstract post state σ' from a given abstract pre-state σ and a transition formula ψ. TAIPAN uses a combination of octagons [11] and sets of divisibility congruences [7] as abstract domain, but for brevity we explain the example using intervals.

In rows 1 to 3 of Table 1, we apply $post^\#$ of the interval domain in sequence to each of the transition formulas from Fig. 1b. In rows 4a and 4b we apply

Table 1. Application of $post^{\#}$ for transition formulas from Fig. 1.

	Pre-state	Transition formula	Post state
1	$\{a : \top, b : \top\}$	$a' \leq 5$	$\{a : [-\infty, 5], b : \top\}$
2	$\{a : [-\infty, 5], b : \top\}$	$b' = a'$	$\{a : [-\infty, 5], b : [-\infty, 5]\}$
3	$\{a : [-\infty, 5], b : [-\infty, 5]\}$	$b' > 5$	$\{a : [-\infty, 5], b : \bot\}$
4a	$\{a : \top, b : \top\}$	$a' \leq 5 \wedge b' > 5 \wedge b' = a'$	$\{a : [-\infty, 5], b : \bot\}$
4b	$\{a : \top, b : \top\}$	$b' = a' \wedge a' \leq 5 \wedge b' > 5$	$\{a : [-\infty, 5], b : [-\infty, 5]\}$

the same operator to the only transition formula of Fig. 1c, but process the conjunction in different orders. Although the logical $\wedge$-operator is commutative, the result differs. This is due to different ways of computing the abstract post state. We can express $post^{\#}(\sigma, A \wedge B) = \sigma'$ either as $post^{\#}(\sigma, A) \sqcap post^{\#}(\sigma, B)$, as $post^{\#}(post^{\#}(\sigma, A), B)$, or as $post^{\#}(post^{\#}(\sigma, B), A)$. The interval domain cannot express the equality relation between two variables (i.e., the conjunct $b' = a'$), therefore, the first way will compute $post^{\#}(\{a : \top, b : \top\}, b' = a') = \{a : \top, b : \top\}$, effectively rendering the constraint useless. The second and third way may succeed, depending on the ordering of conjuncts. In general, the ordering is important, but in our example, it does not matter as long as $b' = a'$ is not first.

In TAIPAN, we solve this problem by introducing the notion of *expressibility* to an abstract domain. We augment each abstract domain with an expressibility predicate ex which decides for each non-logical symbol of a transition formula (i.e., each relation, function application, variable, and constant) whether it can be represented in the domain. For example, the interval domain can represent all relations that contain at most one variable, while octagons can represent all relations of the form $\pm x \pm y \leq c$. We then apply $post^{\#}$ on conjuncts of a transition formula in an order induced by ex, thus effectively choosing a new *dynamic* block encoding. For $post^{\#}(\sigma, \varphi)$, our algorithm computes σ' by first converting the formula φ to DNF s.t. $\varphi = \varphi_0 \vee \varphi_1 \vee \ldots \vee \varphi_n$. For each disjunct $\varphi_i = \varphi_i^0 \wedge \varphi_i^1 \wedge \ldots \wedge \varphi_i^m$, we compute $post^{\#}(\sigma, \varphi_i) = \sigma_i'$ as follows:

1. Partition the conjuncts in two classes. The first class contains conjuncts for which ex is true, the second for which ex is false.
2. Compute the abstract post for the conjunction of all expressible conjuncts first: $\bigsqcap_{ex(\varphi_i^k)} post^{\#}(\sigma, \varphi_i^k) = \sigma''$.
3. Compute the abstract post for all non-expressible conjuncts successively using the post state of the k-th application as pre-state of the $k+1$-th application, and the post state of the last application as final result σ_i' for the disjunct φ_i: $post^{\#}_{\neg ex(\varphi_i^k)}(\sigma_k, \varphi_i^k) = \sigma_{k+1}$.

The result for $post^{\#}(\sigma, \psi)$ is then $\bigsqcup_{i=0}^{n} \sigma_i' = \sigma'$.

2   Project, Setup and Configuration

TAIPAN is a part of the open-soure program analysis framework ULTIMATE[1], written in Java, licensed under LGPLv3[2], and open source[3]. The TAIPAN competition submission is available as a zip archive[4]. It requires a current Java installation ($\geq$JRE 1.8) and a working Python 2.7 installation. The submission contains an executable version of TAIPAN for Linux platforms, the binaries of the required SMT solvers Z3[5], CVC4[6], and MATHSAT[7], as well as a Python script, Ultimate.py, which maps the SV-COMP interface to ULTIMATE's command line interface and selects the correct settings and the correct toolchain. In SV-COMP, TAIPAN is invoked through Ultimate.py with

```
./Ultimate.py --spec prop.prp --file input.c --architecture
            32bit|64bit --full-output
```

where prop.prp is the SV-COMP property file, input.c is the C file that should be analyzed, 32bit or 64bit is the architecture of the input file, and --full-output enables writing all output instead of just the status of the property to stdout. The complete output of TAIPAN is also written to the file Ultimate.log. Depending on the status of the property, a violation [3] or correctness [2] witness may be written to the file witness.graphml.

The benchmarking tool BENCHEXEC[8] supports TAIPAN through the tool-info module ultimatetaipan.py. TAIPAN participates in all categories, as specified by its SV-COMP benchmark definition[9] file utaipan.xml.

References

1. Beyer, D., Cimatti, A., Griggio, A., Keremoglu, M.E., Sebastiani, R.: Software model checking via large-block encoding. In: FMCAD 2009, pp. 25–32. IEEE (2009)
2. Beyer, D., Dangl, M., Dietsch, D., Heizmann, M.: Correctness witnesses: exchanging verification results between verifiers. In: FSE 2016, pp. 326–337 (2016)
3. Beyer, D., Dangl, M., Dietsch, D., Heizmann, M., Stahlbauer, A.: Witness validation and stepwise testification across software verifiers. In: ESEC/FSE 2015, pp. 721–733 (2015)
4. Clarke, E., Grumberg, O., Jha, S., Lu, Y., Veith, H.: Counterexample-guided abstraction refinement. In: Emerson, E.A., Sistla, A.P. (eds.) CAV 2000. LNCS, vol. 1855, pp. 154–169. Springer, Heidelberg (2000). https://doi.org/10.1007/10722167_15

---

1 https://ultimate.informatik.uni-freiburg.de.
2 https://www.gnu.org/licenses/lgpl-3.0.en.html.
3 https://github.com/ultimate-pa/ultimate/.
4 https://ultimate.informatik.uni-freiburg.de/downloads/svcomp2018/UltimateTaipan-linux.zip.
5 https://github.com/Z3Prover/z3.
6 https://cvc4.cs.nyu.edu/.
7 http://mathsat.fbk.eu/.
8 https://github.com/sosy-lab/benchexec.
9 https://github.com/sosy-lab/sv-comp.

5. Cousot, P., Cousot, R.: Abstract interpretation: a unified lattice model for static analysis of programs by construction or approximation of fixpoints. In: POPL 1977, pp. 238–252 (1977)
6. Dietsch, D., Heizmann, M., Musa, B., Nutz, A., Podelski, A.: Craig vs. Newton in software model checking. In: ESEC/FSE 2017, pp. 487–497 (2017)
7. Granger, P.: Static analysis of linear congruence equalities among variables of a program. In: Abramsky, S., Maibaum, T.S.E. (eds.) CAAP 1991. LNCS, vol. 493, pp. 169–192. Springer, Heidelberg (1991). https://doi.org/10.1007/3-540-53982-4_10
8. Greitschus, M., Dietsch, D., Podelski, A.: Loop invariants from counterexamples. In: Ranzato, F. (ed.) SAS 2017. LNCS, vol. 10422, pp. 128–147. Springer, Cham (2017). https://doi.org/10.1007/978-3-319-66706-5_7
9. Heizmann, M., Hoenicke, J., Podelski, A.: Refinement of trace abstraction. In: Palsberg, J., Su, Z. (eds.) SAS 2009. LNCS, vol. 5673, pp. 69–85. Springer, Heidelberg (2009). https://doi.org/10.1007/978-3-642-03237-0_7
10. Heizmann, M., Hoenicke, J., Podelski, A.: Software model checking for people who love automata. In: Sharygina, N., Veith, H. (eds.) CAV 2013. LNCS, vol. 8044, pp. 36–52. Springer, Heidelberg (2013). https://doi.org/10.1007/978-3-642-39799-8_2
11. Miné, A.: The Octagon Abstract Domain. CoRR, abs/cs/0703084 (2007)

VeriAbs: Verification by Abstraction and Test Generation
(Competition Contribution)

Priyanka Darke[✉], Sumanth Prabhu, Bharti Chimdyalwar, Avriti Chauhan,
Shrawan Kumar, Animesh Basakchowdhury, R. Venkatesh, Advaita Datar,
and Raveendra Kumar Medicherla

Tata Research Development and Design Centre, Pune, India
{priyanka.darke,sumanth.prabhu,bharti.c,avriti.chauhan,shrawan.kumar,
a.basakchowdhury,r.venky,advaita.datar,raveendra.kumar}@tcs.com

Abstract. VeriAbs is a portfolio software verifier for ANSI-C programs.
To prove properties with better efficiency and scalability, this version
implements output abstraction with k-induction in the presence of resets.
VeriAbs now generates post conditions over the abstraction to find invariants by applying Z3's tactics of quantifier elimination. These invariants
are then used to generate validation witnesses. To find errors in the
absence of known program bounds, VeriAbs searches for property violating inputs by applying random test generation with fuzz testing for a
better scalability as compared to bounded model checking.

1 Verification Approach

Background. VeriAbs has implemented abstract acceleration [5] and k-induction techniques to scale Bounded Model Checking (BMC) for programs
with loops of large or unknown bounds. VeriAbs abstracts such loops to loops of
known small bounds, which can be proved by BMC. This abstraction is achieved
by accelerating selected variables processed inside loops. Further, VeriAbs applies
incremental k-induction to improve precision. Loops processing arrays of large
and unknown sizes are substituted by abstract loops that execute a small non-deterministically chosen sequence of original loop iterations. The idea is based
on the concept of *loop shrinkability* [10].

1.1 Tool Enhancements

For SV-COMP 2018, VeriAbs has been supplemented with an efficient implementation of output abstraction to prove properties, random test generation
with fuzzing to find errors, and witness generation.

Output Abstraction. The SV-COMP 2017 version of VeriAbs cannot precisely
validate programs with loops in which all variables are modified with non-linear

---

P. Darke—Jury member.

D. Beyer and M. Huisman (Eds.): TACAS 2018, LNCS 10806, pp. 457–462, 2018.
https://doi.org/10.1007/978-3-319-89963-3_32

arithmetic expressions or resets. For such programs, the current version applies an improved output abstraction [13] that simply replaces the corresponding loop with non-deterministic assignments to all the modified variables.

Search for Property Violating Inputs. In order to alleviate the lack of abstraction refinement, VeriAbs adopts an approach to search for a property violating input. To this end, it uses *fuzz testing* to search for the input that reaches the error location. Fuzz testing is a testing technique that aims to uncover run-time errors by executing the target program with a large number of inputs generated automatically and systematically. Grey-box fuzzing [3] is a fuzz testing technique that uses a light weight instrumentation to observe the target program behavior on a test run. It uses this information to generate new test inputs that might exhibit new program behaviors. VeriAbs uses American Fuzzy Lop (AFL-fuzz) [12] as the fuzz testing tool.

Witness Generation. The previous version of VeriAbs used CPAchecker [2] to generate validation witnesses from abstract programs. The SV-COMP 2018 version has implemented techniques for generation of both correctness and error witnesses. If VeriAbs concludes safety of the input program, it generates the correctness witness with loop invariants. These invariants are generated by computing the strongest postcondition equation using methods presented in [8], except for loops where the loop acceleration information is used instead. These invariants can have quantifiers and non-program variables. However, SV-COMP 2017 witness validators recognize only those invariants that are expressed as C expressions in program variables. VeriAbs uses Z3 [6] to eliminate quantifiers and non-program variables from the invariants. These invariants are added to the control flow automaton generated by CPAchecker to generate the validation witness.

The error witness generation technique is decided based on the strategy that was used to falsify the input program. When VeriAbs decides that the input program is unsafe by fuzz testing (i.e., using AFL-fuzz [12]), it generates a violation witness with a valuation of variables at the program points that assign non-deterministic values to program variables. This is achieved by replaying the execution that caused the property violation on an instrumented input program. This instrumented program prints the aforementioned valuation. In order to avoid file latency this instrumented program is only used to replay error execution. The values of variables thus obtained are used to generate error witness. On the other hand, if input program was decided to be unsafe by using BMC, then corresponding error witness is used.

Array Loop Abstraction. We abstract loops that process arrays of large or unknown sizes having quantified property, using the method based on the idea of *loop shrinkability* [10]. We call an array processing loop as *k-shrinkable* when the original program is guaranteed to be correct if execution of every sequence of k iterations of the original loop results in property, which is projected to the chosen sequence, being satisfied. A k-shrinkable loop, is replaced with an abstract loop that executes the non-deterministically chosen sequence of k iterations of the original loop and the property is also translated to be checked

over array elements corresponding to the chosen sequence of iterations only. The
k-shrinkability criterion ensures that if the program is incorrect then the translated property will get violated for some sequence of k iterations, in the abstract
program.

2   Verification Process and Software Architecture

The verification process of VeriAbs is shown in Fig. 1. VeriAbs passes the input
C file to a Tata Consultancy Services (TCS) [1] in-house C front end to generate
the intermediate representation (IR) of the program. It then analyzes this IR
using PRISM, a TCS in-house program analysis framework [9] to perform the
abstractions and instrumentation. It uses C Bounded Model Checker (CBMC) [4]
version 5.8 with MiniSat [7] to validate the abstraction or the original program
of known bounds. VeriAbs generates correctness witnesses by computing loop
invariants using strongest-postcondition. It uses Z3 version 4.5.1 to eliminate
quantifiers as SV-COMP requires invariants to be expressed as C expressions.
These simplified invariants are added to the control flow automaton generated
by CPAchecker version 1.6.1 [2]. VeriAbs uses CRMC version 5.8 for generating
error witnesses. For fuzz testing, VeriAbs uses AFL-fuzz [12] version 2.35b. It
invokes CBMC and AFL-fuzz sequentially, for program falsification.

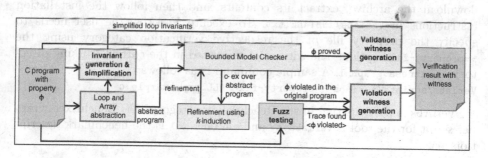

Fig. 1. The verification process of VeriAbs - enhancements are highlighted

The SV-COMP 2018 version of VeriAbs first analyzes every loop to check if
it contains some linear modifications to numerical variables so that they can be
precisely validated by Loop Abstraction for BMC (LABMC) [5]. If this check
passes, it applies a range analysis [11] to identify ranges of those variables. On
the other hand, when all variables are non-linearly modified a simpler output
abstraction is applied. If the loop reads or modifies arrays, then it applies array
loop abstraction as explained in Sect. 1, and then applies BMC to validate the
abstraction. To find errors, VeriAbs uses the new program instrumentation for
violation witness generation and grey-box fuzzing with AFL to generate witnesses for such programs.

3   Strengths and Weaknesses

The main strength of VeriAbs is that it is sound. All transformations implemented by the tool are over-approximations. In case of CBMC, the tool provides an option (`unwinding-assertions`) which ensures sufficient unwinding for proving the property. Hence if the tool reports that a property holds then it indeed holds. Another key strength is that it transforms all loops in a program to abstract loops with a known finite number of iterations, enabling the use of bounded model checkers for property proving. The main weakness of the tool is that it does not implement a refinement process that is well suited to find errors. But it can find errors using fuzz testing and bounded model checking. VeriAbs is dependent on Z3 for quantifier and non-program variable elimination from correctness witness invariants, and it is dependent on CPAchecker for generating program automata. As compared to the results of SV-COMP 2017 version, VeriAbs performed significantly better in Arrays, Loops, ECA, Sequentialized and Recursive sub categories this year.

4   Tool Setup and Configuration

The VeriAbs SV-COMP 2018 executable is available for download at the URL http://www.cmi.ac.in/~madhukar/veriabs/VeriAbs.zip. To install the tool, download the archive, extract its contents, and then follow the installation instructions in `VeriAbs/INSTALL.txt`. To execute VeriAbs, the user needs to specify the property file of the respective verification category using the `--property-file` option. The witness is generated in the current working directory as `witness.graphml`. A sample command is as follows:

`VeriAbs/scripts/veriabs --property-file ALL.prp example.c`

VeriAbs is participating in the ReachSafety category. The BenchExec wrapper script for the tool is `veriabs.py` and `veriabs.xml` is the benchmark description file.

5   Software Project and Contributors

VeriAbs is a verification tool maintained by TCS Research [1], and parts of it have been developed by the authors, Mohammad Afzal and other members of this organization. We would like to thank Charles Babu M and other interns who have contributed to the development of VeriAbs.

References

1. TCS Research. http://www.tcs.com/research/Pages/default.aspx
2. Beyer, D., Keremoglu, M.E.: CPACHECKER: a tool for configurable software verification. In: Gopalakrishnan, G., Qadeer, S. (eds.) CAV 2011. LNCS, vol. 6806, pp. 184–190. Springer, Heidelberg (2011). https://doi.org/10.1007/978-3-642-22110-1_16

3. Böhme, M., Pham, V.-T., Roychoudhury, A.: Coverage-based greybox fuzzing as Markov chain. In: Proceedings of the 2016 ACM SIGSAC Conference on Computer and Communications Security, pp. 1032–1043. ACM (2016)
4. Clarke, E., Kroening, D., Lerda, F.: A tool for checking ANSI-C programs. In: Jensen, K., Podelski, A. (eds.) TACAS 2004. LNCS, vol. 2988, pp. 168–176. Springer, Heidelberg (2004). https://doi.org/10.1007/978-3-540-24730-2_15
5. Darke, P., Chimdyalwar, B., Venkatesh, R., Shrotri, U., Metta, R.: Over-approximating loops to prove properties using bounded model checking. In: DATE (2015)
6. de Moura, L., Bjørner, N.: Z3. an efficient SMT solver. In: Ramakrishnan, C.R., Rehof, J. (eds.) TACAS 2008. LNCS, vol. 4963, pp. 337–340. Springer, Heidelberg (2008). https://doi.org/10.1007/978-3-540-78800-3_24
7. Eén, N., Sörensson, N.: An extensible SAT-solver. In: Giunchiglia, E., Tacchella, A. (eds.) SAT 2003. LNCS, vol. 2919, pp. 502–518. Springer, Heidelberg (2004). https://doi.org/10.1007/978-3-540-24605-3_37
8. Gordon, M., Collavizza, H.: Forward with Hoare. In: Roscoe, A.W., Jones, C.B., Wood, K.R. (eds.) Reflections on the Work of C.A.R. Hoare, pp. 101–121. Springer, London (2010). https://doi.org/10.1007/978-1-84882-912-1_5
9. Khare, S., Saraswat, S., Kumar, S.: Static program analysis of large embedded code base: an experience. In: ISEC, pp. 99–102, ACM (2011)
10. Kumar, S., Sanyal, A., Venkatesh, R., Shah, P.: Property checking array programs using loop shrinking. In: Tools and Algorithms for the Construction and Analysis of Systems (2018)
11. Chimdyalwar, B., Kumar, S., Shrotri, U.: Precise range analysis on large industry code. In: Proceedings of the 2013 9th Joint Meeting on Foundations of Software Engineering, pp. 675–678. ACM (2013)
12. Zalewski, M.: American fuzzy lop. http://lcamtuf.coredump.cx/afl/
13. Darke, P., Khanzode, M., Nair, A., Shrotri, U., Venkatesh, R.: Precise analysis of large industry code. In: Asia Pacific Software Engineering Conference, pp. 306–309 (2012)

Author Index

Printed in the United States
By Bookmasters